G000093611

Günter Grass and His Critics

Studies in German Literature, Linguistics, and Culture:
Literary Criticism in Perspective

About *Literary Criticism in Perspective*

Books in the series *Literary Criticism in Perspective* trace literary scholarship and criticism on major and neglected writers alike, or on a single major work, a group of writers, a literary school or movement. In so doing the authors — authorities on the topic in question who are also well-versed in the principles and history of literary criticism — address a readership consisting of scholars, students of literature at the graduate and undergraduate level, and the general reader. One of the primary purposes of the series is to illuminate the nature of literary criticism itself, to gauge the influence of social and historic currents on aesthetic judgments once thought objective and normative.

Günter Grass and His Critics

From *The Tin Drum* to *Crabwalk*

Siegfried Mews

CAMDEN HOUSE
Rochester, New York

First published 2008
by Camden House

Camden House is an imprint of Boydell & Brewer Inc.
668 Mt. Hope Avenue, Rochester, NY 14620, USA
www.camden-house.com
and of Boydell & Brewer Limited
PO Box 9, Woodbridge, Suffolk IP12 3DF, UK
www.boydellandbrewer.com

ISBN-13: 978–1–57113–062–4
ISBN-10: 1–57113–062–4

Library of Congress Cataloging-in-Publication Data

Mews, Siegfried.
Günter Grass and his critics : from The tin drum to Crabwalk / Siegfried Mews.
p. cm. — (Studies in German literature, linguistics, and culture) (Literary criticism in perspective)
Includes bibliographical references and index.
ISBN-13: 978–1–57113–062–4 (hardcover : alk. paper)
ISBN-10: 1–57113–062–4 (hardcover : alk. paper)
1. Grass, Günter, 1927– —Criticism and interpretation. 2. Grass, Günter, 1927– —Appreciation. 3. Criticism—Germany—History—20th century. I. Title. II. Series.

PT613.R338Z758 2008
838'.91409—dc22

2007047416

A catalogue record for this title is available from the British Library.

This publication is printed on acid-free paper.
Printed in the United States of America.

Contents

Part 3: After Reunification: Old Problems and New Beginnings

Abbreviations

TITLES OF GRASS'S WORKS WILL ordinarily be cited in both German (when the reference is clearly to the original text) and English (when the reference is evidently to the English rendering). Quotations from Grass's writings will generally be given in English and, in comparatively rare instances (for example, for the sake of clarification) in German. The bibliographical details of the translations cited in the text are given below; the editions are listed in alphabetical order according to the abbreviations used. The first date of publication of the respective English translation has been added in square brackets.

CaM *Cat and Mouse.* [1963]. Translated by Ralph Manheim. New York: Signet Books, 1964.

CT *The Call of the Toad* [1992]. Translated by Ralph Manheim. San Diego: Harcourt, Brace, Jovanovich, 1992.

CW *Crabwalk* [2003]. Translated by Krishna Winston. Orlando, FL: Harcourt, 2003.

DS *From the Diary of a Snail* [1973]. Translated by Ralph Manheim. New York: Harcourt, Brace, Jovanovich, 1973.

DY *Dog Years* [1965]. Translated by Ralph Manheim. New York: Harvest Paperback, 1989.

F *The Flounder* [1978]. Translated by Ralph Manheim. New York: Harcourt, Brace, Jovanovich, 1978.

HB *Headbirths, or the Germans Are Dying Out* [1982]. New York: Harcourt, Brace, Jovanovich, 1982.

LA *Local Anaesthetic* [1970]. Translated by Ralph Manheim. New York: Harcourt, Brace & World, 1970.

MC *My Century* [1999]. Translated by Michael Henry Heim. New York: Harcourt, Brace, Jovanovich, 1999.

MT *The Meeting at Telgte* [1981]. Translated by Ralph Manheim. New York: Harcourt, Brace, Jovanovich, 1981.

NL "To Be Continued . . ." Translated by Michael Henry Heim. *PMLA* 115 (2000): 292–300.

PO *Peeling the Onion* [2007]. Translated by Michael Henry Heim. Orlando, FL: Harcourt, 2007.

R *The Rat* [1987]. Translated by Ralph Manheim. San Diego: Harcourt, Brace, Jovanovich, 1987.

SYT *Show Your Tongue* [1989]. Translated by John E. Woods. San Diego: Harcourt, Brace, Jovanovich, 1989.

TD *The Tin Drum* [1963]. Translated by Ralph Manheim. New York: Pantheon, 1999.

TFA *Too Far Afield* [2000]. Translated by Krishna Winston. New York: Harcourt, 2000.

Quotations from Grass's works in German refer to the following editions:

W *Werkausgabe in achtzehn Bänden.* 1997–2003. Ed. Volker Neuhaus and Daniela Hermes. Göttingen: Steidl.

WA *Werkausgabe in zehn Bänden.* 1987. Ed. Volker Neuhaus. Darmstadt: Luchterhand.

Introduction

ALTHOUGH GÜNTER GRASS (b. 1927) was not an entirely unknown entity in the postwar literary scene of the mid-1950s, in which the influential *Gruppe 47* played a significant role, it was the publication of his sensational *Die Blechtrommel* in 1959 (*The Tin Drum,* 1963; see ch. 1) that made him a household name in his native country as well as among literati abroad. The novel was both praised and reviled and has remained his best-known work; it was ultimately *Die Blechtrommel* for which Grass was awarded the 1999 Nobel Prize (Grass's numerous other prizes are listed in Mertens, Hermes, and Neuhaus) in recognition of a singular literary accomplishment after a catastrophic war with its devastating consequences for intellectual and cultural life: "[It] was as if German literature had been granted a new beginning after decades of linguistic and moral destruction" (Swedish Academy 1999). The year 1959 has often been declared to be the *annus mirabilis* of modern postwar (West) German literature, owing to the publication of three significant novels — in addition to *Die Blechtrommel,* Heinrich Böll's *Billiard um halbzehn* (*Billiards at Half Past Nine,* 1961), and Uwe Johnson's *Mutmaßungen über Jakob* (*Speculations about Jacob,* 1963) appeared in the same year. Böll (1917–85), who was awarded the Nobel Prize in 1972, and Johnson (1934–84) are no longer alive and hence do not generate the kind of publicity via the public appearances, interviews, readings, and the like that often precede and follow the publication of works of fiction, but the author of *Die Blechtrommel* has been in the limelight ever since his literary breakthrough. To be sure, the high degree of name recognition Grass can count on is not exclusively attributable to his achievements in the realm of fiction; a contributing factor to his reputation — or, some would say, notoriety — has been his unconventional engagement in grass-roots party politics on behalf of the Social Democratic Party (SPD), which began in earnest in the 1960s and, apart from intervals exclusively devoted to creative pursuits, has essentially continued until today. At the beginning of his literary career, Grass's literary focus was clearly on his hometown of Danzig, as *Die Blechtrommel* and the subsequent works incorporated in the *Danziger Trilogie* (*Danzig Trilogy;* see ch. 4), considered by many to be his crowning artistic achievement, attest. In his fiction he investigated the reasons for the irretrievable loss of Danzig, by exploring the Nazi past and its remnants in postwar West German society. Particularly during the

1980s, critics noted a distinct globalization of Grass's perspective that is evident, for example, in *Der Butt* (1977; *The Flounder;* 1978; see ch. 7) and *Kopfgeburten* (1980; *Headbirths,* 1980; see ch. 9) as well as in his public utterances. Grass's political and literary interventions elevated him to a position in the public sphere in his native country, but also beyond it, that few writers have attained. The entirely unexpected fall of the Berlin Wall in November 1989 and subsequent events refocused Grass's energies on German problems; notably his extraordinarily controversial novel *Ein weites Feld* (1995; *Too Far Afield,* 2000; see ch. 13) was — at least in West Germany — widely perceived as a reflection of his unpopular, strident critique of German (re)unification, a political event of major proportions that for many signified the end of the postwar period and the Cold War. But the (belated) award of the Nobel Prize confirmed his international standing and may be said to have had the effect of minimizing the recriminations he was subject to on account of his nonconformist views about the new Germany.

It is, then, hardly an exaggeration to state that Grass has been engaged in a host of issues of public interest; a short, random list of causes during the last decade or so that induced him to intervene publicly includes his advocacy of the Sinti and Roma, his opposition to the reform of German orthography, his support for the compensation of those who were forced laborers during the Nazi period, his criticism of the policy regarding those seeking asylum in the Federal Republic, and his defense of Turkish novelist Yaşar Kemal, the 1997 recipient of the "Friedenspreis des Deutschen Buchhandels" (Peace Prize of the German Booksellers' Association), who faced oppressive Turkish government policies. All of these activities spring from Grass's self-definition as a democratic socialist and engaged intellectual who deliberately broke with the traditional separation of the spheres of *Geist* (intellect, mind) and *Macht* (power) and refuses to remain silent in the face of unresolved issues or undesirable developments in society at large.

The fact that for several decades his name has been prominently included in German surveys, opinion polls, and rankings of various kinds provides a further indication of Grass's public stature in his homeland. Whatever validity one may attribute to such rankings in general and those of intellectuals in particular, perhaps one should not entirely ignore the results of a listing in the April 2006 cover story of *Cicero,* a magazine for political culture, in which Grass was designated as the most influential intellectual in the German-speaking countries (see Anon. 2006a) — a designation that attests to both his celebrity status and his assumed influential position among his fellow countrymen and countrywomen. In this particular ranking, Grass was followed by late-night talk show host Harald Schmidt in second place; rather paradoxically, Grass's nemesis among critics, Marcel Reich-Ranicki (see below), was ranked third. Ironically, only a few months later, in October 2006, Grass was, for all practical purposes, demoted when literary critics were asked by the editors of the same magazine to name their favorite living author, and Grass was assigned a comparatively lowly twelfth place (see Auffermann 2006).

What may appear as a sudden decline of Grass's fortunes in terms of his reputation among the literati (and the general public) is most likely attributable to the latest "scandal," the fierce debate that erupted in conjunction with the publication of his autobiography, *Beim Häuten der Zwiebel,* in August 2006 (*Peeling the Onion,* 2007; see Epilogue). In his autobiography (Grass dispenses with a generic clarification), the author publicly admitted for the first time that as a teenager, at the end of the Second World War, he had been a member of the *Waffen SS,* an organization of ill repute. The heated discussions that ensued as a consequence of this "confession" are, in a sense, a continuation of those in which the author has been engulfed for nearly five decades. But this particular controversy, which, at least initially, revolved around Grass's position as an allegedly self-appointed upholder of moral standards rather than the literary merits of the autobiography, once again brings into focus the fact that in the public's perception the author's biography is inextricably linked with his work; as a consequence, what in the beginning seemed to be a literary scandal soon evolved into personal attacks on the author. At any rate, the initial reception of *Die Blechtrommel,* today indisputably both Grass's most widely read and critically acclaimed work of prose fiction (see, for example, Baron 1999c), amply demonstrates the potential of Grass's writings to foment impassioned reactions. The heated response to Grass's first phenomenal literary success is indicative of a pattern that was to be repeated with minor variations for almost half a century whenever one of the author's major publications appeared or whenever he forcefully intervened in matters of public concern.

It is common knowledge that the multitalented Grass's artistic endeavors are not confined to purely literary pursuits. As Patrick O'Neill (1987b) puts it: "As well as being a novelist [he is] . . . also a poet, painter, sculptor, stage designer, script writer, dramatist, gourmet cook, one-time jazz musician, and . . . political orator and commentator" (2). Even though Grass has been and continues to be very much in the limelight, a state of affairs that tends to blur the boundaries between political and aesthetic concerns, it is incontrovertible that he is, for the most part, most closely identified with his literary activities in general and his demanding fiction in particular. It is his novels, novellas or *Novellen* (a distinct genre in German prose fiction, which, however, English-speaking critics often tend to erroneously categorize as novels), and narratives of somewhat indeterminate genre such as *Kopfgeburten* and *Zunge zeigen*

(1988; *Show Your Tongue,* 1989; see ch. 11) that have received the lion's share of critical attention, as evidenced by the established cottage industry of scholarly publications, which shows no sign of waning. By no means an ivory-tower recluse, the author has contributed vigorously to the marketing of his writings via public readings and other means (see the bibliography in Mertens, Hermes, and Neuhaus for sound storage media of Grass's works). The present work, a descriptive as well as analytical and evaluative overview of extant scholarship, seeks to cover the pertinent literature from approximately 1959 to 2005. Because of Grass's virtually constant presence in the public view, it is not only the traditional variety of criticism to be encountered in scholarly publications and literary journals that needs to be examined here; rather, additional sources such as the daily and weekly press provide valuable insights concerning the reception of Grass's works.

The task of perusing the press reviews written in German has been facilitated by the collections edited by Gerd Loschütz (1968), which also offers brief excerpts of reviews from abroad, as well as by Heinz Ludwig Arnold and Franz Josef Görtz (1971), which documents Grass's political involvement, and two publications by Franz Josef Görtz: an anthology of reviews exclusively devoted to *Die Blechtrommel* (1984a) and reprinted contributions covering the entire spectrum of Grass's activities, including politics (1984b). As subsequent compilations of reviews of individual works such as *Ein weites Feld* or *Beim Häuten der Zwiebel* attest, the desire to document the journalistic reception of Grass's creative writing appears to continue unabated in the age of the Internet, with its vastly increased possibilities for instant communication and retrieval of information. At the same time, there has been a distinct tendency, by no means exclusively on the part of literary scholars, to take issue with the alleged failure on the part of those entrusted with serving as mediators between the author's works and the reading public to adequately address and explain Grass's prose fiction. In his exceedingly detailed study entitled *Günter Grass — Zur Pathogenese eines Markenbilds* (1978; On the Pathogenesis of a Brand Name), which includes an extensive bibliography of reviews of Grass's first four major prose narratives, Görtz investigated the reception of Grass's works from *Die Blechtrommel* to *Örtlich betäubt* (1969; *Local Anaesthetic,* 1970; see ch. 5) in the mass media by concentrating on prevalent clichés and stereotypes. Such commonly used clichés include blasphemy, cynicism, vitality, exuberance, and scatology; using a computer, Görtz determined their frequency and provided a valuable analysis of the writer's perception by the public.

In a more conventional vein, both Arnold (1997) and Timm Boßmann (1997) scrutinize the coverage of Grass's works by the German-language press and take the *Feuilleton* reviewers to task for having failed to adequately address Grass's literary accomplishments. (Those sentiments, incidentally, are shared by Grass.) The title of Arnold's study (a cooperative venture with his students), *Blech getrommelt* — an obvious allusion to *Die Blechtrommel* — may be roughly translated as "drumming up nonsense." Similarly, the title chosen by Boßmann, *Der Dichter im Schussfeld* (The Poet in the Line of Fire), provides a clear indication of the thrust of his argument. Both considerably more comprehensive and more moderate in his approach — if, despite a voluminous bibliography, less meticulously annotated than Arnold or Boßmann — Harro Zimmermann (2006) chronicles Grass's problematic fifty-year relationship (1955–2005) with Germany and the Germans in great detail and views the continuous media debate with and about the writer-cum-public-intellectual as an element that has significantly shaped the cultural and political history of postwar Germany or, more accurately, West Germany, the pre-unification Federal Republic. Grass reception in the GDR was exceedingly restricted (see Streul 1988, Wittmann 1991); ironically, the readers in the self-proclaimed "Leseland" (land of readers) of the GDR were only selectively permitted to peruse the writings of one of the most famous German writers (see Petzold 2003). This state of affairs changed only after (re)unification; owing largely to the debate about *Ein weites Feld,* Grass was perceived as the spokesperson of those East Germans who were suffering from the economic and social consequences of the demise of the GDR.

In the pre-unification as well as the present Federal Republic (or Berlin Republic) there was and is no dearth of readers of Grass's literary works, nor is there a lack of attention on the part of those charged with observing and commenting on developments in the cultural-literary scene in the *Feuilletons* of major dailies such as *Die Welt,* the *Frankfurter Allgemeine Zeitung,* the *Frankfurter Rundschau,* and the *Süddeutsche Zeitung* — all of which will be fairly frequently cited in subsequent chapters. This array of influential print media with a nation-wide distribution has been supplemented with a host of less well-known (regional) papers as well as prominent, widely circulated weeklies such as *Die Zeit* and influential news magazines, notably *Der Spiegel. Der Spiegel* in particular devoted several cover stories to Grass, beginning with a review of *Hundejahre* (1963; *Dog Years,* 1965; see ch. 3) and (so far) extending to *Beim Häuten der Zwiebel.* There certainly is no dearth of coverage; in fact, the omnipresence of Grass is evident, for example, in the great number of articles devoted to him in the popular magazine *Stern.* But there is, as indicated, a tendency on the part of scholars such as Arnold, Boßmann, and others to charge reviewers with essentially failing in their task of informing and enlightening readers and instead engaging in polemics against the author. In particular, they single out one specific critic, that is, the aforementioned Reich-Ranicki (b. 1920). An extraordinarily influential arbiter in matters of literary taste, who eventually ascended to the position of the presumably infallible "pope" of literary criticism in the German-speaking countries, Reich-Ranicki reviewed virtually all of Grass's works of prose fiction; these reviews have been republished separately (1992a; 2003) and document the decade-long ambivalent relationship between critic and author. From March 1988 to September 2001, Reich-Ranicki reached an impressive number of readers and spectators via *Das literarische Quartett* (The Literary Quartet), a TV show in which he presided over the discussion of new publications and pronounced his verdicts *ex cathedra* (see Wistoff 1996, 188). In the TV show, he was joined by regular hosts, who initially included journalists Sigrid Löffler and Hellmuth Karasek, as well as a number of guest critics. Despite Reich-Ranicki's opening sentence at the beginning of the series, "Dies ist keine Talk Show" ("This is not a talk show"), opponents have charged that the TV medium served Reich-Ranicki as a vehicle for self-promotion and self-dramatization (see, for example, Boßmann, 6–7) — a modus operandi that tended to overemphasize the role of the critic at the expense of the author and to undermine an informed debate about the qualities of the respective literary work discussed.

Even if reviewers may have a propensity to neglect or ignore their chief task, that is, to serve as mediators between the literary text and the reader, it goes without saying that such reviews, particularly those published in print media with a national circulation, play a fairly important role in shaping readers' initial opinions. Mostly penned by professional critics, fellow writers, or other literati such as Günter Blöcker, Joachim Kaiser, and Fritz Raddatz (who republished a number of his reviews of Grass's works [2002a]), they sometimes provide the impetus for further, usually academic or scholarly, studies of a specific literary work; hence they constitute an important aspect of the reception process, which cannot be ignored in a study that seeks to provide a critical survey of the extant literature on Grass.

A multitude of literary studies soon followed the appraisals of individual works of Grass's prose fiction in the *Feuilleton*. A few statistics may suffice to provide an indication of the wealth of secondary literature available. When Patrick O'Neill (1976) published his bibliography, which covers the twenty-year period from 1955 to 1975, he listed about twelve hundred entries relating to Grass's entire oeuvre; approximately thirty years later, well-known Grass scholar Volker Neuhaus, in collaboration with Mathias Mertens and Daniela Hermes, presented a bibliography of more than six hundred and twenty items that were published from 1962 to 2004 (see Mertens, Hermes, and Neuhaus, n.d.). In view of the plethora of critical comment, selectivity becomes a necessity in attempting to provide an informed synopsis of pertinent criticism. As the title of this study indicates, it is the reception of Grass's major prose works — which are, as is generally acknowledged, the best known part of his literary oeuvre — that will be analyzed here. Grass's standing as a widely translated (see, for example, Frielinghaus 2002), truly international writer (in their collection of translated and reprinted essays of 1990, Neuhaus and Hermes provide an indication of Grass's reception abroad) has resulted in a wealth of secondary literature in a variety of languages. Since the attempt to document the Grass reception via reviews on a worldwide scale would present virtually insurmountable linguistic as well as logistic problems, the current appraisal has essentially been limited to that in Germany (and the German-speaking countries), the English-speaking countries (primarily the United States, and, to a lesser extent, England), and, considerably less inclusively, France — a country that accorded *Ein weites Feld* an unusually wide-ranging reception. Unlike reviews, scholarly contributions tend to appeal to an international, if limited, audience; however, the same linguistic constraints are in effect here. Even though scholarly contributions written in German, English, or French most likely constitute the overwhelming majority of the worldwide critical appraisals devoted to Grass's writings, an all-inclusive coverage of (somewhat) pertinent secondary sources remains an elusive, if not unattainable goal; the lament that the literature on Grass has become exceedingly difficult to navigate has begun surfacing with increasing frequency in studies devoted to the writer's work.

In order to provide a broad, general review of the extant literature within the limitations outlined above, the individual chapters of this book seek to document the reception of each work, discussed by proceeding essentially chronologically; that is, I first comment on the critical reaction upon the publication of the German original — or, as the case may be, preceding its official publication — and then survey the reception of the English translation, and, finally, investigate the critical contributions by scholars, which are often informed by more or less clearly defined critical approaches and tend to adhere to specific methodological paradigms and preferences that reflect the ever changing modes of reading literary texts. In fact, one might argue that Grass's texts have been scrutinized using an array of analytical approaches that in their shifting emphases are indicative not only of the development of postwar literary criticism in (West) Germany, about which Boßmann (1997; 10–41) provides a brief sketch, but also of its evolution on an international scale. This evolution, which runs the gamut from sociologically oriented readings to Jungian and Freudian interpretations, from reader response theory to feminist critiques, from structuralism to poststructuralism, to mention only some modes of reading literary texts, may be perceived in terms of postmodernism and the heterogenous elements that it is thought to embrace.

While the critical literature addressing aspects of specific works of fiction will ordinarily be discussed in the individual chapters, in view of the considerable number of publications that deal with Grass's works in general, it is appropriate to provide in this introduction a somewhat cursory survey, in an attempt to outline the evolution of Grass criticism in very general terms.

Whereas sporadic critical notices about his work began to appear in the 1950s prior to the publication of *Die Blechtrommel*, it was the appearance of Grass's *magnum opus* that may be said to have opened the floodgates of comments and interpretations. Among the German-language publications, one of the first collections of essays entirely devoted to Grass was that by Heinz Ludwig Arnold (1963) in an issue of the periodical *Text + Kritik*. The issue has been frequently revised and updated and has stood the test of time. Other anthologies of scholarly writings addressing aspects of all or several of Grass's works in both German and English include those edited by A. Leslie Willson (1971), Manfred Jurgensen (1973), Rolf Geißler (1976), Ray Lewis White (1981) — a compilation of (excerpted) reviews published in the American press — Manfred Durzak (1985a), Rudolf Wolff (1985), Patrick O'Neill (1987c), who collected and edited both reviews and articles written in English, Gerd Labroisse and Dick van Stekelenburg (1992), Hans Adler and Jost Hermand (1996), and Hans Wisskirchen (2002). In addition, there are the anonymously edited conference proceedings from gatherings of Grass scholars in Poland (Anon., 1983; 1990) and a miscellany of articles in the journal *Sprache im technischen Zeitalter* (Ewert, et al. 1999) on the occasion of Grass having been awarded the Nobel Prize.

These collections of essays have been augmented by what may be somewhat indiscriminately termed general assessments — again, both in German and English — which usually take into account both the author's biography and his work and endeavor to appeal to the scholar as well as the general public. To varying degrees, the monographs by Kurth Lothar Tank (1965; rev. ed. 1974; English translation 1969), Norris W. Yates (1967), W. Gordon Cunliffe (1969), Wilhelm Johannes Schwarz (1969, rev. ed. 1971), Irene Leonard (1974), Keith Miles (1975), Hanspeter Brode (1979), Noel L. Thomas (1982), Ronald Hayman (1985), Richard H. Lawson (1985), the repeatedly augmented and reissued biography by Heinrich Vormweg (1986), and the volumes by Michael Hollington (1987), Alan Frank Keele (1988), Polish Grass scholar Norbert Honsza (1989, 1997), Ute Brandes (1998), and Dieter Stolz (1999, rev. ed. 2005), the introductory and pedagogically oriented survey by Theodor Pelster (1999), the very valuable — especially for English-speaking readers — monographs by Patrick O'Neill (1999) and Julian Preece (2001), and the biographically oriented study of Per Øhrgaard (2005), a translation from the Danish, offer a wealth of information. The eminently useful discussion of Grass's works by Volker Neuhaus (1979, rev. ed. 1992) and Sabine Moser's introduction to Grass's novels and other narratives, which examines readings of individual works by various scholars (2000), provide compact analyses. In addition to that of Vormweg, further biographies are those by Neuhaus (1997), Olivier Mannoni (2000), and the two volumes published on occasion of Grass's seventy-fifth birthday by Michael Jürgs (2002) and Claudia Mayer-Iswandy (2002). Whereas Mayer-Iswandy's *Günter Grass* privileges literary analysis intended for a general audience, Jürgs places his emphasis on Grass the citizen rather than on Grass the writer.

The collections of essays, biographies, and general studies began to be augmented by works addressing specific aspects of a significant part of Grass's literary oeuvre; a considerable number of these monographs originated as dissertations, of which only those published will be considered here. Among the first of these investigations is that by Gertrude Cepl-Kaufmann (1975), which addresses, perhaps not surprisingly, the relationship of literature and politics in Grass's work. On the whole, she views this relationship as problematic — owing, for example, to the postulated correspondence between the deficits of political substance exhibited on the part of the social strata depicted on the one hand and the author's lack of theoretical knowledge as well as antipathy to theory on the other. Without doubt, her apparently harsh verdict was inspired by the new orientation of literary criticism that began to assert itself during and after the German student movement of the late 1960s and early 1970s. Almost thirty years later, Sabine Moser (2002) analyzed Grass's *Deutschlandbild* (view of Germany): according to her analysis, Grass saw Germany as a political entity with a disastrous history, and this is what made him reject (re)unification so vehemently, especially, as pointed out before, in *Ein weites Feld*. Timm Niklas Pietsch (2006) takes a somewhat novel approach, rejecting the charge that Grass had a theoretical deficit; he posits that the texts of Grass's political interventions form a significant, independent part of his work, even if they are closely related to his oeuvre.

Although addresses, essays, and interviews devoted to politics constitute a significant part of Grass's output and have attracted considerable attention, other approaches have by no means been neglected. Angelika Hille-Sandvoß (1987) concentrates on the interconnection of verbal and graphic images (*Bildlichkeit*) such as the (in)famous eel episode in *Die Blechtrommel*. After Ann L. Mason had devoted a study to Grass's *Conception of the Artist* (1974), Klaus Stallbaum (1989) explored in great detail Grass's concept of art and his ambivalent portrayal of the artist as both a member of society and an asocial human being. Grass's prodigious innovations in terms of narrative modes and perspectives, structures of syntax, and graphic detail have been researched by Renate Gerstenberg

(1980) who detects in the various narrator-protagonists' stance a shift from individualism to social responsibility and a democratic orientation. Norbert Rempe-Thiemann (1992) goes beyond the general consensus that the texts of the *Danziger Trilogie* form a coherent entity and argues in favor of a unity, based on common motifs, characters, and images, that includes all works of prose fiction from *Die Blechtrommel* to *Die Rättin* (1986; *The Rat,* 1987; see ch. 10). A further, linguistically oriented, study of Grass's prose style is that by Thomas Angenendt (1995) who in his analysis deviates from common practice by assigning a central position to *Aus dem Tagebuch einer Schnecke* (1972; *From the Diary of a Snail,* 1973; see ch. 6) but does take into account stylistic aspects such as unusual word formations, the lengths of sentences and their structures, and various rhetorical devices in texts that range from *Die Blechtrommel* to *Zunge zeigen.* Dieter Stolz (1994) provides a comprehensive analysis of Grass's poetry and establishes links between it and Grass's prose fiction.

Obviously, studies of a linguistic and stylistic bent use Grass's original texts and are primarily addressed to the reader with a command of German. But Grass's success abroad cannot be entirely explained in terms of his verbal dexterity and astounding inventiveness in the original texts; for the foreign reader the quality of the translation of specific works is of prime importance. There are comparatively few systematic studies that address the linguistic, cultural, and other difficulties translators of Grass's notoriously challenging prose face; apart from the collection of essays edited by Frielinghaus (previously referred to), the analyses by Janina Gesche (2003) and Pernilla Rosell Steuer (2004) provide insight into the taxing business of literary translation.

Although there are no comprehensive investigations of the translations of Grass's works into English, the American reception especially of his novels, which began with *The Tin Drum,* is fairly well documented as the aforementioned compilations of reviews by White and O'Neill as well as the surveys by Sigrid Mayer (1978), Patrick O'Neill (1987c, 1992), Siegfried Mews (1989, 1999), and the less comprehensive studies by Walter Ziltener (1982) and Thomas Schaller (1988) suggest. Moreover, the statistical tabulations by Henrik D. K. Engel (1997) reveal that the number of books and dissertations on Grass originating in the United States (and Canada) from 1960 to 1989/90 is second only to those written and published in the German-speaking countries and exceeds the number of published results of scholarly diligence in Great Britain and France by a considerable margin. Similarly, the quantity of essays in scholarly journals of the respective countries that explore Grass's works show a similar statistical relationship: the German-speaking countries account for a total of one hundred and seventy-six contributions, the USA and Canada for sixty, Great Britain for twenty-three, and France for ten (see Engel, 257–59). To be sure, a purely quantitative analysis has to be supplemented by an exploration of the reasons why a specific author or work succeeds or fails in a foreign linguistic, cultural, and political environment. With regard to Grass, O'Neill (1987c, 1992) has offered the intriguing thesis that the decisive difference between the author's reception in the Federal Republic and the United States was, to a considerable extent, motivated by German objections of a political nature, whereas critics in the United States, less attuned to the specifics of (West) German politics, relatively quickly proceeded to promote Grass to the status of a "'world author'" unfettered and untroubled by the business of politics (O'Neill 1992c, 283; see also ch. 1) — in short, in the United States aesthetics supposedly triumphed over mundane matters such as public engagement.

True, the thesis seems persuasive with regard to the *Tin Drum* and, for that matter, with regard to the entire *Danzig Trilogy*. However, as I (1999) have argued, and as the following chapters will bear out, the dichotomous view expressed in the title of a 1977 Grass interview, "Im Ausland geschätzt — im Inland gehaßt" (*WA* 10:206–15; Appreciated Abroad — Hated at Home) does not take into account the gradually shifting perception of Grass on the part of the American press, which is attributable to factors such as the author's increasingly negative view of official US policy, particularly during the Vietnam War, a view that found literary expression in *Örtlich betäubt*. The author's propensity for expounding his negative assessments, which, he insistently reiterated, should not be confounded with Anti-Americanism, in American media or before American audiences during his fairly frequent visits to the United States did not contribute to improving his image.

A case in point is Grass's appearance at the PEN congress in January 1986 in New York City, at which he sharply criticized American Nobel laureate Saul Bellow. Bellow had praised the concept of the "American Dream" and thereby, according to Grass, glossed over the social discrepancies in the United States by taking the side of the establishment. Grass's attacks elicited sharp rebukes and were denounced as "decidedly unliterary denunciations of western capitalism and the American way of life" (Grove 1986). Although there are some parallels in the reception of Grass's works in both Germany and the United States, it is ultimately the question of whether specific American concerns are addressed that provides a clue to the degree of acceptance or rejection of the German writer's fiction. Thus Americans, who were generally favorably disposed towards German (re)unification, did not devote much attention to Grass's pronounced opposition to this historical event; they were able to gather the author's stance from a small volume of essays entitled *Two States — One Nation?* published in October 1990, after united Germany had become a fait accompli. The volume included his lecture "Writing after Auschwitz" (1990), in which Grass argued that the legacy of Auschwitz precluded any desire to achieve national unity — a position that met with severe censure in Germany. This censure was exacerbated by the publication of the anti-unification novel *Ein weites Feld* in 1995; the unusually long-delayed publication of the translation, entitled *Too Far Afield* (2000), came too late to reignite the debate in the United States. But what may be called an officious American view asserted itself on occasion of the award of the Nobel Prize in 1999. Although commentators in both the *New York Times* (Atlas 1999) and the *Wall Street Journal* (Heilbrunn 1999) acknowledged the literary merits of *The Tin Drum,* they attributed the fact that Grass was honored to the left-leaning tendencies of the Nobel Prize committee. In essence then, these commentators promulgated the view that literature and its authors should stay clear of politics — a point of view that novelist John Updike, who reviewed several of Grass's prose narratives, repeatedly articulated. Conversely, Grass was extravagantly praised by novelist John Irving, albeit in the context of Irving's review of *Headbirths,* surely not one of Grass's major fictional accomplishments. Despite Grass's continuing disagreements with official US policy, such as his support for the Red/Green coalition government of Chancellor Gerhard Schröder (1998–2005), which did not support the Iraq War, it is to be assumed that Grass's reputation as the author of a brilliant first novel, which has served many critics as the yardstick with which to measure his subsequent fiction, will not be significantly tarnished by his controversial political views.

Part 1

Danzig, Center of the Universe

1: *Die Blechtrommel / The Tin Drum*

From *Die Blechtrommel* to *The Tin Drum*

ATTRAKTION UND ÄRGERNIS (ATTRACTIVENESS AND NUISANCE), the subtitle of Franz Josef Görtz's 1984 anthology of reviews of *Die Blechtrommel,* which appeared on occasion of the twenty-fifth anniversary of its publication, aptly summarizes the wide divergence and contradictory nature of critical opinion that Grass's first novel elicited. Although *Die Blechtrommel* is today acknowledged as the major work of postwar German literature, its present-day canonical status tends to obscure the decidedly mixed reactions it initially received. True, *Gruppe 47,* that most influential gathering of postwar West German literati, awarded Grass their prepublication prize for reading two chapters from the manuscript of the novel at their 1958 meeting, and the same year critics such as Joachim Kaiser, Marcel Reich-Ranicki, and Hans Schwab-Felisch took notice of an emerging, forceful talent. Upon publication of the novel, reviewers eagerly welcomed a fresh voice that signaled the beginning of a new phase of literary development almost fifteen years after the end of a disastrous war. For example, one commentator, who is identified merely by initials, avers that the epic construct of *Die Blechtrommel* can be compared only to Thomas Mann's *Buddenbrooks,* a novel published in 1901 (hlg 1959). Conversely, among the more than 160 reviews, not all of which are included in Görtz's anthology, there are several that express an unrelentingly negative view. For instance, one physician-turned-critic engages in a pun to voice his disdain — he changes the *Blechtrommel* (tin drum) of the title to *Brechtrommel* (a drum that causes one to vomit) — and warns his readers against the supposedly inferior work because of its voyeuristic, obscene, and blasphemous ingredients (Müller-Eckhard 1959). One of the more conspicuous examples of explicit and officious disapproval of the novel was provided by the city of Bremen: in 1959 the Bremen Senate decided to override the unanimous recommendation of an appointed panel to award Grass the literary prize of the city. The entire affair is amply documented in Arnold and Görtz's *Günter Grass — Dokumente zur politischen Wirkung* (1971, 263–81). By 1965 Grass had been the defendant in some forty lawsuits brought against both *Die Blechtrommel* and *Katz und Maus,* and in the same year a religious youth organization in the Rhenish city of Düsseldorf, the locale of book 3 of *Die Blechtrommel,* publicly burned the novel (O'Neill 1992, 278). These initiatives on the part of opponents demonstrate clearly that the novel was a phenomenon that could not be confined to the niche ordinarily reserved for literary matters; rather, it assumed considerable significance in public discourse.

The influential professor of literature Walter Höllerer (1922–2003), whom Grass was later to memorialize in *Im Krebsgang* (2002; *Crabwalk* 2003) as someone who "captivated the overflowing crowd in the lecture hall with his piercing birdlike voice" (*CW,* 27), tends to draw attention in his reviews (1959a; 1959b) to the strengths of *Die Blechtrommel* — as did other critics, including Kurt Lothar Tank (1959) — and pave the way for its subsequent favorable reception. Perhaps with the major exception of Günter Blöcker (1959), who in his review for the conservative *Frankfurter Allgemeine Zeitung* detects in the novel a program for a highly entertaining nihilism, perceptive critics point to the directions in which scholarship eventually was to proceed. For example, Joachim Kaiser (1959) in the *Süddeutsche Zeitung* directs attention to Grass's depiction of the relationship between the lower middle class and the Nazi dictatorship (56), and Hans Magnus Enzensberger (1959) in his seminal, widely cited review emphasizes Grass's use of traditional elements of the classical *Entwicklungs-* and *Bildungsroman,* terms often used interchangeably. In addition, he notes as a positive feature the absence of the demonic — a category that precludes rational analysis — in the portrayal of Nazism (66) and perceptively observes that the precondition of the city of Danzig entering the realm of German literature was its irretrievable loss.

Despite Görtz's (1984a) laments that reviewers of *Die Blechtrommel* were at least partly to blame for the long-lived clichés about Grass as an author of unfettered imagination, unlimited story-telling skills, excruciating attention to detail, pronounced aversion to modernistic, experimental narrative forms, and preference for traditional narrative modes (10–13), there is no denying the fact that, as Görtz acknowledges (10), these reviewers helped shape the public's perception of an author who was going to dominate the postwar literary landscape. In his review of *Die Blechtrommel,* his first of a work by Grass, Marcel Reich-Ranicki (1960) singles out the author's alleged excessive garrulousness, tastelessness, and desire to shock his readers, but in a 1963 radio broadcast he partially retracted his negative assessment by blaming his errors of judgment on his stance as an "engaged" critic (in Görtz 1984a, 151–52) and admitted to his failure to grasp the significance of protagonist/narrator Oskar Matzerath — whose complexity he now reduced to an embodiment of "absolute inhumanity" (156).

Although the novel was not published in what was then the German Democratic Republic (GDR) until 1986, its first appearance did not go entirely unnoticed there. In 1960 East German writer Hermann Kant hewed to aesthetic conservatism and declared the novel unfit to be called "art" on account of its depiction of repellent incidents. More than a quarter of a century later and approximately three years before the fall of the Berlin Wall, East German critic Ursula Reinhold (1986) took a somewhat more lenient view. She conceded that the novel had the potential to provoke the West German establishment but faulted Grass for harboring anticommunist prejudices and for parodying people's serious quest for meaning because of his own inability to grasp historical processes. In looking back from the perspective of 1996 at the early West German reception of *Die Blechtrommel*, Jost Hermand (1996) observed that, owing to the prevailing postmodern condition of optional — or arbitrary — aesthetic standards in the 1990s, it was difficult to imagine that a literary work could have caused such a violent reaction — an observation that does not take into account that not all parts of the world had been affected by *fin-de-siècle* postmodernism. It can be seen that the reception of literary works depends to a considerable extent on the cultural context within which they are received. The fact that in the 1950s and early 1960s most members of the West German reading public were clinging to a comparatively stable and widely accepted aesthetic, adhering to conservative ideological norms and cherishing an interest in "high" culture, provides a partial explanation for the vehement response to Grass's first major work.

The publication of *The Tin Drum,* in Ralph Manheim's translation, in the United States in February 1963 was widely noticed on account of the acclaim and criticism that the novel had received in Europe. (Wilhelm Johannes Schwarz, 88–89 et passim, provides a brief survey of the initial reaction to the French translation in his 1969 study.) Among the critics who had informed American readers about the publication of the German original was Höllerer with his "Letter from Germany" (1960). The "flood of reviews" (O'Neill 1992, 279) was characterized by the same polarization of opinion that had greeted the German original. But, as the previously cited Patrick O'Neill indicates, there was one decisive difference not counting questions involving the quality of the translation: in the Federal Republic the objections raised were in part motivated by political reasons; reviewers in the United States, largely unfamiliar with the specific issues that German critics responded to, "very quickly elevated [Grass] to the essentially depoliticized status of a 'world author'" (283).

The considerable scope of critical assessments of *The Tin Drum* is evident from Ray Lewis White's compilation (1981). White provides excerpts from sixty-three reviews from publications ranging from those with a national circulation (for example, *Time, New York Times, Christian Science Monitor, Saturday Review*) on the one hand to newspapers with a limited local appeal (such as the Hickory, NC, *Record*) on the other. White's anthology is more inclusive than Sigrid Mayer's 1978 survey of Grass's American reception, in which she refers to approximately two dozen reviews (151) of *The Tin Drum,* and more useful than either Walter Ziltener's (1982) or Thomas Schaller's (1988) narrowly focused and arbitrarily selective reception studies. In my article "'Im Ausland geschätzt?'— Zur Grass-Rezeption in den USA" (1999), I trace Grass's fortunes in the United States and emphasize the central role of *Die Blechtrommel;* Orville Prescott, who reviewed the novel for the *New York Times,* voices both his appreciation ("brilliant") and censure ("very repulsive") of the "picaresque novel," as he called it. He judges the work in traditional terms and faults it for lacking a "modicum of restraint, selectivity and taste" (in White 1981, 3–4). Sigrid Mayer (1978) points out that, in contrast to some of the German comments mentioned above, the critical notices in American publications are rarely unrelentingly negative. However, American critics encounter difficulties in their attempts to define the novel. While the review of *The Tin Drum* together with Heinrich Böll's *Billiards at Half-Past Nine* and Uwe Johnson's *Speculations about Jacob,* which appeared in *Time* magazine (1963) under the title "The Guilt of the Lambs" (in White 1981, 2–3), establishes the thematic links of significant postwar works to the Nazi period, the search for stylistic criteria in and literary antecedents of Grass's novel proves to be more elusive. There is no unanimity as to whether the novel should be called fantastic, romantic, expressionistic, surrealistic, grotesque, absurd, realistic or quasi-naturalistic or, for that matter, whether it was inspired by Rabelais, Grimmelshausen, Goethe, Thomas Mann, Swift, Sterne, Melville, Joyce, Beckett, Nabokov, Faulkner, or Dos Passos (S. Mayer, 152). The considerable number of assumed literary progenitors, however, suggests that critics believed that with this, his first novel, Grass had arrived in the premiere league of fiction writers. In his 1963 review John Simon coins the phrase "The Drummer of Danzig," which emphasizes the importance of both protagonist/narrator Oskar and his Danzig environs as constitutive components of the novel and establishes *The Tin Drum* as the critical yardstick by which Grass's subsequent works are to be judged. Simon praises Grass's "linguistic superabundance," but he is critical of Manheim's translation (Sigrid Mayer also addresses the appropriateness of Manheim's English renderings in her 1976 essay). Furthermore, he calls the novel "a spectacular achievement" and a "German approximation" of that "quintessential modernist novel, James Joyce's *Ulysses*" (26). *The Tin Drum* remained on the bestseller list of the *New York Times* for three months and sold almost four hundred thousand copies during the years 1963 and 1964 (S. Mayer 1978, 153) — surely a propitious beginning for Grass's reception in the United States.

Oskar, "Enigma" and/or "Monster"

Reviews of the novel were gradually supplemented and replaced by more substantive and specialized scholarly articles and monographs as well as dissertations — many of which eventually found their way into print. Not surprisingly, critics tend to focus on the figure of Oskar because of his commanding presence in the events he retells via his drum and photo album. The considerable volume and range of critical opinion cannot be discussed exhaustively here; frequent reference to Oskar will be made in subsequent sections of this chapter. According to Volker Neuhaus (1982, rev. ed. 1988, 121), hardly any other figure in world literature has elicited as much venomous comment as Oskar. To be sure, the text of the novel provides support for condemning Oskar; for instance, Maria, incensed about Oskar's approaching her with the seductive fizz powder shortly after he surprised her and his putative father Alfred Matzerath during their tryst on the living-room sofa, calls him a "loathsome pig, a vicious midget, a crazy gnome, that ought to be chucked in the nuthouse" (*TD*, 290). But in contrast to some reviewers' unenthusiastic assessments, Hans Mayer's exceedingly negative characterization of Oskar (1967) as a "wicked imp [who] presents himself to the reader in the guise of an ugly and awful villain" and lacks "human" qualities (in H. Mayer 1971, 195) is not motivated by moral condemnation; rather, Mayer intimates that the prevalence of "psychotics, fools, criminals, monsters, artists of all kinds" in the novel of the mid-twentieth century seems to "imply something about the condition of a society" (199). Theodore Ziolkowski (1969) elaborates on Mayer's implication and states that Oskar, who begins his narrative with the unsettling admission: "GRANTED: I AM an inmate of a mental hospital" (*TD*, 15), embodies a trend in contemporaneous German literature. The protagonist, in the immediate postwar period most likely a returning soldier or *Heimkehrer* — as, for example, in the early fiction of Böll — has turned into a mental patient. By their choice of setting, such works as *Die Blechtrommel,* Friedrich Dürrenmatt's *Die Physiker* (1962; *The Physicists,* 1964), and Peter Weiss's *Die Verfolgung und Ermordung Jean Paul Marats* (1964; *The Persecution and Assassination of Jean-Paul Marat,* 1966) offer a troubling perspective, in that the insane asylum appears as normal and the outside world as abnormal. Ziolkowski acknowledges that *Die Blechtrommel* makes a valid contribution to the representation of history and credits Grass with a "brilliant move" in that he "has reversed the historical process: his hero moves symbolically back from the world of the grotesque through the madhouse to the everyday world" (357).

Alan F. Bance (1967) considers Oskar an "enigma" who has the potential of becoming "a new archetype of Western fiction" (147). Oskar's "dwarf stature reflects the immaturity and dwarfed morality of society" (151), and his attempt to grow in the chapter "Should I or Shouldn't I?" (book 2) parallels the fate of Germany, a country that, after engaging in destructive "games," is forced to face the reality of the postwar years (Bance expresses similar opinions in his 1980 contribution on *Die Blechtrommel*). Bance's view of Oskar as a representative character — albeit not an allegorical figure — appears to anticipate Robert Maurer's early warning (1968) against "equating Oskar totally with either a resurrected Christ or a contemporary Germany; with either the Artist as Young Dwarf or modern man pursued by Satanic forces and guilt" (102) because such one-sided explanations, albeit not entirely without merit, can hardly do justice to the complex figure of Oskar.

But for W. Gordon Cunliffe (1969) Oskar "serves as a substitute for Hitler" (76), and critic Peter Michelsen (1972) perceives Oskar as a quasi-mythological, virtually inhuman "monster." Irene Leonard (1974) implicitly ignores such readings and states that the Oskar of books 1 and 2 "represents a sane element in a crippled society" (13). She continues: "Oskar's resumed growth possibly symbolizes Germany's coming of age" but cautions that Oskar's "diseased back" may "signal the resurgence of tendencies opposed to a genuine German liberation" (17). In a more encompassing vein, Keith Miles (1975) posits that Oskar, "the satirist, the clown, the picaro, the innocent, the secular Messiah, the practitioner of black arts, the folklore dwarf and the autobiographical figure," is essentially a "historian" whose "challenging task" consists of writing "a report on the character and history of the German people in the twentieth century" (82). John Reddick (1975), who devotes an entire chapter of his book on the *Danzig Trilogy* to "the Meaning of Oskar," reiterates that "the figure of Oskar Matzerath . . . is unquestionably paramount in the novel," because he not only "combines the two outward roles as narrator-cum-protagonist, but is also compounded inwardly of two distinct personas" (58). These two personae are that of the "principled, cerebral, and, above all, detached" picaro (63) and that of what Reddick calls the "Tears' Persona" (63). The latter begins to assert itself "soon after Oskar's recommencement of growth" (73) and expresses itself in "Oskar's forlorn attachment to his mother, [and] his vain longing to have his love for Maria returned" as well as in his pervasive sense of guilt, a "recurrent motif" (77). Reddick also addresses the question of Oskar's credibility, especially in view of the latter's contradictory explanations concerning the key episodes of his jump or fall into the cellar in the chapter "Smash a Little Windowpane" (book 1) and his similarly voluntary/involuntary leap into Alfred Matzerath's grave in the chapter "Should I or Shouldn't I?" (book 2). In the end, Reddick suggests, Oskar's behavior displays a "characteristic note of uncertainty and openness" (86).

Whereas Michael Hollington (1980) credits Oskar with being a "virtuoso exponent of multiple, complex personae" (45), H. E. Beyersdorf (1980) expands on Oskar's unreliability as a narrator in that he "alters reality to suit his subjective conceptions of the moment" (130). Beyersdorf establishes various categories for Oskar's artful deceit but does not reach any overarching conclusion. Reddick's discovery in 1970 of the so-called *Urtrommel* versions in a closet of the Paris flat in which Grass composed *Die Blechtrommel* has spawned several publications on the genesis of the novel by Silke Jendrowiak (1979b), Reddick himself (1981), Detlef Krumme (1986, 19–27), Werner Frizen (1987a, 1987b), and Jochen Wittmann (1989). Most of these have had only a limited impact on the assessments of Oskar. Frizen (1991) points out that the *Urtrommel* does not support conclusions as to the precise origins of or model(s) for the figure of Oskar, because in the course of preparing the final, published version Grass radically changed his concept. He imposed, for example, a numerical symmetry on the novel that accentuates the analogy of personal story and general history. Thus Oskar's narrated life span revolves around the beginning of the Second World War on 1 September 1939. Born at the beginning of September 1924, Oskar is fifteen at the outbreak of the war and ends his narration fifteen years later in 1952.

Neuhaus (1979, rev. ed. 1992), perhaps the most consistent defender of Oskar, uses Oskar's own definition of genuine humanity, "childlike, curious, complex, and immoral" (*TD,* 80), to declare him to be one of the most humane characters in *Die Blechtrommel* because of his solidarity with the victims of society, notably Jewish toy merchant Sigismund Markus (56). Although the memorable figure of Oskar has lately been less intensely scrutinized than in the 1960s, events such as the production and screening of the film version of *Die Blechtrommel* and the publication of John Irving's novel *A Prayer for Owen Meany* (1989) have served to revive scholarly debate, which, however, is not likely to result in a consensus. Despite a host of interpretations, there remains the possibility that Oskar will continue to remain somewhat of an enigma. As one critic puts it: "It remains a moot point whether the dwarfish 'hero' . . . should be regarded as a mirror of his times or an abnormal, distorted caricature, or both" (Ireland 1990, 341–42).

In her investigation of the image of childhood in "literary presentations" (30) of the Third Reich, Debbie Pinfold (2001) proposes that Grass has joined the trend set by others, not only destroying the myth of the good child but also creating a new myth embodied by the "Kind-Dämon" or "Anti-Kind" who exhibits a distinctly hostile view of the adult world. Oskar is then evil, because he is a "pseudo-child with many adult attributes . . . whose very childish, self-centred attitudes parody those of contemporary adults" (90). The "pseudo-child" Oskar represents the "idea of the innocent delinquent"; he assumes the "apparent ignorance [and innocence] of childhood" in order to strike a pose of detachment from events that happen around him or in which he is involved, such as the *Reichskristallnacht* or the occurrences at the "The Polish Post Office" depicted in book 2, ch. 2. Therefore he is able to disclaim "*all* knowledge and responsibility" (147; my italics) — a categorical statement that would require some modification in view of Oskar's genuine lament about Sigismund Markus's death in "Faith, Hope, Love," the last chapter of book 1 (see also Brode 1976). Although Pinfold concedes that Oskar does not function as "an embodiment of Nazi values" (148) — after all, he is in danger of becoming a victim of euthanasia — he certainly cannot (and does not) claim to be a resistance fighter (see Neuhaus 1982), and his motivation for disrupting the Nazi rally is of an "aesthetic" rather than a political nature (Pinfold, 149). In conclusion, Pinfold poses the question of why Oskar, in his function as narrator "an extremely elusive entity" (151), goes to such great lengths "to blacken his childhood persona" (153) and speculates that it is perhaps a strategy to invoke sympathy for Oskar, the (adult) narrator — even though Oskar the child is hardly the "monster" portrayed by other critics.

Bildungsroman, Picaresque Novel, *Künstlerroman?*

From the very beginning, Grass criticism clearly had an international dimension, in that the publication of *The Tin Drum,* as indicated above, was a literary event that attracted considerable notice outside the German-speaking countries. One of the first scholarly endeavors, by William P. Hanson (1963), explores the relationship between "Oskar, Rasputin and Goethe." This relationship, in the words of Oskar a "conflicting harmony . . . [that] was to shape or influence my whole life" (*TD,* 90), is one of the key elements seized upon by those critics eager to relate the novel to the tradition of the *Bildungsroman.* Hanson identifies "Rasputinism" as a central feature that served Grass as the object of social criticism, and he concludes unconvincingly that *The Tin Drum* constitutes an "effort to harmonize violent opposites which is such a characteristic feature of German literature as a whole" (32). Henri Plard (1963) in his spirited, essayistic "defense" of *Die Blechtrommel,* in which he takes issue with previous critics' assumed misperceptions, implicitly modifies Hanson's thesis. He argues that, despite his wavering between Rasputin and Goethe, Oskar's desire for harmony is undermined by his prevalent black humor, which parodies the classical *Bildungsroman* in the tradition of Goethe. In this tradition, the harmonious, humanistic development of the youthful protagonist is of central significance. The "copiously illustrated thick volume entitled *Rasputin and Women*" (*TD,* 90), from which Oskar derived his notions about the primitive monk and "athletic faith healer" (*TD,* 92) at the czar's court, has been identified by Jean-Marie Valentin (1982) as *Der heilige Teufel: Rasputin und die Frauen* (1927; *Rasputin, the Holy Devil,* 1928) by René Fülöp-Miller (that is, Philipp Jakob Müller). Eberhard Mannack (1982) goes beyond Hanson in maintaining that Fülöp-Miller's widely read book encouraged an uncritical reception that catered to the irrational tendencies in the lower middle class to which the Nazis appealed. At the same time, Oskar may have derived the notion of the reincarnation of the savior — in the case of Rasputin a primitive, but mesmerizing seducer — from Fülöp-Miller. This reincarnation was not confined to the religious realm as in Oskar's trying to pass himself off as Jesus; rather, in assuming a religious role, Oskar merely mimicked another seducer who claimed to be a savior, that is, Adolf Hitler. The apparent dualism between Rasputin and Goethe, "the man of the Enlightenment" (*TD,* 91), is less conclusive than Oskar initially avers: death, fear, and superstition are also to be found in Goethe's *Die Wahlverwandtschaften* (1809; *Elective Affinities,* 1963), another text that Oskar cites frequently.

Some critics allude to or specifically mention the fact that *Die Blechtrommel* conforms in several respects to the generic characteristics of the picaresque novel, which had emerged as a distinct genre in sixteenth-century Spain following the fame of the anonymous *La vida de Lazarillo de Tormes* (ca. 1554; *The Life of Lazarillo de Tormes,* 1908) and had found imitators in many European countries, among them Alain-René Lesage's *Histoire de Gil Blas de Santillane* (1715–35; *The Adventures of Gil Blas,* 1807), Hans Jakob Christoffel von Grimmelshausen's *Der abenteuerliche Simplicissimus* (1669; *The Adventures of a Simpleton,* 1912), and Henry Fielding's *The History of Tom Jones, A Foundling* (1749). In a November 1970 interview with Heinz Ludwig Arnold, Grass explicitly acknowledged his indebtedness to the European tradition of the picaresque novel in general and to Grimmelshausen in particular (in H. L. Arnold 1963, 5th ed. 1978, 6). The first, fairly comprehensive attempt to analyze *Die Blechtrommel* in terms of the picaresque novel is Willy Schumann's 1966 article on the return of the picaro, in which he cites Thomas Mann's *Bekenntnisse des Hochstaplers Felix Krull* (1954; *Confessions of Felix Krull, Confidence Man,* 1955) as another conspicuous example of the revival of the genre in postwar German letters. Schumann deals with a number of traits to demonstrate Oskar's affinity to the picaresque tradition, notably his status as a conspicuous outsider — a status that is emphasized by his confinement in a mental hospital — who tells his life story (including his prenatal existence) by looking back from the vantage point of his "white-enameled, metal hospital bed" (*TD,* 15). Further picaresque traits include Oskar's voyeurism and the bawdiness of his depictions of sexual encounters; disapprovingly Schumann remarks that this practice borders on the pornographic (472). Schumann concedes that despite Oskar's travels to France with Bebra's theater troupe in the chapters "Bebra's Theater at the Front" and "Inspection of Concrete" (book 2), he does not entirely meet the requirements of a picaresque "peripatetic antihero" (469), since his existence until the end of the Second World War is firmly rooted in Danzig. The limits of Schumann's approach become evident when he interprets Oskar's use of the fiber rug (see Just 1972) and his assumption of the role of Christ (see Friedrichsmeyer 1965) primarily as efforts to disguise himself. Schumann's conclusion that the return of the picaresque novel, in which Oskar is assigned the function of passive recorder of events, can be attributed to the general lack of religious and ideological (*weltanschaulich*) direction after a devastating war lacks specificity concerning the novel's appeal. To be sure, in 1966 Schumann could not have known that Grass was going to return to Grimmelshausen twenty years after *Die Blechtrommel* and establish an explicit parallel between the end of the Thirty Years' War and that of the Second World War in *Das Treffen in Telgte* (1979; *The Meeting at Telgte,* 1981; see ch. 8).

In a slender volume Wilfried van der Will (1967) follows in Schumann's footsteps and analyzes the metamorphoses of the picaro in works of Thomas Mann, Alfred Döblin, Bertolt Brecht, and Grass. In his short segment on *Die Blechtrommel,* van der Will stresses in particular Bebra's role as mentor. Bebra not only initiates Oskar via a ritualistic kiss on his forehead in the scene at the circus (*TD,* 115); he also serves as Oskar's companion during the latter's foray into the world during his engagement entertaining the troops in France. As a "modern iconoclast" (66), Oskar is impervious to ideologies; as he remarks about his disruption of the Nazi rally, depicted in the often-quoted chapter "The Rostrum" (book 1), he also created turmoil at gatherings of "Reds and Blacks" and even "Boy Scouts" because "it was not only demonstrations of a brown hue that I attacked with my drumming" (*TD,* 124). Van der Will attributes to Oskar the desire for innocence that transcends both his own disillusionment and his disillusioning comments. Ultimately, van der Will ascribes the social satire in *Die Blechtrommel* to the partial identity of author and narrator, a claim contested by other critics, and the fact that Grass productively uses his own biography in a fictional text.

As early as 1967, Hans Mayer, here cited in translation (1971), dismissed the debate about the generic status of *Die Blechtrommel* as irrelevant; he declares Oskar to be a "grotesque artifice" (186) and "monstrosity" (194) fit for "neither the *Bildungsroman* nor the picaresque novel" (187). Mayer then engages in the "confrontation of two borderline cases" that represent the "highest sociability of the irresistible confidence man [Felix Krull] and the extreme lack of socialness [Oskar]"

(188). Their common bond is their existence as artists, evidenced by the "criminal and innate artistry of Felix Krull" (194) on the one hand, and Oskar's tin-drumming (and, one might add, glass-shattering) activities on the other. H. Mayer's cautionary note about the efforts to pin down *Die Blechtrommel* in traditional generic terms did not deter subsequent critics. Dietrich Droste (1969) offers suggestions for approaching Grimmelshausen's *Der abenteuerliche Simplicissimus* and *Die Blechtrommel* in the classroom, and Rainer Diederichs (1971) characterizes both Oskar and Felix Krull as examples of the modern picaro. Diederichs notes that Oskar is essentially a loner (*Einzelgänger*) who hails from the social milieu of the lower middle class and refuses to become a member of society (in books 1 and 2). He insists on his personal freedom, a freedom that he is able to enjoy under the guise of an ostensibly naïve but actually very clever three-year-old child, and rejects adherence to any and all ideologies. Oskar's self-chosen position allows him to view his environment and the world of adults, their foibles, and their susceptibility to political slogans with a critical eye. Conversely, Oskar's retarded growth prevents him from establishing meaningful relationships and gaining a foothold in middle-class life. Diederichs appears to be echoing Schumann when he seeks to establish the close relationship between the picaresque novel and the spiritual malaise of the postwar years. This malaise does not allow Oskar to hope for better times; he resigns himself to the meaningless repetitiveness of life. Even if Oskar does not formulate a moral in the traditional vein of the picaresque novel, Diederich's claim that Oskar does not articulate the question of guilt is hardly valid in view of Oskar's overpowering fear of the "Schwarze Köchin" (literally: black cook; translated by Manheim as "Black Witch") at the end of the novel. Although the episodic character of the picaresque novel is less pronounced in *Die Blechtrommel,* the fact that the narrative is presented as a fictive autobiography may lend some credence to Diederich's cautiously formulated conclusion that the presence of other generic patterns does not invalidate the claim that we are dealing with a modern specimen of an established novelistic genre.

Manfred Kremer (1973), who bases his article on the work of Schumann, van der Will, and other genre studies from the late 1960s and early 1970s, reiterates that one common element shared by Grimmelshausen's and Grass's novels is that they were written after destructive wars. He goes beyond his predecessors in pointing out that *Die Blechtrommel* tends to parody the picaresque novel rather than to naively imitate it (390). G. Richard Dimler (1975) analyses the picaresque novel tradition from a religious perspective. He sees the protagonists in Grimmelshausen's and Grass's works as "alienated heroes" in a triple sense: they are alienated from their environment, from themselves, and from

God. Surprisingly, Dimler surmises that Oskar overcomes his alienation and is united with Jesus at the scene of his arrest in Paris simply because he introduces himself to the detectives as Jesus in three languages (*TD*, 587).

The genre studies continued into the 1980s. Jürgen Jacobs (1983) opines that Grass's work is the most important example of the resurgence of the picaresque novel in postwar German literature and rejects attempts to classify it as either a *Bildungsroman*, a *Künstlerroman*, or a novel that shows the development of an artistically inclined individual who struggles to prevail against his bourgeois environment. In a speculative essay, Laurence A. Rickels (1985–86) situates Grass's work between the *Bildungsroman* and the picaresque novel and attempts to demonstrate the influence of Nietzsche. Hans Wagener (1988) bases his brief remarks about Oskar as a picaro primarily on Kremer (1973). Although the efforts to establish the literary predecessors of Oskar and to define the generic criteria of *Die Blechtrommel* are meritorious, perhaps they fall short in not sufficiently acknowledging, as Helmut Koopmann (1977) notes, Oskar's motivation in remaining a small child: to unmask the pronounced infantilism of an entire epoch (175).

Oskar's relationship to art and his status as an artist have been widely noticed. In her fairly detailed study, *The Skeptical Muse* (1974), Ann L. Mason considers Grass's "acute" problem to be how to define the "nature of the German artist and the form of his relationship to his society" (10), a problem that concerns not only Grass's "artist-figures" but the author himself — who has been attempting to suggest "parodic reevaluations" (10) of, for example, the genius cult. For Alexander Gelley (1967), Oskar is the "abstracted consciousness" of the novel and its "paradoxical, opaque, terrifying" spokesman, who, however, is not only the "teller of the tale but also its victim" (115, 122). In his 1967 essay, Idris Parry implicitly agrees with Gelley about Oskar's role as the "narrating consciousness" and the "arbiter of events." Specifically, Gelley perceives Oskar as an artist figure; without elaborating, he posits that the "nature of art itself" is "one of the most consistently elaborated themes" in the novel (122). Wesley V. Blomster (1969c) offers an intriguing glance at Oskar's artistic preferences. While critics usually praise Grass's attention to detail and historical accuracy, Blomster provides a corrective comment on an episode in the chapter "The Stockturm: Long-Distance Song Effects" (book 1), and, in a somewhat positivistic manner, faults Grass for not adhering to the actual date of the production of Richard Wagner's *Der fliegende Holländer* (1843; *The Flying Dutchman*, 1982) in 1939 as well as for taking considerable liberties with its libretto on occasion of the Matzeraths' and Jan Bronski's visit to the Opera-in-the-Woods at Zoppot, the "Bayreuth of the North," in the vicinity of Danzig. But Blomster credibly shows that the visit to Zoppot — which owing to

Oskar's glass-shattering intervention ends in utter chaos — serves Grass both to poke fun at bombastic grand opera and to parody Hitler's favorite composer by having the Wagner episode take place in "the summer of '33" (*TD,* 109), the year that marks the beginning of Nazi rule in Germany — albeit not yet in the Free City of Danzig.

While Oskar's rejection of Wagner is quite unambiguous, he is more equivocal about Wagner's contemporary Felix Dahn, whose monumental and immensely popular historical novel *Ein Kampf um Rom* (*A Struggle for Rome,* 1878) appeared in 1876, the same year in which the Bayreuth Festival opened, with the first production of Wagner's complete tetralogy, *Der Ring des Nibelungen* (1853; *The Ring of the Nibelung,* 1976). Oskar fondly calls Dahn's novel one of his "old standard works" (*TD,* 169) and identifies with the Byzantine general Narses, who defeated the Ostrogoths, because Narses was "undersized, a dwarf, a gnome, a midget" (*TD,* 319). It is then this identification that provides the main impetus for Oskar's critique of the death-defying nationalistic ideology that *Ein Kampf um Rom* conveys.

Manfred Durzak (1971b) rejects both the label of *Bildungsroman,* because Oskar's intellectual capacities are fully developed at birth, and that of picaresque novel, because Oskar leads a comparatively sheltered existence in the Matzerath family. To his family he appears as a three-year-old whose development has been arrested; actually, he is an "allegorical construction" (263) whose narrative is characterized by a high degree of reflexivity. Rather than dwelling on Oskar as an artist figure, Durzak discusses Oskar's teacher and mentor Bebra, a character who is not usually at the center of scholars' interest. Despite his warning about the advent of the Nazis when he first encounters Oskar in the circus, during the Second World War Bebra makes arrangements with them and entertains the German troops in France. He succeeds in continuing his career in postwar Germany and becomes boss of the West Concert Bureau that employs Oskar after he has resumed his drumming. After Bebra's death, Oskar inherits his business — but also the latter's guilt about remaining passive in the face of evil. Bernd Neumann (1985) endeavors to augment Durzak's approach by concentrating on those features that relate *Die Blechtrommel* to the subgenre of *Künstlerroman.* Neumann largely ignores books 1 and 2; instead he focuses on the postwar period and identifies Oskar as a representative of the "existentialist, skeptical" generation that came to the fore in the 1950s and, primarily via aesthetic means and via a quasi-Bohemian life style, expressed their unfocused opposition to the then emerging *Wirtschaftswunder* or "economic miracle" and its attendant materialistic orientation (49). As an artist and Bohemian Oskar both belongs to and opposes bourgeois society; as Bebra did before him, he experiences the problematic relationship between artist and society. In making available his art to the postwar public for "the pure, resounding gold of the postwar period" (*TD*, 551), Oskar becomes dependent on the economic structure that sustains the production and distribution of art; as a result, his oppositional impulses are stifled.

Coming to Terms with the Nazi Past; the Role of History

Dirk Grathoff (1970) contends that scholars have tended to concentrate on formal and aesthetic aspects of the novel. Yet in his short and rather general article Derek van Abbé (1969–70) is one of the first critics to establish an explicit connection between the novel and the so-called *Vergangenheitsbewältigung*, the postwar endeavors to come to terms with the Nazi past. These endeavors he attributes to the beginning preoccupation with both the literary and political past by a younger generation of writers and intellectuals. Indeed, the 1970s saw the appearance of a number of studies of *Die Blechtrommel* that reflected the new orientation of literary criticism promoted by members of the post-Nazi generation who had been exposed to or participated in the (West) German student movement of the late 1960s and early 1970s. The students' efforts to reform both academia and society at large eventually affected the institution of literary criticism, which in the first two decades of the postwar period had been dominated by the methodological approach of the close readings of texts — a method termed *werkimmanent*. This critical practice tended to regard texts as aesthetic constructs that were divorced from the various facets of their social context, especially their modes of production, distribution, and reception. In a radical departure from traditional modes of literary interpretation, in the late 1960s younger critics began to view literary works in a fashion that stressed the dependency of cultural systems and products on social structures and on socioeconomic conditions. As a corollary of this development, critical emphasis shifted from the producer of literary works and the texts' intrinsic structures to their communicative value and their recipients.

One of the first works written under the auspices of reception theory (*Rezeptionsästhetik*) is that by Georg Just (1972; see also Just 1973). Just bases his study of *Die Blechtrommel* on the work of reception theorists Hans Robert Jauß and Wolfgang Iser as well as that of Jan Mukarovski, a structuralist and member of the Prague School, and analyzes the problem of the novel's intended critical effect. Just sees the contrast between Oskar and the world of adults in the novel as the principle that is also operative in the constellation of reader and work, that is, the novel's portrayal of the pervasive mentality of the lower middle class. The prevailing attitude among the novel's readers constitutes, in Jauß's terminology, their horizon of expectations (*Erwartungshorizont*). The readers' horizon of expectations conflicts, however, with Oskar's narrative stance (which Just discusses in considerable detail), which has the function of criticizing and unmasking the world he describes. Furthermore, although Oskar structures his narrative according to the criteria of the *Bildungsroman*, he is basically a *Kunstfigur* (75), an artifice, and does not invite reader identification. In order to define Oskar's chief function, Just adopts the term *Verfremdung* (76), a key term of Brecht's theory of epic theater, that is variously translated as "alienation," "estrangement," or, in Russian formalist Viktor Shklovskii's use, "defamiliarization." In *Die Blechtrommel, Verfremdung* signifies the author's critical distance from his figure precisely because of Oskar's strangeness, a strangeness that invites a process of reflection on the part of the reader.

While Oskar is the major vehicle on the level of the aesthetics of effect (*Wirkungsästhetik*), Just chooses a two-pronged approach in analyzing those aspects of the novel that pertain to the aesthetics of representation (*Darstellungsästhetik*). He examines rhetorical devices, metaphors, symbols, leitmotifs, and, especially, objective correlatives such as the central motifs of the drum and Oskar's activity of drumming and the fiber rug in the chapter "On the Fiber Rug" (book 3), fizz powder in the chapter "Fizz Powder" (book 2), and the notorious eel episode in the chapter "Good Friday Fare" (book 1). The term "objective correlative" as coined by T. S. Eliot denotes a verbal formula referring to an object or sign that evokes a specific state of emotion at its occurrence and constitutes a complete congruence between object and emotion. Thus the fiber rug (re)kindles Oskar's desire for Sister Dorothea; similarly, the fizz powder is instrumental in Oskar's seduction of Maria Truczinski. In his extraordinary attention to *Dinge* (objects) that he endows with powers of their own (118), Grass radicalizes Eliot's concept. At the same time, the elevation of ordinary, trivial objects (fiber rug and fizz powder) to agents in sexual encounters, Just argues, denies the reader the sensation of titillation — hence the charge of obscenity, which presupposes the intent to titillate, is moot. The eel episode, which eventually leads to the death of Oskar's mother Agnes Matzerath, is more complex than the two other instances mentioned, but it is likewise indicative of Grass's arbitrary and startling use of objective correlatives. Since objective correlatives also function in the mediation of events from the political sphere, Just concludes that *Die Blechtrommel* is indeed a work that engages in social criticism.

However, Just assumed that Grass changed his authorial intent while writing the novel, with a resulting rupture in its structure. For this reason, in contrast to most other critics, he largely excludes book 3 from his discussion. He ultimately rejects the "existentialist" reading of Heinz Ide

(1968), which centers on the terrifying Black Witch, whose imminent arrival Oskar expects with great trepidation when the novel concludes. But Just concedes that there is a basic weakness in his analysis, in that his model of the aesthetics of effect in *Die Blechtrommel* is not applicable in the case of readers who ignore its ethical and critical function and prefer to regard it as a purely aesthetic construct.

Robert Leroy's book-length study of *Die Blechtrommel* (1973) is only marginally concerned with the aesthetics of effect and essentially provides a textual analysis in terms of the intrinsic approach suggested by Roman Ingarden's *Das literarische Kunstwerk* (1931; *The Literary Work of Art,* 1973). Nevertheless, Leroy acknowledges that the social background at the time of the novel's composition informs *Die Blechtrommel,* and he sharply rejects the hypothesis that book 3 is less successful or even superfluous. He singles out Oskar as the medium through which Grass articulates his criticism — a criticism that is directed against both pre- and post-1945 society. As the title of his 1975 essay indicates, Jürgen Rothenberg (see also Rothenberg 1976a) considers *Zeitgeschichte* (contemporary history) to be the constitutive element of the novel. He identifies Oskar's drumming as a sign of protest against the outbreak of the barbarism that becomes fully evident during the events of the organized burning of synagogues and looting of businesses owned by Jews on 9 November 1938 — euphemistically called the *Reichskristallnacht* (Crystal Night or Night of Broken Glass) — and he cites the case of trumpeter Meyn as an example of the perversion of values that was taking place with the ascent of Nazism. Meyn, who had turned from a communist sympathizer and a drunk into an SA man "of rigorous sobriety" (*TD,* 199), was charged with "inhuman cruelty to animals" because he tried to kill his four cats and was finally expelled from the SA "for conduct unbecoming a storm trooper." Oskar sardonically remarks that even Meyn's efforts to redeem himself, his acts of "conspicuous bravery" (*TD,* 201) during *Kristallnacht,* could not save him from disgrace. Meyn's case serves to underline the corruption of the moral value system that punishes cruelty to animals but condones and encourages violence against fellow human beings, in this instance the Jews. According to Rothenberg, Oskar does not confine himself to acoustic protests; inasmuch as he regards his two putative fathers responsible for the political choices they made, he does not allow them to escape the consequences of their decisions but plays an instrumental role in their respective deaths. The fathers are, then, representative of an entire generation's failure to weigh the consequences of their political options. Rather than depicting a private rivalry between father(s) and son, Oskar's deeds underline the political dimension of the novel. In Rothenberg's persuasive reading, Oskar's decision to grow at the end of the war and his unsuccessful endeavor to assume the responsibilities of an adult follows logically from the defeat of Nazi Germany. But the German people do not fully grasp the chance that *Stunde Null*, the zero hour, offers for a new beginning. In fact, Düsseldorf, the Rhenish metropolis where the Matzeraths find refuge (in book 3) after their expulsion from Danzig, epitomizes the business mentality of the "economic miracle" with its emphasis on material reconstruction and consumerism at the expense of probing the past, as Neuhaus (1991b) has shown.

In partial disagreement with Just (1972), Irmela Schneider (1975) stresses the mediation in narrative form of a specific historical-political context and focuses in sometimes heavy-handed Marxist diction on the structure of the novel: it encompasses the period from 1899 to 1953 — a period that in Schneider's view is dominated by Nazism/Fascism. Thus book 1 (1899–1938) deals with the time before the advent of Fascism, which on account of Danzig's status as a Free City did not hold full sway until the first major orchestrated eruption of violence against Jews during *Kristallnacht*. Book 2 covers the Second World War and the demise of Fascism (1939–45), and book 3 depicts the post-fascist era in postwar West Germany and the Federal Republic (1945–53). The importance Schneider attributes to the historical-political context is also evident from the fact that she "confronts" the fictive world of the novel with the ideology of Fascism and *Vergangenheitsbewältigung* as well as other background elements. Rather than trying to determine the novel's adherence to strict mimetic principles, her aim is to explore the aesthetic structuring of the novel's lower-middle-class personnel, their socio-economic status, their political and cultural activities, and so on. Only after elucidating these aspects does she discuss the narrative perspective that is determined by Oskar. Despite her disavowal of Just's reception model, in the final analysis she also acknowledges that Oskar's narration provides important impulses for the novel's reception. For example, in her analysis of Oskar and Jan Bronski's interaction in the chapter "The Polish Post Office" (book 2), Schneider skillfully points to the interdependence of private relations and politically significant events — in this instance the beginning of the Second World War.

In his brief essay, Josef Schnell (1975) states that *Die Blechtrommel* helps to enlarge and sharpen the perception of readers with regard to the historical period depicted, because the novel attacks their preconceived conceptions. Hanspeter Brode (1976; see also Brode 1977; 1979, 66–83) reads *Die Blechtrommel* as social history in fictional guise. While noting that the structure of the novel, in which the Second World War, flanked by the prewar and postwar periods, functions as the focal point, serves to emphasize the novel's sociohistorical and sociopolitical aspects, Brode points out that it is not the only factor; he cites a number of other examples that reflect the interrelatedness of events in the domestic sphere and at the front. Thus Oskar's luring Jan Bronski into the Polish Post Office corresponds to the beginning of the war, Oskar's seduction of Maria with the help of fizz powder signifies the occupation of France by German troops, his "bedroom triumphs" (*TD,* 306) in Mrs. Greff's flat are accompanied by the German invasion of the Soviet Union, and Alfred Matzerath's death signals the end of the Second World War. Oskar is then, according to Brode, an "allegory of the Nazi period" (88). At the same time, Brode turns Oskar into a "caricature of Hitler" (91) primarily on account of his drumming. Hitler was named "the drummer" because of his propagandistic skills and ability to influence the masses, but, as Neuhaus (1982, rev. ed. 1988, 51–53) justifiably objects, Oskar also uses his drum to disrupt Nazi rallies — even if he does not claim to be a "resistance fighter" (*TD,* 124). In addition, Oskar's special relationship with Sigismund Markus reminds him that he too is vulnerable, a potential victim of the Nazis' euthanasia program: "When they took away his [Oskar's] toy merchant and ransacked the shop, he suspected that hard times were in the offing for gnome-like drummers like himself" (*TD,* 203). Brode's reading is more convincing when he characterizes *Die Blechtrommel* as having been written to counteract the widespread tendency during the 1950s to indulge in a kind of amnesia and to suppress guilt feelings about the past and past complicity. It is thus the postwar (West) German reader — implied rather than actual — who is reluctant to remember the past that the novel addresses. Because Oskar does not participate in this general forgetfulness, Brode suggests that society has isolated him and declared him to be mentally incompetent. Such a contention is rather dubious in view of the fact that Oskar was confined because of his falsely assumed involvement in the murder of Sister Dorothea and that he will be released from the mental asylum at the end of the novel.

Brode — in contrast to Just (1972) — sees Maria, who has successfully suppressed all memories of the past and has become the quintessential representative of postwar consumerism during the "economic miracle" in the Federal Republic, as an embodiment of the type of reader whom the novel attempts to reach. It follows that Brode considers book 3 absolutely essential in that it provides an integral part of the narrative framing device. Oskar tells his story from his hospital bed as a warning against the pervasive inability to mourn that Alexander and Margarethe Mitscherlich decried in their *Die Unfähigkeit zu trauern* (1967; *The Inability to Mourn,* 1975). In the "Onion Cellar" chapter of book 3, Grass satirically draws attention to this perceived emotional and affective deficit of postwar society (see also Sabine Richter 2004). Hence, according to Brode, *Zeitgeschichte* provides the focal point of *Die Blechtrommel;* it follows, he claims, that approaches concentrating on elements of the picaresque novel are ultimately wanting.

Less interested in the overt manifestations of *Zeitgeschichte,* Lore Ferguson in her 1976 interpretation, originally a 1967 dissertation, provides specific insights by means of elucidating the function of objects. These objects range from the skirts of Oskar's grandmother to his drum and include a host of other inconspicuous, insignificant "things" that, beyond their purpose to serve as illustrative details of everyday life, have the capacity to cause emotional responses but also highlight the characters' conscious or unwitting involvement in politics and history — as in the scene in which Alfred Matzerath tries to swallow the "party pin" (*TD,* 394). Heinz Hillmann (1976) poses the rarely articulated methodological problem of how literary scholarship, which prefers readings that at first glance seem *werkimmanent* but actually are dependent on implicit, psychologically, historically, and sociologically grounded comparisons, can test the veracity or probability of representations of "reality" in literary texts. Hillmann suggests the "confrontation" of literary text and the corresponding segment of reality via a comparison of literary text and social-science text. The latter presumably entails a higher degree of objectivity than the experience of "reality" as mediated via individual subjects. When compared to more encompassing analyses of Fascism, such as that by Marxist philosopher Ernst Bloch, Grass reduces the motivation of members of the lower middle class — notably Alfred Matzerath and trumpeter Meyn — to join the Nazis to their frustration with a rather meaningless existence and their compensatory desire. Despite this apparently deficient and reductive procedure, Grass's choice of Oskar as narrator signifies a selective, subjective perspective that is circumscribed by his petit-bourgeois-cum-artist's horizon and does not aim at an inclusive representation of his world. In his emphasis on the assumption that literary texts "interpret" social reality (25) and in his tendency to privilege sociological investigations, Hillmann offers a prime example of the methodological shift that was taking place in the 1970s.

Elisabeth Pflanz's 1976 dissertation on the sexuality and sexual ideology of the first-person narrator in *Die Blechtrommel* is a forerunner of the feminist studies of the 1980s and 1990s on Grass's works by critics such as Barbara Garde (1988) and Claudia Mayer-Iswandy (1991). Pflanz suggests that, in contrast to the explicit or implicit assumptions of several reviewers, Grass's violation of bourgeois sexual norms and disregard of sexual taboos is not intended to establish emancipatory sexual practices that gradually evolved as a consequence of the student movement. Rather, Pflanz reasons, Grass's 1968 defense against the charges of blasphemy and pornography in the "Affaire Ziesel" (documented in Arnold and Görtz 1971, 303–27) and his invocation of the mimetic principle essentially serve to preserve patriarchal sexual morality. Despite engaging in some abnormal and even pathological features and practices, Oskar essentially conforms to accepted moral norms. In contrast to Just's (1972) categorical rejection of Oskar as an identification figure, Pflanz stresses the "normalcy" of Oskar's sexual practices, which allows (male) reader identification. Yet in agreement with Walter Schönau's psychoanalytical approach (1974), Pflanz concludes that the reader has several options: morally condemning Oskar, emphasizing the aesthetic qualities of the novel, or acknowledging the existence of infantile sexual fantasies in him- or herself and seeking to come to terms with them.

Gegenwartsliteratur und Drittes Reich (Contemporary Literature and the Third Reich), the title of a collection of essays edited by Hans Wagener (1977), had clearly become a topic of interest even in mainstream Germanistik by the 1970s. In a substantial and repeatedly reprinted article Helmut Koopmann (1977) ignores reception theory and the construction of the reader. Instead he concentrates on Grass's achievement with regard to the literary analysis of Nazism in *Die Blechtrommel:* that is, his encompassing portrayal of the lower middle class as the social stratum that supported Hitler. Unlike Thomas Mann and other exiled writers, Grass dispensed with the demonization of Nazism or the suggestion of the German people's innate propensity for Nazi ideology — an argument that was about twenty years later insistently but unconvincingly advanced by Daniel Jonah Goldhagen in his *Hitler's Willing Executioners* (1996). Rather, Grass shows how Alfred Matzerath, fellow traveler par excellence "who espoused the forces of order at a relatively early date" (*TD*, 115), gradually succumbs to the lure of Nazi propaganda and the spectacle of the Nazi Sunday demonstrations in which he actively participates. Conversely, Oskar, as he explains in the chapter "The Rostrum" (book 1), has seen the rear of the rostrum and has become "immunized . . . against any magic practiced in any form whatsoever on rostrums" (*TD*, 119). Yet Oskar's sober observation and description of the rise of Nazism in Danzig does not induce him to seek an explanation for the causes of the Nazis' success beyond the world of the little people — both followers and eventual victims — that he so masterfully evokes. Although Grass tends to confine himself to the description of historical processes — rather than offering an explanation of their causes — in the milieu of shopkeepers and their ilk, he is, Koopmann argues, vitally interested in the legacy of Nazism and its potential for survival in the postwar period. This potential threat has continued to haunt Grass in subsequent works — and he did not always escape the temptation to use the topic of *Vergangenheitsbewältigung* in the service of party politics also in his fiction (see, for example, ch. 6).

In what amounts to a revisionist stance, Silke Jendrowiak (1979a) foregrounds the artistic qualities of the novel. She proceeds from the hypothesis that *Die Blechtrommel* served Grass as an aesthetically complex vehicle for clarifying his own artistic and social views. Grass had begun developing these views in the late 1950s in an attempt to come to grips with his position as a then largely unrecognized artist, with his origins in the Danzig milieu of the lower middle class, and with his experience of National Socialism. Protagonist Oskar presents himself as an autonomous artist but instead turns out to be a complacent member of the lower middle class. His "hubris" is evident from the fact that his assumed autonomy is merely a peculiar form of conformity, and in his autobiography his actions appear governed by childlike play in book 1, youthful puberty in book 2, and the abortive endeavor to become a mature adult in book 3 (214). According to Jendrowiak, then, it is not a question of discovering parallels between author Grass and first-person narrator Oskar; rather, *Die Blechtrommel* constitutes Grass's process of self-examination, which results in his bidding farewell to the dream of the autonomous artist who transcends his lowly origins (217). In doing so, Grass, in parodistic fashion, takes issue with postwar works that, in the manner of the *Künstlerroman* and, notably, Thomas Mann's *Doktor Faustus* (1947; *Doctor Faustus,* 1948), tend to both demonize Nazism and extol the artist in the classical-romantic mold. Furthermore, Jendrowiak identifies Gottfried Benn as another of Grass's targets. Benn, after his beginnings as an expressionist poet and a brief dalliance with Nazism followed by a kind of "inner emigration," was celebrated in the postwar period as a supreme artist who strove for absolute values (see also ch. 14). She further asserts that the dominant ideology of *Gruppe 47*, generally credited with playing a decisive role in the rebirth of literature after the Second World War, turned out to be a hindrance to Grass's development. After an abortive initiative to formulate a political agenda, many members reverted to the time-honored concept of the artist who proclaims universal truths from the ivory tower of individualism and intellectual elitism. Jendrowiak deviates from critics such as Just (1972) and Brode (1976) in postulating that Grass ultimately fails to provide a convincing socio-psychological explanation that would support his moral appeal to his German readers and enable them to productively reexamine their concept of art and history, because the model he provides — the close interrelationship between middle-class mentality and the artist on the one hand and middle-class mentality and Nazism on the other — proves to be insufficient.

Without referring to Jendrowiak (1979a) and without concerning herself with the problematics of the *Künstlerroman,* Judith Ryan (1983) engages in a fairly extended comparison of *Doctor Faustus* and *The Tin Drum.* She acknowledges Henry Hatfield's 1967 "amusing parenthetical comment" about the "analogy" (Hatfield, 125) between the two novels and conceives of Grass's work as "an answer" to that of Thomas Mann.

As the title of her study, *The Uncompleted Past,* reveals, Ryan follows the well-established pattern of analyzing *The Tin Drum* as an "attempt to come to terms with nazism" (56). She identifies various elements in both novels that signify the shift of emphasis that has taken place from Mann to Grass, among them that of social class: Mann idealizes the country folk among whom protagonist Adrian Leverkühn grows up, Grass caricatures the petit-bourgeois family that forms Oskar's social environment. Ryan persuasively views Oskar's being torn between Goethe and Rasputin as not only a parody of Goethe's *Faust* figure with his proverbial two souls but as a possible radicalization of the dualism inherent in Adrian Leverkühn. Grass "de-mythicizes" the Faustus figure by not having Oskar make a pact with the devil, because he "belongs to the devil's party from the outset" (61). Some of Ryan's assertions are factually incorrect or of dubious validity. For example, Oskar explicitly denies that Agnes Matzerath was "forced" to eat fish again (*TD,* 159), and it is the eel episode rather than Agnes's death that may be called "the most grotesquely repugnant in German literature" (Ryan, 60). In characterizing "Oskar's rebellious grandfather" as "the paradigm of the anarchist" (63), Ryan overlooks the possibility that Joseph Koljaiczek's incendiary acts may also have been motivated by feelings of (Polish) nationalism. Her statement that the "idea of working through guilt by writing about it" is "patently inappropriate in Oskar's case" appears to undermine her assumption of the "inescapable" presence of the Black Witch, particularly in the last chapter (65). These quibbles aside, Ryan's analysis of Grass's "attempt to de-mythicize nazism" (68) appears to be cogent.

Hans Dieter Zimmermann's rereading of the novel more than twenty years after its first publication (1983) largely dispenses with references to other secondary literature and offers a summary survey that does not assign chief priority to the representation of *Zeitgeschichte* but admits it under the heading of "historical novel." Conversely, Donna K. Reed (1985) assigns *Doctor Faustus, The Tin Drum,* and Böll's *Billiards at Half-past Nine* the status of "classics on Nazism" (7) — albeit classics that differ in several respects: "Whereas Mann pursues what he sees as the philosophical sources of Nazi ideology at great length, Grass shows less interest in the search for its alleged intellectual precursors" (26). In previous comparisons of Grass with Mann and Böll it had been pointed out that Grass, in focusing on Oskar's social milieu, is "the most avowedly conscious of the historical significance of his petit bourgeois characters" (30). Reed's arguments against those critics who stress the normalcy of the middle-class milieu are unconvincing: the "dwarf" Oskar is the "'little man' in the extreme" who "provides an exaggerated mirror image of these grotesquely evasive little folk" (28). Basing her arguments to some extent on Mason's essay (1974), Reed further explores the novel's rendering of "the identification of art and politics under Hitler" (69), the "quasi-religious appeal" (73) of Nazism and, perhaps less compellingly, the "psycho-sexual" (76) causes of both "the Dusters' and the SA's acts of belligerence" (77). Reed's claim that Oskar's art, his drumming and shattering of glass, is completely "destructive" (78), requires modification; after all, the tin drum functions, as Reed acknowledges (144), as a tool for evoking the past. In terms of structure, Reed classifies *The Tin Drum* as an "open" (112), "anti-classical" and "anti-Wilhelm Meister" (113) novel that, in combination with stylistic and narrative devices, "foster[s] the desired skeptical attitude in readers" (115) as an antidote "against the widespread postwar tendency to repress guilt" (119). In reiterating that the three works by Mann, Böll, and Grass "continue to stand out as the most successful novels on the Nazi epoch" (149), Reed's study belongs to the category of contributions that analyze the novel in terms of *Vergangenheitsbewältigung*. Her forte lies in the extended comparative analysis of the three works mentioned.

Hannelore Mundt (1989) resumes the discussion about the relationship between *Doktor Faustus* and *Die Blechtrommel* by exploring the "consequences" of the former for the development of postwar literature in general and Grass's novel in particular. She engages in a lively defense of the lower middle class, which, she avers, has received low marks from critics too eager to adopt Oskar's perspective and to overlook positive traits. For instance, Alfred Matzerath genuinely loves Agnes and cares for her despite her adulterous relationship with Jan Bronski, and the members of the Matzerath social circle tolerate greengrocer Greff's homoerotic inclinations. In the final analysis, Mundt adds, these positive traits do not excuse politically irresponsible behavior on the part of the characters, but they do contribute to a fairer assessment. One of the chief factors that prevent Alfred Matzerath and his ilk from comprehending Nazism as a destructive political movement is its unwitting elevation to the position of a pseudo-religion, a position formerly reserved for art. The "most sinister of all confrontations" (*TD*, 116) in the Matzeraths' living room between the "gloomy" portraits of Ludwig van Beethoven, representative of the humanistic-classical epoch, and Hitler, representative of an inhumane, nationalistic ideology, is indicative of the exclusive devotion that both representatives demand. Beethoven appears to give Alfred Matzerath the "strength" for an act of resistance when he hesitates to deliver Oskar into the hands of the Nazi doctors practicing euthanasia. But in the end neither Beethoven's elucidation of "destiny" nor Hitler's expounding on "providence" (*TD*, 185 and 211) can save Alfred Matzerath. In book 3, Mundt claims, the mitigating circumstances in the portrayal of the lower middle class — for example, the display of solidarity — have disappeared because the tension between Oskar's authorial and narratorial perspectives is no longer in evidence. Oskar resumes his career as an artist in the role of a "miracle man, a faith healer, and a little short of a Messiah" (*TD*, 555) and enables his audience to escape the confrontation with their past by reverting to infantilism. Through his grotesquely exaggerated portrayal of Oskar's messianic, artistic qualities, Grass undermines the traditional German view of the artist as leader, a notion perpetuated in *Doctor Faustus.* Yet, Mundt continues, Grass's attitude toward artists is ambivalent because he allegedly claims to represent "the conscience of the nation" (86) — a conclusion that Mundt derives from non-literary texts that Grass penned after the publication of *Die Blechtrommel* while she ignores other utterances in which Grass rejects the label. Grass's ambivalence is attributable to the contradictory elements in his perception: while he parodies the definition of Germany in terms of high culture in the manner of Thomas Mann, his creation of Oskar, the artist, tends to affirm the dominant position of art and its inability to function in a socially responsible way.

In his voluminous and exceedingly detailed study of *Die Blechtrommel,* in which he productively uses the exploration of the intellectual currents of the 1950s for the interpretation of the figure of Oskar, Dieter Arker (1989) establishes the close interrelationship of literature and politics, of artist and citizen. Grass composed the novel in Paris during his "existentialist phase," a phase that was superseded by his engagement for the Social Democratic Party after the novel had been published (xxiii). *Die Blechtrommel* is then a *Schwellenroman* or a novel at the threshold of a new artistic and political orientation, one that combines elements of Grass's work in the absurdist vein, evident in his early lyrics and plays, on the one hand, and his newly found political awareness on the other (xxiv). Hence the reader has to contend with the novel's inexplicable aspects ("Ungereimtheiten"; 58) such as Oskar's "decisions" to be born, to stop growing on his third birthday, and to resume his growth at the end of the Second World War. Arker, who does not refer to Werner Frizen's essay (1986) on the affinity of *Die Blechtrommel* to the theater of the absurd, sees lyric and drama as forms in which Grass experimented and tried out his prose fiction projects. The novel's special place in Grass's artistic development is particularly evident from Oskar's "split" and "synthetic" character; he is both an unreliable narrator and someone who annoys his readers by insisting on remembering the past. In addition, he is also both an amoral monster and one of the most humane characters. History in *Die Blechtrommel* is then largely represented as an absurd, violent process, a concept influenced by Albert Camus. Grass's profound distrust of all ideologies reflects the prevailing attitude of his generation, which is summarized in the title of sociologist Helmut Schelsky's *Die skeptische Generation* (1958; The Skeptical Generation); Grass's adoption of the theory of totalitarianism, which postulates the affinity between Nazism and Communism, is evident, for example, in Meyn's opting for the Nazis. In his painstaking analysis, Arker does not confine himself to *Die Blechtrommel* but traces Grass's further artistic development in order to indicate its connection to his engagement for the Social Democrats.

In a retelling of key passages of the novel, Werner Schwan (1990) perceives as its theme the events of the Nazi period and the efforts in the postwar years to come to grips with it. Curiously at odds with most assessments of Oskar is his observation about a "moving love story" (47) when Oskar is ultimately unable to find fulfillment with regard to the great love of his life, Maria. In a different vein, Hermand (1996) deduces from the initial reception of *Die Blechtrommel,* which concentrated mainly on the charges of obscenity and blasphemy, that during the late 1950s and early 1960s conservative reviewers wanted to avoid discussing the topic of Fascism, which assumed such significance later on. But in contrast to most critics, who view Grass's literary *Vergangenheitsbewältigung* in a positive light and acknowledge its critical impetus, Hermand, in developing ideas he had voiced before (1979), opines that the novel does not offer an analysis of Fascism that is to be taken seriously. Rather, Grass wallows in the representation of "animalistic" aspects of the lower-middle-class milieu — eating, sex, digestion, and bedwetting (15) — at the expense of introducing a moral and intellectual dimension. Hermand's interpretation smacks remotely of the criticism the novel was subject to in the GDR, where scholars objected to the novel's limited intellectual horizon, which did not transcend that of its characters (Streul 1988, 84–87). Oskar himself, Hermand suggests, is a product of his environment and does not significantly rise above it because in the 1950s Grass had not yet overcome the narrow sphere of his lower-middle-class origins. In the final analysis, Hermand opines, Grass wrote his novel from the position of a nonconformist without a firm ideological conviction — an appraisal that tends to deemphasize the consistent pattern of *Zeitgeschichte* underlying the novel, which was considered a strength by various scholars.

In a radical yet unconvincing attempt to reevaluate the literature of the pre-unification Federal Republic, Frank Schirrmacher (1990) of the influential conservative *Frankfurter Allgemeine Zeitung* departs from the widely accepted notion of the oppositional role of writers such as Böll, Grass, and Martin Walser and maintains that their works actually served to exonerate West German society and to provide a reassuring substitute for its lacking engagement with regard to facing and accepting the Nazi past. Hence, Schirrmacher continues, the assumption that these writers had to prevail in a largely hostile public sphere dominated by reactionary and nationalistic voices is inaccurate and was fostered by the writers themselves. Conversely, in 1997 I drew attention to the well-documented literary and political opposition that especially *Die Blechtrommel* encountered upon its publication and suggested that Schirrmacher's attempted reevaluation may be seen as part of an effort to declare postwar literature a closed chapter and promote a "shift in the direction of letters in the new Germany" (31) that both shuns the postwar *Gesinnungsästhetik* (ideological aesthetics) with its alleged emphasis on "extra-literary" topics and embraces pure aesthetics and conservative values instead.

The Holocaust and Its Consequences

German reunification did not put an end to the discussions of the Nazi past in general and Grass's *Die Blechtrommel* in particular. Although both toy merchant Sigismund Markus and the survivor of the Treblinka concentration camp, Mariusz Fajngold, are comparatively minor figures, they, as the only Jewish representatives in the first two books of the novel (for the third, unheralded, representative, see Sabine Richter, below), have received a fair share of attention. Markus, in particular, has been classified as "the best-known Jewish figure in post-war German fiction" (Prawer 1985, 95), a sentiment echoed by Sander Gilman (1988, 272), and has received the lion's share of attention. Yet Markus is "linked" to Fajngold; they "frame the Second World War and neither can be understood without the other" (Preece 2000a, 615). As we know, the history of literary criticism is not without ironic twists. Before turning against Grass, in 1963 Reich-Ranicki, as a Jew a victim of Nazi persecution, credited Grass with having resolved the difficult problem of adequately portraying Jewish figures in postwar letters without succumbing either to conspicuous philo-Semitism or maudlin sentimentality (in Reich-Ranicki 1992a, 38–39) and rejected the charge of anti-Semitism raised against Grass by an East German critic (170–71). In his 1983 essay, Bruce Donahue presents Markus and Fajngold as projecting an "alternative ethos" to the "dualistic" world view embodied in the dichotomy of Goethe-Rasputin, inasmuch as they practice an "earthy humanism" and must therefore be counted as "two of the most positive characters in the novel" (115). Donahue's persuasive argument takes a somewhat unexpected problematic turn when he associates the two Jewish characters with Christ on account of the "suprahuman suffering they have endured" (119).

Hans Dieter Zimmermann (1985) offers a similarly positive view of Markus, whose individual fate he interprets as representative of the collective fate of Jews under Nazism. In Zimmermann's reading, Markus's unrequited love of Agnes Matzerath transcends the personal and reflects the unhappy state of relations between Germans and Jews (296). Positive assessments of Markus such as those by Donahue and Zimmermann are implicitly and disdainfully rejected by Ruth Angress [Klüger] (1985) who summarily and unfairly dismisses the toy merchant as a "pathetic, ridiculous victim" (223). Similarly, Sander Gilman (263–64) concentrates on Markus's speech patterns, which, he contends, reflect Grass's prejudicial notions of Jewish identity — an assertion that is disproved by Preece (619) and put into context by Prawer (100). Angress's contemptuous dismissal of Markus — a "quintessentially human" figure in the dissenting view of one critic (Brody 1996, 99) — serves to buttress Ernestine Schlant's thesis in her book *The Language of Silence* (1999) that Grass displays "an ingrained obtuseness and insensitivity to those who suffered and died" by engaging in "verbal dexterity" (71). Yet, as I suggested in my article of 2001 (203), the register Grass chose for the episode of Markus's suicide is both appropriate and effective in its restraint and understatement. Schlant's argument about the absence of the Holocaust in Grass's fiction is further weakened by her — inexplicable — failure to mention Fajngold at all. Richard Weisberg (2000) discerns in Schlant's argument "a surprisingly unsophisticated notion of the way stories affect readers" and credits Grass with being "unsurpassed . . . in capturing forthrightly and imaginatively an event that his mainstream readers would surely have preferred to forget. . . ." And, as Peter O. Arnds (2004a, 9 n. 14; see also Arnds 2002) has pointed out, Schlant's failure to refer to other, non-Jewish, Nazi victims does not make her claims more convincing.

In fact, the "causal link" (Preece, 618) between the Holocaust and the expulsion of more than ten million Germans from Danzig and the territories east of the Oder-Neisse line, the de facto border between (East) Germany and Poland from 1945 to 1990 (the border was officially recognized by the Federal Republic as a precondition for reunification) is provided by survivor Fajngold, who lost his entire extended family at Treblinka. Haunted by his memories, it is he who takes over Matzerath's store and flat — conceivably as the instrument of retributive justice (see Brandes 1998, 24). Yet, as Scherf (2000, 69–70) argues, when Fajngold's memories of his loved ones begin to dim and he proposes to Maria, she rejects him on account of her latent anti-Semitism. Scherf concedes, however, that the official Polish/Russian policy of expelling Germans may have been a motivating factor — even if the Matzeraths' future in likewise war-ravaged West Germany may not have been a particularly promising prospect. Although the evidence does not necessarily confirm Grass's reading of the historical developments that caused the mass expulsion, the novel clearly conveys his conviction, which has the force of a moral imperative, that "it is because of the Holocaust that the Germans have to leave" (Preece, 618). In fact, as Wilhelm Johannes Schwarz (1969; rev. ed. 1971, 15) briefly points out, Grass delves deeply into the changeful history of Danzig before depicting the arrival of the Poles with "bag and baggage" (*TD*, 398); without doubt, such depiction is intended to enable the reader to perceive the expulsion as yet another chapter in a long chain of wars and destruction.

Not until the 1990s is the controversial topic of expulsion, which Grass was to address more comprehensively decades later in the novella *Im Krebsgang* (2002; *Crabwalk* 2003), tackled by Herman Beyersdorf (1992) in relation to *Die Blechtrommel.* Beyersdorf proposes — not quite convincingly — to violate a taboo of long standing by drawing attention to the act of expulsion that has hitherto been glossed over. He categorizes *Die Blechtrommel* as a work of *Vertreibungsliteratur* (literature of expulsion; 48), but he is at pains to emphasize that Oskar's sorrow about the loss of his home (*Heimat*) also entails an unambiguous rejection of all attempts to alter the status quo (52). Beyersdorf's observations are supplemented by Ervin C. Brody (1996), who provides a different perspective on the "Polish-German conflict" (79) by citing instances of Oskar's unambiguous sympathies for the Poles, such as the magical incantation of the gallant Polish cavalry, which comes to the rescue of Victor Weluhn after he — unlike Jan Bronski — has managed to escape from the beleaguered Danzig Polish Post Office. In the debate about expulsion, the concept of *Heimat* assumes paramount significance, not only in *Die Blechtrommel* but in the *Danziger Trilogie* as a whole, as Gertrude Cepl-Kaufmann (1986) has shown.

As to Jewish figures, Sabine Richter (2004) credibly claims that Jewish figures do not entirely disappear in book 3 of the novel. Although her wholesale characterization of *all* of Grass's figures as caricatures will hardly find universal approval, Richter's observation that the author's relationship to both Poles and Jews is ambivalent seems apt; she paraphrases Reich-Ranicki's observation that the author avoids sentimentalizing Jews, turning Poles into heroes, and demonizing Nazis. But Richter draws attention to a third Jewish figure, the owner of the "Onion Cellar" (see also Brode 1976), Ferdinand Schmuh, who hires the "Rhine River Three." His name gives Schmuh away; it is derived from the Yiddish word for deception or sham; furthermore, his pseudo-servile manner as well as the fact that he spent his childhood and youth in Budapest and Vienna, provide strong hints as to his Jewish origins. Analogously to his habit of killing a specific number of sparrows by shooting them and then feeding the survivors — a procedure that artificially creates a feeling of guilt to be followed by atonement — he makes his guests weep profusely by having them slice onions without causing them to genuinely mourn. By portraying Schmuh, who can be presumed to be a Jew, as an impostor, Richter writes, Grass comes dangerously close to using an anti-Semitic stereotype. It remains to be seen whether the assumption that each victim is also a potential perpetrator will be generally accepted.

The question as to whether or how to write about Jewish figures is part of the larger problem of whether it is possible to write at all after the Holocaust in the face of Theodor W. Adorno's famous injunction, in which he postulated that it was "barbaric" to write poems after Auschwitz — a dictum that Grass sought to refute in his essay "Schreiben nach Auschwitz" (1990; "Writing after Auschwitz," 1990) by insisting on continuing to produce poetry, dramas, and fiction (see also ch. 8). Jin-Sok Chong (2002) takes Grass's thesis as his starting point and compares *Die Blechtrommel,* a work characterized by its openness, with Paul Celan's lyrics, often defined as hermetic, as alternative possibilities of literary responses to the Holocaust.

Mythological, Allegorical, and Psychological Readings

In contrast — but usually not in direct opposition — to scholars who emphasize the dimension of *Zeitgeschichte,* several critics in the 1960s and 1970s opted for an approach that focuses on the mythical aspects of the novel. Erhard M. Friedrichsmeyer explores "Aspects of Myth, Parody and Obscenity" in *Die Blechtrommel* (1965) and interprets Oskar's imitation of Christ in the chapters "The Imitation of Christ" and "The Dusters" in book 2 as a "parody of the divine child myth" (243) as formulated by Carl Gustav Jung and Karl Kérenyi. Friedrichsmeyer states that Oskar is not a "monstrosity" springing from the author's "warped imagination"; rather, he is indicative of the "horror of man's alienation from himself" (252). Somewhat similarly, A. Leslie Willson (1966) conceives of Oskar as a "grotesque Everyman longing for the white of innocence, [who is] fascinated by the red of evil, seeking deliverance from the black witch of guilt" (138). Hildegard Emmel (1963) discusses the problem of Oskar's guilt with regard to the deaths of his mother and his two putative fathers as well as that of Sister Dorothea in less metaphysical terms. She observes that Oskar, although not a criminal in the strict sense of the law, parodies admissions of guilt. Still, his parody allows us to draw a conclusion as to the existential guilt of humankind in general — a conclusion that, for example, diverts attention from the specific historical circumstances under which Alfred Matzerath and Jan Bronski died.

Willson's assessment of 1966 is not shared by David Roberts (in Jurgensen 1973), who sets out to "examine the connexion between Oskar's inner world and the external world" (45) by exploring the "psychological logic and mythological structuring" (46) of the novel in Jungian terms. Although Roberts, in partial agreement with M. K. Sosnoski (1971), dwells fairly extensively on Oskar's Jungian characteristics, he concludes by elevating Oskar the figure (as distinguished from Oskar the individual) to the symbol "of the coming of the Antichrist, of the rise of National Socialism and of the horror of the second world war" (70). While Roberts does not exclude the historical dimension altogether, in the end he sees Oskar and Adrian Leverkühn, protagonist of Thomas Mann's *Doktor Faustus,* as twentieth-century successors of *Faust.* But because of Oskar's failure "to achieve the goal of individuation" (72), there is no prospect of redemption for him, and at the end the Black Witch, the opposite of grandmother Anna Koljaiczek with her protective skirts, is closing in.

The most ambitious, comprehensive, and radical attempt to interpret *The Tin Drum* in terms of its postulated "unique and persuasive mythology" (1) is the late Edward Diller's *A Mythic Journey* (1974), a study that includes a very useful apparatus consisting of a genealogy of the Bronski and Matzerath families, a chronology of events, and a German-English concordance of editions of *The Tin Drum.* Diller, who does not mention either Sosnoski (1971) or Roberts (1973), finds the generic approach practiced by critics such as Schumann (1966), van der Will (1967), and others insufficient in that these critics have a propensity to reduce Oskar from a "hero-deity" to a "mindless picaro" (1). Diller also disagrees with reviewers and scholars who perceive *The Tin Drum* as a novel of "political protestations." According to Diller, "the mythic is the polar opposite of . . . the historical" (2); hence "history and politics are only the mise en scène in this novel, merely of secondary importance as a formal backdrop" (182 n. 6). It follows that in *The Tin Drum* "myth is posited as an attempt to transcend history by shifting focus from measurable time and specific events to paradigmatic ritualized forms of a timeless order" (3). Diller praises the novel highly on account of Grass's art of "mythopoeic symbolizing" (5–6) — a procedure that results in a work full of "supernatural beings, bizarre adventures, complex rituals, and mythic configurations" (7).

As the title of his study reveals, Diller devotes the main part of his analysis to Oskar's "quest," which he views in terms of the three stages of the "monomyth" derived from Joseph Campbell's *The Hero with a Thousand Faces* (1949): the "hero's departure, initiation, and return" (5). These stages unfold in Oskar's development, from his "mythic birth" to his drumming up the Black Cook (Diller, 160, prefers the literal translation of Grass's "Schwarze Köchin") who will lead him back to his mythic origins. Neuhaus (1982, rev. ed. 1988, 100) singles out Diller's reading of Oskar's "homecoming" to Danzig from his stint with Bebra's war-time theater in occupied France as an example of a generally flawed approach. At the beginning of the chapter "The Imitation of Christ" in book 2, Oskar muses in a self-deprecating manner about the inflationary use of "mythological names" and, despite his prolonged travels, declines to present himself as a "Ulysses." Instead, he suggests the return of the Prodigal Son as a potential parallel from the realms of myth and religion, because Alfred Matzerath welcomes him "like a true, not a presumptive father" (*TD,* 346) and sheds genuine tears. On the following day, Oskar's efforts to induce Kurt, whom he considers his son, to follow in his footsteps go completely awry. Kurt demolishes the tin drum that Oskar had brought as a present for his third birthday and gives Oskar a good thrashing to boot. Despite Oskar's disavowal of the role of Ulysses and that of Telemachus for Kurt, Diller interprets this scene as a "kind of burlesque of the Odysseus-Telemachus reunion" (86). In addition, the reference to Cain and Abel (*TD,* 351) provides a further model of interpretation for the homecoming scene and tends to undermine Diller's claim as to the exclusive validity of his mythological approach.

Neuhaus (1982, rev. ed. 1988, 152 n. 194) also faults Diller for his deliberate and openly stated neglect of contemporaneous history as reflected and refracted in the novel. Indeed, Diller devotes little attention to phenomena such as the tensions between Germans and Poles, the politically charged atmosphere in Danzig, the persecution of the Jews, and the postwar "economic miracle." To be sure, Diller does mention, for example, *Kristallnacht* (64) and the concentration camp at Treblinka (96). Curiously, he omits the ideological underpinnings, in part derived from Germanic mythology, of racially motivated persecution when he compares the victim Sigismund Markus "with his [mythological] namesake" Siegfried, "whose death was the signal for the collapse of Valhalla and for the passing away of the old gods" (64). Similarly, Diller turns Fajngold into one of the "shamans and seers" (95) of the novel. In the final analysis, Diller's emphasis on "the primordial states, ritual adventures, and mythological prototypes" (172) as divorced from sociopolitical concerns make his reading incompatible with approaches that see the novel as a vehicle for the representation of *Zeitgeschichte.*

In his reading of "Faith, Hope, Love," the concluding chapter of book 1, in which the events of *Kristallnacht* are depicted, O'Neill (1974) points to the "glaring polarities" on the "Pauline message of spiritual rebirth" and suggests that the phrasing, "there was once a toy merchant, his name was Markus, and he took all the toys in the world away with him out of this world" (*TD,* 206) elevates Markus's death to an "event of mythic significance" (307). Glenn A. Guidry, in his 1991 article on mythic form in *Die Blechtrommel,* goes beyond Diller by grounding myth in history. He wishes to show that the novel, "by means of its own mythic form, suggests socially constructive and ideologically progressive ways for myth to function in literature" (128). Guidry sees Oskar as a trickster who both resembles and differs from Till Eulenspiegel and the picaro in that all three are "historically and culturally adapted metamorphoses of the trickster archetype" (131). According to Guidry, "myth does not occupy a timeless realm divorced from historical reality" (134); consequently, *Die Blechtrommel* is "not only a reflex of the socio-historical context [of catastrophic twentieth-century German history] but also a reflection on it" (137). Guidry maintains that the task of initiating the act of *Vergangenheitsbewältigung* falls to Oskar, because (referring to Brode 1977) he "accepts the adult burden of guilt and responsibility through the act of narration" (139). Through their self-critical identification with Oskar and their projection of infantile and immature traits onto him, readers achieve the purging of these traits both individually and in German society as a whole. Hence Grass's mythopoeic text responds to the need of postwar German society to confront the past.

Postmodern Approaches

The 1980s witness the emergence of approaches that may be loosely grouped under the heading of the rather imprecise term "postmodern." As far as *Die Blechtrommel* is concerned, analyses in this vein tend to deemphasize or disregard entirely the political dimension of the novel and instead stress the aesthetic construct. A case in point is the essay by Werner Frizen (1986) who seeks to establish the novel's affinity to the theater of the absurd. Frizen uses Grass's early lyrics and plays, which originated shortly before or concurrently with the novel, as evidence of Grass's familiarity with modes of the absurd. He cites Fernando Arrabal's farce *Pique-nique en campagne* (1958; *Picnic on the Battlefield,* 1967) as a model for the grotesque and clownesque playlet in the chapter "Inspection of Concrete, or, Barbaric, Mystical, Bored" of book 2. This playlet underlines the pervasive mentality of the lower middle class, a favorite target of the absurdists' derision. Frizen then interprets the 1958 poem "Im Ei" ("In the Egg") from Grass's collection *Gleisdreieck* (1960; *WA* 1:80–81) as a paradigm that reflects the anthropology and epistemology of the theater of the absurd and, at the same time, contains in a nutshell the hermetic world view that finds expression in *Die Blechtrommel.* Whereas Arker (1989) attributes the absurdist elements in the novel to a traditional phase in Grass's artistic development, Frizen confines his analysis to *Die Blechtrommel* and refrains, for example, from drawing inferences from the political twist that Grass gives to Albert Camus's reading of the myth of Sisyphus in *Kopfgeburten* (1980; *Headbirths,* 1982), a work that Frank Brunssen (1997) discusses in detail (see ch. 9).

In her essay on the "visual intertexts" in *Die Blechtrommel,* Ingeborg Hoesterey (1988) focuses on Grass's training as a sculptor and graphic artist. She traces the "knot construction[s]" of Oskar's "keeper" Bruno Münsterberg, whom Oskar is hesitant to call an artist (*TD,* 15), to the creations of Bernhard Schultze. Furthermore, Hoesterey argues persuasively that the disreputable artist Lankes, whose "stuff slants too much" to be endorsed during the Nazi period (*TD,* 335), echoes prominent art critic Will Grohmann. Lankes uses the latter's terminology — for example, "structural formations" (*TD,* 336) — that signifies a form-oriented, international, and modernist concept of art popular in the 1950s and 1960s. Grass's satire of this concept in *Die Blechtrommel* turns subsequently into vehement repudiation, because he perceives it to signify the rejection of a realistic style of representation. Precisely the incompatibility of his artistic views and practice with the prevailing abstract mode causes Grass not to follow a career as a sculptor and to engage in literary pursuits instead, Hoesterey writes. Yet Grass's condemnation of abstract art as politically irrelevant remains problematic in view of its seminal role in the twentieth century and its having been banned during the Nazi period. Nevertheless, Hoesterey surmises that Grass's origins as a sculptor are evident in the much-praised plasticity of his language.

With an amazing display of chutzpah André Fischer (1992) scathingly dismisses virtually the entire body of *Die Blechtrommel* criticism, which, by his count, amounted in October 1989 to more than two hundred dissertations, monographs, and essays. Fischer maintains that the overwhelming majority of critics approach the novel in almost exclusively political terms and investigate its contribution (or lack thereof) to *Vergangenheitsbewältigung* at the expense of a thorough analysis of the aesthetic structures of Oskar's narration (99). Instead of following in the footsteps of previous, supposedly inept, Grass criticism, Fischer reads *Die Blechtrommel* as a self-constituting humoristic novel, a reading that embraces its totality. He sees Oskar naively and eccentrically producing himself as narrator and estranging the represented world in such a fashion that the text essentially amounts to an experiment in deforming those aspects that contribute to constituting "reality." From the very beginning, Fischer avers, the narrator's self-reflexivity concerning the act of narration is at the center; hence this narrator cannot be evaluated according to extrinsic criteria. Rather, he plays a role that is distinct from that of the first-person narrator, and his drumming does not have any other function than being playfully naive ("ludistisch naiv," 119). Furthermore, Oskar's reduction of political, social, and economic factors to the level of sexuality is indicative of the lack of a plausible, extrinsically motivated explanation of the characters' actions. Thus Fischer (122) cites Alfred Matzerath's joining "the Party in '34" as an example of conveying important events and decisions via sexual connotations: "Jan Bronski quickly grasped the new Sunday political situation and, incorrigible civilian that he was, took to calling on my poor forsaken mama while Matzerath was drilling and parading" (*TD,* 116). It may be noted parenthetically that Manheim's translation neither captures the flavor of the phrase "auf zivil eindeutige Art" nor the pun on "Glied" (penis) in Matzerath's standing in "Reih und Glied" (*WA* 2:135).

Similarly, Oskar's reading, his view of religion, and, above all, his "naive presentation" of history (Fischer, 136–48), which arbitrarily focuses on the insignificant, do not make any pretense of establishing a causal relationship between an objective socio-historical context and Oskar's subjective experiences. Fischer uses Mikhail M. Bakhtin's systematic use of the term carnival, notably in his *Rabelais and His World* (1965; translated in 1968) with its emphasis on the body and bodily functions and its disregard of social hierarchies, to buttress his claim that in *Die Blechtrommel* history does not serve to advocate any ideological position, and hence it does not supply a firm basis for producing meaning. Correspondingly, Fischer adopts the category of the grotesque from Geoffrey G. Harpham's *On the Grotesque: Strategies of Contradiction in Art and Literature* (1982). Harpham defines the grotesque as "marked by such an affinity/antagonism, by the co-presence of the normative, fully formed, 'high' or ideal, and the abnormal, unformed, degenerate 'low' or material" (172), and Fischer postulates that both the carnivalesque and the grotesque are narratively "staged" ("inszeniert") by Oskar — thereby enhancing the effect of the failure of language, reason, and history.

For Fischer, then, it is not possible to provide any logical explanation of the events or any coherent pattern of interpretation. The Black Witch, for example, no longer haunts Oskar, as a majority of critics has assumed; rather, her function according to Fischer is to provoke and disappoint those readers who expect the novel to offer a meaningful representation of history. The upshot is that the humor in *Die Blechtrommel* is indicative of an underlying fundamental sorrow ("Grundtrauer," 213); as Grass states in a 1979 interview: "Humour est pour moi un autre nom de désespoir" (Casanova 1979, 180). Despite Fischer's close reading of the novel, the substantial theoretical underpinning of his argument, and a lively, occasionally witty style, there are clear drawbacks to his approach. His radical rejection of virtually all of the scholarly writing on the novel up to 1989, his insistence on its self-referentiality, which does not allow us to draw inferences about the relationship between intrinsic and extrinsic factors, and his entire concept of the "aesthetic simulation of history" have been justifiably called into question. Neuhaus (1979, rev. ed. 1992, 60–61) objected that Fischer's reading denies Oskar any development and ignores the fact that *Die Blechtrommel* is not an isolated work but pertains to the context of the *Danziger Trilogie* (*Danzig Trilogy*). Even more scathingly, Fischer's "apolitical" reading has been rejected as merely "l'art pour l'art" by Rainer Scherf (2000, 46 n.7).

Die Blechtrommel as Film

Films are ordinarily not a subject for discussion in literary studies. But the dominance of film as perhaps the chief cultural medium in the twentieth and the beginning of the twenty-first centuries, the advent of film studies as a discipline, and the decreasing rigidity of disciplinary boundaries tend to favor the inclusion of a brief review of criticism on the film version of *Die Blechtrommel*. The film, produced at various locations in 1978 under the direction of Volker Schlöndorff, is a special case in that it is a genuine *Literaturverfilmung* (a film based on a literary text). This particular *Literaturverfilmung*, which may be termed a collaborative effort between a famous author and a director fully familiar with the problems of adapting literary works (such as, with Margarethe von Trotta, Böll's *Die verlorene Ehre der Katharina Blum* [1974; *The Lost Honor of Katharina Blum*, 1975]), is documented in Grass and Schlöndorff's *Die Blechtrommel als Film* (1979; *The Tin Drum* as Film) and constitutes part of the novel's reception process. The cinematic version of *Die Blechtrommel*, which opened in May 1979 in fifty-five West German cities, revived the debate about the novel twenty years after its original publication. Yet the intellectual and political climate in the Federal Republic had changed; as *Der Spiegel* surmised in a cover story ("Film" 1979, 183–84), the film was unlikely to revive the charges of obscenity and blasphemy that once had been hurled at the author and his work. However, such a view turned out to be somewhat premature with regard to other countries: in June 1997 police in Oklahoma City confiscated video cassettes of the film on acount of its alleged pornographic content involving children (the verdict was later rescinded). In West Germany, the discussion focused on whether a *Literaturverfilmung* could do justice to a notoriously complex literary work. Indeed, one reviewer deemed the film qualitatively sound but summarily rejected it as entirely superfluous because Schlöndorff failed to add new elements (Blumenberg 1979) — an assertion that has not remained uncontested.

The film opened in New York City in April 1980 and subsequently became the winner of the Academy Award for the best foreign-language film. In two major articles the *New York Times* reported on the collaboration between Grass and Schlöndorff (Vinocur 1980) and on child star David Bennent (Lewis 1980), the Oskar of the film version. Although in his review Stephen Harvey (1980) credits Schlöndorff with having created a "satisfactory transplant" from novel to film, he finds the attempt "to refashion densely symbolic . . . works of fiction" into film "quixotic." The prominence of the New German Cinema induces some to wonder "whether the important role played by adaptation" was "conducive or detrimental" to its further development (Head 1983, 348). However, in the case of *Die Blechtrommel* it is difficult to see how the film does not contribute to furthering the fortunes of the New German Cinema. Apart from its popular success and critical acclaim, the film is striking in that it endeavors to follow the "exigencies of cinematic aesthetics" (Head, 360) and not to insist on the primacy of the literary text. Even though Oskar's comments via voice-over in the film involve "a degree of identification with the narrative perspective of the novel" and amount to "more or less direct quotation from the text" (361), the use of captions or intertitles as narrative devices can be traced back to the era of silent films. Hence there is no need in the age of sound to use the camera as "the only narrator," Head claims; in addition to music, for example, the employment of the "spoken equivalent of captions" or "talking captions" is a legitimate filmic means and does not detract from the film's emancipation from its textual source (364–65).

John Flasher (1983) concentrates on the "grotesque hero" Oskar, whom he characterizes as "ambivalent, libidinous, evil, corrupting, alienated, anomalous, satanic, grotesque, freakish, and monstrous." Surprisingly, Oskar is also said to possess a "quintessential humanity" (93). In his brief summary of the film, Neuhaus (1982, rev. ed. 1988, 116–26) finds that the most striking difference between novel and film results from the change in narrative perspective that is dictated by having the film end with book 2. Thus the final scene shows the train leaving Danzig/Gdańsk and passing a Cashubian woman, who resembles Oskar's grandmother, sitting in a potato field — a reference to the beginning of both the novel and the film. Whereas this scene may suggest closure or a circular movement to the spectator unfamiliar with the novel and unaware of Oskar's fate, the train actually carries the adolescent Oskar, who has decided to resume his growth and to assume adult responsibility, beyond the confines of his hometown to Düsseldorf in West Germany and, ultimately, to his confinement in a mental institution where he begins writing his memoirs. Despite dispensing with thirty-year-old Oskar as narrator, Schlöndorff (1979, 25, 72) was at pains to preserve the change between a subjective and an objective point of view, which is expressed in the novel by Oskar's frequent switching from a first-person narrative to referring to himself in the third person. Neuhaus cites Oskar's birth in the chapter "Moth and Light Bulb" of book 1 as one of the instances of an "objective" presentation of an event that is purely subjective in that only Oskar can have experienced it. The film first shows Oskar in his mother's womb, but after Agnes Matzerath has given birth to Oskar, the spectator perceives the scene as turned upside down on the screen — a confirmation that it is seen from the perspective of the newly born baby who has been lifted up by his feet.

Neuhaus further argues that the film provides the basis for a new assessment of Oskar. Portrayed by David Bennent, Oskar appears both more childlike and humane than many literary critics have been willing to concede. But it is precisely the emphasis on the childlike narrator that Arker (1989, xviii) takes issue with. Neuhaus professes to be especially impressed by the scene in which Oskar closes the dead Markus's eyes in a gesture indicating a bonding that lasts beyond death. The minor role of the toy merchant is played by French star Charles Aznavour; his screen presence plausibly underlines the representative character of Markus as a victim of racial persecution. Grass's attention to detail and the plasticity of his language facilitate the transposition of the novel into film; for example, the dismembered dolls in Markus's store evoke in anticipatory fashion the mountains of corpses in the extermination camps. In addition, Schlöndorff notes (1979, 72), the actors derived a wealth of information about their respective roles, ordinarily not to be found in film scripts, from the novel.

The *Literaturverfilmung* debate is revisited by Hoesterey (1996) who bases her essay on Schlöndorff (1979) and pleads for abandoning the criterion of the film's faithfulness to the original literary text that is frequently invoked in reviews of the film. Grass himself acknowledged the requirements of the filmic medium and consented to dispensing with the grown-up narrator and his complex narrative stance, which is analyzed by Neuhaus (1982, rev. ed. 1988, 20–28) by agreeing to substitute the cinematic equivalent of a first-person narrative in the form of Oskar's voice-overs. On the one hand, the film cannot do justice to the complexity (and sheer volume) of the literary text and must necessarily simplify matters; on the other, the dialogic character of the cooperation between author and director, Hoesterey points out, has a most unusual result: Grass uses the film to "correct" his text — notably by upgrading the role of the toy merchant.

Die Blechtrommel in the Classroom

The customary division between scholarly writing and that with a didactic bent is hardly tenable in the case of *Die Blechtrommel.* Apart from a number of articles that specifically address questions related to effectively teaching the novel in the upper grades of the German *Gymnasium* such as that by Droste (1969), there are some book-length studies in German that deserve to be mentioned briefly. To be sure, these studies differ with regard to length, comprehensiveness, and soundness; however, for the most part they are recognized as legitimate contributions to the ever-increasing body of secondary literature on *Die Blechtrommel,* in that they may provide comparatively easy access to a complex work and provide useful information not only for secondary school teachers in Germany but for all of those contemplating to teach (and read) the novel in German or English.

It is instructive to observe that the process of the novel's canonization proceeded rather rapidly; whereas it was condemned at the beginning of the 1960s as *jugendgefährdend* (morally corrupting young people) by conservative circles, as early as 1966 a secondary-school teacher posed the question of whether *Die Blechtrommel* might be suitable for the classroom (Klinge 1966). Although this teacher ultimately refrained from endorsing the novel as appropriate reading for young people, it subsequently gained wide acceptance in the schools of the Federal Republic — a fact that did not remain unnoticed by the suppliers of educational tools for interpretation. To mention some examples: the indefatigable Edgar Neis brought out his commentary, which hardly meets scholarly expectations, in 1970 (continued by Rüdiger 2001), Ute Liewerscheidt's didactic analysis appeared in 1976, and materials relating to both *Die Blechtrommel* and *Katz und Maus* came out in 1981 (Brunkhorst-Hasenclever). Heinz Gockel (2001) and Thomas Rahner (2005) penned similarly general and/or pedagogically oriented studies.

There is then no dearth of information of an introductory nature. A more substantial contribution on *Die Blechtrommel* is the 1982 work by Volker Neuhaus, who is also author of *Günter Grass* (1979), a compact, valuable guide that has been frequently referred to above. Neuhaus recommends *Die Blechtrommel* on account of its formal aspects, its use of a wide variety of narrative techniques, and its status as an eminently political work that seeks to combine the German tradition of the *Bildungsroman* with its emphasis on individual development with that of the under-represented social novel. Neuhaus also provides a shorter introduction to the novel (1993b). Noel L. Thomas's (1985) critical guide provides an indication that *Die Blechtrommel* has also gained a foothold in the classrooms of the English-speaking world. In 1986 Detlef Krumme's commentary, which was not explicitly designed for instructional purposes in secondary schools, was brought out by the reputable publishing house of Hanser, and the publication in 1993 of Walter Jahnke and Klaus Lindemann's "model analysis," which features a detailed tabular synopsis of the various chapters (historical dates, Oskar's biography, leitmotifs, and so on), attests to the fact that the novel has remained a fixture of the literary canon in the 1990s and beyond.

Although a research tool rather than an instructional one, the *Wortindex* to *Die Blechtrommel*, edited by Franz Josef Görtz and others (1990), offers a convenient approach to text-based inquiries. But the full potential of the *Wortindex* can only be realized in a computer-compatible version that is not (yet) available.

Die Blechtrommel as Literary Model

Among contemporary writers of fiction, especially American writer John Irving and Indo-British novelist Salman Rushdie are frequently mentioned in conjunction with Grass in general and *Die Blechtrommel* in particular. Irving, who in his review of *Headbirths, or The Germans Are Dying Out* (1982; see ch. 9) professed his unabashed esteem for Grass — "simply the most original and versatile writer alive" (60) — has not wavered in his admiration. In his 1992 introduction to a reading by Grass in New York City, he essentially reiterated his assessment: "Grass is 'one of the truly great writers of the 20th century'" (in Irving, 1996, 418). Irving relates his struggle with the demanding German language of *Die Blechtrommel*, a struggle that was finally resolved when he got hold of a copy of *The Tin Drum*. After the publication of Irving's novel *A Prayer for Owen Meany* (1989), reviewers were quick to notice the obvious intertextual references: "Meany shares more than initials with Oskar Matzerath, the runt hero of Günter Grass's masterpiece, *The Tin Drum*" (Sheppard 1989). Irving (1994, ix), in fact, confirmed that the choice of initials for his protagonist was intended "as a gesture of homage" to Grass. Neuhaus (1979; rev. ed. 1992, 60) points out that the narrative structure and the motifs of *Owen Meany* relate it to *Katz und Maus, Örtlich betäubt,* and, above all, *Die Blechtrommel.* But whereas Oskar remains essentially noncommittal in the face of evil, Owen Meany acts and sacrifices himself. His memory lives on in narrator John Wheelwright's tale.

In a short, albeit perceptive, essay Ryan (1995) raises the question of the models for dealing with the past, that is, the Vietnam War, in the United States. Although she is primarily concerned with establishing Nathaniel Hawthorne's *The Scarlet Letter* (1850) as a literary model for *A Prayer for Owen Meany,* Ryan does refer to the similarities of the protagonists in *Die Blechtrommel* and Irving's novel: they "share not only the initials of their names, but their short stature, their delayed development (Oskar's childish attachment to his drum and Owen's childlike voice), and their ability to 'see' beyond the façade of everyday adult reality" (43–44). Ryan concludes that Irving's adaptation of Grass may serve as a stimulus for a "somber and thought-provoking reflection of ourselves seen through the lens of German literary models" and "an American exploration of guilt" (47).

In her fairly extensive analysis Katherine Arens (1996) reiterates that "Meany borrows heavily from Grass in both plot and characterization" (65) and adds that Irving has incorporated Grass's stylistic features as well as his "politics, social stance, and authorial intent in use of genre" into his aesthetics (66). In agreement with Hans-Georg Pott (1986b), who considers *Die Blechtrommel* to be a chief specimen of the new, socially aware regional novel that is distinct from the trivial and sentimental *Heimatroman* in the manner of Ludwig Ganghofer (see also Cepl-Kaufmann 1986), Arens emphasizes the significance of, respectively, Danzig and New Hampshire. But whereas Grass's "distinctive antieducational novel," which constitutes "an inversion of the values encompassed in the original genre" of *Bildungsroman,* remains male-centered (Arens overlooks the pertinent work by Pflanz 1976, discussed earlier in this chapter), Irving includes a "feminist gesture" by drawing attention to his male narrator's "unreliability" in authentically rendering women's voices and thereby establishing that "both sexes are victims of the prevailing social construct" (69). Hence, Arens concludes, Irving's criticism "stresses personal identity constructs, while Grass construes politics in largely ungendered terms" (81). While the general thrust of Arens's argument appears persuasive, her reading of Grass's texts is occasionally highly idiosyncratic and misleading. For example, Markus dies in the Danzig version of *Kristallnacht,* not "as the Nazis overran Danzig" (66). Oskar does not tell his story sitting in a "jail" (68), but rather in a "mental hospital" (*TD,* 15), and Arens's assumption that Oskar makes "two" attempts to grow is hardly supported by textual evidence. In fact, Oskar's — partially — successful attempt to grow and to become a responsible adult occurs almost immediately after Alfred Matzerath's death — not "after the death of his [two] putative fathers at the end of the war" (68). Finally, Oskar's mother does not commit suicide "by eating eels because she cannot deal with the conflicts between her German husband and her Polish lover" (79). The eel episode in the chapter "Good Friday Fare" (book 1) constitutes merely the beginning of Agnes Matzerath's devouring all kinds of fish, a self-destructive act that eventually leads to her death. And disgust with her adulterous life as well as the prospect of her giving birth to another misshapen, presumably retarded child qualify as more plausible causes for Agnes Matzerath's suicide than the at least superficially cordial relations between Alfred Matzerath and Jan Bronski, who have accepted their respective roles in the love triangle without rancor.

Whereas Henrik D. K. Engel (1997) in his comprehensive investigation of Grass's prose and its relationship to English-language literature in general does devote a substantial section to the literary and personal associations between the author of the *Danziger Trilogie* and Irving (as well as Salman Rushdie; see below), Iris Heilmann's study (1998) is by far the most detailed analysis of the "transatlantic" intertextuality. This intertextuality is evident in what Heilmann considers, in Bakhtinian terms, Irving's "dialogic" approach to Grass's texts (next to *Die Blechtrommel, Katz und Maus* serves Heilmann as an intertext; see ch. 2). Like Ryan (but without referring to her), Heilmann locates the point of contact in the two authors' concern about, respectively, the Second World War and the Vietnam War — a concern that is an expression of an analogous ethical world view inspired by a feeling of guilt. To be sure, Irving refrains from direct borrowings in the form of, for example, verbatim quotations or duplicating specific courses of action; although the analogies between the two novels are quite compelling, they do not pose any obstacle for the reader of *Owen Meany* who is not familiar with *Die Blechtrommel.* Conversely, readers well versed in Grass's text will not encounter any difficulties in discerning Irving's deliberate intertextual markings, such as the similar physical characteristics of Oskar Matzerath and Owen Meany, the peripheral role of the narrators (actually, the constellation of narrator John Wheelwright and protagonist Owen Meany more closely resembles that of narrator Pilenz and protagonist Mahlke in *Katz und Maus* than that of narrator/protagonist Oskar), and the protagonists' role in assuming a Christ-like stance that casts a spotlight on the desolate state of a world characterized by war, destruction, and death. At the same time, Irving's (pre)occupation with Grass's texts signifies a universalizing tendency that transcends national boundaries.

Like Irving, Rushdie (1985) has acknowledged his profound interest in Grass and *The Tin Drum.* He recalls that the novel had him "hooked" (179) when he read it during the summer of 1967 while a student at Cambridge University, because it confirmed his resolve to become a writer. As in the case of Irving, reviewers immediately noted the similarities between Grass's novel and Rushdie's *Midnight's Children* (1981), but more extensive studies did not appear until several years later. Rudolf Bader (1984) engages in a thematic comparison, and Eric W. Herd (1987), who does not cite Bader, discovers a considerable number of thematic and other similarities: the blue eyes of the protagonists Oskar and Saleem Sinai, the parallel roles of the black goddess Kali and the Black Witch, the transformation of Saleem Sinai into a dwarf at the novel's conclusion, the reflection of general history — that of Germany and India, respectively — in the protagonists' fates, the protagonists' unreliability as narrators who either turn thirty (Oskar) or are in their thirtieth year (Saleem Sinai) at the end of their tales, their propensity for addressing their readers, the authors' comparable attention to the evocation of specific local contexts despite the enormous culture gap between Danzig and Bombay, and so on. Although *Die Blechtrommel* is not Rushdie's only literary model, Herd concludes that Rushdie's adaptation of novelistic techniques from Grass constitutes a cultural transfer of imposing proportions.

Kenneth R. Ireland (1990) concentrates on the "metafictional concern" (343), the reflections on style and narrative that both protagonist-narrators engage in. Oskar, for example, reflects at some length on the question of how to begin his tale before putting his fountain pen to the "virgin" paper (*TD,* 16 and 17). In support of his findings, Ireland quotes

Rushdie's 1985 essay on Grass and terms the former's literary indebtedness to the latter an "inspirational debt" (358) rather than outright borrowing. Patricia Merivale (1990) characterizes *Midnight's Children* as a "translation, as flamboyant as it is skillful, of themes, topoi, events, characters, images, and above all rhetorical and metaphorical strategies, from western fictions" (328) and identifies Gabriel García Márquez's *Cien años de soledad* (1967; *One Hundred Years of Solitude,* 1970) and *The Tin Drum* as Rushdie's chief inspirations. She confines herself to merely suggesting "the astonishing density of allusions to and echoes of *The Tin Drum*" (341) in *Midnight's Children,* which in part have been noticed by previous critics. Rushdie's claim to share with Grass the status of an "international" and "migrant" writer is hardly applicable to Grass inasmuch as, in the German context, the term *Migrantenliteratur* denotes the literature of cultural minorities. However, owing to this status, Rushdie is at liberty to choose his literary parentage: "Saleem's intertextual relationship to Oskar is a genealogical allegory of Rushdie's 'choosing' of Grass" (Merivale, 342) in the mode of magic realism that discovers the marvelous in the real and constitutes one element of the enduring appeal of *Die Blechtrommel.* French novelist Michel Tournier (1975) acknowledges as much when he credits *Die Blechtrommel* with presenting an original mixture of plain realism and black magic. William Cloonan (1986), in fact, analyzes Grass's novel (see also Cloonan 1999) and Tournier's *Le roi des Aulnes* (1970; *The Ogre,* 1972) in terms of their new approach to providing fictional accounts of the Second World War; Grass and Tournier deal with this conflict of unprecedented destructiveness via addressing some of its "moral and intellectual ramifications" (71) from unusual narrative perspectives.

Die Blechtrommel Forever

As we are approaching the fiftieth anniversary of the publication of *Die Blechtrommel,* there is no precipitous decline of critical interest in what is unquestionably Grass's major literary achievement, an achievement that was acknowledged as such in 1999 by the Nobel Prize Committee. It is then not surprising that Rainer Scherf (2000) accords the novel the central place in his collection of essays on Grass's works; at the same time, he engages in polemics against those reviewers and critics who neglect to acknowledge that the author's impetus for writing and for engaging in politics springs from the same source. Behind both lies the desire to confront readers/citizens with their various forms of *Wirklichkeitsverkennung,* or misinterpretations of "reality," which in literary criticism amounts to the dominance of the secondary — for example, via asserting the central role of the critic — over the primary material, the literary text itself. In dismissing the potential charge of succumbing to the intentional fallacy, or the assumption that the meaning intended by the author of a literary work is of primary importance, a concept discredited by New Criticism, Scherf cites from numerous essays by Grass in support of his reading.

Although Scherf concedes that a critical approach to *Die Blechtrommel* would be possible without recourse to Grass's biography, he postulates that a central event in the author's life, the death of his mother in 1954, is reflected in the novel — but not, as one might assume, via the death of Oskar's mother Agnes. Rather, it is the constellation of Madonna and Whore in Matzerath's cellar ("The Ant Trail," book 2) that provides clues. When the Soviet Army began invading Danzig in March 1945, Russian soldiers gang-raped the widow of greengrocer Greff, who, in Oskar's extremely misogynist report initially seemed to welcome the Russians' attention owing to a long period of lacking opportunities for sexual activities. Unexpectedly, they leave Maria, who is holding little Kurt in her lap, unmolested on account of their being "great lovers of children," as Oskar's source Rasputin had revealed (*TD,* 392). Without equating Mrs. Greff and his mother, Scherf speculates, Grass indirectly reveals her fate, of which he learned comparatively late. His mother was raped repeatedly; in order to protect and save her daughter, Grass's younger sister, from a similar fate, she put herself at the disposal of the Russians. As an entirely innocent victim without culpability for Nazi crimes, Grass's mother felt a profound sense of shame — a sense of shame that was eventually shared by her son, and that served as a powerful impetus for his writing.

Unlike Grass's relationship with his mother, that with his father was tense because of his father's resistance to the young ex-POW's artistic ambitions. But instead of concentrating on the relationship between Oskar and his putative father Alfred Matzerath, which ends when Oskar (possibly deliberately) engages in what could be patricide in the aforementioned chapter of *Die Blechtrommel,* Scherf focuses on Oskar's association with the greengrocer Greff. Greff commits suicide in September 1942 because of the loss of contact with his former protégés, the death of his favorite "scout, then squad leader, then lieutenant" (*TD,* 309), and, the final straw, a "summons to appear in court on a morals charge" (*TD,* 317) that, Scherf conjectures, is attributable to Oskar's denunciation of Greff. Perhaps the construct of Greff's role as Oskar's substitute father, who is ultimately punished because he has lost faith in National Socialism and violates its taboos, is indicative of Scherf's propensity to engage in speculative conclusions — a propensity that tends to detract from his many surprising and valid observations.

In his monograph *Representation, Subversion, and Eugenics in Günter Grass's "The Tin Drum,"* Peter O. Arnds (2004a) revisits Bakhtin (see also Fischer 1992, above) and uses his cultural theory, his "focus on the grotesque," on "pornography," and on "blasphemy" to cast Oskar in the role of representative of all "the social groups whom the Nazis tried to silence" (3). Accordingly, Oskar "embodies" a variety of "figures from popular culture" such as the Tom Thumb of fairy-tale origin, the "trickster," and the "harlequin" (4) and is, especially after his return from France, in constant danger of becoming a victim of the Nazis' euthanasia program, a fate from which only Alfred Matzerath's paternal qualms save him. (When Matzerath finally signs the consent form to have Oskar committed, the Danzig postal service has ceased functioning on account of the destruction wrought by the advancing Soviet army.) Arnds supports his argument with copious references to the Nazis' program of euthanasia as well as to studies that have a bearing on his topic but that occasionally tend to detract from the reading of the literary text. Thus, in his chapter "Heteroglossia from Grimmelshausen to the Grimm Brothers" (28–48), Arnds surveys a wealth of materials that sometimes appear to have a somewhat tenuous relationship to the text under discussion; conversely, the looming and frightening "Schwarze Köchin," without doubt a figure of fairy-tale or folkloristic origin, receives short shrift. True, Arnds goes beyond previous attempts to define *The Tin Drum* in terms of the picaresque novel (see, for example, Schumann, van der Will, above) when he emphasizes the "satire and . . . carnivalesque features" (132) of Grimmelshausen's *Der abenteuerliche Simplicissimus.* Even if one may question the universal validity of the concept of an irrational counterculture for a reading of Grass's novel — a concept that, at any rate, would seem to be more relevant to books 1 and 2 — Arnds has extended the boundaries of interpretational possibilities.

Perhaps one of the latest monographs devoted to *Die Blechtrommel* provides an indication as to the virtual inexhaustibility of critical approaches to the novel and, at the same time, testimony to the intricacies and complexities of Grass's masterpiece, which continue to provide interpretive challenges. In her 2004 study, Antoinette T. Delaney seeks to provide a "scientific analysis" that is based on a "cognitive theory of metaphor." There is, of course, no dearth of metaphors and metaphorical expressions in *Die Blechtrommel,* and Delaney painstakingly lists the former according to categories such as "Noun or Nominal Metaphors," "Noun-Composite Metaphors," "Adjectival Metaphors," and so on; furthermore, she subsumes "Personifications," "Idiomatic Expressions," and the like under the heading of "Stylistic Features" (35–63), and summarizes her findings in statistical tabulations that show the frequency of metaphors in the three books of the novel. Without doubt, the extraordinarily detailed tabulations and listings serve to support the prevalent opinion of the amazing richness of Grass's language and constitute a valid scholarly contribution. One wonders, however, whether the identification and analysis of "862 metaphors and . . . 2200 significant words" does not tend to overemphasize the "quantitative, scientific element of language analysis" (151) at the expense of a cohesive interpretation of the text, which has been attempted by scores of scholars and critics but has not prevented others from the publication of their specific readings — a state of affairs that in view of the interpretive challenges posed by the text is not likely to change in the forseeable future.

2: *Katz und Maus / Cat and Mouse*

First Critical Responses

IN HIS COMPILATION AND SUMMARY EVALUATION of Grass criticism, Heinz Ludwig Arnold (1997) devotes just over five pages to *Katz und Maus,* which was first published in 1961, whereas *Die Blechtrommel* merits fourteen and a half pages. While such quantitative measurements do not provide a firm basis for the comparison in aesthetic terms of the two works in question, they do allow us to draw conclusions as to the scope and the intensity of their reception, inasmuch as reviewers understandably tended to refer to Grass' first monumental success when discussing its much slimmer sequel. Arnold's summary is somewhat misleading in that, apart from the discussion of the characteristics of the *Novelle* (see below), it devotes major attention to negative comments, notably those by veterans' associations and former residents of Danzig, Grass's birthplace, who were expelled from their home town as a consequence of the Second World War (for a summary of the criticism, see also Sturm n.d.). The former saw their honor besmirched because protagonist Joachim Mahlke not only steals a Knight's Cross, one of the highest military decorations during the Second World War, which could only be conferred by the Führer himself, but subjects it to inappropriate use by dangling it "in front of his private parts, [where it] concealed no more than a third of his pecker" (*CaM,* 76; see Anon. 1962). A representative of the latter group revived the charge of pornography that had been leveled against *Die Blechtrommel* and applied it to *Katz und Maus* — a work that in his opinion totally discredits the city of Danzig (see Dr. Kö, 1962).

When a right-wing writer went to court in the state of Hesse to obtain an injunction against *Katz und Maus* on account of its being *jugendgefährdend* (morally corrupting) to young people), publisher Luchterhand mobilized literary scholars, writers Hans Magnus Enzensberger (1962b) and Kasimir Edschmid (1962), and a psychologist, who unanimously rejected the charge of pornography on the grounds that salacious details were part and parcel of an intricate literary work by an internationally renowned author, a work that was by no means intended to titillate. In a separate essay ("Zusatz"), Enzensberger (1962c) credits Grass with establishing a balance between his anarchic imagination and his superior artistic ability. In addition, literary scholar Fritz Martini (1962) made the point that mature and sophisticated adults rather than the supposedly threatened young people were the most likely readers of Grass's complex work. In the end, the entire affair came to naught, and the suit was withdrawn (see the documentation in Loschütz 1968, 51–69; Ritter 1977, 127–40). This defeat, however, did not silence Grass's opponents; in 1967 and 1974 respectively, both veterans' associations and expellees from the former German territories to the East of the Oder-Neisse demarcation line sought unsuccessfully to prevent the showing of the film and TV versions of *Katz und Maus* (H. L. Arnold 1997, 31).

Reviewers who did not have a political or ideological axe to grind generally gave *Katz und Maus* high marks on the basis of Grass's superior narrative skills, which resulted in a tightly structured novella — a form analyzed, for example, by Wolfgang Maier (1961) — of moderate length that differs considerably from the expansive novel *Die Blechtrommel.* Concerned with formal criteria, critics showed comparatively little inclination to thoroughly explore the militaristic value system prevailing in Nazi Germany and the fact that Mahlke's compensatory drive forces him to divert attention from his perceived deficiency, his extraordinarily large Adam's apple, by means of the Knight's Cross — an object he obtains first via theft and then earns through his heroism on the Eastern front. To be sure, Marcel Reich-Ranicki (1963b) applauds Grass's appealing specificity in his critique of conditions in Nazi Germany, yet others ignore such criticism. Emil Ottinger (1962), for example, views Mahlke's theft of the Knight's Cross as a criminal act and considers him to be a "constitutionally disturbed" youth (47) who is unable to achieve social rehabilitation and integration despite the moderate response of the representatives of law and order. Whereas West German Ottinger classifies Mahlke as a juvenile delinquent, East German critic Gerhard Dahne (1965), in a brief essay that appeared after considerable delay, takes issue with Grass's propensity for the unabashed depiction of sexual details (chiefly associated with Mahlke). This propensity he attributes to the author's inability to recognize the fundamental laws underlying human society, laws that Marxism claims to have discovered. Dahne does credit Grass with having portrayed the senselessness of war, which does not offer any meaningful perspective to young people, but, not surprisingly, he discerns the same lack of perspective in postwar West Germany's capitalist system. Such a dim view hardly enticed the GDR authorities to permit the publication of *Katz und Maus;* the *Novelle* was not made officially available to readers in the other half of Germany until 1984.

Cat and Mouse — A "Compact Masterpiece"?

The American translation of *Katz und Maus* by Ralph Manheim under the title *Cat and Mouse* appeared in August 1963, only six months after *The Tin Drum,* and its treatment at the hands of critics profited to some extent from the fact that Grass was no longer an unknown in the United States. What the reviewer of the Boston *Globe* called a "compact masterpiece" (Bemis 1963) was not universally hailed as such; in addition, the fact that both Sigrid Mayer (1978) and Patrick O'Neill (1992) in their studies of Grass's American reception devote merely a few lines to the critical responses to the author's second work of fiction seems to indicate a dearth of comment; however, Ray Lewis White's compilation (1981, 39–62) lists sixty-one excerpted reviews versus sixty-nine for *The Tin Drum* and thereby attests to the attention Grass's work continued to receive in the United States. Critics inevitably compare *Cat and Mouse* to *The Tin Drum* — both favorably and unfavorably; Stanley Edgar Hyman (1963) uses more than two thirds of his essay to discuss the *Tin Drum* before he briefly tackles the *Novelle* and finds both "disappointing" on account of their "meaningless" symbols. Although they generally approve of the manageable dimensions of *Cat and Mouse,* which lacks its predecessor's ample proportions, virtually all reviewers resort to calling the prose narrative a short novel and fail to take into account the characteristics of the *Novelle* — a misunderstanding caused by unfamiliarity with its significance in German literary history as well as by the omission in the translation of the generic definition *Eine Novelle* in the subtitle of the original.

In a major review in the *New York Times Book Review* Stephen Spender (1963) compares *Cat and Mouse* and Alain-Fournier's novel *Le grand Meaulnes* (1913; *The Wanderer,* 1928) — a comparison echoed by other reviewers (see also Gross 1979–80, discussed below) — in that both narratives feature an idealistic young protagonist whose idealism embodies that of an entire generation destined to become victims on the battlefields of the First and Second World Wars respectively. Spender's tendency to universalize Mahlke's struggle with society and to deemphasize the specific political circumstances under which he grew up were readily accepted by others. Spender speculates that to Grass "wartime Germany is a metaphor for systems which are enemies of the individual today almost everywhere"; similar views were particularly propounded in publications with a local or regional distribution. While the frequency of reviews attests to the fact that Grass was by no means ignored by critics, one may doubt whether all of these reviews were contributing to informing and enlightening the reader about the work. Thus *Cat and Mouse* is declared to be "an allegory for our times" (Quinn 1963), a "fable of our time" (Lane 1963), "undeniably a parable" (Gilbreath 1963), and even deemed a failed attempt at writing a "Kafkaesque parable" (Rhodes 1963). Explicit references to Nazi Germany and to Grass's evocation of the Danzig milieu during the Second World War are comparatively rare. One reviewer writes about the war's effect on "the city of Danzig and its petty bourgeoisie." He continues that there is "nothing left of Hitler's *herrenvolk* dream" once Grass finishes "telling his ironic and grimly funny tale" (McLaughlin 1963). But then the eagerness to read about "the tragic distortion of the growth of German youth under the Nazis" (Anon. 1963c) appears to be limited; in a compliment of sorts one critic regrets that Grass is a German author whose literary contributions are in the German language. Nevertheless, this critic concedes, Grass has "produced quality fiction that will rank with the best of American writers" (Miller 1963). Josef Bauke (1963) expresses a perhaps more prevalent opinion when he indicates his relief that "the German miracle [was] not limited to the economy" but had found in Grass a representative voice that signaled the rebirth of letters in postwar (West) Germany.

Archetypal, Mythological, and Psychoanalytic Approaches

Academic criticism did not lag far behind the initial reviews of both the German original and the American translation. The first phase of North American criticism may be described as following archetypal patterns. For example, Erhard M. Friedrichsmeyer's exploration of "Aspects of Myth, Parody and Obscenity" (1965) in Grass's first two prose works posits that the "divine child myth" as formulated by Carl Gustav Jung and Karl Kérenyi assumes "central importance" (245) in *Katz und Maus,* in that in the masturbation scene the "sea gulls swallow Mahlke's sperm" (248). On other occasions, during their excursions to the half-sunken Polish minesweeper, the boys chew the sea gulls' "dried excrements" and spit them out so that the sea gulls can snap them up again. Friedrichsmeyer concludes from this cyclical process that human life is presented "in a brutally deranged cycle of creation" — a cycle that entails "one of the starkest repudiations . . . of the hopes of man for a rebirth" (249). Friedrichsmeyer is in part contradicted by Karl H. Ruhleder, who concentrates on "A Pattern of Messianic Thought" (1966) in *Katz und Maus.* Ruhleder emphasizes Mahlke's "Messianic role" (604) with reference to the blackboard drawing of "Mahlke the Redeemer" (*CaM,* 35) and his excessive veneration of the Virgin Mary and opines that Mahlke turns his "sinful act of self-abuse into a meaningful attempt at procreation" by trying to mix his semen with the "conceiving element" (608) of water — an attempt, however, that fails on account of the seagulls' intervention. Ultimately, Ruhleder states in his associative tour de force, "phallic analogies and symbolic procreation" take precedence over the "Christ parallel" (610). Ruhleder's conclusion is disappointing, because he fails to establish the link between Mahlke's role and what at the beginning of his article he calls the German "quest for the Millenium (Third Reich and the coming of a second Savior)" (599) that would have established a valid historical context for Mahlke's messianic aspirations (see also ch. 4: Di Napoli 1980). Helen Croft (1973) hews to Jungian criticism and seeks to demonstrate "the unity of Grass's distinctly ironic archetypal patterning," in which Mahlke functions as a "libido hero-figure," a function that is indicated by his "association with Christ and Christian symbolism" (in O'Neill 1987c, 113). Like Ruhleder, Croft largely disregards the historical and political dimensions of *Katz und Maus*.

In a minor essay, Adolf Schweckendieck (1970) views Mahlke in strictly clinical terms as a neurotic with an unhealthy fixation on his Adam's apple, and Manfred Sera (1977) examines the relationship between Pilenz and Mahlke, albeit in a psychoanalytical and somewhat idiosyncratic mode. He assigns the role of persecutor to Pilenz and that of the persecuted to Mahlke. The antagonism is evident in the act of Pilenz's narration, which merely constitutes a repetitive attempt to "kill" Mahlke (597). Yet Pilenz only "phantasizes" (598) that he is a perpetrator in the fashion of Mahlke by imagining that he put the kitten on Mahlke's Adam's apple, an act that set in motion Mahlke's efforts to divert attention from his physical blemish and to compensate for it by his heroics, and hid the can opener, which would have enabled Mahlke to open the tin cans and eek out a meager subsistence after he had sought refuge on the minesweeper. Pilenz's omnipotence as a narrator — Sera conveniently overlooks the implied author to whom Pilenz defers — compensates Pilenz for his sadomasochistic love of Mahlke but also demonstrates how inextricably linked the two figures are. Although Sera's contribution adds new insights concerning Mahlke and Pilenz's intricate relationship, some of his observations are of dubious validity. For example, the assertion that Mahlke's stealing the Knight's Cross is a sign of protest against being conditioned to die a heroic death (592) attributes to Mahlke a high degree of oppositional consciousness that not many critics are ready to grant him.

"Hero" Mahlke and Narrator Pilenz

The figure of Mahlke has attracted a substantial amount of attention, but not necessarily at the expense of Pilenz, the second major figure in *Katz und Maus*. James C. Bruce (1966) sees Pilenz as an "equivocating narrator" on account of his "ambivalent relationship toward Mahlke" (141), a relationship that is characterized by both admiration and envy and results in "Pilenz' wish to be rid of Mahlke" and "his compelling attraction" (142). Pilenz achieves his goal — never clearly articulated — at the end of the *Novelle* when Mahlke, aided by Pilenz, goes AWOL, and disappears in the partially submerged minesweeper, never to surface again. By introducing the implied author — "the fellow who invented us because it's his business" (*CaM,* 8) — as a separate entity, Pilenz is forced to reveal his motives in telling his tale, and his attempt to "present himself as only admiring and guiltless" fails. It is then not the "author," as Bruce would have it, who "tells us about Pilenz" (149), but the equivocating narrator himself.

Heinz Ide (1968) compellingly analyses the immanent dialectics of *Katz und Maus,* determining that the Adam's apple is the central symbol that characterizes the fall from grace and human beings' susceptibility to death — with the consequence that the threat of death mobilizes man's resistance and turns life into a battlefield. Hence representatives of Nazism play a comparatively minor role in the *Novelle* because the ideology of National Socialism is a consequence rather than the cause of the dominant culture that stresses violence and finds its "apostles" (616) in the air-force officer and the submarine commander — both former students of the institution — who deliver patriotic lectures at the school both Pilenz and Mahlke attend. Catholicism is implicated in this culture of violence, but as the interchangeability of gymnasium — its dressing room is called the "sacristy" by the schoolboys (*CaM,* 65) — and chapel, a former gymnasium, indicate, Catholicism represents any weltanschauung that demands absolute loyalty from its followers. Thesis and antithesis do not result in a synthesis, however, inasmuch as the (phallic) tool of annihilation (Mahlke's tank cannon) turns into an organ of procreation (Mahlke aims for the underbelly of the Virgin Mary whose apparition hovers in front of the Soviet tanks that he is destroying). This process eventually condemns Mahlke to inactivity (and presumable death) — a radical reversal that signals his inability and that of society at large to continue in the customary violent vein. Ide deviates from other critics in maintaining that Mahlke serves as a means to demonstrate this incapability rather than as a figure who ought to be interpreted psychologically.

In contrast to Ottinger (1962), Bruce (1966), and W. Gordon Cunliffe (1969; see discussion below), Johanna E. Behrendt (1969) posits that Pilenz and Mahlke are *Doppelgänger* rather than antagonists (321), and she avers that Pilenz's overriding interest in Mahlke results from his intense desire to find out what makes the latter tick. Inasmuch as Pilenz endows the actually negligible initial cat-and-mouse episode with great significance via his skillful narration, he questions the *Menschenbild* (concept of a human being) as represented by Mahlke (316). What unites Mahlke and Pilenz is their common striving; Mahlke achieves extraordinary feats in the realms of sports and war (and sex), and Pilenz searches intensely for lasting values and faith. While Mahlke perishes because he subscribes to the false ideals of hero and superman, Pilenz cannot rid himself of his admiration of Mahlke; ultimately, he is unable to come to terms with the Nazi past and find peace. Despite trenchant observations on the distinction between Pilenz as a youth and Pilenz as the postwar narrator or on the various layers of interpretation with regard to both Pilenz and Mahlke (Behrendt elaborates on this aspect in her 1968 essay), Behrendt's "metaphysical" reading fails to fully convince. For example, she absolves Pilenz of all personal responsibility with regard to Mahlke's presumed death and declares the former's guilt feelings to be the secularized equivalent of original sin. Furthermore, Behrendt does not provide any indication that Mahlke might have been a victim as well as a perpetrator — nor does she acknowledge that he possessed an at least rudimentary awareness of genuine heroism. In the lecture that he was prevented from giving at his old school, Mahlke had planned to mention his father, a courageous civilian who sacrificed his life in order to prevent the deaths of fellow human beings — hence he could not be claimed by the Nazis as a representative of their version of the Nietzschean *Übermensch* ideology (317).

Following to some extent Robert H. Spaethling (1970), who discusses the complexity of Pilenz's relationship to Mahlke and who observes that Pilenz is a narrator with "a psychological problem" in that he "writes not to communicate but to free himself" of that problem (145, 144), Gertrud Bauer Pickar (1971) attributes the complexity and intentional ambiguity of the *Novelle* in part to Pilenz's "dual role as interested party and narrator" (239). This role induces him "to maintain that his narration is the 'absolute truth'" (241) even in the face of his own "desire for artistic fulfillment" that has him striving for "psychological validity" rather than "actual reality" (242). In another essay, Pickar (1970) extends her investigation of the "pervasive nature" (304) of ambiguity via an analysis of the colors used in *Katz und Maus.* Contrary to "the black, red and white" with their connotations of "sin, guilt and innocence," the grey, fusing black and white, represents "moral ambiguity" (305). The dominant colors "red-white-black," Bauer writes, alert the reader to the world of Mahlke and Pilenz in that they are those of "the flag of the Third Reich" (309), a political entity that has a profound effect on both protagonist and narrator.

Ever since William Empson's validation of the term ambiguity in his *Seven Types of Ambiguity* (1930), its positive qualities have been touted by New Criticism and its adherents and successors. Hence Kurt J. Fickert (1971) takes as his starting point W. Gordon Cunliffe's statement (1969) that Grass's work in general "conspires to propagate uncertainty and a world deprived of meaning" (23) and concludes that Grass's use of ambiguity "principally in style, point of view and narrative obfuscation" results in "a clear and persuasive statement about modern life and the functioning of an uncertainty principle in its religious dimension" (377). To be sure, there is no denying that ambiguity is at work in *Katz und Maus;* however, to elevate it to an all-pervasive principle rather than acknowledging it as a narrative strategy that serves specific ends does not appear to do justice to the text.

One of the first full-length studies of *Katz und Maus* is that by Gerhard Kaiser (1971). Kaiser rejects the approaches taken by Friedrichsmeyer (1965), Ruhleder (1966), and Behrendt (1968) as insufficiently concerned with the specific circumstances under which the Mahlke story unfolds and emphasizes the importance of the fatherless society (Mahlke's father is dead, and Pilenz's father is absent) in which the pubescent boys grow up. In fact, there appear to be no adults with a conscience and a sense of responsibility who could serve as positive role models (31). Hence Mahlke is encouraged to strive for his perfect fig leaf, the Knight's Cross, which will cover his physical blemish. Precisely because Grass presents Mahlke as an extreme case of psychological and physiological aberration, contemporary history remains a foil that obscures the underlying political roots of Mahlke's behavior and does not allow us to explore the question of Mahlke's personal responsibility (35). However, Kaiser seems to have it both ways. In stressing that *Katz und Maus* is a *Novelle,* he mentions the criterion of the *unerhörte Begebenheit* (unheard-of, extraordinary event), which has been an essential part of definitions of the *Novelle* since Goethe (actually, "eine sich ereignete, unerhörte Begebenheit"). Whereas in the text it is Mahlke's theft of the Knight's Cross that is referred to as "a disgraceful thing" (*CaM,* 78; the "Unerhörtes" of the German original alludes to the definition of the *Novelle;* see *WA* 3:86), Kaiser defines Pilenz's entire story of Mahlke as extraordinary (31). Hence the unheard-of events depicted are, to a large extent, determined by Grass's choice of genre, which necessitated his concentration on unusual features (see also Durzak 1993).

Similarly, Noel L. Thomas (1973) sees Mahlke as a victim of a "physical deformity" that is "the externalization of a state of psychological imbalance" (230). But Thomas deviates from most critics in suggesting that the kitten that jumped on Mahlke's "mouse" in the initial scene of the *Novelle* "symbolizes above all the seductive influence of the Virgin Mary" (232). Mahlke's obsessive veneration prevents him from establishing normal relationships with women and leads him to sacrifice "his own humanity in his attempt to become Godlike" (234). In the end, Thomas concludes in a censorious mode, Mahlke's character flaw turns him into "the willing henchman of a murderous political system" (237) — a system that operates within a framework of cooperative Catholicism. In a different approach, Inta M. Ezergailis (1974) proceeds along structural and stylistic lines. He does not refer to Ide's (1968) concept of the *Novelle*'s dialectics and views *Katz und Maus* as "perhaps the most explicit statement of Grass's own sense of dichotomy and balance" (225), which is expressed, for example, in Mahlke's "desperate search for symmetry" (226) as evidenced by the various items he is wearing around his neck. Carl O. Enderstein (1975) sides with those critics who point out Pilenz's ambivalent attitude toward Mahlke, which entails both envy and admiration, but Enderstein's main focus in the initial scene is on Pilenz's teeth, or, rather, on his toothache. Healthy teeth symbolize potency and strength, yet Pilanz's toothache, which is mentioned no less than eight times, suggests the opposite. When the cat attacks Mahlke's "mouse," Pilenz's keenly felt sense of inferiority disappears temporarily, and he experiences a short-lived triumph over his friend and adversary.

In a wide-ranging essay, David Roberts (1976) implicitly contradicts Thomas (1973), whom he does not mention, by stating that the "National Socialist state" misused Mahlke's "idealism and heroism." Mahlke, although "invincible in battle" like the "legendary heroes" Achilles and Siegfried (315), shares with them the fatal flaw of vulnerability — exemplified in his case by the Adam's apple. Yet Mahlke is not, as Cunliffe (1969) maintains, a "true hero" (88). Rather, Mahlke's "Faustian striving" serves Grass as the focal point of his "analysis of national psychology, of the 'public soul' of Germany" (321). In the formation of the national psyche among adolescents, Roberts observes, the institutions of "Church, school, and army" (320) play a pivotal role — a role that has not been sufficiently emphasized by previous critics.

In *Katz und Maus* "Grass makes his most important statement about 'Widerstand' [resistance]," Judith Ryan (1977) asserts, and she declares Mahlke to be, "despite his ultimate failure, its most viable representative in Grass' works" (149–50). Ryan proceeds from the premise that Pilenz's chief motivation for his both deliberate and subconscious concealment in his narrative is "the fact of his own previous involvement with Nazism" (151), but she provides little evidence as to the precise nature of this involvement. As to Mahlke, his "plan" for his personal "redemption" as well as that of the world progresses in the three stages of "inner emigration," "resistance," and "resignation" (153). Unlike critics of a psychoanalytical bent — for instance, Sera (1977), who see Mahlke's diving feats as an immersion into the realm of the unconscious (589) — Ryan writes that Mahlke's inner emigration is "symbolized by his transformation of the radio cabin in the minesweeper into his own personal realm" (154). This realm accentuates Mahlke's identification with the Polish cause via the various objects of Polish origin with which he adorns the cabin. But the theft of the Knight's Cross is Mahlke's "first genuine attempt at an act of resistance" (157) — a questionable assumption in view of his deliberate search for an appropriate object with which to divert attention from his Adam's apple. Similarly, it is not entirely convincing to construe Mahlke's "volunteering for military duty [that is, the Labor Service for which Mahlke was drafted]" as a "crucial part of his 'resistance,'" particularly when Ryan cites Mahlke's sexual exploits with the Labor Service commander's wife as an example of his "subversion of the system" (158). Mahlke's single-handedly smoking out a "partisan ammunition dump" (*CaM,* 101), for instance, would certainly qualify as support of the system rather than as the opposite. Similarly, Mahlke's hubris in assuming that he could have stopped Soviet advances had he not been transferred to a different sector of the front (*CaM,* 121) is not indicative of the mentality of a resistance fighter. It is therefore rather doubtful whether Mahlke would indeed have taken "the final step" (161) of rejecting the Knight's Cross had he been allowed to speak at his old school. In the final analysis, Ryan provides an intriguing, if rather speculative hypothesis with regard to Mahlke's alleged resistance, which is not fully supported by textual evidence.

Katz und Maus and the Schools

As in the case of *Die Blechtrommel,* it is hardly appropriate to seek to separate scholarly writings from those that also are concerned with pedagogical issues. In most instances, the demarcation lines are not clearly drawn; furthermore, the discussion about the suitability of *Katz und Maus* for young people constitutes an important facet of the work's reception. Despite Martini's (1962) assumption that *Katz und Maus* would presumably not cater to young people, teachers at secondary schools soon began to weigh the pedagogical merits of including Grass's text in their curricula. Werner Zimmermann (1965) expresses his qualms about the work's ethical, aesthetic, and religious offensiveness but still advocates the use of this "avant-garde" work. He does so for the curious reason that Mahlke (whom he calls Gustav rather than Joachim) was a genuine hero and, presumably, worthy of emulation. In a later, substantive article Zimmermann (1969) modifies his perception of Mahlke slightly and considers him basically human, in contrast to Oskar in *Die Blechtrommel.* Hans Lucke (1969) appears to concur with Zimmermann (1965) that *Katz und Maus* should be taught at schools. He does not offer any significant observations except to note that the *Novelle* deals primarily with developmental problems of male pupils at the expense of political aspects. A somewhat cursory essay by Ulrich Karthaus (1971) supplements Lucke's approach by drawing attention to the political and historical aspects of the

Novelle, which transcend the purely individual; hence Mahlke's fate stands for that of an entire generation. Pilenz's narrative is motivated by a feeling of guilt and is an attempt to come to terms with the Nazi past — an attempt that the political situation of the postwar years appears to call for. Karthaus defines the pedagogical goal of interpreting *Katz und Maus* as the elucidation of Grass's concept of history, which implies a warning against ideologies of the right as well as the left.

The most thorough interpretation of the *Novelle* from a pedagogical point of view is that by Ingrid Tiesler (1971) who sets out to defend it against the charges of pornography and nihilism (10) that were launched upon the publication of *Katz und Maus.* In her investigation, Tiesler takes into account facets such as the reception history of the work, its place in Grass's total output, the characterization of figures that have received relatively little attention (the teachers Klohse and Mallenbrandt, the girl Tulla), the function of the narrator, and the historical background. A novel feature is her emphasis on the comical aspects of *Katz und Maus:* that features Mahlke, a comical hero and a comical figure who desires to become a clown (118, 123). Tiesler, unlike most other critics, does not endeavor to promote one particular point of view that virtually excludes other readings. Instead of advancing a thesis or claiming to have found the key to the *Novelle,* Tiesler opts for a latitudinal approach and the multivalence of the literary work of art; hence she is prepared to accept various and even contradictory readings (39–41). Tiesler's main thrust, however, is designed to justify the inclusion of the work in the curriculum for the upper classes in the West German *Gymnasium,* or secondary school. As an important text of contemporary German literature and a historical document, Tiesler points out, *Katz und Maus* has provoked debate about critical issues, which in part have been used as arguments to advocate the banning of the text from schools. According to Tiesler, the charges of pornography, nihilism, blasphemy, and anti-authoritarianism can be invalidated by a careful literary evaluation that will enable students to appreciate the work.

It is not ideology that concerns Annette Delius (1977). In her empirical study she delineates a problem of reading comprehension and attributes some of the difficulties students encounter in reading the complex text to its lack of a clear-cut evaluation on the part of the author — thereby confirming the point Martini (1962) made about the lack of attraction of *Katz und Maus* for youthful readers. The frequently reissued compilation by Alexander Ritter (1977), which includes copious explanatory notes, a thorough commentary, and a useful documentation of the *Novelle*'s reception, is a valuable guide that can be used with profit by both youthful and adult readers. Similar guides that are primarily intended for schools include those by Annegrit Brunkhorst-Hasenclever and

Martin Brunkhorst (1981), Martin Neubauer (1998), Widar Lehnemann (2001), and Wolfgang Spreckelsen (2001). Grass's publisher Steidl has announced the publication in 2007 of a volume of commentary, edited by Volker Neuhaus — a further addition to the steadily increasing literature on *Katz und Maus.*

Narrative Aspects, "Gastro-narratology," and Critique of the "Male" System

During the 1980s and 1990s the number of analyses of *Katz und Maus* declined markedly in comparison to the preceding fifteen years or so. Inevitably, critics continue to follow some of the same approaches their predecessors employed. Notably, they are preoccupied with aspects of narratology or, more specifically, the role of narrator Pilenz. Ruth V. Gross (1979–80) contributes the only genuinely comparative study in her an analysis of both Alain-Fournier's *Le grand Meaulnes* (1913; *The Wanderer,* 1928) and *Katz und Maus* — albeit through adding a new twist in presenting both narrators and protagonists in the respective texts as "demonic" figures: The narrators "have created both the myths and the demonic heroes of these myths" in order to obscure "their own genuine demonism" (626). As to Mahlke, "ironically, [he] is special because he is average," and some of Pilenz's descriptions of him make it difficult "to take Mahlke seriously" (628). Such statements seem to undermine rather than support Gross's thesis of Mahlke's demonic nature, which, according to Grass, Pilenz is supposedly at such pains to portray. Furthermore, it is open to debate whether Mahlke possesses the "neptunic" power of controlling the element of water simply because of an incident in the winter of 1941–42, when he succeeds in having Pilenz's visiting female cousins as well as Pilenz and another classmate urinate on the ice above the sunken minesweeper so that the ice will melt and he will be able to reach the forward hatch. It turns out that the protagonists' "demonism is illusory" (631) because it is "manufactured" (634) by the unreliable narrators in the two texts under discussion. The creation of the narrative is then the hallmark of Pilenz's "truly demonic nature" (637) inasmuch as he is controlled by an outside force, that is, the implied author to whom he makes reference. Such an assertion is tantamount to saying that works that "are related through characters involved in the plot" (639) are of a demonic nature — hardly a tenable position.

Werner Krueger (1980) accepts the critical consensus that Pilenz's narrative is motivated by a pervasive sense of guilt; however, in noting the parallels between the biographies of Pilenz, Mahlke, and author Grass, he elevates Pilenz to the role of representative in the "paradigmatic" confrontation with both past and present (187). Yet he does not pursue the parallels between author Grass and his figures — a line of reasoning that rarely surfaces in the critical literature. Rather, in time-honored fashion Krueger devotes attention to Pilenz and Mahlke — albeit under the auspices of group dynamics. He states that in the initial episode Pilenz chooses to join the group of boys rather than siding with outsider Mahlke, by using the cat that embodies the group's latent aggressiveness. Mahlke's abnormal sexuality, narcissism, and unorthodox religiosity contribute to his position as outsider; his "fear" of the group (193) is actually the chief impetus for his compensatory efforts in the realm of sports. Pilenz, ever the alienated conformist, again engages in an act of aggression at the end of the *Novelle* when Mahlke does not return to the front and needs his help. It is Pilenz's fear of becoming implicated in Mahlke's desertion that causes him to abandon the friend he both admires and envies — a final testimony to the societal pressures at work on a weak individual.

The Rhetoric of Fiction (1961) by Wayne Booth serves Roger Hillman (1981) as a starting point in his characterization of Pilenz as an unreliable narrator. He finds the application of Booth's criteria to *Katz und Maus* problematic in that there is no perceivable difference between the perspectives of narrator and implied author. In fact, the author demonstrates his sovereignty by having tin drummer Oskar make a brief appearance in the narrative and dropping the name of Matzerath. Hillman differs from the majority of critics in seeing these figures from other parts of the *Danziger Trilogie* as not really relevant in terms of the Pilenz-Mahlke interaction, which for him is determined by Pilenz's double role as (retrospective) narrator and participant in the action of Grass's work, which, Hillmann contends, flouts the conventions of the *Novelle.*

Detlef Krumme (1985) returns to the figure of the narrator Pilenz. He writes that the narrator's insecurity — Pilenz offers three separate versions of the initial kitten episode — affects the reader, who views the figure of the narrator with suspicion and, at the same time, is inclined to keep his or her distance from protagonist Mahlke. According to Krumme, Pilenz embodies the difficulties inherent in the act of narration by an author such as Grass, who is skeptical about closed fictional systems that pretend to adequately represent the world in a nutshell. Pilenz's plaintive question, "Who will supply me with a good ending?" (*CaM,* 126), demonstrates his inability to suggest a meaning and leaves it up to the reader to make sense of the *Novelle.*

Taking Gérard Genette's distinction between narration, *récit* (text), and *histoire* (story) as well as Freudian and other psychoanalytical insight as a point of departure, Shlomith Rimmon-Kenan (1987), who does not cite any previous Grass criticism except for one unpublished dissertation, distinguishes between "narration-as-reporting and narration-as-performance" (177). The performative aspects of Pilenz's narration indicate that, as several other critics have noted, it is "his own story" (179) rather than that of Mahlke that he is telling. Rimmon-Kenan goes further than most of those critics by suggesting that Pilenz kills Mahlke "twice figuratively" (180) by erasing the chalk drawing of Mahlke the Redeemer and by removing Mahlke's carved name from the latrine in the Labor Service camp, before he proceeds to "the literal eradication" (181) of Mahlke. Rimmon-Kenan casts the story in the stark terms of "persecution and murder"; hence Pilenz's act of narration amounts to "killing Mahlke again" rather than to an act of "evoking and expiating past crimes" (183).

In her close reading of the first twenty-nine sentences of *Katz und Maus,* Daniela Hermes (1991) shows convincingly that this initial passage includes all the motifs that are more fully developed in the course of the narration. A rather different approach is taken by Lawrence O. Frye (1993) who chooses the term "Gastro-narratology" for his method of interpretation. Based on the frequent occurrence of "references to food, sex and bodily functions" in all of Grass's works, Frye sets out to show that the "apparently scattered references" form "coherent, body-defined constructions" (176) that influence the entire action of *Katz und Maus.* Thus Mahlke's ascendancy to a position of unquestioned superiority among his classmates corresponds to the unproblematic functioning of his "body cycling system" despite his eating the spoiled canned goods he brings up from the "belly" (177) or, rather, as the text has it, the "galley" of the minesweeper (*CaM,* 25). Conversely, in Mahlke's final hours his bodily system breaks down, as evidenced by his stomach ache, his vomiting and sweating, and his shaking knees. Although the overall pattern, which Frye establishes, seems to be conclusive, he does not account for Mahlke's complete recovery when approaching the minesweeper on his last trip. Frye agrees with Rimmon-Kenan (1987) that Pilenz wants to eliminate Mahlke but shifts the focus to Mahlke's being "consumed and reprocessed as vocalized matter" (184) through Pilenz's narrative act.

Whereas during the early reception phase of *Katz und Maus* the sexual preoccupations of readers and critics, who assumed heterosexuality to be the norm, often resulted in the condemnation of the work because of its explicit depiction of sexual acts, Leonard Duroche (1994) reads *Katz und Maus* as a "critique" of "the male system" (74) and compares Grass's work to Mark Twain's *The Adventures of Huckleberry Finn* (1884) in terms of an initiation story. Instead of taking sides in the debate about the main figure in the *Novelle* — Mahlke or Pilenz — Duroche argues that it constitutes "specifically an exploration of male relation" (78) with "undeniably strong homoerotic overtones" (81). The "possible cognitive tool for the examination and reconstruction of masculinity" that Duroche purports to offer in his reading is also intended to set free the inherent "political potential" (92) of the narration via the reader's conscious interaction with the text. Duroche's activist stance may be overly optimistic in view of the partially negative reader response to *Katz und Maus* in the 1960s and 1970s, but his observation that Grass's literary texts should not be taken as normative descriptions of the way things are but rather as an indication of historical conditioning is not without merit.

Although the number of analyses of *Katz und Maus* delined in the 1980s and 1990s, the text continues to attract critical notice. A case in point is the study by Rainer Scherf (1995), which borders on interpretive overkill, in that Scherf's monograph (originally a dissertation) consists of three hundred and fifty-seven densely packed pages of small print — a volume that exceeds the length of the *Novelle* by a considerable margin. In the time-honored fashion of writers of dissertations, Scherf castigates those who differ from the approach that he advocates and that he paraphrases in his lengthy subtitle, which may be roughly translated as "Literary Irony after Auschwitz and the Unspoken Appeal to Engage Politically." Although it is not possible to do complete justice to Scherf's argument here, a brief and necessarily limited synopsis is in order. Scherf proceeds from the strict separation of actual author and fictive narrator and argues that Grass's narrative has an ironic structure that should warn readers not to trust Pilenz's narration. The narrator's motivation is complex in that he wishes both to confess and, at the same time, to engage in the freedom of a budding writer to fictionalize events. For example, Pilenz is suggesting that the world is subject to an eternal cat-and-mouse game and strongly hinting at the fall from grace via the allusions to Mahlke's Adam's apple — a fall that applies to the erroneous assumption on the part of Mahlke and Pilenz's generation that they were born in the paradise of National Socialism as well as to the perception of those postwar Germans who regarded their complicity in or acceptance of Nazism as a loss of innocence. While the narrator's main interest is directed toward coming to terms with his guilt, or suppressing it, the author aims at uncovering exculpatory statements as an attempt, even after the fact in the postwar period, to vindicate the assumption that it was futile to resist Nazism. Scherf's analysis pertains then clearly to the category of criticism that seeks to secure Grass's place as a politically aware and engaged writer. Scherf's contribution, by far the most thorough and extensive (the bibliography includes more than two hundred entries), is, however, not the last word on *Katz und Maus*.

Frank F. Plagwitz (1996), who does not take into account Scherf's findings, concentrates on the Knight's Cross as the central symbol of a depraved heroism — a symbol to which Scherf devotes fairly little attention. The choice of a concrete object supports Grass's efforts to counteract the demonization of Nazism, a reading of history that fosters the rejection of responsibility for the past on the part of individuals, he claims. The Nazis' choice of an anachronistic term for a military medal that they created seeks to establish an ideological kinship with the medieval crusaders who fought against the infidels. Conversely, by omitting both the swastika and the origination date of the Knight's Cross (1939) on the cover illustration of *Katz und Maus,* Grass wanted to expose the long tradition of the abstract concepts of heroism, bravery, and honor. According to Plagwitz, Mahlke functions as the paradigm of a general societal deterioration of values — a view that has merit but disregards entirely Pilenz's ambivalent role.

In his essay "Showing, Telling, and Believing" (2001), K. F. Hilliard refers to the passage in which Pilenz mentions the "fellow who invented" (*CaM,* 8) both him and Mahlke as an indication of the "structural symmetry" of the *Novelle,* which rests on the two main characters, whose relationship changes from "observer and observed" to that of "narrator and hero of the tale" (Hilliard, 422). Pilenz's scopophilia or voyeurism is almost exclusively directed at Mahlke and expresses an element of latent aggressiveness that Mahlke senses in his juvenile cohorts and counters by his display of unsurpassed feats, notably in the masturbation scene and via the theft of the Knight's Cross. Mahlke's masturbation feat takes place on the minesweeper (see *CaM,* ch. 3) before an audience of schoolmates (and Tulla Pokriefke) that represents a kind of "carnivalesque counter-society" to the assemblies that take place in the school auditorium and are governed by rules designed to instill "orderly, hierarchical, authoritarian" values (Hilliard, 427). Both the size of Mahlke's penis and the theft of an object venerated in Nazi Germany contribute to Mahlke's elevated standing among his classmates. Even though it "preserves the power of the phallus" and represents the "ultimate proof of iron male potency" (429), the stolen object cannot be displayed in public by Mahlke, who is ultimately driven by an "adolescent, overcompensating neurosis, with a strong element of sexual pathology" (430) in pursuit of the supreme distinction at the Eastern front. Hilliard departs from the majority view with his assertion that when Mahlke is denied permission to speak at his old school, he does not die but simply disappears. He, who had been highly visible, becomes invisible — a not entirely plausible reading owing to the considerable difficulties Mahlke would have encountered in the attempt to reach a neutral ship and escape from Danzig and Nazi Germany. Furthermore, Hilliard avers that Pilenz has not contributed to Mahlke's death; rather, his narrative serves as "self-aggrandizing self-incrimination" (433), with which he seeks to disguise his own insignificance, but it does not amount to any "insight into the [Nazi] system" (434). Thus an exploration of the "narratological conditions" of the *Novelle* induce the reader to "reflect on the moral and political conditions that produced [such a] stunted moral growth" (436).

There are several studies that analyze *Katz und Maus* in the context of the *Danziger Trilogie* (see ch. 4) and/or other works by Grass that will ordinarily be discussed in different contexts. Iris Heilmann (1998) in her investigation of "transatlantic" intertextuality suggests that the constellation of narrator John Wheelwright and protagonist Owen Meany in John Irving's *A Prayer for Owen Meany* (1989) fairly closely resembles that of narrator Pilenz and protagonist Mahlke. Although Irving's novel is most frequently compared to *Die Blechtrommel* and protagonist Owen Meany to narrator/protagonist Oskar Matzerath (see ch. 1), *Katz und Maus* contributed to Irving's intertextual borrowing, albeit with one decisive difference. Whereas Mahlke presumably commits suicide, Owen Meany sacrifices his life in order to save the lives of Vietnamese children (see also Engel 1997, 181–83).

3: *Hundejahre / Dog Years*

A Literary Sensation?

THE PUBLICATION OF Grass's second novel, *Hundejahre,* which appeared in September 1963, was preceded by advance publicity: prior to its availability in bookstores excerpts were published, and Grass read from his manuscript in a TV broadcast — a distinctly uncommon practice at the time. If the novel did not, perhaps, become quite the "literary sensation" that at least one reviewer predicted (Ungureit 1963), the resonance it achieved in terms of both critical acclaim and sales figures — three hundred thousand copies were sold within three months, owing in part to the skillful publicity campaign on the part of Grass's publisher, Luchterhand — was quite remarkable, particularly in view of the work's complexity and considerable length of more than seven hundred pages. The influential journal *Der Spiegel* (4 September 1963) featured a substantial cover story — the first of several others that were to follow in the course of the decades — by an anonymous contributor about the then thirty-five-year-old "bestseller author" Grass. The story combines biography and literary criticism with an emphasis on Grass's Danzig roots; in a pattern adopted by most critics, *Der Spiegel* engages in a comparison of *Die Blechtrommel* and *Hundejahre,* but unlike other reviews, the magazine deems Grass's second novel the equal of his first in terms of its abundant length, attention to detail, exuberantly fantastic elements, and drastic recklessness (65). Apart from acknowledging the literary merits of the work, the story also signals that Grass had reached what was then the zenith of his fame; the author's eminence was to continue to grow both independently of and in conjunction with his literary activities (see H. Zimmermann 2006, 117–22). In the same *Spiegel* issue, Hans Magnus Enzensberger presented a brief but laudatory review, in which he praised Grass's unfettered imagination: Grass evokes the lost world of Danzig and succeeds in making it relevant to readers totally unfamiliar with the formerly German city. Yet Enzensberger anticipated the objections of other critics by pointing out the lack of a central figure in the vein of Oskar Matzerath, a figure that would have imposed unity on the novel (71).

The almost immediate commercial success of the work was accompanied by a generally affirmative reception on the part of reviewers. Heinz

Ludwig Arnold (1997) estimates that, of the eighty-five reviews that he and his students analyzed, about 25 percent were unequivocally positive, approximately 60 percent mention both negative and positive facets, and the remainder are clearly negative (265 n. 143). Comparing *Hundejahre* with *Die Blechtrommel* turns out to be one of the favorite ploys critics use to come to terms with the novel. Some of the difficulties that the reviewers encountered are evident from Heinrich Vormweg's (1963) ambivalent appraisal; he calls *Hundejahre* an obscene, unjust, and blasphemous book. At the same time, he acknowledges Grass as an original writer who has written a great novel that captures the essence of the epoch. Roland H. Wiegenstein (1963) deems the work significant enough to compare its evocation of Danzig to that of James Joyce's Dublin, Marcel Proust's Combray, and William Faulkner's Jefferson, Mississippi — a comparison that is by no means limited to *Hundejahre* and that has become one of the staples of Grass criticism. Günter Blöcker (1963) similarly perceives that Grass's convincing narrative owes much to his overpowering ties to his old *Heimat*, but he detects definite flaws in book 3 of the novel, in which Matern functions as an avenging angel — a development, Blöcker implies, that has been inspired by the author's hatred of the *status quo* in the Federal Republic. An even harsher condemnation is that by literary historian Walter Jens (1963) in the weekly *Die Zeit*. While Jens concedes that the Danzig portions of the first two books are reasonably successful, he considers book 3, which takes place in West Germany and West Berlin, a failure. Furthermore, Jens opines that *Hundejahre* is essentially a repetition of *Die Blechtrommel* and criticizes Grass's idiosyncratic approach to contemporaneous history in which the demise of the Third Reich is merely a footnote to the loss of a dog — albeit not an ordinary canine but the Führer's dog Prinz. Jens's criticism is not shared, for instance, by Rudolf Hartung (1963) who points out that the view from below (from the doghouse, so to speak) is an appropriate response to the grandiloquence of Nazi rhetoric. Furthermore, Jens misses the unified narrative perspective of Grass's first novel — a perspective that has been replaced by that of the "authors' consortium" (*DY*, 54 et passim), which consists of Brauxel/Brauksel/Brauchsel (the former Eddi Amsel), Harry Liebenau, and Walter Matern. Joachim Kaiser (1963) reaches a similar conclusion, and Jost Nolte in the conservative daily *Die Welt* (1963) adds that the "authors," or rather narrators, have a tendency to mask and disguise themselves — a narrative device that is likely to contribute to the difficulty of the text. Nolte also finds book 3 less compelling than books 1 and 2 and surmises that Grass's real strength is to be found in the depiction of the Danzig past — a conjecture that certainly is not without validity but does not do justice to the range that he was to demonstrate in subsequent works. Klaus Wagenbach (1963) contradicts Jens and defends the novel's "excessive" length, considers the choice of three narrators justified in terms of the three periods they write about, and deems Grass's parody of the diction of philosopher Martin Heidegger (1889–1975) entirely apt. Not surprisingly, GDR critic Hugo Braun (1963) acknowledges Grass's brilliant analysis of West German society, a society that concentrates on the "economic miracle" but ignores the Nazi past. Yet Braun considers the analysis to be absolutely non-committal; it does not offer any future-oriented perspective.

In the Christian cultural magazine *Stimmen der Zeit,* which was and is edited by Jesuits, Paul Konrad Kurz (1964) provides a fairly extensive review, together with a detailed summary in which he surmises that Grass's role as enfant terrible or bogeyman (*Bürgerschreck*) inspired him and increased his courage to transgress the borders of legitimate contortion by totally condemning the economic status quo of the Federal Republic, failing to distance himself sufficiently from his characters, especially Matern, and indulging in the undifferentiated use of language as, for instance, in Harry Liebenau's negation of the existence of purity, in which he equates "pigs . . . Jesus Christ, Marx and Engels" (*DY,* 296). There is then, Kurz observes, a nihilistic tendency that tends to aim not only at the destruction of Hitler but also that of religion.

From the vantage point of 1967, Marcel Reich-Ranicki offers a kind of postscript to the reviews of *Hundejahre* and grants the novel the status of one of the important works of the 1960s; however, he also notes that the narrative represents an earlier stage in Grass's artistic development that the author had already overcome in *Katz und Maus,* a work in which he successfully strove for a synthesis combining artistic discipline and moral responsibility. In part, Reich-Ranicki reiterates previous critical comments by calling the introduction of three narrators less convincing than the single perspective provided by Oskar in *Die Blechtrommel.* Furthermore, Reich-Ranicki faults Grass for using a profuse number of gags, which detract from the work's social criticism.

A Writer of International Repute

An anonymous review in the *Times Literary Supplement* (1963d), which preceded the novel's publication in the English translation by Ralph Manheim, is unencumbered by German sensibilities and takes a more positive stance than several German appraisals. The reviewer praises Grass for having written "by far the fullest and most convincing critique of Nazism yet achieved in fiction" because, unlike Thomas Mann in *Doktor Faustus* (1947; *Doctor Faustus,* 1948), he succeeds in "demythologizing, de-heroizing and . . . de-demonizing" (68) the Nazis. The commentator also lauds Grass for "retracing the topography, folklore and idiom of his native region" with "incomparable verbal ingenuity and zest" and expects "further developments" with regard to Grass's "capacities as a novelist" (71). In a 1964 essay, George Steiner essentially agrees, but he assumes a combative stance when he writes that Grass in singular fashion makes the Germans "face up to their monstrous past" (in O'Neill 1987c, 31) and reiterates that "like no other writer he has mocked and subverted the bland oblivion, the self-acquittal which underlie Germany's material resurgence" (36).

When Ralph Manheim's English rendering of *Hundejahre* was published in the United States in the spring of 1965 as *Dog Years,* it received approximately the same critical response in quantitative terms as its two predecessors. Ray Lewis White (1981) lists seventy-six reviews in his compilation of excerpts, a number that is somewhat larger than the counts for either *The Tin Drum* or *Cat and Mouse.* Needless to say, more important than the quantitative yardstick is the fact that with the publication of *Dog Years* Grass became established as a writer of international repute, as Sigrid Mayer (1978) notes in her survey of Grass's reception in this country. The most visible sign of the author's increasing stature, which was no longer confined to literary circles, is perhaps the extensive coverage Grass received in the 4 June 1965 issue of *Life* magazine, a coverage that includes photos of Grass and family as well as an assessment by David E. Scherman. While Scherman calls Grass the "most startling German novelist since Thomas Mann" and compares his writing to that of T. S. Eliot, Faulkner, and Joyce, Anthony West in *Newsweek* (24 May 1965) puts the case rather more strongly: "Günter Grass today is acknowledged as the author who put postwar German literature back in the world market. He is fast becoming a director of much of his country's creative movement, a keeper of old myths and new methods" (117). Yet *Dog Years* falls short, the reviewer writes, because the novel is "not up to nailing down the evasive essence of Nazi horror," and Grass contends himself "with mere substitutes and symbols" (118).

British writer and critic D. J. Enright (1965) offers a somewhat ambivalent opinion in the *New York Review of Books* by stating that there is "no end of excess fat," but, at the same time, the novel is a "muscular piece of flesh and blood." Enright surmises that "central" to the book is the "idea of the bloodbrotherhood of German and Jew" but intimates that by portraying Amsel as a willing victim, Grass appears to dabble in "old racist theory." Furthermore, Enright takes issue with the reviewer of the *Times Literary Supplement,* questioning the writer's success in "dedemonizing" Nazism by referring to the "ambiguous Wagnerism" in *Dog Years.* Yet in the end Enright concedes that, on the whole, the novel represents a "staggering performance."

Less ambivalent than Enright, John Simon (1965), occasionally given to acerbic comments, prefers *Dog Years* to *The Tin Drum* because it hovers between Homer, who brings "the huge down to human size," and Joyce, who makes "the minute immeasurable" (13). Paul West (1965) is similarly appreciative and considers the novel "a work of genius, no matter how cantankerous, willful, filthy, tedious, brutal, nihilistic, long-winded, importunate, self-conscious or Germany-obsessed you find it" (84). British poet Stephen Spender, writing on the front page of the *New York Times Book Review* (1965), is less flattering. Although he acknowledges that Grass successfully conveys "how modern propaganda and power politics" can corrupt traditional patterns and concedes that the novel "contains scenes more powerful than those by any other contemporary novelist," he finds it ultimately "far too long" and even "turgid." In the *New Yorker,* Anthony West (1965b) praises Grass's "exemplary courage" in arriving at what may be perceived as an undifferentiated conclusion of dubious validity, in that Nazism is declared not to have been an aberration but a "logical" product "of the Germanic tradition" — a tradition against which the author invokes "individual responsibility." Earl Rovit (1965) places Grass's achievement in the context of a (West) German postwar "literary renaissance" (678), which because of the Nazi legacy dispenses with a "literature of entertainment, of decoration, of even mild social criticism" (679) and, in the case of Grass, develops an "authentically revolutionary" structure "in its attempt to comprehend the jaggedness of our contemporary world" (682).

During approximately three weeks in the spring of 1965 Grass visited New York City and other cities along the East coast, read from his works, granted interviews, was to be heard on radio and to be seen on TV, and received an honorary doctorate from Kenyon College in Gambier, Ohio — activities and events that attested to and confirmed Grass's status as an author of international repute.

Weininger, Heidegger, Wagner

On the whole, *Hundejahre* has attracted less critical notice than either of its two predecessors in articles or monographs that are exclusively addressed to the novel. There are, however, sometimes fairly detailed discussions to be found in other contexts, that is, in works proffering analyses of the totality of Grass's work and in studies devoted to the *Danziger Trilogie* as a whole (see ch. 4).

One of the first academic critics to concern himself with *Hundejahre,* Wesley V. Blomster (1969b), examines the function of Otto Weininger's influential *Geschlecht und Charakter* (1903; *Sex and Character,* 1906). Weininger's study surfaces at crucial junctures in the lives of the Amsels, father and son, and "appears to remind" each of them of "his [Jewish] progenitors." On the one hand, they find in Weininger "an escape mechanism" by learning "that being Jewish is essentially only a mental state, a psychological concern"; on the other, especially Eddi Amsel is reminded by Weininger that his attempts to "overcome" his Jewishness have not been entirely successful. As a consequence, he renews his unsuccessful battle for complete acceptance (125), which carries him to the extreme of wanting to identify with the storm troopers. Inasmuch as Weininger postulates that Jews lack a metaphysical *Sein* or essence, Eddi Amsel seeks to fill this perceived void in his life by joining a movement that demands sacrifices from its adherents in the service to a cause. At the same time, Weininger is also of relevance for the "Aryan" Walter Matern, Eddi Amsel's blood brother, because Weininger writes that the Jew serves as a warning to the "Aryan" who may find "Jewish elements in his own character" (Blomster, 137).

Blomster detracts from the persuasiveness of his argument about Weininger's significance in *Hundejahre* by then shifting his analysis to a different plane and concluding that Grass demonstrates "the operation of demonic forces within the historical phenomenon" (138). Actually, in a brief essay (1969a) Blomster investigates "The Demonic in History" further by elucidating the differences between Grass's novel and Thomas Mann's *Doktor Faustus*, somewhat in the vein of the anonymous reviewer of the *Times Literary Supplement* (1964) cited above. While Grass opts for the "'dedemonization' of history," in dealing with the Third Reich, in the eyes of Mann the "allegorical ability," which leads to the "formulation of mythology," is "the very greatness of artistic creativity" (79). Blomster perceives Grass's alleged unwillingness to transcend surface realism as evident in the episode involving Tulla Pokriefke, when she finds and identifies a "pile of [human] bones" (*DY*, 295 et passim) from the concentration camp at Stutthof near Danzig. Tulla's matter-of-fact observations are accompanied by Harry Liebenau's comments in Heideggerian diction (see *DY*, 306–7) — a "process of abstraction" (Blomster, 80) that, as might have been added, serves to obscure and obfuscate the Nazi crimes that have been committed.

The incorporation of Weininger's work in *Hundejahre* is also investigated by Lyle H. Smith, Jr. (1978). Smith observes that Grass uses Weininger to develop, with "ironic gravity," the "structure of Eddi Amsel's German-Jewish identity" (78). Amsel makes an effort to overcome some stereotypical Jewish traits singled out by Weininger: to counteract the aversion to physical exercise, he acts as middleman in the physically undemanding sport of *Faustball* (see *DY*, 170 et passim), and he seeks closer contact with the world of art by acting in a managerial capacity as ballet master of the "German Ballet" (*DY*, 255). Yet ultimately he fails to rid himself of those traits when, for example, he disrespects the sacred, as Matern disapprovingly notes (*DY*, 239). But, paradoxically, it is his "sense of ironic detachment" in particular that makes Amsel "both stereotypically 'Jewish' and vastly more complex . . . and interesting than the inarticulate and pugnacious Matern" (Smith, 89). True, Amsel also "manifests a sinister side" (92), particularly when in the postwar period he assumes control of his subterranean realm, which is populated by scarecrows and characterized by Matern as "hell itself" (*DY*, 541 et passim), but by "appearing to substantiate anti-Semitic doctrines" in the case of Amsel, Grass succeeds in deflating "Nazism's chief myths" about Jews (Smith, 94 and 95).

H. Peter Stowell (1979) views *Dog Years* as an apocalyptic novel in which a "rich mythic anthropology [is] combined with the Jungian psychological interpretation of . . .[the trickster] archetype [and culminates] in Claude Lévi-Strauss's structural model of the dioscuric trickster" (79). Amsel and Matern are then siblings and "antinomic doubles" (84), in that they form a "symbiotic relationship" as long as they act in accordance with their respective astrological signs. Amsel's sign, Pisces, associates him with water, creativity, femininity, planning, and Christ-like self-sacrifice, and Matern's sign, Aries, associates him with fire, aggressive behavior, destructiveness, masculinity, impulsiveness, and opportunism (see the chart in Stowell, 88–89) — a contrast that is only dissolved when both Amsel and Matern emerge from the underground "hell" and assume their old identities. Thus, instead of the "dioscuric trickster," a "dioscuric Messiah" embracing "good and evil" seems to emerge (93) — a reading implying an optimistic ending of the novel that is not shared by a majority of critics (see, for example, Di Napoli 1980; ch. 4).

Like Weininger, philosopher Martin Heidegger served as a target of Grass's polemics; these polemics are the focus of Sascha Kiefer's essay (2002), in which he plausibly suggests that Heidegger's affiliation with National Socialism made the philosopher a convenient target. Heidegger's style relies on neologisms and homonyms, and when quoted out of context, such a mode of writing appears comical. Although, Kiefer maintains, Grass's parody is neither original — Heidegger's style had served as fodder to elicit laughs in cabarets — nor subtle, it does have a provocative edge, in that it serves as a means to suppress and deny unpleasant facts as, for instance, when Liebenau verbally obscures what is obviously the aforementioned "pile of bones." Moreover, Grass establishes a clear intertextual reference between the seductive melodies the legendary Pied Piper of Hamelin plays on his flute (see also ch. 10) and the enticing words of Heidegger when the students serving in the antiaircraft battery attribute Liebenau's success in catching rats to his murmuring incantatory phrases akin to the philosopher's words (see *DY*, 303). An obvious parallel is then established between the Pied Piper's pervasive influence on young people and that of Heidegger, who induces them to follow Hitler. Moreover, the use of "'Heideggerdeutsch'" (Kiefer, 249) borders on the absurd at the end of book 2, when in April 1945, in the waning moments of the Second World War, Hitler's favorite dog, the German shepherd Prinz, runs away and is searched for by "Führerdog-searchgroups" who communicate with headquarters in Heideggerian terminology such as: "The original manifestness of the Führerdog is attuned to distantiality'" (see *DY,* 324–53). The grotesquely disproportionate effort that is expended on the dog search in conjunction with the obfuscating language used contributes to obliterate any trace of pathos and heroism that may be associated with the fall of the Third Reich.

Although one could question his excessive use of the Heidegger parody, Kiefer writes, one should not underestimate Grass's contribution in tackling a sensitive topic that was not widely discussed in the Federal Republic during the Adenauer era: that the common roots of both Heidegger's thinking and that of National Socialism were irrationalism, a precarious romanticism combined with nationalism, and intolerance vis-à-vis those holding different opinions. Grass may then be said to be attuned to Theodor W. Adorno and the Frankfurt School's critical theory; in *Mein Jahrhundert* (see ch. 14) he moderated his polemical stance and offered a more balanced view of the philosopher.

Whereas the references to Heidegger are prolific, but not necessarily overt (his name is explicitly mentioned nine times; for the numerous textual allusions, see especially Kiefer, 246–47, and Harscheidt, below), Richard Wagner merits merely two entries by name (see *DY,* 185 and 494), but the reference of Goldmouth (the former Eddi Amsel) to Weininger, Heidegger, and Wagner (via the "Siegfried motif"; see *DY,* 528) in virtually the same breath is indicative of the composer's importance. Actually, as Hanspeter Brode (1984) has surmised, Grass may, like Thomas Mann, a Wagner enthusiast, have derived the leitmotif technique from Wagner. There are, at any rate, allusions to *Der Ring des Nibelungen* (1853; *The Ring of the Nibelung,* 1976; see also ch. 1) via the "so-called Hoard of the Nibelungs" (*DY,* 524) and, less obviously, to *Götterdämmerung* or *Twilight of the Gods* ("world twilight"; *DY,* 349), the last opera of the tetralogy, which, Brode claims, serves to underline the demise of the Third Reich with mythological props — albeit, it should be added, hardly with the intent to endow its downfall with grandeur.

In her short study on Wagner reception in Günter Grass's *Hundejahre,* Mary A. Cicora (1993) takes Brode's suggestion that the prelude of *Twilight of the Gods,* in which the three Norns spin the rope of Fate, recalls Wotan's days of power, and predict the end of the Gods, has been adapted by Grass, in that the three narrators evoke past and present (somewhat) in the manner of the Norns. Cicora states that in *Hundejahre* Grass uses the Nazis' "obsession with death," as expressed in their identification with *Götterdämmerung*, by parodying the "apocalyptic aspect" of the "Wagnerian model" (55) and cites as a further instance of the author's parodistic intent the scene in which Matern and the escaped dog he (re)named Pluto are questioned by the participants in a postwar "Open Forum" (see *DY*, 471–506). In order to determine the dog's previous owner the panelists test the dog's reactions to various pieces of music; Pluto does not react to Mozart, wags his tail when "*Deutschland, Deutschland über Alles*" is being played (not Händel, as Cicora, 55, has it), and howls throughout when he hears the music from *Götterdämmerung* — irrefutable proof that the dog "must have belonged to an admirer of Wagner," that is, Hitler (*DY*, 494).

In a more encompassing vein, Cicora perceives parody at work in the overall design of the novel, which, unlike Wagner's dealing with the "beginning and end of the world" confines itself — albeit hardly exclusively — to the telling of the "story of a family of dogs." The future is foretold not by Erda, goddess of wisdom/Earth, but by lowly (meal) worms. In what might be called a bold transposition, Wagner's "Rhine has become the Vistula," the blood brothers Amsel and Matern recall Siegfried and Gunther, who are bound by an oath, and Matern's tossing his pocket knife into the Vistula may allude to Siegfried and Brünnhilde's "refusal" to hurl the ring of the Nibelungs into the Rhine (58). Yet the explicit and implicit parodistic allusions to Wagner should not entirely obscure the serious, albeit playfully presented intent underlying *Hundejahre*.

Fantastic Realism, Mythmaking, Intertextuality

In his 1972 publication, which originated as a dissertation and was preceded by a very brief article (1970), Albrecht Goetze chooses an unusual format, presenting his ten theses in numerical order and a style that dispenses with traditional concessions to readability in the form of transitions and the like, in order to better enable the reader to check the results the study has achieved. Goetze's radical stance is not only evident in matters of form; he does not confine himself to acknowledging the social dimension of literature via its potential for reflecting and portraying social mores; rather, he defines literary studies as a prospective tool for intervening in societal practices (vi). Hence Grass's choice of three narrators is a good way of displaying the simultaneous recapitulation of past and contemporary history from differing positions and levels of consciousness (xviii). The three narrators are then not figures that can serve as objects of psychological analysis; rather, they exhibit the deformations resulting from the pressures exerted by the capitalist and imperialist socioeconomic structures. Especially Matern has turned into a phenotype that persists in contributing to the reproduction of the prevailing socioeconomic system.

In Goetze's Marxist-inspired view, which reflects the orientation of the student-protest generation, this system survived the Nazi period and is flourishing in postwar West Germany. Whereas Goetze makes relevant observations on the structure and language of *Hundejahre,* his "depressing" conclusion is less convincing. He uses the general lack of awareness of the deformations wrought by society and the absence of class consciousness in the novel to add an implied activist twist to his argument. The acquisition of class consciousness, he opines, will set people free. This is hardly a proposition that Grass, radical opponent of all ideologies, would have endorsed, as for example, Volker Neuhaus (1979, rev. ed. 1992, 90–91) notes.

Breon Mitchell (1973) sets out to defend the novel against those reviewers who charge that it lacks structural unity. Mitchell suggests as a model Dante's *La divina Commedia* (1472; *The Divine Comedy,* 1993), a model Grass uses in "a formal and literary reworking of certain of its characteristics" (Mitchell, 66) that amounts to a "parodic inversion" (75). Grass retains structural features of the *Comedy* such as the thirty-three "Morning Shifts" in book 1, which indicate the importance of numbers in Grass's scheme and correspond to the thirty-three cantos in each book of Dante's work. *Hundejahre* ends with the visit of Brauxel (the former Eddi Amsel) and Walter Matern to the underworld mine in "The Hundred and Third and Bottommost Materniad" (*DY,* 535–61) — whereas Dante's *Divine Comedy* concludes in paradise. A complete inversion would require a beginning of *Hundejahre* in paradise; in view of the absence of such a beginning, Mitchell proposes that a "relative state of innocence" prevails in book 1 "prior to the betrayal" (75) of Eddi Amsel by Walter Matern in book 2 and the dominant sense of guilt pervading book 3. *Hundejahre* retells the story of the Fall "from innocence, through 'sin,' to guilt" — albeit by providing a "commentary on history" rather than one in a cosmological-theological vein.

Less concerned with historical forces, Carl O. Enderstein (1975) focuses in his short survey on the significance of teeth for the characterization of both Eddi Amsel and Walter Matern. The latter is nicknamed the "Grinder" because he is in the habit of grinding his teeth (*DY,* 7 et passim) — primarily in order to signal his aggressiveness to potential opponents; at the same time, his healthy teeth are indicative of sexual potency. Conversely, Eddi Amsel loses all thirty-two of his teeth when he is viciously attacked by the storm troopers in disguise, among them Matern. Although Amsel's lack of potency had been established before this incident, the loss of his teeth may be interpreted as a symbolic castration in accordance with Freud. After Amsel has been reincarnated as Haseloff and has acquired gold teeth, he is nicknamed Goldmäulchen or Goldmouth and begins to act more decisively. Yet he remains essentially a man who inclines toward contemplation rather than action.

Michael Harscheidt (1976) identifies "fantastic realism," the co-existence of Grass's almost pedantic penchant for rendering historical, geographical, political, and other details with a high degree of accuracy on the one hand and his desire to explode this surface realism with elements of parody, satire, and the fantastic on the other, as one of the key aspects of *Hundejahre:* "There is no contradiction between playfulness and pedantry" (*DY,* 3), as the novel has it. In his voluminous study of more than seven hundred pages, which features an extensive bibliography and detailed index, Harscheidt explores stylistic and rhetorical elements at great length. He also traces Grass's original sources and other minutiae; thus he specifies the quotations from Martin Heidegger that Grass parodies (189–90). However, as the title of the work suggests, Harscheidt's main thrust is the symbolism of numbers, which he finds to be pervasive and which form the "macro structure" of the novel. In a segment on the secularization of the sacred number three, for instance, he offers a wealth of textual evidence that goes far beyond the obvious, such as the division of the novel into three books and the narration by three "authors" (258–73). Ultimately, the numbers signify the conflict between the sacred, which is associated with the number ten as in the Ten Commandments on the one hand, and the Hitler-inspired, sinfully profane on the other, which is represented by the number nine, which has a long pedigree of "evil" connotations and comes to the fore in the aforementioned attack of the nine masked storm troopers on Eddi Amsel as reported in book 2. Yet there is such an overabundance of informative detail in Harscheidt's encyclopedic study that, as Neuhaus (1979, rev. ed. 1992, 97) remarks, the results of his labors tend to become diminished on account of his inability to separate important from less important points.

In her essay on *Dog Years,* largely overlooked by other scholars, Hamida Bosmajian (1979) reads the novel as a "message" from the dark side of "the utopias of Nazism, West German consumer democracy, and, to a lesser extent, East German socialism" (83). In agreement with other critics, Bosmajian grants Grass his demythologizing impetus, his desire to rob "evil of its sublimity, its hot-air hyberboles"; however, she deviates from accepted opinion by declaring Grass, in alluding to the subtitle of Hannah Arendt's *Eichmann in Jerusalem* (1963), to be a mythmaker of his own: "[Grass] is the mythmaker of the banality of evil, the petty evil of every man that leads . . . to murder" (89). Inasmuch as "Hitler, the greatest power" (111) in the novel, is virtually absent, and inasmuch as Grass's predilection for the milieu of the lower middle class has not been seriously questioned, Bosmajian's observation seems apt. Her equation of author Grass and narrator Harry Liebenau — both supposedly succeed in "burying a real mound made of human bones under medieval allegories" (109) — seems rather far-fetched in view of the fact that the pile of bones from the

Stutthof concentration camp actually "cried out to high heaven" (*DY*, 311). Although Amsel's postwar reincarnation Brauxel specifically instructs Harry Liebenau to write about the bones (see *DY*, 295), Bosmajian infers that Amsel/Brauxel is not genuinely interested in coming to terms with the past. Referring to Goetze, she categorizes all three narrators as phenotypes, "distinguished by visible and external rather than internal traits" (92), and, furthermore, as tricksters who seek to deceive others but also deceive themselves. It is therefore fitting that Eddi Amsel assigns the writing of book 1, the Morning Shifts, to himself, because this book describes the youthful friendship between him and Walter Matern and is not primarily concerned with the "far more complicated and implicating years of the Nazi era" (93) — a legacy with which both Amsel and Matern fail to cope adequately.

"The Dilemma of Freedom" in *Die Blechtrommel* and *Hundejahre* is the topic addressed by William Slaymaker (1981). Slaymaker distinguishes between the "bold and decisive pronouncements" in Grass's political and literary essays and the "mind boggling complexity" of Grass's presentation of the "problem of human freedom" in his fiction. This problem arises from overburdening the two novels with "conflicting forces and counterforces" (66). In a rare admission of critical impotence, in which one encounters faint echoes of the objections raised by early reviewers, Slaymaker admits that Grass's suggestion of a "world of cooks and robots who stir the soup of life and keep the mechanisms of human tragedy percolating" (48) causes the critic "to throw up his hands in despair" (66) — an honest but not particularly helpful statement. Scott H. Abbott's (1982) approach augments that of Slaymaker by focusing on the three narrators and thereby offering a key to an understanding of the novel. He calls the tripartite narration by Eddi Amsel, Harry Liebenau, and Walter Matern "confessions of misled, defensive, and representative minds" (218). Abbott attributes both the "innumerable references to astrology, myth, superstition, magical transformation, divination of the future, and other supernatural activities" (212) and the novel's numerological structure to the narrators' "demonization of the Nazis" (218) — the very activity that Grass wishes to expose.

Without referring to Abbott, Marc Silberman (1985) extends part of Abbott's argument when he writes that the three narrators are not characters in a traditional sense. Rather, they represent separate perspectives and initiate the process of remembering in the face of postwar (West) Germany's tendency to suppress the past. The narrators' differing perspectives are one strategy devised by Grass to induce the reader to enter into a dialogue with the text; the deliberately complex structure of the novel, its both fragmentary and ambivalent character as well as its clearly exhibited intertextuality are designed to motivate the reader to begin the task of coming to terms with the past via recollecting. In this way, Grass's politics and aesthetics intersect, and the fundamentally distinct modes of his political writings and fiction, lamented by Slaymaker, serve the same purpose of enlightening various segments of the (reading) public.

In his study of works by Jean Genet, Louis Ferdinand Céline, and Grass (*Die Blechtrommel, Hundejahre*), Frederick J. Harris (1987) bases his comparison on the fact that all three authors "provide graphic scenarios of the end of World War II in Europe" that are narrated "from very personal, almost idiosyncratic, points of view" (257). While Harris seeks to shed light on the relationship between "literary and historical truth," his analysis appears to be stating the obvious: Genet, Céline, and Grass "presented historical situations" (273) for different reasons and chose unrelated manners of presentation.

It may well be appropriate to assume, as Jutta Goheen (1996) does, that the narrative complexity of *Hundejahre* explains its place at the "periphery" (155) of the critical debate about the *Danziger Trilogie*. A contributing factor to this complexity is Grass's use of intertextual references, among which Goheen singles out the mention of nineteenth-century novelist Wilhelm Raabe, whose novel *Stopfkuchen* (1891; *Tubby Schaumann,* 1983) is one of the favorites of Dr. Oswald Brunies, teacher of both Eddi Amsel and Walter Matern (see *DY,* 92 et passim). On the basis of the similarity of names, Goheen discovers in Eddi, whose full name is Eduard Heinrich Amsel, similarities to both Eduard, whose last name is not given, and Heinrich Schaumann, the two friends in Raabe's novel. Narrator Eduard seems to be adventurous and daring: he has emigrated to South Africa, where he leads the existence of a European colonialist; conversely, his friend Schaumann never leaves home but acquires a remarkable degree of wisdom, which enables him to solve a baffling murder mystery. Yet both Eduard and Heinrich represent variations of patterns of behavior to be found among the petty bourgeoisie — reason enough for Grass, Goheen argues, to resurrect Raabe's figures and to endow Eddi Amsel with traits of these literary forebears. However, instead of having the option to undertake Eduard's exploratory journey, Eddi Amsel is coerced to flee for his life; conversely, instead of being able to choose Schaumann's voluntary seclusion, he is forced into the role of an outsider and becomes a victim of discrimination. In short, as several other critics have also noted, Raabe's humorous idyll has turned into a veritable nightmare in *Hundejahre,* and the petty bourgeoisie has become the breeding ground for Nazism.

Artists, Children, Dogs, and "Magic Spectacles"

The ambivalent function of artists and artist figures in both *Die Blechtrommel* and *Hundejahre* is examined by Ann L. Mason (1973), who states that both Oskar Matzerath and Eddi Amsel reflect "what the Nazis revered as well as what they rejected" and alludes to the difficulty arising from the attempt to disentangle the "various artistic roles" Eddi Amsel plays (355). Notably the parade of his scarecrow storm troopers, during which he assumes the role of the Führer (*DY,* 209–11) may express his desire to participate via his art "in the spirit of the Nazi movement" or, conversely, to present "a grotesque satire of Nazi reality" (Mason, 356). In using "parodic variations of the traditional artist-figures" (362), Mason concludes, Grass has endowed Eddi Amsel with traits that "symbolically epitomize" (361) those forces that shaped German history.

In her 2001 study Debbie Pinfold characterizes Tulla Pokriefke, a figure who makes her first appearance under that name in *Katz und Maus* (see ch. 2), as a "predatory female with an overwhelming sexual drive"; in contrast, her complementary figure Jenny, the foundling reared by Dr. Oswald Brunies, represents "innocence and vulnerability." But in her highly questionable conclusion, Pinfold states that the "tensions inherent in the children of *Hundejahre* suggest that Grass wants to believe in the child's positive intellectual and moral potential" and that "within every Grass child, no matter how apparently monstrous, a Romantic child is struggling to get out" (135–43). Before Pinfold's study appeared, Volker Neuhaus had published his illuminating essay on Tulla (1970). Neuhaus associates her with the realm of the dead via the irrepressible and "infernal" smell of "bone glue" that she exudes (*DY,* 121 et passim), her virtually murdering Jenny in the snow — an act of extreme savagery from which Jenny miraculously recovers — and her living, eating, and sleeping with the dog Harras. Harras "sired" the Führer's dog Prinz (*DY,* 15) but was called Pluto by Amsel — an unmistakable reference to the realm of the dead. According to Neuhaus, Tulla's sojourn in the kennel resembles Orpheus's descent into the underworld, in that she seems to be intent on resurrecting her drowned, deaf-mute brother, the only person she genuinely loved (see *DY,* 141). When she returns to the realm of humans, her family, she has turned into a strangely attractive demonic creature that is instrumental in spreading doom and misery.

Ursula or, rather, Tulla, the nickname that probably has been "derived from Thula the Koshnavian [derived from Koshnavia or Koschneiderei, an area southwest of Danzig] water nymph" (*DY,* 118), also merits a brief mention in Rimvydas Šliažas's essay (1973). Although the name appears to reinforce the associations about Tulla's "demonic" nature, Šliažas focuses primarily on "Elements of Old Prussian Mythology" in the novel, such as the gods Perkunos, Pikollos, and Potrimpas, who are revived in Amsel's scarecrows. Perkunas, "the Lithuanian god of thunder and lightning" (41), lends his name to the black dog of "mystical origins in Lithuania" (40), who heads the line that includes Senta, Harras, and, finally, Prinz, the dog that "will make history" (*DY*, 36). Grass's well-substantiated choice of such lineage in conjunction with his evocation of or allusion to other elements of Old Prussian mythology, Šliažas claims, signifies the resurgence of "old pagan myths [and] ancient barbarism" during the Nazi period that Christianity had not entirely succeeded in annihilating (40).

Another approach Grass takes to the "occult and irrational" world of National Socialism is explored by Alan Frank Keele (1987, 58) who traces the occurrence of "Magic Spectacles and the Motif of the Mimetic Mantic" in postwar texts such as Wolfgang Borchert's *Draußen vor der Tür* (1947; *The Man Outside*, 1952) and Martin Walser's *Ehen in Philippsburg* (1957; Marriages in Philippsburg). In *Hundejahre* the so-called "'miracle glasses'" (*DY*, 453 et passim), which are marketed by Brauxel, make it possible for members of the postwar generation to see the flaws and misdeeds of their parents. Whereas Frank-Raymund Richter (1979; see ch. 4) views Brauxel as representing an unrealizable alternative to the existence of actual artists in the Federal Republic, Keele stresses Amsel's role as a "mimetic mantic, an aesthetic seer" (53) who passes on his vision of horrors to younger people. When Amsel as a young boy is virtually forced by his "bigoted and superstitious neighbor" (54) to burn his arsenal of scarecrows, among them the especially fear-inspiring specimen, the "Great Cuckoo Bird" (*DY*, 85 et passim), he envisions his future role as a creator of scarecrows that embody the "apocalyptic realities of holocaust and doomsday" (Keele, 54). Thus Walli Sawatzki, presumably Matern's niece, "sees" the savage attack on Amsel by the storm troopers, among them her uncle and her father, through the glasses (see *DY*, 209–11; see also Enderstein 1975) — a haunting vision that causes her to be hospitalized. The "miracle glasses," Keele concludes, do then seem to function as a kind of mirror "held up to the Third Reich and to postwar German society" by dealing with these phenomena on their "own occult and irrational terms" (58).

4: *Danziger Trilogie / The Danzig Trilogy*

A Genuine Trilogy?

ALTHOUGH COMPARISONS BETWEEN Grass's first three major narratives had been made before, John Reddick (1975), taking a cue from the author, who supposedly complained about the lack of critics' recognition of the interrelation of the three works (see Reddick 1971), was the first to state explicitly that *Die Blechtrommel, Katz und Maus,* and *Hundejahre* belong "together as a kind of trilogy" (xi), show a "genetic relationship" (xii), and "amount to a distinctive complex" (xiii). He based this claim on the virtually simultaneous origin of concepts, drafts, and plans that then evolved into the three related yet separate texts, which he named the *Danzig Trilogy.* The title caught on and is now widely used; Luchterhand, then Grass's publisher, brought out a special edition of the three texts as *Danziger Trilogie* (1980), and in 1987 Harcourt Brace Jovanovich followed suit with the first American edition of the entire trilogy. As Volker Neuhaus and Daniela Hermes in their miscellaneous collection on the *Danziger Trilogie* (1991, 7) point out, the trilogy evolved into a pentology through the addition of the later works *Der Butt* (see ch. 7) and *Die Rättin* (see ch. 10); Grass's current publisher Steidl advertises *Das Danzig-Sextett* (2006), which in addition to the volumes of the trilogy includes *Der Butt, Unkenrufe* (see ch. 12), and *Im Krebsgang* (see ch. 15). The significance of Danzig for Grass's oeuvre is thus incontestable; to point out its importance has indeed become a commonplace in Grass criticism. In his 1975 monograph, Reddick proposed to subject the three works of the *Danzig Trilogy* to a "straightforward interpretation" (174); this resulted in a comprehensive analysis in which he scrutinizes each text individually but also takes into account the relationship of each text "to the others" (xiii) while acknowledging the distinct differences among the various works. For example, Reddick stresses that "death figures . . . prominently and insistently" in *Die Blechtrommel* but not in *Hundejahre* (31–32). Yet one obvious common denominator, that is, the importance of the lower middle-class Danzig milieu as "a German microcosm . . . [where] events in the Reich were repeated in slow motion," as Hans L. Leonhardt, a possible source for Grass, wrote in his *Nazi Conquest of Danzig* (1942, vii) does, perhaps, come less clearly into focus than the emphasis of other critics (see, for example, Koopmann 1977) would lead one to expect. Conversely, Reddick does mention that in the "strongly localised" parts of *Hundejahre,* which mostly take place in the Vistula delta and in Danzig, a convincing "lucid pattern" prevails (267); moreover, in his brief conclusion, which is exclusively devoted to the last novel of the trilogy and dispenses with a summary comparison of the three works in question, Reddick finds *Hundejahre* full of "hollow contrivances" such as the escape of Hitler's dog Prinz, which is presented in a "grossly artificial manner" (268). Nevertheless, he asks rhetorically, is the trilogy "perhaps the finest body of fiction in modern German literature?" (270).

Reddick's monograph was preceded by his 1971 essay, in which he posed the question of whether the three works formed a trilogy of suffering ("Leiden"); both essay and monograph are based on Reddick's 1970 Oxford dissertation. Apart from the common origin of the three works, Reddick emphasizes the factors of time and place they have in common — as evident in the correspondence of the three books of *Die Blechtrommel* and *Hundejahre:* books 1 and 2 take place during the prewar period and the Second World War in Danzig and environs, the respective third books deal with postwar history in West Germany. The considerably shorter text of the novella *Katz und Maus* corresponds essentially to the middle parts of the two novels in that it deals with the wartime period. It is then justified to speak of a trilogy, even if the three works do not cohere in the sense of a serialized novel. In fact, the differences with regard to the narrative stance would seem to undermine the assumption of a trilogy; furthermore, whereas *Katz und Maus, Hundejahre,* and *Örtlich betäubt* (see ch. 5), a text that Reddick frequently cites in conjunction with the trilogy, each feature a pair of antithetical protagonists, *Die Blechtrommel* does not. But what ultimately justifies the term "trilogy," Reddick avers, is the assumption that all three texts are laments about the state of the world in general and a society in particular in which destruction, persecution, and disintegration predominate. (In his 1999 tribute to Nobel laureate Grass, Reddick seems to have modified his opinion when he writes, without further elaboration, that the "great trio of books" is generally, "if misleadingly" [!], known as the *Danzig Trilogy.*)

More specifically than Reddick, Gertrude Cepl-Kaufmann (1986) emphasizes the concept of *Heimat,* which, in conjunction with the debate about the postwar expulsions of Germans from the territories to the East of the Oder-Neisse line, assumes paramount significance in the *Danziger Trilogie.* Cepl-Kaufmann defines Grass's perception of this central category as diametrically opposed to that of the *Heimatkunstbewegung* around 1900 (an artistic movement focusing on the representation of *Heimat*) with its opposition to the big city and its culture, science and technology, anti-intellectualism, and anti-Semitism (62). Rather, Cepl-Kaufmann argues,

Grass's socio-critical intent is evident in his lack of idealizing and sentimentalizing his former *Heimat* Danzig: inasmuch as the lower middle class, in whose milieu the novel takes place, supported Nazism, its members are implicitly or explicitly responsible for the loss of their *Heimat* (72).

In what might be considered a questioning of the coherence of the *Danzig Trilogy,* Wayne P. Lindquist (1989) reiterates previous critics' sentiments in stating that the three "novels" [!] leave readers with "ambiguous and contradictory conclusions." Lindquist differs from those previous critics because he does not endeavor to resolve these contradictions or to "reduce" them "to greater clarity" (179). Rather, in a fairly detailed analysis of book 3 of *Hundejahre,* the "Materniads," Lindquist interprets the brief exchange between Amsel/Brauxel and Walter Matern before they leave the mine in the last "Materniad" as one instance of an insoluble paradox: Matern suggests that the "mine-joyous" inscription "'*Glück auf,*'" the traditional greeting of miners wishing each other good luck, ought to be exchanged for the famous quotation from the third canto of Dante's *Divine Comedy,* "'Abandon hope all ye who enter here!'" (*DY,* 561). Grass does not make any attempt to reconcile these conflicting maxims, nor, for that matter, does he offer a "system, answer, formula, and ideology" (191) — with the presumable result that he will disappoint readers' expectations and will leave them dissatisfied. Whereas Silberman (see chapter 3), whom Lindquist does not refer to, suggests the possibility of the reader's active engagement with the text, that would, ideally, counteract the postwar tendency to suppress the past, Lindquist also appreciates the work because of its capability to initiate reflection on the part of the reader. Lindquist does not, however, provide any indication as to the direction in which such reflection might proceed.

Detailed studies of the reception of Grass's works outside the German-speaking countries and the English-speaking lands are quite rare. Janina Gesche's monograph (2003) about the critical resonance the *Danziger Trilogie* achieved in two different countries, Poland and Sweden, constitutes an exception. While such juxtaposition may appear odd, it brings to the fore the fact that the postwar European reception of Grass's works was, to a considerable extent, dependent on historical conditions, specifically the reaction to the two successor states to Nazi Germany on the part of other European countries — a reaction that was influenced by the political situation during the Cold War in a Europe divided by the Iron Curtain. In Sweden, a neutral country during the Second World War and not a member of any postwar alliance, the volumes of the trilogy appeared in translation within a few years of the publication of the German originals and were generally well received by Swedish reviewers, who, by and large, arrived at their evaluations by emphasizing literary and aesthetic criteria. It was quite a different matter in Poland, Gesche writes; apart from the political considerations mentioned above, Polish sensibilities were affected by the topic of Danzig, the former German and now Polish city, with the result that a Polish translation of *Die Blechtrommel* was not published until 1983 — although an underground edition appeared in 1979 — and *Hundejahre* appeared as late as 1990, almost thirty years after the German edition. The Polish rendering of *Katz und Maus,* however, became available comparatively early, in 1963. Polish critics tended to include in their reviews questions about Grass's attitude toward Poland in general and the Oder-Neisse line, since 1990 the officially recognized border between Germany and Poland, in particular (see also Gesche 2004 for the significance of "national clichés" in Polish criticism). Polish critics' preoccupation with *Die Blechtrommel,* especially the chapter "The Polish Post Office" in book 2, constitutes what is presumably a singular phenomenon in international Grass criticism, inasmuch as the work was not officially available in Poland for more than twenty years (280).

The Messiah and the Absurd Process of History

In one of the comparatively rare contributions that focuses exclusively on the role of religion or, more specifically, on the "Christ Figure" in the *Danzig Trilogy,* Thomas Di Napoli (1980) posits that Grass is concerned "with the possibility of the archetypal messiah figure emerging in our own troubled age" (25) and displays an "almost obsessive interest in the Christ figure" — a proposition the majority of critics would probably be reluctant to subscribe to. Nevertheless, Di Napoli's analysis of Oskar's role in *The Tin Drum,* which revolves around his "identification with the *Infant* Jesus rather than with the adult Christ" (30) is not without credibility, in that this identification allows Oskar to assume the stance of a sheltered yet irresponsible child. Oskar maintains this stance until the very end, when he seeks "security . . . [within] the walls of an insane asylum" (33) and is most likely not to "play the messiah they see in me" (*TD,* 585).

Whereas the coming of the Messiah does not occur in *The Tin Drum,* Joachim Mahlke in *Cat and Mouse* is identified with the Messiah via the "mocking idolatry" (Di Napoli, 34) of his classmates, who scornfully notice his superficial resemblance to Christ in his appearance as a "redeemer" (*CaM,* 43 et passim). Yet Mahlke is particularly drawn to the Virgin Mary, a figure he tends to confuse with Eve because of his increasing sexual awareness — an aberration that finally leads him "to return to the sea," that is, the sunken minesweeper. Ironically, this happens on a Friday, "the day on which that figure died from whom he has tried in vain to detach himself" (Di Napoli, 40). In order to complete the "parody of the scriptural Christ's life," Di Napoli maintains, Grass would have had to portray Christ's return in the third part of the trilogy. Although the

"Christ figure . . . is less clearly defined" in *Dog Years* than in either *The Tin Drum* or *Cat and Mouse,* Di Napoli sees Walter Matern as an unlikely "emissary of the Lord," who inflicts "retribution" on former Nazis (by infecting their wives and daughters with venereal disease) even if he is motivated by "unconscious, personal considerations" (41). The absence of a "true Messiah" is underlined by the conclusion of *Dog Years,* where Amsel and Matern emerge from the former's "inferno-like, underground factory" and, "in desperate need of redemption," seek to cleanse themselves as best as they can (42).

The premise of redemption and a Messiah is implicitly rejected by Dieter Arendt (1989) in his essay on the cipher of the absurd in the *Danziger Trilogie.* In his observations, which incline toward the aphoristic, Arendt singles out individual scenes from the three texts and views them in the context of Gras's lyrics and plays. The memorable (and revolting) scene in which Oskar is forced to eat the unsavory broth that his playmates have concocted (see *TD,* 97–104) assumes significance in that Oskar is not allowed to act as a bystander but must swallow the "soup" that others have cooked up and the preparation of which he was unwilling or unable to prevent — a situation that reflects the fate of an outsider on the fringes of a totalitarian society. Similarly, in Oskar's nightmare about the unstoppable merry-go-round (see *TD,* 411–12) God is revealed as both effigy and bugbear of man/woman in his role as the mechanic and director of the absurd circular movement of history. In book 3 of *Dog Years* the question is asked: "If man was created in God's image and the scarecrow in the image of man, is the scarecrow not the image and likeness of God?" (*DY,* 552) — an ultimately unanswerable question, which, however, implies the absence of meaning and the prevalence of nihilism as the philosophical concept of the absurdity of historical processes. The function of art is then to represent this process, the absurdity of which is in part attributable to the contributory negligence of many, in order to provoke a confrontation.

Zeitgeschichte and *Vergangenheitsbewältigung*

Die Blechtrommel is clearly the focus of Hanspeter Brode's investigation (1977); although Brode does refer to the *Danziger Trilogie* in the title of his study about the *Zeitgeschichte* in Grass's texts, he only occasionally discusses *Katz und Maus* and *Hundejahre* and does not offer a detailed examination of these works. Among the handful of monographs that are explicitly devoted to the *Danziger Trilogie,* several of which originated as dissertations, Frank (Raymond) Richter (1979), in general follows Brode's approach (although he does not list him in his bibliography). Richter, who uses the uncommon term "Danzig-Trilogie," insists on the interconnectedness of aesthetics and ideology, of literature and society, and finds John Reddick's emphasis on the aesthetic qualities of the trilogy wanting. However, in his first publication on the trilogy (1977), he concedes that the difficulties of arriving at a conclusive reading of *Die Blechtrommel* in particular are considerable, because of the "Verfremdung" of the narration via Oskar's strangeness and negativity, which leave it to the reader to draw conclusions as to cause and effect, possible directions to follow, and potential courses of action to be taken. In his 1979 study on the *Vergangenheitsbewältigung* in the three prose texts in question, Richter hews to the stance of literary critics of the post-Nazi generation, who had been influenced by the (West) German student movement of the late 1960s and early 1970s (see ch. 1), when he defines as the focus of his investigation the aesthetic reflection of a late-bourgeois reality by a late-bourgeois writer. The question Richter poses is whether Grass succeeds not only in making transparent the mechanisms that caused the rise of Nazism but also in showing the possibility of their transformation with the aim of creating a praxis-oriented perspective for both artists and readers (13).

In accordance with his stated goal and in contrast to most other studies, Richter provides a rather detailed and fairly systematic analysis of the trilogy by making a genuine comparison between specific aspects of the three texts. Thus he shows that the predominant social milieu of the lower middle class in *Die Blechtrommel* is extended in *Hundejahre* to what may be called a panorama of society; as exemplified especially by the figures of Matzerath and Matern, the prevailing separation of the private realm and politics in the first novel is abandoned in favor of an explicitly political perspective in the last novel; and in both works the adherents and supporters of National Socialism have traits in common. Thus musician and former-Communist-turned-Nazi Meyn appears as a radicalized Matzerath; Matern, in turn, changes from Communist to Nazi and then anti-Fascist. These changes however, Richter maintains (61), are not depicted as sufficiently motivated and do not offer the reader any insight into the causality of historical processes, because Grass's ideological pattern of thought proceeds from the assumption of the identity of Fascism and Bolshevism (63) and is based on the assumption of hopelessness as the basic experience of human existence (79) — a premise that Grass began to modify in *Hundejahre,* albeit within the framework of bourgeois society, when Amsel/Brauxel emerges as the intellectually superior in comparison to the extremist Matern (85).

Amsel's artistic development results in his stature as a competent, superior artist. This development, however, is fostered by means of a utopian design when the "real," overweight Amsel emerges from the severe beating he receives from the disguised Matern and his cronies as a slender young man and turns into an artificial figure, later named Brauxel, in the "double miracle in the snow" (*DY*, 222), during which Jenny underwent a similarly miraculous transformation process. Even though Brauxel's way of life represents an unrealizable alternative to the existence of an artist in the society of the Federal Republic, Richter argues, Grass points out the socioeconomic conditions under which artists work when he has Brauxel market the so-called "'miracle glasses'" (*DY*, 453 et passim) that enable members of the postwar generation to perceive the flaws of their parents — a function similar to that of the scarecrows Brauxel produces for sale in the former mine.

However, by endowing Brauxel with a superior intellect, Richter avers, Grass essentially subscribes to the concept of culture prevalent in bourgeois society, which fosters the notion of the intellectual independence of the artist and, by doing so, obscures the conditions prevailing in a class society. Richter seeks to underscore his insights in the concluding chapter on Grass's realism and an appendix about National Socialism.

Less inspired by Marxist theory than Richter, Susanne Schröder (1986) investigates narrators and narrative perspectives in the *Danzig Trilogy;* she bases her interpretation primarily on Heinz Hillmann's *Alltagsphantasie und dichterische Phantasie* (1977; Everyday Fancy and Poetic Imagination), which proceeds from the assumption that literary texts are dependent on or derived from implicit, psychologically, historically, and sociologically grounded comparisons, which may serve as a means to test the veracity or probability of the representation of "reality" in specific works. In her detailed analysis of the three texts, Schröder reemphasizes the parallelism of events in Oskar's private sphere and those in the larger, historical context — for instance, Jan Bronski's death in book 2 marks the defeat of Poland — as well as his view from below, and his being rooted in the environment of the lower middle class. Schröder then poses the question whether, owing to the numerous biographical correspondences with which Grass endows his narrators, not only Oskar's comparatively narrow perspective but also the perspectives of the other narrators in the trilogy are akin to that of the author. Schröder concludes that the *Danziger Trilogie* does demonstrate the novelist's affinity to a perception of history that relies on moral categories but does not enable the reader to perceive the larger political, historical, and economic context that ultimately determines the characters' behavior — a conclusion that is somewhat reminiscent of that of Richter. Yet what may be characterized as a resigned stance on the part of Grass is both negated and supplemented by his pragmatically oriented political activity that, in part, is reflected in works such as *Aus dem Tagebuch einer Schnecke.*

Unlike Richter, Klaus von Schilling in his study of the "Schuldmotoren" (2002), a term used by Grass in an interview to define guilt as the narrators' impetus in *Danziger Trilogie*, perceives literary *Vergangenheitsbewältigung* not as a problem related to questions of the contents and modes of representation of National Socialism but as one that is intimately related to the aesthetic form ("Gestalt") of the respective works. The narrators' desire to express their guilt transcends their individual culpability and is related to the delegitimization of art in postwar society as a consequence of the Holocaust. This state of affairs was expressed in Theodor W. Adorno's famous dictum (and implicit postulate) of 1949, "To write poetry after Auschwitz is barbaric." Schilling devotes approximately two-thirds of his reading to *Die Blechtrommel*, and he attributes the cohesion of the *Danziger Trilogie* not only to the unity of time, place, and characters in the microcosm of Danzig-Langfuhr but also to the narrators' (sporadic) comments about their predecessors and their works, for example, when Harry Liebenau, the second narrator in *Hundejahre*, confirms the accuracy of Oskar's description of the Danzig "Stadttheater" in *Die Blechtrommel* (*DY*, 231). But Schilling perceives Grass's "artistic" narration as his chief accomplishment, that is, a type of narration that does not foreground the realistic mode of representation but rather the reflection about the catastrophe of the Holocaust, and the conditions that determine the writing of prose texts in the shadow of Auschwitz and provide an antidote against forgetting.

Adorno's dictum is also used as a starting point by Benedikt Engels (2005) in his analysis of the lyrical environs ("Umfeld") of the *Danziger Trilogie*. In his lecture on poetry on 13 February 1990 in Frankfurt am Main, entitled "Schreiben nach Auschwitz" ("Writing after Auschwitz"; in *Two States — One Nation?* 94–123), Grass looked back at the 1950s, when he began writing poems. He quoted his "programmatic" poem "Askese" (*WA* 1:98; "Askesis"), in which the color gray predominates, as evidence of his then not fully comprehended status of being a member of the "Auschwitz generation" — a generational experience that, in Adorno's terms, did not explicitly prohibit writing poetry but, rather, called for a new mode of expression that dispensed with the entire apparatus of conventional imagery, metaphors, and rhymes and engaged in an ascetic substitution of objects of daily life. But, Engels writes, whereas unconventional, frequently recurring motifs such as nuns, cooks, and birds (all of which he discusses in their appropriate contexts) tend to create a certain degree of cohesion in Grass's writings, they often leave the reader or interpreter at a loss owing to their novelty and idiosyncratic use. Yet Grass's lyrics may be considered an experiment in which he tests the suitability of materials to be used in his prose works.

Engels provides a rich array of textual evidence, enhanced by reproductions of Grass's illustrations; his book clearly demonstrates the interdependence of Grass's lyric and epic as well as his pictorial and sculptural work. To cite only a few examples of the many that Engels discusses in considerable detail, in *Die Blechtrommel,* Oskar's notorious, glass-shattering, "annihilating" screams (*TD,* 66 et passim) are prefigured in the poem "Die Schule der Tenöre" (*WA* 1:18–19; "The School for Tenors"), and an entire poem entitled "Der elfte Finger" (*WA* 1:36; "The Eleventh Finger"), anticipates Oskar's "eleventh finger" (*TD,* 280), which signifies his sexual arousal, in the chapter "Fizz Powder." Although *Katz und Maus* offers far less copious evidence of the interrelationship of lyrics and prose text, Engels cites Grass's poem "Racine läßt sein Wappen ändern" (*WA* 1:99–100; "Racine Has His Coat of Arms Altered") as proof of the irreconcilable antagonism between hunter and hunted, perpetrator and victim, good and evil, beauty and ugliness: Racine's changing of his coat of arms by having the rat removed and retaining the swan does not eliminate the fundamental rift in creation. Similarly, both (stuffed) cat and Mahlke's "mouse," his oversized Adam's apple, are still present when, highly decorated, he returns to his old school with the abortive plan to give his speech (see *CaM,* 154–55) — an incident that narrator Pilenz relates with an explicit reference to Racine.

In *Hundejahre* Grass continued to use lyrical passages in a narrative text, Engels observes, when, for instance, Harry Liebenau, who had been writing poetry, concludes book 2 with a very extensive passage in which each paragraph begins with an introductory sentence derived from fairy tales: "Once upon a time . . ." (*DY,* 295–353). But especially in the case of *Hundejahre,* Grass reversed the process of using lyrics as a source of inspiration for his prose works by having poems published independently from their original context. A case in point is "Mein Onkel" ("My Uncle"), a poem spoken by Matern's niece (see *DY,* 504) during the "open forum," in which Grass uses a variety of forms usually not associated with a novel, and which reveals Matern's complicity in the savage beating of Eddi Amsel.

In his thorough and systematic study Engels adds a new dimension to the readings of the *Danziger Trilogie.* While not overtly concerned with *Zeitgeschichte* and *Vergangenheitsbewältigung,* he offers new insights into the interdependence of epic, lyric, and sculptural as well as pictorial elements in Grass's work that enable the reader to perceive intricacies of the texts that address questions such as coming to terms with the past — but do so in a complex and highly sophisticaed artistic manner.

Part 2

From Danzig to the Global Stage: Grass's Fiction of the 1970s and 1980s

5: *Örtlich betäubt / Local Anaesthetic*

A Farewell to Danzig

THE PUBLICATION OF *ÖRTLICH BETÄUBT* in the summer of 1969 was preceded by the (West) Berlin premiere of Grass's play *Davor* (WA 8:479–555; translated as *Max,* 1972) in February of the same year. *Davor* essentially corresponds to the second part of the novel, in which the secondary-school teacher Eberhard Starusch — nicknamed "Old Hardy" by his students — seeks to dissuade his favorite student Philipp Scherbaum from going through with his planned protest, which consists of dousing his beloved dog Max with gasoline for the purpose of a public immolation. Scherbaum's drastic and cruel measure is intended to sharpen dog-loving (West) Berliners' awareness about the use of napalm by American troops in Vietnam. On the one hand, it has been pointed out that by 1969 Grass had become firmly established on the literary scene (see H. L. Arnold 1997, 111) so that the mere announcement of a forthcoming new work by the author of *Die Blechtrommel* signified an important literary event. On the other, the mixed to poor reviews that *Davor* had received tended to diminish readers' and critics' high expectations. Yet the coincidence of the book's publication date and the beginning of Grass's renewed active involvement in politics, which resulted in his speaking at 190 rallies during the 1969 election campaign on behalf of the Social Democratic Party (SPD) and Willy Brandt, candidate for Chancellor of the Federal Republic, served to draw additional attention to the novel. His literary fame caused the concerned citizen Grass's political interventions to be widely noticed; he was propelled from the comparative obscurity of the cultural section, the *Feuilleton,* of the West German press to its front pages. In short, Grass attained "the publicity rating of a star" in the areas of both literature and politics (Kurz 1969) and was anointed by one publicist as the "heraldic animal" of the Federal Republic, a role that entailed a representative role at home and abroad and guaranteed — similarly to the Mercedes star — a quality product (Krüger 1969). Inevitably, Grass's much debated political activities served to boost his recognition as a writer (see H. L. Arnold 1997, 110); as a result *Örtlich betäubt* achieved a high ranking on the bestseller lists during the fall of 1969.

To judge by the more than one hundred and twenty articles in newspapers and reviews in radio broadcasts (see H. L. Arnold 1997, 274 n. 62), there was a significant critical reaction to the novel. However, the reading public's preferences, as indicated by the substantial sales figures of *Örtlich betäubt,* are not reflected in the largely negative responses by critics — an indication, perhaps, of the limited influence on the book market of those entrusted with providing literary value judgments. Although the dire prediction of one journalist that the novel would prove to be Grass's "Waterloo" proved incorrect (Lichtenberg 1969), *Örtlich betäubt* did not find favor with most of the reviewers writing for the major dailies and weeklies. In his review in *Der Spiegel,* Rolf Becker (1969) articulates the criteria that were to play a significant role in the subsequent debate such as the (mostly unfavorable) comparison of Grass's then latest work with *Die Blechtrommel,* his alleged reliance on stating his topics rather than incorporating them into a riveting narrative, his excessive attention to detail, with regard, for example, to Starusch's extended dental treatment, which results in straining the central metaphor of "local anaesthetic," and the unwarranted dependence on the narrative device of the TV screen in the dentist's office, onto which first-person narrator and protagonist Starusch projects his "memories, associations, imaginings, episodes, and arguments from the past and present" (Kurz 1977, 87). Writing in *Die Zeit,* Marcel Reich-Ranicki (1969) deplores what he considers to be Grass's lack of imagination, temperament, and originality: the once innovative storyteller has fallen silent and is now resorting to the techniques of montage and collage. Reich-Ranicki finds the figure of the dentist, in Starusch's unflattering opinion a "competent idiotic specialist" (*LA,* 194), particularly unconvincing, in part because of the dentist's habit of delivering long disquisitions on the history of dentistry and quoting the ancient philosopher Seneca as well as Friedrich Nietzsche. Reich-Ranicki also addresses — albeit rather cursorily — the issue of politics, which is prominently mentioned in other reviews. Inasmuch as *Örtlich betäubt* deals with the comparatively new phenomenon of the youth movement, the New Left, and the so-called *außerparlamentarische Opposition* (opposition outside of parliament) in the Federal Republic, the novel may be considered a "political" text. Unlike other critics, who prefer to approach the novel from a non-political perspective (see Boßmann 1997, 56), Reich-Ranicki, although hardly a political radical, chastises Grass for playing down the significance of the new movement and endowing it with an infantile dimension by selecting as its representatives the seventeen-year-old Scherbaum and his coeval girlfriend Veronika Lewand (Vero), two youngsters in the throes of puberty. This novel, Reich-Ranicki concludes, represents a low point in Grass's career.

In another contribution to *Die Zeit* — the weekly carried several reviews by different authors to Grass's work — Hellmuth Karasek (1969), after having perused a host of reviews, summarizes critics' main objections to *Örtlich betäubt* and establishes the four most common criticisms. First, Grass appears to be no longer the author who wrote *Die Blechtrommel;* Karasek characterizes this unexpected change as the mutation of an anarchist to a writer of bestsellers and that of a provocateur to a volunteer in election campaigns. Hence the figure of teacher Starusch appears to be an attempt at a melancholy self-portrait — a view that was not universally shared by subsequent critics. Second, Grass is reprimanded for publishing his novel in the midst of an election campaign, a reproach to which Karasek does not attribute major significance. Third, Grass's narrative is assumed to be uninteresting on account of its unexciting central characters. Here Karasek implicitly agrees with Reich-Ranicki when he considers Scherbaum and Vero to be cartoon-like figures and unsuitable representatives of the opposition outside parliament. Fourth, in view of the ensuing mythologizing of the rebellious 1960s, Karasek seeks to refute the rather curious argument that *Örtlich betäubt* is uninspiring because of the comparative dullness of the period in question by noting that Grass's precise depiction of the Danzig milieu in the first two books of *Die Blechtrommel* was not matched by that of West Germany in the third book. Thus, Karasek implies, Grass's real strength rests squarely in his Danzig roots. Karasek's review appeared in September 1969, at a time when the novel had sold more than eighty thousand copies; yet he refrains from speculating about the apparent divergence between its poor reception by the press on the one hand and its commercial success on the other. In his fairly substantial comparison of the play *Davor* and the novel *Örtlich betäubt,* Paul Konrad Kurz (1969) does not significantly deviate from the majority opinion, and he goes so far as to predict — prematurely, as later works were to prove — that "the materials and themes of the Danzig saga have been exhausted." Yet even though he misses the "vehemence and plasticity" (Kurz 1977, 94) of the Danzig scenes, whose lack is largely seen as the chief factor contributing to the assumed failure of the novel (for example, H. L. Arnold 1963, 4th, rev. ed. 1969), in his nuanced reading Kurz attributes "exemplary" features to the novel in that it reflects the "crisis of moderate, almost unideological reason. . . . the identity crisis of society, the identity crisis of a man of forty" (Kurz 1977, 95).

Although Manfred Durzak in his 1970 essay, one of the first of the academic variety, asserts that the allusions to Danzig in *Örtlich betäubt* are mere "arabesques" (1979, 292), he shifts his perspective from a geographical and cultural approach to one that favors a sociological orientation and considers Grass's departure from the Danzig milieu of the lower middle class an asset rather than a flaw. Durzak postulates that the "farewell to the petty bourgeoisie" (289) and the shifting of the author's focus to Starusch who, along with his female colleague Irmgard Seifert and the nameless dentist, represents the university-educated (West) Berlin middle class, signals a deliberate engagement on Grass's part with the contemporaneous Federal Republic — an engagement that is filtered through Starusch's consciousness (293). Whereas the dentist represents the type of the pragmatic intellectual and technocrat who believes that scientific progress will solve all societal problems, Starusch is less given to such overly optimistic belief. His skepticism, Durzak (296–97) indicates, is attributable to the fact that in Starusch Grass has created the figure of a teacher who differs starkly from the traditional, authoritarian model depicted in numerous literary texts, but perhaps most memorably in Heinrich Mann's novel *Professor Unrat* (1905; *The Blue Angel,* 1932), in which the protagonist counterbalances his abject obeisance toward officialdom and higher authority with his autocratic conduct in the classroom. In contrast, Starusch is a new kind of teacher; he is plagued by past failures, lacks the certainty of moral righteousness, and is fully aware of the tenuous nature of his attempts to solve Scherbaum's and his generation's problems. Hellmut Becker (1969) even goes so far as to claim that in *Örtlich betäubt* Grass creates memorable figures of a (male) teacher and a (male) student — as well as the supplementary figures of a female teacher and a female student — that readers will not forget and educators should ponder. As to Durzak, he in part reiterates objections that had been previously voiced, such as the caveat about the TV screen as an artificial and unsuitable device to sustain the narrative — in Durzak's view, TV functions as a manipulator of consciousness and thereby undermines the ability to reflect (298) — and the insufficiency of the dog-burning motif as a potential writing on the wall in the face of adults' consumerism, political apathy, and general indifference (300). But all in all, Durzak sums up, Grass's departure from the topic of Danzig constitutes a step in the right direction.

"The Dentist's Chair as an Allegory of Life"

Before *Örtlich betäubt* appeared in English translation, an anonymous contributor to the London *Times Literary Supplement* provided a fairly detailed analysis of the novel in the light of Grass's political activities and writings — the latter were translated by Ralph Manheim as *Speak Out! Speeches, Open Letters, Commentaries* (1969) and extensively reviewed by Neil Ascherson in the *New York Review of Books* (1969) — under the title "Grass and His Nation's Burdens" (1969b), in which s/he surmised that the book, "completely made in Germany," would most likely encounter success "in the English-speaking-and-reacting world." The contributor's assumption certainly proved correct with regard to the American reception of *Local Anaesthetic,* which was published in the spring of 1970, less than a year after the German original. Ray Lewis White's 1981 compilation of fifty-seven excerpted reviews provides a useful overview of critics' reactions to the novel in the daily and periodical press. Although most of the reviews are clearly positive, there are a number of unflattering comments — albeit mostly in local or regional newspapers. For instance, Paul Kiniery (1970) dispenses the following advice to prospective readers: "You may begin on any page and read either forward or backward, since there is no action for you to follow." Webster Schott in *Life* (1970) opines that "Grass the novelist talks about everything in *Local Anaesthetics* and settles nothing." Other complaints include the assertion that the novel will put readers to sleep and that its perusal requires a painful effort, or, as a punster has it, reading the work is "deadening. You might try it the next time you have a tooth pulled" (Porterfield 1970). While such carping may be dismissed as idiosyncratic and ultimately inconsequential, one is at a loss as to how to respond to such obvious misreading as that by a commentator who is only identified by his/her initials and claims that Grass's "wild humor, imagination, indignation, sarcasm, and irony" are as "conspicuous" in his latest work as in his previous fiction (D. T. 1970). Similarly unconvincing is praise based on erroneous assumptions. In a formulation reminiscent of philosopher Martin Heidegger, whom Grass satirizes in *Hundejahre* and parodies in passing in *Örtlich betäubt* (for example, "'The nothing nihilates unremittingly'"; *LA,* 10), one reviewer claims that the author "is more interested in capturing essence and being than in pegging social and political values" (Raab 1970).

In contrast to the misinterpretations and misconceptions cited, critics of publications with a national circulation incline toward positive appraisals, frequently reassessing and reasserting Grass's stature as a novelist of world renown on the basis of his just-published novel. John Leonard (1970) writes in the *New York Times* that the author belongs with Julio Cortazar, Doris Lessing, Vladimir Nabokov, Norman Mailer, Jean-Paul Sartre, and Alexander Solzhenitsyn "among that handful of contemporary Western writers we must either read or else confess our cultural illiteracy." Freelance critic Anatole Broyard (1970) headlines his review on the front page of the *New York Times Book Review* "Günter Grass demonstrates that fiction is not only alive but healthier than ever" and considers the book "a brilliant *tour de force,*" the "form" of which or "the relation of its parts to each other, he adds, is as efficient and as economical as a Volkswagen." A slightly sour note is struck in the *New Yorker* by Grass's fellow novelist John Updike (1970) who, in particular, objects to Grass's "device of aping television" as a feature that has been "superimposed." Although he categorizes Grass as "one of the very, very few authors whose next novel one has no intention of missing," D. J. Enright (1970) in the *New*

York Review of Books finds *Local Anaesthetics* "a little on the tired side," but, unwittingly echoing some German critics, attributes this drawback to the theme of "the apparent homelessness in the affluent state of passion and ideals." By far the most salient tribute is that by an anonymous reviewer in a publication that does not specialize in literary matters and therefore had the potential of making Grass known to an audience beyond that of readers of novels. *Time* magazine's cover story of April 1970 featured, for the first time since 1945, a German writer, proclaiming "Germany's Günter Grass" the "Novelist Between the Generations: A Man Who Can Speak to the Young." Quite in contrast to the at-best-lukewarm response that *Örtlich betäubt* elicited in Germany, a response that resulted in the questioning of Grass's stature (Lietzmann 1970), the novel's author is elevated to the pinnacle of literary fame: "At 42, Grass certainly does not look like the world's, or Germany's, greatest living novelist, though he may well be both." Grass's status is attributed less to formal criteria than to his genuine concern about "the Generation Gap, the morality of revolutionary protest, the apparently helpless and surely tragic bankruptcy of liberalism" (68).

Durzak (1971a) ponders the implications of the astoundingly different reactions to *Örtlich betäubt/Local Anaesthetic* in the German press and that of the United States and pleads for an aesthetics of reception (*Rezeptionsästhetik*) that will induce critics to reflect on their premises, presuppositions, and intentions and convey them to their readers. According to Durzak, the traditional German model of the solitary arbiter in matters of literary taste, whose authoritatively rendered judgment is, depending on the degree of his or her media access, unquestioningly accepted by the reading public, is an idealized construct. This model has come under attack by the student movement and has lost its validity because it ignores the specific historical, socio-cultural, and political conditions that determine the respective national reviewing practices. Whereas in Germany Grass is condemned for what appears to be his cavalier treatment of the student opposition, in America both the lack of knowledge about the specifics of the German protest movement and Grass's pronounced opposition to the rebellious students — he "worries about the moral absolutism of the revolutionary young who seem willing to destroy society in order to cure it" (Anon. 1970, 74) — fosters readings bordering on the allegorical as expressed, for instance, in the title of *Time* magazine's story about Grass, "The Dentist's Chair as an Allegory of Life" (68). Furthermore, in Germany *Örtlich betäubt* has been frequently compared to *Die Blechtrommel* in particular and is found wanting on account of the assumed dwindling of Grass's creative powers; conversely, in the United States the comparison is deemed less compelling because the previous fiction presents (German) history in a somewhat exotic guise by "using dwarfs and drums and scarecrows to explore the nightmare dominion of Nazi Germany. . . . To many readers, particularly in the U.S., all this was fascinating. It also seemed very long ago and far away" (Anon. 1970, 68). In addition, the presumed topicality of *Örtlich betäubt* tends to override aesthetic considerations. As the anonymous reviewer in *Time* puts it: "Is it a mark of German progress or American decline that Grass's anguished study of a contemporary German student, his teacher, and a threatened antiwar demonstration seems as American, and as unsettling, as the latest homemade-bomb scare?" (69). The curious implication that the German author is capable of articulating most clearly American apprehensions and anxieties relating to the war in Vietnam and, perhaps, proposing solutions, leads Durzak to surmise that Grass has been indirectly turned into a mouthpiece of American middle-class ideology on the basis of his suggestion that, as demonstrated by Starusch and Scherbaum, communication between the generations on the basis of common sense may be possible. There is, no doubt, a hefty dose of wishful thinking involved in pinning American hopes for the resolution of generational and other conflicts on Grass, who is stylized as "a fanatic for moderation. He is a moderate the way other men are extremists. He is a man almost crazy for sanity" (Anon. 1970, 70). True, Durzak's attempt to provide an explanation for the glaring discrepancies between the German and American assessments of *Örtlich betäubt* and his appeal for reception studies that are cognizant of their ordinarily unstated presuppositions establish a constructive framework for approaching and evaluating literary works in their respective contexts; perhaps less convincing are the far-reaching conclusions Durzak draws — such as his assertion that the novel functions as a subliminal vehicle of affirmation for a generation that feels threatened by the protest of the young.

Violence, Pain, and Politics

As the two aforementioned 1970 and 1971 articles by Durzak indicate, scholars began to devote their attention to *Örtlich betäubt* comparatively early. Erhard Friedrichsmeyer's cogent essay "The Dogmatism of Pain," first published in 1970, is a further case in point. Friedrichsmeyer, who does not refer to the reviews in the American press, engages in a fresh approach, one that had been either neglected or given short shrift by previous critics. He starts out by defending the novel against its detractors, noting that Grass has made a conscious choice, based on his rejection of the concept of "the separation between artist and citizen" — a choice that is reflected in the "form" of the text, which exhibits, in comparison with Grass's previous fiction, "more restraint and a greater interest in ideas, particularly political ideas" (in Willson 1971, 35). But rather than engaging in overtly political writing, Friedrichsmeyer seems to imply, Grass actually focuses on "violence and its correlative, pain" — a "theme" (36) that is evident in Starusch's agonizing dental treatment and his fantasies about murdering Sieglinde (Linde) Krings, whome he fancies to have been his fiancée. She is the daughter of the former "fight-to-the-finish" (*LA*, 40) Nazi field marshal by the same name who, after his return from a Soviet POW camp, indulges in sandbox war games, in which he seeks to win the battles he had lost on the Eastern front during the Second World War. Furthermore, Starusch's reminiscences about his youth in Danzig as Störtebeker (the name is taken from a fifteenth-century pirate who attacked the ships of the Hanseatic League in the Baltic) also hinge on violent actions. As the leader of the Dusters, he make his appearance in the *Danziger Trilogie,* where he commands a band of juvenile delinquents rather than a group dedicated to opposing Nazism. Furthermore, violence — both potential and actual — is evident not only in Scherbaum's abortive protest but also in "the violence of the world at large in terms of the Vietnam war" (36). Violence and the accompanying pain are, then, a given of the human condition; attempts to eradicate it, notably on the part of the dentist but also, on a different level, on the part of the rebellious students, amount to creating an unsustainable and unacceptable utopia or a "final solution" (37) by radically eliminating the old order and its adherents. Unlike Starusch, who "continues to be a lover of false therapy," secretly approving of Scherbaum's plan but ostensibly opposing it, the latter "sublimates his pain, anaesthetizing it in meaningful work" (43) by becoming editor of his school's newspaper and opting for persuasive arguments rather than violent action. There are a very few and very minor flaws that tend to detract from Friedrichsmeyer's argument. It is not because of pressure from "school officials" (43) that Scherbaum withdraws his article on Kurt Georg Kiesinger, a former Nazi and Chancellor of the Federal Republic during the grand coalition from 1966 to 1969; rather, he gives in to "the representations of his fellow students" (*LA*, 259). Curiously, unlike several other commentators, Friedrichsmeyer attributes a "beneficial function" to television in that it sensitizes the public by "pointing to social disorders" (40) — a debatable claim.

John Reddick (1972) finds the pattern of "action and impotence" to be pervasive in all of Grass's novels that had been published up to that time. In particular, Starusch is "haunted . . . by a driving sense of failure" (566) that compels him to seek refuge in surrogate activities such as the "'bulldozer' sequence" in which he imagines "the demolition of consumer society in graphically revolutionist-anarchic terms" (569): "Housecleaning on TV. Bulldozers . . . set themselves in motion, attack gadgets and cosmetics, crush upholstered groups and camping equipment, sweep second cars, home film projectors, and built-in kitchens into great heaps . . ." (*LA*,

204–5). Starusch's orgiastic desire for destruction and annihilation also finds expression in a series of murderous fantasies about seeking revenge for his having been slighted by his supposed ex-fiancée Linde. These fantasies culminate in "the novel's penultimate — and longest — subsection" (567) in which Linde and her family are smashed to pieces in the "Wave Pool" (*LA*, 279–84). Despite Reddick's characterization of Starusch as a failure whose "private frustrations" correspond to his "total pessimism about social-political change and hence about all political activity" (570), he considers Starusch and "the convolutions of his lot" as the chief aesthetic attraction of "this quietly magnificent novel" — a value judgment that differs starkly from the novel's unenthusiastic early German reception. Yet it is Starusch's "antithesis, the nameless, faceless dentist" (572) whom Reddick views as an entirely positive figure, in that he articulates "what amounts to a philosophy of action" and advocates "an enlightened and liberal tolerance" (574) via his both utopian and whimsical "worldwide and socially integrated Sickcare" (*LA*, 86). Moreover, Reddick argues, the political implications of the "philosophy" the dentist espouses correspond essentially to Grass's own (Reddick, 577). There is then, in the end, no solution to the apparent paradox that, although the constructive solutions suggested by the unobtrusive and anonymous dentist may exert their appeal, in aesthetic terms it is Starusch who contributes greatly to "the book's curious power" — a dilemma that leaves the reader in a "labyrinth" of unresolved questions (578).

Peter J. Graves (1973) follows a similar line of argument, albeit in a slightly more metaphysical vein, when he posits "man's inability to reconcile the two conflicting natures within himself," that is, the tendency to strive for either "action and creativity" or "reason and order" — or, put differently, the impossibility of striving for a synthesis of the "Nietzschean dichotomy of the Dionysian and the Apollonian" (133). While Grass may engage in politics for the sake of his own "salvation," as a writer he confines himself to "interpreting the world" (141) as he sees it and does not offer much hope: indeed, the last words of the novel are: "Nothing lasts. There will always be pain" (*LA*, 284).

Starusch, a Failure?

As the protagonist-narrator, the figure of the hapless Starusch has attracted its fair share of attention, and several scholars have concentrated on elaborating on his shortcomings. James C. Bruce (1971), who dispenses with references to secondary literature on the novel altogether, nevertheless establishes a convincing link between the two elements in his title, "The Motif of Failure and the Act of Narrating in *Örtlich betäubt*." In his article Bruce elaborates on those failings of Starusch that were noted — usually in passing — by previous critics and draws attention to Starusch's lack of endeavor "to carry things through to their proper end" (in O'Neill 1987c, 145) — as is evident, for instance, in his inability to complete his book project on Nazi general Ferdinand Schörner, the historical model for the above-mentioned field marshal. Furthermore, Starusch shows signs of "sexual inadequacy" (146) in his relations with his colleague Irmgard Seifert, to whom he eventually becomes engaged without, however, having married her by the end of the novel. Similarly, he presumably lacks sexual prowess during what seems to have been a seduction attempt by his student Vero, and his claims to have had intercourse with Linde rest on shaky grounds, inasmuch as what he tells the dentist about his engagement and his employment as an engineer in a cement-producing plant is most likely a "fanciful story" (147). Starusch is also given to embellishing other parts of his past when, for instance, he casts himself in the role of leader of an anti-Nazi resistance movement during his time with the Dusters. Perhaps the most telling indication of Starusch's general failure is Scherbaum's ultimate motivation for not sacrificing his dog. Scherbaum refrains from the sacrifice not on account of Starusch's attempts to dissuade him but rather because he does not cherish the prospect of becoming like Starusch, "peddling the feats of a seventeen-year old when he's forty" (*LA*, 242). The "linkage" between "the failure motif and the act of narrating" (Bruce, 150) is then Starusch's "creativity" as expressed in his "talent for free invention," especially under the influence of the anesthetic and painkillers. Starusch's adroitness in verbalizing his "vicarious, imagined experience[s]" and providing an "extemporized narrative" (151) for the dentist is surely motivated by his compensatory desire to minimize or hide his failings — an aspect of interrogating the text that Bruce does not at all allude to. At the same time, according to Bruce Starusch is also the narrator of his own "actual experience and lived reality" in his written account. Although this account includes his "wild, obvious flights of fancy," it serves as a vehicle for Grass's "treatment of social, political, and moral questions" (151), which Starusch is forced to face without forever being able to rely on the "local anesthetic of narcotizing ideologies or the palliative of moral, social, and political delusions" (155), as the final words of the novel suggest. In direct but unstated opposition to some German reviewers, Bruce suggests that, therefore, the "major import of the combined motifs of failure and creativity" is perhaps that they are indicative of "an art" that reflects "the inadequacy of the time" (155).

In "The Fiction of Fact and Fantasy" (1977) Gertrud Bauer Pickar analyzes Grass's new mode of presenting a narrator-protagonist who is no longer endeavoring to provide a somewhat objective view of his past; rather, Starusch "presents the reader with a multiplicity of fictional levels in which reality is interlaced with fantasy and is often indistinguishably fused with it" (289). In a later, rather detailed essay, in which she takes into account virtually all the secondary literature on *Örtlich betäubt* available at the time, Pickar (1985) provides a thorough examination of Starusch in terms of the (self) portrait of a failure that emerges from the latter's conscious utterances and subconscious impulses as well as from the thoughts and attitudes that he attributes to the other figures. Whereas other critics have acknowledged Starusch's failure as a teacher — an opinion that is not universally shared (see, for example, Durzak 1970, 233) — Pickar goes to considerable lengths to cite examples that support her thesis. As a teacher of history and German, he questions — and is questioned by his students about — the viability and usefulness of his subjects. For example, despite his constant ruminating in his own past, Starusch admits (to himself and the dentist) that "history . . . can teach us nothing" (*LA,* 89), an insight that is used against him with a vengeance when the activist and Maoist Vero, paraphrasing one of Karl Marx's theses about philosopher Ludwig Feuerbach, tells him: "All you know how to do is to interpret, you don't know how to change things" (*LA,* 162). Likewise, the subject of German literature is discredited when Starusch seeks to persuade Scherbaum to voice his protest by means of ballads in the manner of poets Bertolt Brecht or Wolf Biermann or, for that matter, protest singer Joan Baez — a proposition the latter flatly rejects: "Only lulls people to sleep. You don't believe in it yourself. . . . It only affects the tear glands" (*LA,* 174). Yet, as Pickar herself indicates, the assumed ineffectiveness of words is only valid in the context of an alternative consisting of presumably effective political action; consequently, when Scherbaum becomes editor of the school paper — a position he is qualified to assume because he is an excellent student in the subject of German — he appears to validate one of Starusch's fields of expertise that he previously scorned. Starusch, at any rate, clearly perceives his susceptibility to the pain caused by his dental problem. When fretting about his aching teeth and indulging in self-pity, his complete indifference toward global problems manifests itself clearly — another flaw in his personality that is succinctly articulated by Scherbaum: "'You and your toothache. But what is going on in the Mekong Delta? Have you read?'" (*LA,* 11, 44). In the final analysis, Starusch's relationship to Scherbaum remains ambivalent; Pickar suggests that it has the characteristics of a love-hate relationship. Ultimately, Starusch is unable to rid himself of his self-perception as a failure and will presumably continue to be haunted by it.

More than two decades after the majority of articles on *Örtlich betäubt* had appeared, Stuart Taberner (1998) revisits the issue of Starusch's failings and, in agreement with others, concedes that he displays glaring defects as a "school teacher by default, self-confessed flop, and compulsive falsifier of personal biography" (69). Yet Taberner wonders, in referring to Reddick's 1972 essay about Starusch as an aesthetically pleasing character, why precisely Starusch "engages the reader's sympathies more compellingly than the dentist" (69) — even though the dentist is generally assumed to act as Grass's mouthpiece. Starusch's "supreme control over the telling of his story," Taberner contends, invalidates his own complaints about his "impotence" (70) as well as, it might be added, those of his critics. In a rather radical departure from what may count as the majority opinion, Taberner then ascribes a didactic intent to Starusch "who sacrifices his putatively authentic self for the sake of educating both other characters in the novel and the reader" (71). Such an endeavor results in fashioning himself as a "public intellectual" (75) in a role that transcends that of teacher. Starusch's assumed "fictionalizing and staging his own person as a warning to others not to repeat his errors" (79) would seem to be contradicted, for example, by his boasting about his youthful exploits in Danzig and Scherbaum's explicit rejection of Starusch's tales. Conversely, his supposed attempts to "frame himself as representative of generation, and of nation" (79) correspond to Grass' authorial intent with regard to establishing the indispensability of the artist, as elaborated in Starusch's tale about the seventeenth-century Danzig painter Anton Möller: "'The artist as savior. He helps sin to safety'" (*LA*, 277), that is, in his representations the artist preserves "sin" because "to eliminate human failings" means "to eliminate man" (*LA*, 86).

The Symbolism of Teeth

Independently of early contributions such as those by Friedrichsmeyer (1970) and Bruce (1975), Carl O. Enderstein in his 1975 essay on the symbolism of teeth in *Katz und Maus, Hundejahre,* and *Örtlich betäubt* reaches similar results with regard to Starusch's failures, but he establishes a persuasive causal link between the latter's periodic impotence, his lacking energy as a writer, and his deficits as a pedagogue on the one hand and the state of his teeth on the other. Starusch's constant toothaches are then the symbolic expression of his frustration about an essentially failed existence and the symptom of a tormented psyche as evidenced by his subconscious jealousy of his former fiancée because of her unfaithfulness and his (barely) suppressed feelings of aggression against her. Enderstein takes the forty-year-old Starusch's unmarried status as a sign of a less than satisfactory sex life; Starusch himself offers unequivocal proof that his impotence is related to his toothache, when he confesses to the dentist that "after two hours of strenuous effort that first attempt to include sex in my relations with Irmgard Seifert proved a failure" (*LA,* 263). Conversely, three weeks after the (temporarily) successful "dental treatment," a self-confident Starusch "managed for the first time to have intercourse" (*LA*, 269) with her. His newly restored virility, however, does not last; his misaligned jaw, a congenital condition, cannot be permanently healed, and the prospects for Starusch to invalidate Linde's unflattering characterization of him as a "coward failure superwashout" (*LA*, 12) remain dim indeed. In contrast, Enderstein writes, the fact that Scherbaum's dental problem is not congenital provides an indication that he is of an entirely different mettle.

Whereas Hanspeter Brode (1978) agrees implicitly with Enderstein, whom he does not cite, about the relationship between Starusch's crisis of identity and his dental treatment, he is — presumably under the influence of the activist political program of the student movement — less inclined to acknowledge Scherbaum's positive development. In attempting to read the novel from the latter's position, Brode sees Scherbaum as the eventual product of a socialization that amounts to conformity and capitulation. In contrast to Enderstein, who emphasizes the limited duration and ultimate cure of Scherbaum's dental problems, Brode interprets the dentist's corrective intervention as indicative of the pathogenic process of conforming to societal expectations that the student undergoes. Although Brode admits that Scherbaum's editorial work at the school newspaper may amount to the kind of tedious, demanding kind of grass-roots work that the campaigner Grass advocated, he ends his analysis on what might be considered a pessimistic note by inferring that the novel also suggests the possibility of Scherbaum's failure in his efforts at enlightening others and promoting democratic processes. It may be parenthetically noted that in his book of 1979 Brode revised his somewhat negative view of Scherbaum by drawing attention to his selection of the seventeen-year-old Helmut Hübener (a historical figure) as a model of correct political action. Hübener distributed flyers, provided information gleaned from foreign broadcasts, and engaged in other underground activities against the Nazi regime. Hübener was arrested and executed in 1942 (155).

Theodore Ziolkowski in "The Telltale Teeth: Psychodontia to Sociodontia" (1976) recommends *Local Anaesthetic* as an "appropriate graduation present for a new dentist" despite his unconvincing claim that "the action of the novel can be recapitulated with no mention of teeth or dentists" (9). After all, the external structure of the novel is based on Starusch's visits to the dentist in the spring of 1967; in the first book his lower jaw bone is taken care of, in the second book there is a break in the treatment, and in the third book the treatment is resumed with work on the upper jaw bone. Furthermore, as Ziolkowski acknowledges, there is "much about the history, theory, and practice of dentistry" in addition to a "catalog of dental technology" and a "thumbnail sketch of the history of dentistry" (9–10) to be found in *Local Anaesthetic.* Although, at first glance, this information might seem unimportant or superfluous, its significance derives from the fact "that Grass develops the odontological material into a consistent image for society as a whole" (10). Ziolkowski then delves into the history of literature and the arts to sketch the development of "human attitudes toward teeth" (11). Of particular interest for our purposes is Thomas Mann's *Buddenbrooks* (1901), a novel that deals with the gradual *Verfall* — a term that may be translated as either "decline" or "decay" — within four generations of the wealthy Buddenbrook family in the North German city of Lübeck. As an inheritor of "the belief prevalent in German thought at least since romanticism that art and beauty are somehow related to, even a product of, disease" (16), Mann lets Thomas Buddenbrook die as a result of the botched extraction of a rotten molar; Thomas's artistic son Hanno is also afflicted by violent toothaches. The recurrence of the motif of harmful teeth "suggests that Mann is using the decay of teeth for a larger purpose, to signify the decay of an entire family and, by implication, of civilized European society as a whole" (17). The change that has taken place from Mann to Grass, Ziolkowski argues on the basis of other texts that need not concern us here, is the "shift in emphasis from psychodontia to sociodontia: decaying teeth now represent with increasing frequency society as a whole." Thus "Eberhard Starusch's agonies in the dentist's chair correspond to the agonies of an entire people trying to come to terms with its past" (19) — a statement that, perhaps, requires modification in that Starusch is chiefly the representative of his generation, the forty-year-olds, rather than that of the entire nation, which includes, of course, the generation of the Scherbaums.

Ziolkowski claims that an "organismic view of society," as well as the appropriation of the tooth metaphor by various writers, underlies the shift to "sociodontia." This "organismic view" runs counter to the "mechanistic theories of the Enlightenment" (20) and gains wide currency in the twentieth century. Ziolkowski ends his enlightening essay with a rhetorical flourish: "Grass's sociodontist can peer into his patient's mouth and see society largely because so many generations of postromantic sociologists and cultural historians have looked at society and seen an organism" (21).

What is not taken sufficiently into account in the preceding quote as well as in other essays discussed above is the role of the dentist, whose "real" existence as a purveyor of opinions about the state of the world or as "the anonymous and impersonal social engineer of the modern welfare state" (Ziolkowski, 10) is categorically denied by Volker Neuhaus (1979, rev. ed. 1992, 107), who rejects all notions about an actual dialogue between Starusch and the dentist. Rather, Neuhaus writes, Starusch ascribes his views to the dentist, and the latter remains an abstract principle without an individual life of his own. This is not to say that there is no dentist at all — obviously, we must assume that the dental treatment did take place — but his role is far more limited than most scholars would assume. Hence the endeavor of Hans Wisskirchen (2001) to rather belatedly elevate the dentist to the role of narrator — albeit in conjunction with Starusch (205) — is hardly convincing. Although Wisskirchen sees the dentist as the alter ego of Starusch (207) and emphasizes the collaborative effort of the two figures (208), he tends to grant the former a degree of independence and authenticity that may be reasonably questioned.

The Image of Women and the Role of Pop Culture

In her 1985 essay Pickar alludes briefly to Starusch's association with the women in his life, that is, the possibly fictional Linde as well as Irmgard Seifert and Vero. These associations are characterized by Starusch's predominantly negative attitude and his aggressive behavior. Thus the prospects for a happy future of the couple Starusch-Seifert are hardly promising, because he does not love her, treats her condescendingly (not vice versa as Pickar writes), and does not find her particularly attractive. A few years later, Pickar (1989), perhaps under the influence of feminist scholarship that asserted itself particularly vigorously in the case of Grass's novel *DerButt* (1977; *The Flounder,* 1978), returns to the topic of women in a lengthy article. In addition to the three women mentioned above, she briefly draws attention to Starusch's mother, the only female figure that he remembers fondly. Otherwise, Pickar contends, Starusch's hardly flattering view of (German) women in general is shared by both Scherbaum and the dentist (if, indeed, he can be assumed to voice opinions that are not ascribed to him by Starusch). Yet when she cites one of the dentist's utterances as proof — "the German woman voted first for Hitler, then for Adenauer, and eats too much cake" (*LA,* 192) — she adds the caveat that such a statement may be a somewhat simplistic generalization and should not be taken at face value. More convincing are Pickar's analyses of the three women in Starusch's life. But whether Vero represents a new variant of the unsympathetic girl, a type that is represented in Grass's previous prose fiction by Tulla Pokriefke, may be doubted — even if both of them exercise their sexual allure on men despite their unattractiveness (see Neuhaus 1979; rev. ed. 1992, 105) — on the grounds that the reduction of female characters to stereotypes denies them their distinctness, which, in Tulla's case, is largely determined by her Danzig lower middle-class environment during the Second World War, whereas Vero represents one version of the politically committed, middle-class secondary-school student during the 1960s. In the eyes of Starusch and Scherbaum her propensity for slogans, emotionalism, and sensational happenings, such as Scherbaum's planned protest, characterize her as immature. Similarly, Irmgard Seifert is given to displays of excessive emotionalism in rhetoric that borders on the ecstatic in the style of late expressionism; not without reason do her students call her "'archangel'" because "her manner of speaking often evokes the flaming sword" (*LA*, 57). Although Pickar does not explicitly mention it, Irmgard Seifert corresponds to some extent to the "authoritarian personality" as defined by Theodor W. Adorno, that is, someone who is susceptible to subordinating him- or herself to an idea, a political system, and/or a charismatic leader. Whereas she formerly, in a kind of youthful aberration, was dedicated to the Führer and regarded "Bolshevism as a Judaeo-Slavic alliance," she now supports, "in flamboyant adjectives," a "left-wing creed" (*LA*, 58); her predisposition to believe in (changing) causes and sacrifice has remained unchanged. At the same time, Grass conveys through her his conviction that left-wing and right-wing extremism are comparable in their rejection of a course of action that hews to gradual reform rather than revolution. However, social processes ultimately cannot be steered via public welfare and prophylaxis, as the chaotic conditions in Irmgard Seifert's well-tended aquarium demonstrate (see Brode 1979, 156 and 157).

Without doubt, as Pickar points out, Linde remains for Starusch the most important woman in his life, as her almost constant presence in his memories and fantasies, including her frequent imaginary appearances on the TV screen, show. She, more than the other two female characters, contributes to Starusch's self-image as a loser, a perception that is closely linked to his reluctantly professed lack of sexual prowess. True, "Lost Battles" (*LA*, 20), Grass's initial working designation for both novel and play (Brode 1979, 149) as well as the title that Starusch has selected for a projected film about his time at the Krings cement works, does not exclusively refer to his abortive affair with Linde, as Pickar seems to imply, but also encompasses the aforementioned sandbox war games played by Linde's father. Beyond that, "Lost Battles" is an apt description of Starusch's failures in general, which, in the sexual arena, manifest themselves by the joylessness of sex. The bleak picture of the largely unsuccessful relationships of Starusch and, to a lesser extent, Scherbaum is compounded in Starusch's case by his distinct propensity for brutality toward women. Although Starusch slaps Irmgard Seifert in the face, and Scherbaum does the same to Vero, both women accept such a treatment meekly and without protest. Pickar takes Starusch's macabre, apocalyptic fantasy about killing Linde and her family in the "Wave Pool" as an unambiguous indication of Starusch's sadism and latent violence toward women in this distinctly misogynist novel, but, by concentrating on Starusch, she refrains from drawing any conclusions as to the presumable authorial intent.

Less concerned with the role of women, Chloe E. M. Paver (1997) strikes out in a hitherto largely uncharted direction by exploring Grass's use of "popular culture and protest culture" (53). Indeed, there are numerous references in the novel to, for instance, Lois Lane, the girlfriend of Superman in the comic strip of that name, to Donald Duck, and, on a somewhat different level presumably, to protest singer Joan Baez. In fact, Paver finds such references to be so pervasive that she maintains: "Popular culture saturates the whole narrative of *Örtlich betäubt*" (54). Such a claim is credible in view of her inclusive approach, which takes into account Starusch's allusions to or his use of mass media such as TV, cinema, magazines, and other print products as well as "a very broad range of popular genres and forms" (54) ranging from spy thrillers to protest songs. As an intellectual, Starusch is on occasion given to parodying the practices of the popular media; a case in point — albeit one with potentially devastating consequences for his career — is his imagining the reaction of the notorious mass-circulation daily *Bild-Zeitung,* which depends on titillating sex scandals as a "stock ingredient" (56) to boost circulation, to his assumed dalliance with a female student. After his abortive encounter with Vero on the rug in his flat he visualizes headlines: "'Education on Berber Rug!'" "'Senior Schoolteacher Likes Absinthe-Green Tights!'" (*LA,* 233). Despite the façade of "earnest intellectualism" that he maintains by publicly treating "popular culture with condescension," it actually exerts "a powerful fascination" (Paver, 58) on him. This fascination is particularly evident in his fantasizing about Linde, whose affair with the electrician Schlottau he casts in terms of the spy thriller: "'Like in a spy picture: The pleasures of the flesh in return for military secrets'" (*LA,* 82). Although in Paver's view Starusch "is very clearly a comic exaggeration," he serves as an object for demonstrating the "psychological mechanism" in which "popular culture offers a surrogate for real experience" (60; in her 1999 study, Paver stresses Starusch's propensity for "fictionalization"). The surrogate experience extends to the realm of politics, as is evident in Vero's using the revolutionary cult-figure of Che Guevara as a pin-up, an inconsequential act that provides instant gratification and serves as a surrogate of meaningful political action. Needless to say, Vero's pseudo-engagement confirms the dim view of her character prevalent among those who know her. Conversely, Scherbaum's unglamorous decision to accept the editorship "refuses the reader the gratification of a climactic ending" precisely because stories entailing the "spirit of democracy," which strives for reform rather than revolution, "must necessarily end with a whimper rather than a bang" (62).

6: *Aus dem Tagebuch einer Schnecke / From the Diary of a Snail*

The Author as Campaigner

LIKE THAT OF *ÖRTLICH BETÄUBT,* the publication of *Aus dem Tagebuch einer Schnecke* (*Tagebuch*) in the fall of 1972 elicited a response that emphasized Grass's political commitment and activities. Such a response was not without justification inasmuch as the "semi-fictive" prose text (Moser 2000, 97) is in part a somewhat fictionalized account of the author's engagement in the campaign of 1969 on behalf of the Social Democratic Party (SPD), an engagement that resulted in that party's strong showing (Grass cites the "figures on our close victory" in *DS,* 5). As a consequence, the so-called grand coalition then in power, a partnership of Christian Democrats (CDU) and Social Democrats under CDU Chancellor Kurt Georg Kiesinger, during the Third Reich a member of the Nazi party, was dissolved, and Willy Brandt became Chancellor of a new coalition government formed by the SPD in alliance with the Free Democrats (FDP) — a rather momentous event in the postwar history of (West) Germany, in that for the first time in twenty years the CDU was excluded from the control and administration of the Federal Republic. In addition, a new election campaign had begun when the book appeared, and some critics erroneously assumed that *Tagebuch* had been timed to go on sale at a moment when its impact on the outcome of the 1972 election would be greatest (H. L. Arnold 1997, 121). In a preview of *Tagebuch* in August 1972, the news magazine *Der Spiegel* published an anonymous review, which acknowledges Grass's stature as both a public persona and a writer. At the same time, the article comments briefly on the nearly unmanageable number of critical notices as well as secondary literature devoted to Grass — a remark that, in retrospect, appears quaint in view of the outpouring of literature on the novelist in subsequent decades. In addition, *Der Spiegel* emphasizes the novelist's engagement as a campaigner and intimates that such activity might detract from and be harmful to his craft — a recurring criticism, particularly on the part of conservative reviewers, who prefer to keep the realm of art (or, for that matter, the artist) unsullied by politics. Despite critics' general tendency to view Grass's then latest work in political terms, Hans Egon Holthusen's review in the conservative *Die Welt* of August 1972 — one of the first in a major newspaper — is largely devoted to an analysis of a text that cannot be defined in terms of conventional genre classifications. Holthusen, who in a lengthy 1966 essay had defined Grass as a political author, does not find fault with the novelist's intellectual commitment and his work on behalf of the SPD; rather, he refrains from inveighing against the comparatively new concept of the politically engaged artist that Grass represents and simply accepts it. Holthusen further discards the notion that the tasks of novelist and pamphleteer-cum-campaigner are incompatible. According to Holthusen, seven interwoven strands or levels may be discerned in the complex structure of *Tagebuch*. The first of these consists of the aforementioned literary-political journal about the election campaign. Yet the journal or diary does not correspond to the customary form of a monologic text, because the narrator carries on a dialogue with his four children (second strand) — a feature that points in the direction of a pedagogical guide. Third, the participation of the children in the conversation opens up another dimension so that the narrative includes elements of a family chronicle. Fourth, there is the documentary report about the persecution, expulsion, and annihilation of the Danzig Jews during the Second World War. This report is related to the story of fictional teacher Hermann Ott, named "Zweifel" or Doubt, who worked with Jews (he was not a Jew himself, as Holthusen incorrectly assumes) and survived Nazi persecution by going into hiding. Fifth, there is another story, which is based on an actual occurrence that Grass witnessed, about the apothecary Augst (a pseudonym) who commits suicide in public after provocatively proclaiming his solidarity with his former comrades of the SS out of a misguided sense of idealism and the desire to belong. Sixth, the text can also be read as a continuous meditation about the problem of how to achieve progress in history; a problem that is exemplified by the central metaphor of the snail as the embodiment of extraordinarily slow forward movement. Hence the choice of the snail entails Grass's rejection of the utopianism of the student revolutionaries and their ilk; he voices similar sentiments in his public lecture on Albrecht Dürer's copperplate engraving *Melencolia I*. The address, which Grass delivered in 1971 on the occasion of the five-hundredth anniversary of Dürer's birth in the artist's hometown of Nuremberg, is somewhat enigmatically entitled "Vom Stillstand im Fortschritt" ("On Stasis in Progress," *D*, 286) and is appended to *Tagebuch* as the last chapter. Although Holthusen approves of Grass's condemnation of both Communism and the ideology of the radical students, he faults him for ignoring that *melencolia* is supposedly an essentially arch-conservative disposition; consequently, Holthusen rejects Grass's purportedly idiosyncratic attacks on the political opposition, the CDU. Despite Holthusen's careful reading, it is then ultimately politics that provides the yardstick for his assessment of the text.

Günter Blöcker (1972), writing in the liberal *Süddeutsche Zeitung,* sees the main strengths of the *Tagebuch* in Grass's portrayal of actual events and then present-day conditions in what appears to be a departure — albeit not a complete one — from his fixation on Danzig, the place of his origin, in previous texts. Grass's development, Blöcker states, has felicitously resulted in the overcoming of the hitherto unresolved tension between his politicking and his literary pursuits. On the one hand, Blöcker applauds the author for not confining himself to a conventional reportage about his campaign activities but promoting, via his snail metaphor, a world view that emphasizes that which is possible; on the other, he censoriously faults him for indulging in excessive virtuosity by partially succumbing to his presumed compulsive habit of returning to Danzig via the Ott story and giving in to his penchant for depicting "unappetizing" erotic scenes — a standard complaint by reviewers of a conservative bent since *Die Blechtrommel* — particularly in Ott's successful endeavor to cure the daughter of his (reluctant) host from her depression by reawakening her sexual desire via the use of snails. Moreover, Blöcker takes umbrage at Grass's "egomaniacal" propensity for portraying himself (and his family) in a central and representative role through the device of having his children ask him questions about the election campaign and other matters on which he then expounds. Yet in a slightly surprising twist, Blöcker concludes that *Tagebuch* is the most relaxed, humane, and kind-hearted "novel" Grass has written so far and that it should be welcomed despite its flaws.

Less inclined to take offense than Blöcker, Rolf Michaelis (1972), writing in the conservative *Frankfurter Allgemeine Zeitung,* finds it comical rather than distasteful that Grass assumes the role of "magister Germaniae" (schoolmaster of Germany) and displays his acquaintance or friendship with well-known politicians via name-dropping, and he praises the "pedagogical novel" as a significant achievement — even if it falls short in comparison to the *Danziger Trilogie.* In a somewhat different vein, in his extensive review for the weekly *Die Zeit,* Dieter Zimmer (1972) reflects on the multiplication effect of the mass media, which promote the tendency to turn writers of Grass's fame and notoriety into veritable monuments. Nevertheless, Zimmer views Grass's revelations about himself and his family — revelations that Zimmer deems free of both exhibitionist traits and false modesty — as a new departure for an author who ordinarily prefers to discuss the political prospects of the SPD rather than the details of his personal life. But Zimmer is not enamored by Grass's metaphor of the snail and his use of actual snails of various kinds in the narrative; he deems them to be of limited value and not a sufficient substitute for a political philosophy. Although Günther Schloz (1972) finds Grass's stated motivation for his self-portrayal — that is, the curiosity of his children — "touching," he anticipates Zimmer's argument about the unwieldiness of the snail metaphor, which tends to distract from Grass's vivid observations about, for example, his political friends. However, Schloz's overall conclusion is entirely supportive; he considers Grass's text, which he characterizes rather imprecisely as a *Gelegenheitsroman* (a novel arising from a special occasion), the most graphic, least solemn, and most enjoyable textbook ever written about the shared responsibility of citizens in a democratic society. In his essay, Paul Konrad Kurz (1973) similarly accentuates Grass's positive and conciliatory self-portrayal as well as the symbiosis of the pedagogical and political. Kurz also draws attention to teacher Ott and claims that the latter's nickname "Zweifel" (Doubt) suggests that he is akin to the skeptical teacher Starusch in *Örtlich betäubt* and serves as an alter ego of the narrator.

If *Tagebuch* achieved a measure of recognition even in the conservative press, the text and its author did not fare as well in the liberal daily *Frankfurter Rundschau*. Writing from a leftist perspective, Wolfram Schütte (1972) classifies Grass as a member of the liberal bourgeoisie who propounds the ideology of that segment of society. In particular, Schütte reprimands Grass for portraying teacher Ott, who is usually given good marks by other critics because he helped Jews and, as a result, was persecuted by the Nazis, as essentially apolitical and considers the depiction of Ott hiding in a cellar during the Second World War tantamount to a justification of the non-resistant "inner emigration" during the Third Reich on the part of such bourgeois writers as Gottfried Benn and Ernst Jünger. Grass's lack of active engagement — a curious charge in view of the author's tireless labors on behalf of the SPD — is also evident, Schütte argues, in his wholesale rejection of social theories and utopian designs. Such rejection, Schütte opines, reflects the lower middle class's attitude of resignation and skepticism. Underlying Schütte's criticism is his concern that Grass's views might correspond to those prevalent in the SPD, a party that he deems in danger of turning its back on one of its founding fathers, Karl Marx. Hence Schütte's contribution is a reflection of the ideological debates raging within the Left: on the one hand, literature is considered a political issue, inasmuch as it may reflect the political state of affairs or even contribute to a change in societal conditions; on the other, literature is being increasingly perceived as an ineffectual means to achieve fundamental change (see Arnold 1997, 125).

Subsequent reviews in mainstream journals are, perhaps predictably, mixed. Hans-Schwab-Felisch (1972) discerns two antithetical narratives in the stories of teacher Ott and apothecary Augst respectively, and considers the metaphor of the snail an apt motto for conveying not resignation but the determination to carry on in spite of considerable odds (1029–30). In his 1972 essay, Horst Krüger surmises that with his disguised *Zeitroman* (contemporaneous novel) Grass has overcome a crisis in his literary development, and he distinguishes between three interrelated levels of *Tagebuch* — considerably fewer than those enumerated by Holthusen. The weakest of these levels, Krüger suggests, is the narrative stance assumed by Grass the father when talking to his children. Conversely, the second level, which is formed by Grass's experiences and encounters during the election campaign, appears to be the most vivid, inasmuch as it includes a genuine engagement with Grass's new *Heimat* — the postwar Federal Republic rather than Danzig — and its manifold regional differences that became familiar to Grass during his ceaseless election-campaign travels (742). The third level entails the story of the Danzig Jews, which serves, Krüger plausibly indicates, as the largely unarticulated, yet underlying cause of Grass's active participation in politics and his rejection of a mode of existence that is exclusively devoted to literary pursuits (744). Hence the metaphor of the snail, which suffers from excessive use on Grass's part, may explain the developing antagonistic relationship between Grass and, for example, fellow writer Hans Magnus Enzensberger (745–46), an early supporter of Grass's fiction (see ch. 1), but now a spokesperson for the New Left, propagating revolutionary change. In a sarcastic aside, Grass contrasts his grass-roots work with the carefree existence he ascribes to Enzensberger, an existence that is not sullied by worrying about the thorny details of social progress: "Look what fun Enzensberger is having: hops off to Cuba without a care in the world while you knock yourself out trying to drum up enthusiasm for the activation of pensions for war victims" (*DS*, 73). Yet Grass's labors do not go entirely unrecognized; for example, Thomas Kielinger (1972) acknowledges Grass's unquestionably meritorious, pioneering partaking in the day-to-day business of politics (158), but he deems *Tagebuch* a failure on the grounds that it does not represent a genuine symbiosis of engagement and literature (156) and is marred by an obtrusively pedagogical stance.

A "Strange" Book

American readers were informed about Grass's latest work a few months after its publication in Germany by the essayist and journalist François Bondy (1972), an erstwhile exile from Nazi Germany, in the magazine *World*. Bondy categorizes *Tagebuch* as "unquestionably a work of creative fiction," which is "opinionated, polemical, argumentative" but rooted "much more" in "present-day reality" than any of Grass's previous works (in O'Neill 1987c, 50). At the same time, Bondy credits the author with offering his "German contemporaries," who are mostly "indifferent" to history and are content to live in the present while "blotting out the past" (51), a "new intense consciousness of history." While Bondy finds Grass's disparagement of the Hegelian *Weltgeist* and his "concomitant admiration for Hegel's enemy Schopenhauer" on account of the latter's lack of interest in even glacially slow progress and history "rather odd," he applauds Grass for presenting "a tale of suffering, humiliation, and destruction" in the face of the "economic miracle" — a materialistic boon that tends to distract Germans from reliving the past "in memory and awareness" (51). Bondy closes his engaged review by briefly and necessarily inconclusively speculating about the standing of this "brave . . . piece of work" (52) in future years. As the following discussion of the body of ensuing criticism will show, several decades later the status of Grass's work is no longer entirely conjectural.

Ralph Manheim's 1973 English rendering of *Tagebuch* as *From the Diary of a Snail* (*Diary*) was promoted in a half-page advertisement in the *New York Times Book Review,* which cites Allen Bruce (1973) of *Library Journal.* Bruce writes that Manheim's translation "is an obvious and triumphant success" and that *Diary* is "an essential book . . . the best one Grass has written" (644) — an astounding assessment that is hardly widely shared. To be sure, there are exceptions to the rule; the reviewer of the *Christian Century* finds *Diary,* despite its discursiveness, "a scintillating novel of high distinction" (Fyne 1973, 1259). And John Reed (1973) of the *Christian Science Monitor* classifies Grass's work as "political journalism" in which Grass is "at his baroque best" and offers a "bountiful feast." Conversely, the review in the prestigious *New York Times Book Review* is far less effusive than the advertisement that ran in the same publication. In fact, there seems to be a palpable sense of puzzlement on the part of Mavis Gallant (1973) who, after enumerating the various strands of the narrative, comments: "These accounts, recitals, pieces of fiction and reportage have been sliced like a loaf of bread and reassembled in an order that seems random, but that probably was carefully planned. Whatever the intention, one has the feeling of reading a number of short and incomplete magazine pieces with the page turns gone mad" (4–5). On the plus side, Gallant praises Grass for the story of teacher Ott, which she deems "rich, mad, funny, violent and dreamlike" (5) — precisely the qualities that the author exhibits in his earlier Danzig works and for which he had been taken to task by some German reviewers. Melvin Maddocks (1973) of *Time* magazine is more affirmative in his review. He views *Diary* as "less the expression of a political platform or even a philosophy than of Grass's character" and stresses the difficulties of conveying his unglamorous, "undramatic . . . snail fables" to his children (and readers), who are most likely accustomed to more spectacular fare in the manner of *Bonanza:* "No white hats, no showdown at the O.K. Corral." Yet,

Maddocks avers, "Grass still has more endurance, wit, sheer cantankerousness than a pair of polarized extremists half his age" (110). Like most critics before him, Neal Ascherson (1973), writing in the *New York Review of Books,* seeks to define the generic qualities of the text and concludes: "We get a novel, a central narrative, and interleaved with it an assorted mass of diary, fantasy and reflection." Such a work, in which "at least four themes succeed each other paragraph by paragraph," can become "irritating at moments" (10). Reiterating complaints voiced before, Ascherson faults Grass for his "indulgent asides" and a "fair amount of mildly boastful stuff" about his "personal intimacy with presidents and chancellors" but acknowledges that the text displays an essential unity: The "book is a whole" (10–11). Ascherson reserves his most stinging criticism for Grass's presumed inability to provide a proper perspective on the activities of the Left — despite his "imaginative power" — and attributes this presumed inability on the writer's part to his lacking "experience of resistance to tyranny." In support of his rejection of Grass's "many diatribes against the revolutionary left" (11) in *Diary,* Ascherson refers to the events leading up to and following the death of leftist Chilean president Salvador Allende, who was the victim of a military putsch on 11 September 1973, two weeks before the publication of *Diary* in the United States. During these events, Ascherson reports, the well-to-do students of Santiago de Chile distinguished themselves not by adopting the tactics of the snail but by fighting defiantly and sacrificing their lives for a just cause. As justified and noble as the actions of the Chilean students may have been, Ascherson seems to be missing Grass's point, that is, his incessant and insistent endeavor to promote democratic behavior and values in the Federal Republic, an essentially stable political entity in which the potential threat of violent upheaval emerges from the Left rather than the Right.

Grass's fellow novelist John Updike (1973) in the *New Yorker* puts the matter rather succinctly: A "German is speaking to Germans, intimately and urgently. For Grass . . . has the local duty, with all the German writers of his generation, of guarding and barring the path back into Hell" (185). Updike observes that "a portrait of Germany filters through the jottings — the Germany of the postwar economic miracle" (182). In apparently ignoring the (not entirely sufficient) explanatory footnotes of the American translation, Updike concludes regretfully that such a portrait may not be fully comprehensible to the American reader because "exceptionally much has been lost in translation" (185). In what by then amounts to a quasi-obligatory exercise, Updike seeks to come to grips with Grass's unconventional "authorial method" and its result, that is, a product that cannot be called "a work of art" (182) — a value judgment that may have been inspired by the unspoken, conventional assumption that art and politics are entirely separate entities. Furthermore, Updike singles out Grass's "primary conceit" (183), his narrative stance, which rests on the assumption that *Diary* is addressed to his children, as wearing out quickly; but, in concurrence with others, he considers "Ott's invented story" to be the "most characteristically Grassian, and most easily followed." Here again, the preference for the Grass of *The Tin Drum* asserts itself. According to Updike, a further strong point is the concluding lecture about "Melencolia and her sister Utopia" (182), whereas he finds, in agreement with several previous critics, that "the unifying metaphor and theme of this farrago," the snail, "symbolizes too many things; Willy Brandt, the vagina, melancholy embodied, the human masses, moderate progressiveness, the author himself" (184).

Like Updike, Paul Zweig (1973) in the *New Republic* judges *Diary* to be "a disappointing book" and a "calamity" (28) and singles out the episodes of the Ott story as the "best portions"; they are, however, ultimately insufficient to "save the book." Zweig, with his recourse to *The Tin Drum* and his implicit thesis that "citizen" and "artist" are incompatible (29), follows a pattern that has become well established in the American reception of Grass. Daniel Coogan (1973) in *America* cannot muster much enthusiasm about "this strange book" and "curious web" that is told "in apparently random fashion" and is full of "confusing and obscure references to German political and literary figures"; in short, "readers . . . have come to expect better things" of Grass. Despite some initial complimentary comments about Grass's ceaseless endeavors to "let the past tumble guiltily out of the nation's pocket" (15) and his assuming a "moderate, antiapocalyptic, antiextremist position on social change" in *Diary,* in the end Pearl K. Bell (1973) in the *New Leader* is put off by the book's "lazy anything-goes organization" and its "formlessness," which make it "difficult to read and not worth the effort" (16). Not surprisingly, she deems the story of Doubt or teacher Ott to be the work's only redeeming feature. It is, then, fair to say that the initial American critical response to *Diary* was at best lukewarm; somewhat positive reactions were generally mitigated by a sense of bafflement or annoyance about a text that neither conforms to traditional notions of genre nor appears to be a book in the familiar mode of *The Tin Drum.*

Politics and Aesthetics

Although of an essayistic rather than a scholarly nature, Fritz Raddatz's 1973 reading of *Tagebuch* may be considered one of the first attempts to provide a somewhat comprehensive approach to the text after the wave of book reviews in (West) Germany had ebbed. In contrast to some earlier interpreters, Raddatz posits that Grass's text features a self-examination and self-interrogation that aims at communication and instruction rather than at self-representation in the vein of self-glorification (192). Hence Grass's choice of the form of the diary, Raddatz argues, is an expression not of artistic impotence (actually, a charge rarely leveled) but rather of sadness and loneliness (194–95). Raddatz emphasizes the private dimension of the text far more than other critics, without, perhaps, paying sufficient attention to its public aspects. Conversely, beginning in the late 1960s, a number of articles (and monographs) investigating Grass's political role began appearing, in which the analysis of the writer's politics occasionally overshadows his accomplishments as a writer. Among these contributions, the one by Kurt Lothar Tank (1973) may be mentioned as an example of an unqualified acceptance of Grass's unprecedented political engagement.

In a more distinctly literary vein, Ann L. Mason in her 1976 contribution focuses on Grass's "presentation, in a new and overtly autobiographical form of an artist-hero and an investigation of the interrelationship of politics and aesthetics" (in O'Neill 1987c, 159) in an effort "to develop an explicitly post-Nazi and democratic conception of the artist in an increasingly self-conscious, didactic manner" (160). She emphasizes the continuity and consistency of Grass's concept of the artist as citizen, a concept that is reinforced by the interspersed anecdotes about the author's family life — a device that undermines any inclination to regard the writer as an "aloof artist" (161) removed from the humdrum routine of daily life. In teacher Ott, Mason sees a further mutation of Grass's previous artist figures, such as Oskar Matzerath in *Die Blechtrommel* and Eduard Amsel in *Hundejahre;* Ott engages in "quasi-artistic activities" because he was "forced to relate ever new stories and improvise dramatic productions in order to entertain his host," the bicycle dealer Stomma, so as to prevent the latter "from turning him over to the Gestapo." Unlike Oskar and Eduard, however, Ott does not display any ambivalence in his attitude toward or dealings with the Nazis; furthermore, unlike his artistically inclined predecessors, Ott is no longer a narrator who is "at least partially entrenched in fascist fantasies of power." Grass's preoccupation with Danzig and his recourse to "recent German history," which was viewed dimly by reviewers such as Blöcker, serves ultimately as the "impetus for his activity of engaged artist in postwar [West] Germany" (162) — a point made previously, albeit in considerably less detailed fashion, by other critics, such as Krüger.

As an artist, Mason writes, Grass's "preoccupation with Dürer as a humanist" contributes to his "own self-image as neo-Enlightenment man" (163) in the realms of both art and politics; hence the concluding lecture, "On Stasis in Progress," covers both realms, providing "a theory of socio-political practice and of artistic expression" (164). With regard to the latter, Mason plausibly suggests that Grass's "meandering style" in *Tagebuch* is a reflection of his "aversion to goal-directed, ideological social and political action and his emphasis instead on slow social reform" (165). Hence Grass uses Dürer's *Melencolia* "to criticize the extremes of capitalistic and communistic political and social practice"; furthermore, Grass extends his polemics to inveigh against both the "European literary tradition and Marxist literary theory" (169) in general. Specifically, Grass rejects Marxist literary historian and critic Georg Lukács's doctrine of realism as well as Thomas Mann's "hero-worship of the anti-bourgeois artist" and his concept of art with an "irrationalistic and daemonic bias" (171) as displayed in the passages on *Melencolia* in Mann's novel *Doktor Faustus* (1947; *Doctor Faustus,* 1948). Rather than assuming that the book's resistance to "genre classification" constitutes a drawback, Mason conceives of it as Grass's "experimentation with genre that will allow him to unify the diverse aspects of his . . . artistic and intellectual interests and social activities" (172). From Mason's thorough and detailed discussion there emerges a virtually unmitigated positive assessment of a text that, as has been shown above, has not found universal favor among critics.

In his brief remarks in a 1974 essay that traces Grass's artistic development from *Die Blechtrommel* to *Tagebuch,* John Reddick postulates that after *Hundejahre* Grass needed to find a new form for the novel, one in which he could address the compatibility (or incompatibility) of writing fiction and at the same time becoming involved in meaningful social (and political) contributions. Reddick sees the constitutive elements of this new form in the pervasive irony of *Tagebuch* as well as its openness (51) and marvels at the trajectory of Grass's artistic development, in which the unspectacular snail has replaced the fear-inspiring specter of the "Schwarze Köchin" in *Die Blechtrommel.* Mark E. Cory (1983) briefly explores the snail as a metaphor for the political process in this "campaign novel" (519) — a metaphor that works on the "essayistic," "autobiographical," and "narrative" levels (521) — and brings into focus the unresolved tension between politics and aesthetics by crediting Grass with displaying a "talent for metaphor better received by literary than by political critics" (522). But then, as the author himself and other critics have made abundantly clear, Grass does not consider literature to be a prime tool for achieving political progress.

In her analysis of Grass's total oeuvre under the aspect of the relationship between literature and politics, which precedes Cory's remarks, Gertrude Cepl-Kaufmann (1975) justifiably singles out *Tagebuch* as the work in which the nexus between a specific election campaign and the author's literary production is most pronounced (185). Grass's starting point is the assumption that the writer is also a normal citizen who actively participates in politics rather than standing disdainfully aside — as many authors had done during the Weimar Republic. Yet Grass rejects any "progressive literary concept" (192) in the sense of a specific future-oriented, socio-political function of literature and distinguishes clearly between the tasks of the novelist and that of the campaigner. He makes this clear by his demonstration of what may be called the juggling of two beer mats for the benefit of aspiring writers who consider the involvement in politics detrimental to their craft: "'This is my political work that I do as a Social Democrat and citizen; this is my manuscript, my profession, my whatchacallit.'" The juggling act, during which a perfect balance of the two components is neither intended nor achievable, is "hard, but it can be done" (*DS*, 284). Consequently, neither of the two activities Grass engages in is privileged; Cepl-Kaufmann argues that he establishes the connection with his potential readers by endowing his personal problems with a comparatively high degree of social relevance (193). Yet, she continues, Grass's definition, "A writer, children, is someone who writes against the passage of time" (*DS*, 141), transcends the alleged fixation on the purely personal and explains the author's task as writing against the forgetfulness induced by the passage of time as well as against deliberate attempts to falsify history (here, the crushing of the "Prague Spring" of 1968 by the Soviet Union and its allies): "It's time that makes terror habitual: time is what we must write against" (*DS*, 139).

A Children's Book?

Since the appearance of *Tagebuch,* studies comparing one specific facet in several texts by Grass have become more frequent. A notable example is Hanspeter Brode's essay (1980b) in which he investigates the communicative structures and position of the narrator in *Die Blechtrommel, Tagebuch,* and *Der Butt.* Inasmuch as *Tagebuch* presents both a clearly identified narrator, who is immanent to the text and closely related to father and electoral campaign activist Grass, and an immanent audience (or, to use narratological terminology, the narratee), the four children, this particular work is especially suitable for an analysis in terms of communicative structures. In the case of *Tagebuch,* Brode notes the lack of a genre classification such as "novel" or "novella," which Grass provides as subtitles in his previous works of fiction, but contends that *Tagebuch* follows the conventional composition pattern of a novel in that two levels of narration are evident: the *Erzählzeit* (discourse time, time of the narrating) and the *erzählte Zeit* (story time, time of the narrated). The former refers to Grass's involvement in the election campaign, the latter entails the Ott story. The two narrative strands are closely related to each other because Grass pursues the theme of the persecution of the Jews up to the present by tracing the fates of survivors — an endeavor that takes him to Israel. Moreover, Brode explains, the Danzig past is established as a didactic model of elucidating historical processes for a youthful audience with limited capabilities of absorption and abstraction and is thereby made significant for the present: "Preparations for the universal crime were made in many places . . . in Danzig, . . . the process was slowed down, which made it easier to record later on . . ." (*DS*, 12).

Abstract history comes alive for Grass's children in two stories they can relate to, that of Ott and the complementary one of Augst. Both men have been seriously affected by the Nazi period and encounter difficulties in adjusting to the postwar "economic miracle" — Ott has to spend several years in a Polish sanatorium and Augst, as previously mentioned, commits suicide. Particularly effective in demonstrating the susceptibility of young people to totalitarian ideologies is the narrator's indication of his own potential culpability. In quoting and paraphrasing Erwin Lichtenstein's "documentation," *Die Juden der Freien Stadt Danzig unter der Herrschaft des Nationalsozialismus* (1973; *The Exodus of the Danzig Jews*, *DS*, 280), his main source, Grass writes about "the last Jewish emigrants" leaving Danzig in 1940. The exodus was accompanied by "laughter, malicious jingles, spitting" from bystanders: "The young people showed particular zeal. (I wasn't there; but — children — I was thirteen and could have been there)" (*DS*, 152). Hence, Brode suggests, Grass seeks to establish a link between former "SA students" and "Maoists" (*DS*, 25), albeit somewhat tentatively; the author also does not refrain from admitting the possibility that his own children might be led astray: "It may be, . . . that when you're in search of something later on, Communism will give you hope; it lives holding out hope of the true Communism to come" (*DS*, 143). Grass's narrative stance, needless to say, is intended to prevent his children's potential attempt to embrace a totalitarian ideology; lest persuasion should prove insufficient, he adds a forceful warning against their aspiring to "the goal of forcing the liberation of mankind by Communism . . .: at any price. . . . I say: over my dead body" (*DS*, 144).

If, as Brode surmises, in 1972 *Tagebuch* conforms to a prevailing tendency of the West German book market, in that books for children penned by authors of serious literature are in vogue, the question arises why the intended reception did not materialize and the anticipated recipients — the very first sentence begins with "Dear children:" (*DS*, 3) — were not reached. It is to be assumed that Grass, an established writer of demanding, complex, and controversial fiction, simply does not fit the image of an author of a children's book. Moreover, the intricate structure of *Tagebuch* is presumably far too challenging for children or adolescents. Consequently, Brode concludes, the internal communicative structure and narrative stance are not sufficient to influence the actual reception on the part of actual readers in the way that Grass may have hoped for.

Without mentioning Brode, Armin Arnold (1985), who characterizes *Tagebuch* as a "mixed salad" because of its various components, appears to challenge Brode's basic premise by insisting that the book is not intended for the author's children, because he tells his stories in such a fashion that no real child would listen to him for more than a minute. But, Arnold concedes, the children do not only seem to listen; as their repeated questions indicate, they actually seem to follow and comprehend what they are being told. Hence Grass has created *Überkinder* or super-kids (131) whose succinct queries, however, do provide a stylistic contrast to the narrator's self-professed circuitous narrative: "Be patient. . . . If my sentence twists, turns, and only gradually tapers to a point, don't fidget and don't bite your nails. Hardly anything, believe me, is more depressing than going straight to the goal. We have time" (*DS*, 9). Arnold, who does not fully address the question of the intended audience, tends to confirm Brode's view that *Diary* does presumably not appeal to readers of a young age.

In his 1991 essay "History-Writing as Hybrid Form," in which he completely dispenses with references to previous scholarship, Philip Thomson views Grass's opting for presenting himself as the father in his domestic realm as a "typically disarming ploy," inasmuch as he, the "teller," shows himself in the "most intimate and vulnerable role possible." "Paradoxically," however, this narrative device "maximizes the authority of the teller" (187) in that he shows himself struggling with the questions of his children and provides answers that draw attention to the "uncertain, provisional, and altogether dubious nature of story-telling" (186). Thomson seems to provide an implicit answer to Brode when he — presumably correctly — assumes that Grass's answers are not exclusively addressed to his own children but also to children in general. Yet Thomson's appropriate observation that "Kinder" (children) is also used in German as a "familiar way to address adults in a group" (187) does not support his contention of the existence of a text-immanent adult audience, because none is identified. At any rate, the discontinuities of the narrative, which Thomson considers the "most distinctive feature" of *Diary,* turn out to be — strangely enough — "Grass's guarantee of historical relevance" (183) because history does not evolve in a linear pattern; moreover, both modern historiography and historical fiction are afflicted with the "hermeneutic insight into the inseparability of fact and interpretation" (182). It follows that Grass's text is an "antidote to the unreflected narration of history that rests upon a naïve notion of representation" and, via its very method of narration, is directed against all absolutes: "absolute faith, absolute certainty, absolute demands."

According to Thomson, the very title — *From the Diary of a Snail* rather than just "The Diary of a Snail" — suggests the incomplete character of the story and its "fragmentary, excerpted or selected nature" (184), which is evident in the way Grass moves "uncertainly between fiction and fact" (185). An obvious case in point is that Ott's fictional story overlaps in part with critic Marcel Reich-Ranicki's real-life experience. As the narrator reveals, a "story" told him "years ago by Ranicki as his autobiography" stayed with him and "insists on an invented name, established origins, and a cellar to take refuge in later on" (*DS*, 18). Thomson ends his essay by drawing attention, in unspoken agreement with others, to "On Stasis on Progress" as a "philosophy of history." Less persuasive is his contention that *Diary* represents the "end of the first large phase" (189) of Grass's work, in that in his subsequent fictional writing he was to abandon his "grand project of narrating the history of his time" (190). In view of the Grassian prose texts of the 1990s and the early twenty-first century, which will be discussed in later chapters, such an assertion seems untenable.

The Persecution of the Jews and the Question of German Guilt

Virtually all the critics mentioned above refer to the persecution of the Danzig Jews — although they tend to do so somewhat summarily because of their different emphases and specific approaches to the text. Hans-Dieter Zimmermann's 1985 essay is the first to explicitly address an important topic that gained increased relevance in public discourse during the late 1970s. Zimmermann elevates the luncheon table in Grass's Berlin home, where the conversations between the author/narrator and his children take place, to the central locus, a place of discussion and reflection, of the two narrative strands, that is, the present-day election campaign and the past discrimination of the Jews in Danzig. Grass, Zimmermann points out, gives an accounting of and to himself, to his children, and to the young people of the *außerparlamentarische Opposition* (opposition outside of parliament) in the Federal Republic, who reject his recipe for slow social progress in favor of striving for a revolution (302). Whereas the luncheon table provides a clearly defined space (and audience) for the telling of the tale(s), it is Ott who serves as a means to merge the two narrative strands. While justifiably drawing attention to the figure of teacher Ott, who represents the allegory of doubt against all ideologies, as well as to his function and his activities — Zimmermann suggests that Ott's selflessness and willingness to help the Jews are motivated by human kindness rather than the principle of doubt (304) — Grass's depiction of the actual persecution of the Jews receives comparatively short shrift. True, Zimmermann aptly characterizes Grass's basic stance as "laconic but sympathetic" (303) and attests to the latter's firm intention to provide an accurate historical record in order to counteract the tendency to forget. Furthermore, Zimmermann writes, Grass does not seek to embellish the historical record by suppressing such incidents as the conflict between Orthodox Jews and Zionists in 1939 — an occurrence that might detract from the perception of the Jews' status as victims. Ultimately, however, Zimmermann's subtitle "The Persecution of the Jews in the Works of Günter Grass" appears to be slightly misleading because of his major emphasis on Ott rather than on the actual persecution. Ott serves, as Jürgen Rothenberg (in both his 1976 monograph and his 1976 article, 147) argues, primarily as a means to convey to the narrator's children the fate of the Jews in the form of a personalized but fictional story rather than in abstract terms.

In a 1983 essay, the late critic and novelist Winfried Georg Sebald (1944–2001) acknowledges that Grass succeeded in reducing the "deficit" (38) of postwar German literature with regard to memorializing the Danzig Jewish victims, but he considers the figure of Ott a product of Grass's wishful thinking — although Sebald admits the possibility that such "good" Germans did, indeed, exist. Hence, he concludes, Ott is a figure with an alibi function that prevents the exploration of and genuine engagement with the deformed emotive state of those who unquestioningly let themselves be integrated into the Nazi system. The dominance of fiction (the Ott story) over actual occurrences then tends to detract from the attempt of proper memorialization. Even the portrayal of the SPD, the party on which Grass pins his hopes, does not escape Sebald's censure; he faults the author for presenting too rosy a picture of the SPD's history in general and for not providing an explanation as to how the party was "embraced" (40) by Fascism. (Even though Sebald uses the phrase "dem Faschismus in die Arme lief," which suggests an accidental rather than a deliberate encounter, the critique appears to belittle the resistance to the Nazis of those SPD members who suffered in concentration camps.) True, Sebald grants that without Grass's "contrapuntal excursus" into mourning via Dürer's *Melencolia* the *Diary* would have been a less judicious and understanding book; yet he still considers this excursus to be a laborious, quasi-compulsory exercise (42) intended to give voice to the inarticulate collective conscience.

Somewhat along the lines of Sebald and in contrast to Zimmermann, whom she does not cite, Ernestine Schlant, in her nuanced reading of *Diary* in *The Language of Silence* (1999), makes Grass's portrayal of the suffering of the Danzig Jews the centerpiece of her analysis. She acknowledges the difficulties the "father/I-narrator [first-person narrator]" (74) is facing in seeking to answer his children's questions about the Jews without tolerating "jumps entailing a frivolous departure from history" and without becoming bogged down in the "mechanism" of numbers and other "technical details" (*DS*, 11) of the mass killings. Potential evasions on the narrator's part might be prompted by questions such as "'exactly how many were they?'" or "'How did they count them?'" (*DS*, 11) and, on a slightly different note, "'Did it always work?'" or "'What kind of gas was it?'" (*DS*, 12). Furthermore, Schlant concedes that it is "a rare occurrence in German postwar literature for a gentile character [Ott] to acknowledge what was happening to the Jews, let alone help them for no reasons other than altruistic ones." She also draws attention to the narrator's efforts both to follow "the dispersal of the Jewish community in significant detail" while Ott "is still in Danzig" (Schlant, 75) and to juxtapose "the fate of the Danzig Jews with the campaign against Chancellor Kurt [Georg] Kiesinger and for Willy Brandt" — a juxtaposition that allows Grass to underscore "the persistence of ideological fanaticism (instead of the SS it is now the SDS)" (76).

Yet in keeping with her general thesis that "in its approach to the Holocaust" (West) German literature has been "a literature of absence and silence contoured by language" (1), Schlant is bound to find fault with Grass's approach. Her main charge is that in a book, "purportedly written to tell his children about the decimation of the Danzig Jewish community" (76), the narrator fails to mention the Danzig Jews after chapter 17 (approximately in the middle of *Diary*) and only refers to them briefly in the (pen)ultimate chapter. Hence, Schlant argues, just as Jews "have vanished from German territory, so they have vanished from the narrator's consciousness" — a "serious shortcoming" (77) in terms of memorializing the suffering of the Jews. There are several flawed assumptions underlying such an argument. First of all, despite the importance of the subject matter, the doom of the Danzig Jews is by no means the only topic about which the narrator wishes to enlighten the children. Therefore, the children's "urgent" (76) questions "'And then what? What happened then?'" do not refer to the Danzig Jews but to the narrator's activities at the Evangelical Church Congress in Stuttgart, at which he "inveighed against ritualized protest" (*DS*, 161) — although a group discussion about "Jews and Christians" is mentioned parenthetically. Second, Schlant's charge that the Augst story "in fact replaces the Jews of Danzig" (77) loses its sting when one considers Augst's function as the polar opposite of Zweifel or Doubt, as the first letters of their respective last names, which form the beginning and the end of the alphabet, indicate. Whereas Augst serves as the representative "witness of the absolute" with his belief in "ultimate goals" (*DS*, 162) and thereby displays a mental predisposition that is akin to that of the young radicals, Doubt functions as an exemplary, if somewhat allegorical character (see Neuhaus 1979, rev. ed. 1992, 119) by adhering to the principle of rejecting totalitarian ideologies. Inasmuch as Augst and his ilk are largely responsible for such phenomena as the persecution of the Jews in the first place, it is then appropriate that the narrator go to considerable lengths to explain Augst to his children — precisely to warn them against the consequences of blindly dedicating oneself to one cause. Third, Schlant deplores Grass's almost exclusive reliance on Lichtenstein's documentary account, since it does not allow him to enter "unknown territory and create individuals or imagine their suffering" (78). If we may assume that, as Brode and others have shown, Grass's pedagogical bent propels him to search for constructive solutions that will prevent the recurrence of the past, then a factual account may indeed impress his youthful audience more than expressions of grief. That Grass is quite capable of articulating sorrow and mourning in his fiction has been demonstrated, for example, in the chapter on *Die Blechtrommel*. That the Augst story retains its relevance is demonstrated by Augst's daughter Ute Scheub (2006), who frequently cites from *Tagebuch* while recounting her relationship with her father, whom she seeks to understand and whom she perceives as a member of a misguided generation incapable of coming to terms with the past as well as unable to adjust to postwar society. Even as astute an observer and consummate an artist as Grass, who in *Tagebuch* not only pinned his hopes for a better future on the SPD but also conveyed to his readers his efforts to bring about such a future, carried the undisclosed burden of his military service during the Third Reich with him for decades (see Epilogue) — evidence of the long-lasting, traumatic effects of the Nazi past on an entire generation and, perhaps, a reason for the keen interest Grass took in the fate of Augst, according to Scheub.

7: *Der Butt / The Flounder*

Book of the Century?

NEARLY FIVE YEARS AFTER THE PUBLICATION of *Aus dem Tagebuch einer Schnecke,* a period that Grass mostly spent working assiduously on his new novel, *Der Butt* appeared in August 1977. Its publication was preceded by extraordinarily intense media interest, which was in part fuelled by critics' expectations that after *Tagebuch,* which had been less than enthusiastically received (see ch. 6), Grass would redeem himself by presenting a "genuine" novel in the manner of *Die Blechtrommel:* that is, without straying too far into the realm of contemporaneous politics. In addition, the reading public's curiosity about *Der Butt* was aroused by a skillful advertising campaign on the part of Grass's publisher Luchterhand — a campaign that included the mailing of four thousand advance copies to various recipients. Although some observers deemed this an excessively large number, others note that Luchterhand's marketing strategy cannot be considered unwarranted in view of a huge first printing of a hundred thousand copies (Durzak 1982, 70). The author himself contributed significantly to the marketing effort; during the last eight weeks before the official publication date he gave thirty readings from the novel, and in the eighteen months preceding this intensive reading effort, Grass had come face to face with more than ten thousand potential readers via his presentations (H. L. Arnold 1997, 135).

As befitted the stature of Grass, virtually all major critics writing for the main dailies, weeklies, and other review media took notice of *Der Butt.* But in contrast to the popular success of the novel, which dominated the bestseller charts for months (Boßmann 1997, 57), reviewers' reactions are by no means unanimously laudatory. One of the first commentators, Hellmuth Karasek in *Der Spiegel* (1977), bases his criticism on Grass's alleged flight from the present into the scurrilous Danzig of times past. Karasek's dismissive characterization of the question of women's emancipation, one of the central themes of the novel, as a mere "Wehwehchen" (103), or very minor complaint, betrays a rather cavalier attitude with regard to a highly charged topical issue that was to assume major significance in subsequent discussions. Conversely, Rolf Michaelis of *Die Zeit* (1977) professes at the beginning of his review not to have read anything as beautiful in a long time and proceeds to enumerate and describe various ingredients of *Der Butt,* a work that may be read as a novel of romance, a cultural history of nutrition based on the kitchen, a proletarian cookbook, a feminist fairy-tale parody, a domestic story of a separation, a history of an emancipation, and so on. Furthermore, Michaelis provides a sound analysis of the novel's intricate structure and innovative narrative stance — both rest on the time frame of nine months that elapse between the conception and birth of the child (a girl) whose parents are the present-day, first-person narrator (who, however, is also present in all other time phases) and his wife Ilsebill. The fact that Ilsebill eventually is going to give birth to a daughter impels the narrator to figuratively deliver himself of his nine, or eleven, cooks, his "ersatz babies" (*F,* 396–97). He tells the stories of the nine historical cooks — from three-breasted Awa, priestess-cook in 2211 B.C., to Lena Stubbe (d. 1942) — in the first seven chapters (the first chapter features three cooks) or months (the nine months of the pregnancy provide the external structuring principle); the two contemporaneous cooks appear in the last two months. The eleven cooks correspond to and share traits with the members of the "Womenal" or female tribunal (*F,* 515), including the prosecutor and defense counsel (see the structural diagrams in Neuhaus 1979, 144; Russell 1979–80, 256; Zimmermann 1982, 462–63; Mews 1983c, 198–99). They have put the talking, omniscient, and superhuman fish, the masculine *Butt* (the English translation "Flounder" is not gender-specific) of fairy-tale origin on trial because (in the fairy tale collected by painter Philipp Otto Runge and given to the Brothers Grimm) he has finally put a stop to the ever more extravagant wishes of Ilsebill, the insatiable and ambitious fisherman's wife, and because (in the novel) he has stalwartly advocated the male cause from Neolithic times to the present.

Michaelis's praise is not entirely unadulterated, however; especially in "Father's Day" (that is, Ascension Day, a legal holiday in Germany), the eighth chapter, in which Billy, a self-styled Lesbian, is first sexually exploited by her lesbian friends and then raped and murdered by a gang of male motorcyclists, he detects an unwarranted atmosphere of loutishness and a denunciatory, misogynist tone. At the same time, Michaelis defends Grass against the expected charge of having written a book that is directed against endeavors to achieve women's emancipation and concludes his overwhelmingly positive review with the blessing "The Flounder be with you" as well as an appeal to his readers to peruse *Der Butt.* The lack of unanimity among major critics is evident when one compares this with Marcel Reich-Ranicki's review in the *Frankfurter Allgemeine Zeitung.* Whereas Michaelis considers the eighth chapter a deplorable lapse in taste, Reich-Ranicki deems it, next to the depiction of the encounter of the two seventeenth-century poets Martin Opitz and Andreas Gryphius in the fourth month, to be one of the high points of the novel, owing to its fierce evocation of a sinister anti-idyll that amounts to a critical study of a contemporaneous milieu (1977, in Reich-Ranicki 1992a, 116). Although he concedes that *Der Butt* is an extraordinarily rich work by an author whose imagination does not seem to know any limits, in general, Reich-Ranicki's tone tends toward the negative. All in all, he finds the novel disappointing, because Grass attempts to achieve too much (111) and ultimately fails in his attempt to design a private mythology and to present world history from the vantage point of the cooks (116).

The "Father's Day" chapter turns out to be a touchstone of sorts; another major critic, Joachim Kaiser of the *Süddeutsche Zeitung* (1977) remains ambivalent in his evaluation of Grass's both horrific and grandiose representation of the contemporaneous scene briefly described above — in the end, the aforementioned Billy is murdered for violating traditional gender roles (1977, in Kaiser 1988, 284). Kaiser's critique of the novel specifically entails the unsuitability of the Flounder, an essentially abstract principle, as a vehicle for creating suspense; furthermore, Kaiser — somewhat in the manner of Karasek — blames Grass for unnecessarily delving deeply into local Danzig lore and historical minutiae; finally, Kaiser is displeased with Grass's allegedly profoundly conservative ("grundkonservativ") stance that is supposedly evident in his ironic and skeptical distrust of the women's movement, his castigating men for their use of force against women (while, at the same time, Grass has an enlightened woman ask for corporal punishment), and Grass's rejection (as demonstrated in the ninth month) of the propagandistically embellished claim of communist states to have abolished exploitation and set people free (282–83).

Although, in general, most reviews have a moderately positive slant (H. L. Arnold 1997, 135), there are less flattering appraisals. For example, Swiss journalist Dieter Fringeli (1977) characterizes the novel as one of the most whimsical literary expeditions since the end of the Second World War. He posits, somewhat astonishingly, that *Der Butt* is not really about equal rights of men and women, female emancipation, the matriarchy, and feminism; rather, he reduces the complex work to a profoundly private statement that reflects a personal crisis in the life of author Grass who, as the ever-present narrator, undergoes several reincarnations throughout the centuries (1977, in Fringeli 1982, 86). The result, according to Fringeli, is then that the novel is essentially a failure, albeit one on a grandiose scale (87). Next to hilariously comical chapters and scenes, Fringeli finds several he deems to be of a puerile nature; he considers the recipes rather than the work's literary quality to be one of its redeeming features (90). Another Swiss journalist, Anton Krättli (1977), voices reservations of a different kind and takes issue with Grass's generic classification; while acknowledging Grass's extraordinary gifts, he proposes that the enormous wealth of material amassed between the covers of the book would have been more suitable for a collection of novellas rather than a novel (489).

As the foregoing discussion has shown, *Der Butt* is by no means regarded as a general failure; yet Heinz Ludwig Arnold (1977) feels called upon to defend the novel against its detractors by contrasting its popular success — in October 1977, before the beginning of the Christmas shopping season, the novel had sold nearly two hundred and fifty thousand copies — with its less than fervent endorsement on the part of the critical establishment. Arnold perceives the reviews of Grass's third *opus magnum* (after *Die Blechtrommel* and *Hundejahre*) that he takes into consideration to be highly subjective, rashly formulated, and prescriptive, in the sense that authorial intent is blithely ignored in favor of critics' preconceived notions of how and what Grass should have written. A recurring point of critical discontent, Arnold observes, is that *Die Blechtrommel* continues to provide an unsurpassed model of the author's creativity. In particular, Arnold singles out one of the few female critics, Marielouise Janssen-Jurreit in the Zurich *Weltwoche* (1977), author of *Sexismus: Über die Abtreibung der Frauenfrage* (1978; *Sexism: The Male Monopoly on History and Thought,* 1982), who rejects the assumption that *Der Butt* evinces sympathy for the women's cause; instead, she charges, Grass relies on melodramatic effects, which he achieves via violating taboos, in order to titillate his bourgeois reading public. Janssen-Jurreit's engaged contribution may be counted as one of the first decidedly feminist critiques that challenge male reviewers' presuppositions. (In July 1977, before the book's publication, the newly founded feminist magazine *Emma* declared Grass to be "Pascha des Monats" [pasha of the month]). Whereas in 1977 Arnold essentially rejected Janssen-Jurreit's appraisal, twenty years later feminist criticism had become a fully accepted and legitimate part of the critical spectrum — a development that is reflected in a far more moderate assessment of Janssen-Jurreit's piece in a 1997 survey of Grass criticism edited by Arnold; he now finds her questioning of the author's assumed unwillingness to probe the traditional gender roles entirely valid (139). In general, however, when commenting on the complex relationship between author and critic, literary scholars tend to take the side of the author. This is evident, for example, in a 1977 interview (in H. L. Arnold 1963, 5th ed. 1978, 1–39) in which Grass ironically characterizes his association with dominant representatives from the realm of literary reviews such as Reich-Ranicki and Kaiser as a forced marriage that cannot be dissolved despite the incompatibility of his and their respective views regarding his literary production (36). Both interviewer Arnold and scholar Manfred Durzak (1982, 68) essentially concur with Grass's view.

Yet this dominant position of established critics in forming and shaping the reading public's opinion has its limits. Heinrich Vormweg (1978, 94) notes that the phenomenal success of *Der Butt* is based on readers' genuine interest rather than on critical acclaim; the novel is actually being read rather than merely bought and then displayed as a kind of intellectual status symbol. Moreover, the readers themselves were given the chance to express their opinion, thanks to an experiment conducted by the Cologne station of the radio network Deutschlandfunk during the summer of 1977, in which readers were asked to write reviews of *Der Butt.* The statistical analysis of the three hundred and fifty submissions yielded evaluations of which 50 percent are predominantly positive, 20 percent are ambivalent, and 30 percent reject the novel as imitative, boring, and a failure (Durzak 1982, 73–75). The two best contributions, selected by a jury, were broadcast and subsequently published — surely an important step in democratizing the process of reviewing by giving the average reader a voice and a forum. The published essays by the two prize winners show considerable sophistication and tend to be somewhat more positive than the general tenor of literary experts. Although not quite as "enthusiastically" as Durzak claims (75), Christoph Perels (1978, 90) judges the novel to be Grass's best book since *Die Blechtrommel,* but Gunzelin Schmid Noerr (1978, 92) is more cautious in his praise and finds Grass's women figures peculiarly "pale" in that they seem to function as projections of male wishes and anxieties.

Apart from the ranks of professional literary critics and members of that opaque segment of general readers who were exposed to the author and his work via the ubiquitous medium of TV (Jaumann 1982), there are others of a literary bent who have a particular axe to grind — a hardly surprising development with regard to a volume of encyclopedic scope that challenges preconceived notions in several areas. Religious issues, which do not play a significant role in discussions of the works immediately preceding *Der Butt,* surface again but remain essentially a peripheral concern. The article by Anneliese Triller (1977) is a case in point; she focuses on Grass's portrayal of one of the numerous historical figures (albeit the only cook with a clearly defined historical precedent) and objects to his presumed misrepresentation of fourteenth-century saint Dorothea von Montau in the second month — a falsification, she avers, that transgresses the boundaries of poetic license. Triller conveniently ignores that, in essence, Grass adheres to the ascertainable facts of Dorothea's life but reaches conclusions that are unlike those — but similarly fictitious — of Dr. Stachnik, one of the main proponents of Dorothea's sainthood (see *F,* 164–68; H. D. Zimmermann 1982, 468).

Although not as vehemently and pervasively as in the case of *Die Blechtrommel,* charges of blasphemy are also leveled against *Der Butt.* The original review of the staunchly conservative *Bayernkurier* notes that the novel is rife with obscene and blasphemous utterances; in contrast, the official newspaper of the Vatican, the *Osservatore Romano,* sees matters differently and praises both Grass's artistic creativity and his affinity with Catholicism — in spite of the author's status as a lapsed Catholic; not surprisingly, the *Bayernkurier* heatedly rejected the novel's benign categorization by the papal publication (W. J. Müller 1978).

Whereas *Der Butt* is generally considered to constitute a departure from the diary-cum-fiction mode of *Tagebuch,* Fritz J. Raddatz (1977b) emphasizes that both texts are an expression of increasing loneliness on the part of the author and draws attention to the structural principle of the novel, which rests on the number three (three times three yields the nine chapters or "months") as, for example, in the first cook, the aforementioned three-breasted Awa. Hence Raddatz posits the importance of the narrator who, despite his various historical manifestations through the ages — "I, down through the ages, have been I" (*F,* 4) — is essentially a present-day writer akin to author Grass (Raddatz, 895), disposing of his assiduously and meticulously acquired wealth of historical material in sovereign fashion and in the manner of the picaresque novel, the social novel of William Makepeace Thackeray and Lawrence Sterne, and the psychological study of Marcel Proust (898). Raddatz's high praise is further enhanced by his acknowledgment of the importance of the interspersed poems, which ordinarily receive comparatively little attention in reviews; they function as the least disguised statements about the writer's self (899). In agreement with some previous critics, however, Raddatz considers the "Father's Day" chapter (the eighth month), in which the Lesbians are presented as caricatures, to be farcical and not in keeping with the overall tone of the novel (900). In the end, Raddatz returns to his starting point and interprets the novel's conclusion as an expression of the narrator's futile endeavors to prevent the disintegration of his relationship with women (901): "Ilsebill came. She overlooked me, overstepped me. Already she had passed me by. I ran after her" (*F,* 547).

Raddatz's laudatory review is surpassed by that of writer Wolfgang Hildesheimer (1977), an erstwhile member of *Gruppe 47,* who in his open, congratulatory letter on the occasion of Grass's fiftieth birthday calls *Der Butt* a veritable *Jahrhundertbuch* (book of the century) comparable to James Joyce's *Ulysses* (1922) and *Finnegan's Wake* (1939). Hildesheimer's approach is somewhat akin to that of Raddatz, in that he discerns a supreme melancholy in Grass's insight that matters in both the public and private realms have gone terribly wrong, but he views such insight as part of Grass's greatness (971). In contrast to Triller, Hildesheimer finds nothing offensive in the depiction of Dorothea von Montau and declares it to be a genuine saint's legend (971). As the previously mentioned dissenting opinions of several critics, as well as the ensuing discussion of the "Father's Day" chapter show, Hildesheimer may have been motivated by wishful thinking when he wrote that Grass's critical portrayal of male terror in all of its disgusting details will find the appreciation of engaged feminists (967).

As the broad spectrum of critical voices has shown, *Der Butt,* not surprisingly, does not meet with unequivocal approval. However, this work evokes a response on the part of readers that has not only been reflected in their attending Grass's readings in impressively large numbers and in the bestseller status of the novel; they were actually given a forum to voice their opinions. This new development led Grass to assume — decidedly prematurely in view of the controversies in which he was to become engulfed in the following decades — that the major critics had lost their influence and were not taken seriously anymore by the public (H. L. Arnold 1963, 5th ed. 1978, 39).

Grass "Floundering"

The Flounder, in Ralph Manheim's translation, was published in England and the United States in November 1978. For all practical purposes, it is on Manheim's work that "Grass's image in the English-speaking world is based" (Butler 1980/81, 3). Hence it is in order to briefly dwell on the quality of the English rendering. John Simon (1978), writing in the *Saturday Review,* is that rarity among American reviewers who is capable of knowledgeably assessing the quality of Manheim's translation. Although, in general, he gives the translator good marks in view of the "high demands" made by Grass's "imaginative power and stylistic variety and verve," he does draw attention to a number of inaccuracies and flaws in the English version. In a similar vein, Sofus Simonsen (1979) deplores the insufficiency of the English translation in coping with Grass's innovative use of language. The most comprehensive appraisal of the English rendering is that by G. P. Butler (1980/81), who praises its indubitable strengths but also detects "sufficiently varied and numerous" shortcomings that invite comment (3). As an Englishman, Butler feels uncomfortable with Manheim's Americanisms, which "non-American readers may find hard to catch" (5); he admits, however, that "certain concessions must be made to the target readership." Butler notes, for instance, the translator's tendency to shy away "from colloquialism and vulgarity" (6) — a rather difficult task in view of Grass's irrepressible zest and linguistic exuberance — as well as his making unwarranted "concessions to Anglo-American ignorance" by inconsistently elaborating on or omitting certain of Grass's profuse "cultural-cum-historical references and allusions" (8, 9). While conceding that Grass's "novels are not reading matter for the scant of breath, of any nation" (9), Butler pleads for as faithful a rendering as possible — in view of the complexity and "mind-boggling problems for translators" (Russell 1979/80, 255) of *Der Butt* perhaps an unattainable goal. Certainly, the author sought to aid and support translators in their difficult undertaking. Beginning with *Der Butt,* Grass, in cooperation with his domestic and foreign publishers, instituted a novel practice that resulted in the first weeklong seminar for translators of *Der Butt* in February 1978. It was conducted by the author and has become a regular occurrence after the appearance of each new work. In *Der Butt spricht viele Sprachen* (2002; The Flounder Speaks Many Languages), Helmut Frielinghaus has edited the reminiscences, comments, and reflections of those concerned with the extremely challenging task of making Grass's texts available in other linguistic mediums.

The American reception of *The Flounder* was very different from the German response. In contrast to the enormous fanfare that greeted the appearance of the original, both the prepublication notices and the initial reaction in the United States were muted. True, Grass gave a reading from the novel at the New School in New York City in April 1977, which attracted some attention, and in September 1977 the *Christian Science Monitor* had a report about a reading by Grass, "the magic master of the German language," in Bonn (S. Simon 1977). In addition, some interviews with the author were conducted. Herbert Mitgang (1978) of the *New York Times* tells of such an interview, which was held in the New York office of Helen Wolff, Grass's American publisher (*The Flounder* was published by Harcourt Brace Jovanovich as a "Helen and Kurt Wolff Book"). In this interview, the writer concedes that "he had satirized some female radicals" but rejects charges of antifeminism. In the fall of 1978 Grass appeared on the now defunct Dick Cavett TV show for an interview (S. Mayer 1983, 180), but the interviewer spent virtually the entire time questioning the novelist about his memories of the Nazi past, to the extent that *The Flounder* received virtually no attention — an indication that Grass was primarily seen as the author of *The Tin Drum,* a work that continues to hold sway as the unchallenged exemplar by which all of his other literary efforts are to be measured.

British novelist Anthony Burgess, writing in the *Times Literary Supplement* (1978), strikes several chords that resonate with subsequent reviewers, to wit, Grass's "Rabelaisian . . . monstrous exaggeration," particularly with regard to the "devotion to eating" — a devotion, however, that highlights the importance of nutrition, so readily ignored by historians, in world history. Grass's preoccupation with food also allows Burgess to indulge in the propensity of particularly British reviewers to ferret out traits perceived to be genuinely German. In a clever pun, Burgess modifies the slogan "Kanonen statt Butter" (cannons instead of butter), attributed to Hitler's Commander-in-Chief of the Luftwaffe, Hermann Göring, which emphasized the Nazis' priorities on the eve of the Second

World War, to "*Butt* not gunners" and observes that Grass warns "the German people to beware of the abstractions that have too often made them flounder in a nordic mist" and to pay attention to the "needs of the stomach" instead. Burgess relates his speculations about Grass's subject matter to questions of genre and maintains that the writer does not produce what "Thomas Mann would call novels" because the adoption of "naturalistic fictional technique" would have required him to depict "with gloomy accuracy" the "shameful" prehistory, history, and posthistory of the Second World War — the war and its legacy tends to be another British preoccupation when it comes to things German. On a different note, it is not quite clear whether Burgess considers Grass's aforementioned "Rabelaisian" mode of representation a valid substitute for a more conventional generic approach.

One of the first, comparatively brief and almost entirely laudatory, American reviews is that by Karl Keller in the *Los Angeles Times* (1978): "Grass has never been better at working up a long series of bawdy tales, all of them thoroughly German, in a rich fantasy with serious political overtones. . . . Grass's novel is extremely fanciful, funny, political, contemporary." Keller's only minor qualification concerns the "silly" device of using the Flounder as "Grass' stand-in" — a debatable point inasmuch as the author may be more closely identified with the narrator than the extraordinary, fabulous fish. Moreover, Keller's reading of the novel as taking issue with "all national myth-making" and German "nationalism" seems to underestimate the central battle of the sexes, which cannot be defined in exclusively national terms.

It is a measure of Grass's stature that both of the leading general news magazines, *Time* (Sheppard 1978) and *Newsweek* (Clemons 1978), reviewed *The Flounder* and paid tribute to "Germany's finest living novelist" (Sheppard) and the "greatest living German novelist" (Clemons) in their respective essays. They both strike a tone of praise, albeit rather cautious on the part of Clemons, who called it an "encyclopedic" novel and a "tedious" but "formidable achievement," while Sheppard wrote that it was a "joyfully indulgent book" by a "robust genius." In general, the critics of major dailies and periodical publications are predisposed to view the novel with varying degrees of approval. Perhaps most effusive is Morris Dickstein, writing in the *New York Times Book Review* (1978), who cites Grass's "monstrous miscellanies," which "serve as inflatable vessels of bizarre information, vehicles for all kinds of encyclopedic, mythological, and historical lore" in the manner of Rabelais's multivolume *Gargantua et Pantagruel* (1532–52; *Gargantua and Pantagruel,* 1653–94) and Sterne's *Tristram Shandy* (1759–67). Once again, Dickstein evokes Joyce's *Ulysses* as a comparable achievement. Yet, he surmises, *The Flounder* surpasses those novels (as well as *The Tin Drum,* usually favored by American literati) in that it is "by far the most audacious product of [Grass's] historical imagination" owing to the author's obsession as a "serious socialist" with exploring history via an "original conception," that is, the use of both "culinary" and "sexual history" as a "vehicle" for promoting the causes he supports.

William McPherson (1978), book critic of the *Washington Post,* likewise positions *The Flounder* in the context of world literature, when he refers to the "Rabelaisian novel by the German *wunderkind* (now 51)" Grass, a veritable "Baltic *Ulysses.*" McPherson, who quotes extensively from the novel, praises it as a "bravura performance . . . by a brilliant virtuoso, a vastly intelligent, sensitive and humane writer"; yet he finds the "brilliance more dazzling than radiant" and feels overwhelmed or "stuffed" by the wealth of material. Rabelais (in addition to Claude Lévi-Strauss) also serves John Leonard (1978) in the *New York Times* as a reference point in this novel, which looks like a "mess" but is "actually shapely." As a minor criticism that originates from a distinct misreading, Leonard rejects what he considers the interspersed "*burlesques* of epic poetry" [my italics] as "to no one's advantage." Yet he shows insight in interpreting the novel's conclusion, women's takeover from the bankrupt patriarchy, as ambivalent: "Who knows whether the world of the New Woman will be braver or better than the old world of restless Goths with final solutions?"

In a different vein, John Simon, cited above, sees Grass "gracefully" accepting the "coming of a new age of female hegemony"; at the same time, he sums up the complex issue of how Grass — whom he simply identifies with the narrator(s) by referring to him/them as "G.G." — deals with the battle of the sexes both authoritatively and succinctly: "*The Flounder* is the first major satirical feminist novel; it is also the first major satirical anti-feminist novel" (59).

Although he professes that there is "much to admire" about *The Flounder,* whose author displays "great aplomb, erudition, and energy," fellow novelist, short-story writer, poet, and critic John Updike (1977), writing in the *New Yorker,* reiterates other critics' complaints about feeling "stuffed" after wading through the "nine-course . . . feast" of more than five hundred pages. Updike paraphrases objections that he had voiced previously, saying that Grass's "fictional imagination" has been dominated by his politics at a stage in his development as a writer when he is "at the extreme of his virtuosity" but in danger of overextending himself on account of his "strenuous career as celebrity-author-artist-Socialist." As a dire warning, Updike refers to Thomas Mann's protagonist Gustav von Aschenbach in the English version of *Der Tod in Venedig* (1913; *Death in Venice,* 1930). Whereas Grass, as the jacket flap of *The Flounder* states, decided "five years before his fiftieth birthday . . . that he would write a major novel as a present to himself," Aschenbach achieves the pinnacle of his official recognition as a writer by being ennobled on his fiftieth birthday. But ultimately he breaks under the strain of his incessant labors and ceases to resist his infatuation with a Polish boy while vacationing in Venice, ignores the obvious signs of the outbreak of the plague in order to stay close to the object of his desire, and dies as a consequence. Needless to say, Updike avers that he does not wish a similar fate to befall Grass; nevertheless, his reference to Aschenbach appears to be motivated by Updike's reservations about Grass's conspicuous role in the public sphere — a role that requires a considerable investment of time and effort and is ultimately detrimental, Updike infers, to Grass's craft of fiction.

English writer and critic Nigel Dennis's ill-defined and idiosyncratic "personal approach" to *The Flounder* in the *New York Review of Books* (1978) results in an exceptional bashing of what he calls "a very bad novel." The work was praised by German critics, Dennis opines, because Germany seemed to "need" Grass in order to be able to tout presumably "'great prose'" again in order to overcome the aftermath of the Second World War. Dennis seems unable to resist the temptation of indulging in speculations about national traits — indicative, perhaps, of a certain degree of 'Germanophobia" (Butler 1979, 23) — when he surmises that the "soft and flaccid element" of the novel, particularly evident in the maternal Neolithic world of the first month, is "what has pleased the Germans." But the "warm sense of bed and *Schmalz*" that, according to Dennis, *The Flounder* conveys cannot be construed as a sign of Grass's "rich imagination" — rather, he believes that it is indicative of a lack of original faculties. The dubious validity of Dennis's arguments is further undermined by a number of errors that are most likely attributable to careless reading. For example, he underestimates the role of the Flounder, who is appropriately identified by Simon and Updike as a kind of Hegelian *Weltgeist* (*F,* 38 et passim) of a male-dominated world, by calling him the "mock villain of the piece." The Flounder is said to be put on "trial at the hands of the libbers in Bonn" rather than those in (West) Berlin, and the fish's origin is traced to "one of Grimm's [sic] fairy tales" rather than to that of the Brothers Grimm. Although Dennis finds some "impressive" sections in the "general muddle" of the novel, his tendency is to damn Grass with faint praise. For instance, he writes about the "Father's Day" chapter: "This story would make a fine short novel — in the hands of another writer." To add insult to injury Dennis explicitly expresses his preference for Manheim's translation, which he finds superior to Grass's original. It is odd, indeed, that Manfred Durzak (1985b) praises Dennis's review as a "brilliant" piece of work that he found it a pleasure to read (107). But then Durzak is at pains to demonstrate the shortcomings and biases of German star reviewers, especially Kaiser, Karasek, and Reich-Ranicki, and uses Dennis as a foil — albeit an ill-chosen one.

The controversial "Father's Day" chapter serves Jessica Benjamin (1978) in *Ms.* magazine as an indication of Grass's "troubling cynicism" with regard to the "feminist challenge" and his disturbing answer to the "monumental antagonism [between the sexes]," in that he shows "'the new woman'" to be an "unspeakable imitation of men: her real desire is to rape her sister." In a psychoanalytical vein, Benjamin conceives of "Grass's treatment of women" as boiling down "to a child's conception of the all-powerful mother who is really a projection of his own omnipotence fantasy"; furthermore, Grass is "deviously purporting to take seriously the questions raised by contemporary feminism in order to ridicule it." Such a posture, Benjamin intimates, represents a departure from Grass's progressive politics and his efforts to "scandalize the establishment with his scurrility and bawdiness."

Benjamin's engaged feminist perspective is an isolated instance among major American reviews. In a more conventional mode, William Cloonan (1979) belatedly revisits some of the issues raised by his male colleagues (discussed above) in his ambiguously titled essay "Günther [sic] Grass Floundering." He dwells extensively on the prose texts of the *Danzig Trilogy* and Grass's assumed "pedagogical dimension" and his "didactic propensity," which compel him to explain the significance of "German history, myth, and fairy tales" (3) in order to expose the "infantile fantasies" and "juvenile narcissism" grown-ups tended to cling to during the Nazi period in general and the Second World War, which he assumed to be Grass's favorite subject, in particular. Hence Cloonan seems almost disappointed that "little is made" of the war in *The Flounder,* but he detects an "eerie resemblance" of the trial of the Flounder by the feminist Womenal to that of Hitler's bureaucratic henchman Adolf Eichmann in Jerusalem in 1961. Cloonan shares his fixation on the Second World War with other American critics; in contrast, German reviewers such as Karasek and Kaiser fault Grass for again delving into Danzig lore. Ultimately, of course, it is *The Tin Drum* that serves as Cloonan's yardstick of Grass's achievement. To his apparent relief he discovers in the Flounder's "combination of intelligence, amorality, self-irony, and curiosity" traits that make the fish "almost the equal of Oskar" (4) — an assertion of dubious validity in view of the two totally dissimilar figures' role in their vastly different fictional universes. Ultimately, Cloonan concludes, *The Flounder* does not completely succeed as a novel because it is weighed down by a "plethora of literary and historical figures"; furthermore, Grass fails to avoid the danger of "sounding fashionably chic on the subject of women's liberation" (4) — surely, a rather superficial view that completely underestimates the significance of the issues articulated in the novel.

Fairy Tale and Myth

In addition to investigatios of Grass's innovative use of both culinary and emancipatory proverbial sayings (Mieder 1978; Simonsen 1979), a considerable number of substantive scholarly contributions were to follow in the late 1970s, early 1980s, and beyond. It is indicative of the general, sustained interest on the part of literary scholars, for example, that three collections of scholarly essays on *The Flounder* (not all contributions to the volumes in question can be discussed fully here) were published within fifteen years or so of the novel's publication (Pickar 1982, Mews 1983a, Brady, McFarland, and White 1990). Among the first to analyze the novel in terms of its fabulous or magical (*märchenhaft*) properties, Durzak (1979a, 1979b) does not begin his discussion with the most obvious linkage of *Der Butt* to the fairy tale, that is, the source of the fish's origin to which the Flounder himself draws attention in an intertextual reference when he rhetorically asks the "three hard-boiled females" (*F*, 35) by whom he lets himself be caught a second time whether they "are familiar with the fairy tale of 'The Fisherman and his Wife'" (*F*, 38). Rather, Durzak dwells first — albeit briefly — on the fabulous achievement of the novel in terms of both critics' response and its commercial success. Even if Durzak is stretching the analogy a bit when he applies the conventional fairy-tale moral to author Grass by implying that good people are rewarded in the end, there is no doubt that *Der Butt* was noticed, as indicated previously, far beyond the German-speaking lands.

Durzak tackles a more intriguing subject when he draws attention to Grass's initial attempt to disregard traditional generic categories and call *Der Butt* a fairy tale — only the intervention of Luchterhand, then Grass's German publisher, finally persuaded him to abandon his plan. In an interview, the author cites one reason in particular for not insisting on his preferred genre classification: the presumed inability of publishers, critics, and scholars to abandon their conventional notions about the homey German fairy tale (Raddatz 1977). Durzak elaborates on Grass's distinction — in part derived from the latter's "teacher" Alfred Döblin — between the customary psychological novel, which is based on a rationalistic outlook, and the Grassian form, which incorporates a metafictional dimension. This dimension is evident, for example, when the Flounder assumes a "professorial" (*F*, 44) air and dispenses "literary advice" (*F*, 413). Furthermore, Durzak plausibly argues, the fairy tale also functions as a device that serves to integrate the various strands of the text. Thus the narrator's relationship with his wife Ilsebill, who constantly voices her — albeit comparatively modest — wishes, resembles that of the henpecked fisherman and his insatiable and power-hungry wife by the same name in the fairy tale. Furthermore, the name of "Billy" (that is, Sibylle Miehlau), the rape victim in the aforementioned "Father's Day" chapter, is clearly akin to that of Ilsebill. But unlike the narrator's wife Ilsebill, who is somewhat equivocal about becoming a fully emancipated woman, Durzak observes, Billy and her friends provocatively tout their total liberation from male society. Less convincing is the parallel that Durzak establishes with regard to Billy and the fisherman's wife: shortly before her death, the former reasserts her femininity when she parts company with her exploitative friends; conversely, the latter appears to be entirely devoid of conventional feminine traits in her single-minded striving for ever more power and by relegating her husband to the role of messenger who conveys her wishes to the Flounder.

In yet another respect the fairy tale operates as a device for integrating the diverse elements of the novel. Grass actually presents (or, mostly, refers to) several versions of the fairy tale: first, the already mentioned extant original in Pomeranian dialect as penned by Runge and made famous by the Brothers Grimm — as a homage to Grass, fairy-tale specialist Heinz Rölleke (1978) has collected a number of variants and published them with a brief introduction — second, the "story of the Flounder" (*F,* 483) about a sexually voracious Ilsebill who consumes men of increasingly higher social standing until the Flounder puts a stop to her promiscuous behavior when she demands to have intercourse with Beethoven — "classics" are off limits (*F,* 485). This "story" is told by one of Billy's lesbian friends to console her about her irrepressible femininity. Third, there is the presumably lost version that proclaims "the other truth" (*F,* 20) by showing "a modest Ilsebill and a fisherman with immoderate wishes" (*F,* 349). Yet, as several scholars have shown (for example, Adolph 1983, 131; Mews 1983c, 174–75), both the "misogynistic propaganda tale" (*F,* 20) by the Brothers Grimm and its opposite with its "apocalyptic tone" (*F,* 353) and depiction of man-made utter disaster embody only one aspect of the larger truth; although they appear to be mutually exclusive in their indictment of one sex, they must be read together in order to obtain a sense of the ultimate truth.

The incorporation of the two aspects of the fairy-tale tradition in his novel, Durzak argues, constitutes Grass's response to the postulates and ideologically fixed positions of the representatives of the women's movement and cannot be reduced to a satire of the efforts to achieve female emancipation; rather, the satire should be seen in the context of Grass's acknowledgment of women's genuine, life-sustaining contributions to historical development through their activities of procreation, cooking, and nourishing. Ultimately, Grass is motivated by a utopian desire, Durzak concludes, a desire that entails the hope for a new, enlightened phase of history without the restrictions imposed and antagonisms fostered by rigid gender roles. Such a hope, however, may be unfounded and pertain to the realms of the fairy tale and wishful thinking. Conversely, Walter Filz (1988, 96) categorically rejects the notion that *The Flounder* in general and the fairy tale in particular represent a utopia; rather than projecting the opposite of catastrophic reality, the fairy tale serves as a corrective of the traditional view of history as developing progressively.

Like Durzak, Edward Diller (1983) postulates that Grass and his narrator "remain preoccupied . . . with the idea of a larger and lost unity that eludes logic but remains [Grass's] major goal and artistic intention" (99). This original unity can be grasped in the myth of three-breasted Awa, who keeps men safe and content in a state of childlike dependency. The unity is lost when the Flounder decides to liberate men by serving as the adviser to the male cause, an act whose consequences are akin to those following the "Fall from paradise" and result in the "conscious division of the male and female principle" (100). The narrator-protagonist's efforts to reconstruct the "alternate version" (99) of the fairy tale both refer to and supplement the myth, Diller suggests, in that they set the (pre)historical record straight and offer a chance — if remote — to reestablish the lost unity. Because the novel tells of "origins and destinies" and seeks to explain the "nature and destiny of man," Diller (104) draws on René Wellek and Austin Warren's terminology in their *Theory of Literature* (1949) and calls *The Flounder* a "mythic novel" (105). In his 1982 contribution, Friedrich Ulfers similarly elucidates the underlying mythical structure by basing his argument on the writings of Johann Jakob Bachofen on the matriarchy and those on the development of consciousness in historical manifestations by Erich Neumann. Ultimately, Ulfers views the novel in psychoanalytical terms as "an elaboration of the Freudian dialectic of repression" (39), which the narrator demonstrates by delivering himself of his nine or eleven cooks. Such an act suspends the "inferior, negative, deadly role" of women as symbols of "nature and the body" and indicates, as the novel's conclusion suggests, the integration of the "mythical, ahistorical orientation of the age of the Great Mother" (40) into history that is no longer exclusively driven by the idea of (male-dominated) progress. Ulfers's reading of an ultimately benign resolution of the male-female antagonism is not universally shared by critics.

Concerned primarily with "narrative technique" and the "intertwining themes" (810, 820) in the novel, Osman Durrani (1980) ignores mythical structures but discusses the importance of the fairy tale and distinguishes four key concepts that Grass's use of "The Fisherman and His Wife" conveys — concepts that unite "the principal ideological strands" and allow the reader to draw conclusions with regard to the "author's attitude to history" (817). First, there is the "idea of progress," as evident in the increased production of material goods, which is stimulated by consumers' demands such as the persistent wishes of the fairy-tale Ilsebill as well as her present-day counterpart. Second, the "idea of futility" is expressed in the unceasing "chain of demand, consumption, demand" in which Ilsebill becomes "trapped." Third, the history of consumption is presented as a "cyclical process," a process that is eventually "terminated by a 'big bang.'" Fourth, Durrani goes beyond the realm of socio-economics, which offers a far too restrictive framework for a reading of the relationship of the sexes, and briefly addresses what may be described as the quasi-political dimension of the "historical process," that is, the fairy-tale Ilsebill's aspiration to assume traditionally male roles such as king, emperor, or pope; her "extreme" ambition "anticipates the events" of the "Father's Day" chapter (817–18).

Yet Durrani rejects the argument that the fairy tale is the "anti-feminist backbone" of the novel; rather, it is essentially a "variation on the Paradise Lost theme." Moreover, the "alternative version," about which we are informed in "The other truth," a subchapter of the sixth month (*F*, 345–54), is suppressed precisely because it "cruelly demolishes man's strivings and dreams of greatness" (*F*, 350) and hence would discredit the male cause. Conversely, the "show trial" of the Flounder, which resembles that of the terrorist Baader-Meinhoff Red Army faction in 1976–77 (for a different interpretation of the trial, see Cloonan, above), is suffused with a "carnival" atmosphere and offers a both "lighthearted" and "serious" statement "on the excesses of the [West German] emancipation movement in the early 1970s" (819). Whereas Durrani tends to view Grass's incorporation of the fairy tale in general and the "episode" about "The other truth" in particular as a "brilliant" invention (818), Gunther Pakendorf (1980) considers the fairy tale to be primarily a confirmation of the insights gained by the women's movement; that is, the fairy-tale Ilsebill is punished because she transgresses the political, economic, and legal boundaries established for women by men. Pakendorf's reading does not explain, however, why the fisherman's wife is allowed to assume traditionally male roles of power and influence without repercussions — until she succumbs to extreme hubris and desires to be godlike. According to Pakendorf, these boundaries are being established after the Flounder has his first grand entry and engineers the historical change from matriarchy to patriarchy (in his second grand entry, during his trial, he eventually reverses course). The — invented — alternative version of the fairy tale does then not contradict the ideology of the version published by the Brothers Grimm; it is, in fact, an affirmation of the existing social division of gender roles, inasmuch as both fairy-tale variants are based on the assumption of irreconcilable differences between male and female. What Grass's schema with its emphasis on biological factors fails to address, Pakendorf suggests, is that male and female are primarily social categories that evolved historically and are subject to change. Hence the grotesque happenings of the "Father's Day" chapter are based on a caricature of the women's movement — a caricature that suggests anxiety and hopelessness on the part of the author rather than the possibility of a constructive solution, the third way that the present-day narrator briefly refers to at the beginning of the novel: "Maybe we've simply forgotten that there's still more. A third something. In other respects as well, politically for instance, as possibility" (*F*, 7).

In essence, Hanne Castein (1990) tends to agree with Pakendorf (whom she does not cite). She begins by drawing attention to the fact that during the 1970s a veritable "Märchenwelle" or wave of fairy-tale adaptations swept over both German states and constituted a genuine, "widespread literary phenomenon" so that, in a sense, Grass participated "in a firmly established trend" (97). But Castein gives Grass credit for making an "unusual choice" in selecting a fairy tale that does not feature one of the "almost obligatory miraculous happy endings" (100) owing to his conviction, expressed in the aforementioned interview (Raddatz 1977a), that fairy tales, far from indulging in a flight from reality, actually (re)capture it. In the 1970s, Grass's stance was rather "unusual," Castein states, because the dominant inclination — without doubt, one may assume, inspired by the anti-authoritarian student movement — was to battle the presumed "pernicious influence" (100) of fairy tales in conveying a false sense of harmony.

Moreover, Castein credits Grass with being the first German writer of fiction to address the significance of gender roles "in the shaping of world history." As the author states in an interview, the beginning of the nineteenth century, when "The Fisherman and His Wife" was published, represents a kind of "watershed" in the "power struggle" (102) between men and women. This struggle resulted in women's "absolute" loss of control during the age of industrialization (H. L. Arnold 1963, 5th ed. 1978, 36–37). Although Castein acknowledges that Grass puts the fairy tale to "strikingly original use" (101), in the end she does not attribute major significance to the suggested synthesis of the two versions of the fairy tale and avers that ultimately Grass does not seem to progress beyond the perception of the "continuation of matriarchal and patriarchal patterns" (104). Hence she implicitly denies the utopian dimension of the novel alluded to, for example, by Durzak and Durrani and maintains that Grass merely advances the notion that the feminist movement seeks to substitute domination by females for that by males.

As Volker Neuhaus (1979; rev. ed. 1992, 144–45) has pointed out, the fairy tale also comes into play in the last three chapters of the novel. The seventh month concludes on a note of resignation owing to the protagonist-narrator's sense of having been "written off" — a perception that induces him to refer to male-dominated history as a past epoch in the fairy-tale term "once upon a time . . ." (*F*, 453). The eighth month appears to offer a radically pessimistic ending in that the emancipated women fail to put forward a genuine alternative to the failed experiment of the opposite sex; the ninth month presents a modicum of hope on account of the birth of a new human being (a girl) — but one may be skeptical whether the crafty Flounder's assuming the advisory role for the women's cause will indeed result in the realization of the third way, as Neuhaus seems to suggest.

The Flounder

As the creature that lends the novel its name, the Flounder has, as the foregoing discussion has shown, justifiably attracted considerable attention on the part of reviewers and critics. Yet there are very few analyses that are exclusively devoted to an overall analysis of the fabulous fish's significance and function. (Oddly, the title of Hans Dieter Zimmermann's 1982 essay, "Der Butt und der Weltgeist," is entirely misleading because Zimmermann discusses the role of the Flounder hardly at all.) But Ingeborg Hoesterey's 1981 article is an exception to the rule in that she analyzes the figure of the Flounder in the poetological terms of fairy tale and myth as well as those of allegory and symbol. She posits the affinity of the fairy tale to myth on the basis of the fairy-tale Ilsebill's perennial dissatisfaction and ever more extravagant wishes; this dissatisfaction, a common human trait shared by both men and women, leads to the striving for more possessions, knowledge, and insight, and thus constitutes the fodder for myth. Hoesterey goes beyond Diller's definition of myth and singles out Grass's explicit reference to Claude Lévi-Strauss's anthropological study *Le Cru et le Cuit* (1964; *The Raw and the Cooked,* 1975) at the beginning of the novel: ". . . some two thousand years before the incarnation of our Lord, when myths were beginning to distinguish between raw food and cooked food" (*F*, [3]). But she does not elaborate on the significance of fire, which is stolen by Awa from the Sky Wolf and which enables her to establish her power over men. Scott H. Abbott (1983) has convincingly shown that in *The Flounder* Grass derives the myth about the origins of fire from those myths Lévi-Strauss found to be prevalent among Amazonian Indians and transposes it — replete with Grassian bawdy details — to the delta of the Vistula, the location in which the city of "Danzig, or Civitas Danczik" (*F*, 109) was founded in 1236.

In contrast to scholars viewing the Flounder primarily in the context of the fairy tale, Hoesterey regards the Flounder as an essentially mythical creature that lacks all the endearing features usually associated with the German fairy tale. As we know, "The Fisherman and his Wife" does not fit the traditional fairy-tale mold in this regard; rather, as Hoesterey suggests (465), the tale may be considered the secularized, popular, and late form of myth. The Flounder himself explains that he has "couched a centuries-long and hence complex historical development . . . in simple words appropriate to the popular tradition" (*F*, 43–44). This development began when the Flounder sought to provoke, albeit in an ironic mode (as Adolph 1983, 122, 129, in particular points out), the males enthralled by the benign matriarchy of Awa into shaking off their yoke and begin creating "a masculine myth, a Jovian head-birth" (*F*, 98) as an essential precondition as well as the ideological underpinning of their eventual domination. Inasmuch as the Flounder is instrumental in initiating the process of male liberation, the fish is also the originator of the "masculine myth" (Hoesterey, 466). In addition, because of his multivalent status, the Flounder may be perceived as an allegorical or symbolic figure — although the argument that he is grounded in myth seems to be more compelling.

In my article "The 'Professorial' Flounder" (1983c), I approach the protagonist from a different perspective and discuss Grass's pervasive use of literary and intellectual history, which is reflected in the talking fish's "combination of omniscience and self-indulgent garrulousness" (Mews 1983c, 164). Thus the Flounder is eager to display his wide knowledge, which includes "all the intellectual giants from Erasmus to Marxengels" (*F*, 517), with "scintillating arrogance" (*F*, 516). Not content with merely dispensing advice to his Neolithic male protégées, whom he instructs about far-away, advanced cultures until they gain "informational superiority" (*F*, 45) as a prerequisite for escaping women's rule, he wishes "to be quoted" (*F*, 103) and insists that the present-day narrator name the book after him (*F*, 413). Moreover, the "rational" Flounder, the "patron of progress and order" (Crick 1990, 35), advises the narrator to proceed chronologically (see *F*, 18) — advice that, in principle, the narrator heeds. In fact, he has done everything the Flounder has instructed him to do since the fish first addressed him as "my son" (*F*, 40) and thereby assumed the role of "stepfather" or father substitute, because in Awa's matriarchal society fathers are unknown and Oedipal conflicts do not exist (see Crick 1990, 40).

The text of the novel does, indeed, provide brief but explicit glances at Grass's intentions in writing it, when, for example, the narrator refers to the Flounder's indispensability by suggesting that introducing him provided a "counterweight" to the originally intended story about the cooks as well as "some kind of a history of human foodstuffs" (*F*, 147) and turned the novel into the "great historical accounting" (*F*, 413) of the male-female antagonism throughout the centuries. The textual evidence of Grass's design is corroborated by his utterances in several interviews (Mews 1983c, 164 n.7).

During his trial, the Flounder draws on a wide variety of literary sources, to the dismay of the members of the Womenal, for whom all forms of traditional academic learning are highly suspect, since they tend to uphold the patriarchal order; hence the radical feminists dismiss the Flounder as a "shitty Germanist" (*F*, 23). For example, they take umbrage at the Flounder's suggestion to elevate the lusty "cooking nun" Fat Gret of the third month by touting her as "a female companion piece" (*F*, 218) to Rabelais's Gargantua and securing her a place in the pantheon of literary figures of world renown. Furthermore, the Womenal humorlessly accuse the Flounder of cracking "literary jokes at the expense of the world's oppressed women" (*F*, 219). Yet the Flounder's attempts at elevating the (literary) status of women are not entirely selfless; in his endeavors to support the male cause, he had promoted love as "an ideational superstructure" (*F*, 262) to ensure female emotional dependence and secure male dominance. Curiously, through their selfless devotion and love, figures such as Shakespeare's Juliet demonstrate that what the Flounder had intended to be an "instrument of oppression" could be turned "into a symbol of eternal womanly greatness" (*F*, 267) that extols womanhood without, however, changing the basic equation that, in the realm of art, assigns to women a "passive, servile, manuring mediation" (*F*, 255), and to men the creative role that produced great accomplishments such as "Handel's *Messiah* [and Kant's] categorical imperative" (*F*, 256). Their creativity notwithstanding, men are given to suppressing unpleasant truths as, for example, in the pivotal scene "The other truth" of the sixth month, in which the fairy-tale version inimical to men is burnt in a "romantic" setting near Danzig (see Mews 1983c, 171–72, and Øhrgaard's 1983 brief essay on the significance of Romanticism in contemporary letters).

Women's mediatory function is perhaps most evident in the cook Agnes Kurbiella in the fourth month. She serves both Baroque poet Martin Opitz and painter Anton Möller, both residents of Danzig, as an unconventional, albeit unsung "muse." She functions as but one example of counteracting the prevailing "injustice of neglecting and suppressing women's contributions in both historical accounts and literary histories" (Mews 1983c, 169). (The fourth month has attracted attention — often in connection with *Das Treffen in Telgte* — particularly on the part of Baroque scholars such as Haberkamm 1985, Preece 1994, A. Weber 1995, and Moeninghoff 2001.)

The alleged (and, within the fictional context, actual) dearth of artistic talent on the part of the cooks, which the members of the Womenal condemn as extraordinarily unjust and highly objectionable, cannot necessarily be considered a flaw in the Grassian scheme of things. To put it simply, Grass ascribes to women the realm of nature and to men the realm of culture (Mews 1983c, 168–69) — an assignment of apparently immutable gender roles that, understandably, is roundly rejected by feminist critics in particular (see below). The Flounder's declaration of the bankruptcy of the male cause, which he proclaims in his grand self-indictment (*F*, 518–23), and his prediction that the future will belong to the female sex do seem to indicate the ancient fish's ability to change his views (G. S. Williams 1980, 187) — even if his "tactical conversion to the women's cause" may be "spurious and self-interested" (Prochnik 1990, 158) because he is facing the death penalty. But from the authorial perspective, women's superiority can be attributed to the fact that they represent a life-sustaining force by giving birth. Men's accomplishments, their aforesaid "ersatz babies" (*F*, 396–97), which include literary products and other artistic endeavors, definitely pale in comparison. The beginning of the novel makes this abundantly clear: the act of procreation has precedent over the act of narration (*F*, 3): the demands of nature must be satisfied before one can engage in cultural pursuits (Mews 1983c, 169).

In his more recent investigation of the role of the Flounder, Dieter Arendt (2001) engages in what amounts to a rather detailed month-by-month retelling or paraphrasing of the novel, a retelling that is buttressed by copious quotations from the text. Arendt poses the question of whether Grass's Flounder is different from that in the fairy tale ("ein anderer Butt," 333), but he initially fails to elucidate the specific aspects that might distinguish the sage fish from his famous predecessor in the Brothers' Grimm tale. Apart from the Flounder's vastly expanded function in the novel, there is, of course, the obvious difference, stated earlier, that the fairy-tale creature functions as the omnipotent agent who carries out — up to a point — the wishes of the fisherman's wife; conversely, in *The Flounder* the fish serves as a promoter — again up to a point — of the male cause. (Helmut Koopmann, 1983, 83, makes the valid observation that the fairy-tale Flounder and Grass's Flounder share their "immortality"; however, the latter lacks the "omnipotence" of the former.) More than other critics, however, Arendt devotes attention to the significance of the trial that the Flounder is subject to and draws attention to the vague desire of the feminists, who are listlessly fishing in the Baltic, for an "ideologically acceptable prop for [their] superegos" (*F*, 36). Their wish is eventually fulfilled when, after the trial, the fish is set free and begins to assume the role of women's advocate. Initially perceiving the Flounder as a potential "embodiment of Hegel's *Weltgeist*" (*F*, 38), the members of the Womenal continue to associate him with Hegel's philosophy, which is presumably based on reason and rationality — precisely the qualities that have led to the disastrous results of male-dominated history and are consequently rejected by the female veterans of the rebellious student movement (Arendt 330–33). Contemptuously dismissed as a "super-Hegel" (*F*, 333) in the service of the patriarchy, the Flounder will apparently continue to function as the "*Weltgeist*" in promoting female issues to the exclusion of his former active sponsorship of the male agenda (for the influence of Schopenhauer's philosophy, see Best 1983). At any rate, there is little textual evidence to support Arendt's suggestion (334) of a tangible power-sharing arrangement between women and men that would, in terms of Hegelian dialectics, indeed resemble a kind of synthesis. True, there is the apparently utopian hope for a better understanding (see Durzak 1979, above); but as John Sandford (1990) in particular, whom Arendt in his selective use of secondary literature does not take into account, has argued rather persuasively, the possibility of a "third way" that would overcome the prevailing antagonism between the sexes is never articulated in any concrete fashion and tends to recede into the background as the narrative progresses: "The future, it seems, has nothing to offer except a reversal of the power relations between the sexes, with no room for a third possibility" (173). We may then assume that the Flounder as the architect of this reversal is incapable or unwilling to deviate from the prevailing antagonistic pattern. As to the question of the Flounder's origins, which may be expanded to include a query as to his quintessence, Arendt has it both ways. On the one hand, the fish is declared to be of fairy-tale origin; on the other, he is said to represent a myth that transcends recorded history and is ultimately a creation of the novelist's boundless imagination (338–39).

Narrative Perspectives and the Time Structure

Hanspeter Brode (1980b) investigates rather succinctly the narrator's position in terms of the novel's internal communication structure, which rests upon the relationship between the narrator and his wife Ilsebill and their various manifestations throughout the ages; the close association between husband and wife reflects the liaison of the sexes, which has become increasingly problematic. But Brode draws attention to the potential discrepancy between the gist of the text-immanent communications and the novel's actual reception by critics and readers — even if in the case of *Der Butt* there appears to be a correspondence between authorial intention as evidenced by the hardly unambiguous communicative pattern on the one hand and the critical response, which dwells extensively on the definition of gender roles and male-female partnerships, on the other (448).

Whereas Brode merely touches upon the role of the narrator, Guy Stern (1982), in his rather brief contribution, identifies the presence of a "protean" and "multiple" narrator, who appears in many guises but is essentially a writer and artist, as one of the "compositional devices" that holds the novel together (51–52). Furthermore, Stern emphasizes the clearly autobiographical feature of the narrator's assuming the identity of

Portuguese explorer Vasco da Gama in the third month ("Vasco Returns") and surmises — correctly, as Grass's corroboration in an interview shows — that Vasco's voyage to India posed a "compositional problem" (Stern, 53) inasmuch as it is couched in terms that seem to describe Grass's own journey to that country in 1975 (for a more detailed discussion of the subchapter, see Ulrich 2004, especially 166–71). In part, this problem has been resolved by the author's choice of a third-person narrative for the Vasco segment instead of the dominant first-person account. Moreover, Stern observes, owing to the author's "eschewal of chronology" (a salient feature that is discussed at greater length by other critics; see below), the ubiquity of Danzig and environs becomes a "structural necessity" (54) — although, presumably, the choice of Grass's birthplace was hardly exclusively determined by structural considerations.

Patrick O'Neill (1982) casts his net wide and engages in a thorough analysis of narratorial strategies. He characterizes Grass as an "iconoclast" who, in the face of the "postmodernist apocalyptic mode" of the 1970s and 1980s, engages in a "critical humanism" that is informed by a "blend of social satire and metaphysical skepticism" and compels the author, an "inspired and untiring artificer," to submit to the Scheherazade syndrome of keeping talking or, rather, writing. The result is a "meganovel" (14), in which the reader encounters the "author as narrator and protagonist" as well as his "fictional counterparts" (3) in various time phases. More insistently than other critics, O'Neill emphasizes the role of Ilsebill, who on the one hand is an individual and yet, simultaneously, represents all women, as the "rhetorically projected receiver of the narrator's soliloquy" (4). In a perhaps overly systematic manner vis-à-vis a novel that defies easy classification and systematization, he distinguishes "five distinct narrative levels," which, however, have permeable boundaries. First, there is the Flounder's narration before the Womenal; second, the narrator tells his/their story to his wife in predominantly monologic fashion; third, the narrator occasionally addresses the reader directly; fourth, a "semi-fictionalized Günter Grass" (who is not entirely identical with the present-day narrator) does the same; fifth, the author "speaks for himself" in the interspersed lyrics that critics usually treat with benign neglect (for exceptions, see, for example, C. Mayer, 1988; Brady, 1990). Hence the complex narrative stance pertains to a novel that displays the hallmarks of "a highly self-reflexive, self-questioning metafiction" (11). At the same time, the "multi-fractured narrative consciousness" is indicative of a concealed, "deep-seated crisis of male identity" (13) — a crisis, one might add, that shows a male far more vulnerable than the macho image that the feminists in the novel love to hate.

In her essay "The Prismatic Narrator: Postulate and Practice" (1983), Gertrud Bauer Pickar proceeds from the assumption of an "apparent multiplicity of narrative perspectives"; this multiplicity, however, is "the manifestation of but a single, narrative consciousness" (55). The previously cited third sentence of the novel "I, down through the ages, have been I" (*F*, 4; see Raddatz, above) signals a shift from the "narrative preterite" of the first two sentences and introduces a "new temporal dimension" in that it refracts "the narrative consciousness into previous existences" that predate the beginning of (written) human history (Pickar, 56). Similarly, since the narrator's wife Ilsebill also has been existing "from the beginning" (*F* 3), she is presented by the narrator as the "eternal female" (Pickar, 56). The prevalence of a refracted narrative consciousness results in a variety of its embodiments and allows the protagonist-narrator to assume multiple identities such as those of "Blacksmith Rusch, Franciscan monk Stanislaus, Preacher Hegge, rich man Ferber, and Abbot Jeschke" (*F*, 173) — "all of whom share a relationship with the central cook Fat Gret" (Pickar, 60) in the third month.

Pickar convincingly argues that "the historicity of sequence is suspended by the creative fantasy" (62) in that the narrator occasionally assumes an identity that resembles that of author Grass. For instance, during a filming for television in postwar, reconstructed Danzig, now Polish Gdańsk, the narrator, who like author Grass serves as a commentator in the 1975 film, switches between the present and the past and seeks to ascertain the traces of fourteenth-century Dorothea von Montau's environment. The freely roaming narrative consciousness allows the narrator to merge the city of the present with that of the past; but the fluidity of "temporal dimensions" is not used by Grass to promote a progressive view of historical development. Rather, the novel presents, as other critics have noted, "the cyclical, repetitive nature of history itself" (Pickar, 64), as, for example, the line frequently cited in reviews and essays about the changes in Danzig or Gdańsk since 1378 — "today the [oppressive] patricians have a different name" (*F*, 120) — as well as the comparison of the May 1378 and December 1970 uprisings in that city (see *F*, 114) make abundantly clear.

Yet despite her general praise of Grass's intricate narrative design, Pickar finds fault with the narrator's occasionally assuming an unexplained omniscient stance that appears to undermine what is essentially a first-person narrative (or, conceivably, a series of first-person narratives). For example, in the seventh month the author of an (unpublished) proletarian cookbook, Lena Stubbe, travels to an international conference in Zurich unaccompanied; hence the reader is informed about her activities by an omniscient "I" or, rather, a narrator who appears to be distinct from the omnipresent first-person narrator. Similarly, the much debated "Father's Day" chapter in the eighth month lacks the "benefit of a participatory perspective"; in both instances, the "narrative options" provided by the novel tend to be marred (Pickar, 68) — a criticism generally not voiced by others. All in all, however, Pickar judges *The Flounder* to be "a rich and fascinating work" owing to the "most complex narrative structure" that Grass has yet tackled (71).

Helmut Koopmann (1983) also notes the suspension of the traditional sequence of time and the substitution of the simultaneity of events recorded by the narrator but finds the "omnipresence of characters" (76) and the juxtaposition of happenings that are separated by centuries (see *F*, 77), to be "anything but a compelling parallel" (Koopmann, 77). Yet the "arbitrarily proceeding narrative subjectivity" (79), which resides in the narrator's consciousness, is held in check by structuring devices such as the nine months that elapse from conception to birth — a limited period during which the narrator has to deliver himself of his "'headbirths,'" and, at the same time, the period during which the trial of the Flounder proceeds. A further dimension is added by the story of the Flounder, which begins in Neolithic times when the fish is first caught by the initial embodiment of the narrator. To fit into the nine-months time frame, no attempt is made to recreate history in its totality; rather, it "occurs only paradigmatically in nine significant examples," so that the novel proceeds on the "four planes" of "[w]orld history, history of the birth, history of the novel's origin, history of the trial" (80). (In his 1990 investigation of the "conceptions of history," David Jenkinson similarly speaks of the "lack of a continuous narrative" and "teleological significance" in the historical episodes that reside in the "highly egocentric consciousness" of the narrator [51] who displays a "provocative indifference to textbook history" [54]).

Koopmann further posits that *The Flounder* pertains to the category of "novels of consciousness" in the manner of James Joyce, Marcel Proust, or, in the tradition of German-language literature, Arthur Schnitzler and Alfred Döblin (83). The "simultaneity of the unsimultaneousness" functions as a "formula" for displaying the "development of consciousness" particularly on the part of the narrator. The narrator's developing consciousness serves also to "enlighten the reader" about a vital but misrepresented or underrepresented part of human history that must necessarily dispense with the "colossal figures" of conventional, male-dominated historiography (84–85) and focus instead on its reinterpretation — a process made possible by a both omnipresent and omniscient narrating "I" (Koopmann does not share Pickar's reservations about the introduction of an omniscient narrative perspective) that, at the same time, also functions as a narrated "I."

Michael Minden (1990) strikes out in a somewhat different direction by going beyond the role of the "I" as a "narrative device" and interpreting its pervasive presence also as a "gesture of [moral] commitment" (187) on the part of Grass, who seeks to "dispel the aura of the artist" by using his own voice and "entering a debate" about feminism (189) that is predicated on the fact that the author of *The Flounder* is a man. As a result, the process of story-telling by the "I" is "necessarily vitiated by male sexuality and its attendant attitudes" (192). Hence story-telling, which is related to the "oral phase," may serve as a "*substitute* for satisfaction" after the males have been weaned from Awa's third breast in prehistoric times; thus it is necessarily "narcissistic and self-indulgent" (192–93). Yet story-telling assumes a different dimension when it becomes the "*product* of dissatisfaction" and men resort to "'brutality'" to compensate for their being disgruntled. In this context, Minden singles out three instances of rape (the actual number is considerably higher because of the involvement of multiple perpetrators) in the subchapter of the first month ("What I don't want to remember"), the rape of Agnes by the Swede Axel and others in the fourth month ("It seems his name was Axel"), and the "artistic linchpin," Sibylle's being violated in the infamous "Father's Day" chapter. However, Minden insists that this incident cannot be construed as a "disguised wish fulfillment" on the part of the author (194), since not all rapes conform to the pattern of male violence against women (see 197).

Yet whereas the "invention of the eleven cooks is the key operation of fantasy" that shows the various "projections of the 'I'" in "abject, subordinate, or despicable" positions, the "compensatory gesture" of re-inventing the cooks as the Womenal results in a reversal of roles of sorts: the "I" now appears as a "single, inexhaustible seducer" who has affairs with all the members of the feminist tribunal although he realizes the inherent meaninglessness of such womanizing (196). Perhaps this mea-ingless activity may be construed as a last, futile assertion of male power and prerogative before "man is dismissed from [his] own history," as the poem "Man oh man" (*F*, 538) proclaims.

Ronald Speirs (1990) perceives the novel as a "dualistic unity" in that it mixes up the "identities of the narrator and the cooks" (20) when, for example, at the beginning of the novel the narrator ascribes to his and Ilsebill's joint efforts of procreation an "ätherische Nebenzeugung" (*WA* 5:6) or ethereal offspring as a byproduct (that is, the story of the cooks) rather than the "ethereal union," as Manheim's translation (*F*, 4) has it. But ultimately, the "dualistic unity" is not only evident in Grass's portrayal of the narrator; rather, Speirs interprets the "complex, 'polysemic' image" of the estuary (primarily that of the Vistula) as a device "that binds together much of the novel's thematic material in an extensive network of parallels and antitheses" (Speirs, 28). In deemphasizing the antagonistic aspects of the male-female relationship in his careful and detailed analysis, Speirs offers a balanced view that deviates from the occasionally partisan utterances of other critics. Joyce Crick, in her contribution on "Future Imperfect: Time and the Flounder" (1990) reaches somewhat similar conclusions (for example, 48 n. 19).

Feminist Approaches

As has been shown in the first section of this chapter, hardly any reviewer of either *Der Butt* or its English translation fails to address the central issue of feminism in the novel; predictably, literary scholars followed suit. There are comments such as those by Geoffrey P. Butler (1979), who attributes the "revival of [Grass's] flagging notoriety" (23) to his treatment of women, who are presented "with at best a mixture of affection and condescension" (26–27), or the brief remarks by Thor A. Larsen (1983), who ascribes to Grass the intent to offer to modern women a feminine, motherly alternative to the pursuit of power. It is hardly surprising that the "Father's Day" chapter, which had played such a prominent role in the initial phase of the novel's reception and beyond, resurfaces in the scholarly debates about feminism. Noel L. Thomas (1979) somewhat unspecifically views the chapter as an "integral part of the uninterrupted flow of history" (81) as it is depicted in the preceding seven chapters and the concluding ninth chapter. Billy's three female friends who rape her "not only attempt to behave like men, but to think like men" (82) — a disposition that is reflected in the Womenal's decision not to carry out the death sentence against the Flounder but to keep him alive so that he may serve as the women's adviser. The "provocative" eighth chapter is then intended to invite the reader to ponder "man's attitude to history"; at the same time, he or she is asked to contemplate the distinct possibility of women "pursuing emancipation" in the disastrous male fashion (84).

Although not explicitly concerned with feminist issues, John Reddick (1983) provides a cogent reading of the "Father's Day" chapter, which, he convincingly shows, constitutes a drastic "climax" that is not only totally "different in rhythm, tone and impact" from both the preceding and following chapters but is also more "carefully and intensively prefigured" (143) than any other sequence of events. The repeated references to Billy (Sibylle Miehlau) create an ominous "sense of ultimate disaster" (144) and relate her fate to the novel's "abiding motif of death and destruction" (146) both in the private realm and the world at large, in which "violence, oppression, starvation" are "outward manifestations" of Grass's central theme, "the struggle for freedom and emancipation" (147). This struggle goes terribly awry, however, in that the four female protagonists of the "Father's Day" chapter have opted for an "aggressive lesbianism" (148) and succumb to "grotesque hubris" (149) when Maxie climbs the "phallic pine," proclaims herself to be the "'new sex,'" and wants to "beget a son" whose name shall be Emmanuel (*F*, 473; see the prophesy in Isaiah 7:14). On the basis of the recurrence of the number three with regard to Sibylle and her gruesome fate, Reddick claims that Grass is presenting a "grotesque mockery of the redeemed world of the Holy Trinity." Even though he admits that such claim may appear "far-fetched," Reddick uses the repeated references to "Ascension Day" (*F*, 454 et passim) as his main argument to postulate that Grass uses Sibylle's "suffering and death" as a "most mordant and agonizing re-enactment of the vain passion of Christ" (154) — a reading with distinct religious overtones that deviates from the majority of comments but certainly cannot be dismissed out of hand.

At any rate, reading *The Flounder* in religious terms is of little concern to feminist academics. Not entirely coincidentally, the first major salvo in the ensuing battle about the alleged antifeminism of *The Flounder* was fired by a female literary scholar. Ruth Angress [Klüger] (1982), credits Grass with displaying a "Dickension" quality — Dickens is hardly ever invoked as a literary precursor or kindred spirit of Grass by other commentators — especially by demonstrating his "spontaneous sympathy at the sight of suffering." Yet, Angress claims, this positive quality is rendered ineffective by an assumed "curious intellectual poverty" on the part of the author, who seems to "wear blinders" when confronted with the suffering of a considerable part of humankind — that is, women. Consequently, Angress views the novel as evidence of Grass's "basically hostile" attitude toward the women's movement and his ignorance of its "aspirations" (43).

Although she acknowledges the significance of *The Flounder* as the "first major novel in any language" that deals with "organized feminism in our time," she charges Grass with depicting women in typically male fashion as "all tits and cunts" — a procedure that is far removed from any endeavor to treat men and women on equal terms (43). For example, the very brief appearance of socialist Rosa Luxemburg in the seventh month ("The trip to Zurich") serves Angress as an indication of Grass's inability to deal with "a certified woman intellectual" (44). Such criticism is not entirely convincing in view of the fact that Grass's focus in this segment is on Lena Stubbe, cited above, who unobtrusively deflates both Luxemburg's and her male companion's arguments in favor of revolution. In a similar vein, Angress uncompromisingly chastises Grass for misrepresenting Dorothea von Montau, who, as I have pointed out, is repeatedly invoked in reviews and criticism (see especially Timothy McFarland, 1990). Her poetry tends "towards sexual metaphor" in the customary mystic vein, but her poems are allegedly denigrated in a "particularly idiotic set of [Grassian] verses" (Angress, 45; see *F*, 156). In her openly militant stance, Angress, who dispenses entirely with references to other opinions expressed in secondary literature, arrives at the conclusion that Grass is "either sincerely homophobic" or caters to the "pornographic tastes of his male readers" (49) — a scathing verdict that must be considered extreme.

Far less belligerent than Angress, Irmgard Elsner Hunt (1983) shifts her focus to women as mothers as well as the myth of mothers in *The Flounder* and systematically investigates the female cooks from Awa, the first one, to Maria Kuczorra, the last one. In addition, she includes the narrator's wife Ilsebill, who merely pretends to be an emancipated woman (160), in her detailed survey. She reasonably argues that in emphasizing the biological aspects of motherhood — rather than stressing the social role of maternity in the manner of, for example, Bertolt Brecht — Grass appears to adhere to an old-fashioned concept, which, however, enjoys wide currency among male writers (191). Yet, coupled with the life-sustaining force of motherhood, there is also a destructive element that results in the misuse of power, as most notably demonstrated by the Ur-mother Awa (193–94). Conversely, Agnes Kurbiella of the fourth month represents the selflessness of motherhood to an extent that suggests wishful thinking on the part of the author (197). Ironically, the paragon of motherhood does not prevail: Agnes eventually perishes at the stake. Sibylle Miehlau of the eighth month, an emancipated career women and would-be Lesbian, initially rejects motherhood and realizes only shortly before her violent death that her child needs her (199). In Grass's mythologizing of motherhood women seem to function as mothers to their male partners rather than as mothers to their children, about whom the reader learns comparatively little (202). Hence the mother serves as a somewhat narrowly circumscribed source of faith, hope, and love; although Grass made occasional attempts to downplay and satirize the mythical concept of motherhood reflected in *The Flounder,* Hunt considers Grass's views to be largely anachronistic — particularly when contrasted with feminists' strenuous rejection of traditional notions and their attempts to arrive at a new definition of motherliness (204). However, Hunt concludes on a note of optimism by singling out the possibility of precluding the dominance of either sex, which is inherent in the elusive third way alluded to in the novel (see especially Sandford, above).

Despite the title of Erhard Friedrichsmeyer's essay, "The Swan Song of a Male Chauvinist" (1983), a title that appears to signify the narrator/author's resignation and abdication, Friedrichsmeyer's article ends somewhat optimistically by holding out hope for a "workable approximation of balance" (160) between the sexes in the manner of the much debated "third possibility." Although he says that the novel concludes in a "threatening, even . . . somewhat apocalyptic" fashion (152), and that Sibylle at the end of the eighth chapter embraces the concept of being a "'total woman' as the alternative to surrogate masculinity" (157), Friedrichsmeyer, in contrast to, for example, Angress, absolves Grass from the charge of being an "unabashed male supremacist" (154).

In her dissertation, which deserves more attention than it has received in the critical literature, Barbara Garde (1988) investigates the role of women and the women's movement in *The Flounder* and *The Rat* (see ch. 10) in the context of the West German female emancipation initiatives of the 1970s. In particular, Garde goes beyond such critics as Angress and Friedrichsmeyer and analyses the various factions within the Womenal on the basis of those groupings that actually existed within the movement. But she judiciously points out that the novel does not deal exclusively with feminist issues; hence Grass's treatment of such matters should not serve as the exclusive yardstick for evaluating his prose work. Rather, it should be viewed as the (fictional) articulation of a male stance, which does not entirely correspond to that of the author, at a time when all men are confronted with the disquieting consequences and problems caused by the women's emancipatory endeavors. In the end, however, Garde finds the novel lacking because it does not advocate changes in the relationship of the sexes and fails to depict a genuine feminist utopia — a perhaps unrealistic expectation that appears to negate her insight about the narrator's discomfort in the face of male tribulations in the wake of the women's liberation efforts.

In a somewhat different vein, Claudia Mayer-Iswandy (1991) proceeds from the distinction between (biologically determined) sex and (psychologically grounded) gender and, beginning with the Bible, delves fairly deeply into the historical development of (traditional) female roles. In a far more detailed, systematic fashion than other critics, Mayer-Iswandy provides an analysis of Grass's representation of women figures from the *Danzig Trilogy* (see ch. 3) to *The Flounder* and posits that, in principle, female figures correspond to what man imagines or wishes them to be. It follows that women are only of consequence when and if they play a role in the lives of men and are not allowed to lead individual existences of their own (96). Yet in *The Flounder* it is women who, for the first time in Grass's fiction, assume a central position — albeit collectively rather than individually, it would seem, in contrast to the single narrator-protagonist in his various manifestations or reincarnations. Since the women (above all, the cooks) are primarily identified as mothers, the role of the fathers also comes into focus. The Flounder succinctly summarizes the deficiencies of paternal parentage as compared to the nurturing, life-giving function of the mothers: "Persons who can't give birth to children are at best presumptive fathers; nature has not done well by them" (*F*, 397). The dichotomy of nature versus culture does not only result in male "headbirths," Mayer-Iswandy argues, but also in men's proclivity to use force against women and to consider them primarily as sex objects (143–44). Hence there are hardly any positive male role models to be found in *The Flounder* — an implicit criticism of the traditional self-image of men that, however, does not result in a full-fledged endorsement of the women's movement. Mayer-Iswandy shows in a nuanced reading, based on Neuhaus, of the three open endings of the novel, that it is rather the unresolved question of whether the women's movement will be capable of developing alternative models that may ultimately decide the future course of events.

In contrast to feminist readings (among them those by Synnöve Clason 1988), which tend to emphasize the sociopolitical and cultural implications of emancipation, critics such as Speirs and John J. White in his "The Body as Battleground" (1990) shift their emphasis to the relationship of the narrator and his wife Ilsebill. In White's reading, the novel displays a "fundamental contrast" that is "impure" or flawed on account of Grass's reduction of virtually all women to their "reproductive function," whereas it appears that the Flounder argues that the entire male species should be considered "capable" of major "achievements" on the basis of the stellar accomplishments of some (114). Hence the narrator functions as a "figurative mother" who gives birth to "metaphorical children (or cooks)." The (largely imaginary) existence of the cooks then serves the narrator as a reference point and argument in his protracted "sexual conflict with the real mother-figure" (120), that is, his wife Ilsebill. Indubitably, White's approach has merits, but one wonders whether what appears to be a privileging of the domestic sphere does complete justice to the larger issue of the power struggle between men and women in general.

Most critics have implicitly or explicitly acknowledged that *The Flounder* may be considered a "cornucopian text" and a "metaphorically culinary work" that is "loaded" with sociopolitical and other "meanings" (Phelan 1990, 151). Although not explicitly concerned with feminist issues, Alois Wierlacher's brief elaboration of the significance of eating in his examination of prose texts from Goethe to Grass (1987, 188–89), provides a somewhat different perspective on the role of the cooks: he devotes attention to the ingredients as well as the preparation of meals as indispensable prerequisites for achieving a harmonious and peaceful atmosphere during dinnertime as, for instance, during the "solidarity" meal prepared by Lena Stubbe for Social Democrat August Bebel in the seventh month ("Bebel's visit"). Conversely, Noel L. Thomas (1988) also addresses the sinister side of eating, that is, food poisoning, in his essay. In her abortive attempt to poison General Rapp, Napoleon's representative in Danzig, the eighth cook Sophie Rotzoll (in the seventh month) is in part inspired by revolutionary ideas.

In their rather unconventional approach, Dieter and Jacqueline Rollfinke (1986) investigate the role of scatology in German literary texts and arrive at the startling conclusion that the "revolting message" of *The Flounder* is that "excrement is all that is ever really produced through thought, word, or deed" (176). Although the body and its various secretions are liberally used by Grass both literally and metaphorically — as, for instance, in the "pile of shit that God dropped and named Calcutta" (*F*, 186) — the Rollfinkes' assertion that what the novel conveys is that "we are totally imprisoned by our excremental existence" (175) constitutes the reduction of the extraordinarily complex work to a simple message that cannot conceivably do justice to *The Flounder*.

8: *Das Treffen in Telgte / The Meeting at Telgte*

"Gruppe 1647"

APPROXIMATELY A YEAR AND A HALF after the publication of the vast and controversial novel *Der Butt,* the much less voluminous "Erzählung" or prose narrative *Das Treffen in Telgte* (*Treffen*) appeared in the spring of 1979; rather surprisingly in view of Grass's political and aesthetic stance, which contravened official GDR doctrine (see A. Weber 1995, 149 n. 66), an edition became available a few years later, in 1984, in that part of Germany. The volume is dedicated to Hans Werner Richter (1908–93) on the occasion of his seventieth birthday; Richter was the guiding light, chief organizer/coordinator, and chronicler (see H. W. Richter 1986) of *Gruppe 47,* the famed and influential but loosely structured association of postwar writers such as Heinrich Böll, Hans Magnus Enzensberger, Martin Walser, and, since 1955, Grass himself. The group's meetings were also attended by critics, and (eventually) publishers. During the heyday of its existence, from 1947 to 1968, the informal discussion group strove for a democratization of society and a rejuvenation of literature. In an obvious reference to *Gruppe 47,* Grass's narrative presents a fictional meeting of German poets and writers of the Baroque period in the small town of Telgte near the cities of Münster and Osnabrück in 1674, where the long and complex negotiations were conducted that eventually led to the Westphalian Peace Treaty and finally ended, in 1648, the major European conflict known as the Thirty Years' War. Grass follows the normal procedure of *Gruppe 47* in that the assembled writers read from their works and subject them to their colleagues' often scathing criticism; in addition, they compose an appeal for peace, which, however, perishes in the flames when the Bridge Tavern, their gathering place, burns down.

In contrast to the contentious reception of *Der Butt,* the reviews of *Treffen* by critics of the major dailies, weeklies, and monthlies are overwhelmingly affirmative. The conservative daily *Die Welt* applauds the narrative as excellent and lauds Grass's "Baroque phantasmagoria" as well as his faithfulness to literary history (Ferber 1979); Fritz Raddatz (1979), writing in the renowned weekly *Die Zeit,* which published *Treffen* in advance, speaks of the admirable perfection of the small volume, noting

Grass's effortless organization of a vast historical as well as literary material — an achievement that is distinguished by the accuracy and correct attribution of each quotation. Such an endeavor, Raddatz somewhat erroneously assumes, would seem to require the toiling of many participants in seminars on German literature (Verweyen and Witting, 1980, identify Grass's main source; see below). Raddatz further finds that the text expresses a melancholy "truth" and masterfully evokes a hypothetical meeting that establishes a link between past and present in the midst of the horrors and devastations caused by the war.

Marcel Reich-Ranicki (1979), writing in the *Frankfurter Allgemeine Zeitung,* questions Grass's premise that all invited writers followed the summons of poet Simon Dach despite their habitual self-absorption and despite the fact that travel was both exhausting and dangerous in those perilous times of rampant carnage and destruction as well as widespread shortages of the necessities of life. Moreover, Reich-Ranicki notes a bit pedantically, the seventeenth-century poets lacked the self-assurance, solidarity, and sense of responsibility for national affairs that would have enabled them to begin enlightening the public about their concerns. In particular, Reich-Ranicki objects to the "hair-raising" anachronism of having the poets declare themselves the representatives of the "true" or morally superior Germany (a claim made by exiled writers during the Nazi period). Yet Grass, looking backward, has created a bold and original utopia that is populated by figures of considerable plasticity and has succeeded in merging the biographies of Simon Dach and Richter to create a convincing portrait of the latter. Dach acts as a mild, conciliatory taskmaster — precisely the role Richter played in the often fierce debates of *Gruppe 47.* Reich-Ranicki insists that, apart from Dach, none of the seventeenth-century poets can be considered as portraying (or caricaturing) any of Grass's colleagues — hence *Treffen* does not qualify as an "'Inside[r]-Story'" (in Reich-Ranicki 2003, 111) or *roman à clef* about *Gruppe 47.* There is no unanimity on this point among reviewers, however; in fact, August Buchner, the friend of Martin Opitz and professor of poetry at Wittenberg, has been said by some to represent Reich-Ranicki himself (for example, Rolf Schneider 1979, see below). At any rate, Reich-Ranicki bestows high praise on Grass's recreation of Libuschka, called Courasche or Courage, a minor figure in Hans Jakob Christoffel von Grimmelshausen's *Der abenteuerliche Simplicissimus* (1669; *The Adventures of a Simpleton,* 1912) but the heroine (and the earliest female first-person narrator in German literature) of Grimmelshausen's subsequent novel, *Trutz Simplex oder Die Lebensbeschreibung der Erzbetrügerin und Landstörzerin Courasche* (1670; *Runagate Courage,* 1965). The resurrection of the figure in Bertolt Brecht's play *Mutter Courage und ihre Kinder* (1949, first produced in 1941; *Mother Courage,* 194-?) is well-known but bears little resemblance to the original; Grass emphasizes the down-to-earth attitude of Grimmelshausen's Libuschka — a feature that Reich-Ranicki views as providing a counterweight to the aesthetic concerns of the poets. In short, Reich-Ranicki sums up, the implausible story of "'Gruppe 1647'" is without equal in contemporaneous German prose fiction — a somewhat unexpected tribute in view of the critic's negative assessments of Grass's previous works. As to Richter, Reich-Ranicki opines, he has truly achieved immortality via Grass's fiction.

Other reviewers of nationally distributed newspapers and other publications generally concur in the almost universal positive appraisals. (Then) GDR writer Rolf Schneider, writing in *Der Spiegel* (1979), implicitly contradicts Reich-Ranicki by seeking to identify various Baroque poets, such as Andreas Gryphius, whose encounter and debate with the older Martin Opitz in *Der Butt* (see ch. 7) is often cited as the nucleus that gave rise to *Treffen,* as well as Paul Fleming, Johann Scheffler, the aforementioned Grimmelshausen (Grass names him Gelnhausen after his place of birth), and numerous others, as counterparts of members of *Gruppe 47.* (Rühle, in his 1979 review, similarly engages in the guessing game of "who's who?"). Schneider is considerably less effusive in his comments than, for example, Reich-Ranicki, but as an author who suffered from repressive measures in the GDR, he is more keenly attuned to the political dimension of *Treffen.* Ultimately, Schneider avers, Grass's immense labors in populating his text with historical figures, many of whom are only known to scholars of German (Baroque) literature (*WA* 6:293–302, includes a cast of characters and brief explanatory notes; see also Füssel, below), are testimony to his patriotic concern about both divided German letters and the divided country. Somewhat in the same fashion, Hans Scholz (1979) acknowledges Grass's propensity for philological fun that does not make any concessions to the reader, and discerns a patriotic trait in the author's evocation of (literary) history. Similarly, Wolfram Schütte (1979) dismisses the notion that Grass is interested in mining the past for inconsequential figures and facts; rather, Grass is creating a kind of utopia by projecting the contradictory idea of a German national literature into the past.

Anton Krättli (1979) deems the speculations about which participants in the meetings of *Gruppe 47* the Baroque poets represent unproductive; he also credits Grass with articulating the problem of the writer's existence between (political) engagement and an ivory-tower way of life in terms that make the narrative relevant for the present. (Another Swiss author and journalist, Dieter Fringeli, 1979, goes further and declares *Treffen* to be a product that conveys ideas to be found in Grass's political speeches and essays.) The demands on the reader with only a passing knowledge of the Baroque period are considerable, Krättli writes, but

Grass's evocation and transformation of the material of literary history is so full of life as well as wit and humor that *Treffen* will find its public. As other critics have done (for example, Schneider 1979), Krättli singles out as characteristically Grassian features of wide appeal to a prospective audience the vigorous lovemaking of the younger poets with the maids in Libuschka's inn in Telgte, the writers' meeting place, and the lavish meal that has been provided by Gelnhausen.

One of the rare exceptions in the chorus of congratulatory voices is Reinhard Baumgart of the *Süddeutsche Zeitung* (1979); he acknowledges Grass's artistry, but in the end he dismisses the narrative as negligible because it engages in insider jokes that will not appeal to the general public — in particular, he does not find the analogies between the Baroque and postwar periods compelling. If one searches for reasons for the comparative unanimity among major critics as to the quality of *Treffen,* one should, perhaps, not dismiss out of hand the argument that the text's comparative brevity of about one hundred and eighty pages (in the German hardcover edition) may have influenced its benign reception by the critics. Pressed for time in the face of an unceasing flood of books, a manageably brief and well-written publication may have gained the favor of professional reviewers — especially after they had had to face the formidable challenge of *Der Butt* (see Boßmann 1997, 65). A perhaps more incisive reason for the friendly reception may be the fact that most reviewers had been directly or indirectly involved in the affairs of *Gruppe 47* and had continued to hold the association in high esteem (J. Schmidt 1985, 144).

A "Strange New Production"?

In contrast to the fairly significant number of translations of *Der Butt,* there are only three publications in foreign tongues (in English, French, and Italian: see the listing in Füssel 1999, 159–60; see also Wertheimer 1983, for a brief review of the difficulties in translating particularly this text). Ralph Manheim's English rendering, *The Meeting at Telgte* (*Meeting*), became available in print approximately two years after the German original; it features an afterword and notes on the dramatis personae by British Baroque scholar Leonard Forster that inform English and American readers about matters that are most likely unfamiliar to them. As in the case of *The Flounder* (see ch. 7), the English version did not escape criticism. Sigbert Prawer (1981), writing in the *Times Literary Supplement,* accepts the omission of the genre classification "Eine Erzählung" as understandable (owing, perhaps, to the more flexible categorization system for prose narratives in English) but objects strongly to Manheim's exclusion of Grass's dedication of the narrative to Richter — particularly in view of the fact that the opening paragraph explicitly mentions a "friend . . . [who] is soon to celebrate his seventieth birthday" (*MT,* 3). Prawer notes that despite the translator's "slight American accent," the English rendering "reads smoothly and makes imaginative use of English idiom." Yet there are several instances in which a "more literal rendering" would have been more effective (in Füssel 1999, 122) — a problem that most likely is of little concern to the reader without knowledge of German.

In one of the first American reviews, Princeton scholar of German literature Theodore Ziolkowski (1981), writing in the *New York Times Book Review,* refers to *Meeting* as Grass's "strange new production." Commendably, Ziolkowski provides concise background information about *Gruppe 47,* the Thirty Years' War, and some seventeenth-century writers — matters most likely of remote interest to the American reading public — and terms the work "not so much a historical novel (or novella) as a celebration of Group 47 in the form of a fictional historical analogy" that Grass has chosen "with brilliant precision" owing to the persuasiveness of the premise that writers might have gathered in 1647 and did gather in 1947 in the wake of devastating wars, foreign occupation, and the need to refashion the German language after its corruption. Yet, in the end, "the story remains a lifeless literary construct" that is "likely to be a mystifying disappointment" for the general American reader but may fascinate a select group, that is, "students of German Baroque literature." In time-honored fashion, Ziolkowski evokes *The Tin Drum,* a "powerful creation," as the standard by which Grass's work is to be judged.

Paul Gray (1981) in *Time* draws a different conclusion from the inevitable comparison of *Meeting* with *The Tin Drum,* "a sprawling, picaresque vision" of "a later war" (the Second World War) than the Thirty Years' War, by assuming that "rascally Gelnhausen" provides a poetic program that "jibes perfectly with Grass's own fictional method" — especially, when Gelnhausen delivers a speech in which he proclaims that he intends to write as "a chronicler" who will "let loose gruesome laughter and give the language license" in an idiom that is "always drawn from the casks of life" (*MT,* 112–13). Surprisingly, and in obvious contrast to Ziolkowski, Gray does not deem the somewhat esoteric subject matter, which gave even some German critics pause, an obstacle. He writes that the book "is easily accessible . . . even to those unfamiliar with the details of German life in [the twentieth] or the 17th century." In a dissenting, very brief piece, the reviewer of *Saturday Review* (Newlove 1981) finds many passages that "provoke an Olympian boredom" and detects too much material that "fades into encyclopediana." Such an opinion presumably reflects the view of actual readers more precisely than that of Gray.

In his substantive review in the *New York Review of Books* under the title "Elbe Swans and Other Poets" (1981), British poet and literary critic

Stephen Spender (1909–2005), discovers in the conditions that prevailed during the Thirty Years' War a foreshadowing of those that George Orwell describes in his novel *Nineteen Eighty-Four* (1949), that is, a permanent state of war with constantly shifting alliances. Spender notes that the "projection back into the past" of the meetings of *Gruppe 47,* at which the writers discussed the status of the German language and literature after a disastrous war, does fit "comfortably into what is plausible in history" and serves as a "powerful historic construction" that relies solely on "one piece of historic invention." The persuasiveness of the text is enhanced by the presence of a "featureless, anonymous, timeless 'I'" — a narrative device in which the author functions as an "abstract tricentennial witness." In addition, Spender draws attention to the figure of Gelnhausen as the violent and rhetorically gifted "embodiment . . . of the soldier-adventurer-troubadour" of the period. At the same time, Gelnhausen is a portrait of Grimmelshausen, with an additional "certain degree of self-portraiture" by the "ebullient" Grass, whose frequent depiction of tavern scenes Spender finds a bit distasteful. (John Leonard, in his 1981 review, likewise mentions Grass's identification with Grimmelshausen.) Nevertheless, Spender judges *Meeting* to provide "brilliant entertainment" — not least because there is the "consoling demonstration" that in spite of the poets' inability to effect change, poetry may survive, as demonstrated by the dust jacket (a drawing by Grass), which shows a hand clasping a quill pen and thrusting upward through what appears to be rubble (see also *MT,* 129).

Grass's image of the "hand holding a goose quill [and] rising triumphant from a heap of stones" serves fellow novelist Salman Rushdie (1981) to reaffirm the notion that the writer is "taking arms . . . against a sea of rubble" created by war. In the persona of the lying, cheating, and brawling Gelnhausen Grass manages to be "his own best character" who dispenses advice to the overbearing poets. Although Rushdie considers *Meeting* to be "astonishingly restrained," written by Grass "in second gear," he ends his review with unmitigated praise: a "fascinating, entertaining book" by "one of the few great ones around" — an endorsement with which novelist John Updike (1981) implicitly disagrees. Updike objects, like Ziolkowski, that *Meeting* has not been written "for the general reader" but as a "homage" to Richter and hence is "less a novella" than "an extended pleasantry" (91–92) that excludes the ordinary (American) booklover. As is his custom in reviews of books by Grass, Updike dismisses the political engagement of those gathered at Telgte as "narrow Germanness" (93), disapproves of the rhetorical fervor in the use of the term "fatherland" (93) in the manifesto (see *MT,* 67), and, in casting an ironic glance at his own profession, declares the purpose of the 1647 meeting to be not much different from that of any other literary get-together, that is, "to gossip, to drink, and . . . to fornicate" (92).

In contrast, a further positive voice is that of Guy Davenport (1981) in the *Washington Post* who terms *Meeting* "smartly shaped" as well as "critical, witty, bright," and, in a brief comparison of dubious merit, elevates Grass, "the first German novelist of modern times," above Thomas Mann on account of the former's "rebuilding a ravaged language," whereas the latter followed foreign models. All in all then, the American reception in influential review organs appears to be more affirmative than Grass's "strange" subject matter would lead one to expect. Moreover, it is to be assumed that the publication of *Meeting* resulted in an at least moderate commercial success; approximately one year after the marketing of the hardcover edition a paperback version was published; for advertising purposes, it featured a considerable number of laudatory comments from various reviews of the book.

The Narrator; Narrative Strategies

Scholarly contributions began to appear in the same year in which *Treffen* became available in bookstores. Hungarian Katalin Fenyves (1979) addresses the tendency of German writers of fiction in the 1970s to delve into literary history for the creation of their works; in particular, he singles out Christa Wolf's *Kein Ort: Nirgends* (1979; *No Place on Earth,* 1982), which entails a fictitious 1804 meeting between dramatist and prose writer Heinrich von Kleist and poetess Karoline von Günderrode during the period of Romanticism, and Grass's narrative. (In his 1979 essay, Krättli engages in a similar comparison.) In summary fashion, Fenyves bases his comparison of the two literary texts on the general premise that history is viewed by both authors as a continuum whose effects determine both present and future (433). At the same time, the narrative mode of *Treffen,* which relies on the proclaimed omniscience of the narrator that, as the ending shows, turns out to have been exaggerated, constitutes an indirect appeal for self-reflection to the reader — a process, Fenyves maintains somewhat unconvincingly, that is most likely going to be as fragmentary and confused as the narrative mode itself (440).

In his careful analysis, which he modestly calls a "gloss," Klaus Haberkamm (1979) implicitly takes issue with Fenyves's characterization of Grass's narrative stance. Haberkamm starts out by positing the fairly obvious similarity of the author as narrator with the "reporter" of the happenings at Telgte. In fact, the first paragraph of *Meeting* provides what amounts to a programmatic statement about such similarity or identity: ". . . I am writing down what happened in Telgte . . ." (*MT,* 3). Following this, Haberkamm does not devote his attention to elucidating further parallels between the first-person narrator and author; rather, he turns to the figure of Gelnhausen, who, he claims, displays a great affinity with the "reporter," with the result that in some instances the narrative perspectives of the two seem to be indistinguishable. As his chief evidence, Haberkamm cites a playfully serious passage from the beginning of the ninth chapter in which, under the benign influence of the moon, the three poets cohabiting with the maids in the hay change their sexual partners not once but twice; consequently, they are oblivious to what is happening in their surroundings (see *M,* 44–45). While the "reporter" appears to assume an omniscient perspective, it is difficult to see the merging of his perspective with that of Gelnhausen, because the two characters appear as distinctly separate entities in the passage following the sexual frolicking; in fact, it is the "I" that observes and reports on Gelnhausen's activities. In addition, the narrator explicitly states that he was not Gelnhausen (see *M,* 84).

Furthermore, Haberkamm writes, Gelnhausen, who characterizes himself as "endowed with all the wisdom of Saturn" (*MT,* 11), displays an affinity for astrology in the manner of both Grimmelshausen and his eponymous protagonist Simplicissimus. For example, when Gelnhausen proclaims his intention to become a writer, he does so by invoking "Jupiter, Mercury, and Apollo" (*MT,* 113) — precisely the gods whom Grimmelshausen designates as benefactors of those aspiring to become devotees of letters (Haberkamm, 72). Thus Grass has succeeded not only in honoring his friend and mentor Richter but also, by attempting to fuse the figures of the unobtrusive "reporter" with that of the far more flamboyant Gelnhausen, in casting a glance backward to the beginning of his own literary career and his first appearance before *Gruppe 47* (which, incidentally, took place in 1955 rather than 1956, as Haberkamm has it).

In his analysis of the narrative perspectives, Ruprecht Wimmer (1983, 1985) both elaborates on and partially disagrees with Haberkamm's findings. He rejects the notion of assigning the narrating "I" to "all figures simultaneously and none exclusively" (1983, 25). Despite the "paradoxical aphorism" with which *Meeting* begins — "The thing that hath been tomorrow is that which shall be yesterday" (*MT,* 3) — Wimmer suggests that the initial three chapters may be read as a conventional frame story in the manner of a nineteenth-century novella, albeit with an occasional interruption by a narrator with "omniscient ambition" (1983, 26). Yet in the fourth chapter the "I" establishes itself as a bona fide participant in the proceedings by an interjection: "Someone (I?) asked . . ." (*MT,* 21) and continues to present itself as a "distinct *persona*" with a "specific presence" that is not to be confused with the presence of any other writer present (Wimmer 1983, 27). Yet the attempt to identify the "I" as one of the participants of the meeting turns out to be unproductive, inasmuch as a separate presence cannot be established for each one of them. We are then faced with an "I" that "travels through time" (1983, 29) — a narrative device that immediately brings to mind the predecessor of *Meeting, The Flounder* (see ch. 7). But Wimmer goes further and, after a brief examination of Grass's works of prose fiction that precede *The Flounder,* concludes that Grass tends to establish his various narrators' "points of view" within their respective narratives "in only a precarious and approximate fashion" (1983, 32). In *Meeting,* Wimmer posits, the "authorial 'I' dwells principally and sovereignly" in the Baroque period in order to establish a "history suitable for analogy" without serving as a mere "prefiguration" of events that were to follow three hundred years later (1983, 35).

In her essay on the "Narrative Dialectic," Judith Ryan (1983a) singles out as a pivotal scene that inspired *Meeting* not the often cited get-together of Opitz and Gryphius in the fourth month of *The Flounder* ("The burden of an evil day") but the secluded gathering of Romantic poets and fairy-tale lovers near Danzig in the sixth month ("The other truth") that, somewhat anachronistically, bears not only several of the hallmarks of "modern writers' conferences" but is also "placed in a political context" (Ryan, 43) — even if, it might be added, the fairy-tale version depicting overweening man is burnt deliberately in *The Flounder,* whereas the Telgte manifesto perishes accidentally in the fire at the Bridge Tavern, which was set by someone unknown to the otherwise omniscient narrator (see *M,* 132).

As others have done, Ryan briefly speculates about the persona of the narrator and concludes that he is a highly unconventional "'omniscient narrator'" because he speaks in a very "personal" tone. At the same time, the narrator constitutes a "narrative construct both omniscient and omnipresent" (47) that reveals the gaps and disjunction between 1647 and 1947 and results in "ironic comparisons" (49) between the Germany of *Gruppe 47* and that of Simon Dach. In this way, Ryan contends, the "novel" — a term of uncertain legitimacy she uses throughout her essay — invites reflection on the contemporaneous tendency to view the "present as . . . a subtle variant of the past" and challenges the notion of the text as merely a "private reflection" (52; see also Verweyen and Witting, below).

Without denying the existence of parallels or resemblances between the narrator and individual figures appearing in *Meeting,* Alexander Weber (1986) dismisses all previous attempts to ascribe the narrator's role to a specific participant in the gathering as inconclusive. Rather, he proceeds from the distinction between the authorial "I" and the fictive "I" that assumes the mask of one of the members of the group and reports on the proceedings and happenings. In a 1977 interview (in H. L. Arnold 1963, 5th ed. 1978, 28), Grass himself points out the distinction, which resulted from a novel narrative strategy that he used extensively in *The Flounder.* As to *Meeting,* Weber singles out Johann Mathias Schneuber, a professor of poetry in Strasbourg and the least known among those assembled at the Bridge Tavern, as the narrator — in part because he shows an affinity with the Baroque "emblem of the moon and the howling dog" (Weber 1995, 10), which characterizes him as a less than stellar character. The fact that Schneuber appears as a detractor does not disqualify him from being considered the narrator, Weber (1986, 109–10) writes, because Grass habitually tends to discredit his first-person narrators and emphasize their unreliability.

Weber's attempt to establish the identity of the narrator did not end the debate. Andreas Graf (1989) posits, without acknowledging Weber, that the persona of the first-person narrator is a cleverly calculated playful fiction within the fiction of the text, and that all efforts to decide whether we are dealing with, in the terminology of Franz K. Stanzel in his *Typische Formen des Romans* (1964; Typical Forms of the Novel), an authorial or a first-person narrative must ultimately remain inconclusive (Graf, 292).

Writing and Politics

Theodor Verweyen and Gunther Witting (1980) initially review the *Feuilleton* criticism and, in particular, take issue with Reich-Ranicki's assertion (1979) that the German Baroque poets and writers lacked a sense of national responsibility and were not keenly interested in the state of the German language, citing clear evidence for their case. In a partial repudiation of journalistic claims that Grass's extensive use of quotations required Herculean labors (see Raddatz 1979), Verweyen and Witting demonstrate that the author relied heavily on excerpts from the second, revised edition of Albrecht Schöne's literary anthology *Das Zeitalter des Barock* (1968; The Age of the Baroque) and even largely followed the sequence of texts in the anthology by having those gathered read from their works and discuss the texts according to the arrangement in Schöne's compilation (the 1981 paperback edition of *Treffen* includes the cited texts in an appendix; a 1994 paperback edition includes forty-three Baroque poems). Yet, Verweyen and Witting aver, Grass's considerable borrowings do not diminish his artistic achievement, which consists in the creative and innovative use of extant texts, in the slightest. Moreover, in articulating the writers' — ultimately impotent — desire to have an impact on politics via their manifesto as well as in assigning the first-person narrator a fairly insignificant and inconspicuous role, Grass provocatively opposes the "New Subjectivity," a tendency prevalent in the literature of the 1970s, with its emphasis on introspective soul-searching.

Angelika Menne-Haritz (1981) goes further than Verweyen and Witting in emphasizing the political aspects of *Treffen* and insists that despite Grass's disavowal of direct political action, for which literary texts are an unsuitable vehicle, the poets and writers have an important function via their command of the written word. Like the members of

Gruppe 47 three hundred years later, they strive to preserve in writing "for all time whatever truly deserved the name of German" (*MT,* 129), as Simon Dach vividly puts it in his concluding speech.

Werner Hoffmeister (1981) shifts the emphasis and views the figure of Gelnhausen, which is indebted to the picaresque tradition, as Grass's implicit tribute to Grimmelshausen, the literary chronicler of the Thirty Years' War. Moreover, Gelnhausen represents the tension between literature and life, between imagination and empiricism. Hence, Hoffmeister argues, *Treffen* is not an esoteric virtuoso performance based on an imaginary event that takes place in idyllic seclusion. Rather, Grass's text is clearly an exception in the literature of the 1970s in that it does not participate in the prevailing mood of the "New Sensibility," which attributes prime importance to the individual's inner life (see also Verweyen and Witting 1980) and neglects the fundamental issues affecting and shaping society as a whole.

Michael Hollington (1980) contributes in passing to the much debated issue of "who's who?" going beyond the generally accepted configuration of "autodidact picaro Grimmelshausen/Grass" as well as the "rather paternalistic diplomat Dach/Richter" and very briefly mentions "Gryphius/Böll" on account of the two writers' assumed melancholic disposition. Furthermore, Hollington advances his main thesis that according to Grass's poetics writers have a dual function, that is, to "transcend ephemerality" via their chosen medium, the written word, on the one hand, and to renounce the use of "verbal art" as a "kind of substitute for life" on the other (172–73). Hollington surmises that in Baroque poet and novelist Philipp von Zesen Grass satirically portrays one of his old adversaries, philosopher Martin Heidegger (see ch. 3 and ch. 14), as well as, conceivably, a "more recent *bête noire*" at that time, the influential poststructuralist psychoanalyst Jacques Lacan. For example, in one scene, which is also quoted by other critics, Zesen encounters the bloated corpses of a man and a woman, tied together, on the shore of a river; yet his desire to create poetic metaphors predominates over his potential feelings of horror and disgust — the pursuit of art has suppressed human emotions and compassion (see *M,* 35).

In a relatively rarely practiced approach, Richard Schade (1982) goes beyond a purely literary analysis and investigates the "iconographic images" (200) that Grass, both writer and graphic artist, derived from Grimmelshausen's novel about Courasche or Courage. Schade observes that Grass's use of graphic art in elucidating and informing literary texts is by no means a new feature; notably in *Aus dem Tagebuch einer Schnecke,* the writer employs Albrecht Dürer's engraving *Melencolia I* (see ch. 6) as an "intellectual touchstone" (201) of politics in the Federal Republic. Although the dust jacket, briefly discussed above (see Spender, Rushdie), is Grass's own creation, Schade endeavors to prove in somewhat circuitous fashion that the drawing showing the hand holding the quill (reproduced in Schade, 203) is Grass's "homage" (205) to Grimmelshausen. For example, Schade takes Gelnhausen's reference to his sword as his "goose quill" (*MT,* 11) as an implicit invocation of the "image of the writing hand" to be encountered in the seventeenth century (Schade, 205; Rempe-Thiemann refers to Grass's graphic work as a revealing commentary without mentioning Schade [1992, 138–39]). More persuasive is Schade's demonstration of the significance of the thistle; Grass derived this symbol from the emblematic frontispiece of *Courasche,* which depicts Courasche's mule feeding on a thistle (the reproduction of the frontispiece in Schade, 206 is not detailed enough to recognize the thistle). The thistle, which Libuschka has taken from her garden and planted in an "earthenware pot" (*MT,* 53), assumes symbolic significance when Dach praises it as "that latter-day flower and symbol of adverse times" (*MT,* 34, 53). In expressing the "spirit of the times" (Schade, 208), it then represents chaos and disorder in general but also, as Gryphius eloquently states, the poets' fatherland. Miraculously, the thistle survives unscathed when Gryphius deliberately drops it to the floor — a sign, as Zesen claims, that the fatherland will eventually emerge similarly "unscathed" (*MT,* 125). With this "theatrical" act, Schade suggests, the thistle has "fulfilled its function," inasmuch as the future of Germany henceforth appears to rest on the manifesto, which, however, burns and remains unknown. Thus the "image of the thistle" is being replaced by and "transformed" into that of the dust jacket, which defines the thrust of the narrative "in terms of visual art" (Schade, 209–10). (For a deviating reading of the significance of the thistle in terms of Grass's "parodistic" intent, see J. Schmidt 1985, 149–51.)

In a different vein, Andreas Graf (1989) emphasizes the "literary" character of the text, a character that is more pronounced in *Treffen* than in any previous work by Grass because of its internal network of textual references, which provides important clues for the interpretation and, at the same time, illuminates the intricate interrelationship between literature and "reality" (284–85). Graf considers the scene in which Zesen encounters the floating corpses (see Hollington, above) of particular importance because the poetically verbalized experience of a horrific encounter distances him from the immediate impact of what he has witnessed and tends to diminish its authenticity. The scene gains in poignancy because it is a direct literary borrowing from Edgar Hilsenrath's *Nacht* (1960; *Night,* 1966), a novel about a ghetto in the Ukraine during the Second World War. In passing, Graf contends, Grass casts a satirical glance at the concept of *Betroffenheit* (a term akin to "profound concern"), which was ostentatiously displayed particularly in women's literature during the

1970s (286), and contrasts it with the unspectacular determination of the poets to make their voices heard and carry on despite all odds. In the words of composer Heinrich Schütz, also a participant in the meeting, it was important to "wrest from helplessness" — including that in the political domain — "a faint 'and yet'" (*MT*, 69).

It may be noted here that *Treffen* has also stimulated the interest of pedagogues and scholars engaged in providing didactic tools for the teaching of literature at German secondary schools. Like Werner Zimmermann (1988), Ralph P. Crimmann (1986) emphasizes the powerless and, at the same time, defiant attitude of the poets, who endeavor to find a common German language in order to represent the unity of the riven nation. Crimmann also provides a useful schema of the events transpiring at the symbolically named Bridge Tavern, where the attempt is being made to unite the disparate literary societies and poets, with their different poetic concepts and dialects. Similarly, in her wide-ranging, slightly aphoristic essay, Swenta Steinig (1992) touches upon the relationship of literature to politics, but her main concern is of a pedagogical nature: how to make Grass's prose narrative relevant for discussions of *Gruppe 47*. Despite the promising title of Helgard Mahrdt's more recent essay (2000), which refers to the significance of the symposium as an elucidation of the relationship between eating, drinking, and writing poetry, she essentially summarizes the findings of previously published research; perhaps noteworthy is her reiteration of Steinig's suggestion about the relationship between the "butcher's feast" (*MT*, 104), a plentiful meal in which the poets indulge before realizing that Gelnhausen acquired the food through violent means, and Grass's essay "Schreiben nach Auschwitz" (1990; "Writing after Auschwitz," 1990), in which he modifies Theodor W. Adorno's famous dictum that it is barbaric to write poems after Auschwitz by insisting that Adorno's "imperative could be refuted, if at all, only by writing" (103). Although an analogous situation seems to obtain by virtue of the fact that the poets at Telgte ultimately opt for continuing to compose their "morally motivated appeal for peace" (*MT*, 104) in spite of their unwitting complicity in a criminal act, construing an analogous situation between the Telgte meal and the post-Auschwitz period tends to ignore the vastly different scales of the crimes committed.

Dramatis Personae

To some extent, the guessing game of "who's who?" indulged in by some of the first reviewers of *Treffen* has been continued by scholars. In addition to investigations seeking to establish the identity of the narrator, the functions of several other figures have been researched. Noel L. Thomas (1980) analyzes the central role of Simon Dach in the narrative and points out that the meeting convened by Dach cannot be considered "fanciful at all" in view of the existence of a number of seventeenth-century literary societies that "sought to promote the German language and literature" (92). Among these was the *Kürbishütte* or Cucumber Lodge in Königsberg (Kaliningrad since the end of the Second World War) of which Dach was a member (see *M,* 146). Dach's central role in *Meeting* is evident from the fact that he convenes and organizes the conference and acts as its chairman — hence his function corresponds to that of Richter. But Thomas goes beyond Dach's managerial competence and credits him with literary merit; he considers Dach's reading of his poem in the twentieth chapter as the "climax of the literary readings" (98) in that it combines the laments about the "destruction of Magdeburg" with that about "Germany's self-dismemberment" as well as the poets' aspirations for "immortality" (*MT,* 120).

Yet the interventions of Gelnhausen and his small military unit, which secure the poets' lodging and sustenance, serve as a "constant reminder" of their powerlessness, as does Dach and his fellow writers' dependence on "military protection" (Thomas, 105). In the face of such helplessness, Dach's parting words about the "invincibility of literature" (106) in words that elucidate the aforementioned drawing on the dust cover (see *MT,* 129) inspired hope in 1647 as well as three hundred years later.

Without doubt, Gelnhausen has been a source of major interest among critics and scholars (see, for example, Haberkamm 1979) — even though there are hardly any essays exclusively devoted to that figure. Wimmer (1983, 1985; see also the discussion above) stresses the point that Grass fuses two diverse sources in creating Gelnhausen by having him appear as "Grimmelshausen's character Simplicissimus" but also endowing him with details of Grimmelshausen's biography and letting Gelnhausen "invent himself" in this figure. He does so notably by proclaiming his aforementioned firm intention of wanting to become a writer (Wimmer 1983, 36; see *MT,* 113); he thereby essentially adopts the (in 1647) as yet unwritten story of Grimmelshausen's protagonist as his own. What distinguishes Gelnhausen from the other poets, Wimmer writes, is that he appears as a "personified, poetological confession" by embodying the "'truth of art'" rather than that of surface realism. Gelnhausen's "literary counterpart," Courasche/Libuschka differs from Gelnhausen in that she springs "entirely from literature." Both figures depart from the scene once their mission of conveying a truth that encompasses more than the "adage of the necessity and frailty of the poet's word in troubled times" (37) has been accomplished.

Next to Gelnhausen it is Libuschka who has attracted considerable interest. Silke Umbach (1992) posits that Grass shows Libuschka in a phase of her life that closely corresponds to that of Grimmelshausen's Libuschka/

Courasche in his novel. The correspondence of the figures in the respective literary texts extends to the way they dress, but there is no complete identity (11–12). For example, by simply using the name Libuschka or the designation "landlady" with or without her name far more frequently than that of Courasche or Courage (Umbach, 114, provides a statistical tabulation about the frequency of the names' occurrence), Grass is, as should be fairly evident, less interested in reconstructing the (hi)story of Libuschka than creating a portrayal that suits the dramaturgy of his narrative. Thus the comparatively rare use of the name Courasche, which has a sexual connotation in Grimmelshausen's text (see the translator's note, *MT,* 36–37), is presumably attributable to her chief function in *Meeting,* that is, to serve the poets and to provide for them without showing any interest in financial gain for the services she renders. Although Grimmelshausen's Courasche engages in prostitution, Umbach curiously appears to defend Courasche against what she seems to view as disparagement of the figure on the part of Grass by claiming that Courasche could not have engaged in the obscene behavior depicted in *Meeting* when she farts into Gelnhausen's face after he has offended her by referring to her infertility (see *MT,* 37). In sum, Umbach does not find many features that Grass's and Grimmelshausen's figures have in common; as a consequence, Libuschka in *Meeting* is hardly suitable as an interpretive tool for *Runagate Courage* — but then, despite his indebtedness to Grimmelshausen, it is presumably not Grass's intent to provide an explanatory elucidation of an acknowledged literary masterpiece, a point also made by Battafarano and Eilert (2003, 212 n. 517).

In fact, Battafarano and Eilert argue that it is precisely the creative adaptation of two of Grimmelshausen's figures that demonstrates Grass's appreciation of his literary forebear and emphasizes the importance he attributes to fiction in the process of coming to terms with history (209). Hence, in portraying Libuschka, he conflates traits of the literary figure and those of Grimmelshausen's biography, a method similar to the one he uses in creating the figure of Gelnhausen (213). Via the relationship of Gelnhausen and Libuschka — she serves as Gelnhausen's lover, confidante, and mother figure — Grass provides a demonstration not only of the interrelatedness of history and fiction but also of one of its central aspects, the problematic relationship between man and woman (216). Although the treatment of the war of the sexes is far less expansive in *Treffen* than in *Der Butt,* Battafarano and Eilert justifiably stress that both Gelnhausen and the poets, among whom there are no females (see also Graf 1989), are given to claiming to be the exclusive representatives of the human race and treating women as (sexual) objects, as is evident, for example, in the aforementioned episode of the younger poets' frolicking with the maids.

Gelnhausen and Libuschka are united by a love-hate relationship that is often on the verge of erupting into violence, particularly when Libuschka displays her verbal skills, which are superior to those of Gelnhausen (226). Although the composer Heinrich Schütz advises Gelnhausen to write down his "murderous fictions" (*MT*, 92) rather than putting them into practice, it is Libuschka's scornful speech, in which she ridicules his assumed lack of literary talent (*MT*, 101–2), that provokes Gelnhausen into resorting to violence — he hits Libuschka in the face. But, Battafarano and Eilert suggest, Libuschka's provocation ultimately serves to foster Gelnhausen's process of introspection, which results in his gradual maturation when he begins to prepare seriously for his desired profession (229–33). In a sense, Libuschka also contributes directly to Gelnhausen's becoming a writer; in the scene in which Libuschka, who is dancing on a table, farts into Gelnhausen's face (see Umbach 1992), Battafarano and Eilert detect the ingredients of a non-verbal theatricality that emphasizes the corporeal as an important element of literature — an element that, Grass indicates, cannot be ignored in favor of the spiritual and intellectual favored by the poets.

By no means a paragon of virtue, Libuschka displays her merciless acquisitive instinct, a character trait that appears to have been inspired by Brecht's Mother Courage rather than Grimmelshausen's Courasche, when she recounts how she enriched herself by robbing corpses during the siege and ensuing destruction of the city of Magdeburg in 1631 by the troops of the imperial general Tilly. By means of her unabashed confession, Libuschka serves notice that in war there are perpetrators and victims, an insight that the poets are reluctant to accept but one that Gelnhausen, who morphs into the historical Grimmelshausen, adopts by creating a "strong" seventeenth-century female figure who poses a challenge to the twentieth-century writer Grass (247).

General Assessments

Evidently, the text under discussion has not attracted quite as large a volume of criticism as, for example, *The Tin Drum* (see ch. 1) or, for that matter, *The Flounder* (see ch. 7). But there are some very substantive contributions that may be said to aim at establishing the general significance of *Meeting* rather than elucidating one or several specific aspects. In her revised dissertation, *Grass and Grimmelshausen: Günter Grass's "Das Treffen in Telgte" and Rezeptionstheorie* (1987), Susan C. Anderson views the relationship between Grass and Grimmelshausen, which she defines as the authors' participation "in a dialogue through their works" (24), in terms of Hans Robert Jauß's theory of reception. But Anderson also provides additional material such as a very short and hence sketchy introduction to Grass's major prose fiction prior to 1979, a rather brief survey of *Gruppe 47*, and a more detailed analysis of *Meeting* (which may serve as a competent, useful introduction to the text) as well as Grimmelshausen's pertinent writings. In her conclusion, Anderson seeks to demonstrate how *Meeting* contributes to changing the "reader's perception" not only of "Grimmelshausen's narratives" but also of the functioning and significance of *Gruppe 47* (94) — an endeavor in which she generally succeeds. Last but not least, she inclines toward both overstating and simplifying her interesting findings by suggesting that art, which, in the case of *Meeting*, consists of a highly complex, intricate "double-layered tale," will necessarily result in "socialistic propaganda" if the artist happens to be an "activist" (96–97). Needless to say, it is doubtful whether the terms "activist" and "socialistic propaganda" are entirely applicable to Grass, an admittedly committed and engaged writer who uses his prominence to participate vigorously in public discourse.

In contrast to Anderson, in his monograph *Günter Grass's Use of Baroque Literature* (1995) Alexander Weber devotes a substantial chapter to *Treffen*, in which he focuses on Grass's "active use of literary tradition." He concentrates specifically on the "manner of writing which evolves from the use of baroque literature" (138 n. 43) and goes far beyond the brief contribution on a similar topic by Adolf Haslinger (1985). In his detailed analysis of Grass's linguistic archaism and other devices, Weber justifiably confines himself to the German text — although an occasional reference to the English translation might have contributed to further elucidating both Grass's innovative use of language and the difficulties it poses for readers of both the original and renderings in other tongues. True, Weber mentions in passing the reception of *Meeting* in England and argues that the "strange [Baroque] guise of the story" does not pose an obstacle to its understanding owing to Grass's "indirect and ironic mode of writing" (165).

Apart from his insistent use of the generic term "novel" (114 et passim), which hardly corresponds to Grass's designation "Erzählung," Weber engages in a systematic discussion of the "baroque context" (107), in which he stresses Grass's indebtedness to recent baroque research (see Verweyen and Witting, 1980), Grass's aforementioned use of baroque language, which amounts to a virtuoso performance, and also the structure of the novel and the character of Gelnhausen. Although necessarily dependent on previous research, Weber adds insights concerning, for example, the structure of the text (129–34) and suggestions such as as that the poets' "sexual round dance" (132 n. 36) in the scene repeatedly referred to previously may have been inspired by Arthur Schnitzler's *Reigen* (1903; *Hands Around*, 1920). Less convincing is Weber's description of Libuschka, the "leading female figure," as a "negative character" who represents a "negative variation of the theme of women's liberation in *Der Butt*" (140) — an assessment that does not appear to be tenable in view of the later findings by Battafarano and Eilert about the "strong" woman Courasche (2003). More plausible is the connection Weber establishes between the two Germanys on the basis of Grass's notion of the German *Kulturnation* (nation united by a common culture), rather than one defined by the encompassing boundaries of a nation-state (Weber, 158–59; see Mews 1994) during a time when the reunification of Germany seemed, at best, to be a remote hope. Weber refers to an additional element, often overlooked by other critics, that forms a "decisive link between the two Germanies": language and art (159). Specifically, there is a relevant passage in *Kopfgeburten* (see ch. 9) in which Grass and other writers from West Berlin meet with their East Berlin colleagues during the 1970s to discuss literature and politics in the divided city and divided country — precisely the kind of undertaking in which the poets at Telgte are engaged. At the same time, the poets' seemingly irrelevant activities serve Grass as an argument to counter the notion of the "death of literature" (*MT,* 33) that Gryphius eloquently proclaims. But Weber (152) does not go far enough in attributing the prevalence of such notions to the postwar years, when the members of *Gruppe 47* had to contend with them. For different reasons, the student movement of 1968 considered the pursuit of literary matters irrelevant and superfluous; Grass, an avowed opponent of the rebellious academic youth (see ch. 5), was surely aiming at discrediting such claims. These quibbles aside, however, it must be said that Weber's painstaking analysis of Grass's "employment of baroque literary devices" (138n. 43) goes far beyond an arid scholarly study of influences and succeeds in demonstrating the relevance of these devices for an adequate understanding of a modern text.

A handy tool for accessing the text is Stephan Füssel's small volume on *Treffen* (1999), which appeared in the series *Erläuterungen und Dokumente,* issued by the Reclam publishing company in Stuttgart. Following the format of the series, the book includes a brief introduction, a helpful line-by-line commentary-cum-explanatory notes, interviews with Grass relating to the origins of the text, reprints (mostly in excerpts) of reviews and scholarly articles, materials relating to *Gruppe 47,* and a bibliography. In short, Füssel's compilation represents a sound starting point for any serious study of *Treffen.*

In an interview (Siemes 2005b) more than twenty-five years after the first publication of *Treffen* and more than thirty-five years after the demise of *Gruppe 47,* Grass returned, with a trace of nostalgia, to the topic of that famed postwar literary association and suggested that there might be a need to reconvene such gatherings in view of the relative isolation of younger German writers and their comparative abstinence from politics. A meeting named "Lübeck 05" did indeed take place in the northern German city, the erstwhile home of Thomas Mann and at the time that of Grass, which gave the get-together its name. But Grass's revival attempt was not greeted with universal acclaim; journalists (for example, Fuhr 2005) objected to Grass's condemnation of one of his *bêtes noires,* the *Feuilleton,* and pointed out — not entirely without justification — that journalists had contributed significantly to making his name a household word by reporting on his manifold activities and initiatives. On a positive note, *Treffen* experienced another reincarnation when the text was adapted by composer Eckehard Mayer and librettist Wolfgang Willaschek and premiered in March 2005 at the Dortmund Opera House (see Fasel 2005). However, one may conclude that the feud between the author and his critics is one of the constants of the reception process.

9: *Kopfgeburten oder Die Deutschen sterben aus / Headbirths or The Germans Are Dying Out*

A Contribution to the 1980 Election Campaign?

In June 1980, less than a year after the publication of *Das Treffen in Telgte* and shortly after Grass's return from his second extensive journey to Southeast and East Asia in the fall of 1979, on which he was accompanied by Ute Grunert, his second wife, *Kopfgeburten* (*Headbirths or The Germans Are Dying Out,* 1982) appeared on the book market. The weekly *Die Zeit* published the entire eighth chapter in May of the same year, accompanied by a laudatory introductory note by Fritz J. Raddatz (1980), one of the few major critics who fairly consistently took Grass's side and who had been defended by Grass against attacks by other critics prior to the publication of *Kopfgeburten* (see Mews 1983b, discussed below). Raddatz praises the narrative, which cannot be classified in traditional terms of genre, as a masterful product of the author's virtuosity. Unlike other reviewers, among whom the renowned Marcel Reich-Ranicki is conspicuously absent, Raddatz does not seem to be bothered by the lack of recognizable generic distinctions; on the contrary, he sees in the text, which is neither a film (Grass's plans to produce a film based on his travel experiences in cooperation with Volker Schlöndorff, director of the 1979 film version of *Die Blechtrommel,* did not materialize), a film novella, nor a novella, but a prose study full of scurrilous humor, cheerful grotesqueness and, at the same time, serious nonsense.

Not all journalists are inclined to agree with Raddatz. Particularly damning is Urs Jenny's appraisal in *Der Spiegel* (1980) inasmuch as Jenny considers the text the product of the "Großschriftsteller" Grass (188) — an English rendering such as "major writer" does not fully convey the numerous connotations the German term evokes — who is enamored by his historical greatness and condescendingly dispenses advice about German and world problems to his readers as well as his figures Harm and Dörte Peters, two tenured teachers and politically engaged veterans of the student protest movement of the 1960s, who hail from the federal state of Schleswig-Holstein. They experience the problems of developing countries on their journey which, in part, corresponds to the itinerary of Grass's

Asian voyage of 1978 rather than his lecture tour to China and other countries in 1979.

Joachim Kaiser (1980), writing in the *Süddeutsche Zeitung,* puns in the headline of his article that Grass's "headbirth" regrettably turns out to be both a premature birth and a stillbirth. Kaiser is less harsh in condemning Grass's superior attitude toward his creations Harm and Dörte, whom, Kaiser remarks, the author treats with paternal irony; rather, the critic attributes the dullness of the Grassian headbirths to their origin as figures in a sketchy, incomplete film treatment. Hence the two teachers tend to be typecast and their dialogues, particularly whenever they inconclusively debate whether to have a child or not (it is on the island of Bali rather than in India, as Kaiser has it, that Dörte falls temporarily under the spell of religion and is ready to conceive but is disappointed by Harm's momentary failure to perform) are unsuccessful in conveying any suspense. On the positive side, Kaiser mentions the moving tribute to Nicolas Born (1937–79), Grass's writer friend who was dying when *Kopfgeburten* originated and to whom the book is dedicated, and the polemics against Bavarian Franz Josef Strauß (1915–88), candidate for Chancellor of the CDU/CSU (Christian Democratic Union/Christian Social Union) in the 1980 federal elections, whom Grass brilliantly portrays as a (potentially) potent writer rather than an (actual) misguided politician. In the end then, Kaiser opines, *Kopfgeburten* hardly amounts to more than a modest contribution to the election campaign.

Swiss journalist Dieter Fringeli (1980) likewise emphasizes the significant role of Strauß in Grass's text but is more explicit in pointing out the intersection of literature and politics, which is not only evident in Grass's hypothetical portrayal of the Bavarian candidate for Chancellor. Despite a miscellany of topics that Grass addresses, topics that would appear to be the province of journalists rather than that of writers of serious literature, such as overpopulation in the Far East or, closer to home, the resistance against the construction of a fast-breeder nuclear reactor at Brokdorf on the lower Elbe river, it is evident that his main concern is (West) Germany and the problems it faces. Hence Fringeli, the neutral observer from abroad, fairly accurately predicts that *Kopfgeburten* will not elicit unmitigated praise from German reviewers. Even though Fringeli deems the book to be a poor product — if one applies the yardstick of other works by Grass — he ultimately concludes that the text provides a readable analysis of the political mood in Germany and acknowledges Grass's endeavor to elevate writers over politicians (see also chapter 8).

Grass's political instinct and involvement also provide the starting point for Horst Krüger's critique in the *Frankfurter Allgemeine Zeitung* (1980). Krüger professes not to be surprised by the publication of *Kopfgeburten,* because of Grass's well-known activities as a passionate campaigner in federal elections. Yet, surprisingly, the author refrains from writing pamphlets and engaging in polemics; instead, he surprises his reading public with a cheerful, ironic, and even witty book in the form of a fictive film script, in which he displays his dreams, utopian designs, travesties of, for example, the Germans' low birthrate, and grotesque distortions, including chipping away at his own, figurative, monument by presenting an imaginary autobiography in which he turns into a Nazi bard. Even if Grass's fantastic notions about politics and society lack stringency, he is at his best as a congenial storyteller. Unlike Jenny and Kaiser, Krüger views Harm and Dörte as typical representatives of their generation, who reflect on and articulate the problems with which they and their world are confronted; they are portrayed adroitly yet sympathetically. Krüger believes that the vision of a multicultural future in Germany, which emerges in the final scene after Harm and Dörte have returned home and are faced with a swarm of children from various continents, was inspired by former Chancellor Willy Brandt of the SPD, who is not mentioned by name in *Kopfgeburten* but whose concern about the impending conflict between wealthy and impoverished nations informs the text throughout.

Somewhat in the vein of Krüger, Wolfram Schütte (1980) dismisses the notion that Grass's text constitutes a playground for his private "changelings" (that is, "headbirths"); rather, the text constitutes a piece of autobiographical prose that has been constructed in sovereign fashion. The text, moreover, has remained deliberately sketchy and allows the reader to witness its gradual construction. The thread that holds the piece together is the story of Harm and Dörte; their discussions revolve around the central theme of the book, that is, the future of humankind in Orwell's decade, as Grass pessimistically terms the 1980s (see *WA* 9:775–88). Among the numerous topics, the "apotheosis" of German unity in the realm of letters in the manner of *Das Treffen in Telgte* is noteworthy, Schütte observes. In the end, Schütte queries Grass's tendency to adopt in his text a somewhat smug stance that allows him to be impervious to doubt and irony — an approach that is akin to that of Jenny, albeit formulated in a less abrasive manner. From the critiques discussed above it seems obvious that the initial reception of *Kopfgeburten* on the part of the *Feuilleton* is fairly mixed or, to put it somewhat differently, restrained. It is, then, not quite accurate to state that the book was panned with a rarely encountered unanimity by German reviewers charged with the critique of Grass's later works (see V. Neuhaus 1979, rev. ed. 1992, 157; see also Armin Arnold 1985, 140). Other summary comments on the validity of the critical response do not necessarily reflect the tenor of the cited critics' arguments either. For example, Heinz Ludwig Arnold (1997, 157) implies that the divergence between Grass's literary pursuits on the one hand and his articulation of political statements on the other induced reviewers who secretly objected to mixing literature and politics to disqualify *Kopfgeburten* on the basis of its journalistic tendencies — the opinions of critics such as Krüger (cited above) notwithstanding.

"Brilliant Improvisations" or "Unproductively Irritating"?

The English translation of *Kopfgeburten* was published in the spring of 1982, nearly two years after the appearance of the German edition; as had become customary, *Headbirths or The Germans Are Dying Out* in Ralph Manheim's rendering served as the edition for both the British and the American book markets. Like *The Meeting at Telgte,* Grass's newest publication posed difficulties for the English-speaking reader — albeit difficulties of a different sort. Whereas the subject matter of *Meeting* was considered by some critics to be comparatively obscure and arcane on account of its historical dimension (see chapter 8), in *Headbirths* Grass seems to indulge, in addition to addressing a host of other topics, in an excessive concern that "with current conditions in both Germanys . . . the non-German reader is likely to find little of relevance or even comprehensibility in the text," as the publication notice in the formerly Boston-based monthly literary-cultural magazine *Atlantic* states (Adams 1982). Presumably in anticipation of complaints of this nature, a "publisher's note" with a brief explanation of the pre-election situation in the Federal Republic precedes the text of *Headbirths* proper; in addition, there are several explanatory footnotes.

Perhaps because of Britain's comparative geographic proximity to Germany, the issues being debated in conjunction with the election in the latter country did not seem quite as remote to British reviewers. Writing in the *Times Literary Supplement,* Gabriel Josipovici (1982) notes that Grass is going "from strength to strength" by becoming "at once more German and more international" via taking "the responsibility of the writer" seriously and raising complex questions of general concern, for example about the "the miseries of the Third World." In alluding to Adorno's famous saying about the barbarism of writing poetry after Auschwitz, Josipovici suggests that Grass began writing after the Second World War in order to "live up to the heritage of the great émigré writers, [Thomas] Mann and [Bertolt] Brecht" — a statement of somewhat dubious validity, especially in view of Grass's play *Die Plebejer proben den Aufstand* (1966; *The Plebeians Rehearse the Uprising,* 1966), which was widely interpreted as a criticism of Brecht's reaction to the GDR worker's strike and ensuing unrest on 17 June 1953. Josipovici concludes his review with high praise: artists cannot tear down walls, yet an artist of Grass's caliber can make the walls about which he writes (the Berlin Wall, the Chinese Wall, the wall around the construction site of the Brokdorf nuclear reactor, or the walls around slums to hide them from sight) transparent by poking holes in them in his fiction that, in the case of *Headbirths,* amounts to "an exhilarating performance."

Not surprisingly, the reviewer of the now defunct British humor magazine *Punch* views *Headbirths* as "not just thought-provoking but also funny" and "wonderfully, wittily embroidered with symbolism"; he adds that Grass's thrust amounts to a "questioning" of the "fundamental tenets of Western values" by means of "finely balanced" arguments that will not leave the reader "in despair" (Boston 1982). Initially less enthused than Boston, John Sutherland (1982), writing in the *London Review of Books,* begins his evaluation with a comparison "of a national kind" by surmising that the "representative British novelist" would presumably be too inhibited by "decorum" to "smuggle front-page . . . material" into his or her literary text and publish what amounts to "a novelist's diary or quarry, unprocessed working materials." However, what would seem to be an advantage of British fiction is counteracted by the gradually emerging "recognition" that Grass "is fashioning a new discourse and claiming . . . new territories for modern fiction" — a difficult task of Sisyphean proportions, Sutherland observes, referring to the myth that is invoked in *Headbirths,* and he sums up by referring to Grass's "main literary-historical datum," that is, the laying waste of the German language through the "ideology of National Socialism." In order to revive the language German writers have to create their own tradition via a kind of "headbirth," and Grass "manages to do that very well."

The positive reception in Britain differs to some extent from that in the United States despite a propitious beginning. Before the release of *Headbirths,* the *American Poetry Review* printed the second and fifth chapters and featured a Grass photo on the cover of the January/February 1982 issue. One of the first extensive American reviews is that by novelist John Irving (1982) who reiterates his admiration for *The Tin Drum* by stating that "*Die Blechtrommel* . . . has not been surpassed, it is the greatest novel by a living author" (57). Irving extends his high regard to the author's entire *œuvre* by insisting that "you can't be well-read today if you haven't read him. Günter Grass is simply the most original and versatile writer alive" (60). Surprisingly, Irving recommends *Headbirths* as a "*general* introduction to the methods of [Grass's] genius" (57) and proceeds to provide a fairly detailed analysis of the various plot elements of Grass's heterogeneous subject matter, including those relating to German affairs, which may serve as an aid to the uninitiated reader. In a sense, Irving seeks to do justice to the fine points of *Headbirths* in the manner of Grass, whose "scrupulousness to detail" (58) is evident, for example, in the subplot of the liver sausage that Harm and Dörte take along on their journey. Implicitly, Irving rejects the charge that Grass's book is addressed only to German readers (Adams 1982) in pointing out that, for example, the fixation on growth and productivity is hardly a unique German phenomenon. He also introduces a personal note when he identifies himself as a former member of the student protest movement and hence someone who can identify with Harm and Dörte. As one of the "hard core" of Grass fans he unambiguously recommends *Headbirths* to any kind of reader, no matter how much or how little exposure he or she has had to the author's previous work.

John Leonard (1982), writing in the *New York Times Book Review,* strikes a note of bemusement that occasionally borders on exasperation in his discussion of a text that is "part fiction, part travelogue, part screenplay and part political pamphlet" — in short, "a wise, sad, witty mess" (11), one that Leonard discusses and explains in ironic fashion. But his bemusement does not prevent Leonard from ending his review on a laudatory note; in alluding to some of Grass's previous works such as *Cat and Mouse* and *Dog Years,* and in essential agreement with Irving, he deems the "by turns grief-stricken, bemused, hortatory, punprone, furious, dreamy, fishy, catlike and dogyeared" work "minor Grass," which, however, "would be major for almost any other writer." Hence Leonard surmises that the award of the Nobel Prize to Grass is only a question of time; he also deems Manheim, an "admirable translator" (20), worthy of the same distinction without mentioning that there is an inexplicable (and unexplained) omission of a passage of several pages in chapter 9, a passage that relates to the aforementioned candidate Strauß (see *WA* 6:262–69; *HB,* 135).

The coincidence of the nearly simultaneous publication of the translations of Heinrich Böll's novel *Fürsorgliche Belagerung* (1979; *The Safety Net,* 1982) and *Headbirths* induced several editors to commission joint reviews of the two titles. D. J. Enright (1982) of the *New York Review of Books,* the first critic to publish such a combined assessment, acknowledges that both Grass and Böll have "amply demonstrated their staying power" and their "versatility"; he detects as a common thread in both texts their authors' intense worrying about the current state of affairs at that time; in Grass's case the "matter of Germany (including the world)" looms large. Enright characterizes *Headbirths* as a "collection of footnotes, endowed with Grass's free-spluttering intelligence, satirically pointed out, but not too sharp" and concludes rather benignly in view of his previous off-the-mark attack on *The Flounder:* "Major writers must be allowed a general helping of solipsism, but here Grass seems to be cannibalizing himself."

Another critic to address the quality of the translation, Joel Agee (1982), writing in the *New Republic,* acknowledges the difficulty of the translator's task, such as working under time pressures, yet he judges

Manheim's prose to be "comparatively bland" when compared to the original, which was written by the "vigorous, colorful stylist" Grass, an "inventive" user of words and manipulator of "themes," whose sentences abound with "puns and wordplay." As the title of Agee's review indicates, he focuses in particular on Grass's "headbirth," in which, when faced with huge masses of bicycle riders in the city of Shanghai, the author entertains the notion of the existence of 950 million Germans (instead of Chinese) and its implications. Unlike other critics, most of whom are not enamored by Harm and Dörte, Agee is captivated by Grass's "homunculi," who gradually "take on an ever more human appearance."

An additional positive voice is that of David H. Richter (1982) in *Commonweal,* who credits Grass with "brilliant improvisations" and the "lunatic vitality of his prose" and focuses on a topic that has received less attention from others, that is, the central role of literature in the text or, to put it differently, the "difficulties of being a writer, and specifically a German writer today." Indicative of these difficulties are Grass's and some of his West German colleagues' futile attempts to continue the dialogue with their East German counterparts via meetings in East Berlin in the hope of preserving the unity of German culture and literature in the face of the political division.

Whereas the majority of reviewers seem to accept Grass's text with varying degrees of approbation as a bona fide, if unconventional, literary text, there are discordant voices. Richard Gilman (1982) in the *Nation* stridently proclaims: "Today there is no writer more swollen with self-importance or, if that's too harsh, more convinced of his responsibility for the whole of his culture than Günter Grass, who has begun to think of himself as identical with the fates of German literature, German politics, and German mores." Accordingly, Grass uses Harm and Dörte as well as the planned movie as "pretexts for a wide, rambling, unwitty, at times nearly incoherent attack" on all kinds of German problems. One of the few saving graces that Gilman detects is that Grass shows an occasional awareness of his "unproductively irritating" stance; on the whole, however, a "lofty, hectoring tone predominates." As the passage in which capitalism and Communism are being equated shows (see *HB,* 68), the author's "headbirths" advance "neither the cause of literature nor that of political understanding."

The underlying premise of Gilman's scathing critique, the incompatibility of literary pursuits on the one hand and journalistic or political statements as well as public appearances on the other, is even more apparent in John Updike's acerbic review in the *New Yorker* (1982). Updike wishes to draw the attention of those who "urge upon American writers more social commitment and a more public role" to the "cautionary case" of Grass, a writer who has become a public persona to such an extent that "he can't be bothered to write a novel; he just sends dispatches . . . from the front lines of his engagement." As a consequence, there are only a "few dollops of fiction" relating to the adventures of the "imperfectly animated dolls" Harm and Dörte, and Grass openly shares his problems about "inventing a story" with the reader of whose "indulgence" he appears to be "ingenuously confident." Unexpectedly, even Updike detects an optimistic feature in the final scene, which was briefly discussed above, in that the influx of a multitude of foreign-born children conveys to the reader "an authentic pang as Germany surrenders its barbaric old notion of racial purity" and seeks to determine its place in a "mongrel," multi-ethnic and multicultural world.

In the final analysis, the contrasting views of especially American critics and their irreconcilable differences concerning the literary quality of *Headbirths* may be attributed to their underlying incompatible concepts as to what constitutes fiction. Whereas some emphasize Grass's innovative features and his exploration of new subject matter, others insist on a more conventional approach and a more narrowly defined role of the writer of fiction, who is expected to exclude certain topics such as politics and refrain from liberally experimenting with narrative modes.

Narrator and Narrative Structure

As the foregoing discussion has shown, Grass's innovative narrative stance was not universally acclaimed by reviewers of either *Kopfgeburten* or its English rendering. In his scholarly contribution on the narrative structure, Jochen W. Rohlfs (1982) proceeds from Grass's concept of *Vergegenkunft,* translated by Manheim as "paspresenture" (*HB,* 103), a fourth time dimension embracing past, present, and future that the author employs in his attempt to suspend the "inevitability of linear narration," in order to simulate *Gleichzeitigkeit* or simultaneity by "discarding chronology as a structural principle." Yet "syntax and logical progression" remain essentially unaffected (Rohlfs, 886). It might be added, though, that Grass's experimentation with the simultaneity of past (the Grasses' journey to East Asia in the fall of 1979), present (the Peterses' tour in the summer of 1980), and future (the final phase of the 1980 election campaign after the Peterses' return to Germany) and their postulated simultaneous presence both in the author's consciousness and on paper (see *HB,* 84) can at least claim a certain degree of verisimilitude (see Mews 1983b, 505).

Although the Peterses' journey forms the "central narrative strand," it is the narrator in his dual function of "authorial voice" and "storyteller" who expresses Grass's "global concerns" (Rohlfs, 886–87) and his anxiety about the future. There are, then, topics pertaining to the level of "authorial reflection" from which the purely "fictional" Peterses are "barred"

(891), such as the report about Nicolas Born, Grass's writer friend. While one may agree that the text "has a much stricter structure than the narrator's comments suggest" (892), Rohlfs's suggestion that the structural unity of the text is enhanced by the frame of its nine chapters, which correspond to the nine months of the pregnancy in *Der Butt* (see ch. 7), is unconvincing in that there is no compelling evidence of a pregnancy in *Kopfgeburten*.

Writing nearly twenty years after the publication of *Kopfgeburten*, Stuart Taberner (1999) declares it to be "axiomatic" that the "recurrent textual resonances" in the text have been exhaustively explored (84). One may well question the validity of such a statement in view of the fact that Taberner fails to mention Gruettner's 1997 study on intertextuality (see below), which goes beyond the obvious references to Orwell and Camus and suggests that further explorations of Grass's use of other texts may not be entirely unproductive. But then Taberner is interested in pursuing a different approach, one that he deems more germane to coming to grips with the unorthodox work; he reads *Kopfgeburten* as Grass's "personal manifesto" with regard to the necessity of reconfiguring "the relationship between the politically engaged intellectual and his reading public" by specifically initiating a "dialogue" between the "fictional" Grass and the Peterses because they represent a socially progressive and "liberal" segment of the population that the author must win over as readers to successfully promote both his literary and political agendas (85). As has been noted by other critics, Harm and Dörte are unable to muster much enthusiasm for Grass's concept of the *Kulturnation* (see below) and his "championing of the interconnectedness of writing and politics" (Taberner, 86). The notion of the *Kulturnation* is, in part, intended to combat the "escapism" and the "withdrawal into depoliticized aestheticism" that is characteristic of the *Neue Innerlichkeit,* or new inwardness, prevalent in the 1970s (87) and to which, despite their self-professed political engagement, the Peterses succumb.

In order to escape the "complexity and ambivalence" of their own social environment as well as their indecision with regard to having a child, Harm and Dörte venture on their journey where their "scrutiny transforms the Third World into a stage upon which their flight from personal crises can be acted out" (89; similarly Feldmann, 3, who stresses the voyeuristic element in Harm's filming of slum dwellers). In contrast, Grass manipulates his "personal biography" so as to be able to deal with the complex issue, topical at that time, of writers' "complicity" in National Socialism (91; see Mews 1983b, below) and to assume a position in which he, in his function as narrator, becomes arguably the "true protagonist" (Taberner, 93) of the story. However, the question, which Taberner does not pose, is how Grass — by presenting either his actual or his fictive biography — can bridge the generational gap that exists between himself, the former member of the Hitler Youth and draftee in Hitler's army, and the condescendingly portrayed Peterses, who are unencumbered by the Nazi past. Taberner acknowledges that Grass's "aesthetic strategies," which aim at convincing his potential audience of the necessity to combine writing and politics, are open to criticism. An even more serious shortcoming may be that the text conveys the writer's "aura" and "authority" as well as his representative role — qualities that hardly encourage "democratic participation" (97).

Literature and German Cultural Unity

In one of the first scholarly or, rather, essayistic contributions, Hanspeter Brode (1980a) takes his cue from several German reviewers and states that Grass is wont to contribute a narrative work, which usually hovers uneasily between fiction and documentation and includes a pronounced autobiographical element, to each election campaign. But the only pertinent predecessor of *Kopfgeburten* that Brode cites is *Aus dem Tagebuch einer Schnecke* of 1972, a mixture of travelogue, essay, and campaigning. While Brode's observation that the private conflicts and tensions experienced by Harm and Dörte are indicative of larger problems is apt, his suggestion that there is a triangle of couples consisting of the two teachers, Grass and Ute, and Volker Schlöndorff and Margarethe von Trotta (the filmmakers are also traveling in Asia) is less persuasive, because the women companions of Grass and Schlöndorff have been assigned fairly passive roles.

More convincing is Brode's comment about Grass's multifaceted narratorial role as a world traveler, observant tourist, lecturer at various Goethe Institutes, the (West) German cultural institutions abroad, spinner of tales, autobiographer recalling past events, and note-taking chronicler — a role that allows him to address a large number of topics from overpopulation in India (see also Ulrich 2004, especially 172–75) to the perceived threat emanating from Strauss in the Federal Republic. Above all, however, Brode plausibly avers, Grass is concerned with the prospects of a German *Kulturnation* in the divided country, a topic addressed in different guise in *Das Treffen in Telgte* (see Richter 1982). Yet in unambiguous words of disapproval, which anticipate Gilman and Updike's censure cited previously, Brode condemns the excessively elevated stature that Grass ascribes to writers (see *HB*, 83–84) because of his gratuitous personal "vanity" (256), which manifests itself in his presumptuous assumption that he represents the entire realm of literature and culture in Germany. Although Brode judges *Kopfgeburten* to be a weak and mediocre book, in the end he acknowledges that several of Grass's comments are to the point — for example, his observations about the essential failure of the reform of the educational system in the Federal Republic.

In my article on *Kopfgeburten* (1983b), I likewise emphasize the centrality of Grass's literary concerns (as does Cory 1983, 528; see below) but I extend my discussion beyond the concept of the German *Kulturnation* and address the "role and function of literature in society" or, in terms especially relevant for Germany, the "precarious relationship between 'Geist' [spirit, intellect, mind] and 'Macht' [power]" (506). It is the Peterses who serve Grass as examples of the beneficial effects of reading fiction. As former student protesters, they are used to considering literature irrelevant for solving social problems and to attributing validity to the slogan about the "death of literature" (see chapter 8). Not ordinary tourists passively viewing the customary sights but citizens concerned about Third World problems related to overpopulation and malnutrition, they wish to rationally explore social conditions in the countries they visit. Yet ironically, on Bali, their last stop before returning home, they succumb to "irrationalism and wishful thinking" (508) — largely under the influence of two novels, Vicki Baum's *Liebe und Tod auf Bali* (1937; *Tale of Bali,* 1937) and Eric Ambler's thriller *Passage of Arms* (1959), which they read voraciously and which lead them to temporarily imagine themselves in the roles of the respective novels' protagonists. Grass's fairly extensive use of intertextual references to the two novels, as well as a host of past and present writers (Armin Arnold 1985, 139, and Gruettner 1997, 23–24, provide a complete listing of names and titles), serves as a means to demonstrate that especially in their capacity as teachers Harm and Dörte, who rely almost exclusively on "specialized knowledge . . . tables, summaries, and fact sheets" (*HB,* 124–25) and are thus representative of a general intellectual malaise, need powerful stimuli to reinvigorate their withered faculties of imagination.

Not surprisingly, the Peterses are not able to muster much enthusiasm for the author's major concern: "the threat to the continuity and unity of German culture and literature in a politically and ideologically divided nation" (Mews, 511), which culminates in the unrealized project of a "National Endowment" (*HB,* 122), originally proposed by former Chancellor Willy Brandt. As in *Das Treffen in Telgte,* Grass, albeit in uncharacteristically modest fashion, "naïvely" postulates that German writers have proved to be "better patriots than their separatist rulers" (*HB,* 14); in view of the two German states' inability to conceive of themselves as parts of one "cultural nation," Germany remains essentially a "literary concept" a (*HB,* 6), a concept that Grass and his friends such as Nicolas Born sought to promote in semi-clandestine meetings with their East Berlin colleagues in the 1970s, until the GDR's expatriation of singer-poet Wolf Biermann in 1976 put an end to those gatherings and initiated a new phase of repression for GDR writers. In the Federal Republic, Grass's opposition to Strauß, whom he perceives as a formidable threat to writers' independence, focuses on the latter's characterization, in the manner of an "East German apparatchik, a Chinese Red Guard, or [Nazi minister of propaganda Josef] Goebbels" of (dissident) writers as "rats and blowflies" (*HB*, 43 et passim). The author's resolve, in Manheim's infelicitous translation, to "gnaw at consensus and shit on the newly laundered tablecloth" (*HB*, 121) derives in large measure from Grass's conviction that writers have an obligation to speak out — precisely because of the lessons of the past in general and the debate about *Stunde Null* or, as Manheim has it, the "fresh start or zero point" (*HB*, 19–20), which took place in the fall of 1979 and which Grass integrated into his text (see Mews, 511–14), in particular. On the one hand, Grass rejects the notion that there was an entirely new literary beginning after the Second World War; on the other, he shows a certain degree of understanding for the writers of the so-called "inner emigration," that is, anti-Nazi writers who continued publishing during the Third Reich — at the risk of having to make compromises with the regime — and who continued their literary activities after 1945. In defense of his older colleagues Grass offers his own fictive autobiography (see also Krüger, 1980), and he reiterates his opposition to and disdain of the "New Subjectivity" (see *HB*, 68–69; see also chapter 8), which so thoroughly contradicts his own concept of literature.

Sisyphus in "Orwell's Decade"

In her short essay, which appeared before the publication of the English translation of *Kopfgeburten* and was presumably intended as a general introduction for the American reader interested in world literature, Judith Ryan (1981) posits that *The Flounder, The Meeting at Telgte,* and *Headbirths* form, after the *Danzig Trilogy,* Grass's second, "dystopian" trilogy on account of their common features such as their indulgence in "flights of fancy," their hewing to the "primacy of narrative" without entirely absorbing "fragments of reality," and their bold and playful hovering "between fictional and historical or 'real' time" (564–65). But her thesis, which Ryan advanced before Grass's other texts of the 1980s were available, is based on rather broad criteria and has not found any adherents. As to the Orwellian features of *Kopfgeburten* — Orwell and "Orwell's decade" are invoked repeatedly (*HB*, 67 et passim) — Ryan concludes unflatteringly and not entirely correctly that "Orwell's nightmare of bureaucratic despotism has been reduced to the dithering of a featureless couple over whether to have a baby" (567).

Mark E. Cory (1983), who disregards generic distinctions and calls the text a "novel" (525 et passim), argues that Grass has shifted his emphasis concerning the problems to be addressed in the 1980 election campaign. Whereas in *Aus dem Tagebuch einer Schnecke* (1972), which is based on Grass's strenuous involvement in the 1969 pre-election activities (see ch. 6), the snail served as an apt metaphor for the slow progress of societal reforms in the Federal Republic, the new focus on problems in the developing countries, particularly "overpopulation and chronic undernourishment" (524), require a different approach, which comes to the fore, for example, in Harm and Dörte's journey. This plot element allows Grass to contrast the high birthrate in Asia (China represents somewhat of an exception owing to its strict regulations with regard to the number of children a family is allowed to have) with the Peterses' vacillation with regard to their potential offspring. The "specter" (525) of the Germans "dying out," alluded to in the subtitle, is directly attributable to the indecision of Harm and Dörte (and to that of other couples/women of childbearing age). Grass's startling "headbirth," which has received considerable attention on the part of reviewers and critics, is neither an entirely idle speculation nor an exclusively politically motivated ploy to poke fun at the "doomsayers and fearmongers of the CDU/CSU" (Mews 1983b, 502), who are so concerned about the insufficient number of children born to sustain a stable population.

Although Grass reserves his "most cutting satire" for the Peterses as representatives of an entire "generation of liberal, politically active young professionals" (Cory, 525), he also acknowledges their sincere desire to explore global problems firsthand by having them sign up for a travel agency with the atypical name of "Sisyphus" — a reminder of the author's previous engagement with Albert Camus's *Le mythe de Sisyphe* (1942; *The Myth of Sisyphus,* 1955; see also ch. 1). Hence Harm, undeterred by Orwellian threats (temporarily), adopts Sisyphus as his model in his labors to promote the cause of democratic socialism and advances to the status of the "absurd hero battling the absurd; he is the hero of history [and of the story]" (*HB,* 80). In implicitly rejecting claims — for example, those by Gilman and Updike, cited above — that "politics and art do not mix" (532), Cory finds the "speculative novel" (531), which is indicative of the narrowing gap between Grass's "public and narrative personae" (532) an appropriate medium for the author's participation in the election campaign.

In "An Orwellian Decade?" Heinz D. Osterle (1985) is one of the first critics to address the Orwellian features of Grass's text in some detail. Osterle seeks to demonstrate that, although Orwell's "nightmare vision" (481) has not materialized in the 1980s, Grass's adoption of a terminology of "apocalyptic fear" results from a "pronounced radicalization of his political views" as well as a "darkening of his creative vision" (482).

Osterle bases his analysis largely on chapter 5, the "ideological and structural center" (486), which has references at the beginning to Orwell and at the end to Camus and presents a "satirical view" of the convergence between East and West, between Communism and socialism (487). Whereas the Orwellian references tend to invite despair, those to Camus offer a modicum of hope owing to the "existential activism and humanism" that Sisyphus projects (490; see *HB,* 80–81). Osterle supplements his essay with a discussion of Johano Strasser's essay, "*1984:* Decade of the Experts?" (1982), which, he convincingly claims, may be profitably used as a "commentary" (491) to *Kopfgeburten,* inasmuch as Strasser addresses concerns, such as the arms race, that are also articulated in Grass's text. Furthermore, Osterle establishes the close correspondence between *Kopfgeburten* and the author's public speeches — "Orwells Jahrzehnt" (*WA* 9:844–52), the second of Grass's election campaign addresses by that name, given in February 1983, is appended to the essay.

In his detailed textual analysis, Frederick Alfred Lubich (1985) singles out Grass's preoccupation with the future as the feature that distinguishes *Kopfgeburten* from his previous work, in which he sought to negotiate the political problems of the present by delving into the past via his narratives. Both Orwell's Big Brother and Camus's Sisyphus advance to figures on which Grass projects his hopes for and fears of the future. In the Peterses Grass has created his first prototypical couple of the postwar period; Harm and Dörte are unfettered by the Nazi past (unlike, for instance, teachers Eberhard Starusch and Irmgard Seifert in *Örtlich betäubt*) and have experienced their socialization as adherents of the student protest movement; in contrast to their Grassian forbears during the Third Reich, they radically question the legitimacy of their state, the Federal Republic. In another departure from the orientation of previous generations, the Peterses are more worried about their assumed responsibility for contributing to the solution of Third World problems than with their consideration of national affairs; in addition, Dörte's wishful thinking about becoming pregnant by a dark-skinned Asian amounts not only to a complete rejection of the Nazi doctrine of racial purity but also offers an ironic comment on Orwell's savior myth, which is based on the unconquerable and incorruptible proletarian (Lubich, 398–99).

German history, Lubich suggests, provides illustrative features of the Orwellian dystopia in that both the Third Reich and the GDR represent totalitarian regimes, albeit of a distinctly different nature. Since Grass's "headbirth" of a regular exchange of the two German states' socioeconomic and political systems proves to be impossible to realize (see *HB,* 71), the author substitutes the aforementioned endeavors to preserve German cultural-literary unity (see Mews, 1983b) and to overcome the differences between capitalism and Communism — an endeavor that met with the defensive reactions of both states and induced Grass to resort to the myth of Sisyphus to characterize the toils of his existence as a politically committed writer. At the same time, the absurdity of striving for individual self-realization in the Orwellian state suggests that both Big Brother and Sisyphus have become the representative figures of a civilization in which the powerlessness of the individual and the omnipotence of the (both ideological and repressive) state apparatus is increasing (Lubich, 403).

As discussed previously, ever since the term *Danziger Trilogie* became established in Grass criticism in the 1970s (see ch. 4), there have been occasional attempts to find traits shared among three of Grass's subsequent works that would justify the use of the label "trilogy." The thesis Ryan presented in her article of 1981 did not gain wide currency; from the vantage point of 1997, Frank Brunssen, who concentrates on Grass's prose texts from the 1980s, rejects her claim that *Kopfgeburten* is a failed "updated version of Orwell's *1984*" (63) and both implicitly and explicitly proposes a different kind of trilogy consisting of *Kopfgeburten, Die Rättin,* and *Zunge zeigen* (see ch. 11), on account of the significant globalization of Grass's perspective in these works. Thus Grass now pays increasing attention to the future of our world, a world that is threatened by nuclear holocaust and other catastrophic events, and anticipates it in his fiction. Related to this new orientation is Grass's radicalization of narrative structure, which he achieves by ignoring conventional genre distinctions. According to Brunssen, it is the absurd in general and Grass's reception of Camus in particular that provide the key for the understanding of the Grass texts from the 1980s (16). Although several critics have addressed absurdist features in *Kopfgeburten* (see, for example, Lubich 1985) and other works, Brunssen justifiably claims that a thorough investigation of Grass's appropriation of Camus has been lacking. He sets out to fill this lacuna in considerable detail and concludes that the ambivalent tension resulting from the specific dialectic of enlightenment and absurdity (196) informs the entire trilogy but that this specific dialectic can be most easily grasped in Sisyphus's full awareness of the futility of his incessant attempts to return the rolling stone to its starting position in *Kopfgeburten*. Grass explicitly invokes the Sisyphus myth as interpreted by Camus and ultimately identifies with the mythic figure by asserting the ideas of rational enlightenment in the face of the absurdity of rampant progress that is heading for self-destruction — even though, it might be added, not all of Grass's fears have materialized in the post-Wall world.

Like Brunssen, but independently of him, Mark Martin Gruettner (1997) emphasizes that subjects articulated in *Kopfgeburten,* such as the arms race, overpopulation, poverty, and starvation in the so-called Third World or developing countries, and potential ecological disasters (not yet foregrounded by Grass) point toward Grass's other texts of the 1980s rather than backward to his previous works; hence the narrative constitutes a turning point in his orientation and creativity (21–23). Unlike Brunssen, Gruettner postulates the interconnectedness of Grass's extraordinarily frequent intertextual references on the one hand and his both literary and political concerns on the other. It follows that the various modes of intertextuality, the theoretical basis of which Gruettner briefly explores in his introduction (23–24), serve Grass as a means of *Zeitkritik,* the appraisal and analysis of contemporaneous issues that embrace, as indicated before, both global problems and those of a domestic nature. To the latter category pertain, for example, the 1979/80 election campaign in the Federal Republic, the dangers of a potential police state in the Federal Republic, the relations between the two German states, the highly controversial NATO *Doppelbeschluss* (twin-track decision) of 1979 about the stationing of medium-range nuclear missiles in the Federal Republic, and the Federal Republic's relations to developing countries (24).

Gruettner goes beyond the customary analysis of the significance of both Orwell and his counterpart Camus in *Kopfgeburten* and includes a brief section on Nicolas Born that is more extensive than the remarks about Grass's friend which are to be found in other criticism on *Kopfgeburten.* In the same vein, Gruettner relates the aforementioned novels, Baum's *Liebe und Tod auf Bali* and Ambler's *Passage of Arms* (see Mews 1983b) more closely to contemporaneous political and social events; in addition, he examines the intertextual markings related to the German classic authors Goethe and Schiller — the former is cited by cited Dr. Wenthien, the nearly omniscient tour guide who recommends *Liebe and Tod auf Bali,* "a subtle masterpiece" (*HB,* 93), and lends Dörte his copy of the novel. Moreover, Gruettner includes other, non-literary, reading matter of the Peterses, such as the publications of the Club of Rome, a non-profit, non-governmental global think tank, in his analysis, which refers both to literary texts (including Grass's own) as well as non-literary writings (59). Both kinds of writing serve as a vehicle for the writer to voice his manifold concerns in an original fashion. Although, in view of the richness of intertextual allusions, Gruettner finds it necessary to be selective, he offers a fairly substantial contribution on Grass's use of intertextuality, a literary device that the author uses deliberately in order to voice his concerns; hence the exploration of intertextual references is of central significance for the study of *Kopfgeburten.*

10: *Die Rättin / The Rat*

A "Catastrophic" Book

IN NOVEMBER/DECEMBER 1985 *Die Zeit* published the first and fourth chapters of *Die Rättin,* Grass's new prose narrative of indeterminate genre (the author deliberately omits any classification), and the Berlin newspaper *Der Tagesspiegel* serialized it (see H. L. Arnold 1997, 160). The printing of the first chapter in *Die Zeit* was accompanied by a brief but highly laudatory review from the pen of Fritz Raddatz (1985) who praised the book as a work of fiction of extraordinary power and unfettered imagination that presents a prophecy of doom of global dimensions and still manages to create suspense despite its complicated structure. The narrative, available in bookstores at the beginning of March 1986, pertains, it has been argued, to the category of "Katastrophenliteratur" prevalent in the 1980s, a period named "Orwell's Decade," and seems to be the "literary expression" of the "doomsday scenario" (O'Neill 1987a, 213) that Grass projected in his Rome address of November 1982, "Die Vernichtung der Menschheit hat begonnen" (*WA* 9:830–34; "The Destruction of Mankind Has Begun"). Literary texts dealing with (anticipated) catastrophes on a major scale, such as Christa Wolf's *Kassandra* (1983; *Cassandra,* 1984) and even more so Grass's dark vision about the future of humankind in *Die Rättin,* appeared to be vindicated by, for example, the world's worst nuclear power accident at the reactor at Chernobyl in the Ukraine, then part of the former USSR, in April 1986 (see H. L. Arnold 1997, 159; Ignée's 1986 contribution on *Die Rättin* appeared, not entirely coincidentally, in a volume devoted to the apocalypse in twentieth-century literature).

It is an indication of Grass's fame or notoriety that his new publication attracted attention of a dubious kind: even before the book was available in bookstores, a full-fledged parody by an anonymous Günter Ratte under the title *Der Grass* became available. As was to be expected, the reviews of *Die Rättin* in major newspapers and periodical publications are mixed, inasmuch as Grass once again challenges critics' presuppositions. Joachim Kaiser (1986) of the *Süddeutsche Zeitung* writes less effusively than Raddatz but essentially in a complimentary vein about Grass's abundant imaginative faculties, which are said to enable the writer to create an apocalyptic feature, a mixture of picaresque novel and saga (Kaiser does not follow the habit of others who insistently use the term "novel"), which, however, cannot be perused effortlessly. Kaiser deems it an ingenious idea to have the narrator engage in a running dialog with the rat, a survivalist par excellence who appears as both omniscient "Lese-Ratte" (bookworm) and doom-saying Cassandra — an indication of Grass's genuine concern about the future of humankind. In short, Kaiser believes that *Die Rättin* surpasses both its immediate predecessors *Der Butt* and *Kopfgeburten*.

In contrast, Beatrice von Matt (1986), writing in the *Neue Zürcher Zeitung,* maintains that *Die Rättin,* although an important work both profound and brooding in its presentation of hideous variants of the demise of the human species, ultimately does not measure up to *Der Butt,* a novel named after a creature that does not engage in the loquacious rat's trendy talk of impending disasters. On the positive side, von Matt attests that Grass shows an extraordinary flair for the women who embark on *The New Ilsebill,* named after the fairy-tale fisherman's wife as well as the narrator's wife in *Der Butt,* for their voyage on the Baltic, thereby compensating for the misogynist "Father's Day" chapter in the latter novel (see ch. 7). Although she feels that the dreams and tales are overstrained, von Matt acknowledges Grass's dexterity in using film techniques. Another Swiss journalist arrives at a similarly ambivalent analysis (Krättli 1986).

Not surprisingly, there is no dearth of negative voices. Günter Schäble (1986) in *Der Spiegel* polemicizes against the author by invoking the cliché of Grass, the inveterate harbinger of ill tidings, and condescendingly paraphrases passages from the text in order to hold them up to ridicule. Marcel Reich-Ranicki (1986), writing in the *Frankfurter Allgemeine Zeitung* — his review appeared uncharacteristically late (six weeks after the book's official publication) and had been preceded by Franz Joseph Görtz's supportive report in the same newspaper (1986) about Grass's reading from *Die Rättin* in Switzerland — characterizes the narrative as a "catastrophic" book by declaring it to be the desperate effort of an author who is all too conscious of his national as well as universal responsibility and whose strenuous but futile labors have resulted in an indigestible book for which he deserves pity rather than scorn. Reich-Ranicki dismisses Grass's major themes, such as the threat to the human species emanating from the arms race, the destruction of the environment, and other causes, as suitable for an essay or a speech and considers them far too topical for a work of fiction — an argument that is encountered frequently in Grass criticism and that rests on the conservative aesthetic notion of the incompatibility of literary and topical pursuits. There is hardly any feature that the critic finds praiseworthy; he does not leave the slightest doubt that he considers *Die Rättin* an unmitigated failure.

Other reviewers writing in important *Feuilletons* formulate their objections less harshly. Wolfram Schütte in the *Frankfurter Rundschau* (1986) considers *Die Rättin* a serious disappointment; Grass's listing of factors contributing to the anticipated annihilation of the human race in catalogue fashion — with the notable omission of AIDS — such as the dying of forests and the resultant disappearance of fairy tales, the pollution of rivers and the Baltic, hunger, exploitation, and overpopulation in the Third World, the threat posed by atomic weapons in general and the neutron bomb in particular, and so on, lack the power and imagination that the author has displayed previously as a spinner of Kashubian tales. Even more derisive is the verdict of Günter Zehm (1986) in *Die Welt,* who opines that potential readers do not miss anything by not perusing the work on account of the banality of the figures and constellations as well as the pseudo-topicality of the subjects raised, which are really yesterday's news.

Whereas the somewhat disingenuous complaint on the part of some critics that Grass merely recycles old headlines forms part of the argument with which they seek to pan *Die Rättin,* the environmental magazine *Natur* takes the author's doomsday vision seriously and devotes considerable space to a discussion of *Die Rättin.* Jürgen Schreiber (1986) initially emphasizes the author's customary stellar performance at public readings from his text, which allows the listeners to indulge in both apprehension and fascination, but he cautions that the actual ecological damage surpasses even the imaginative faculties of a writer of Grass's caliber. Schreiber deems the choice of a rat, the hitherto despised and feared creature (in Orwell's *Nineteen Eighty-Four* the threat emanating from a hungry rat suffices to turn terror-stricken Winston into a collaborator; see also S. Mayer 1988, below; for Grass's further borrowings from Orwell, see Neuhaus 1979, rev. ed. 1992, 164–65), a masterstroke in that rats have proved their hardiness despite all attempts to eradicate them; in fact, they thrive in our throwaway society, which is accustomed to heedless consumption and is courting environmental debacle. But the rat, which plays a minor role in some of Grass's previous works (see V. Neuhaus 1999), is only the latest addition to Grass's "literary zoo," which includes eels, a (metaphorical) cat and mouse, a German shepherd, a dachshund, snails, and a flounder, and invites further study. (H. Mayer 1988, does not go significantly beyond a mere listing of Grass's animals; he makes the point, which is not entirely applicable to *Die Rättin,* that they are not symbolical, allegorical, or emblematic, but simply animals. Neuhaus 1993a and 1999 provides a detailed account of the "Rat-Motif"; the title of Köpf's 1987 study is misleading because it does not address the animals in Grass's fictional universe in any detail.) That Grass has rats rather than humans survive Schreiber views as an indication of the author's increasing skepticism with regard to the prospects for a reversal of the course leading to ecological disaster.

According to an overview of one hundred and twenty-one reviews, statistically there is no preponderance of either positive or negative opinions (see H. L. Arnold 1997, 281 n. 9); however, the prevalence of rejections in prestigious publications such as *Der Spiegel, Die Welt,* and the *Frankfurter Allgemeine Zeitung* tends to foster the impression that *Die Rättin* does not generally fare well in the *Feuilleton* — an impression shared by Grass, who once again deplores the state of literary criticism, which prefers personal attacks on the author to a dispassionate analysis of the work in question (see Arnold 1997, 161). In his ominously entitled essay "Literaturkritik: Hinrichtungs- oder Erkenntnisinstrument" (Literary Criticism: A Means of Execution or Insight), Heinz Ludwig Arnold (1986) seeks to scrutinize the cacophony of dissonant and often shrill voices and to ascertain their underlying standards, criteria, and rationales. Arnold goes so far as to suggest that critics who reject *Die Rättin* or discourage the reading of it (see Zehm, above) arrogate the position of censor by discouraging potential readers from coming to grips with the book. Traditional aesthetic norms such as the closed form of a literary text do come into play in rejecting innovative features; for example, Reich-Ranicki consistently and erroneously speaks of a "novel" — a perhaps unwitting ploy that enables him to discard the narrative as not measuring up to its assumed generic requirements. Arnold cites a number of other critics, in addition to Kaiser, who are more attuned to Grass's innovative open-narrative form, even though some of them perceive the occasionally playful, ironic treatment of the apocalyptic scenario as inadequate to produce genuine concern and shock. Those reviewers take a differentiated approach that is a far cry, Arnold maintains, from the desire of some to ridicule and ultimately muzzle a writer whose obstinate political engagement is a thorn in the side of reviewers, in particular conservative reviewers.

Volker Lilienthal (1988) challenges Arnold's thesis that politically motivated resentment is at the bottom of the negative opinions about *Die Rättin* by presenting his analysis of fifty-five reviews, of which he finds only three clearly inspired by a conservative political stance. On the whole, he claims, the response of the critical establishment has been largely favorable, owing in part to a successful public-relations campaign by the Luchterhand publishing company, which resulted in the appearance of the vast majority of reviews almost simultaneously with the availability of the narrative in bookstores. In contrast to both the author's public declarations and Arnold's thesis, Lilienthal discards the notion that Grass has become a victim of a conservative reversal of trends (on the political scene, in 1982, the governing social-liberal coalition of SPD and FDP was replaced by the so-called black and yellow coalition of CDU/CSU and

FDP); rather, as many contributors to the *Feuilleton* (as well as Arnold) point out, there does exist a textual tension between the prophecy of doom on the one hand and the considerable entertainment value of the narrative on the other.

The issue of the validity of the journalistic criticism in general and the criteria applied in the case of *Die Rättin* in particular is revisited by Hans-Christoph Graf von Nayhauss (1990; see also Boßmann 1997, 68–70) who examines forty-one newspapers, thirteen magazines, and two radio broadcasts in terms of their appraisal of the text. Nayhauss summarizes his findings in two statistical tables. In the first of these he categorizes headlines according to key terms used (in descending order of frequency): rats, apocalypse, fairy tale, dream, hopelessness, aesthetics, and miscellaneous. While such statistical approach may appear to be too mechanical a tool for complex literary analysis or, rather, the analysis of criticism, the table does provide, at a glance, the focal points on which the discussion of the narrative hinges (in her detailed analysis, Sabine Gross, 1996, argues that Grass's use of language in *Die Rättin* contributes to unsettling the reader by reinforcing the prevalent skepticism of the narrative.) The second, rather detailed, table provides basic bibliographical information (publication, author, date of publication, and title), assigns to each review a positive, balanced, or negative marker, and summarizes the theme, genre, and number of strands of the plot identified by the respective critic. In general, Nayhauss tends to agree with Arnold (1986) in finding the quality of reviews seriously wanting — as is evident, for example, in their previously mentioned inclination to interpret *Die Rättin* in terms of a novel. The inability of the critical establishment to analyze the text properly then gravely undermines the function of those charged with mediating between author/text and readers.

"The Age of the Rat"

Upon the publication of the German original, G. P. Butler (1986) paid tribute in the *Times Literary Supplement* to Grass, the "prolific artist" who has been "long regarded as Germany's most remarkable, living writer." At the same time, Butler adds a cautionary note by proposing that the author should make an effort "to make the accessibility of [his] messages a higher priority than before" in order to attract that segment of potential readers who still need persuading that the wholesale "destruction," depicted in the narrative, is a real danger. "Ideally," Butler writes, persons wishing to peruse *Die Rättin* — although the English translation had not yet appeared, it is to be assumed that Butler primarily had in mind English-speaking readers without knowledge of German — should prepare themselves by reading, "at the very least," *Die Blechtrommel* and *Der Butt*, because, for instance, of the resurfacing of both Oskar Matzerath and his grandmother, Anna Koljaiczek, from the former novel and the "talkative turbot" or Flounder from the latter. Hence he proposes the publication of an annotated edition, which, indeed, became available (for German readers) shortly after in the *Werkausgabe* of 1987 (see *WA* 7:466–93). As to the persuasiveness of Grass's dark vision, the "prospect of annihilation," Butler would have wished for a sharper focus; however detrimental the devastation of forests by acid rain, for example, may be, shining a spotlight on the supreme "threat of extinction" would seem to have called for "less sophisticated resources, wiles and tools" than those the author has at his command.

One of the first, extraordinarily short, American reactions is that by literary historian Henry Hatfield (1986) who, curiously and without further elucidation, states that Grass continues his drift toward the "European left, further away from his former attachment to the USA" — conceivably, a reference to Grass's widely commented militant stance at the International PEN Congress, held in February 1986 in New York City (see Mews 1989, 327–28) — and, in dubious fashion, classifies the text as a satire of excessive length.

In response to the English translation by Ralph Manheim under the title *The Rat* (in the text, Manheim uses the more appropriate term "She-rat"), which came out in the summer of 1987, Butler (1987), in a note in the *Times Literary Supplement,* objects not so much to the occasional Americanism to be found in the text as to the presumable "policy decision" on the part of the publisher(s) (according to an established practice, Secker & Warburg in London, and Harcourt, Brace in San Diego, CA, formerly of New York City, published the book) of shielding the "Anglophone public from the full impact of Grass's wordy ways" by omitting words and phrases on a fairly consistent basis. In an article that appeared in a scholarly journal the following year, Butler (1988) provides a non-inclusive list of specific examples of how the text has been "doctored" (491) and pleads for the inclusion of "succinct notes" that will direct the readers' attention to the fact that they are not perusing the complete narrative. In view of the pronounced dearth of explanatory annotation (*The Rat* includes only two pertinent notes; see *R* 171, 348), Butler reiterates his previous suggestion of providing instructive aids to help the reader understand and enjoy the text. Despite his assumption that "*The Rat,* like *Die Rättin* is unlikely to become part of any literary canon" (492), Butler emphasizes the significance of translation as a "creative activity" (495) that tends to become ever more important in view of the (English-speaking) reading public's increasing unfamiliarity with foreign subject matter. Whether market pressures, among other factors, will allow translators sufficient time to practice their craft to the fullest extent of their abilities and produce a product along the lines indicated by Butler remains to be seen.

Michelene Wandor (1987), writing in the *New Statesman,* is not concerned with problems related to the translation; she provides a brief, albeit fairly complimentary, summary of this "apocalyptic novel [sic] which goes further" than any of Grass's other works "in plumbing the dangers of our nuclear age." Yet the reviewer detects a ray of hope in the narrator's stance and the interspersed poems.

The American responses to *The Rat* range from highly complimentary to (benignly) critical. Writer Eugene Kennedy (1987) in his review in the *Chicago Tribune* is most effusive in his praise by characterizing the narrative as a "dazzling book" in which Grass "like the magician Merlin . . . touches his wand to the Waste Land of the contemporary imagination and sets it blooming vigorously" in a bold evocation of the "post-human era" that arises from "his poetic vision of the present." Unlike some other American reviewers (see, for example, Gray 1987), Kennedy tends to agree with the political thrust of the narrative, which is evident in Grass's "scalding, ironic attacks on the leadership that has already led us into the post-human era" and deems, in anticipating current debates about national security versus civil liberties in this country, his "bitterly sardonic examination of a world that loses its freedom by betting everything on security [to be] among the most provocative in modern literature."

Like Kennedy, Christopher Lehmann-Haupt (1987), writing in the *New York Times,* does not consider the apparently "impossibly jumbled and confusing" plot elements a drawback; on the contrary, he regards the narrative as "seamlessly welded together." As to the underlying politics, Lehmann-Haupt poses the rhetorical question of whether Grass's satirizing and complaining about such familiar issues as the "cold war, mutual deterrence, nuclear arms, radioactive fallout, art-loving neutron bombs" and similar phenomena are boring and concludes that the author's irrepressible exuberance prevails in the end — albeit not to the extent that *The Rat* is of a quality comparable to that of his major works, *The Tin Drum, Dog Years,* and *The Flounder.*

Lehmann-Haupt's review in the *New York Times* is followed by a second one in the *New York Times Book Review,* authored by Jeanette Turner Hospital (1987). She concentrates on the astonishing structural features of the narrative, on "all six story lines," which are "encroaching on each other, . . . doubling back on themselves" in a manner resembling advanced film techniques but are still able to hold the attention of even middle-aged readers "averse to special effects and avant-garde intellectual tricks." All in all, Hospital judges the narrative to be a major achievement, an "exhilarating, exhausting, maddening, brilliant, funny and profoundly disturbing novel [sic]." (It may be noted that Butler's call for explanatory notes, cited above, would also have benefited critics; Hospital erroneously locates the Bundestag in Danzig — not a sign of great familiarity with postwar German history.)

Far less flattering than Hospital is Richard Locke (1987), writing in the *Washington Post.* Although he grants that the work "shows every sign of high seriousness," albeit in the "form of grotesque historical comedy and self-reflexive narrative technique," it displays a fatal "combination of leaden whimsy, indefatigably garrulous debate, and glum narcissism," which ultimately dooms the narrative despite some evident strong points, such as Grass's offering a "modern Book of Revelation" as well as a "loud and clear" message by calling for solidarity in the face of impending dangers. Polish writer Jaroslav Anders (1987), writing at some length in the *New Republic,* is perhaps even more negatively inclined than Locke. Whereas other critics stress the rich array of plot elements, a structural feature that implies a surfeit of action, Anders professes to have experienced the "odd feeling that very little happens" in the narrative and dismisses the exhortations of the She-rat as "crude generalities" that appear to parody the "radical indignation of the '60s." Furthermore, Anders opines, "there is nothing . . . that makes this contribution to the literature of moral anxiety artistically compelling and intellectually credible." In particular, he singles out the not entirely far-fetched "absence of any sense of proportion" on the part of Grass that comes to the fore in his equating the Federal Republic with the Third Reich, the United States with the Soviet Union, and the Federal Republic with the GDR.

In a similar vein, but ratcheting up the scale of disapproval, Paul Gray (1987) in *Time* attributes the perceived failure of *The Rat,* its "endless jeremiad about the despoliation of the earth" as well as its "preachiness" that "grows fatiguing and self-negating," to Grass's increasing tendency not to be able to keep "literature and crusades" separate — a familiar criticism that emanates from a somewhat restrictive concept of what constitutes the boundaries of the realm of letters. D. J. Enright (1987) of the *New York Review of Books* returns to structural concerns and distinguishes "four main narrative strands" (there is no unanimity among reviewers as to the exact number of plot lines), of which he finds the one concerned with deforestation and the disappearance of fairy tales the "liveliest and most original." On the whole, however, the "dislocated and tangled narratives make arduous reading," even if "Grass's inventiveness remains unsurpassed." Hence Grass is the writer who can undertake the task of depicting the results of the anticipated "Big Bang" with "panache, gusto, wild and gritty humor, with numbing bitterness, and with traces of pathos . . ." (46).

There are no analyses or statistical compilations with regard to the American response in newspapers and review organs comparable to those of the German reactions discussed above. However, it is fairly apparent that there are, apart from questions concerning the quality of the English rendering, no fundamental differences in the critical spectrum of voices, which range from wholesale acceptance to unadulterated rejection.

Apocalypse and (Feminist) Utopia

Although the demarcation line between reviews, examined above, and first scholarly responses to *Die Rättin* is somewhat in flux, as the article by Jürgen Grambow (1986) in the prestigious GDR publication *Sinn und Form* demonstrates, academic literary critics did not hesitate to tackle *Die Rättin*. At any rate, Grambow does provide a fairly detailed account, which surpasses the customary length of reviews, together with a general overview of the narrative. He relies on extensive references to Grass's previous work but also alludes to the highly selective practice of the GDR authorities with regard to making Grass's texts available to readers in that part of Germany. In general, Grambow's account is not marred by overt toeing of the party line; perhaps as a minor concession to official doctrine, he singles out the episode of painter Malskat's forgeries (see S. Mayer 1988) as an instance of Grass's succumbing to viewing postwar German history non-dialectically in terms of vulgar Marxism ("vulgärmarxistisch").

Wolfgang Ignée (1986) uses the uncanny coincidence of the appearance of *Die Rättin* a few weeks before the disaster at Chernobyl as a starting point for his argument that the work anticipates the future in "realistic" fashion (386) by foretelling the entirely imaginable annihilation of humankind by humans themselves. Grass had articulated his apprehensions in speeches and appeals as well as by participating in protests and demonstrations, notably those against carrying out the stipulations of the NATO *Doppelbeschluss* or twin-track decision of 1979 about the stationing of medium-range nuclear missiles in the Federal Republic, ratified by the Bundestag in November 1983. Hence the endgame in Grass's novel begins in Europe with the exchange of medium-range missiles. The cause for the occurrence of the "Big Bang," Ignée argues, is the doctrine of nuclear deterrence, which has paralyzed the rational faculties of politicians in both East and West; they have suppressed the lessons of the first use of atomic bombs in Hiroshima and Nagasaki. In view of a not-too-distant catastrophe, which Grass, according to Ignée, judges to be inescapable, the author has lost virtually all traces of optimism, even though there are remnants of gallows humor in this remarkable book, a book that requires the reader's full concentration. It is precisely the postulated inescapability of the ultimate debacle that is implicitly or explicitly rejected by other critics, for example by Patrick O'Neill (1990), who emphasizes the parodistic, "postmodernist" element in Grass's "prophecy."

In a speculative vein, Reiner Scherf (1987) posits the possibility that the cycle of the fall from grace and the apocalypse may be reiterated in the posthuman world, which is populated by rats. Speculations of this sort are supported by the narrative structure, which pits the first-person narrator, who is to be distinguished from the authorial "I," against the initially noncommittal creature of his dreams, the She-rat, who, however, assumes increasing importance with her insistent reiteration that humankind merely exists in her memory and has actually disappeared — an assumption that serves as the confirmation of her conviction that the rats' genetic makeup has equipped them to become true survivors. But, Scherf argues, the contradictions inherent in the story of the Watsoncricks, the genetically engineered "rat-men or hominoid rats" (*R*, 308), named after the discoverers of the DNA structure, James Watson and Francis Crick, are indicative of a revolutionary myth underlying the text, which contradicts the goals of the Polish Solidarność or solidarity movement in that Solidarność was based on the renunciation of violence and displayed a specifically Polish variety of Catholicism. However, such an argument is unconvincing in that it is the Watsoncricks' failure to practice solidarity that dooms them — whereas the rats, in most instances, adhere to the team spirit (see Kniesche 1991).

In her feminist investigation of women and the women's movement in *Der Butt* and *Die Rättin*, Barbara Garde (1988) analyzes the staging ("Inszenierung") of women's examination of (male-dominated) scientific research in the latter narrative and notes that Grass chooses atomic overkill, ironically triggered by a computer program called "'Peace Among Nations'" (*R*, 97), rather than ecological disaster or gene manipulation, topics that aroused feminists' concern in the 1980s, as the immediate cause for the demise of humankind. Although Grass takes explicit notice of the research activities of the women on *The New Ilsebill*, he portrays them as essentially following male patterns of scientific inquiry. Similarly, the women's raid on a Danish institute for genetic research is characterized by spontaneity and lack of justification. The fate of both the ratty creatures that the daughter of a well-to-do Hamelin burgher gave birth to and the Watsoncricks is indicative of Grass's rejection of putting into practice everything that is scientifically conceivable and attainable. Yet *Die Rättin* displays hallmarks of political science fiction; for example, the narrator, as the sole surviving human being, is confined to a small space capsule circling the earth, semi-human beings surface, and the dominant human beings are replaced by rats. Inasmuch as science fiction has usurped the topic of female power, Garde notes, the feminist utopia Vineta may be subsumed under that literary category. Although the women on *The New Ilsebill* have learned to express solidarity with their sisters, they have failed to extend it to other creatures. Hence the feminist utopia fails, and the women are incinerated by the nuclear blast; the survival skills of the rats have proved superior to those of the women.

In her wide-ranging essay, in which she investigates the relationship between the concepts of utopia and apocalypse in Grass's work from *Aus dem Tagebuch einer Schnecke* to *Die Rättin* in general and the writer's role as a prophet ("Seher") in particular, Sigrid Mayer (1988) buttresses her arguments with references to the author's speeches and essays, notably the 1987 essay "Im Wettlauf mit den Utopien" (*WA* 9:715–36; Racing against Utopias), which combines impressions from Grass's travels in Asia with an interpretation of the dystopian novel *Berge, Meere und Giganten* (1924; Mountains, Seas, and Giants) by his "teacher" Alfred Döblin. Mayer states that a noticeable shift in Grass's outlook has taken place after *Der Butt*, in that the future rather than the past has become a matter of serious concern. Unlike most literary scholars, Mayer meritoriously and extensively refers to the author's graphic work as an important source of Grass's gradual conceptualization of *Die Rättin* and a significant interpretive aid. She considers the narrator's dreams, which range from nightmares ("Angstträume") to pipe dreams ("Wunschträume"), a traditional means of effectively conveying the many nuances of a spectrum that ranges from apocalypse to utopia. Indeed, "A beautiful dream" (*R*, 371) is the last thing the She-rat says before she dissolves.

In agreement with other scholars, Mayer establishes the important distinction between the She-rat as the narrator's interlocutor — the gender-specific designation suggests a kind of intimate relationship that lacks the appallingly dreadful associations evoked by the rat in Orwell's *Nineteen Eighty-Four* (see Schreiber 1986) — and as an ordinary specimen of the species that are usually referred to in the plural as "Ratten" or rats. In tentatively seeking to unravel the diverse strands of the plot Mayer does not confine herself to a summary listing but endeavors to relate the various elements to the dominant theme of wholesale doom. For example, the incorporation of the forged "Gothic" wall paintings during the 1951 restoration of the Lübeck cathedral, the Marienkirche, which suffered severe bomb damage in the Second World War, by the aforementioned East Prussian Lothar Malskat allows Grass to portray them as indicative of the "'phony fifties'" (*R*, 200) and their chief political representatives, Konrad Adenauer in the Federal Republic, and Walter Ulbricht in the GDR. Mayer argues that the question of the role of political forgers should be extended to the 1980s, the decade of impending atomic disaster, and she reads the motif of "Utopia Atlantis Vineta" (*R*, 70), the hoped-for matriarchal realm that is inhabited by rats, as signifying Grass's farewell to the feminist utopias that are hinted at in *Der Butt*.

Mayer identifies Oskar Matzerath, as the chief connecting link between the narrative strands and the simultaneously approaching end in both East and West. Matzerath is involved in filming the dying forests and their fairy-tale figures and is also associated with the painter Malskat. Most importantly, however, his visit to Poland on the occasion of his grandmother's 107th birthday shortly before the "Big Bang" serves as a means to undermine any notions of salvific history in that the mummified bodies of both Anna Koljaiczek and Oskar Matzerath, whom the rats assume to be her son, become sanctified objects of worship in Danzig/ Gdańsk's Saint Mary's Cathedral. If seen in conjunction with other indications, notably the occurrence of the "Big Bang" on a Sunday, the "seventh day of a bungled creation . . . chosen to cancel out [the previous week]" (*R,* 105), as the She-rat pontificates, this veneration amounts to a reinterpretation of the Judeo-Christian concept of the apocalypse on the part of Grass. The reinterpretation might be seen as a travesty of the conventional perception of both apocalypse and utopia and leaves the door open, Mayer argues, dissenting from other scholars, for questioning the inevitability of humankind's demise.

For Irmgard Hunt (1989) an obvious contrast exists between the profound skepticism with regard to the course of events in the 1980s that Grass expresses in speeches and other public utterances and his far less unambiguous stance in *Die Rättin,* in which he appears to hover between utopia and dystopia, between resignation and guarded optimism, a position that has been influenced by Marxist philosopher Ernst Bloch's *Das Prinzip Hoffnung* (1954–59; *The Principle of Hope,* 1986). Hunt writes that Grass designed Vineta as a utopia with reservations in that, on the one hand, the submerged city inspires hope in the women of *The New Ilsebill* but, on the other, their hopes are undermined by both the narrator's satiric touches in depicting them as well as his tendency to engage in self-mockery. The boat itself appears to represent a secluded, self-sufficient world, and the ship's name, with its reminiscences of *Der Butt,* seems to signal a utopian potential, which, however, is diminished by the quarrels among the women.

In a conciliatory mode (unlike, for example, Pusch in her 1988 review), Hunt cites an instance of outright male chauvinism on the part of the narrator: his description of the women's ritual of getting dressed leisurely in their best outfits, applying their makeup, and so on, in preparation for entering Vineta. Their ceremonial, time-consuming activities are ill-conceived because they will be obliterated by the "Big Bang" before achieving their goal. (Hunt judiciously observes that the women could have hardly lived in Vineta because human beings' existence under water is inconceivable; a compelling if common-sense reason for utopia remaining beyond the women's reach.) Inexplicably, Hunt neglects to mention that the city, which because of male folly was swallowed by water in 1284, seven hundred years before 1984, the year that Orwell chose for his dystopian vision, is occupied by rats (the narrator does not offer any explanation as to how they survive), which prevents the women from achieving their goal of inhabiting it.

Fairy Tales

Walter Filz (1988) briefly elaborates on the significance of the fairy tales and their often noted and explicitly stated connection with forests, the romantic and symbolic locus of the mystical and mythical. Hence the ravaging of the forests does signify not only an ecological but also a cultural debacle: "for fairy tales / . . . / are dying with the forests" (*R*, 9; see also Garde 1988, 254–61). Contributing further to the destruction of the fairy tale is the considerable scholarly attention it has received since the 1970s in disciplines such as *Germanistik,* psychology, sociology, and pedagogy — an attention that tends to reduce the fairy tale to a circumscribed meaning and to limit or destroy its utopian potential. As Filz states, Grass pronounces the death of the fairy tale, which no longer offers any prospects for the future and does not permit a return to a presumed idyllic past.

Although hardly a critic fails to refer to the fairy tale(s) in *Die Rättin,* these references are often rather cursory. Norbert Honsza (1988) in his brief remarks deems the "politicized fairy-tale satire" (178) to be below Grass's standards and lacking an overall design — an opinion that is disproved by the thorough discussion-cum-analysis by Jürgen Barkhoff (2000) who places the fairy tales in their proper context by reminding readers that the various editions of the *Kinder- und Hausmärchen* (1812; *German Popular Stories,* 1823) by the Brothers Grimm are, next to the Luther Bible, the best-known and most widely available book of German cultural history not only in Europe but worldwide. It appears that the fairy tales have even survived the momentous shift from the Gutenberg galaxy to the present pictorially and visually dominated universe. Grass views the fairy tale as a specifically German form of narrative; hence the narrative strand based on the fairy tales constitutes a kind of intertextual updating of the originals by resurrecting the Grimm Brothers' best-known figures, having them revolt against the dying of the forest, march on Bonn, then the capital of the Federal Republic, and form a government headed by the Brothers Grimm.

Barkhoff credits Grass with tackling the ecological crisis in his fiction of the 1970s and 1980s to an extent that remains unparalleled in the imaginative literature of the German-speaking countries (for details, see Hunt 1992a, Morris-Keitel 1996; see also Yalin Feng 2006) — as evidenced in *Die Rättin* by addressing the harmful superabundance of jellyfish in the Baltic, and the decaying woods. Coincidentally 1986, the year in which Grass's narrative was published, was declared the year of the forest (see Barkhoff 157 n. 11–12), and this announcement met with a far greater resonance than any other issue on the agenda of the environmental movement. Such approving reception can only be explained, Barkhoff plausibly argues, by the preeminent place of the forest in German cultural memory, a memory that originated in Romanticism and to which the Brothers Grimm contributed significantly by making the forest the symbolic repository of popular and oral tradition. Hence the demise of the natural realm of the forest also signifies the loss of the identity-forming cultural mode of remembrance that has the fairy tale at its center.

In *Die Rättin,* the fairy-tale figures appear in the context of a film script that Oskar Matzerath and the narrator develop jointly. Initially listless and resigned to their fate, the fairy-tale figures gain a new lease on life through the arrival of Hansel and Gretel, the Chancellor's children, who introduce a new method to counter the threat of extinction by engaging in protests in the manner of the environmental movement. "'All power to the fairy tales!'" (*R,* 272) is the new slogan signifying empowerment in the face of the government's environmental policy, which is driven by purely economic considerations of profit maximization and influenced by special interest groups. The fairy-tale figures' uprising is then a mobilization of cultural memory to thwart the ecological dangers and, at the same time, an evocation of the subversive and utopian potential inherent in the fairy tale.

Grass's intertextual use of the fairy-tale world is quite intensive, Barkhoff notes, and the references are clearly marked so as to enable readers to peruse *Die Rättin* on the basis of their cultural memory and their horizon of expectations and thus to make them receptive to the protest potential that the author provocatively assigns to the fairy tale. In a radical departure from the Brothers Grimm, Grass reinterprets their figures as dedicated to the corporeal in general and the sexual in particular. For instance, the Seven Dwarfs are "rough, noisy fellows, crazy about their dice games" (*R,* 183) who have frequent intercourse with poor, emaciated Snow White; the wicked stepmother acts as the madam of the brothel and collects the coins for services rendered by Snow White. Such emphasis on the sexual clearly runs counter to the editorial intent of the Brothers Grimm, who sought to remove anything from their fairy-tale adaptations that smacked of violating sexual and other norms. It is not only Grass's well-known propensity for the earthy, Barkhoff claims, that induces the author to describe the witch (in Hansel and Gretel) filling the tank of an old Ford with her urine, which serves as a gasoline substitute, in great detail (see *R,* 132); rather, scenes like these serve to emphasize the carnivalesque and grotesque elements that, according to Mikhail

Bakhtin's *Rabelais and his World* (1968), are intrinsic to popular culture and open up a future-oriented dimension.

The fairy-tale figures in *Die Rättin,* at any rate, lead a life that is far removed from that recorded by the Brothers Grimm — a situation that induces them to distance themselves from their reinterpreted creations. In Grass's reading, the Brothers Grimm provide an alibi for the structurally unchanged condition of industrial society; they are unable to prevent the disappearance of the fairy tale and the fairy-tale figures' habitat, which, in the end, is brutally annihilated by huge "'dragon bulldozers'" (*R,* 317). Yet the lack of a happy ending is not to be construed, Barkhoff avers, as resignation; rather, Grass displays the tendency both to enlighten and to warn. Even as he acknowledges the powerlessness of cultural memory, Grass views cultural memory as remaining an indispensable part of human civilization.

Narrative Strategies

The unusual narrative structure of *Die Rättin* has induced several critics to concentrate on the analysis of those features that Grass uses to tell his tale(s). In his essay on the author's "Doomsday Book," which was written shortly after the publication of *Die Rättin,* Patrick O'Neill (1987a) aptly characterizes the "basic narrative structure" as a "narrative duel" between the narrator and the She-rat, a duel that entails a "contest of stories, worlds, realities" in that the narrator adopts "feinting [and] shifting" as a strategy and thereby seeks to postpone the (perhaps) inevitable end whereas the She-rat, in "monolithic and linear" fashion (214), exposes his delusions.

O'Neill goes to considerable length to sort out and identify the "collection of narratives," which are interwoven in a non-linear, "complex, flickering narrative statement" (214); he includes the reinterpretation of the legend of the Pied Piper of Hamelin, who in 1284 liberated the city of a rat plague by enticing the rats to follow him into the Weser river, where they drowned. In the narrator's version, it is not primarily the rats that were lured to their deaths but the nonconformist, counterculture youths of the Middle Ages, albeit with their pet rats. The year 1984 signifies then not only the seven-hundredth anniversary of the event in Hamelin; it is also, ominously, Orwell's year as well as "according to the Chinese calendar . . . the year of the Rat" (*R,* 12) and, in a further linkage to another narrative strand, in 1984 Oskar Matzerath turns sixty.

In the final analysis, it is the "relationship between the narrator and the also narrating rat" that functions as the "driving force" of the narrative (220). Yet O'Neill distinguishes between the first-person narrator, the "Ich" or "I," who cannot be simplistically identified with the writer

Grass, and a "Narrator" or, in the terminology of narrative theory, an "'implied'" rather than an actual, "empirical" author. This distinction is necessary on account of a kind of reversal of roles: in the poem at the beginning of the eleventh chapter (see *R*, 311–12) it is no longer exclusively the narrator who dreams (of) the She-rat; rather, the She-rat dreams (of) the narrator — a constellation that raises the difficult question as to "who is dreaming whom?" This question can be answered, at least to some extent, by resorting to the aforementioned "Narrator," who balances and juxtaposes the two competing "narrative voices" (O'Neill, 221). (It is not entirely coincidental that the ambivalent relationship between narrator and She-rat is articulated in a poem; in her 1988 essay, Claudia Mayer emphasizes the often disregarded significance of poems in *Die Rättin* as thematic structural features that provide important clues.)

Like O'Neill, Erhard Friedrichsmeyer (1989) refers to the term "Doomsday" in the title of his essay, but he discards the notion that *The Rat* corresponds to the perception usually associated with that word, that is, a "prophecy designed to frighten us into [sic] our wits" (29). Rather, Friedrichsmeyer concentrates on narrative aspects, among which he singles out the "narrative preponderance of the rat" (21), which constitutes a remarkable departure from the "traditional literary depiction of rats" in that Grass does not harp on "our primal fear" (23) of that species. On the contrary, Friedrichsmeyer writes, in *The Rat* Grass seems to temporarily "abdicate as a writer" in that he delivers not the customary "stock-in-trade doomsday prophecy"; rather, he offers a book in which there is "little" that is not "funny" (27). The pervasive humor, which Friedrichsmeyer finds so dominant and that, perhaps, might more appropriately be called gallows humor, "highlights the essential ambiguity" of the text that "avoids a teleological finality" (31) and leaves the door open for the hope that, after all, doomsday may not occur.

Inge Diersen (1990) discerns a somewhat different and, presumably, unnecessarily complicated narrative pattern in which the narrating "I" occupies the center of what she terms the two plot lines of the "Realhandlung" or actual story, which consist of Oskar Matzerath's visit to his grandmother and his return and the women's Baltic excursion and their return. The first narrative level is supplemented by a second one, in which the narrator and Oskar Matzerath discuss the latter's video projects, notably those concerning the forger Malskat and the fairy-tale forests. But as the most important level Diersen designates — incontrovertibly — the dialogue between narrator and She-rat, which essentially turns the narrative into a dialogic treatise. The dialogue amounts to a "Warnutopie" or cautionary utopia, in that the end of human beings is evoked in order to prevent it from happening. In view of the overriding importance of conveying his bleak message (which is not conceived of as entirely bleak by all critics; see, for example, Friedrichsmeyer 1989) Grass foregoes originality and uses the clichés of science fiction and horror literature. In order to arrive at a somewhat manageable structure, Diersen surmises, Grass dispenses with delving into Third World problems, which preoccupied him in the 1980s. Rather, in Eurocentric fashion, he has the nuclear catastrophe take place in Europe or, more specifically, in Danzig/ Gdańsk. Yet despite the predominance of a scenario of gloom and doom, the ending, as others have observed with varying degrees of emphasis, remains ultimately ambiguous.

Explicitly or implicitly, the question as to how literature can deal with the "End of the World" — the phrase forms part of the title of Julian Preece's 1990 essay (see the discussion below) — is raised fairly frequently. Franz Josef Görtz (1990) offers a somewhat idiosyncratic reading of *Die Rättin* by dismissing the criticism of the German *Feuilleton,* invoking the image of the writer as Sisyphus, and concentrating on those aspects that relate the narrative to Grass's previous work. By shifting his focus from the arguably central theme of the nuclear holocaust to Grass's texts preceding *Die Rättin,* Görtz is able to declare the narrative to be a continuation and update of the Danzig-saga, one that shows no sign of signaling finality of any sort or constituting a farewell to both letters and life.

Julian Preece (1990) returns to the narrative structure and addresses the "duel of words and stories" between the narrator and the She-rat, an ongoing debate in which the latter assumes the position of "spokeswoman of the rat population." Yet, Preece mentions, in tacit agreement with O'Neill (1987a), it is not entirely clear "who is actually dreaming whom" (321). Although he deems *Die Rättin* to be Grass's "most overtly political book" since *Aus dem Tagebuch einer Schnecke,* Preece finds, somewhat in the fashion of Friedrichsmeyer, the "suitability of the literary means" problematic and inadequate for dealing with the "monumental theme." The results are simplifications and a "loose" structure that is "devoid of any genuine plot and tension" (324). Grass's "fiction against the Bomb" is then a "failure" (325), which, in turn, is indicative of the failure of the Enlightenment with its emphasis on reason. Moreover, the "explanation" of the imminent holocaust (which may have taken place already, if we accept the version of the narrator's surviving in a space capsule circling the devastated earth) that Grass provides in his "parabolic account" is reduced to the "point of banality" (327) — clearly a point on which there is no unanimity. But then the author reacts to the menace of "nuclear extinction" in writerly fashion, that is, "by telling stories" (333). Preece omits to mention Grass's numerous essays that precede and supplement his literary activities, a public engagement that, perhaps, may delay the (inevitable) end.

A different tack is taken by Susan C. Anderson (1991), who seeks to explore the relationship between "fact and fiction" on the basis of the pervasive "struggle for truth" that is occurring on all levels of the narrative and that manifests itself particularly vividly in the "conflict between the authorial narrator and the [She-]rat" (107). Conceivably, Anderson stretches her argument too far when she takes the narrator's plaintive ruminations about the end of human life on earth (see *R,* 268) to be a "questioning of the whole narrative" that betrays not only "its fictionality" but also casts doubt on the "validity of the doomsday message" (Anderson, 108). The narrator's insistent reiteration of "maybe" at the beginning of each of his statements would seem to suggest a high degree of uncertainty with regard to the continuance of life on earth rather than an outright rejection of the catastrophe proclaimed by the She-rat. On the whole, however, Anderson's thesis that Grass "undermines the imminence" of the depicted global disaster by "ironically exposing its fictionality" (111) and subtly encouraging readers to mistrust that which masquerades as truth essentially corresponds to other critics' claims.

In extending his investigation to the reception of *Die Rättin,* Klaus H. Kiefer (1991) stresses the incompatibility of the narrative structure and the critical response on the part of journalists whose traditional training in literary analysis leaves them unprepared for a work that is characterized by a Kafkaesque ambivalence in hovering between nightmare and actuality, takes place in the "Post Futurum," and calls into question — especially after the catastrophe at Chernobyl — the efficacy of both safety measures designed to prevent a nuclear holocaust and texts warning about imminent disasters. Yet Kiefer surmises (correctly in view of the considerable scholarly attention, notably via published dissertations) that, among other factors, the narrative's indeterminate genre will continue to serve as a stimulus for further research. Largely on account of the brief synopses in the manner of Grimmelshausen that precede each chapter, Kiefer opts for the classification of *Die Rättin* as a novel. Although Kiefer does not consider Grass to be a postmodernist writer (see also Kniesche 1991, 60–61), he detects postmodern features such as the use of simulation, a concept developed by French social theorist Jean Baudrillard in his *Simulacres et simulation* (1981; *Simulacra and Simulation,* 1994). Baudrillard holds that, owing to the dominance of images in the media age, the implosion of the boundaries between image (simulation) and reality or, in the Grassian context, the blurring of distinctions between the real and the fictive, is inescapable.

Polyphony and Immanent Poetics

The scholarly essays that appeared in the late 1980s were supplemented by a slew of dissertations published in the German-speaking countries in the decade between approximately 1988 and 1997; they are entirely or in substantial parts devoted to *Die Rättin* and originated mostly independently of each other. The majority of these dissertations may be said to emphasize the formal-structural means the author employs to render his apocalyptic vision — even if, as Friedrichsmeyer and fellow critics have pointed out, Grass's artistic devices may not always be adequate to the task.

Among the first of these dissertations is that by Klaus-Jürgen Roehm (1992). Whereas Preece claims that in *Die Rättin* Grass "has moved away from the polyphony of *Der Butt*" (328), Roehm considers polyphony and improvisation to be the structuring principles of the text (which he questionably calls "Roman," or novel) — albeit not in the Bakhtinian sense of a polyphonic narrative, in which there is no dominant or indisputably authoritative voice among several others. Rather, Roehm posits, Grass uses the formal trick of dividing the authorial perspective among three different figures, none of whom attains the psychological depth of a fully developed character (see 7 n. 4). Roehm begins his discussion with an analysis of the narrative strands more detailed than that found elsewhere (for example, O'Neill 1987a; Kiefer 1991; see Neuhaus 1979, rev. ed. 1992, 172–80, for a detailed account). Like Preece, he recognizes the She-rat's role as the representative and spokesperson of all rats in that she never speaks in the first-person singular, preferring the collective "we." The antagonistic relationship of rats and humans is evidenced by the division of world history into the three phases of human, posthuman, and neo-human; these three phases constitute the first strand. The first phase begins with the divinely ordained mythological Flood and ends with an apocalypse, the man-made nuclear holocaust. The rats survive both cataclysmic events because of their solidarity and cunning. The second phase sees the dominance of the rats and the absence of humans, and in the third phase the "Watsoncricks," the upright-walking human rats, products of genetic engineering, subjugate the common rats until they revolt and exterminate their oppressors.

The second strand, which Roehm entitles "Damroka" after the captain of *The New Ilsebill,* combines the topic of female emancipation from *Der Butt,* which in *Die Rättin* assumes the form of the search for the female utopia Vineta (see S. Mayer 1988), with that of the articulation of ecological problems (the measuring of the harmful jellyfish concentration in the Baltic) that have now assumed paramount importance. Oskar Matzerath, a character whom hardly any critic fails to mention, is at the center of the third narrative strand; as in the case of Damroka, there is a bifurcation in the plot in that, on the one hand, Oskar Matzerath perishes in the atomic blast at his grandmother's birthday party; on the other, he returns from Poland to West Germany and undergoes a prostate operation. The fourth strand is that of the despoliation of the forests, the erstwhile breeding ground of fairy-tales (see Filz 1988 and Barkhoff 2000). As the last narrative strand, Roehm identifies the Malskat affair, the shortest episode, and the only one that is authentic and well-documented. In addition, Grass establishes the connection between Malskat's forgeries and the two postwar German states, which, during the Cold War, have become allies and junior partners of the respective victorious superpowers. In doing so they have managed to distance themselves from assuming accountability for the lost war and coming to terms with the question of guilt, by abandoning their national responsibility to pursue ways to overcome the division of Germany (see also S. Mayer 1988).

Yet the various narrative strands do not exist independently of each other. Roehm analyzes the transitions between them; these transitions are accomplished via stylistic means, which include the use of certain words or phrases associated with two or more segments of the plot, and the employment of a whole array of motifs, analogous to the leitmotif technique in musical compositions. For example, the sinking of the *Wilhelm Gustloff* and the *Cap Arcona* (for a detailed account of the sinkings, see Bond and Preece 1991/92) during the end phase of the Second World War are mentioned in conjunction with the stories about "Damroka," Oskar Matzerath, and the rats. Above all, cohesion is achieved by the three narrator figures, whom Roehm defines differently from O'Neill (1987a) but plausibly as the authorial "I," which assumes diverse roles and engages in dialogues with the She-rat, an equal and persistent partner, and Oskar Matzerath. Matzerath serves mainly as a foil of the authorial "I"; ironically, he achieves a measure of independence by contradicting his creator in the narrative strands in which he is involved. The auctorial narrator's repeatedly invoked lack of omnipotence with regard to his interlocutors then serves the self-referential purpose of drawing attention to the process of narration itself, which is characterized by the commingling of heterogeneous elements, time dimensions, plot elements, and the blurring of logic and causality; analytical thinking has been replaced by an associative, albeit controlled, procedure.

The three narrators' notorious unreliability, while frustrating on the one hand, signifies the spontaneity and arbitrariness of an "open" form on the other. In addition, the often farfetched associative linkages are indicative of a meta-novel that thematically foregrounds its origins and reflects on the manner in which this is done at the expense of a fully cohesive and coherent narrative. Thus Roehm considers the writing of *Die Rättin,* which takes place at the auctorial narrator's desk while he is listening to the Third (cultural) Program on the radio the sixth narrative strand. The process of writing can be observed in the auctorial narrator's playful variations of the Hamelin legend, which betray his desire to improvise and to renounce sober, definitive finality.

Oskar Matzerath's video production draws attention to the film techniques, also noticed by other scholars, which Grass employs as a structuring device of his narrative. Furthermore, the auctorial narrator assumes the role of script writer with regard to the Watsoncricks' flight and annihilation in Gdańsk harbor — an episode that narratologically resembles a filmic rewinding effect in referring back to the Watsoncricks' arrival in the same place. Moreover, in his space capsule the narrator perceives the world through the objective of a camera via the pictures on his monitor. He is, in the literal sense, the "Mann mit Überblick" (*WA* 7:361) or "the man with the panoramic view" (*R*, 293), but, at the same time, the narrator with an overarching perspective (for other examples of film techniques, see Auffenberg 1993). Roehm carries the analogy of narrative techniques and those of film even further by suggesting that the five narrative strands correspond to five TV channels that are constantly being changed. Yet the rapid switching of channels is performed by the auctorial narrator, who remains ultimately in control even in the event of interferences or the brief appearance of phantom images that are indicative of the predominant associative structural principle.

Next to the film technique it is Grass's handling of the dimensions of time that is most characteristic of the polyphonous form. The She-rat reports on the human and posthuman time phases from the perspective of the neo-human period in the present tense, a procedure that signifies that this era is the She-rat's present. Yet there is a tendency to blur the temporal proportions as, for instance, in the auctorial narrator's blending of the story about the Pied Piper of Hamelin with that of the Watsoncricks and thereby intermingling medieval times with those of a dystopian future. This kind of temporal juggling is ultimately attributable to Grass's concept of "Vergegenkunft" (see Auffenberg 1993), which in turn reflects the author's view of the cyclical nature of history, in which most events have been predetermined and human beings are essentially powerless to change its course (see, for example, Oskar Matzerath's speech on the occasion of his grandmother's birthday, in which he refers to his anticipatory video; *R*, 227–28). If the narrative appears to dispense with the criterion of probability, Roehm argues, then the fantastic and fictional become part of the real via its reflection of the mechanisms of imagination that take place in the auctorial narrator's consciousness. Despite his emphasis on formal, structural aspects, Roehm concludes his insightful and convincing study with a brief passage on the apparent contradiction between Grass's sharp, encompassing criticism of tendencies and developments in the early 1980s, when the crumbling of the Berlin Wall and the subsequent end of the Cold War could not yet be anticipated, and the often playful, ironic stance that seems to undermine such criticism but essentially conveys the author's defiant attitude in the face of nearly insurmountable odds.

Separately from Roehm, Christian Auffenberg (1993) provides a comprehensive reading of the "immanent poetics" of *Die Rättin,* which he deals with in conjunction with *Die Blechtrommel,* and offers a detailed analysis of those elements of the narrative that articulate the poetological principles underlying the text and, in their totality, amount to the author's aesthetics, which Auffenberg interprets as being based on the denial of absolute truth as well as the assumption of an ambiguous empirical reality. Hence the She-rat is the embodiment of doubt and skepticism; specifically, she epitomizes qualities such as religious tolerance, faith, altruism, imperviousness to totalitarian regimes, and above all, the ability to learn from mistakes — all traits that human beings lack. Endowed with such characteristics, the rats have become the scapegoats of human history in analogy to the Jews (see *R,* 41), and the Pied Piper of Hamelin has evolved into the paradigm of the political leader as seducer in general and Hitler in particular.

In concurrence with the majority opinion, Auffenberg assumes the concept of *Vergegenkunft* (97) or, in Manheim's translation, "paspresenture" to be central in Grass's concept of time, a concept that is based on seeking to overcome the linear, successive sequence of events and replace it with a depiction of their simultaneous occurrence. Thus the She-rat as the personified future (a position that does not prevent her from casting her glance as far backward as Noah's Ark), the narrator as the representative of the immediate present, and Oskar Matzerath as the agent of the recent past (who, however, also anticipates the future in his video productions) all tell their tales, which are then "synchronized" (105) by the narrator. This narrative procedure is analogous to film techniques in general and that of "'cross-cutting'" (106), the film practice of alternating views of one action with views of another to create the impression of simultaneity, in particular.

At the same time, the continuing narrative signifies the continuance of existence, an existence in which dreams function as a chief means of gaining insight. Similarly, the fairy tales provide an additional perspective, which both supplements and contradicts that of, for example, politicians, who justify their actions by invoking "Sachzwänge" (*WA* 7:62; "appeals to realism," *R,* 48). Hence fairy tales serve as the source of a flexible, dynamic concept of history, yet their chances for survival, as most scholars have pointed out, are slim indeed. As indicated above, Grass considers film techniques an important vehicle for conveying his perception of reality because of the dominant presence of media in the transmission of news and the shaping of insights and perceptions. He goes so far as to include elements of science fiction and comic strips in his narrative so as to promote a mode of novel, enlightened, and insightful thinking that goes beyond that of the Enlightenment goal of the "education of the human race" (*R*, 1) as formulated in Gotthold Ephraim Lessing's *Die Erziehung des Menschengeschlechts* (1780; *The Education of the Human Race*, 1858). Auffenberg's detailed analysis of the elements of such new thinking tends to buttress his claim of having offered evidence of the extraordinary coherence of Grass's narration.

"Post-Apocalypse"?

As pointed out previously, the word apocalypse, which is conventionally interpreted in terms of the Judeo-Christian tradition in general and the Book of Revelation in particular but in the 1980s had become a commonplace in the *Feuilleton*, recurs with considerable frequency in reviews, and it is the term that is used by a significant number of scholars to indicate the focal point of their approach. It may be noted, however, that Grass rejects the applicability of the term to *Die Rättin*, inasmuch as in his text the end of the world has not been ordained by God; rather, it is entirely the result of human failure (see Ubben 2001). Thomas W. Kniesche (1991) takes a different approach from the critics and scholars cited before by seeking to analyze the "genealogy of the post-apocalypse" in *Die Rättin* in a decidedly postmodern investigation that draws liberally on the insights provided by psychoanalysis (notably Sigmund Freud and Jacques Lacan) and intertextuality (Mikhail Bakhtin, Julia Kristeva, and others) in both the text under discussion and other works by Grass.

Kniesche begins his detailed investigation with extended references to the inflationary use of the term "apocalypse" in West Germany in the 1980s and observes that it has become devoid of any religiously or philosophically transcendent meaning and is perceived as a distinct threat without any hope for redemption. Because Grass's conception of the apocalypse is based neither on religious notions nor on those of a postmodern philosophy of despair but clings to the hope of achieving a better world via concrete political engagement in the manner of Albert Camus (see Brunssen 1997), Kniesche finds the applicability of the term to Grass's text problematic. Hence he suggests "post-apocalypse," a term that implies both (partial) dependence on and the rejection of tendencies associated with the expression during the 1980s. Or, as Kniesche states paradoxically, Grass's post-apocalyptic text is an apocalyptic text that is directed against (the traditional notion of) the apocalypse (see 49).

As a writer in the tradition of the European Enlightenment, Grass deplores its aberrations, especially its reduction to technology and the exploitation of nature, the delegation of decision-making to computers, and the exclusion of the subconscious — interdependent tendencies and practices, Kniesche avers, that form the dominant themes of *Die Rättin.* In view of the failure of humankind to live up to the ideals of the Enlightenment, it is the rats, practitioners of a collective way of life in the face of dominant human egotism, that are truly enlightened. Kniesche proceeds from the explicitly stated connection between rats and Jews (see *R*, 41 et passim) as the victims of persecution and devotes an entire chapter to the exploration of the question of individual and collective guilt in conjunction with the so-called *Historikerstreit* or historians' debate that revolved around the assumed singularity of the crime against the Jews and was initiated, he claims, in 1986 (actually, in 1980, although until 1986 the topic was primarily the province of historians without much resonance in the public sphere) by Ernst Nolte and Andreas Hillgruber. Particularly the former put forward the thesis that the holocaust was a reaction attributable to Hitler's fear of the Bolshevik (and Jewish) retribution that would befall Germany if not stopped by drastic means that had their precedents in the Russian Revolution of February and October 1917 and the subsequent establishment of the Gulag Archipelago (The *Historikerstreit* has been documented in the 1987 *Historikerstreit: Die Dokumentation der Kontroverse um die Einzigartigkeit der nationalsozialistischen Judenvernichtung,* edited by Augstein and others.)

In view of the enormous political significance of the dispute, which was seen by leftist and liberal intellectuals and historians as questioning the self-perception of the Federal Republic's democratic foundations, Kniesche plausibly argues that a politically engaged writer such as Grass could not possibly have ignored an issue that revolved around German guilt, a topic the writer had been concerned with since at least *Die Blechtrommel.* However, Kniesche seems to overstate his case when he writes that Grass's (sole?) response to the *Historikerstreit* is to be found in *Die Rättin.* True, Kniesche (87–89) unexpectedly establishes a link between Hitler's alleged fear of a torture method involving rats in the manner of Orwell's *Nineteen Eighty-Four,* which was used by the Bolsheviks, and Grass's use of rats as a metaphor for fear-inspiring creatures. Yet the function of rats cannot be reduced to one role, inasmuch as Grass applies both the terminology and the motifs derived from Freud's psychoanalysis and endows his creatures with multiple and often contradictory meanings — from the dirty, disgusting, parasitic carriers of the plague to the seemingly harmless "rat under the Christmas tree" (*R*, 1) as a substitute for the Christian myth, to mention only two examples. Hence the She-rat in her function as a narrating voice serves as a means of Freudian projection via the subject's transfer of uncomfortable thoughts or feelings onto others, thereby assigning his/her repressed thoughts to convenient alternative targets. Since dreams are a favorite means of projection, the "dreamed" She-rat is eminently qualified to serve as such a target because she enables the "dream narrator," whom Kniesche (142), in proposing a different taxonomy of narrative voices, considers more important than "author" or "narrator," to reject the apocalyptic dream vision. But if the She-rat exists only as a figment of the (dream) narrator's imagination, the narrated apocalypse becomes meaningless, and *Die Rättin* indeed constitutes a "post-apocalyptic" text as defined in deconstructionist Jacques Derrida's *D'un ton apocalyptique adopté naguère en philosophie* (1983; "Of an Apocalyptic Tone Recently Adopted in Philosophy," 1984): it is an apocalypse without vision, truth, or revelation (see Kniesche 147).

The She-rat and her opponents then move in a space beyond chronology and apocalypse; her first words are: "You people used to be . . ." (*R*, 3). Hence the "dream narrator" imagines that he is floating in a space capsule — an indication of his oedipal desire to return to the maternal womb (see Kniesche, 167) but, at the same time, it signifies a fantasy of rebirth that, on the individual level, corresponds to the collective fantasy of a new beginning with a clean slate after each apocalypse, from the biblical Flood and Noah's Ark, to the catastrophe of the Second World War and the subsequent 1950s, to the atomic holocaust and the survival of the rats. Yet the posthuman rats in Danzig merely reiterate human history by ignoring the demands of Solidarność and engaging in confessional wars (see also Scherf 1987). Actually, Kniesche claims, obsessive repetition is, next to the aforementioned positioning of the apocalypse in the past, a defining feature of the post-apocalypse. Therefore Grass tells his stories in various versions so as to establish the supremacy of the ever changing oral tradition vis-à-vis the fixed meaning of the written account. As a result, the author disappears (or assumes a diminished role) and, by disappearing, undermines the effort to convey the meaning of the apocalyptic vision.

Kniesche concludes his rewarding analysis with a discussion of Anna Koljaiczek, a figure he declares to be at the center of events. Oskar Matzerath crawls under the skirts of his grandmother, where he finds warmth and peace at the moment of total destruction. With Oskar's return to the refuge of his childhood in *Die Blechtrommel*, Grass brings to an end a (continuous) narrative that for nearly thirty years had been the cause of heated controversies.

In a rare instance of a direct reply to a preceding scholarly publication, Volker Neuhaus (1992), without questioning the insights proffered by Kniesche, deems the term "apocalypse" more appropriate than "post-apocalypse." Neuhaus proceeds from the designation provided by Klaus Vondung in his *Die Apokalypse in Deutschland* (1988; *The Apocalypse in*

Germany, 2000): the apocalypse is not an event but a text that depicts and interprets an event — precisely the task *Die Rättin* accomplishes. Grass modifies the schema of Judeo-Christian salvific history by omitting the first stage (paradise) and the third stage (the realm of God) and concentrates instead on the second stage, the fall from grace (see V. Neuhaus 1988), the "aion houtos," or eon in which we are living, which is to be followed by the "aeon mellon," or the coming eon after the apocalypse. It follows that the apocalypse holds the promise of salvation for the faithful according to God's inscrutable and inexorable plan. Yet in *Die Rättin* it is the computer programs that have taken over the role of God; in contrast to the anthropocentric apocalypse, there is no salvation for human beings; rather, it is the rats, after they have overcome the remnants of the human legacy, notably in form of the Watsoncricks (Neuhaus 1992, 136, detects an intertextual reference to Orwell's *Animal Farm,* 1945), that offer the only hope for a regeneration of the earth. Humankind's only chance is to learn from the rats (for a differing view, see Kniesche 1991), as Neuhaus (1993a; see also Neuhaus 1999) puts it in one of two articles in which he elaborates on the significance of rats in the work of Grass: ". . . it is up to the rats, which had been excluded from the ark, to rescue creation from man" (1993a, 462). As timeless creatures — they are impervious to human measurements of time — rats are devoid of individualism and think in terms of the collective. Yet there remains an unresolved tension between the "'very last chance'" that may be given to humankind, and the tenor of the She-rat's pronouncements, which amount to a "'too late for ever'" (1993a, 461); this tension is evident, for example, in the different (and mutually exclusive) versions of the Oskar Matzerath and *The New Ilsebill* plots. Moreover, Neuhaus writes, *Die Rättin* features a characteristically open ending that entails both (limited) hopes for the future and abhorrent doom.

More vigorously than Neuhaus, Rainer Scherf (2000) questions Kniesche's position by charging that Kniesche's predilection for postmodern theories as an interpretive tool obscures the underlying appeal of *Die Rättin,* that is, to counter the total destruction caused by humankind via the collective resolve to counter the tendencies fostering total annihilation (see esp. 15 n. 8). Scherf seems to impute to the text an activist thrust that, as has been shown, is not generally accepted.

Intertextuality, the Absurd, Melancholia

Whereas Kniesche's intertextual approach relies largely on psychoanalytic insights, Arnd Flügel (1995), who repeatedly takes issue with Kniesche's conclusions, bases his findings on philosophical premises in general and Theodor W. Adorno's negative dialectics in particular. The title of Flügel's extraordinarily detailed study refers to the various modes of conceptualizing experience ("Konzeptualisierung von Erfahrung") to be found in *Die Rättin.* In Franz von Kutschera's *Grundfragen der Erkenntnistheorie* (1982; Basic Questions of Epistemology), "experience" is defined as a specific kind of the reception (perception) of reality via cognitive processes that enable observers to examine it critically and communicate their experiences via language.

Grass's perception of reality and poetics in the 1980s, Flügel argues in agreement with several other critics, is mostly influenced by his preoccupation with the myth of Sisyphus in Camus's version; for both Camus and Grass, Sisyphus represents the anti-idealistic protester par excellence (see 44). The unceasing labors of the mythical figure resemble those of the writer, who mobilizes the imagination, including the unconscious, as well as both individual and collective repressions and projections and claims them as the legitimate province of literature in order to counter reductive observations of empirical reality.

Following his initial extensive methodological section, Flügel devotes considerable space to the dialogic relationship that exists between narrator and the She-rat with their competing claims. Although, in the final analysis, it is the auctorial narrator who has ultimate control over the narrative, the narrator's self-imposed limitations serve the purpose of overcoming self-imposed defense mechanisms. In a further extensive segment, Flügel deals with the figures that appear in the various narrative strands in *Die Rättin,* which he classifies in essentially the same manner as the majority of scholars. These figures are characterized by ironic refractions; moreover, it not always entirely clear who is speaking (the narrator or the She-rat). It is the poems that allow the narrator to combine the multiple narrative perspectives and let the disparate episodes appear as an ensemble.

In addition to the part of the title cited above, Flügel uses as his motto the often quoted phrase from the initial poem in *Die Rättin,* in which the first-person narrator expresses his desire to tell his story "in an attempt to put off the end with words" (*R*, 8) — a sign of his confidence in the power of language, which may be able to delay the impending catastrophe, even if the words have to be supplemented by other means in order to achieve results. Flügel, who devotes considerably more space to the reading of the poems than virtually any other critic, states that both a poetological and a political claim is implicit in such confidence. As indicated, he views the poems as a form that combines the two narratorial positions, that is, that of the She-rat, who is both the counterpoint of the first-person narrator and a facet of his psyche, and the narrator himself. Thus both the "dreaming" and the "awake" narrator have their say in those poems that reflect the defiant attitude of Sisyphus in the face of terrors to come.

In his 1997 work on intertextuality and its relationship to Grass's *Zeitkritik,* or critique of politics and the public sphere, Mark Martin Gruettner systematically explores the manifold intertextual references according to thematic foci. He begins with the multiple quotations from and allusions to the Bible (see also V. Neuhaus 1992), which the author often uses as a means to represent past, present, and future events in a simplified, black-and-white manner, and proceeds to a brief examination of modern texts in which rats serve as the harbingers of ill tidings and represent the non-human Other, such as Camus's *La Peste* (1947; *The Plague,* 1948) and Jean Paul Sartre's *La Nausée* (1938; *Nausea,* 1949). In a further subchapter, Gruettner discusses the heritage of the Enlightenment, notably on the basis of Lessing's aforementioned treatise, to which the narrator clings. The perversion of Enlightenment ideals makes rats the true inheritors of those ideals; but both Orwell's *Nineteen Eighty-Four* and his *Animal Farm* show the animals' unenlightened, destructive behavior.

In a comparatively extensive section, Gruettner explores the intertextual use of specific fairy tales as well as collections of fairy tales in general (see also Filz 1988 and Barkhoff 2000). In addition to the Brothers Grimm, often cited by other critics, he mentions Hans Christian Andersen, Johann Karl August Musäus, and Wilhelm Hauff; occasionally, however, there seems to be a mismatch between the assiduously listed, plentiful sources and the gain in novel interpretive insights. For example, while it is entirely tenable to argue that the fate of the fairy-tale figures is indicative of the death of literature, such a conclusion does not go beyond what has been generally accepted. Gruettner extends his investigation to Grass's drawing on his own works, notably *Die Blechtrommel* and *Der Butt.* Yet his assertion that Oskar Matzerath has been endowed with an entirely new identity as a "'business man'" and "'concerned citizen'" (116) is unconvincing in that the direction of Oskar's course had been set in book 3 of *Die Blechtrommel* (see ch. 1). Commendably, Gruettner extends his analysis to non-literary sources, including the reports of the Club of Rome, a global think tank, that Grass uses — in addition to the speeches by ex-Chancellor Willy Brandt about the East-West as well as North-South conflicts — to convey to his readers the dire statistics on population growth, hunger, and the environment in literary form. On the basis of Gruettner's findings, it is difficult to disagree with his conclusion that *Die Rättin* constitutes the (preliminary) highpoint of Grass's profuse employment of intertextual means in order to pronounce his warning.

More specifically than Gruettner and without explicitly invoking the concept of intertextuality, Frank Brunssen (1997) focuses on Grass's reception of the absurd in general and of Camus in particular as a key to understanding the writer's texts from the 1980s (16), that is, the trilogy of *Kopfgeburten, Die Rättin.* and *Zunge zeigen.* Brunssen begins his discussion by postulating that an absurd world view is being constituted by the radical negation of three essential passages from the Old and New Testaments: the Christmas story (instead of an ornamental Jesus in a crib, the narrator receives a rat in a cage), the story of the Flood (the rats were excluded from Noah's Ark), and the Sermon on the Mount (it is the She-rat who preaches from a pile of rubbish). The dream sequences serve the important function of demonstrating the absurdity of human history, by having the She-rat relate the end of humankind after the final catastrophe — a result that elicits the dreaming narrator's comment: ". . . that's absurd" (*R*, 100); his assessment is confirmed by the She-rat.

Brunssen, who does not mention Kniesche's study, suggests that Bloch's *Das Prinzip Hoffnung* (se also Hunt 1989) rather than Freud's *Die Traumdeutung* (1900; *The Interpretation of Dreams*, 1913) provides the key for an analysis of the dream sequences in *Die Rättin*, inasmuch as Bloch distinguishes between dreams at night and daydreams or waking dreams. The latter do not ordinarily require an excessive amount of interpretation; their transparency enables the reader to recognize them as daydreams originating in author Grass's imagination. Inherent in Bloch's definition of the daydream is a wishful, utopian component that is also present in Grass's text; however, we learn that the hopes and expectations associated with Vineta come to naught — utopia has turned into dystopia, and the dreams anticipating the future of humanity have turned into nightmares. At the same time, the dream structure serves as a means of reflecting on the discontinuities in the narrative and the lack of a closed form, bemoaned by several critics. As noted before, the abandonment of a linear chronological development is attributable to the concept of "Vergegenkunft" in which past, present, and future occur simultaneously.

Apart from Döblin, whom Grass appreciates for his anti-idealistic depiction of historical processes with their inherent absurdity, Brunssen singles out Samuel Beckett and his *Fin de partie* (1957; *Endgame*, 1958) as a key for the understanding of the absurd course of human history until the "Big Bang." Despite Grass's frequent intertextual references to Beckett's one-act play, there is a decisive difference. Whereas Hamm and Clov are physically and intellectually passive and completely ignorant about the causes of the catastrophe, in *Die Rättin* it is the humans who inflict the final disaster upon themselves. With regard to Camus, Brunssen claims that the participants in the endgame, that is, the human race, have given up Sisyphus's act of rebellion and succumbed to nihilism (for a different view, see Flügel 1995) — a state of affairs that becomes particularly evident in the narrated staging of what amounts to an absurdist play, when the Chancellor and his retinue visit a dead forest in which the semblance of unspoiled nature is created by stage decorations of trees, the sounds of songbirds are piped in, and so on (see *R*, 34–37). Even the

Third Program is not a bastion of Enlightenment; at best, it serves to divert attention from the general rush to wholesale destruction. A further instance of narrated absurd theater is the narrator's dreamed appearance on the rostrum (stage) of the Bundestag, where he gives a speech in Orwellian Newspeak to the delegates (audience) in which he extols the benefits of the "art-loving" (*R,* 179) neutron bomb that kills human beings but leaves works of art, museums, and similar institutions intact. In the final analysis, it is the rats who follow the rebellious tradition of Sisyphus; in a kind of Brechtian estrangement technique Grass portrays the rats as the opposite of what they appear to be in popular perception — a procedure, Brunssen writes, that has not met with universal approval and diminishes the appeal of *Die Rättin* to readers — particularly because the catastrophe happens in a dream rather than in "reality" as, for example, in Franz Kafka's *Die Verwandlung* (1915; *Metamorphosis,* 1946). Furthermore, the narrative is largely removed from contemporaneous events by dwelling extensively on the past and the future. While Brunssen's findings are credible and cogently argued, perhaps an attempt to ascertain the validity of Grass's dark vision in the light of post-Wall events is missing.

Sisyphus is also invoked by Andrej Schulz (1997) in his analysis of *Die Rättin,* in which he initially surveys the development of the concept of melancholia from antiquity to the twentieth century. Schulz posits that Grass's critical examination of *Zeitgeschichte,* or contemporary history, as well as the content, form, and narrative stance of the work, is largely dependent on the "melancholic structure" of Grass's text, and he relates melancholia to the modern theory of utopia, which has assumed a decidedly temporal dimension rather than signifying, as in the Christian tradition, the other(wordly) place, paradise. Yet in order to be able to sound a warning in the face of the dangers threatening the existence of the human species and to achieve a collective change of consciousness to ward off these dangers, Grass foregoes the temptation to dwell in future realms — Schulz's assumption ignores, for instance, the tripartite historical scheme with its future dimension(s) discerned by Roehm.

Melancholy, Schulz claims, springs from the discrepancy between the ideal (utopia) and the real. Far from indulging in a disposition that induces passivity, author Grass believes in the ability of a melancholically disposed collective, which consists of individual readers whose consciousnesses have been affected by perusing *Die Rättin,* to change things for the better. Hence there is a chance of "active resignation" in the process of striving for utopia.

As the preceding discussion has shown, *Die Rättin* has attracted a considerable amount of critical comment, which is based on a wide variety of approaches and underlying assumptions. Perhaps, to use Roland Barthes's terminology in *S/Z* (1970; *S/Z,* 1974), the narrative may be called a "writerly text" rather than a "readerly text"; therefore, it poses a challenge to critics and their interpretive faculties. A further factor that most likely contributes to the continuing interest in Grass's work is the foregrounding of the doomsday vision that, as has been amply demonstrated, was a German preoccupation, particularly during the 1980s, but also resonated in other countries. (Unlike the film version of *Die Blechtrommel,* the 1997 TV adaptation of *Die Rättin* by Martin Buchhorn received only moderate notice.) For example, Henrik D. K. Engel (1997) cites Bernard Malamud's *God's Grace* (1982), a conventionally told novel about the consequences of the nuclear holocaust that is not comparable to Grass's intricate text, as a further instance of the preoccupation with the end of the world in fiction. Surprisingly, writing from the vantage point of 2001, Manfred Durzak assumes a revisionist stance by maintaining (in the face of evidence to the contrary) that Grass with *Die Rättin* suffered his "first great disaster" (186) at the hands of reviewers and critics. Instead of viewing Chernobyl (see, for example, Ignée 1986) as a justification of the fears expressed in the text, Durzak dismisses *Die Rättin* as a homey spine-chiller based on trivial science fiction and recommends Christa Wolf's *Störfall: Nachrichten eines Tages* (1987; *Accident: A Day's News,* 1989) as a vision of genuine horror rather than Grass's cabaret-like doomsday scenario. It does not require a surfeit of imagination to predict that Durzak's assessment will hardly be the final word on this work.

11: *Zunge zeigen / Show Your Tongue*

"The Revenge of Goddess Kali"

ZUNGE ZEIGEN, WHICH WAS PUBLISHED in the fall of 1988, is the result of Grass and his wife Ute's extended sojourn in India from August 1986 to January 1987. They stayed predominantly in Calcutta (Kolkata), capital of British India from 1772 to 1912 and today's capital of the state of West Bengal, a city that also plays a prominent role in the subchapter on Vasco da Gama in *Der Butt* (see ch. 7). Even more so than *Die Rättin*, *Zunge zeigen* is of indeterminate genre, inasmuch as it encompasses, in the German original, a prose text of approximately ninety pages, eighty drawings that are concentrated at the beginning, in the middle, and at the end, and a long epic poem of approximately twenty-three pages — in short, a text that confounded the expectations of some reviewers. Particularly those writing for the leading newspapers and magazines voiced their disapproval, which tends to be considerably more pronounced than in the case of *Die Rättin*. Thus Peter von Becker (1988) in *Der Spiegel* compares his own impressions of Calcutta with those of Grass and finds the author's text seriously wanting; in fact, he characterizes it as a "fantastic disaster" (154), even though he acknowledges Grass's recognition of Calcutta's role as a mirror of the global conflicts between the Third World and the First World, a place that displays the heritage of colonialism, the excesses of capitalism, and the helplessness of the socialist government in West Bengal.

In particular, Becker objects to Grass's dwelling on German literary affairs, notably his wife's incessant reading of Theodor Fontane, the nineteenth-century writer who was going to be resurrected in *Ein weites Feld* (see ch. 13), and his attack on star critic Marcel Reich-Ranicki (who, atypically, did not review *Zunge zeigen* but discussed it in his TV show *Das literarische Quartett* and characterized it as a minimally successful minor work; see Busche, Karasek, Löffler, and Reich-Ranicki 1988). As a result, von Becker notes, the reader learns little about the functioning of Calcutta, a chaotic urban complex with its prevalence of roughly three thousand abominable slums and constant displays of abysmal human misery. Furthermore, von Becker charges, Grass evinces little interest in the astonishingly rich cultural life of Calcutta — a neglect that the reviewer attributes to the revenge of the goddess Kali. On the dust jacket and in a drawing at the beginning of the book, Kali is sticking out her tongue, a gesture that lends the book its title and that Grass interprets as a sign of shame (Shafi 1993, 349 n. 30, contends that Kali is associated with fear and terror but not with shame). Becker applies Kali's gesture to Grass: the author has presumably been robbed of his tongue, that is, his ability to speak and write. Grass's alleged neglect of Calcutta's literary and intellectual life is, at least in part, contradicted by the collection of essays assembled in Martin Kämpchen's *My Broken Love: Günter Grass in India and Bangladesh* (2001). Furthermore, Günter Zehm (1988), writing in *Die Welt,* pointedly rejects Becker's assessment and declares that it cannot be taken seriously; rather, Zehm finds the drawings sensational in a positive sense and discerns sympathy, pity, anger, and desperation as the motivating forces underlying *Zunge zeigen.*

In a comparable vein to Becker, Volker Hage (1988), writing in *Die Zeit,* characterizes *Zunge zeigen* as a failed mixture of diary, travel journal, sketches, and political commentary, intended to instruct readers in Germany but unsuccessful in presenting plastic figures. The quality of the poem at the end seems to surpass that of the prose; in the final analysis, the text betrays helplessness in the face of the phenomenon of Calcutta. Günter Metken (1988) of the *Süddeutsche Zeitung* compares *Zunge zeigen* unfavorably with Salman Rushdie's *Midnight's Children* (1981) on the basis of his own experiences in India, and Harald Hartung (1988) of the *Frankfurter Allgemeine Zeitung* finds the work to be based on mere impressions; he sees Grass's lack of solutions as to how to combat the indescribable misery as a flagrant sign of weakness. Perhaps most acerbic is Peter O. Chotjewitz (1988) who accuses Grass of indulging in trivial loquaciousness and traveling as a voyeur who cannot tear himself away from the misery in Calcutta. To be sure, there are exceptions to the rule of unenthusiastic assessments and downright rejections. As Heinz Ludwig Arnold's summary of sixty-three reviews (1997) shows, the responses do not amount to an entirely bleak picture: Arnold judges thirty-six assessments to be negative, seven neutral, and twenty positive (284 n. 118).

One of Grass's habitual supporters, Fritz Raddatz (1988), defends the author against the charge by some critics that he has fled to India on account of an inhospitable intellectual and political climate in Germany — in part attributable to the reception of *Die Rättin* — by pointing out that Grass's travel plans had been of long standing. Although he finds the attack on the unnamed but easily identifiable Reich-Ranicki unnecessary, Raddatz considers the lack of a genre designation to be unproblematic, in that the combination of diary, sketch book, and poetry provides a balanced view of three of Grass's artistic abilities. Yet, there seems to be an increasing tone of resignation when the artist is faced with the writing on the wall that Calcutta represents. Ultimately, then, *Zunge zeigen* is not so much a work about India in the manner of reportage as it is a testimony to the author's own development and his striving for his self-conception as a writer. Heinrich Vormweg (1988), writing in *Der Tagesspiegel,* implicitly agrees with Raddatz that the work is not a book about India that searches for completeness and objectivity but an account that seeks to recapture those impressions and experiences that made a lasting impact on the writer.

In his survey of reviews, Sjaak Onderdelinden (1992) points out that critics' expectations and judgments have been indubitably shaped by their perceptions of *Zunge zeigen* as either a work of German literature or a contribution to the literature about India — albeit from a Eurocentric or German perspective. Apart from this somewhat artificial distinction, which emphasizes the separateness of two closely interrelated aspects, Onderdelinden uncontroversially concludes that there is no common denominator to be found in the wide spectrum of reviews, which range from complete approval to total rejection. Onderdelinden makes no attempt to adduce criteria for the validity of individual assessments; rather, he views the diversity and incompatibility of critical opinion as an indication that the institution of literary reviewing is alive and well.

While the number of reviews of *Zunge zeigen* in the German-speaking countries cannot match that of works such as *Der Butt* or *Die Rättin,* the critical notice the work received in the English-speaking countries in general and the United States in particular is perhaps even less noteworthy. In May 1989, Grass spent two weeks on a promotional tour that led him from New York City to San Francisco to read from his new book (see Streitfeld 1989). Before the release of *Show Your Tongue* in May 1989 in this country in both hardcover and paperback (in the translation of John E. Woods rather than Ralph Manheim), a descriptive paragraph by an anonymous reviewer in *Publishers Weekly* (1989) concludes that we are dealing with a "radical anti-coffee-table book [that,] though less original in manner and matter than [Grass's] fiction, vigorously protests the complacence of the common traveler, Westerner and reader." Yet, if India is a foreign subject matter to the "Westerner," so are German writers Fontane and Georg Christoph Lichtenberg as well as Grass's play *Die Plebejer proben den Aufstand* (1966; *The Plebeians Rehearse the Uprising,* 1967), which was produced in Calcutta during the author's sojourn, relatively unknown to the American reader — hence the explanatory half-page "Postscript" in the English translation (*SYT,* 222). In the *New York Times,* Clark Blaise (1989), author of the journal *Days and Nights in Calcutta* (1977), writes under the heading "Calcutta is the Measure of all Things" that *Show Your Tongue* is "Mr. Grass's tribute to Calcutta's unparalleled ability to move and engage" — a tribute that, "despite its virtuosity, [is] a modest, very personal book" charting the author's "inner journey to a kind of fundamental, uncomplicated political esthetic." Blaise finds evidence for this aesthetic, for instance, in the book's dedication to the "Calcutta Social Project," an educational undertaking for the children of the most abject of Calcutta's garbage handlers and garbage dwellers. By no means a "softheaded lover of India, not even of Calcutta," the writer has engaged in presenting images that are "unexpungeable" and "invoke an apocalyptic mood." Similarly, Eugene Wildman (1989) in the *Chicago Tribune* deems the "combination of text and images . . . powerful" and the writer driven by "pangs of self-reproach" in the face of the "sheer volume of deprivation" on the one hand and the "complacent apathy of both the middle class and the ruling Communist Party" on the other. In a bold, albeit apt, comparison, Wildman declares scenes such as the description of the inept and self-absorbed government bureaucrats in the Writers' Building to be "pure Kafka" — surely a testimony to Grass's craft.

There is then a marked difference between the rejection of the work on the part of several German critics and the far more sympathetic approach taken by the reviewer in the *New York Times.* It is a truism that the cultural, national, or geographic perspective influences — at least to some extent — critics' opinions about a specific literary text. Whereas, in the case of *Zunge zeigen/Show Your Tongue* the reviews cited above show a considerable range of opinions, the (available) Indian reactions are virtually unanimous in their rejection. In his essay on Grass and India, Vridhagiri Ganeshan (1992) cites Pramod Talgeri (1988) of *The Times of India,* who adamantly refuses to attribute any merit to the "travelogue" and states that the "quality of Grass's writing has degenerated . . . into a piling of nonsensical details about the Indian way of life, in order to generate voyeuristic interest in Calcutta's material plight." Less stridently, but still resentful, Amita Malik (1989), writing in the *Indian Express Magazine,* acknowledges the possibility that Indians familiar with the misery of Calcutta have lost the capacity to be moved by it and then continues: "What irks one most about Grass is that such a gifted writer, one of the most outstanding in our generation, should go about single-mindedly searching for muck."

Not surprisingly, Ganeshan's argument follows similar lines when he maintains that Grass is unable to adjust to India, despite his willingness to do so, on account of his European virtual "niche" that offers refuge and is formed primarily by his wife's constant resorting to reading Fontane and other German writers (according to the concordance provided by Amazon.com, "Fontane" ranks among the one hundred most frequently mentioned terms in the text; his name occurs twenty-eight times). Ganeshan reiterates the objections voiced before, that is, Grass's perceived lack of interest in Indian literary and cultural matters as well as his misinterpretation of Indian politics, as evidenced by his neglect of poet and mystic Rabindranath Tagore, Nobel laureate in 1913 (actually, a passage deals with the Grasses' visit to Tagore University; see *SYT,* 49–54) on the one hand and his misunderstanding of the Bengalese politician Subhas Chandra Bose on the other. These flaws are attributable to the writer's chief interest: the depiction of garbage, slums, and filth (indeed, according to the aforementioned concordance, both "garbage" with sixty entries, and "slum" with seventy occurrences rank very high on the frequency list). However, without offering any explanation of his own, Ganeshan blames Grass for a lack of understanding when faced with the inexplicable cheerfulness of the slum dwellers and concludes that India remains for the author essentially the alien Other that he is ultimately unable to comprehend.

Intertextuality; Mythical Determinism

Whereas Ganeshan relies almost exclusively on the prose text for his findings, Sigrid Mayer (1992) elucidates the "intertextual" relationship between graphics, prose, and poetry and points out that the graphics function dialogically rather than illustratively within the context of the entire work. In addition, there is a pronounced literary discourse, which, Mayer concedes, is primarily focusing on German authors who have virtually nothing to do with modern India and seem to be a distraction rather than an integral part of the text. Yet via his fictive presence Fontane advances to the position of companion and interlocutor of the Grasses; he also provides (indirect) comments on Indian colonial history from the perspective of a contemporary who in the 1850s reported from London on Britain's colonial empire for Prussian newspapers. In fact, Fontane has assumed such an important role that he will again serve as a traveling companion in the event that the Grasses should return to India (see *SYT,* 97; Grass did indeed return to Calcutta in 2005 for a brief visit; see Kämpchen 2005). In addition to Fontane, a host of other writers provide a rich array of intertextual literary dialogue (see S. Mayer, 262–63 n. 30), which is supplemented by that with visual artists and their works, especially with indigenous painter Shuvaprasanna (Shuva). In the end, Mayer states in partial agreement with Ganeshan, it appears that Calcutta cannot be grasped by relying on European standards that are largely derived from the authors mentioned.

Mayer elaborates on the intertextual aspects of the text in a further article (1993), in which she traces the origins of *Zunge zeigen* through its three stages — an artistic endeavor that results in an "explicit discourse on the aesthetics of poverty" (142) by deliberately focusing "on the dialogue between drawing and writing" (145). In deviating from other critics (see, for example, Ganeshan 1992), Mayer credits the author with a "predilection for ways of survival available to the poor" (147). In this context, she notes that Grass's interest in garbage or "Müll" has been of long standing and declares it to have been a "standard resource for [his] graphic and literary inspirations" (147). But Calcutta presents Grass with an entirely new dimension of the garbage problem, in that multitudes live in and off the refuse that they recycle assiduously and for which they have to compete with the ever-present black crows. In the often invoked juxtaposition of slum hovels and the Deutsche Bank "highrise" in Frankfurt am Main (see *SYT,* 21) Mayer does not perceive this passage, as the text suggests, as an "attack on capitalism" or, in a different vein, as a token of the Third World future that may befall countries of the West; rather, she interprets it as a celebration of the "ingenuity of the slum hovel and its insistence on independent survival" (Mayer, 151). Yet it seems to be incongruous to read "the great Calcutta poem" at the end of *Zunge zeigen* as projecting the "vision of a *liberating* [my italics] revolution" initiated by Kali, the goddess of destruction. After all, the survivalist spirit of the slum dwellers is, we may assume, devoid of political or socioeconomic motivations. Hence Kali's concluding words, "I make / an end" (*SYT,* 215), have an apocalyptic rather than a liberating ring (see also Brunssen 1997).

In his investigation of the absurd in Grass's texts from the 1980s, Frank Brunssen (1997) includes an analysis of *Zunge zeigen* in addition to that of *Kopfgeburten* and *Die Rättin* and reads the text as evidence of the "Absurdität des mythischen Determinismus" (absurdity of mythical determinism) as represented by the destructive goddess Kali who, according to Hindu scriptures, dominates the last (and present) of four Yugas or Ages; this age is characterized by sin, disease, and heresy, and it will end with the destruction of all life on earth via a conflagration and floods. Grass's stance vis-à-vis the ever-present Kali, Brunssen argues, is not to accept and to lend credence to the Hindu myth but to demonstrate that Calcutta represents a manifestation of the destructive myth — as evidenced, for example, by the identification of the city's inhabitants with Kali as they assume her favorite position of squatting (the majority of drawings in *Zunge zeigen* showing humans depict them as crouching).

Furthermore, the "black goddess" (*SYT,* 20) determines not only the color of Grass's drawings, for which he selected a particularly black ink; she is also present in the frequently invoked motif of the black night. The metaphorical use of "black" also contributes to the mood of impending doom; the last drawing of *Zunge zeigen* shows "A flock of [scavenging] crows" (see *SYT,* 220–21) as harbingers of coming disasters. Kali's sickle, a tool of destruction, is omnipresent, particularly in the hammer-and-sickle emblem of the Communist Party of India that can be found on the walls of houses. Grass suggests the existence of an unholy alliance between the governing Communists, Kali, and the aforementioned politician Subhas Chandra Bose, who during the Second World War sought to establish an alliance with both Stalin and Hitler in order to gain India's independence from Great Britain. Brunssen remarks that, in contrast to Grass's earlier and later works, the three texts that he is discussing show a "signifikante Globalisierung der Perspektive" (16; significant globalization of [Grass's] perspective) and a concomitant diminishing of the importance of Danzig — a dubious proposition in view of the fact that *Unkenrufe* (see ch. 12) takes place almost entirely in Danzig. Nevertheless, he finds the similarity between Kali and another fear-inspiring mythical figure, the "Schwarze Köchin" of *Die Blechtrommel* (black cook; translated by Manheim as "Black Witch") compelling.

In keeping with the Kali myth, Grass interprets the flooding of Calcutta, which is caused by heavy rain and is reminiscent of the Flood, in apocalyptic terms: the rising waters flush the corpses of victims of religious and political strife to the surface. Hence Calcutta becomes the measure of all things (see also Blaise 1989); it serves as the yardstick for future developments worldwide. At the same time, Calcutta defies reason and a rational approach; the city evokes horror and revulsion — in short, it represents the absurd rather than the unfathomable (for Westerners) mysteries of India. The author's experience of Calcutta as incomprehensible and inaccessible via reason is then an indication of the prevalence of the absurd rather than, as postcolonial critics are wont to claim (see, for example, Murti 2001), of Grass's obtuseness and inability to relinquish his ingrained Eurocentric perspective. Far from romanticizing or poeticizing Calcutta, Grass assumes the realist perspective of Fontane, in whose words India "seems as unmysterious as Denmark" (*SYT,* 12), and he goes beyond Fontane by criticizing the political power structure as well as the socioeconomic conditions that result in the widespread exploitation of the poor and underprivileged. Ultimately, then, it is the dialectic of enlightenment and the absurd that, in Brunssen's persuasive view, dominate Grass's attempt to come to grips with the phenomenon of Calcutta and informs *Zunge zeigen.*

Postcolonial Discourse; Orientalism

Monika Shafi (1993) expresses surprise at the paucity of scholarly contributions devoted to *Zunge zeigen* — she does not take into account the contributions by Onderdelinden, Ganeshan, and Sigrid Mayer, discussed above, which were presumably not yet available at the time of her writing — and proposes to read the text as a "postmodern" travelogue despite the ambiguous nature of the term, a travelogue that entails elements of parody, pastiche, intertextuality, and an engagement with the constructedness of historical tradition, which is no longer perceived as linear and teleologically oriented. Furthermore, the observer's basis, which transgresses boundaries and is far removed from Europe (rather than the Western hemisphere, as Shafi has it), is another indication of the text's postmodernity, which allows the questioning of concepts such as home, identity, and a hierarchical value system via both affirmation and negation.

Zunge zeigen, Shafi acknowledges, is a further expression of the German fascination with India that began during Romanticism and was continued, for instance, by Hermann Hesse with *Siddharta* (1922; *Siddharta,* 1951). The fascination with India resulted in aesthetic constructs from a European perspective that emphasized the exotic and that largely excluded social and political problems. Grass deviates from this tradition precisely because he focuses on Calcutta's enormous social troubles (as several reviewers and critics have disapprovingly pointed out) but he perceives them in Eurocentric terms — a cognitive process that leads to a paradoxical result of which Grass is fully aware. Despite his attempts to adjust or, rather, lower his living standard and to shun the convenience and luxury that is available to the well-to-do, he remains a tireless and keen, albeit somewhat distanced, observer who perceives the inhabitants of Calcutta as representatives of unrelenting misery rather than as individuals. Grass's approach thus differs markedly from that of his wife who, despite her incessant reading of Fontane, evinces more genuine sympathy with the poor and downtrodden than her husband. Actually, Fontane's novel *Effi Briest* (1895; *Effi Briest,* 1914) serves as the model for the relationship of husband and wife: just as Effi Briest has been brought by her husband von Innstetten to a place that she dislikes and that makes her uncomfortable, so Grass like von Instetten subordinates the comfort and happiness of his wife to his professional (and artistic) interests, ultimately failing to influence his wife's perspective — even if, in the case of *Zunge zeigen,* there is no tragic end. Nevertheless, Shafi (346) contends, Grass extends his "colonial" gaze, which subsumes the foreign under one's own perspective, to his wife; in fact, his perception with regard to Ute remains more rigid than that with regard to Calcutta, a city that forces him to rethink his poetics — even though language is inadequate to make sense of the pervasive misery. What remains is the "ironic articulation" (Shafi 348) of the author's limitations — a stance that radically distinguishes author and text from other more conventional travelogues.

In a comparison of *Zunge zeigen* with the travelogues of two other (West) German visitors to India, Shafi (1997) explores the descriptions of a "culturally and economically very distinct reality" (40) in Grass's text, Ingeborg Drewitz's *Mein indisches Tagebuch* (1983; My Indian Diary), and Hubert Fichte's *Wolli Indienfahrer* (1978; Wolli, Traveler to India).

She concludes that in contrast to both Grass and Drewitz, who are ultimately unable to overcome their "binary . . . mode of viewing India" from a Eurocentric, "(neo)colonial perspective," Fichte's protagonist conceives of India as an "aesthetic challenge to be mastered" (53) by full-scale immersion in its culture and daily life rather than relying on a somewhat distanced German-centered observation that precludes a wholesale engagement with the foreign Other (see also Shafi 2001, and Ulrich 2004, who in her analysis of the portrayal of India in *Der Butt, Kopfgeburten,* and *Zunge zeigen* reaches similar conclusions).

Reasoning in a similar fashion, Kamakshi P. Murti (2001), who professes to admire Grass's work and to share his "socio-political views and concerns . . . to a large extent" (123), places him in the tradition of nineteenth-century German and Western Orientalism that promulgates the "binary opposition of a 'spiritual India' and a 'materialist West'" (118) — an unacknowledged and unrecognized deficit that is evident in the commodification of the "disease-ridden Indian body" and the fetishization of the "slum/pavement dweller" and results in what amounts to an "erotics of poverty and disease." Murti, a native of India, curiously suggests that the individuals in Grass's text actually "have choices" and are far less "static" (124–25) than portrayed but fails to provide specific examples as to which options slum dwellers have at their disposal to improve their lives. True, the "massive ink smudges" (126) of the sketches strongly suggest the "eternal recurrence of poverty, filth, and disease"; at the same time, the shock of the "(unwritten) aesthetics of poverty" (*SYT,* 58) belies the author's alleged distanced attitude. Murti's list of Grass's sins include his misrepresentation of and "almost obsessive preoccupation with the Indian freedom fighter" Subhas Chandra Bose (Murti, 129; see also Ganeshan 1992) and his "insinuation[s] and generalization[s]" about the "corrupt lifestyle of the bureaucracy, the middleclass, and the business community" (132) — assumed failures that seem to be attributable to the critic's national sensibilities rather than to the shortcomings of the text.

Another contribution in the postcolonial mode is that by Thomas W. Kniesche (1998) who engages in a somewhat more nuanced analysis than Murti and draws on theoreticians of the postcolonial era such as Edward Said, Homi Bhaba, and Gayatri Chakravorty Spivak as well as on Theodor W. Adorno and Max Horkheimer's *Dialektik der Aufklärung* (1947; *Dialectic of Enlightenment,* 1972). Kniesche also emphasizes that Grass's interest in the Third World has been of long standing. Although he credits Grass with a rejection of the European views of India that made the subcontinent the subject of romantic idealization and the primary source of the mysterious and mystical, he also states that the writer has not entirely overcome the basis of Orientalism, that is, a dualistic view of the world that adheres to the separateness of the Other. At the same time,

Kniesche is cognizant of the difficulties and problems inherent in the author's ultimately futile attempt to abandon his Western orientation and standards and distinguishes the rational, objective discourse that predominates in the prose section from the mythologizing tendency that prevails in the concluding poem.

Hence the prose sections may be subsumed under a heading such as "India seen through the lens of German literary and intellectual history," as evidenced by the arrival of the voluminous "steamer trunk" (*SYT,* 1) filled with mostly German reading material that has arrived before the author and his wife set foot in Calcutta — an indication of the inescapability of the intellectual baggage of preconceived notions that serves as a frame of reference for the unaccustomed and foreign. Yet in contrast to Shafi and Murti, Kniesche concedes that there is a change of perspective in the poem in that the "I" of the observer/poet changes to the "I" of the mythical goddess Kali, a gradual process that is indicative of the reclaiming of myth in the sense of Adorno and Horkheimer's enlightenment dialectic, but also of the substitution of the ethnological, registering gaze through a genuinely "postcolonial" gaze (290) that exposes the observer to the scrutiny of the Other.

In a partial departure from the views put forward by the proponents of postcolonial theory, who tend to charge Grass with engaging in an "imperialistic discourse" and assuming a "patronizing stance of superiority," Daniel Reynolds (2003) finds the characterization of Grass's stance as "Eurocentric . . . particularly troubling" on account of his credentials as a "stalwart . . . critic" of "Western European capitalism." Reynolds sensibly asks whether "postcolonial theory" must inevitably lead into the "cul-de-sac" of a "moralistic condemnation of everything Western" (245) and suggests that the author's often loosely defined, but by virtue of upbringing and socialization practically inevitable, "Eurocentrism" should be accepted as a given; the important question is then one of narrative strategy; that is, whether he articulates his "European bias" and how he communicates it to his readers. On the one hand, Reynolds disagrees with critics such as Shafi, Murti, and John Hutnyk, who in his study of the politics of representation, entitled *The Rumour of Calcutta* (1996), chastises Grass for engaging in "intellectual voyeurism" (102) as well as reinforcing and contributing to the global circulation of "stereotypes of Calcutta as a city of cows, garbage, sleepers and ghosts" (103) by producing marketable books. On the other, Reynolds finds that Grass "reaffirms certain Western cultural predispositions" (246) despite having penned a text (Reynolds ignores the drawings) that is "self-reflexive [and] self-critical" (252).

In greater detail than most other critics, Reynolds analyzes the function of Fontane as the vehicle that enables Grass to establish a connection to India's colonial past because of Fontane's aforementioned activity as a Prussian correspondent in London. By depicting Fontane as an anti-colonialist and as a "model of the engaged writer," Grass sets him up as a model that Indian writers should emulate. However, like some other scholars (see, for example, Ganeshan 1992), Reynolds charges that Grass's "interest in contemporary Indian literature," is rather limited and "patriarchal"; it amounts to an "Orientalist desire" to perceive Indian culture in terms of "Western expectations" (254). Among these underlying expectations is the notion that the European/German enlightenment as represented in the text by Lichtenberg, Kant, Lessing, and Einstein, with its "concepts of reason and equality," is opposed to the "chaos [and] irrationality" as embodied by the "goddess of destruction, Kali" (258). As Kniesche (1998), whom Reynolds does not mention, has shown, the lines between rationality and myth are not as clearly drawn as Reynolds would have it. Moreover, his censorious conclusion that Grass merely recycles "images of poverty, chaos, and despair" and falls victim to the legacy of colonialism is undermined by his misreading of *Unkenrufe*, in which Mr. Chatterjee is not the harbinger of the European "crisis coming from the subcontinent" (260) but rather the herald of hope (see ch. 12).

Adherents of the fashionable methodologies of the day, which in this instance may be summarized under the general heading of postcolonial discourse, tend to emphasize the inadequacy and insufficiency of Grass's observations. A totally opposite point of view emerges from the assessment of Bengali writer Subhoranjan Dasgupta (2002a) who applauds the "inspired prose rising to the heights of magic realism" of *Zunge zeigen* and observes that "not even a Bengali . . . has paid Calcutta such an eloquent tribute." Dasgupta further refers to the writer's "unflinching commitment, both political and human" (76) and singles out Grass's discovery of a tiny school in the midst of garbage heaps, an incident that brings out the poet in the writer: he turns "melodious and lyrical" (77; see *SYT,* 203). The school is run by the NGO, the Calcutta Social Project, to which the entire volume is dedicated; Grass has continued to take an interest in the project — as he demonstrated during his visit in 2005 — and to support it financially (Siemes 2005a).

Part 3

After Reunification: Old Problems and New Beginnings

12: *Unkenrufe / The Call of the Toad*

The Return of the Dead

A LITTLE OVER A YEAR AFTER the publication of *Zunge zeigen* (1988), momentous historical events took place in Germany: the opening of the Berlin Wall in November 1989, subsequent German (re)unification in October 1990, and the dissolution of the Soviet Union and the Eastern Bloc. Grass, who since the 1960s had addressed various aspects of the "German question" in speeches, essays, and public debates, emerged — in contrast, for example, to his friend and mentor Willy Brandt (1913–1992), former Chancellor of the Federal Republic — as a prominent intellectual opponent of reunification and vigorous advocate of a confederation of the two German states, which was supposed to be based on the concept of the *Kulturnation,* or nation bound together by its cultural heritage rather than united within a nation state defined by a boundary setting it apart from other nation states. Not unexpectedly, Grass's uncompromising stance against reunification, which is reflected in some of the essays assembled in his *Two States — One Nation* (1990), elicited widespread censure, which in the beginning was fueled by the euphoria (which eventually subsided) generated by the prospect of a re-united nation and the ensuing reestablishment of one German state.

Unkenrufe, which officially went on sale at the beginning of May 1992, had been energetically promoted by the writer's new publishing company, Steidl in Göttingen, months before the book became generally available (see Arnold 1997, 188). The publication of a genuine work of fiction (subtitled *Eine Erzählung* [narrative] in the German original, but not categorized in the English translation) by Germany's most representative writer, coupled with unfounded press rumors about an insufficient number of review copies, which created tension and dissension, was bound to arouse the interest of both critics and the reading public, and the underlying question as to how the author was going to weave his political concerns into the fabric of his fiction could not help but stimulate curiosity.

Among the first reviews was that of Grass's nemesis, Marcel Reich-Ranicki (1992b) in *Der Spiegel,* who acknowledges the writer's elevated status in German letters but then proceeds to pan the narrative, both because he chose to set it in Danzig or rather present-day Gdańsk, a venue that is thoroughly lacking in the scurrilous features the reader is familiar with from *Die Blechtrommel,* and because of the very strange venture planned by the two main figures. Widowed (West) German Alexander Reschke, professor of the history of arts and an expellee from Danzig, and likewise widowed Polish Alexandra Piatkowska, restorer of objects of art and also uprooted, in her case from a part of Lithuania that during the interwar period belonged to Poland, begin to establish a "German-Polish Cemetery Association" (the name that prevails; see *CT,* 30 et passim), which will enable all those who were expelled from their homes during the "Century of Expulsions" (*CT,* 27 et passim), as Reschke puts it, to be buried in their native soil. Curiously, Reich-Ranicki (b. 1920) singles out the restrained depiction of the love affair between Alexander and Alexandra as unconvincing, in that it is both palatable to seniors and G-rated for youthful readers. He ambivalently concludes that further (literary) surprises may be expected of Grass. In *Das literarische Quartett* Reich-Ranicki essentially paraphrased and reiterated his opinion (see Karasek, Löffler, Mayhöfer, and Reich-Ranicki 1992).

Presumably in the interest of offering a balanced view, in addition to Reich-Ranicki's review *Der Spiegel* includes comments by Polish author Andrzej Szczypiorski (1992), who offers a far more positive assessment, in the same issue. For Szczypiorski, Grass is ensnared in German problems; his involvement induces him to scoff at German insufficiencies and to moralize, whereas he tends to be far more lenient with regard to the flaws of Poles. Iris Radisch, writing in *Die Zeit* (1992), identified by Irmgard Elsner Hunt (1992b, 583) as the "usual token woman" among the males of the critical establishment, suggests various possibilities as to how to read *Unkenrufe:* as a German-Polish sentimental comedy, a parable of reconciliation for students in the upper classes of secondary schools, or a book on the well-intended *Ostpolitik* of the Social Democrats. Even if the aspired reconciliation ends as a farce when the maximization of profit becomes the chief motive of the Cemetery Association, the idea of establishing such an organization is both hair-raising and convincing, in that the actual hero of the tale is death. Unlike Reich-Ranicki, Radisch finds the portrayal of the erotic scenes delicate as well as ironic, yet she faults Grass for failing to find appropriate words for his double, Alexander Reschke, when the latter speaks at an important celebration of the fall of the Berlin Wall. Similarly, Radisch considers the introduction of the enterprising Bengali Mr. Chatterjee, who promotes bicycle rickshaws as an economically as well as environmentally sound alternative to automobiles, an insipid idea, in that he appears to represent the salvation of moribund old Europe through the Third World. (Martin Kane 2002, 187, surmises that Mr. Chatterjee "bears some resemblance" to Salman Rushdie.)

Less harsh than Reich-Ranicki, Frank Schirrmacher (1992), writing in the *Frankfurter Allgemeine Zeitung,* also inclines toward a negative assessment. While he discerns the occurrence of strangely touching melancholic passages and acknowledges the two main characters as representatives of their respective nationalities, Schirrmacher finds fault with the narrative, which reads like an instruction manual in which readers are told how they are supposed to think and to feel rather than a prose text. While the narrative illustrates the idea of reconciliation, it does so by extensively relying on topical props. A distinctly sardonic commentary is that by Willi Winkler (1992) who largely confines himself to sarcastically paraphrasing the plot.

Unkenrufe does not constitute an exception with regard to the *Feuilleton* reception of Grass's work in general: Heinz Ludwig Arnold's 1997 brief statistical survey of ninety-one reviews actually reveals a preponderance of positive views; whereas forty-three critics tend to be affirmtive, eighteen pan the narrative, and fifteen remain undecided (186 n. 18). Among the encouraging voices is that of Fritz Rudolf Fries (1992b,), a writer of the former GDR, who detects resemblances to both Heinrich Böll and Uwe Johnson in protagonist Reschke and is pleased — unlike several West German critics — about Grass's return to the familiar milieu of Danzig.

Predictably, Grass derived little consolation from encouraging opinions; with characteristic and perhaps excessive forcefulness he states in the popular magazine *Der Stern* that the critical establishment is intent on finishing him off — in part on account of his leftist convictions and his critique of the unification process (see Frank 1992). It attests to Grass's controversial status that his attack on his critics elicits further responses: one journalist in *Der Spiegel* accuses him of political mystification by intermingling political and literary criteria in elevating the negative reviews of *Unkenrufe* to personal, politically motivated assaults (Schreiber 1992).

In a kind of postscript to the debate stimulated by the publication and reviews of Grass's narrative, Fritz Rudolf Fries (1992a) notes that the evaluations in the former GDR as well as those published in the regional press tend to be far more sympathetic than those that appear in (West) German review organs instrumental in shaping critical opinion. At any rate, as Fries also observes, the negative publicity has not proved to be detrimental to the commercial success of *Unkenrufe,* a work that, after the customary meeting of author and translators (see Verdofsky 1992), was also rendered into a considerable number of languages (Arnold 1997, 188–89).

"Geriatric Love Story" and "Graveyard Utopia"

The English rendering of *Unkenruf* as *The Call of the Toad* (*Call*) by Ralph Manheim, Grass's distinguished, long-time translator, who died in September 1992 (see the tribute by British Germanist Leonard Forster [1993]), was offered in bookstores in October 1992. Although Manheim's literal version of the German title lacks the connotation of the prophesy of doom that is associated with *Unkenrufe*, the text itself provides an explanation. In the words of Reschke: "'The call of the toad foreshadows disaster. . . . Toads became the harbingers of calamity'" (*CT*, 103). Manheim's translation is critiqued by G. P. Butler (1994) in a review in which he cites copious examples of questionable renderings that pertain to the interconnected categories of "Americanisms," "shifts in register," "common or garden mistakes," and "repetitions." Butler, who does not wish to detract from Manheim's merits, concedes, however, that a considerable number of errata and infelicities may be attributable to time pressures and to the translator's working with a corrected manuscript, galleys, and page proofs rather than with the published German original.

Even before *Call* became available, British publications informed readers about Grass's new work. In her perceptive commentary in the *Times Literary Supplement*, Anne McElvoy (1992) interprets the "attacks" on Grass as heralding a "wider re-valuation of modern German literature" — a formulation that is reminiscent of Frank Schirrmacher's 1990 article in the *Frankfurter Allgemeine Zeitung* in which he proclaims a general farewell to the literature of the postwar period in the Federal Republic and charts a course for literary developments in the new Germany that would be free of "extra-literary" concerns such as those espoused by the members of *Gruppe 47* (see, for example, Mews 1997). Schirrmacher's critique constitutes another phase of the post-wall *Literaturstreit,* or literary feud, that initially focused on Christa Wolf, generally perceived as the chief representative of GDR letters. McElvoy singles out the generational difference (Schirrmacher, for example, was born in 1959), the alleged declining "literary quality" of Grass's texts — although his "narrative skills are still bright, . . . there is a distinct sense of *déjà lu,"* she puns — and the assumed "role of the German author as highpriest and moral arbiter" as essential factors contributing to the rejection of *Gesinnungsästhetik,* or the "aesthetics of conviction," and the decoupling of literary merit from the "moral standpoint" a work represents. This elevated role had enabled both Heinrich Böll and Grass to function as the "prototype of the Good German."

In a less encompassing vein, British journalist Blake Morrison (1992) of the London *Independent* foregoes the attempt to chart the German post-unification intellectual and political landscape and concentrates on a discussion of *Unkenrufe* with the author. Unaffected by McElvoy's dismissal of the juncture between literature and politics, Morrison characterizes the author as the "lumbering conscience of the German nation," condemns Reich-Ranicki's "hatchet-job," and attributes the writer's "current unpopularity" to his not generally accepted stance in the reunification debate. The critic considers *Unkenrufe* a "geriatric love story," Grass's "simplest, most touching novel [sic] for many years," and a "lovely, late Utopian idea for . . . the 'Century of Expulsions'" that, however, might give offense as an "allegory of German economic might and eastward expansionism." But then Grass is as eager as his detractors to play the political card, that is, to discuss his narrative in political terms.

Michael Hofmann (1992) of the London *Times* likewise expresses mild amazement at the contentious German reception of a book that is "quite unshrill, a comfortably slack and likeable tale, told with ironic humour by an effortlessly dexterous and experienced puppeteer" who uses the "extraordinary and intimidating historical events" of recent German history to pen a "derisory little parable" about the "idealistic scheme" of the "Gdansk Cemetery of Reconciliation" that "ends as a grotesque re-invasion of Poland." In implicitly dissenting from Radisch, Hofmann considers Mr. Chatterjee's "bicycle rickshaw" enterprise the "crowning glory" of Grass's imagery. In short, the author remains a "great master." As the figure of an "entertaining sub-plot," the "entrepreneurial" Mr. Chatterjee also receives good marks from D. J. Taylor (1992) in the *Sunday Times,* who judges the "novel" to be "elegant, but in the end intensely depressing" on account of Grass's message that "money, not liberty" has prevailed East of the former Iron Curtain — a message that is clearly conveyed by the well-intentioned yet eventually failed project of the "Cemetery of Reconciliation." Consequently, in a rather sweeping generalization, Taylor casts the author in the role of "liberal intellectual" who is "unrepentant in his desire to bite the hand that feeds him." Another reviewer, Philip Brady (1992), writing in the *Times Literary Supplement,* contents himself with remarking that *The Call of the Toad* adds yet "another creature to [Grass's] menagerie," is "pointedly topical," and "lacks the grotesques and . . . stylistic pyrotechnics" of the writer's previous fiction.

A divergent view is offered by W. L. Webb (1992) in the London *Guardian.* Webb posits that Grass renders with "almost confessional accuracy and discomfort" the prevailing mood of those who experienced the Second World War as youths: "battle fatigue, disorientation, a sense of having been outmanouevred [*sic*] by history" — a phenomenon that Webb considers strange indeed in view of the author's reputation as a "famously pugnacious writer." As Morrison, cited above, as well as Grass's combative stance vis-à-vis his German critics indicate, Webb's apprehensions may not be entirely justified; nevertheless, he offers a sensitive reading of the text, one that takes into account the narrative point of view by means of a brief analysis of the "writer-narrator," who constructs the story on the basis of a "collection of diaries, tapes, bills and photographs" sent to him by Reschke, a former Danzig classmate, and engages in self-reflexive ruminations that include the self-criticism of the "banal" love story and the "contrived" idea about the "business with the dead" (*CT,* 80).

The review in the *New York Times Book Review* is penned by Englishman John Bayley (1992), Professor Emeritus of English at Oxford, who on account of the manifestations of "ebullient life surrounding the rituals of death" in *Call* compares Grass's work with Evelyn Waugh's satirical novel *The Loved One* (1948). Moreover, although he acknowledges that Grass's chief "purpose is political," Bayley considers him to be the "only magic realist today."

Yet in this "darkly comic political satire," the reviewer seems to sense that the activities of the Cemetery Association may be driven by a somewhat sinister vision: the "cozy myth of a united Europe" that will be unified by "German zeal and efficiency." In the end, however, the narrative is a "tour de force" that disproves German critics' misgivings. Another review in the *New York Times,* by Herbert Mitgang (1992), strikes a similarly positive note. Mitgang declares *Call* to be Grass's "most linear and readable novel in recent years," and claims that the "author permits himself to be romantic" about his couple hailing from two nations. But hopes for a "new, more sentimental Grass" will be disappointed because the question of guilt about Nazi crimes, familiar from *The Tin Drum,* hovers in the background. In a third article in the *New York Times.* Esther B. Fein (1992) summarizes the results of her interview with Grass on the occasion of his promotional tour for his new publication at the end of 1992 and the beginning of 1993 (see Streitfeld 1993). Fein only peripherally comments on *Call* and instead briefly explores the author's role as a "citizen writer," who considers his long-standing, continuous engagement in politics as inevitable — particularly in view of the apprehensions he voiced in *Two States — One Nation,* referred to above.

In the *New York Review of Books,* Gabriele Annan (1992) similarly acknowledges Grass as "the grand old man of German literature and its liberal conscience" yet perceives in *Call* a "wan, valedictory ring," which makes the text a "novel of political disillusionment" that is not improved by the "pretty schematic" characters to whom Grass allocates "one or two national characteristics or professional deformations apiece." Thus Alexandra is a disenchanted former member of the Communist Party and Alexander is "ridiculed" by his students as a "veteran of '68" (*CT,* 84); the failure of their hopes they associated with these movements leaves them with only one option in the "post-Communist, post-German-reunification . . . world": to construct their "utopia . . . in a graveyard" (Annan

19). When the cemetery project assumes an "unstoppable capitalist momentum," Alexander and Alexandra are forced to resign, and it is the former who offers a "ray of hope" in his resignation speech when he declares Mr. Chatterjee's successful bicycle rickshaw enterprise to be a harbinger of the "predestined Asian future of Europe, free from nationalistic narrowness" (*CT*, 233). Annan's comment that this speech represents a "caricature" of what Grass has stated in previous "public utterances" is not quite convincing; especially in *Zunge zeigen* he has articulated the significance of Asia for Europe and the world at large.

Annan's at best lukewarm endorsement is surpassed by that of Joseph Coates (1992) in the *Chicago Tribune*. Not without justification, Coates views the vision of Mr. Chatterjee, who introduces himself to Reschke as a "forerunner or billeting officer of the future world society" (*CT*, 37), as heralding a "radical, much needed rejuvenation cure" of old Europe (*CT*, 40) — one of the (then recent) favorite themes developed by the "perennial enfant terrible" Grass (Coates), who became a victim of vilification upon the publication of the German original. Under the ominous title "Grass and the Fourth Reich" (1992b) — a reference to the notion propagated by reunification opponents that the new, united Germany would follow in the footsteps of the Third Reich — Irmgard Elsner Hunt gives her opinion, without further elaboration, that the book is "perfectly wonderful in its powerful language" and uncritically and indiscriminately perceives all objections that have been raised as motivated by the impetus to critique the author's "political opinion" (583) rather than the desire to engage in a discussion of literary merit.

In striking contrast to Hunt, Robert Taylor (1992), writing in the *Boston Globe*, is quite unambiguous in his rejection. He judges that the intent of the "mordant and morose satire" is to "demonstrate the life-denying qualities of capitalism and show a free-market economy degenerating into the sepulchral call of the toad" and dismisses the narrative as burdened with a "schematic plot" and a "lugubrious tone." Less scathingly, Donna Rifkind (1992) in the *Washington Post* strikes a familiar note when she maintains that since *The Tin Drum* Grass's "novelistic power has declined while his self-appointed role as his country's liberal conscience" has increased; she cites as evidence Alexander and Alexandra's "peace-promoting" enterprise, which turns into a "symbol of German greed and tyranny in the wake of reunification." Ultimately, Rifkind opines, the "farcical novel" does not lend itself to treating weighty issues.

The article by Gudrun Boch (1992) in the *Frankfurter Rundschau* may serve as a kind of summary of the initial reception of *Call* in the United States. Boch correctly observes that Grass continues to be the most important living German author and also functions as the spokesperson of the critical Left and represents the unofficial conscience of

Germany. Although not as widely read as before — a situation partly attributable to a decrease in the number of readers with a knowledge of German, that is, refugees from Nazi Germany and emigrants who tend to assemble at his readings, especially in New York City — he finds an audience that, negative reviews notwithstanding, tends to be more attentive than his listeners, readers, and critics in Germany.

Swallowing Toads

Among the first of the comparatively few scholarly contributions that deal with *Unkenrufe* is that by Hans-Werner Eroms (1993), who engages in a relatively rarely encountered linguistic analysis and begins by pointing out that the calls of the toad, which accompany the reader throughout the text, provide sufficient hints that the utopia of reconciliation the Cemetery Association initially adheres to cannot be seen in an unequivocally optimistic vein. The prevailing mood of uncertainty is reinforced by the plethora of speculations ("Mutmaßungen") that reduce the degree of certainty inherent in specific statements, as for example when the narrator says: "It is possible that just once . . . I actually did swallow a toad" (*CT,* 33) — an avowal that undermines the (involuntary) role of the narrator as chronicler in that it implies doubt in the accuracy of his tale.

As a prevalent stylistic figure Eroms singles out the personification of inanimate objects, such as: "All the photos . . . speak of January frost . . ." (*CT,* 157), a technique that leads to the condensation or compression ("Verdichtung") of the text, which is also evident in the information-packed sentences of far above-average length (see, for example, "Then flowers . . .," *CT,* 126) as well as in Grass's habit of changing the normal word order of sentences for the sake of emphasis. His frequent employment of the anaphora is another means that emphasizes the artful and artistic, non-spontaneous character of the author's prose. In his concluding section, Eroms examines the speech of the main characters and posits that the German-Polish relations are articulated via a parallelization of the two main figures; in their speech patterns they convey national characteristics as well as those of gender. Whereas Alexandra in her grammatically incorrect but creative German betrays practical intelligence, warm-heartedness, spontaneity, and creativity, Alexander tends to lecture, converse in a circuitous fashion, use bureaucratic jargon, and strictly adhere to grammatical rules. In fact, Eroms suggests, Alexandra's manner of speaking is related to that of the "Kashubian fossil" Erna Brakup, whose dialect is near extinction and is rendered by Grass in a phonetic transliteration not recaptured by Manheim (see *CT,* 107). Inasmuch as Erna Brakup is the last survivor of Grass's Slavic-German fictional universe (and the only critic of Polish policies with regard to the tiny German minority that survived in Danzig/Gdańsk after the Second World War), Alexandra gains in stature because she speaks somewhat similarly. On the whole, Eroms concludes, *Unkenrufe* represents a further example of Grass's inimitable style.

It goes without saying that *Unkenrufe* could not have been written without the historic changes in the political landscape of Central and Eastern Europe briefly referred to at the beginning of this chapter. In her essay on *Unkenrufe* (1993b), Sigrid Mayer seeks to foreground these changes by noting that Grass's narrative constitutes a reversal of the motif of the separation of two lovers on account of the Iron Curtain — as evident, for example, in Christa Wolf's *Der geteilte Himmel* (1963; *Divided Heaven,* 1965). Although the story takes place from 2 November 1989 to the end of May 1991, Reschke's letter to the narrator asking him to write the (hi)story of the Cemetery Association (see *CT,* 9) is dated 19 June 1999 and opens up a future time dimension (see Neuhaus 1979; rev. ed., 1992, 187–88). Evidently the seminal events of 1989/90 are the prerequisite for the "headbirth" of the cemetery that, Mayer (217) states, cannot possibly contribute to unmaking the mass murders and destructions of the recent past (then more than forty years earlier) and renders the idea of reconciliation via the cemetery enterprise implausible. The underlying skepticism is evident in the lack of enthusiasm on the part of the narrator when he is faced with the task of recording the history of the association; he unequivocally expresses his opinion: "'Look here, Reschke, this idea stinks'" (*CT,* 41). Moreover, Alexander and Alexandra's (initial) commitment is not shared by their respective children; two of Reschke's daughters accuse him of indulging in an "'anachronistic homeland cult'" and "'revanchist necrophilia'" (*CT,* 80); Piatkowska's son, who studies in Germany, is similarly dismissive. These reactions Alexandra attributes to a different generational experience: the children, now grown-ups, have never been "chased out, never had to flee in cold" (*CT,* 154). Yet it is also Alexandra, accompanied by the ubiquitous calling of a toad, who in vain suggests to Alexander that they abandon the cemetery project while it is still in its initial stages — a moment that in retrospect signifies "a turning point in their story" (*CT,* 119) and that appropriately occurs in the fourth of the seven chapters, in the middle of the narrative (Mayer, 221). The couple's actual resigning from the Cemetery Board of Directors occurs too late; their error of judgment, Mayer argues, consists in launching the idea of the reconciliation cemetery embellished with humanitarian grounds — Mayer's negative assessment appears to preclude any kind of reconciliation. Mayer views Mr. Chatterjee's rickshaw business as a kind of counter-utopia to the burial scheme (see also Dasgupta, below) in that the Bengali's enterprise offers an ecologically sound as well as economically profitable alternative to the clogged traffic in European cities. Yet there remains some ambiguity, depending on whether Mr. Chatterjee will follow in the footsteps of the sound businessmen on his mother's side or his forbears on his father's side, admirers of the "legendary Bengali national hero" (*CT,* 177) Subhas Chandra Bose, after whom Chatterjee has been named and after whom he names the former Lenin Shipyard in Gdańsk. In Reschke's (and Grass's) opinion, Bose is "a more dubious than exemplary individual" (*CT,* 177; see also ch. 11).

The new, post-wall political constellation has created the opportunity for a dialogue between Germans and Poles and provides a new context for Grass's commemoration in fiction of his lost home, as Hans-Christoph Graf von Nayhauss (2000) observes in his essay on *Unkenrufe,* but he rejects the opinion voiced by some critics that Grass uses the narrative as a vehicle to promote his political agenda via fiction rather than engaging in public interventions via speeches, interviews, and articles. Even though the first-person narrator displays several features of the author himself, he is ultimately dependent on Reschke's likewise first-person account and Reschke's materials, which he puts on paper in the manner of a chronicler, albeit with a certain degree of ironic detachment. In fact, von Nayhauss suggests, one of the distancing devices Grass employs is the narrator's assumption of a quasi-auctorial stance, which enables him to address a variety of political, environmental, and other issues. Yet the narrator's actual swallowing a live toad as a schoolboy assumes a figurative meaning (see Neuhaus 1979; rev. ed. 1992, 187; "Kröten schlucken" may be translated as "to swallow a bitter pill") in that he feels obliged to write about a distasteful matter.

Conversely, in his juggling of time dimensions, which emphasize the utopian character of the narrative, Grass portrays a paradisiacal, Asian-dominated future in Poland in which religious strife has disappeared and the "Black Madonna of Wilno" and Calcutta's "black Kali" (*CT,* 215) coexist in harmony; Mr. Chatterjee is then merely the harbinger of things to come. More specifically than Mayer, von Nayhauss points out that it is not the underlying idea of reconciliation but rather its limitation to the dead and dying that makes the cemetery project a bad idea. In addition, the "ghastly incarnation" of the "beautiful idea" (*C,* 150) on account of the predominant commercial interests and prevailing acquisitiveness discredits something that sprang from a noble impulse. It remains debatable, however, whether Grass's ironic dissociation from the (re)settlement of land by the dead signifies that the concept of home resides, as von Nayhauss puts it, in the realm of utopia and is not bound to any specific place. Yet it seems obvious that Grass's vivid evocations of Danzig contradict Nayhauss's notion.

The *Wende* in Grass's Fiction

Mark E. Cory (1998) observes incontrovertibly that *Unkenrufe* is the "first narrative in the Grass canon to thematize German unification" (181) via a "story of love and death" that can be read as an "allegory of European relations" (182) at the end of the twentieth century. Cory plausibly suggests that the text may not only be interpreted as dealing with German-Polish relations but also as encompassing "German-German" relations in addition to the "role of a united Germany in European relations" (183). German and European problems are put into perspective by Mr. Chatterjee, representative of one billion "living souls." Even though there were more than ten million "displaced and deceased Germans," not "several hundred thousand," as Cory puts it, the disparity in numbers is both startling and reason enough to contemplate the vision of a "pluralistic Europe" rather than a "Europe dominated by a unified Germany" (184). Yet in keeping with the "mournful cry of the toad" that emanates from Mr. Chatterjee's bicycle bell, Grass does not present an unmitigated utopian vision of a multicultural European future; rather, there are "unmistakable *fin-de-siècle*" (185) echoes that lend the tale its charm.

In her somewhat misleadingly entitled article "Günter Grass since the *Wende*," Beatrice Petz (2000) briefly touches upon Grass's status as a controversial German author of international repute but then devotes the main thrust of her argument to an elucidation of "the problematical nature of the representation of historical events and processes" (68) in general and her well-substantiated claim about the emergence of a largely anonymous, unobtrusive narrator in Grass's fiction of the 1990s, that is, *Unkenrufe* and *Ein weites Feld*. The new type of narrator is a far cry indeed from memorable characters such as Oskar Matzerath, who populate Grass's early fiction. Precisely because there is neither a clearly defined narrator — a narratorial "I" emerges briefly at the end of the third paragraph of *Unkenrufe* (see *CT*, 1) — nor any discernible attempt on the part of the author to establish any kind of frame, Petz's claim (71) that the narrative amounts to a *Rahmenerzählung* or framed story in the conventional sense is not tenable. Far more convincing is her observation that in *Unkenrufe* "the constructed nature of historical accounts is foregrounded" (71) primarily via the narrator's presenting himself as a somewhat reluctant "historian" (73) who has been charged by Reschke with writing a "history or report" (*C*, 247) — or, as the original German has it, a "Chronik oder einen Bericht" (*W* 12:244), despite or perhaps because of, his propensity for deriving enjoyment from being "more factual than the facts" (*CT*, 244).

Grass's foregrounding of narrative options corresponds to some extent to the choices a historian is faced with when seeking to determine "the true or most plausible story," as Hayden White puts it in his *The Content of the Form* (1987:27). There are distinct differences in the way in which Reschke and the narrator interpret events: whereas the former casts his meeting with Alexandra in terms of "fate," the latter prefers to view the encounter in terms of "chance" (*CT,* 1; see Petz, 74–75). The term "Chronik," which, Petz erroneously states, occurs "five times in a page and a half of text" (see *W* 12:244; Petz compounds her error by providing incorrect page references to *Unkenrufe*), brings into focus a mode of historiography that essentially relies on a teleological orientation and establishes causal links in order to present historical events in the form of a plot. The narrator's "emplotment," Petz contends using White's terminology, follows the pattern of tragedy that culminates in Alexander and Alexandra's accidental deaths, which the narrator ultimately attributes to chance. As to the narrator's "history" of the Cemetery Association, it corresponds, albeit in a fictional context, to the "fictive character of historical reconstructions" that Hayden White in his *The Historical Imagination in Nineteenth Century Europe* (1973, 1–2; see Petz, 81) discerns as the characteristic mode of historical discourse. With the introduction of a new type of narrator in his post-*Wende* fiction, Petz argues persuasively, Grass has achieved a shift of emphasis from the clearly defined individual identities to "unnamed, relatively undefined narrators" who elucidate the difficult task of the historiographer vis-à-vis the "chaotic events" (82) that define history.

"Jesus in the Market Place"

In her original approach, in which she deemphasizes politics in favor of economics, Chloe E. M. Paver (2000) uses as a starting point of her discussion the painting entitled *The Tribute Money,* which, as the reader of Grass knows from the fourth month of *Der Butt,* was created by seventeenth-century Danzig painter Anton Möller and hangs in the Danzig/Gdańsk Rathaus where Alexandra and Alexander are getting married. The painting shows Jesus "with a Biblical retinue" (*CT,* 241) standing in the Long Market, the "hub of commercial activity in seventeenth-century Danzig," with the Rathaus, the seat of the city's administration, behind him and thereby, the painter seems to suggest, endorsing Danzig's "mercantile spirit" (Paver, 71) as well as the tithing privileges of those in charge of the city's affairs. The painting, Paver maintains, provides a hint as to the "central importance" of economics in what she inaccurately calls a "novel" (72). In fact, Reschke and Piatkowska's initial meeting happens to occur not only in the market place but "between St. Dominic's Market and the Church of St. Nikolai" (*CT,* 4) and therefore between "God and Mammon" — an indication that they eventually will develop a project that is seeking to "reconcile economic with moral aims." Paver is specific in singling out the "villain of the piece" (Paver, 73), German industrialist Gerhard Vielbrand, who becomes the dominant force on the Board of Directors and tends to couch his relentless search for profit in moral sentiments — and whom most other critics fail to mention. When the Cemetery Association becomes increasingly profit-oriented, the wishes of "German nationalists" seem to be near fulfillment; in a scenario in which "Grass's imagination runs amok" (74), a reversal of the postwar expulsions takes place by virtue of child-bearing women from Germany giving birth when attending funerals in Gdańsk (an interesting about-face with regard to Grass's treatment of the fertility problem of teachers Harm and Dörte in *Kopfgeburten,* a topic that Paver does not address).

In addition, Paver sheds new light on the function of Mr. Chatterjee's enterprise, which she views as a signal that "money-making and ethical concerns" (75) may not be entirely incompatible, inasmuch as the rickshaw business is portrayed as representing a "deliberate contrast" (75) to the Cemetery Association, particularly once the association has fallen under the control of Vielbrand. Yet the vision of an Asian-dominated future is open to criticism in several respects: the underlying assumptions about the "less exploitative" nature of Asian free enterprise or the lack of nationalistic and religious tensions (Paver, 76, justifiably cites *Zunge zeigen* as a counterexample) seem to rest on shaky foundations. Grass's ironic stance, Paver claims, is designed to shake his readers' confidence in their preconceived notions by, for example, examining the "limits of their liberalism and . . . racial tolerance" and "confront[ing] their Euro-centric prejudices" (of which Grass himself has been accused) when faced with the prospect of an "Asian colonization of Europe." At the same time, Paver tends to minimize the emotional significance of *Heimat* and notes somewhat condescendingly that Grass implicitly attacks the presumably very small number of "chauvinistic" *Heimatvertriebene* (Paver, 77) among his readers, who tend to be organized in "refugees' associations" (*CT,* 28 et passim). Ultimately, the narrative is highly "playful" in juxtaposing and contrasting various positions so that even the ominous calling of the toad may not be taken at face value. Such a narrative strategy avoids the "pitfalls of a *roman à thèse*" or a novel that seeks to make a political or other point (Paver, 82) on the one hand; on the other, one may add, critical consensus will presumably be difficult to achieve.

Subhoranjan Dasgupta (2002b) reads the text as a "novel protest against globalization" (60) owing to the victory of global capitalism after the collapse of "state socialism," the only "contending ideology" (61), in the post-wall world. Reschke and Piatkowska's project serves as a "counter-paradigm of reconciliation," which is designed to soften or offset the effects of victorious capitalism. As most critics have noted, the "humanist enterprise" eventually turns into a "crass, money-spinning machine" (62) under the guidance of the aforementioned Vielbrand — a development that forces the originators of the all-too-successful venture to resign. Poland succumbs to the "assault of the market" and becomes "mired in chaos and despair" (65). Rather surprisingly, Dasgupta discerns a distinct "element of rosy naiveté" in Mr. Chatterjee's vision of the great unstoppable Asian migration that will flood Europe; as to the rickshaw business, he surmises that Grass could not think of a better "counterpoint" to the "aggressive avarice" (66) of global capitalism. Hence, Dasgupta avers, not quite convincingly in view of the author's rejection of hero worship of any kind, Grass indulges in an almost "childlike adulation" (67) in portraying the Bengali, the central figure of a "subtext of fantasy" that serves as a "redeeming example of interculturalism" (68) and entails the "human and redemptive" vision of a world without frontiers.

A "Time of Reconciliation"

In September 2005, the film *Unkenrufe — Zeit der Versöhnung* (Time of Reconciliation), a German-Polish-British coproduction, was released. Inasmuch as the script adhered fairly closely to the narrative, a modest revival of the debate about Grass's text ensued, primarily in the daily press. It comes as no particular surprise that the reception of the movie was similar to that of Grass's original text in its lack of unanimity. Bert Rebhandl (2005) in the *Frankfurter Allgemeine Zeitung* registers the frequent flashbacks and, in summing up, opines that the film has a tendency to return to the past as represented by Erna Brakup but does not quite succeed in doing so; hence it is neither adequate for the present situation nor suitable as a historical document. Far more scathing than Rebhandl's review is that of Joachim Lottmann in *WAMS.de* (2005). Lottmann dismisses the film as "Ultimativer Trash für die Generation 50 plus" (ultimate trash for the fifty-plus generation) in a strained youthful diction, blithely declares the relationship between Germans and Poles to be unproblematic, and considers the only redeeming virtue of the film to be that it is better than the book, a veritable "Machwerk" (thoroughly botched effort). At the other end of the critical spectrum, Katrin Hillgruber in *Der Tagesspiegel online* (2005) praises the work of Polish director Robert Glinski, who professes to have been intrigued by the parallel biographies of the two expellees and has succeeded in creating a work of art entailing a love story that is linked to the German-Polish history of the last fifty years or so, a story that sweeps the spectator along.

Another reviewer, Stephan Speicher in *Berliner Zeitung* (2005), tempers his criticism with favorable remarks. While he questions Grass's propensity for editorializing (see also Schirrmacher 1992) and draws attention (as most critics do) to the ominous presence of the toad, he remarks that the film fails to reproduce the prevailing mood of deliberate, slow-paced humor that prevails in the original text — a mixed blessing owing to the vitality of the main actors, especially the "wonderful" Krystyna Janda in the role of Piatkowska. It remains to be seen whether the film will contribute to enhancing the fortunes of the prose narrative.

13: *Ein weites Feld / Too Far Afield*

"My Dear Günter Grass . . ."

THE COVER OF *DER SPIEGEL* (21 August 1995) shows critic Marcel Reich-Ranicki literally tearing apart a copy of Grass's *Ein weites Feld,* and the condescendingly rather than cordially phrased caption reads, "Mein lieber Günter Grass. . . ." In what amounts to a review of the novel in the form of a purportedly open letter in the same journal, Reich-Ranicki proceeds to assure Grass that he esteems him as an extraordinary writer, but, at the same time, he professes to be unable to hide the fact that he considers *Ein weites Feld* an utter failure, because Grass has tackled a highly charged political topic, the so-called *Wende* and the aftermath of German (re)unification (for a definition of these two terms, see Frank Thomas Grub 2003). Not without justification, Reich-Ranicki points out that Grass's negative views on the (re)union of the two postwar German states, as he deems them to be reflected in the novel, are not shared by the majority of his fellow citizens; hence Grass finds himself among a distinct minority (for a cogent summary of the development of Grass's stance with regard to German unification, see Jan-Werner Müller 2000). Apart from the all-important politics that underlie many of the negative reviews, the critic considers the writer's ploy to introduce Fonty, a kind of doppelgänger — or, as the English translation has it, "revenant" (*TFA,* 347) — of nineteenth-century novelist Theodor Fontane (1819–98), a complete disappointment and the figure of Fonty itself an artificial construct. Theodor Wuttke, nicknamed Fonty, although chronologically separated from his idol by a hundred years (Fonty was born in 1919), identifies with his predecessor to such an extent that he incessantly cites quotations from his letters and works, dresses in a similar fashion, and adopts his habits. Similarly, Reich-Ranicki opines, the figure of Hoftaller, as a member of the state security apparatus the embodiment of the loyal servant throughout the centuries regardless of the specific regime he happens to serve, functions as a marionette. Moreover, Hoftaller has been derived from the novel *Tallhover* (1986) by Hans Joachim Schädlich (see the discussion below) and hence lacks originality. Although Reich-Ranicki credits Grass with passably imitating Fontane's *Plauderton,* or gift of striking the right conversational tone, he objects to the mixing of texts, that is, the indiscriminate juxtaposition of the author's words, phrases, and sentences and those that have been derived from Fontane without indicating their source — a curious charge indeed that entirely ignores the widespread use of intertextuality as an accepted literary practice.

But Reich-Ranicki reserves his most damning critique for the political views that he discerns in the novel. In particular, he objects to the author's tendency to portray the defunct GDR as a comparatively normal entity by, for example, having Fonty question its characterization as an "illegitimate state" and proclaiming it to have been "a comfy dictatorship" — albeit one that constituted a "world of want" (*TFA*, 270). Furthermore, Reich-Ranicki, who is Jewish, strongly disagrees with Grass's characterization of (re)united Germany as hostile to Jews: Professor Freundlich, a former GDR citizen, is eventually driven to commit suicide on account of his conviction that "'There is no room here for Jews'" (*TFA*, 556).

Whereas Reich-Ranicki acknowledges Grass's masterful handling of the obviously fictional encounter between writer Uwe Johnson (1934–84) and Fonty in the city of Neuruppin, Fontane's birthplace as well as that of Fonty (see *TFA*, ch. 30), his subsequent assessments of *Ein weites Feld* proved to be unrelentingly negative. Ironically, the critic had introduced Grass at the author's first public reading from the novel in the sold-out Frankfurt am Main Jewish Community Center in February 1995 and had applauded along with the audience. The first press reports — in 1995, dpa, the German news service, issued approximately fifty dispatches about the novel (see Hermes 1996, 481) — tended to arouse the reading public's curiosity by referring to Grass's tackling of a major topic (see, for example, Lüdke 1995). However, owing to the publicity campaign on the part of the Steidl publishing company, which resulted in the distribution of a considerable number of advance copies, reviews began to appear in the major and many minor dailies before the originally envisioned official publication date of 28 August, Goethe's birthday (for details of the "orchestrated publicity and marketing campaign," see Preece 2000b, 217–18). The tenor of these reviews in (West) German dailies with a national circulation such as *Die Welt* (Tschapke 1995), *Frankfurter Allgemeine Zeitung* (Seibt 1995), and the weekly *Die Zeit* (Radisch 1995) is predominantly negative. Iris Radisch classifies the book as unreadable because it propagates the myth of the opposition to reunification on the part of the GDR population and the takeover of the GDR by a colonial power in the manner of the *Bitterfelder Weg,* the cultural policy that briefly flourished in the GDR during the 1960s and sought to promote closer ties between writers and artists on the one hand and workers on the other, with the aim of building socialism.

In the TV broadcast of *Das literarische Quartett* on 24 August 1995, which was watched by more than a million viewers, Reich-Ranicki reiterated and intensified his attacks on both Grass and his novel. He was supported by critics Hellmuth Karasek and Karl Corino; only the fourth participant in the discussion, Viennese journalist Sigrid Löffler, attempted to introduce the elementary notion of narrative perspective by distinguishing between Grass's views and those of his figures and sought to question — without much success — the validity of Reich-Ranicki's condemnation of the book as totally worthless and boring because of its failure to adequately address an event of historic proportions (see Corino, Karasek, Löffler, and Reich-Ranicki 1995).

Perhaps not unexpectedly, the panning of *Ein weites Feld* by Reich-Ranicki and others did not have any noticeable effect on the demand for the book by potential readers — nor, for that matter, did the opinions of Reich-Ranicki and his ilk remain uncontested. More so than in previous publications of fictional works by Grass, the critical reaction, which was by no means confined to the literati and tended to ignore the aesthetic merits of the work, assumed extraordinary proportions — as two compilations of reviews, interviews, and letters amply demonstrate (see Negt 1996b; Oberhammer/Ostermann 1995). For example, Klaus von Dohnanyi (1995), then mayor of the city of Hamburg, wrote an open letter to Grass in which he warned that the writer was in danger of forfeiting his standing as a public figure owing to his severe censure of the "failed" reunification in general — which according to von Dohnanyi amounted to a misjudgment of historic proportions — and his attack on the *Treuhand* or "Handover Trust" (*TFA,* 131 et passim), the authority created to dispose of GDR state property, in particular. Von Dohnanyi advanced the dubious argument that Grass lacked the competence and experience necessary to engage in such a far-reaching denunciation of post-unification economic policies. Similarly, Birgit Breuel (1995), who succeeded the first head of the *Treuhand,* Detlev Karsten Rohwedder (1932–91), after he had been murdered and remained in that position until the *Treuhand* was dissolved in 1994, expressed her great disappointment in Grass's depiction of an agency that was faced with the difficult (and unprecedented) task of saving the remnants of an entire socioeconomic system, a system that had depended for its functioning on the Eastern Bloc and had suddenly collapsed, and of seeking investors who would keep the economy afloat.

Whereas critics such as von Dohnanyi and Breuel are clearly motivated by non-literary considerations, not all professional reviewers were inclined to condemn *Ein weites Feld.* For instance, the reviews in the *Süddeutsche Zeitung* (Busche 1995) and especially in the *Frankfurter Rundschau* (Schütte 1995) tend to be more even-handed than the authors of scathing critiques in other publications. Wolfram Schütte considers *Ein weites Feld* the exemplary novel of the *Wende,* which would serve future generations as a veritable treasure trove or archive of contemporaneous clichés of speech, thought, and opinions in its essentially successful mirroring of the two German (re)unifications in 1871 and 1990. Especially readers in the former GDR appreciated Grass's novel far more than their counterparts in the West (see Dieckmann 1995), because the author succeeded in recapturing the existential orientation and sense of alienation of former GDR citizens. Several GDR writers also praised *Ein weites Feld,* among them former cultural functionary Hermann Kant (1995), who professed not to be offended by Fonty's remark about Kant's "'cynicism'" (*TFA,* 502) and similar unflattering comments. Fritz Rudolf Fries (1995), writing in *Neues Deutschland,* the erstwhile official organ of the SED, the Socialist Unity Party, which has retained its socialist orientation and is widely read in East Germany, expressed his satisfaction with Grass's trenchant observations about, for instance, the literary scene in the East-Berlin district Prenzlauer Berg. Rolf Schneider (1995), another East German writer, claims to have read the text with pleasure and deems the integration of Fontane's biography successful. Statistical compilations — regardless of the objections one may raise against their use as a tool of literary analysis — do tend to support the thesis that former GDR citizens liked *Ein weites Feld.* The examination of one hundred and sixty-one reviews in German-language publications from September to December 1995 shows that of the thirty-one unambiguously positive reviews (21.1% of the total) 28.6% were published in the East and 20.7% in the West. Conversely, entirely negative assessments comprise fifty-four contributions or 33.5%; however, with regard to unenthusiastic responses the difference between East (19.0%) and West (34.7%) is quite pronounced (see Hermes 1996, 482–83).

Scrutinizing the Critics

While reviewers — foremost among them Reich-Ranicki — who judged *Ein weites Feld* to be a general failure were not unanimously supported in all the *Feuilletons,* a more systematic critique on the part of scholars and literary historians began to surface approximately one year after the novel's publication. In his introduction to the aforementioned compilation of reviews and other pertinent materials, entitled *Der Fall Fonty* (The Case of Fonty), Oskar Negt (1996a) posits that it is not the rejection of Grass's work that is scandalous; rather, it is the lack of invoking aesthetic norms and the substitution of political criteria as the ultimate standard of evaluation that is appalling. Specifically, Negt discerns three foci that predominate in negative assessments: the absence of genuine narration, the author's lack of dedication to a truthful depiction, and citizen Grass's deficient patriotism (14). Negt blames critics for neglecting what should be their chief task, which consists of elucidating the novel's complex structure, the interlacing time levels, and the role of the anonymous members of the Fontane Archives, who function as a narrative collective. Yet despite the assumed failings of the critical establishment, Negt reiterates that the negative comments have not noticeably diminished readers' interest in the novel and reaffirms the prevalent notion that Grass the writer cannot be separated from Grass the concerned and intervening citizen, whose prominence enables him to have his voice heard in the public sphere. Negt's condemnation of the critical establishment should be taken with a grain of salt, one critic (Frank 1998, 85–86) observes, in that Grass's publisher Steidl vigorously participated in the debate, not only via its promotion of the book, referred to above, but also by publishing *Der Fall Fonty,* a compilation that includes Negt's commentary, letters of fellow writers such as Christa Wolf and Christoph Hein, and statistical data about the tenor of reviews as well as the novel's placement on bestseller lists — tactics intended to create the impression that Grass has become the innocent victim of a media circus gone wild.

Clearly a defender of Grass, Florian Kirner (1996) ascribes a new, unconstructive quality to the criticism of *Ein weites Feld,* a negativism that surpasses that on the occasion of previous Grass publications; such negativism is attributable to the author's violation of taboos cherished by conservatives, who fail to acknowledge Grass's differentiation between the GDR and the Third Reich and object to his views on (re)unification. In a somewhat similar manner, Wolfgang Gabler (1997) expresses his disenchantment with the "misery" and assumed failures of journalistic reviewers, who tend to dismiss the novel as weak and unreadable and often pronounce judgment without actually having read the text. He singles out Reich-Ranicki as the chief manipulator in a shift of emphasis from what ought to be the primary object of discussion, the novel, to a secondary object, the review (but see Frank 1998, discussed below) — a procedure that results in the virtual disqualification of Grass's political views instead of an extensive analysis of the artistic merits of *Ein weites Feld* (309). (Andreas Wistoff, 1996, advances related arguments but concentrates exclusively on Reich-Ranicki's role in the debate.) Gabler traces the dissatisfaction with the novel not to a concerted campaign by major and minor critics but rather to the politically motivated but frustrated desire for the great "Wende- und Vereinigungsroman" (373; a novel about the *Wende* and unification), which appears in the guise of literary criticism. Essentially, Gabler contends, *Ein weites Feld* takes issue with a topic prevalent in (West) German public discourse, the theory of totalitarianism, which entailed the designation of the GDR as the "second dictatorship" on German soil — a dictatorship that disappeared as a consequence of (re)unification. In establishing a parallel between the first unification in 1871, which resulted in the establishment of the German Empire, and the second unification in 1990, Gabler argues, Grass emphasizes the continuities and analogies of different periods in German history in general; he reinforces the parallels by specifically comparing the *Gründerjahre* or "Founders' Era" (*TFA,* 447) of the early 1870s, a time of rapid economic expansion that caused detrimental socioeconomic consequences, with the 1990s in particular. Hence Grass severely disappoints the expectations of those who had anticipated a depiction of (re)unification based on the proven model of the Federal Republic.

In indirectly responding to Reich-Ranicki's charge that the figures of the novel are lifeless constructs, Gabler dismisses the notion that all characters must correspond to the realistic or naturalistic pattern prevalent in nineteenth-century novels. But he concedes that, for example, the characters' adoption of Fontane's aforementioned leisurely *Plauderton* may pose problems for readers at the end of the twentieth-century (and beyond), because they are accustomed to comparatively concise communications as well as inclined to succumb quickly to boredom. Likewise, Gabler conceives of the device of the "'paternoster,'" or "an elevator that is open at the front and moves in two directions, a chain of cabins in constant motion passing turning points in cellar and attic, rising and falling, never stopping . . ." (*TFA,* 60), as an embodiment of the principle of repetition that is also evident in the characters' conversations. (Berit Balzer, in a 2001 essay, provided a more encompassing analysis of the "paternoster" as a *Dingsymbol* indicative of the ups and downs of history as evidenced in the fate of individuals without, however, providing a conclusive answer as to the significance of the destruction by fire of the device at the end of the novel; see *TFA,* 643–44.)

Klaus Görzel (1996), who cites several reviews in their entirety, perceives the publicity surrounding the publication of *Ein weites Feld* merely as a repetition of the occurrences familiar from the appearance of *Unkenrufe:* reviews began appearing before the official publication date, these reviews generated headlines in other publications that were not necessarily based on the reading of the book, the marketing strategy of Grass's publisher in promoting the novel was being questioned, and the public clamor began with a scathing review by Reich-Ranicki — a chain of events that is indicative of the new media landscape, in which the task of reviewing literary texts fairly appears to be less urgent than producing news that borders on the sensational. Although only the first part of Werner Schwan's essay (1996) is devoted to the press reception of *Ein weites Feld,* Schwan provides a detailed discussion of Fontane's significance as a model for the creation of Fonty and suggests that Fonty's critique of (re)unification remains, on the whole, rather moderate, both because of his age — he turns seventy on 30 December 1989 — and because he is following in the footsteps of Fontane, a writer who was not given to embracing radical views. Furthermore, Fonty is a figure in the picaresque tradition (see also Wellnitz 2002c). Hence Grass's novelistic contribution to the widely discussed question of (re)unification appears far less strident than many *Feuilleton* writers would have it and his speeches and essays on the same subject would seem to indicate.

Whereas Timm Boßmann (1997, 93–156), Heinz Ludwig Arnold (1997, 205–37, 288–91), Harro Zimmermann (2006, 530–40), and, to a lesser extent, Robert Weninger (2004) provide fairly comprehensive discussions of the novel's reception in the press of the German-speaking countries, Dirk Frank (1998) establishes a rather encompassing theoretical framework with regard to the reception of *Ein weites Feld* by singling out the novel as the chief impetus for a somewhat frenzied discourse about the role of the media, which was primarily fuelled by the underlying fear on the part of some participants in the debate that the new media landscape would hasten the loss of a genuine reading culture based on an individual reading of the text in virtual isolation. But the preponderance of medial intervention, which embraces a variety of activities ranging from the conventional *Feuilleton* review to academic studies, tends to divert attention from the original text, which is further removed from the center of interest in the event that it turns out to be a bestseller — which, indeed, happened to be the case with *Ein weites Feld*. Hence the "*Öffentlichkeitswert*" (76) of a literary work, the degree of public esteem with which it is regarded, tends to overshadow the intrinsic value of the original text discovered by the individual reader without media access. Professional critics, who continue to play a major role as mediators between text and reading public, instigated the debate about the novel; according to Frank, their arguments may be reduced to one of the following positions: *Ein weites Feld* is boring, it is politically incorrect, or it is an artistic failure. Frank notes an increasing tendency among reviewers to reflect on their own activities, a process that entails a shift of emphasis from the inherent strengths or weaknesses of a work to be discussed to its reception. As a consequence, such reviewers come into conflict with astute observers (and critics) of the *Literaturbetrieb* (80; literary scene) such as Grass who on the one hand gave vent to his derision in the satirical scene involving a West German student in chapter 14, "Martha's Wedding" (see also Kniesche 2001, Staiber 2001b, and Bartl 1997) but on the other abetted the shift from text to *paratext* (the term is taken from Gérard Genette's *Seuils* [1981; *Paratexts,* 1997]). *Paratext* consists of *epitext,* or texts separated from the book but related to it, and *peritext,* such as introductions, titles, dedications, epigraphs, footnotes, and so on, which serve as a form of mediation between author and reader. It is particularly in his revival of the protagonist in Hans

Joachim Schädlich's novel that Grass resorts to the not entirely uncontroversial use of *peritext* (see Schädlich, discussed below).

Far more succinctly than Frank, Julian Preece (2000b) in his pointed "Seven Theses on 'Der Fall Fonty,'" both summarizes the arguments of critics and seeks to refute them. First, Preece claims, the novel failed to convince on account of the absence of the expected *"clichéd mixture of sex, food, grotesquerie, and linguistic bravura"* (215); second, Grass's anti-unification stance contributed to the "vendetta" against the writer, and third, "Grass became a victim of his own immense fame" (216) when the enormous publicity campaign, referred to above, went awry. Like numerous other observers who disagree with the treatment of Grass at the hands of the media, in his fourth thesis Preece singles out Reich-Ranicki as the chief villain, and, fifth, in partial agreement with the detractors of *Ein weites Feld,* he concedes that the length of the novel, which exceeds the volume of other works of fiction by an author well-known for his long narratives, may be an impediment in "contemporary culture" that "celebrates youth and values speed" (221). Sixth, in a partial restatement of his second thesis, Preece attributes the negative reception to Grass's allegedly "ill-informed and unoriginal" views (223), such as the contention that German history endlessly repeats itself, "crudely symbolized" in the eternally returning "paternoster" (225). Finally, Preece addresses the charge that Grass takes the side of the GDR and portrays the Stasi in a favorable light by pointing out that *Ein weites Feld* can be considered a "GDR-work" in that "it deals *exclusively* [my emphasis; "predominantly" might have been a more appropriate term] with GDR-characters in GDR or ex-GDR settings . . . from a recognisably pro-GDR perspective" (227). In a sense, the novel is "the first GDR-work by a West German" — a statement of somewhat dubious validity if one considers, for example, Friedrich Christian Delius's prose narrative *Die Birnen von Ribbeck* (1991; *The Pears of Ribbeck,* 1991), which, incidentally, takes one of Fontane's best-known ballads, one that is repeatedly referred to in *Ein weites Feld* (see *TFA* 130 et passim) as its point of departure. Nevertheless, *Ein weites Feld* may be considered a remarkable feat in view of Preece's perception that the "division of Germany . . . is nowhere so blatant as in its literature." Furthermore, Preece, in essentially following Frederic Jameson (1996) and Dieter Stolz (1997), plausibly explains Grass's virtual bracketing out of the pre-unification FRG by indicating that establishing the "historical parallels and continuities" (227) is far more convincing in the case of the GDR, a state that underwent a gradual process of Prussianization, in contrast to the Westernization of the Federal Republic. Hence, Preece suggests, from a political vantage point the critics' "glib judgements" and "hysterical reaction" were quite "astute," because Grass refuses to demonize the GDR in general and the Stasi, elevated to "diabolic" status (228) in the West, in particular. Yet despite the novel's implication that German history after unification will follow a disastrous course, Preece surprisingly inclines toward a positive interpretation; he maintains that *Ein weites Feld* has "by far the most optimistic ending of any" of Grass's prose works. He surmises without further elaboration that "Germany can escape from its past, just like Fonty slips away to France" (227–28). In what is essentially a restatement and an elaboration of his "seven theses," Preece (2001a) maintains that in the less than two years of the *Erzählzeit* or discourse time (from 17 December 1989, shortly before Fonty's seventieth birthday on 30 December, to the middle of October 1991) Fonty learns how to come to terms with himself, his biography, and German history — even though Preece concludes, paradoxically, that despite its ambivalent ending the novel exudes optimism. (For a more comprehensive reading, see Preece 2001b, 194–207. Martin Kane, in his 2002 survey, essentially recapitulates the negative assessments of German Grass critics during the 1990s.)

"Germany against Günter Grass": The French Reception

As in the English-speaking countries, in France Grass is well-known as the chief representative of postwar German literature. *Die Blechtrommel,* translated by Jean Amsler as *Le tambour* (1961) and awarded the prize for the best foreign book ("Prix du meilleur livre étranger") "made" Grass in France (Mannoni 1996, 138). Virtually all of Grass's prose works, in addition to plays, essays, interviews (notably those by Nicole Casanova in 1979 and Françoise Giroud in 1989) as well as other writings have been rendered into French. Olivier Mannoni, in his book-length, engaged study, *Un ecrivain à abattre: L'Allemagne contre Günter Grass* (1996), drew attention to the debate raging in Germany about *Ein weites Feld,* placed the arguments in the context of German history and politics, and polemically declared Grass to be the victim of a political-literary lynching because he had violated the taboo against criticizing German unification, a political process that once more had brought to the fore questions about Nazism in general and Auschwitz in particular, Communism, and the "Jewish question." (In his 2000 essay about memorialization and Auschwitz, Edgar Platen insists, as does Grass, on the centrality of Auschwitz for postwar literature.)

To be sure, Mannoni does summarize the reaction of the German press in considerable detail and dwells to some extent on the literary merits of the narrative, which, he declares, cannot be entirely subsumed either under the rubric of satire or under that of politics. Rather, Mannoni astoundingly declares, *Ein weites Feld* is also a novel about

German happiness ("le bonheur allemand"; 48), about an ideal and idyllic Germany that Grass regards with tenderness and nostalgia — a perception that he ultimately derived from Fontane. Hence Fonty appears as the incarnation of the German spirit ("l'esprit allemand"; 51) with all its virtues and faults. Rather than a comprehensive literary analysis, Mannoni provides a detailed exploration of the unlikely, complex, and paradoxical situation that pitted Grass against Reich-Ranicki, Germany's "national writer" ("l'écrivain national") against its literary "pope" ("[le] pape de la littérature allemande"; 101). After a propitious beginning at the aforementioned reading by Grass in the Frankfurt am Main Jewish Community Center, Reich-Ranicki's devastating review in *Der Spiegel,* as well as his panning of the book in *Das literarische Quartett* relations between critic and author quickly began to sour. As a result, Reich-Ranicki, a Polish Jew, survivor of the Warsaw ghetto, postwar Polish secret agent, and, ultimately, literary critic with a profound appreciation of German literature, appeared as the defender of German unification; in contrast, Grass, a former member of the Hitler Youth and firm believer in Nazi ideology (and, as he was to reveal in his 2006 autobiography, *Beim Häuten der Zwiebel,* a member of the *Waffen SS;* see the epilogue) as well as an exile from the former Eastern German territories who during the unification debate professed to be without a fatherland, was cast in the role of traitor. Yet Reich-Ranicki's criticism, Mannoni contends, was not only motivated by his habit of engaging in literary polemics; rather, the critic appeared to be genuinely concerned that Grass, the representative of a democratic and vigilant Germany, would turn his back on German affairs at a moment when his presence as well as his constructive interventions were sorely needed. In elucidating the complex relationship between writer and critic to an extent not encountered elsewhere, Mannoni has shed new light on the controversy caused by *Ein weites Feld.*

The novel's translation by Claude Porcell and Bernard Lortholary was published as *Toute une histoire* in 1997; in her thorough analysis of five translations of Grass's narrative, in which she emphasizes the problems inherent in rendering culture-specific words and concepts, Pernilla Rosell Steuer (2004) points out that, owing to the intertextual reference to a well-known phrase from Fontane's novel *Effi Briest* (1895; *Effi Briest,* 1914), the title poses special difficulties (see also Winston, below). Yet she finds Porcell and Lortholary's rendering quite acceptable in that it refers to both story and history, obviously pervasive elements in the narrative (307). At any rate, neither Grass nor his text escaped the attention of French critics and scholars during the following decade or so. After the award of the Nobel Prize in 1999, *Magazine Littéraire* devoted its November 1999 issue, edited by Lionel Richard, to Grass. The following year, Mannoni's voluminous biography, *Günter Grass: L'honneur d'un homme,* which includes a chronology and an annotated bibliography, appeared. In his combination of biography, literary analysis, and political history, Mannoni provides a sympathetic portrait of the author, whom he declares to be the figurehead of those writers who have dared to leave the ivory tower and engage in issues affecting society. Three further collections of essays and conference presentations by French and German scholars devoted to *Ein weites Feld,* edited respectively by Marie-Hélène Quéval (2001a), Françoise Lartillot (2001a), and Philippe Wellnitz (2002a), were published in France within a short time span and testify to the considerable interest the novel has attracted in that country — even if, one may surmise, both the academic orientation and the substantial number of articles written in German will not facilitate the French general reader's access to the three volumes. Owing to some thematic and methodological overlapping, which is in part attributable to several scholars contributing to more than one collection, as well as the impressive total of approximately forty articles in the three collections, a somewhat cursory discussion of individual essays, some of which will be referred to in different contexts, is in order.

In her brief introduction to the collected readings of *Ein weites Feld,* Quéval underscores the paradoxical fact that it is the young Frenchwoman, a foreigner, who is in favor of German national unity, but Quéval adds the cautionary note that only by renouncing any desire of conquest will Germany be able to retain its place in the European Union. The contributions by Volker Neuhaus (2001a, 2001b) briefly explore one historical dimension of the novel by interpreting the figure of Fonty as the vehicle by which the dusty archival materials regain life and impart meaning to the archivists' work; *Das Treffen in Telgte* functions as a kind of precursor of *Ein weites Feld* in that the former text provides ample evidence of Grass's (re)constructing a figure such as Gelnhausen from the works of Grimmelshausen, just as the creation of Fonty attracts the attention of the members of the Fontane Archives as someone "more alive . . . than the original compressed in our filing cabinets" (*TFA,* 374).

In a previously published article, Michael Ewert (2001) investigates Fonty and Hoftaller's numerous walks, mostly in reunited Berlin, and perceives them as a sign of openness, the desire to explore the urban landscape and to establish connections between past and present. (Ursula Reinhold, 2000, stresses the significance of Berlin as the past and then future capital and observes that Fonty and Hoftaller's walks take place within a triangle that is formed by the historical building occupied by the *Treuhand,* the locus of politics, the Tiergarten, a place for reflection and leisure, and the flat in Prenzlauer Berg, the not entirely private realm of the Wuttkes. Stéphanie Vanasten, 2006, explores the significance of the Tiergarten.) Sabine Moser (2001) elaborates on the interplay of imagination and historical events in the novel and suggests that Grass's imaginative reconstruction of history is driven by the desire to enlighten and to avoid the mistakes of the past; Anne-Sofie Dideriksen (2001) follows somewhat similar reasoning, arguing that the fictionalization of historical events in the novel is achieved by a conflation of Fonty's narrative and that of the narrators of the Fontane Archives, whereby the latter lend the story a documentary flair. In her investigation of history and memory, Sophie Lorrain (2001a) questions the appellation of *Ein weites Feld* as a novel about German unification and proposes instead the more encompassing designation of historical novel, in that literature is the locus *par excellence* to establish the connection between past and present, a connection that is particularly frequently invoked by Fonty, for example, when in one of his leaps in time he titles one of his lectures "'From [Prussian] Junker Estates to [GDR] Agricultural Collectives'" (*TFA,* 130). Yet the baleful course of German history, the German *Sonderweg,* seems to have come to an end when the symbol of endless repetition, the infernal "paternoster," is destroyed by fire. In another contribution, Lorrain (2001b) meticulously establishes the novel's topography of places in both present and past that are visited and/or evoked by Fonty and Hoftaller. They range from Berlin and its districts, buildings, monuments, parks, cemeteries, and bridges to other cities, both domestic, such as Neuruppin, and foreign, such as London; Fonty and Hoftaller's walks and explorations come to an end when they depart from Berlin. (In her essay of 2005, Helena Da Silva reads Berlin as the locus of a history of simultaneity that serves as palimpsest and archive.)

The close interplay of word and image in *Ein weites Feld* has been mentioned by several critics, but on the basis of Grass's sketches and drawings in the planning stages of the novel, which are primarily to be found in his book *Fünf Jahrzehnte: Ein Werkstattbericht* (2001), Florence Bancaud demonstrates that they cannot be separated from the written text and that they serve as a means to expose the contradictions of both history and art — evident, for example, in Fonty's supposedly uncritical veneration of Fontane. Biographer Mannoni (2001) briefly recapitulates the controversy caused by the publication of *Ein weites Feld* and predicts, alluding to the reception history of *Die Blechtrommel,* that twenty or thirty years hence the novel will no longer be read as a pamphlet but as a gigantic literary metaphor of a malaise that affected Germany. Thomas Serrier (2001) emphasizes the French component in the narrative, which is overtly concerned with the "German question" — a question, he contends, that has not been resolved by the opening of the Berlin Wall and (re)unification. There are evocations of the Franco-Prussian war of 1870–71 as well as the Second World War, during which Theo Wuttke supported the activities of the French resistance. Yet the issuance of an edict of tolerance by the Great Elector of Brandenburg in 1685 (see *TFA,* 118 et passim) enabled the persecuted French Huguenots to settle in Berlin and the region that was to become the state of Prussia; this historical event and its consequences offer an example of a non-aggressive element of German history and reveal a liberal concept of the nation. Independently of Serrier, Thomas W. Kniesche (2001) singles out France as an important constituent part of the "symbolic topographies" in the novel. Whereas Scotland signifies the dominance of historical forces beyond human control and England represents the unbroken belief in rational political action, France stands for Enlightenment, as evidenced, for example, by Fonty's frequent visits to the Rousseau Island in Berlin's Tiergarten (*TFA,* 13 et passim) — an Enlightenment, however, that went terribly astray during the French Revolution when Robespierre established his bloody reign of terror (see *TFA,* 96). Although Fonty's granddaughter Nathalie Aubron, who unexpectedly arrives in Berlin and insists on being called Madeleine after her grandmother, Fonty's lover during the German occupation of France (see *TFA,* 344), is frequently invoked by critics as the foremost representative of the French concept of nationhood (see Osinski 1996 and Lorou 2003), Kniesche stresses her role as a meticulous, exceedingly knowledgeable reader of Fontane's writings, who, in contrast to the German student Martina Grundmann (see also Bartl 1997) with her indifferent attitude toward the reading of primary texts, is the product of the "French educational system . . . [that is] characterized by a veritably Prussian rigor" (*TFA,* 446). (Maryse Staiber [2001a] contributes a spirited comprehensive study of the wedding celebration, at which the German student mindlessly displays her ignorance and her preference for abbreviated versions of secondary literature; Staiber persuasively attributes the satirical thrust of chapter 14, "Martha's Wedding," to Grass's repeated insistence in interviews on the importance of reading primary texts in the face of the prevailing tendency, especially among professors of literature and critics, to privilege theoretical writings.) In addition, via the connection to Marcel Proust (see Zschachlitz 2001), Kniesche refers to Madeleine as the agent who liberates Fonty from his circular, unproductive process of recollection about personal and collective guilt, by enabling him to leave Berlin — even if the search for truth continues to remain a laborious task.

The last contribution in the collection edited by Quéval is that by Dieter Arker (2001), who perceives the basic structure underlying this novel about Berlin, Fontane, and politics to be a strategy of doubling that is most noticeable in the often noted leaps in time — primarily those between 1871 and 1990 — as well as the doubling of the protagonists in Fonty/Fontane and Hoftaller/Fonty. The leaps in time are supported by the device of repetition, which is evident in the motif of the frequently recurring "diving duck" (*TFA* 86 et passim), which signifies Fonty's desire to escape, and the repeatedly invoked "paternoster," the mechanical device of endless reiteration.

The subtitle of the collection of essays assembled by Lartillot (2001a) refers to the political, historical, and literary aspects of *Ein weites Feld,* but the first two contributions begin with the last of these, addressing the artistic and literary views of Alfred Döblin, whom Grass repeatedly acknowledged as his "teacher," even though he has hardly been inclined to follow Döblin in adopting the latter's metaphysics of the universal spirit of life ("Metaphysik des universellen Lebensgeistes"; Koehn, 18). Perhaps more germane to the topic under discussion, Isabelle Solères (2001b) investigates Fontane's political views, which changed from revolutionary to conservative, in general and his attitude toward the (first) German unification in 1871 in particular. Although Fontane was a (not entirely uncritical) admirer of the towering figure of Chancellor Otto von Bismarck (1815–98), Solères contends that he never quite abandoned the idea of freedom that he had cherished during the bourgeois revolution of 1848 and that had been preempted by unification. A useful chronology of biographical and political/historical data and events during Fontane's lifetime concludes Solères's article.

In an unusual departure from what might be termed the prevailing scholarly consensus, Theo Buck (2001) views Grass's narrative construct, which is based on the equation of historical and contemporaneous events such as the two German unifications, as an indication of a crisis in the author's writing, in that it tends to simplify and render harmless a complex development. As one of several specific examples of a lack of coherence, Buck cites the episode of the reinterment of the two eighteenth-century Prussian kings Friedrich Wilhelm I, the "Soldier King," and Friedrich II (the Great), also known as "Old Fritz" (*TFA,* 592), in their original resting places in Potsdam (see *TFA,* 611 et passim) as a gratuitous effort to discredit Helmut Kohl, then Chancellor of the Federal Republic. Yet, Buck concedes, any reader interested in the events of 1989/90 will hardly be able to ignore *Ein weites Feld.* A more thorough assessment is offered by Cécile Millot (2001), who questions whether the novel is really the grand novel about the *Wende,* in view of the fact that, strictly speaking, the narrative encompasses a polemic rather than a work of "documentary fiction" (65) — as evidenced, for example, by the frequent references to the unjust but certainly not illegal acquisition of real estate in the (former) GDR by Heinz-Martin Grundmann (see also Bartl 1997). As a prime example of Grass's lack of "realism," Millot cites Fonty and Hoftaller's visit to one of the enormous and ghastly open pits from which the GDR obtained its chief source of energy in the form of lignite (ch. 25, "On the Edge of the Abyss"). Although the vast wasteland might have served as a perfect visual demonstration of the economic bankruptcy of the GDR, Hoftaller uses the occasion to launch into a kind of delirious, paranoid discourse that amounts to an "apotheosis of the Stasi" (Millot, 71); he claims that it was ultimately the Stasi that engineered the fall of the Berlin Wall (see *TFA,* 432–35) — a sign of Grass's lack of ability in *Ein weites Feld* to tell a spellbinding story. Yet, as other critics have noted (see, for example, Schwan 1996, 456–57), Hoftaller does acknowledge the bankruptcy of the GDR (see *TFA,* 433); Irmgard Elsner Hunt (1997) considers the bleak episode a warning about the future but also an indication that a course reversal may be imminent.

Like Volker Neuhaus (2001a), Evelyne Schmitt refers to *Das Treffen in Telgte* in her contribution about Grass's use of time and chronology in *Ein weites Feld,* but suggests that the novel in its totality assumes a function for the present similar to that of the poets' burned manifesto during the Thirty Years' War; that is, it is claiming the superiority of the written word over a dismal political reality in a divided Germany. Inasmuch as Grass's novel about the *Wende* has been widely read as opposing (re)unification, a political goal implicitly pursued by the powerless participants in the Telgte meeting, Schmitt's comparison does not appear to be entirely apt — even if Grass's notion of the *Kulturnation* underlies both texts.

In her analysis of one single episode, Fonty's birthday party at McDonald's in the second chapter (see *TFA,* 22–33), Maryse Staiber (2001b), a contributor to all three collections, demonstrates the interlocking of historical and literary allusions that establishes the relationship between the two epochs (2001b), and Philippe Wellnitz (2001), who in a contribution to a different volume poses the question whether *Ein weites Feld* qualifies as a picaresque novel (2002c), discovers aspects of the comical and satirical in the novel, such as Fonty's unsuccessful attempts to find a more appealing term for the negatively connoted verb "abwickeln," which describes the activities of the *Treuhand* and has been translated as "winding down" (*TFA,* 542). (In his 1997 linguistic analysis, Karl-Heinz Siehr perceives Fonty's futile efforts to find less negatively perceived terms for the verb "abwickeln" and the noun "Abwicklung," both of which occur with extraordinary frequency, especially in book 4, as indicative of the deliberate manipulation of the unification discourse on the part of West German politicians. Such a discourse seeks, via the use of euphemisms, to divert attention from the harsh economic consequences of the (re)unification for East Germans.)

Departing from the approaches of other contributors, Françoise Lartillot (2001c) explores the function of images in *Ein weites Feld* in general and the "omnipresence" of the world of art as an indication of a programmatic engagement in particular. Noteworthy is the appearance of and integration in the novel of artist figures such as Daniel Chodowiecki (1726–1801), born in Danzig and of both Polish and Huguenot descent, Adolf Menzel (1815–1905), and Max Liebermann (1847–1935), as well as the occasional remarks relating to the role of the cinema (but see Labroisse 1999)), TV, and photography. Among the creators of images and their manifestations, Lartillot devotes special attention to the frequently mentioned, enormously popular "colored pictorial broadsheets" (*TFA*, 479 et passim) that were produced in Neuruppin and greatly appreciated by Fontane. They are an "expression of a responsible but imaginative and naïve realism" (Lartillot, 148) — an artistic concept that is not to be confused with the complex artistic notion underlying *Ein weites Feld.*

In their contributions to Lartillot's collection, both Achim Geisenhanslüke (2001) and Ralf Zschachlitz (2001) discuss instances of Grass's allegorical narration that appear to contradict modern and postmodern modes of writing fiction; yet Geisenhanslüke claims that precisely the parallelism of past and present enables the narrator to maintain an ironic distance. Thus the *Wende* does not appear as tragedy but rather as comedy — as evidenced by the fact that two antediluvian actors play the leading roles — and the novel validates in the field of literature what Karl Marx postulated for politics, that is, great events occur first as tragedy and then as comedy. A further aspect of "the French connection," which primarily revolves around the repeatedly mentioned Madeleine, is discussed by Zschachlitz. He defines the French student, a mixture of cliché and perfection (179) who makes her first appearance in book 3, not only as a symbol of the broadening of the German-German framework that evolves into a French-German as well as European context but also as an allegorical figure representing a literary concept in the form of the "*petite madeleine,*" the tea biscuit that in the first volume of Marcel Proust's multi-volume novel *À la recherche du temps perdu* (1913–27; *Remembrance of Things Past,* 1932–34) stimulates the "*mémoire involuntaire*" of the first-person narrator and enables him to remember and tell about things past. Similarly, Madeleine inspires the archivists as well as Fonty, who ultimately leaves Germany to find a new home in the Cévennes in the South of France — the region in which he taped broadcasts for the French resistance movement against the German occupation during the Second World War and also where the persecuted Protestant Huguenots found refuge before many of them, Fontane's forbears among them, left France after the revocation of the edict of Nantes (1685).

The essays edited by Wellnitz (2002a) explore and summarize the (German) reception of *Ein weites Feld* (Stolz, Genton), investigate the intersection of literature and German history, especially with regard to its legacy in the face of (re)unification (Tambarin, Benoit, Bancaud), engage in intertextual approaches that go beyond Grass's use of Fontane (Scherf, Lartillot, Wellnitz), elucidate the significance of landscapes and specific places (Meffre, Bréthomé), and provide a close reading with an emphasis on the role of the archivists in their role as narrators (Staiber). In their totality, the contributions assembled in the three volumes constitute an impressive achievement of scholarly cooperation without regard to national boundaries.

"Germany's Last Heretic"

Owing primarily to the death in 1992 of Ralph Manheim, long-time translator of Grass's works, the English rendering of *Ein weites Feld* by Krishna Winston, entitled *Too Far Afield,* did not appear until the year 2000. The translator reported on the considerable problems she encountered in rendering the difficult text (Winston 2002), but in contrast to translations in other languages Winston opted for a proverbial saying familiar to English and American readers that retains the connotations of "ein weites Feld" in the German original, the well-known phrase from Fontane's *Effi Briest,* which the heroine's father evasively utters whenever he wishes to avoid discussing unpleasant matters. Rather than following the practice of two of the translations of *Effi Briest* (1967, 1995), which use variants of the phrase "That's too big a subject" (Steuer 2004, 309–10), Winston clearly establishes the intertextual reference to Fontane by using old Briest's favorite phrase, which, at the end of the novel, is slightly modified as "das ist ein zu weites Feld," "retranslates" it as "that takes us too far afield," and uses it as the novel's motto (*TFA,* [vii]).

During the long interval between the publication of the German original and that of the English version, English and American critics and, to a lesser extent, reviewers referred to it by its German title. (Hendrik D. K. Engel [2000] provides a somewhat cursory survey about Grass's reception in the English-speaking countries.) Even before the novel became available, Roger Boyes (1995) of the London *Times* provided information about Grass's aforementioned reading in the Frankfurt am Main Jewish Community Center — an event "akin to Oscars night" or, as Rick Atkinson (1995) put it, a "prizefight or rock concert." Boyes briefly addresses the theme of treachery by writers, which comes to the fore when both Fontane and Fonty betray their ideals and serve as informers, and concludes from the enormous publicity that preceded and accompanied the publication of the novel that "skepticism about German unity . . . [is] an acceptable platform for a potential bestseller."

Stephen Kinzer (1995), writing for the *New York Times* from (East) Berlin where Grass had read from his novel in the *Kulturbrauerei,* a former brewery that was turned into a cultural center and which also serves as the venue of Fonty's last, inspired, lecture before he leaves Berlin forever (see *TFA*, 628–40), reported that Grass was accorded a reception of a magnitude that "most authors can imagine only in their most extravagant fantasies." Yet the reading was not exactly a "love feast"; rather, many of the hundreds present had come to see and hear how the author would react to a "vituperative assault [that was] probably without parallel in the recent history of European literature." This assault was attributable to Grass's "highly critical vision of Germany," which appeared to undermine the view of modern Germany as a "vibrant and healthy society" and marked the novelist as one of Germany's "last unreconstructed leftists," or, as Kinzer titles his review, "Germany's Last Heretic." While critics' reactions, based on Grass's assumed political views, tend to predominate in Kinzer's review, he does provide a brief introduction to the novel for the uninitiated. His suggestion that Fonty is "evidently an alter ego" of Grass is distinctly a minority opinion.

A substantial review by Frederic Jameson appeared first in the *London Review of Books* (1996) and was republished (with added annotation) in the *South Atlantic Quarterly* (1997). Jameson's title, "Prussian Blues," indicates the reviewer's emphasis on the Prussian component of *Ein weites Feld;* he claims that Grass is rewriting "the German past on the basis of a Prussia of which East Germany (the German Democratic Republic) was the rightful heir." Accordingly, Jameson concludes that the thrust of the novel is to portray unified Germany as having to "assume the legacy of the socialist and Prussian Germany as its imaginary other." As indicated above, such a proposition met with vehement reactions by (West) German critics; Jameson perceptively attributes the vigorous opposition to Grass's apparent discrediting of unification via the 1871 analogy to the desire to separate art from politics, abandon "engaged" literature, and reinstitute "the untroubled cultivation of the aesthetic" (1996; repr. 1997, 717). Given that Grass explicitly drew attention to the parallels between the Bismarckian founding of the Empire and German (re)unification, it seems astonishing that Jameson implicitly contradicts prevalent notions about Prussia and its baleful influence on the course of German history — notions that are obviously shared by Grass; instead, he credits Prussia with having sustained a "tolerant Protestant culture" that was not to be found in "Catholic and provincial West Germany" (717). On a different note, Jameson hews to conventional wisdom and provides a brief sketch of Fontane's novelistic achievements for the English-speaking reader (but he excludes any discussion of Fontane's views of Prussia) and outlines the striking similarities between Fonty and his idol Fontane — a symbiotic relationship that makes it sometimes difficult to "tell the two apart" (719).

Of the "pseudo-couple," Fonty and Hoftaller, Jameson takes a somewhat benign view, comparing them to Samuel Beckett's Vladimir and Estragon, Miguel de Cervantes Saavedra's Don Quixote and Sancha Pansa, and even Mutt and Jeff (722). Such a portrayal, Jameson suggests, may perhaps amount to minimizing the role of the Stasi; indeed, the Stasi-observed protagonist's anguished ruminations in Christa Wolf's *Was bleibt* (1990; *What Remains,* 1993) offer quite a different perspective. In the end, Jameson returns to his overriding theme, the postulated reincorporation of the "older Prussia" into the "so-called West" — a process whose effects are "as yet unforeseeable" (726).

When *Too Far Afield* was published at the end of the year 2000, the historical events in the center of the novel had lost some of their immediacy and topicality; at any rate, British and American reviewers had little reason to revive the fierce debate that had raged in Germany five years earlier. Writing in the *Times Literary Supplement,* Hugh Macpherson (2000) discerns the "desire for a great German novel" on account of the "events of last century, culminating in reunification." Although Grass's work would seem to satisfy such desire, it is a "curious and quirky book" that does convey some sense of history in the making but cannot be called "user-friendly" on account of its length and because it leaves the reader with "perceptions that seem as unpredictable and random as the birds." Maya Jaggi (2000) in *The Guardian* sees the novel exploring the "warnings encrypted in a longer, repetitious national history" but the technique of leaping "across centuries, sometimes within a sentence" result in a work that is "complex and at times mystifyingly allusive" particularly for those readers "not steeped in 19th-century German literature" and, it might be added, history. (As a concession to the English-speaking reader, *Too Far Afield* features a "Brief Chronology," ix–xiii, which, regrettably, erroneously lists 1918 instead of 1898 as the year of Fontane's death.) Yet the "gentle comedy of Fonty . . . is part Kafka, part Chaplin."

The reviews of two leading American publications arrived at opposite conclusions. Writing in the *New York Times Book Review,* James J. Sheehan (2000) judges *Too Far Afield* a "rich and complex book" that deals with "'the German Question,'" that is, the "painful intrusion of the past into the present that remains part of the Germans' national consciousness." The novel displays decidedly "autumnal hues" and is about "growing old rather than growing up" as in Grass's earlier fiction. Yet Sheehan detects "hope and affirmation" in the text, which he attributes to the author's belief in "literature's enduring power to overcome the obdurate power of time, history and death." Gabriele Annan (2000) offers quite a different opinion in the *New York Review of Books,* in that she deems *Too Far Afield* a "tract disguised as a novel" and says that it uses ill-defined "postmodern methods" and is therefore "not easy to follow," indulges in a "downpour of dropped names," has "almost no story line," suffers from "endless conversations," especially those between Fonty and Hoftaller, and uses the "symbols" of the aforementioned "paternoster" and the previously cited "diving duck" with "quite irritating frequency." Although Annan concedes that the "mood becomes more upbeat" once Fonty's granddaughter Madeleine has entered the story, she concludes that the book is "so self-important, so self-indulgent, and so repetitive too" that Grass has succeeded in condemning "his giant opus to oblivion." Annan's harsh verdict is undermined by some blatant factual errors and questionable readings. For instance, she confuses the member(s) of the "Archives" in Potsdam (*TFA*, 80 et passim) with those of the "Stasi organization" in Berlin, located in the "State Security fortress on Normannenstrasse, [which] had been stormed [after the fall of the Berlin Wall] and then immediately sealed" (*TFA*, 61). Similarly, Annan's suggestion that the "diving duck . . . symbolizes the political turncoat," who survives all regime changes by temporarily going underground (something Fonty hardly does), is less persuasive than the assumption that in the duck Fonty sees a manifestation of his desire to escape from Berlin, as evidenced by his two unsuccessful attempts to evade Hoftaller's clutches before Madeleine succeeds in spiriting him away to France.

A far more knowledgeable appraisal than that by Annan is offered by Dennis Drabelle (2000) in the *Washington Post*, who professes to "love" Fontane and to have read all of his works available in English translation; even so, he was not able to decipher all references to the writings of the "Immortal" (*TFA*, 21 et passim) in *Too Far Afield*. Moreover, Drabelle draws attention to Heinrich von Kleist, "the other Prussian" (*TFA*, 612) whom Fontane/Fonty respects but does not feel not close to. Ultimately, the combination of "modern German history" and the dominant presence of Fontane via his mouthpiece Fonty present Grass's "non-German readers with a hugely long, fitfully engaging book that can't stand on its own."

In what surely must count as a minority opinion, Thomas McGoniggle (2000), writing in the *Los Angeles Times*, suggests that Grass "has delivered a creation worthy of Oskar" in the "intriguing and sympathetic" Fonty — even if, it goes without saying, their disparity is all too obvious. Although "hopelessly literary, hopelessly entangled with German history," *Too Far Afield* can still lay claim to the status of a "witty humanistic novel"; it features the unlikely pair of Fonty and Hoftaller, a reprise of Laurel and Hardy, and is "a fitting companion" to *The Tin Drum* — an assertion that presumably does not find much support. In implicitly inviting a not entirely persuasive comparison between the Third Reich and the GDR, McGoniggle sees Fonty serving as "a memorable witness to the rise and fall of another regime which was to have lasted forever."

Fonty and German Unification

Literary critics writing in scholarly journals tend to be less inclined than reviewers in the *Feuilleton* to give *Ein weites Feld* poor marks. Hans Kügler (1995) reads Grass's text as radically countering the convictions of national conservatives, who celebrated the successful (re)unification after forty years of separation; (re)unification would, they expected, lead to a "normal" state of affairs unhampered by the liability of the Nazi legacy. In particular, Grass employs the device of "erinnerndes Erzählen" (302), a commemorative act of narration that, via the technique of leaps in time, presents history in terms of contemporaneous events seen as a repetition of past events. For example, Fontane first experienced the founding of the German Empire in 1871 as a national awakening and wrote about it in this vein; however, he increasingly began to perceive the Bismarckian project as the cause of general torpor. Analogously, Fonty first greets the GDR's "'Bloodless revolution'" of 1989 (*TFA,* 472) as the point of departure for a more humane future; but he soon begins to discover that the process of transformation, which had begun with high hopes, turned into the so-called *Anschluss,* a politically loaded term signifying the takeover of Austria by the Third Reich in 1938, or, in the context of 1989/90, the "annexation [of the GDR by the FRG that was] officially termed a 'voluntary accession'" (*TFA,* 382). In fairness, it must be said that in March and May 1990 the majority of the GDR population voted for a conservative alliance that was in favor of (re)unification; hence the term *Anschluss* is not entirely apt (see Zschachlitz 2001, 178).

Specifically, Kügler singles out three "myths" that were frequently invoked during the unification process. Grass exposes them by drawing attention to historical parallels: the myth of a reawakened, purified nation, the myth of the redeeming qualities of the West German hard currency (philosopher Jürgen Habermas spoke of "DM-Nationalismus," a nationalism based on the currency of the German Mark), which Grass exemplifies by resorting to the aforementioned *Gründerjahre* or *Gründerzeit* of the 1870s, and the myth of the abdication of leftist intellectuals in both parts of Germany. In fact, the debate about the role of intellectuals in the GDR exposed the ambivalent attitides of writers such as Christa Wolf and Heiner Müller who after the fall of the Berlin Wall were harshly criticized on account of their (partial) collaboration with the GDR regime. But, as Grass makes clear, both Fonty and Fontane have accepted compromises and have engaged in opportunism. Kügler concedes that the recreation of a twentieth-century Fontane-like figure is not entirely unproblematic; in contrast to Fontane, both prominent chronicler and critic of the Empire, Fonty is confined to his niche and not in a position to exert much influence. In the end, he is dismissed by the *Treuhand,* the institution he served as a lowly messenger, and disappears from Germany.

In her investigation of aspects of the Fontane reception in Grass's novel, Jutta Osinski (1996) justifiably draws attention to the erroneous assumption of some previous reviewers, who blithely ignore the elementary distinction between author, narrator, and characters in order to mistakenly suppose that the novel serves as an unmitigated reflection of the author's political stance. For example, Fonty's pessimistic ruminations about German nationhood are counterbalanced by the views of his French granddaughter, for whom the unified nation state represents an entirely normal and desirable entity. Furthermore, Osinski emphasizes the self-referentiality of the literary text, which makes it an unsuitable vehicle for political purposes. Thus Fontane, who is never mentioned by name but instead referred to as the "Immortal," continues to exist via the veneration of his present-day readers as well as in the figure of Fonty, who does not serve as a mere copy of the original; rather, he extends the existence of Fontane into the present by, for instance, reinterpreting and rewriting the latter's novels. A case in point is the new ending he devises for *Irrungen Wirrungen* (1888; *Entanglements,* 1986): weak-willed baron Botho von Rienäcker no longer marries the "aristocratic ninny Käthe" but disregards "class barriers" and takes proletarian Lene as his wife (*TFA,* 593).

Although a cipher and a construct rather than a psychologically drawn character, Fonty embodies the spirit of literature; he is the medium through whom the "Immortal" continues to exist. Thus Fonty is a favored guest in the Fontane Archives, where he provides insights that augment the assiduously collected materials of the "diligent footnote slaves" (*TFA,* 4) and bring them to life. (Germanist Dieter Stolz conducted research for Grass "undercover" in the Fontane Archives; see Bielefeld, Grass, and Stolz 1996.) Grass's emphasis is then clearly on the biographical; the frequent references to works such as Hans-Heinrich Reuter's standard biography of Fontane (1968; see *TFA,* 47 et passim) do tend to invalidate theories about the "death of the author" advanced by Roland Barthes (1968) or the dissolution of the author in a variety of discourses suggested by Michel Foucault (1969). Actually, Osinski posits that the essence of the text lies in the interplay between the biographies of Fontane/Fonty. But its very playfulness undermines the biographical mode; without further theoretical underpinning, she maintains that the author Fontane is constructed by the act of the reader's perusing the novel.

Less concerned with textual intricacies, Andrea Bartl (1997) reads the novel as a text that conveys Grass's views about the *Wende,* which he articulated in numerous essays, speeches, interviews, and public debates, in literary form. The marriage of Fonty's daughter Martha and the widowed owner of a construction firm may be seen as establishing a union between the Grundmanns from the West and the Wuttkes (Fonty's family) from the East (see *TFA,* ch. 15). But what is supposed to be a time of harmonious togetherness at the wedding feast brings into focus the disparate experiences and expectations of the inhabitants of the two parts of Germany when Martina Grundmann, the previously mentioned student of *Germanistik* from Cologne, expresses her indifference not only to Fontane, of whom she has barely heard, but also to Dresden and says that she prefers Paris or Amsterdam to the East German city (see *TFA,* 234, Kniesche 2001, and Staiber 2001a). True, such sentiments were not entirely uncommon among West Germans of the postwar generations — Patrick Süskind (b. 1949), author of the acclaimed novel *Das Parfum: Die Geschichte eines Mörders* (1985; *Perfume: The Story of a Murderer,* 1986), may serve as a prominent example — but Bartl opines that Grass resorts to trite clichés and cites the figure of the aforementioned *Wessi* (that is, someone hailing from West Germany), Grundmann (see Millot 2001), as proof: Grundmann represents the prototypical wheeler-dealer, for whom the unification is merely a euphemism for the pursuit of economic interests. (On a different note, in an essay he wrote in 2000, Walter Hinck reads *Ein weites Feld* as Grass's homage to Fontane and considers the wedding scene a prime example of Grass's success in recreating Fontane's ambiance.)

In partial agreement with other critics (see, for example, Osinski 1996), Bartl views the representation of Fontane in the novel as both a historical and a literary-fictive figure as a device that allows Grass to establish the predominant nexus between past, present, and fiction. Via the figure of Hoftaller Grass succeeds in ascertaining the subversive power of words in particular and "literature in general" (*TFA,* 392). Yet in *Ein weites Feld* literature is largely used to provide insights into the present; the dimension of the future, which figures prominently in political and journalistic statements about the *Wende,* is virtually ignored. Although Bartl's main insight, that Grass puts forward his political critique of unification via literary means, is hardly novel, her fairly detailed elucidation of the narrative techniques employed and her critical stance, which seeks to strike a balance between widely divergent views, would seem to do justice to a complex work.

Like virtually all other critics, Manfred Misch (1997) takes issue with Reich-Ranicki's review and emphasizes the most important role of allusions and quotations in the novel. He views Fonty's fate as that of a typical GDR intellectual in his relationship to the state, since Fonty had served as a speaker at gatherings of the *Kulturbund* or "Cultural Union" (*TFA,* 3 et passim) and was first honored as a "cultural activist" (*TFA,* 128) but ultimately demoted on the grounds of his being viewed as critical of the GDR; subsequently he served temporarily as an informant on the oppositional writers of the East Berlin "Prenzlauer Berg 'scene'" (*TFA,* 63; see also Fries 1995). Yet in his speech from the Neuruppin Fontane monument (see *TFA,* 499–502), which he addresses to Hoftaller, Fonty delivers a severe indictment of the GDR's cultural policies. But Misch considers the frequent allusions, especially to Fontane's *Irrungen Wirrungen,* a feature that attest to the status of the novel as an intricate literary text rather than an unrefined political statement.

Lutz Kube (1997) discusses the role of the GDR intellectuals in more detail than Misch and sees the figure of Fonty as a vehicle for minimizing the culpability of writers in their subservience to the state — a reading that is also supported by Hoftaller's ambivalent role as both oppressor and protector of Fonty and his family. It should be noted, Kube points out, that it is precisely Fonty's critical stance vis-à-vis the GDR authorities, which is based on his veneration of the positive traditions of Prussia, that places him in a position that is subject to repression and censorship by Hoftaller and his ilk. Yet Grass is not proposing an undifferentiated acquittal of all GDR intellectuals; for example, the aforementioned Hermann Kant who, despite his "distinguished name" (*TFA,* 185), which evokes that of philosopher Immanuel Kant, actively participated in repressive measures against his fellow writers, does not find favor with Grass. Although Fonty characterizes the results of the excessive care of the GDR regime for its writers as leading to a subtle form of dependency — "Between the lines of the most courageous appeal one reads commissioned protest . . ." (*TFA,* 501) — Kube argues that in view of his idiosyncratic stance and minority opinion with regard to reunification (see Reich-Ranicki 1995), Grass is eager to garner the support of critical GDR intellectuals as allies in his critique of recent political developments in Germany.

"Tallhover/Hoftaller/Revolat/Offtalère"

Next to Fonty, it is the figure of Hoftaller/Tallhover who has aroused the greatest interest of critics and scholars. Yet the controversy between Hans Joachim Schädlich and Grass about the legitimacy of the latter's "borrowing" of the protagonist of Schädlich's novel has undeservedly received comparatively little notice. In his autobiographical note, Schädlich (1998) reconstructs Grass's interest in his creation of Tallhover, a figure who surfaces as early as 1988 in *Zunge zeigen* (see *SYT,* 24 et passim) and who, Grass insisted, should not have been allowed to die after the uprising of 17 June 1953 as (presumably) happens in Schädlich's novel. Hence Grass asked Schädlich's permission to update Tallhover, whom he eventually renamed Hoftaller; Grass also uses the names of Revolat (Tal[l]hover spelled backward) for the brief period when turncoat Tallhover served as a West German agent in the Federal Republic (see *TFA,* 10) and, in Madeleine's pronunciation, Monsieur Offtaler (*TFA,* 349 et passim). Schädlich, who felt indebted to Grass because the latter supported him during his difficulties in the GDR and enabled him to obtain permission to leave the GDR in 1977, granted Grass's request but gradually began to object to Grass's borrowing of his figure. Although Schädlich is frequently referred to in *Ein weites Feld* either by name (*TFA,* 38 and 291) or as the "biographer" of *Tallhover* (*TFA,* 5 et passim), he found Grass's explicit acknowledgment of his source in a *paratextual* note (see D. Frank 1988, above) at the very end of the novel (the note has not been included in the English translation) insufficient. Furthermore, he objected to Grass's portrayal of Tallhover/Hoftaller, because it implied that the methods and goals of Stasi and Western secret services were entirely compatible; in an exchange of letters, Schädlich broadened his critique by positing that Grass's anti-unification resentment had led him to trivialize both the Stasi and the entire system of surveillance prevalent in the GDR — a charge that Grass rejected.

Although the interest of critics and scholars in the figure of Tallhover/Hoftaller is quite pronounced, there are only a very few studies that are exclusively devoted to this character, for the obvious reason that Tallhover/Hoftaller is usually discussed in conjunction with Fonty; in fact, the appearance of the unlikely pair has resulted in the search for literary forbears, which include, in addition to those mentioned (see Jameson 1996) Goethe's Faust and Mephistopheles, Diderot's Jacques the fatalist and his master, and Laurel and Hardy. But taking Fonty's remark "Hoftaller is better than Tallhover" (*TFA,* 455) as her starting point, Britta Kallin (1997–98) confines herself essentially to Hoftaller and his literary antecedent by engaging in a brief comparison of the two figures, a comparison that does not go much beyond registering comparatively insignificant features such as smoking and eating habits, without elucidating in any detail the respective figures' similar political and moral views or their function within the systems they serve. More comprehensively, and with close attention to the historical context, Hélène Boursicaut (2001) traces the career of Tallhover from the *Vormärz,* a period preceding the March revolutions of 1848 in the German states and Austria, to the extension of his existence in *Ein weites Feld.* Without resorting to Schädlich's autobiographical note, Boursicaut reads *Ein weites Feld* in terms of Genette's theories, as a *hypertext* that is based on the preceding *hypotext* by Schädlich — a form of intertextuality that is evident in Grass's use of quotations, summaries, and allusions. Since verbatim and/or slightly modified quotations are, without doubt, the most obvious form of intertextual references, Boursicaut cites Tallhover's plea for help when he is at the point of committing suicide (see *TFA,* 87) and Lenin's 1917 travel through Germany from Switzerland to Russia in a sealed train (see *TFA,* 110 et passim) as examples of Grass's use of quotations from Schädlich's novel. On the whole, Grass engages in a subtle and ironic game with a preexistent literary text, a game that cannot be reduced to the claim that Hoftaller's fictive existence is simply an extension of that of Tallhover; rather, Boursicaut writes, the Grassian *hypertext* has a decidedly creative dimension.

Hoftaller, by virtue of functioning as Fonty's "day-and-night shadow" (*TFA,* 3 et passim), evokes not only the word "beschatten" (closely observe) but also Adelbert von Chamisso's tale *Peter Schlemihls wundersame Geschichte* (1814; *Peter Schlemihl,* 1823), in which the protagonist sells his shadow to the devil. Grass, not content with merely reviving a literary figure, humanized Hoftaller and turned him into a multifaceted character, both watchdog and Fonty's "guardian angel" (*TFA,* 19 et passim) at the same time. Boursicaut singles out two scenes of symbolic import that emphasize Fonty and Hoftaller's interdependence. The first of these shows the two old men exchanging places in an unsteady rowboat, a precarious maneuver that results in "an embrace of the sort that is based on the well-known assurance: We're in the same boat" (*TFA,* 340); the second scene, the reenactment of the exchange of agents during the Cold War at Glienicke Bridge (see also Labroisse 1999), emphasizes the inseparability of Fonty and Hoftaller (see *TFA,* 410–14). In the final analysis, Grass's text offers a palimpsest in which the *hypotext* is transparent in the *hypertext,* in which the author appears as reader, and in which the genesis of the novel is revealed. Objections such as that by Frauke Meyer-Gosau (1997), who claims that Grass violated the norms of collegial behavior vis-à-vis Schädlich, place too much emphasis on ethical rather than literary aspects; after all, *Ein weites Feld* is open to rereading and reinterpretation just like any other literary text.

The importance of reading is likewise stressed by Thomas W. Kniesche (2001; see also the discussion above) in Tallhover/Hoftaller's case; compared with the readers and archivists in Potsdam, Fonty is "the better archive" (*TFA,* 170), but Hoftaller reads voraciously in order to be able to manipulate and control potential adversaries of the state — an endeavor that ultimately fails because of Hoftaller's single-minded, non-comprehensive approach to reading, as Fonty gleefully points out to him (see *TFA,* 532). Julian Preece (2001a) goes so far as to elevate Hoftaller to the "Geist der Geschichte" (220; embodiment of the spirit of history), who, in his complex relationship with Fonty, symbolizes the state of affairs in Germany during the *Wende,* while the country is dealing with its past. For Dieter Arker (2001), Tallhover/Hoftaller is a figure out of a fairy tale, albeit a somewhat sinister character who is motivated by his fanaticism for order at all costs and whose deliberate inconspicuousness contrasts starkly with the flamboyance occasionally displayed by Fonty. Yet Arker traces the origins of Tallhover/Hoftaller's type back to the early 1880s when, under the guidance of Chancellor Bismarck, laws regulating welfare and social policies as well as those aimed at suppressing the Social Democratic Party were passed. The combination of public welfare institutions and police-state methods was also to be found in the GDR, Arker claims; Hoftaller, in both aiding and obtrusively shadowing Fonty, is then the typical representative of such a system.

Narrative Strategies; "Aesthetization"

According to Dieter Stolz (1998), by changing the novel's working title *Treuhand* to *Ein weites Feld*, the familiar phrase from *Effi Briest*, Grass replaced a designation that bears the "unmistakeable signature of the angry critic of unification" with one that opens the "spaces of the imagination" (150). Yet in choosing a collective of narrators, among whom an individual voice can only occasionally be discerned, Grass opts for a narrative that is told from a "GDR perspective" (151) inasmuch as the Fontane Archives are located in Potsdam near Berlin, in the former GDR. Old habits die hard; although they prefer anonymity, the archivists do not shy away from shadowing Fonty and producing veritable "*Stasi* reports dressed up in literary language." But their incessant labors are ultimately in vain owing to the "unlimited possibilities of wide open spaces" (152) and the endless possibilities they evoke.

In a bold interpretive move, Stolz hypothesizes that the true import of the text is to be gleaned from a virtually hidden subtext, that is, Fonty's mention of the nearly forgotten editor of the reactionary Prussian newspaper *Kreuzzeitung* (*TFA,* 27 et passim) by the name of Hesekiel, a name by which Fonty also calls a stray dog. The name Hesekiel evokes Martin Luther's translation of the Old Testament; in chapter 37 of the Book of Ezekiel (not coincidentally, *Ein weites Feld* counts thirty-seven chapters — see Stolz, 155), the Lord sets down Ezekiel "in the midst of the valley which was full of bones," a passage that Stolz plausibly reads as signifying the field or realm of the dead ("'Totenreich,'" 155). This realm is suggestive of the victims of Nazism, the remembrance of whom will not be obliterated by unification. Similarly, the huge "abyss and moonscape" (*TFA,* 426; see also Millot 2001) created by surface mining in the GDR is indicative of the dead resting "on a barren wasteland" (Stolz, 156). However, far less convincing is Stolz's reference to the passage in the Book of Ezekiel that tells of the resurrection of the dead as a premise for uniting "the children of Israel" and making them "one nation" under "one king" — thus ending all division. It is then difficult indeed to see how the passages cited could be construed as a negative reflection on unification in the face of "harmonizing" official versions (Stolz, 156).

More persuasive are Stolz's attempts to tease out intertextual references or, rather, allusions. For instance, he cites Heinrich Heine's poem "Nachtgedanken" (1843; "Night Thoughts," 1982), written during his exile in France, as a possible inspiration for Fonty's love for his "enchanting French granddaughter" (Stolz, 157). The granddaughter ultimately enables him to escape from Germany and the influence of Hoftaller — who, ironically, had arranged the meeting of Fonty and his granddaughter in the first place — so that at the very end of the novel Fonty is seeking to prove Effi Briest's father wrong by proclaiming — perhaps unfoundedly — that despite his having "gone far afield, an end is in sight . . ." (*TFA,* 658). The creation of Fonty as well as Fonty's frequent references to Fontane, Stolz contends, add up to a "biography of Fontane" (159). But the encyclopedic novel also incorporates elements of the picaresque, makes use of satirical humor, and relies on the invoked "power of fiction" (*TFA,* 645). Grass's work is then neither a leading article nor a *roman à these* but "an ambitious work of art" and a "daring formal experiment" that is filled to the brim with "quotations and allusions," incorporates "poetological self-reflection[s]," and, Stolz concludes in self-deprecating fashion, ultimately defies a "concluding résumé" even by learned Germanists (159, 160, 161, and 162).

In the epilogue to his *Das Kunstwerk im Zeitalter seiner technischen Reproduzierbarkeit* (1936; complete version 1963; *The Work of Art in the Age of Mechanical Reproduction,* 1976), Walter Benjamin famously observed that Fascism strove for the "Ästhetisierung des politischen Lebens," the aesthetization of politics, in order to divert the attention of the masses from the political process and ultimately disenfranchise them, a phenomenon to which Communism responded with the "Politisierung der Kunst" or the politicizing of art. However, when Mark E. Corey (1998) appears to unintentionally refer to Benjamin by entitling his article "Ein weites Feld: The Aesthetization of German Unification in Recent Works by Günter Grass," he obviously does not have in mind a blatant abuse of aesthetics by Grass in the service of discrediting unification; rather, Cory seeks, somewhat along the lines of Stolz, to demonstrate that *Ein weites Feld* is "the most developed aesthetization of the unification" (177) and hence not an explicit political statement.

Cory takes into account Grass's works from the 1990s, among them *Unkenrufe,* but considers *Ein weites Feld* incontestably the author's "major literary statement on German unification" because of the creation of the figure of Fonty/Wuttke, a device that essentially allows him, Cory points out in agreement with others (see, for example, Gabler 1997), to "simultaneously juxtapose two turning points in German political history," that is, the *Gründerjahre* and the "collapse of the GDR" (Cory, 188) as well as, one might add, its attendant socioeconomic consequences. Fonty's "double identity" as both a "retired civil servant" and Fontane's "cultural soulmate" results in an "extraordinarily dense set of palimpsests" that serves as a "reminder" of successes and failure of the past and their potential implications for the future (188).

Although several critics have expounded on the ambivalent relationship between Fonty and Hoftaller, Cory, more than others, inclines toward emphasizing both their symbiotic association and Hoftaller's role as Fonty's "'guardian angel'" (*TFA,* 89 et passim). Particularly the "insensitivity of the Treuhand" and the "crass commercial exploitation [of the former GDR] . . . generate considerable sympathy" for Hoftaller and make it ultimately "impossible," Cory claims, to decide which of the two figures is "more subversive" (189 and 191). Yet Cory discovers a "subtly optimistic dimension" in the novel that emanates from Fonty's bond with his charming French granddaughter, a bond that spans generations and nationalities and may entail Grass's "stubbornly hopeful vision" (192) of a European integration that would end the pernicious cycle of German history, symbolized by the eternally returning "paternoster."

The "paternoster" is singled out by Gerd Labroisse (1999) as one of the conspicuous devices by which Grass achieves the evocation of visual images via verbal means. A case in point is the scene when Fonty sees the chief of the *Treuhand* descending in the "paternoster" and sees himself "transported back in time by half a century" (*TFA,* 474) to his encounter with *Reichsmarschall* Hermann Göring, who was then leaving the cabin. Fonty immediately begins "to film the historical transition" from the Third Reich to the "first German Workers' and Peasant's [sic] State" when "Party secretary" Walter Ulbricht comes into view riding the "paternoster" (*TFA,* 475; see Labroisse, 363–65). Grass's recourse to and reliance on film techniques is evident throughout the novel, Labroisse observes. Thus Fonty and Hoftaller's walk at the beginning of the novel — the first of many — is depicted as a "silent film [that] unreeled in the direction of Potsdamer Platz" (*TFA,* 6); Fonty and Hoftaller reenact the plot of "actual and invented spy stories and secret-agent thrillers" (*TFA,* 411) at that famed locus of Cold-War lore, Glienicke Bridge, which connects (West) Berlin and Potsdam; and during their farewell Fonty and Hoftaller ride on a Ferris wheel, a scene with explicit references to Graham Greene's novella *The Third Man* (1950) and the film of the same name (1949) starring Orson Wells (see *TFA,* 654). Yet the pronounced tendency of striving for visual effects, Labroisse avers, is ultimately problematic, because Grass's approach does not lend itself to a sober analysis of political and historical developments.

Without recourse to Labroisse, Jutta Heinz (2002) investigates Grass's concept of history. *Ein weites Feld* is couched in a kind of oral history that tends to shun events destined for the history books, such as the negotiations preceding (re)unification, and favor daily occurrences and common people such as the "picking peckers" (*TFA,* 107), who are slowly but surely taking the Berlin Wall apart. History is then depicted in the manner of the aforementioned "colored pictorial broadsheets" (*TFA,* 479 et passim; see also Lartillot 2001c) as a series of poetic images that ascribe "immortality" (*TFA,* 19 et passim) not only to Fontane and his work but to all those involved in the daily toil of life.

The *Wende;* Literature and National Unity

Unlike other scholars, Rolf Geißler (1999), who entirely dispenses with citing previous analyses of the novel and casts his study in philosophical terms as a subject-object relationship, adamantly insists that reading the text as a novel about the *Wende* amounts to a superficial appraisal, inasmuch as *Ein weites Feld* neither adds to Grass's arguments against unification, which he set forth in essays and addresses, nor depicts the collapse of the GDR in striking, memorable scenes. In fact, reading the novel as a *Wenderoman,* Geißler suggests, amounts to adopting the perspective of Hoftaller, a scientific bean counter who completely lacks an understanding of poetry with its openness, inconsistency, and multiple dimensions. This poetic quality is to be found in Fontane's *Effi Briest,* a narrative that cannot be convincingly classified as either a social novel or a novel about women and marriage.

By immersing himself totally in the past life of Fontane, Fonty creates a space in which he is comparatively free from the strictures of the increasingly totalitarian tendencies in the GDR, of which the nonentity Hoftaller and his sort are indicative. Neither an ideologue nor a "bloodhound" (*TFA,* 332 and 653), Hoftaller prevails via complementing his obtrusive observation of Fonty with assisting and caring for him. But it is not the extraneous events of one hundred and fifty years of German history that are important, Geißler contends; rather, the meaning of the novel can only be discerned by the way it is narrated, which encompasses and intertwines Fontane, the Fontane Archives, Hoftaller, Fonty, and the literary and political history of the nineteenth and twentieth centuries. A case in point is chapter 5, "Deep Down in the Sofa," in which the sofa is suggestive of the psychiatrist's couch and serves as a repository of manually shredded documents as well as Fonty and Fontane's torn personal papers, which serve Hoftaller as a source for reconstructing the past of both Fonty and his idol. In addition, Hoftaller considers Fontane's aforementioned novel, *Irrungen Wirrungen,* a *roman à clef* that enables him to ferret out the indiscretions of the "Immortal," such as his illegitimate offspring.

To counter the dominant themes of "*Einheit und Identität*" (unity and identity), on various levels that range from the personal to the political, Geißler (74) proposes, Grass employs a narrative mode of polyperspectivism, which results in the dissolution of biographical and historical continuities and yields a kaleidoscope of fragmented bits and pieces. Yet after leaving Germany, Fonty, who has abandoned his role as an imitator of Fontane and accepted his responsibility as grandfather Theo Wuttke, sees, as other critics have pointed out, an end to the wide, open field. To some extent, Geißler's findings are corroborated by Beatrice Petz (2000), who, although she is primarily discussing the narratorial position in *Unkenrufe,* draws attention to the emergence of an anonymous "new type of narrator" (82), one quite distinct from memorable narrators such as Oskar Matzerath in Grass's early prose fiction.

Whereas most commentators who investigate the press reception of *Ein weites Feld* confine themselves to taking issue with the treatment of the novel on the part of the predominantly West German *Feuilleton,* Bernd Wittek (1997) establishes the connection between the *Literaturstreit* that erupted upon the publication of Christa Wolf's *Was bleibt* in 1990 and that generated by Grass's text. Wittek discerns as the aesthetic principle underlying the attacks on Grass the desire to depoliticize literature, to steer clear of any kind of literature that even remotely smacks of *littérature engagée.*

The controversies surrounding *Ein weites Feld* have become muted, and the individual studies seeking to analyze various aspects of the novel have been augmented, as Wittek's reception study also shows, by more recent scholarly contributions, which tend to grapple with the question of how literary texts address the question of national unity by comparing a number of pertinent narratives. In his voluminous investigation of this complex problem, in which he analyses literary texts from the French Revolution to the present, Stefan Neuhaus (2002) uses as his basic criterion the juristic entity of the state, in that constructs such as "nation" and "people" are ultimately indefinable (61). But Neuhaus begins his analysis by questioning the assumption on the part of several critics and scholars (see, for example, Stolz 2002) that the narrators are either affiliated with the Stasi or use surveillance methods derived from that organization, albeit for a presumably beneficial purpose. Perhaps more importantly, Neuhaus challenges the generally assumed existence of a narrators' collective — referred to in the very first sentence of the novel: "We, the Archives staff, called him Fonty" (*TFA,* 3) — and claims that only one female functions as the narrator. Her rudimentary biography (see, for example, *TFA,* 658) serves Neuhaus to establish parallels between her fate and that of several of Fontane's heroines, among them Effi Briest. While such parallels may appear persuasive, it strains plausibility to assume that the arduous, time-consuming task of observing Fonty could be performed by a single person whose livelihood depends on archival work. But then the credibility of the narrator is undermined by her unquestioning acceptance of Fonty's imitation of Fontane or the existence of Hoftaller/ Tallhover, who began his career in the early 1840s (see *TFA,* 5 et passim). Both Fonty and Tallhover are essentially inauthentic, implausible figures; however, they contribute to the humor of the narrative, which, Neuhaus avers, occasionally approaches the level of a *Kolportageroman* or dime novel (467) when, for instance, Hoftaller acknowledges the victory of the West by appearing in an unconventional, "American" outfit including "baseball cap and T-shirt, . . . [and] sneakers" (*TFA,* 303).

In deviating from those critics who accused Grass of glorifying the GDR (for example, Reich-Ranicki), Neuhaus suggests that *Ein weites Feld* presents the failure of that state as a desirable outcome and cites the partial — but, as others have also noted, hardly harmonious (see, for example, Symons 2005) — reunion of the separated Wuttke family after the fall of the Berlin Wall as well as Fonty's being kept "for decades under ideological supervision and badgered" (*TFA,* 444) in support of his reading. Furthermore, Fonty's rejection of the classification, in GDR parlance, of the "workers' uprising" on 17 June 1953 (*TFA,* 174) as "counter-revolutionary" and a "putsch instigated by the West" (*TFA,* 470) provides another indication of Grass's critique of the GDR. This critique loses its edge, one may argue, by the prevailing tendency in *Ein weites Feld* to view German history in its entirety in a negative light; inasmuch as the history of the GDR must be perceived as an integral part of the baleful German past, the hopes for a better future appear to be dim.

But Grass employs a differentiated approach that is evident, for example, in the portrayal of the sympathetically drawn workaholic first chief of the *Treuhand,* with whom Fonty is on such friendly terms that in one of their several joint rides in the "paternoster" they "were closer to one another than a father and son can be" (*TFA,* 513). At the same time, Fonty is concerned about the "colossal amount of power" (*TFA,* 476) that the chief wields, which is bound to cause resentment and enmity and finally leads to his being murdered. In support of his nuanced reading of the novel, Neuhaus conjectures that there is an indication of an incestuous relationship between Fonty and Madeleine — a relationship, however, that should be viewed symbolically as a plea for a symbiosis of the German tradition, which Neuhaus does not define, and French "esprit" (*TFA,* 383), past and present — a symbiosis that may result in European unification. *Ein weites Feld* is then, Neuhaus concludes, not to be read as a rejection in fictional form of (re)unification and the presumably outdated nation state but rather as a constructive questioning of the premises underlying the beginning of a new phase in German and European history.

A more negative assessment is offered by Blé Richard Lorou (2003) who limits himself to the analysis of three works of prose fiction; in addition to *Ein weites Feld* he discusses narratives by two East German writers: Erich Loest's *Nikolaikirche* (1995) and Brigitte Burmeister's *Unter dem Namen Norma* (1994). Lorou deals with Grass's novel in considerable detail and at great length without consulting or citing more than a modicum of the extant literature; however, the expansive treatment is largely attributable to a fairly extensive retelling of the contents, some repetitions, and quite inclusive quotations. On occasion, Lorou's conclusions are misleading; one example concerns the massive building in the center of Berlin, which after the *Wende* housed the *Treuhand* and was equipped with the above-mentioned "paternoster." Lorou erroneously assumes (179, 211) that the building, located in what was called the Otto-Grotewohl-Strasse during the GDR's existence but renamed Wilhelmstrasse in 1993, had served from the Empire to (re)unification in various capacities and thus provided evidence of the unbroken continuity of the disastrous German history. However, Grass's assiduously researched text states quite clearly that the imposing edifice was not built until the 1930s and began serving as the Reich Aviation Ministry in 1935 (*TFA,* 54, 58 et passim).

Although he acknowledges Grass's use of intertextuality with regard to the two figures of Fonty and Hoftaller as well as the reference to other texts, notably Fontane's novels, Lorou seeks to weaken the anti-unification sentiments frequently uttered by the two main characters by citing in great detail historical documents that shed a different light on the *Wende.* In addition, Lorou rhetorically asks — not unreasonably — whether equating the unification of 1871 with that of 1990 does not amount to an anachronistic approach, inasmuch as the institutions of the Empire and those of the Federal Republic are quite incompatible. Similarly, Lorou does not consider the postulated continuity from the Empire to reunified Germany in general and the attempt to cast then Chancellor Kohl in the mold of Bismarck, the "Iron Chancellor," persuasive. In fact, he speaks of the demonization of unification and its ridiculing by Fonty, who however, as others have pointed out, is contradicted by his granddaughter Madeleine, to whose forthright exclamation "'Vive la France!'" Fonty meekly responds with "'Long live Brandenburg!'" (*TFA,* 385). Such a response, Lorou surmises, evades the question as to how to define the German nation and smacks of Grass's concept of the *Kulturnation;* on the basis of Grass's numerous speeches about unification, Lorou maintains that in the final analysis this remains a utopian concept and serves as a hindrance to the goal of achieving an undivided nation.

There are unmistakable indications that the stridency of the initial reception of *Ein weites Feld,* which was intimately related to the general perception of the *Wende* and (re)unification, has abated. Handbooks such as that by Frank Thomas Grub (2003) are usually not designed to stimulate controversy; rather, they tend to summarize and evaluate the state of the discussion on a given subject, in Grub's case the "mirroring" of "'Wende'" and "'Einheit'" in literary works, rather than seeking to promote controversial views. In his voluminous two-volume compendium, Grub establishes the literary context of the *Wende* and (re)unification debate in great detail and establishes a useful distinction between these often indiscriminately used terms, in that he defines the *Wende* as the period from summer 1989 to the elections for the *Volkskammer,* the GDR parliament, on 18 March 1990; he applies the term *Vereinigung* (unification) or *Einheit* (unity) — Grub does not sufficiently distinguish between these concepts — to the following period, from the March elections to the official date of unification on 3 October 1990 (8). It should be noted that Grub, perhaps too scrupulously, rejects "reunification" as a misnomer, on the basis that the two postwar German states had never before formed a political entity (1 n. 2). With regard to the terms *Wendeliteratur* and *Wenderoman,* Grub seeks to establish a number of criteria, the most common of which is obviously that literary texts subsumed under such headings are dealing with the events in 1989/90 in some fashion. Not surprisingly, the quite brief analysis of *Ein weites Feld* and its reception does not provide any new insights; the analysis is preceded by a short summary of the chief arguments of Grass and his opposite number in the (re)unification debate, Martin Walser.

Postmodernism and Intertextuality

Adopting a line of reasoning that has been pursued by hardly any other critic, Heinz-Günter Vester (1997) seeks to show in a comparatively brief essay, in which he dispenses entirely with explicit references to the text of *Ein weites Feld* as well as to pertinent secondary literature, that the novel exhibits pronounced "postmodern elements" (238). Vester cites as examples the prevalence of pastiche evident in "Fonty's self," because he was endowed with "feelings and . . . reflections borrowed from Fontane and his fictional character" (239), Fonty's dependence on "cultural frameworks" such as Fontane's writings, the obvious intertextuality that relates various texts to each other, the "decentering of self or subject" (242), which comes to the fore when both Fonty and Hoftaller disappear, the ambivalence toward "Germany's reunification process" (243) diplayed by both Fonty and Hoftaller, and, finally, the prevailing "anti-heroic and ironic" emotions vis-à-vis the "nation-state" on the part of the protagonists. As Dirk Frank (1998; see also above) has shown, Grass's use of Schädlich's text amounts to a tacit acknowledgment of the assumptions underlying postmodernism; the author's considerable intervention in the reception process via interviews, readings, and providing biographical details similarly indicates the virtual impossibility of discussing a text on the basis of its assumed intrinsic merits in a new media environment that does not foster reading in isolation.

Without contributing to the debate about postmodernism, in her *Room for Manoeuvre* (2005) Morwenna Symons explores the role of intertext in *Ein weites Feld* as well as some other texts and concentrates on "deciphering the central character, Fonty" (61) and his relationship to Fontane, a task that is made difficult by the novel's "central narrative feature," that is, "a willful strategic refusal to be constrained" (62). The lack of restraint is primarily evident in the "inherent slipperiness" (63) of Fonty, an "instance of pure intertext" (66) in that Fontane's "world is brought to bear variously" on Grass's text (74), notably in the secretly arranged meeting between Fonty and Uwe Johnson in front of the Fontane monument in Neuruppin (see Reich-Ranicki 1995; Christine Ivanović, 1996, has provided a detailed analysis of the scene, in which Johnson is depicted as following in the footsteps of Fontane even though the real and the fictionalized Johnson, unlike either Fontane or Fonty, tended to be rigidly uncompromising). Both this meeting and Fonty and Hoftaller's excursion to the same location (see *TFA*, ch. 28–29) serve to establish a "critical political perspective" (Symons, 74). But Fonty's appearance in the *Kulturbrauerei*, mentioned above, "represents the culmination of the intertextual project" (74) when, by means of his extemporaneous speech, Fonty accomplishes a complete fusion of figures from Fontane's novels with relevant persons of post-unification Germany and Berlin. Notably Fonty's vivid and imaginative revival of Frau Jenny Treibel, a rapacious bourgeoise *par excellence* and the protagonist of Fontane's eponymous novel (1892), a character who in her modern reincarnation appears as the second chief of the *Treuhand*, the above-mentioned Birgit Breuel, is indicative of Grass's "absolute integration, via the Fontane intertext, of literature and politics" (76). The guests of Treibel/Breuel appear, as Symons states not without exaggeration, as a "metaphorical representation of a cultural colonialism of unimaginable proportions" (80).

In contrast to other critics, who view the ubiquitous "paternoster" as a device expressing a (resigned) sense of "historical inevitability" and a "preference for the old over the new," Symons also discerns an underlying "deep, . . . obsessive, concern with the past and its consequences" (88), which comes to the fore in Fonty who, after all, is not only a "historical witness to events" but also "complicit in their making" (89) by avoiding outright acts of resistance. On the personal level, Symons adds, he is no less culpable; for example, he does not make any attempt to contact the mother of his child in France when, after the war, there might have been a chance to do so. He is similarly evasive in the wedding scene, which has been briefly discussed in different contexts, when his son Friedrich from the West demands a confession of guilt from his father for his collaboration with the GDR authorities without his "usual bobbing and weaving" (*TFA,* 245). From incidents such as this Symons concludes that the wedding is "a heavily allegorical episode" representing the difficulties facing the "union of the two German states" (93) rather than a private affair. Other elements, such as Father Bruno Matull's highly unconventional affirmation of doubt, which contrasts strongly with the bride's unbroken desire for indiscriminately believing in political doctrine or religious dogma, or the classical-mythological allusions in conjunction with Jacques Offenbach — the wedding celebration takes place in a restaurant named after the nineteenth-century French composer — emphasize the "intertextual performance" of the scene. The "cohabitation" (97) of the two German states is then fraught with uncertainties, and the invocation of the "vast domain of German cultural significances" serves the purpose of a "political critique," in that the "extraordinarily dense nexus of significations" obstructs the desire to quickly traverse the "vast literary space" (101) of *Ein weites Feld* and undermines the expectation that a genuine union of the two (former) German states will be achieved quickly. It remains to be seen whether such a pessimistic prediction proves to be valid.

14: *Mein Jahrhundert / My Century*

A Media Event

As happened in the case of *Ein weites Feld* four years earlier, the official publication on 7 July 1999 of *Mein Jahrhundert,* in both a text version and an edition with watercolors, was accompanied and preceded by Grass's readings from his new work (Schade 2004 provides an account of one Grass's performances; see below), radio and TV broadcasts, interviews, exhibits, an advance publication in the weekly *Die Zeit* (1 July 1999), and a meeting of translators in Göttingen as early as April 1999 during which Grass sought to explain difficult passages and terms in this specifically "German" work (H. Zimmermann 1999). The Steidl publishing company's skillfully arranged book launch in general and the numerous happenings in conjunction with the publication in particular suggest a media event and shifted attention, as Ulrich Baron (1999a) asserted in the daily *Die Welt,* from the literary text to the "Großschriftsteller" (eminent writer) Grass himself. Since the publication of *Die Blechtrommel* Grass had increasingly begun to dominate the literary scene and had gained in international stature in the face of the often unenthusiastic and even hostile response to his later works on the part of the German *Feuilleton.* The text itself, Baron wrote in another review in the same paper (1999b), is based on the principle of stringing together beads: it features mostly unknown protagonists without regard to any overarching historical context.

In comparison to the uproar that accompanied the publication of *Ein weites Feld* (see ch. 13), critics' reaction to *Mein Jahrhundert* was muted both in terms of the number of reviews published and the prevailing, comparatively moderate, tone. Major critics such as Marcel Reich-Ranicki, Joachim Kaiser, and Wolfram Schütte did not take notice of *Mein Jahrhundert* in print (see H. Zimmermann 2006, 571) — although Reich-Ranicki somewhat belatedly held forth on the book in *Das literarische Quartett* (13 August 1999; see Fliedl, Karasek, Löffler, and Reich-Ranicki) and deemed, essentially in agreement with the other participants in the discussion, its structural device of devoting one short story to each year of the twentieth century a failure. It should be added that Karasek (1999) had also voiced his disappointment in the daily *Der Tagesspiegel,* but in the same issue of the paper Bruno Preisendörfer characterized *Mein Jahrhundert* as a notable work of contemporary literature. What to other critics appeared as blemishes, that is, the concentration on German themes, the wide variety of topics, and the variants of form (monologues, dialogues, letters, miniatures, confessions, short stories, and so on) Preisendörfer viewed as positive features; the only drawback he perceives is the author's choice of first-person narratives that are permeated by the "Grass sound" and lack variety. Summary dismissals such as those by the *Literarisches Quartett* then do fail to take into account the considerable formal range of these short stories, which are designed to establish a link between individual fate(s) and history writ large in an unobtrusive, entertaining, as well as slightly didactic fashion (see H. Zimmermann, 572).

Differing viewpoints were offered in an article in *Die Zeit* by Fritz Raddatz and Ulrich Greiner (1999). Raddatz praised the pastiche character of the stories, although he found their arrangement somewhat arbitrary, in that the imagined and the experienced did not form a unity; furthermore, the author's voice tended to sound like that of a dogmatic Cassandra. Yet ultimately Raddatz judged the work to be deserving of interest. Conversely, Greiner considered only those stories that were based on Grass's own experiences to be of importance; according to him, *Mein Jahrhundert* could not claim to be *the* book about the twentieth century because the author had succeeded in writing such a work before, notably when he published *Die Blechtrommel.* Whereas some critics miss the grand design on the part of the author, others, such as Ingo Arend (1999), believe Grass's strategy of having the century come alive via mosaics to be a strong point. In his extensive review Arend also notes the exclusively German perspective, which is indicative of Grass's love-hate relationship with Germany, in the narrative as well as the prevalent view from below via the perception not of the movers and shakers but that of the common folk (a feature termed by Hans-Peter Kunisch, in the *Süddeutsche Zeitung* in 1999, a Social Democrat realism) — a concept that displays the sophistication of a colored Neuruppin broadsheet.

In the *Frankfurter Allgemeine Zeitung,* Helmut Böttiger (1999) observes that Grass strives for authenticity by including elements of folklore and, occasionally and somewhat artificially, the use of dialect; the author also relies on a wealth of sources (which he assembled and consulted with the help of a jobless historian) in order to achieve authenticity. He takes into account events of historical significance such as the First World War and the fall of the Berlin Wall but avoids the danger of lapsing into journalism.

The title *Mein Jahrhundert* is perceived by Volker Hage (1999), writing in *Der Spiegel,* as somewhat presumptuous, particularly since the book does not pertain to the category of memoirs or autobiographies — the author is only present in thirteen of the one hundred chapters. On the whole, despite the horrors that were perpetrated in the twentieth century, the one hundred years as viewed by mostly random witnesses appear surprisingly harmless and almost idyllic. In the end, neither the mosaics of the times nor the autobiographical elements come clearly into focus; the result is a rather arbitrary sheet of pictures that do not make excessive demands on the reader. Hans-Dieter Schütt (1999) of *Neues Deutschland* observes that the divided public (and journalistic) opinion is a customary phenomenon in the case of a book publication by Grass; in the center-left *Berliner Zeitung* Robin Detje (1999) took exception especially to Grass's brief depiction of Wolf Biermann, the GDR singer-poet who was expatriated in 1976, in one scene and the characterization of Biermann's pro-war stance during the first Gulf War in 1991 in another (see *MC,* 207–8, 247). Such criticism, Detje polemically posits, is entirely inappropriate for a writer who felt offended because he was unable to prevent (re)unification.

In a comparatively late review, philosopher and political science professor Iring Fetcher (1999) takes exception to the claim advanced by several journalists that the perspective of the little people predominated to the virtual exclusion of other viewpoints. He cites as a notable exception business woman Birgit Breuel, whose name is not given, but who is clearly identifiable as the chief of the *Treuhand* (see also ch. 13) and who describes herself as "hard as nails" (*MC,* 258). The 1960s meeting between Erich Maria Remarque (1898–1970), author of the famous anti-war novel *Im Westen nichts Neues* (1929; *All Quiet on the Western Front,* 1929), and Ernst Jünger (1895–1998), whose *In Stahlgewittern* (1919, rev. ed. 1924; *Storm of Steel,* 1929), an account of trench warfare during the First World War that has been criticized as a glorification of war, is presented in a somewhat more amusing vein, Fetcher suggests. The two writers meet in Zurich at the invitation of an unnamed young Swiss woman who has been asked to write a report for a Swiss company that produces weapons for export. But Fetcher expresses his preference for scenes such as the one featuring then Chancellor Willy Brandt kneeling down in front of the Warsaw Ghetto memorial in December 1970 — a widely reported occurrence that in *Mein Jahrhundert* is maliciously and resentfully told from the perspective of a reactionary journalist opposed to Brandt's *Ostpolitik* (but see Schade 2004, discussed below). Although Fetcher acknowledges the author's right to select the episodes that were included in the volumes, he would have preferred the insertion of more historically poignant and consequential moments such as, in the story of 1956, Soviet leader Nikita Khrushchev's secret speech about Stalin's crimes, which inaugurated the far-reaching process of de-Stalinization, rather than the (fictional) encounter between Gottfried Benn (1886–

1956) and Bertolt Brecht (1898–1956), then perceived to be the respective laureates of letters in West and East Germany during the Cold War. Lastly, basically concurring with other reviewers, Fetcher finds *Mein Jahrhundert* unsatisfactory — not least because of its penetrating aforementioned "Grass sound."

An additional, rather disappointing, essay, which amounts to a brief summary of reviews without annotation, is provided by Norbert Honsza (2000), who relies on extensive quotations from *Mein Jahrhundert*. He misses the baroque exuberance as well as the obscenities in the manner of *Die Blechtrommel*, acknowledges that Grass provides history lessons in the form of a journal, but finds his excursions into pop culture and sports such as soccer eccentric, grotesque, and even tasteless — a standpoint that is untenable in view, for example, of the enormous significance for the German psyche of winning the 1954 World Cup. Honsza cites as an example the 1936 Berlin Olympic Games, an event that is told from the perspective of a "political" prisoner at the concentration camp Sachsenhausen in the vicinity of Berlin. Although the prisoner realizes that foreign visitors attending the games are largely oblivious to what is going on in Nazi Germany, he takes great interest in the contests and seeks to catch snippets of the radio broadcasts from Berlin, notably during the "broad-jump duel" between Jesse Owens and German contender Lutz Long. But, ironically, he is deemed "unworthy" and explicitly "forbidden to celebrate" (*MC*, 93) German successes — a complex and ambiguous situation whose depiction, contrary to what Honsza says, rises considerably above the level of provincial journalism.

"Germany's Many Faces"

Several weeks after the publication of *Mein Jahrhundert*, on 30 September 1999, the Stockholm Nobel Prize Committee announced that Grass, a candidate in waiting ever since the appearance of *Die Blechtrommel*, had finally been selected as the recipient of the coveted award — an honor that was widely noted in the international press (see, for example, Jürgs 2002, 421–29; H. Zimmermann 2006, 576–89). In November 1999, *My Century*, translated by Michael Henry Heim, became available before the English rendering of *Ein weites Feld* as *Too Far Afield* (see ch. 13), with the result that critics in the English-speaking countries were confronted with the problem of dissecting a Nobel laureate's literary text that had received comparatively poor marks from their German colleagues. In one of the earliest American reviews, Bill Marx (1999) of the *Boston Globe* adopts a surprisingly benevolent stance with regard to *My Century*, "an exhilaratingly panoramic view of the past century in Germany" in which "individuals from all segments of society" are given a voice. It is precisely these "apolitical voices" that contradict the claim by James Atlas (1999) in the *New York Times* that the Swedish Academy tends to reward "radical lefties" (a similar opinion was voiced by Jacob Heilbrunn, 1999, in the *Wall Street Journal*). In extending his attack on the critical establishment, Marx breezily dismisses Ernestine Schlant's claim in her *The Language of Silence* (1999; 968–79; see also ch. 1) that "there aren't enough Jewish characters" in Grass's fiction as part of a "politically correct debate" that may result in "ethnic or religious one-upmanship." Unlike other reviewers, Marx does not consider the "chronological" form of *My Century* a flaw — even if the "bounty of [Grass's] fantasies" appears to be restrained by the format of the predominantly first-person short tales that deal with both "trivial events and national crises" and display the writer's talent as a "dazzling mimic of different voices" but show little of the "hallucinogenic richness" of his other works. Traces of this richness, of a "tragicomic spirit," are to be found, for example, in the whimsical tale of the Jewish survivor who built the "bulletproof cell" that was used during Adolf Eichmann's 1961 trial in Jerusalem: "I think he liked his bulletproof cell. Why else would he have smiled the way he did?" (*MC,* 162). (Schade 2004 points out the irony inherent in the fact that Eichmann, the representative of a system responsible for the "Night of Broken Glass," is now protected by unbreakable glass.)

In the *New York Times Book Review,* cultural historian Peter Gay (1999) elegantly avoids the potential pitfall of having to pan the Nobel laureate's latest work, by commenting at some length on Grass's literary accomplishments, foremost among them, needless to say, *The Tin Drum,* as well as his role as an "eminently political animal" before "sadly" concluding that the author's latest work is most "likely" not going to be either a commercial or critical success owing to its basic flaw — that it constitutes a "collection of fragments that fail to cohere." Furthermore, Gay points out the difficulties the English or American reader would presumably face in reading a text that dispenses with explanatory notes — which, at any rate, would destroy the "spontaneity" of Grass's "witnesses" — for example, about historical events such as the "Kapp Putsch" of 1922 (which was directed against the elected government of the Weimar Republic) and its perpetrators (see *MC,* 51–55). "Howlers" such as the mistranslation of the song "Wir sind die Moorsoldaten" (1933; text: Johann Esser and Wolfgang Langhoff; music: Rudi Goguel) as "Song of the Moorish Soldiers" (*MC,* 91) rather than as "soldiers of the swamp" or "bog" do not facilitate the understanding of the text. Actually, the song was not "first sung" during the Spanish Civil War, as Gay has it, but originated in 1933 in an Emsland concentration camp in Northern Germany, where the inmates had to work in the peat bogs. In concluding his review, Gay intimates that it might not have been necessary to translate

My Century at all, but he does not suggest any failing of Grass's powers of imagination, and hopes for a future "masterpiece."

Less circumspect than Gay, Richard Bernstein (2000), writing in the *New York Times,* declares at the outset that, presumably owing to the fact that *My Century* was specifically written for the occasion of the "passing of a millennium," the work "falls . . . flat" and exhibits only "flashes of brilliance." Bernstein reiterates a complaint, which also has been expressed by other reviewers, that the voices relating their various experiences "are similar in tone and very similar in their storytelling technique." Thus the narrators tend to suffer from a kind of "historical myopia" as evident, for instance, in the postwar gathering of former war correspondents, now gainfully employed by the media of the Federal Republic, on the Isle of Sylt in the North Sea. There they swap war stories, and some unredeemed Nazis among them complain about missed opportunities for winning the Second World War as if it had been merely a "lost football game." Bernstein, who erroneously writes that Grass was born in 1937 rather than 1927, similarly judges episodes from the 1960s student movement involving, among others, sociologist and philosopher Theodor W. Adorno and student leader Rudi Dutschke as coming across as "arcane, tangential, unfocused." In sum, *My Century,* although in part "gripping and uniformly intelligent," essentially consists of "mostly forgettable fragments" that do not offer a "coherent, gripping or illuminating whole."

The opposite view is advanced by Robert Boyd (1999) of the *St. Louis Post-Dispatch,* who considers Grass "the literary conscience of his country" (not necessarily a positive term; see Buruma, below) with whose characters American readers can identify, even if the stories or "'vignettes'" follow the disastrous course of twentieth-century German history. The particular lessons Americans perusing the volume may learn consist of viewing especially the "first half" of the twentieth century from a "radically different point of view" and revising cherished stereotypes of "The Enemy" — an insight that may lead to the recognition of the fragility of democratic systems, as evidenced by the fact that Auschwitz-Birkenau was the abominable creation of the "same nation that produced Martin Luther, Beethoven's Ninth Symphony and Kant's 'Critique of Pure Reason.'"

John Simon (1999), writing in the *Washington Post,* finds Grass's stance "both self-effacing and arrogant" and, paradoxically, considers *My Century* a "flawed" book despite its "sassily original" concept, which exhibits "undeniable charm and lasting fascination" — albeit primarily for the reader who happens to be a "bit of a sleuth" and well-versed in German affairs (like Gay, above, Simon dismisses explanatory notes as "off-putting"). Simon, at any rate, provides an unwitting demonstration of the difficulties of the text by falling victim to a factual error when he attributes the 1970 Warsaw memorial visit to Chancellor Konrad Adenauer (1876–1967) rather than Willy Brandt (1913–92). (The *Washington Post* published a correction on 19 January 2000.)

Simon finds the "many representatives of different disciplines" that make their appearance in the text striking, among them "various scientists, athletes in different sports, politicians." But despite the diversity and richness of topics and figures, the task of seeking to encapsulate an entire century is overwhelming and "involves making choices." Furthermore, it raises the question whether the text is "inclusive and shared enough" — a question that obviously will be answered differently by different critics. Like Gay, Simon briefly addresses the "daunting" task of translator Heim, but unlike Gay, he does not single out mistranslations. In the end, Simon bestows unadulterated praise on Grass and his work, which he characterizes as "rampant with bravura showmanship [and] rife with impudent trickery."

In a less effusive vein, Michael Arditti (2000), writing in the London *Independent,* offers an assenting assessment of the "composite portrait, made up of a myriad of voices." He provides a succinct overview of the stories and credits Grass with having captured the essence of the century of contradictions, a century that hovered between the achievements of "technological invention" on the one hand and despair caused by "institutionalised brutality" on the other — a phenomenon that is captured in the words of Grass's mother, who is revived at the very end of the century and who mostly remembers "war, war with breaks in between" (*MC,* 273). Indeed, war is a dominant theme and is articulated in the very first story told by a Bavarian participant in the German expeditionary corps that in 1900 participated in suppressing the Chinese "Boxer Rebellion" (*MC,* 2) and chose to send home an executed rebel's pigtail as a souvenir. Arditti deems the "most powerful story" to be that about the *Kristallnacht* ("'Crystal Night'") of 9 November 1938 — a story that is not, as Arditti erroneously assumes, about an "East German schoolgirl" but rather a girl whose father escaped from the "Soviet occupied zone before the wall went up" and who was born in Swabia in West Germany. But the main point of the story is that the girl's teacher is criticized for his "'obsession with the past'" when, instead of celebrating the fall of the Berlin Wall, which, coincidentally, occurred on 9 November 1989, he seeks to explain to his pupils that the events of *Kristallnacht* were an indication of things having "gone wrong" (*MC,* 96–97) and — here the teacher serves as Grass's mouthpiece — were to be seen as one of the causes contributing to the postwar division of Germany. Yet the story ends on a somewhat optimistic note when the students, whom their teacher had informed about the fate of the Jewish children in their community, decide to stage a protest when they learn that the authorities plan to deport one of their classmates, a Kurdish boy, and his parents.

"Great national and international events" are then interspersed with "domestic accounts," Arditti justifiably observes, and Grass "provides a richly varied cast." Despite the "unduly personal title" of *My Century,* the collection is "fascinating" and "wide-ranging" — an unmitigated positive assessment rarely encountered among German reviewers. Similar approval is voiced by Hugo Barnacle (2000) of the London *Sunday Times,* who calls *My Century* the "most readable publication [Grass] has produced for some time." Even if the collection of a "hundred short stories" is not the "most conventional" literary form, most of the "vignettes are witty and sharp," displaying "different voices" that present the "interplay of parochial and universal concerns."

Writer and academic Ian Buruma (2000), author of, among many other publications, *The Wages of Guilt: Memories of War in Germany and in Japan* (1994), casts his review in the *New Republic* in terms of the "German problem," that is, Germans' persistent preoccupation with "darkest German barbarism" in the face of "brilliant German achievement" (31; see also Boyd, above). Buruma reiterates some objections voiced before by other American and English critics, such as that the translation offers a "rather wooden English text" and that the events depicted may be well known in Germany but "will not have much resonance" in other countries. For example, the (West) German soccer team's 1954 victory over Hungary at the world championship in Switzerland resulted in a revival of national pride in West Germany but will presumably remain a "rather obscure" affair for foreign readers. But Buruma's real target is the prevailing "Grassian perspective," which he defines in explicitly political terms and which, he implies, springs from the writer's "position as Germany's self-appointed conscience" — a position that resulted in his "intemperate use of Auschwitz" as a warning signal during the (re)unification debate. Although Buruma concedes that Grass "could be a vociferous critic of the GDR," he also points out that there was a tendency on the part of the Left to speak about East Germany "with a degree of nostalgia" (32) that is evident in the ambivalent or outright negative portrayal of the aspirations of the GDR population, especially at the Leipzig Monday demonstrations in the fall of 1989. Curiously, the story in which those demonstrations are mentioned is the short narrative about the Falkland War of 1982, in which an anonymous agent retrospectively voices his concern about the political implications of the sale of (West) German submarines to Argentina and recalls the 1914 Falklands battle at which the German Pacific Fleet was sunk by the British. It is the "military flag of the Reich," which was flown at that battle, that surfaces again at the Leipzig demonstrations and is used by skinheads to replace the "empty slogan 'We are the people' with the . . . politically effective cry of 'We are one people'" (*MC,* 223). Indeed, one cannot entirely disagree with Buruma when he states that in this scene Grass has "contrived to smear . . . the East German people demonstrating for freedom [and (re)unification] with the tar of extreme nationalism and mass violence." Grass's apparent inability to "conceive of a united Germany" without "Nazism or imperialism," Buruma scathingly concludes, "represents a colossal failure of imagination" on the part of one of the "most celebrated writers of the twentieth century" (Buruma, 33–34).

"Narrative(s) and History"

One of the first essays to transcend the customary confines of a book review is that by Wolfgang Weber (1999) who analyzes *Mein Jahrhundert* from a decidedly partisan perspective. Although he counts the volume among Grass's successful writings because of its narrative technique and overall conception, Weber finds it ultimately wanting. On the one hand, he acknowledges the advantages of the prevalent view from below, which results in "unforgettable" scenes such as that for 1946, which shows the indomitable spirit of the "Berlin Rubble Woman," one of many charged with the formidable task of cleaning up the "ruins" and "rubble" that were "everywhere." She finds a dead man among the ruins of bombed-out houses and unscrupulously keeps his "perfectly usable" coat of "prewar" quality (*MC,* 116, 118), which will keep her warm in the winter and offer her a better chance for survival. On the other, Weber points out — somewhat in the vein of Fetcher — that Grass has not given any indication as to how human actions influence social relations as well as the course of history and vice versa — a tendency that is evident, for example, in the omission of significant historical events, among them the 1917 Russian October Revolution, the 1918 German November Revolution, or the worldwide economic crisis of 1929. These omissions are also indicative of "national blinders," which come to the fore in the last story and, Weber claims, essentially constitute a withdrawal into the private realm of the family (see also Shafi, 2002); moreover, the last story fails to establish a link to the beginning of the century and its story about the Bavarian soldier's role in the Chinese "Boxer Rebellion" (see Arditti, 2000). In a highly questionable analogy, Weber compares the gruesome suppression of that rebellion to the participation of the *Bundeswehr,* the German army, in the United Nations mission in Kosovo — a farfetched comparison indeed, which tends to bring into question the validity of some of Weber's other observations.

Although Hans Weber's essay (2001) is primarily pedagogically oriented, offering advice to instructors of German at non-German institutions, the potential problems that students at such institutions are likely to encounter when reading the texts resemble those that, as several critics have noted (see, for example, Gay 1999), English-speaking readers are likely to face. Obviously, students have the advantage, depending on the degree of their respective instructor's preparedness, of having access to vocabulary aids, explanatory notes, summaries of historical events, and the like. Precisely the fact that *Mein Jahrhundert* is not a novel, as is occasionally assumed by critics, but a narrative that consists of one hundred more or less independent parts offers the chance to abandon the strict chronological sequence and devise reading strategies that are based on combining individual stories in sequences of thematic clusters, such as the division of Germany (1951, 1961, 1979, 1989). The sequencing offers the advantage of demonstrating (German) "history" via stories in which the view from below and unusual perspectives prevail, stories that supplement or contradict official historiography.

Monika Shafi (2002) similarly addresses "Narrative and History" in *Mein Jahrhundert* and emphasizes that the highlighting of subjective experiences on the part of the various narrators has been perceived as a "textual oddity," in that the text offers an exploration of the "interplay between story-telling and history-writing" (40). But the very first sentence, "I, TRADING PLACES WITH MYSELF, was in the thick of things, year in and year out" (*MC,* 1), is indicative of Grass's attempt to combine the "dual role of chronicler and autobiographer" (41) by enabling a multiplicity of often discordant voices to be heard. These voices in their totality, as well as the anecdotal form chosen, privilege *Alltagsgeschichte* or the (hi)story of daily life — albeit without the admixture of sentimentality that is often associated with the term *Heimat* — rather than the *grands récits* or the great narrative constructs of a mythological, religious, philosophical nature that undergird the self-perception of societies and nations.

Yet despite the diversity of narrative voices, Shafi finds women in particular underrepresented, in that only twenty stories are told by them. The argument about the lack of adequate representation of certain groups should not be dismissed out of hand, but there is the danger of applying the yardstick of political correctness to literary works (see also Marx 1999) and elevating statistics to a criterion of literary criticism, a procedure that may not find universal approval. Shafi attributes the fact that virtually all the women characters are "firmly anchored in the domestic realm" (54) in their conventional roles as mothers, daughters, and housewives not to Grass's recreation of (then) prevailing conditions in society but to his "unabashedly male perspective," which precludes any articulation of a "critique of patriarchal rule" (55) on the part of female characters. In fact, Shafi implies, the final scene, in which Grass's mother is resurrected, presents an almost "idyllic" conclusion to the tales about a troubled century, an ending that projects "optimism, resilience, and reconciliation" (56) — a conclusion that is called into question by the mother's previously cited words about seemingly constant war. In the same issue of the annually published journal *Gegenwartsliteratur* (2002) in which Shafi's article appeared, Amir Eshel maintains in an essay on *Mein Jahrhundert* and Alexander Kluge's *Chronik der Gefühle* (2000; A Chronicle of Feelings) that, in a radical departure from the "notion of history as chaotic and absurd" as evinced in *Die Blechtrommel* (70) and insistently reiterated by the author in pronouncements of various kinds, Grass's "fictionalized historical narratives . . . unfold . . . a Hegelian concept of history as a cohesive, intelligible process" (64) and posits that all the events depicted in the various stories are interrelated via the "book's focal center, the narrating 'I'" that is both "omnipotent and omnipresent" (69). True, the first sentence of the text, cited above, lends some credence to the claim of the narrating I's omnipresence (for a more complex and challenging construction of the narrating I in *Der Butt,* see ch. 7); however, its assumed omnipotence is confined to its ability to appear in different guises and speak in different voices. As Shafi (2002) and most other critics have pointed out, the predominant view from below and the prevalence of the voices of the powerless in the stories virtually preclude the emergence of any grand teleological design in the Hegelian manner, but not the retrospective pondering of past events by different figures (see S. Kiefer 2002) — an insight that Eshel seems to ignore.

Heidegger and Celan; The Student Movement

The depiction of influential philosopher Martin Heidegger in *Hundejahre* and *Mein Jahrhundert* serves Sascha Kiefer (2002) as chief evidence of Grass's remarkable departure from his narratological roots. Kiefer emphasizes the radically polyphonic narrative principle underlying the latter text, a principle that enables author Grass to remain in the background, to provide only flashes of insights into his biography (for example, for the years 1959, 1976, and 1998), and to deal with historical events such as the Second World War, which happened during his lifetime, in a distanced, somewhat detached manner that lacks the immediacy of personal involvement and results in an objectifying, politically correct reconstruction of German history — a task more appropriate for a historian than a writer of fiction.

Whereas Martin Heidegger (1889–1976) appears in *Hundejahre* as the target of aggressive parody, primarily on account of his professed sympathies for Nazism, *Mein Jahrhundert* offers a far more differentiated view of the philosopher, via the depiction of his (actual) 1967 encounter with poet and Holocaust survivor Paul Celan (1920–70) in Heidegger's cottage in the Black Forest, which resulted in Celan's poem "Todtnauberg" and was followed by further meetings, which ceased when Celan committed suicide. The three years from 1966 to 1968 are narrated by a former student protester, now a docent of German literature offering a seminar on Celan's poetry, who witnessed the first encounter at a time when he was torn between engaging in activism and his attraction to the "great shaman" Heidegger (*MC,* 173), whose influence he has not managed to escape. Kiefer views the three texts as presenting a historical panorama that includes the student rebellion and the Prague Spring, mirrors the mentality of the Sixty-Eighters, symbolizes the difficult postwar relationship between perpetrator and victim, and (surprisingly) hints at parallels between Heidegger and Theodor W. Adorno (1903–69), chief representative of the Frankfurt am Main school of critical theory. He bases his conclusion on the fact that the docent exchanges the "jargon of 'essentiality' for the jargon of the dialectic" (*MC,* 178); this seems to indicate the interchangeability of one philosophy or ideology with another — a somewhat deplorable objectifying tendency in presenting historical contexts and personages on the part of Grass, Kiefer infers, which lacks the vigor of the writer's previous feisty attacks on the philosopher.

"Memories of 1968 in Recent German Novels" (2006), Monika Shafi's essay, singles out the student movement of the 1960s as one of the most important topics in *Mein Jahrhundert,* because only the "two World Wars are accorded a similar multi-year time span" (212). The docent's reminiscences about his past and his ideological twists and turns, referred to above, are flanked by the author's report on his election campaign activities on behalf of the SPD in 1965 and a woman's recollections of 1969, a year that she spent in a student-run "'antiauthoritarian'" play group (*MC,* 183), but also the year of the moon landing and the Social Democrats' victory at the polls. Grass's opposition to left-wing radicalism is well known, but Shafi suggests that via the introduction of Adorno, whose much discussed dictum about the impossibility of writing poetry after Auschwitz Grass used as an argument against (re)unification, as well as the aforementioned 1967 encounter between Heidegger and Celan, it is the Holocaust rather than the "students' political demands" that provides the "key" to an understanding of Grass's reading of the student movement (Shafi, 212). In "Todtnauberg," Celan expresses his "'hope . . . for a thinker's coming word'" (*MC,* 177), a hope that remained unfulfilled and is indicative of the silence that tended to prevail with regard to Nazi crimes in postwar (West) Germany. Furthermore, the students' misguided radicalism is underscored when they turn against Adorno, their formerly revered teacher. The docent's failure to "come to terms" with his past, his errors and failures — "'You've got nothing more to give'" (*MC,* 182), one of his students dismissively remarks — is tantamount to a wholesale censure of the "student movement, of its representatives, their actions and goals [and] their aspirations" (Shafi, 213). Although such perception would seem to correspond to that of Grass, it is perhaps too bleak a view of an entire generation. After all, one may argue, members of this generation (partially) redeemed themselves by assuming constructive roles in the Berlin Republic when the "Red-Green coalition" came to power in 1998 (see *MC*, 269–72).

"Histories, Paintings, and Performance" (2004), the title of Richard E. Schade's essay, is indicative of a rarely applied approach that goes beyond textual analysis and seeks to establish the relationship between stories and watercolors in *Mein Jahrhundert* as well as to elucidate performative aspects. In his overview of the "decidedly anecdotal narrative," which is akin to a "micro-historical presentation of events" (410), Schade's observations are not always supported by the textual evidence of the various stories. For instance, the 1903 soccer match between the Leipzig and Prague clubs — admittedly hardly a well-known event — was not a "*Länderspiel*" or a contest between two national teams but the (first) game that decided the German championship (in 1903, German clubs from abroad were permitted to participate). One may also question whether Grass "humoristically deconstructs" then Chancellor Willy Brandt's "moving Kniefall" in Warsaw, which, Schade claims, is "deftly ironized" (411), as unconvincing; the reading of this incident by Fetcher appears far more compelling in view of Grass's admiration and support for Brandt. In his reconstruction of the "anecdotal" literary history in *Mein Jahrhundert* that results in an "unusual literary canon," Schade (412–13) misses writers such as Alfred Döblin, Heinrich Böll, and Uwe Johnson but grants Grass the privilege of creating "his own canon" that, evidently, does not have to follow academic criteria. But in the context of discussing literary figures, Schade appears to misconstrue the narrative perspective of the aforementioned (former) member of the student movement of the 1960s, who does not hold his seminar at the "height of the student demonstrations," is no longer "caught in the crossfire of radicalized debate," and has attained an academic rank considerably above that of a lowly "*Assistent*" (413). Rather, as the text explicitly states, he ponders the question: "What has become of the once 'being-heedless' yet still radical sixty-eighter . . .?" (*MC*, 171) — without finding a satisfactory answer (see also Kiefer 2002, Shafi 2006).

More convincing is Schade's analysis of the paintings, which "reinforce the message of the text visually" (415) and display Grass's talent as an artist who recreates his own dust-jackets, notably those of *Die Blechtrommel* for the year 1959 and *Der Butt* (1975–77). The great variety of watercolors corresponds to the diversity of topics, but Grass's "creative interaction of representational art and literary textuality" goes beyond a mere illustration of contents and serves as a structuring device via, as Schade terms them, "variously colored tangle-paintings." (Kniesche

2002 provides a general assessment of the relationship between Grass's writing and his visual art.) Placed on double pages, they exhibit a jumble of numbers in shifting colors that demarcate various time periods and provide "coherent historical units" imparting "historiographic meaning" (Schade, 418). Rather than emphasizing the aspects of a media event in the fashion of various critics (see Baron 1999a), Schade stresses Grass's performative achievement in his report about the author's reading of selected chapters on 4 June 1999 in Dresden. Accompanied by percussionist Günter Sommer and illustrated by projections of watercolors from the volume on a screen, Grass's performance privileged the autobiographical and underscored the writer's or actor's taking "possession of *sein Jahrhundert*" (420). A dramatized version was produced in 2000 by the Thalia Theater in Hamburg — a further indication that the appeal of Grass's texts is not limited to the reading public (see Burkhardt 2000).

15: *Im Krebsgang / Crabwalk*

"The German *Titanic*"

SHORTLY BEFORE THE PUBLICATION OF *Im Krebsgang,* the influential news magazine *Der Spiegel* published a laudatory cover story-cum-review by Volker Hage (2002a), which featured this new book by Grass. Hage's extensive, favorable essay constitutes a somewhat startling reversal, inasmuch as star critic Marcel Reich-Ranicki had mercilessly panned Grass's novel *Ein weites Feld* in another *Spiegel* cover story several years earlier (1995; see ch. 13). Yet in 2002, the same critic extravagantly praised *Im Krebsgang* in his *Solo* TV show (Fries 2002), and he celebrated its canonization (H. L. Arnold 2002, 38). Rudolf Augstein (1923–2002), the founder of *Der Spiegel* and one of postwar Germany's preeminent journalists, who had vigorously opposed Grass's anti-unification stance (Augstein 1990), also acknowledged the text as a significant work (Augstein 2002). *Im Krebsgang* rapidly rose on the bestseller charts and was eventually translated into more than thirty languages; the work was also discussed in classes in German schools (Fieberg 2003, 34; Pelster 2004). There was an outpouring of reviews: Herman Beyersdorf (2002, 581) counts close to sixty and, later, almost one hundred (2006, 159 n. 13); approximately two months after the publication of *Im Krebsgang,* in May 2002, Heinz Ludwig Arnold (38) estimated that there were hundreds of them. The conservative *Die Welt,* a daily with a national distribution, returned to *Im Krebsgang* repeatedly; the various contributors, among them Grass's fellow writer Rolf Schneider (2002), find the success of Grass's work fully justified; conversely, they question Grass's premise of exploring an allegedly neglected topic (for example, Wittstock 2002).

In addition to the customary response in the *Feuilleton* of all major and many minor newspapers and magazines, the literary text served to inspire a "'media event'" that focused on "German wartime [and post-wartime] suffering" (Taberner 2002, 161), as predominantly exemplified by two events: the wholesale allied bombing of German cities during the Second World War, and the flight-cum-expulsion of ten to fifteen million ethnic Germans from the German territories East of the Oder-Neiße line at the end of or after the war. The essay *Luftkrieg und Literatur* (1999; "Air War and Literature," in *On the Natural History of Destruction,* 2003) by the late W. G. Sebald (1944–2001), which is based on a 1997 lecture series, raises the question of why so few postwar German writers of the legendary *Gruppe 47* had been willing to confront the traumatic aspects of the past related to the bombing; Jörg Friedrich's documentary *Der Brand: Deutschland im Bombenkrieg, 1940–1945* (2002; *The Fire: The Bombing of Germany, 1940–45*) further intensified the debate about whether Germans are entitled to claim the status of victims rather than that of perpetrators. This debate was also fueled by other literary works; in a second major *Spiegel* article (8 April 2002b), Hage deplored the "bizarre" discussion that led critics inspired by political correctness to subject novels such as Bernhard Schlink's international bestseller *Der Vorleser* (1995; *The Reader*, 1997) to the suspicion of playing down German guilt and rejected their attempts to view literature in purely ideological terms. In this context, the sinking of the *Wilhelm Gustloff* on 30 January 1945 by a Soviet submarine, a gruesome chapter of the broad theme of expulsion that forms the central event in Grass's *Im Krebsgang*, received renewed attention. The demise of the *Gustloff* had been the subject of the "forgotten" (*CW*, 119) black-and-white film *Nacht fiel über Gotenhafen* (1959; *Night Fell over Gotenhafen; CW*, 63 et passim); two new film projects were announced, by the UFA production firm and, as *Die Welt* (15 February 2002) reported, by the Polish director Agnieszka Holland.

In *Im Krebsgang*, Grass appears to provide a response of sorts to the problem stated by Sebald (in *Mein Jahrhundert*, the fate of the *Wilhelm Gustloff* merits only a few lines; see *MC*, 114). *Der Spiegel*, at any rate, supplemented its cover story with some additional contributions in order to draw attention to the "suppressed tragedy" of the *Gustloff*, a former cruise ship of the Nazi organization *Kraft durch Freude* (*KdF;* Strength through Joy), which departed from the port then called Gotenhafen (Gdingen) near Danzig and was carrying close to ten thousand refugees, but also several hundred submarine sailors and female members of the navy auxiliary. The refugees were fleeing from the onslaught of the Red Army in East Prussia in January 1945 to presumed safety in the West. Only about twelve hundred people survived the sinking, including approximately one hundred infants, children, and teenagers of the several thousands on board — a catastrophe of unimaginable proportions, which induced the editors of *Der Spiegel* to dub the *Gustloff* "Die deutsche Titanic" (The German Titanic) on the cover of the magazine. Actually, in the statistical "balance of terror" (*CW*, 142) as indicated by the death toll, the comparison entails an understatement, inasmuch as it has been estimated that about fifteen hundred lives were lost when the *Titanic* sank. Hence there is a startling incongruity: on the one hand, the *Gustloff* catastrophe is simply "the greatest maritime disaster of all times" (*CW*,

10) but, on the other, "the ship's name" does not "carry global significance as the epitome of disaster" (*CW*, 143).

Both the textual message conveyed by the caption "Die deutsche Titanic" and the visual stimulus of the cover layout of *Der Spiegel*, which features a portrait of Grass in the upper right-hand corner and a sinking ship in the bottom half, clearly alert the reader to the subject matter Grass is dealing with, that is, the sinking of the *Gustloff*, rather than to the aesthetic construct of his work — a state of affairs bemoaned by some commentators (Engler 2002). To be sure, *Spiegel* critic Hage does emphasize Grass's literary achievements, such as his masterful and appropriate use of the compact form of the *Novelle* as well as his skillful combination of the various narrative strands, which involve the fates of Wilhelm Gustloff, a Nazi "martyr" after whom the cruise ship was named, David Frankfurter, the Jewish student who murdered Gustloff in Switzerland, and Aleksandr Marinesko, the commander of the Soviet submarine that sank the *Gustloff*. Furthermore, Hage points out the uncanny coincidence of dates: Gustloff was born on 30 January 1895; exactly fifty years later, on 30 January 1945, the *Gustloff* was torpedoed. Moreover, on 30 January 1933 Hitler seized power and set in motion the chain of events that resulted in the unprecedented disaster at sea. Grass adroitly seizes on the opportunity to mingle historical fact and fiction by letting reluctant narrator Paul Pokriefke be born on the same day.

Hage further comments positively on Grass's unorthodox narrative stance — albeit one that the writer had used in previous works — which lets the narrator introduce the unnamed author's alter ego or "'super-narrator'" (Taberner, 171) as "this person not to be confused with me" (*CW*, 1) and "the old man" who has pressured him into serving as his "ghostwriter" (*CW*, 28). Pokriefke, a mediocre journalist without pronounced political convictions — he "always sang along" (*CW*, 227) — had refused for several decades to embark upon writing about the fate of the *Gustloff*, despite the constant nagging of his mother, Tulla Pokriefke, a memorable figure from *Cat and Mouse* and *Dog Years*, who supposedly died when the *Wilhelm Gustloff* sank, as reported in *Die Rättin* (see *R*, 66), turns out to be very much alive. In fact, in an interview Grass professed that it was the idea of having Tulla survive that led to the shaping of the documentary material in literary fashion (Jeismann and Schlögel 2002, 21). As one of the survivors of the *Gustloff*, Tulla, who gave birth to Paul shortly after she was picked up from the icy waters of the Baltic by a German torpedo boat, continues to remind her son that he owes his existence to chance and has an obligation to tell the story of the *Gustloff*.

Violating Taboos?

Paul Pokriefke's reluctance, Hage argues, is indicative of the unwillingness of an entire generation to address controversial topics that might blur the both clear and convenient distinction between the perpetrators of the Nazi crimes and their victims — a dichotomous scheme in which the parent generation of those born during or shortly after the Second World War was indiscriminately classified as culpable. Hence *Crabwalk,* which foregrounds German misery, amounts to Grass's violation of a long-standing taboo. The textual evidence supports Hage's reading; as the narrator tells it, for a long time there was no interest in the story in either West Germany or in the GDR: "For decades the *Gustloff* and its awful fate were taboo, on a pan-German basis, so to speak" (*CW,* 29). A number of reviewers agree with Hage; they find it particularly noteworthy that it is Grass who dares tackle a presumably unmentionable subject. After all, the Nobel laureate has been widely known as an author of leftist convictions with impeccable credentials in shaping the collective memory of his fellow compatriots by attuning them to the horrors of the Nazi past. Furthermore, Grass had — on perhaps somewhat dubious grounds — opposed German (re)unification on account of the moral imperative of Auschwitz, which forbade the creation of a unified and more powerful country with the potential to repeat the mistakes of the past (see Mews 1994). Indeed, one critic calls what amounts to a shifting of Grass's stance "quite unexpected" (Grambow 2002, 135), and another reviewer finds Grass's treatment of a hitherto ignored topic not only surprising but bordering on a "miracle" (Franzen 2002).

Less surprised than some of his colleagues, author Peter Schneider (2002) set out to provide an answer to the question posed by the narrator's employer at the very beginning of the text: "Why only now?" (*CW,* 1). Schneider, a prominent member of the rebellious student movement of the late 1960s who, however, began to distance himself from his comrades in the early 1970s, critically examines the blind spots and failures of that movement. In their fixation on Nazi crimes, the students were oblivious to German torment; through their identification with the victims of racial persecution they sought to establish their own innocence — which, one might add, was attributable to the accident of their births around 1945. Yet despite Schneider's critique of the student movement, he avers that in the political climate of the Federal Republic of the late 1960s and early 1970s it was a moral imperative for the students to lift the veil of silence surrounding their parent generation's active involvement or silent acquiescence in the horrors committed during the Third Reich; the time for a differentiated approach to the Nazi past that also would take into account German suffering had not yet come. Schneider, who cites *Im Krebsgang* as an example of the amazing ability of literary texts to change an entire generation's perception of history via the representation of a singular case, does indeed speak of and about his own generation — in *Crabwalk* represented by such figures as Paul Pokriefke and his ex-wife Gabi — and explores the causes of their indifference toward German victims. Schneider pays scant attention to the preceding, so-called *Flakhelfer,* generation, which derived its name from the fact that its members were usually too young to be drafted for full-fledged military service during the Second World War and served instead as anti-aircraft gunner assistants on the home front. As the chief literary representative of this generation, Grass may be said to have displayed a similar disinclination to deal with an emotionally charged and highly contentious issue. In an interview (2002b), critic Fritz Raddatz (b. 1931) considers himself a member of the student protest movement and, despite his general approval of the meticulous structure and complex dramaturgy of the narrative as well as Grass's restraint in meting out blame, detects traces of the author's prejudice against the kind of revolutionary activities in which the students engaged. At any rate, the text seems to suggest Grass's long-lasting disinclination to tackle a controversial subject: Pokriefke's employer refers to his "regrettable omission, or, to be quite frank, failure" (*CW,* 80) — a failure aggravated by his conviction that all matters "having directly or loosely to do with the city of Danzig" (*CW, 79*) ought to be of paramount concern to him.

Whereas Schneider implicitly tends to agree with those critics who view *Crabwalk* as challenging a taboo — although he minimizes the assumed surprise effect of this challenge — others scoff at the notion that a taboo imposed by the guardians of political correctness has been broken. In the prominent weekly *Die Zeit,* Thomas E. Schmidt (2002) roundly rejects the thesis of the prevailing silence about the abhorrence of the "area bombing" of German cities and the gruesome flight and expulsion of millions of Germans from the Eastern territories, maintaining that the oral tradition of family history as well as conservative historians kept the memory of these events alive over the decades. At the same time, Schmidt acknowledges the constraints that hampered the memory discourse and prevented it from becoming dominant: the pronounced aversion of the student movement to regard Germans as victims, the *Ostpolitik* of Chancellor Willy Brandt in the 1970s, which aimed at reconciliation with Germany's Eastern neighbors, and the inopportune policies of the associations of refugees and expellees in the Federal Republic — policies that entailed the revision of de facto postwar borders and the restitution of property. In contrast to Schneider, Schmidt opines that Grass's grand gesture, with which he wants to reassert the power of literature to shape public consciousness, has come too late. He adds a cautionary note for those who would rashly draw moral lessons from the *Gustloff* tragedy, juxtaposing it to another event: only one day after the ship's sinking, the SS forced five thousand inmates on a death march from the concentration camp Stutthof near Danzig and into the surf of the Baltic, where they were executed.

Some critics go considerably further than Schmidt in warning of the conceivably fateful consequences for the German national psyche that might be caused by the "spectacular success" (Welzer 2002) of *Crabwalk*. They claim that it might result in a paradigm shift that privileges the German victims rather than the perpetrators, which carries with it the risk of minimizing or ignoring the relationship between cause — the Third Reich's aggressive policies and the Holocaust — and effect, that is, German suffering. Although such views are not universally accepted, inasmuch as they seem to dispense with the category of individual responsibility in favor of a collective attribution of guilt or innocence (Gillessen 2002), they do find their advocates. Journalist Ralph Giardano (2002), a survivor of Nazi persecution, acknowledges the literary qualities of *Im Krebsgang*, a work that, he surmises, may be counted as one of the best works in Grass's total *œuvre*, emphasizes the necessity of telling stories such as those of the *Gustloff*, and absolves Grass of any responsibility for the emerging discourse that foregrounds the victimization of Germans. Yet Giardano forcefully insists on reiterating one fundamental historical truth: Nazi Germany began the war of aggression that resulted in such highly deplorable consequences for the German population. He is particularly adamant in rejecting the officious 1950 charter of those Germans who lost their homes in the East and labels it an instrument perfectly suited for repressing historical facts — an instrument that might still exert its baleful influence approximately fifty years later. Some evidence that Giardano's apprehensions are not entirely unfounded may be gleaned from the fact that British reviewers of the German original focus on the "forgotten victims" of "'ethnic cleansing'" and interpret the newly found "sense of loss" as signifying the "'normalisation of Germany'" (Cowley 2002) after (re)unification. Similarly, the *Daily Telegraph* reports that the "9,000 people who died — six times more than in the Titanic disaster — were largely ignored by the country's literary elite and to an extent by its historians" (Helm and Gunther 2002). Actually, how to cope with the past in general and with the legacy of the Second World War in particular is not conceived of as an exclusively German problem; the British newspaper *The Guardian* adds an international perspective by writing that Britain has yet to engage in a "final reckoning" of its "own war crimes" and cites as an example the "bombing of Dresden" (Cowley 2002).

Whereas Frank Brunssen (2006) acknowledges the centrality of the problem of whether or not a taboo about German victimization has been broken in the debate about *Im Krebsgang*, he offers a new approach to the hotly debated issue by suggesting that the *Novelle* is essentially a continuation of Grass's decades-long discourse about German culpability. As evidence Brunssen cites the fact that Grass devotes comparatively little space to those major figures such as Tulla that may be and have been considered victims. Tulla's status as victim in particular may be questioned in that she was and continues to be both a proponent of the classless society propagated by Nazism and, contradictorily, an adherent of Stalinism. Rather than breaking the presumed taboo about the sinking of the *Gustloff*, Grass foregoes foregrounding the suffering of the victims and instead draws attention to the culpability of those who through their support of the Nazi system contributed to the catastrophe.

The Expulsion of Germans from the East and the Normalization Debate

It is evident then from the foregoing discussion that the initial impact of *Crabwalk* is attributable to reviewers' inclinations to view the text in the context of an appropriate interpretation and commemoration of the past — the importance of this process is emphasized by Martina Caspari (2002, 108), among others — rather than to concentrate on an analysis of the text's intrinsic literary merit. The aforementioned contribution of Arnold is somewhat of an exception in that he not only rejects the notion that Grass has broken a taboo but also applies an excessively narrow definition when he questions the text's generic classification as a *Novelle* on the grounds that it involves several intertwining narrative strands rather than proceeding in linear fashion.

The first full-fledged scholarly contributions continued to address issues raised in the reviews. Herman Beyersdorf (2002) claims Grass to be a writer of *Vertreibungsliteratur* (568; literature of expulsion), a category he derives from Louis F. Helbig's pertinent publication (1988). Helbig devotes only two brief segments to the relevant chapters at the end of book 2 of *Die Blechtrommel* (Helbig 1988; rev. ed. 1996, 149–53) and to the poem "Kleckerburg" (*WA* 1:206–9; Helbig, 247–49), an avowal of Grass's commitment to his place of birth that resulted in attacks from functionaries of expellee organizations, but Helbig emphatically states that, although ultimately the deaths and expulsion of Germans are not comparable to the mass murder of innocents by the Nazi regime, it remains an injustice that cannot be hushed up. Beyersdorf, at any rate, concludes from his analysis of Grass's pertinent works that the author's stance has changed from a rather critical and distanced approach to the problem of *Vertreibung* — as evidenced, for example, by Oskar Matzerath's preponderantly pitiless gaze in *Die Blechtrommel* — to his stance in *Im Krebsgang,* in which understanding of and even compassion with the sufferers predominate (568). A case in point is the narrator's inability to adequately render the fate of the refugees trapped in the interior of the sinking ship, although his employer urges him "with words of horror, [to] do justice to the full extent of the catastrophe": "But what took place inside the ship cannot be captured in words" (*CW,* 145). Although Beyersdorf faults critics for having ignored or underestimated the important *Vertreibungsliteratur* component of Grass's prose fiction (581), the validity of his argument is undermined by his reference to the author's longstanding inability — as voiced by the "old man" (*CW,* 80) — to come to grips with the *Gustloff* tragedy. While Beyersdorf makes a convincing case for the presence of thematic elements of expulsion in the majority of Grass's fictional texts, he tends to underestimate Grass's qualitatively new approach in *Im Krebsgang,* which does assign a significant role to the unsung victims and strikes a most responsive chord in the changed cultural and political climate of the Berlin Republic. In fact, the (internalized) taboo that prevented most writers — or, at least those affiliated with the Left — from articulating controversial subjects was also observed by literary historians and critics; the term *Vertreibungsliteratur* itself is of comparatively recent vintage and remains somewhat problematic, in that it invites comparisons with another kind of *Vertreibungsliteratur,* that is, the works written by exiles from Nazi Germany such as Thomas Mann and Bertolt Brecht.

Ultimately, as Beyersdorf points out, in agreement with other critics, Grass breaks the taboo of silence for political reasons, because he realizes that the sinking of the *Gustloff* might serve the radical right and neo-Nazis as a pretext to rewrite history as a narrative of injustices and deprivations endured by Germans. Indeed, the narrator only overcomes his reluctance to tell the *Gustloff* story once he discovers a "right-wing extremist Stormfront home page" that leads him to the site www.blutzeuge.de about Nazi "martyr" Gustloff and the ship that was named after him (*CW,* 29); the creator of the site turns out to be his son Konrad (Konny). The relationship between father (figure) and son, both Beyersdorf (587) and Stuart Taberner (173–75) suggest independently of each other, has been prefigured in *Örtlich betäubt* (see ch. 5) in that the father (figure) narrates his parental failure, which comes to the fore when he is unable to temper the left-wing (*Örtlich betäubt*) or right-wing (*Im Krebsgang*) radicalism of his protégé or offspring via a sense of political moderation. The posited continuity of *Im Krebsgang* with Grass's previous work is valid only up to a point, however. For example, student Scherbaum in *Örtlich betäubt* ultimately abandons the planned action of publicly burning his dog as a sign of protest against the American use of napalm during the war in Vietnam largely on account of the dentist's moderating influence (see ch. 5) — a figure with no parallel in *Im Krebsgang* — whereas Konrad Pokriefke resorts to violence and commits murder by killing the philo-Semitic Wolfgang Stremplin, an "internet rival" (Taberner, 173) who sympathizes with Gustloff's killer Frankfurter and assumes a Jewish identity. Somewhat surprisingly, both Beyersdorf (587) and, before him, Hage (2002a, 190) consider this murder the obligatory, unheard-of, extraordinary, and central event that the strict form of the *Novelle* demands — in Goethe's famed definition, "eine sich ereignete, unerhörte Begebenheit" — a contention that is not fully supported by the text. If it is reasonable to assume that the comments of the "old man" accompany the various stages of Paul Pokriefke's writing process, which initially is almost exclusively concerned with the fate of the *Gustloff,* then his employer's observation, at the beginning of chapter 6, that Paul's "report would make a good novella" (*CW,* 130) clearly refers to the ship's actual sinking. Although Paul reacts indifferently to this "literary assessment" (*CW,* 130) of his efforts, he proceeds to reconstruct the *Gustloff's* destruction, which his employer characterizes as a "unique event, an exemplary event, an event worthy of being told" (*CW,* 30), in the same chapter. Hage's hypothesis (190) that Grass added the (fictional) murder of the assumed Jew by the neo-Nazi Konrad Pokriefke as a kind of afterthought in order to conform to the mandate of political correctness and to forestall any chance that Konrad might be perceived as too sympathetically portrayed hardly does justice to Grass's narrative skills and presumable conceptualization of the *Novelle,* which both articulates German victimhood and warns of a revival of the attitudes and allegiances that caused it to begin with.

Whereas Beyersdorf's approach foregrounds the treatment of expulsion in Grass's work, Stephan Braese (2003) concentrates on the question of guilt and the knowledge of guilt ("Schuldwissen") as well as their "transgenerational transmission" (170). In more detail than other critics, Braese analyses the parental failure of both the narrator and his ex-wife as well as that of the parents of "David" (actually Wolfgang Stremplin), who adopted the name David (as in Frankfurter) and "became so obsessed with thoughts of atonement for the wartime atrocities . . . that eventually everything Jewish became . . . sacred to him" (*CW,* 199). Both Konrad Pokriefke, the fanatic neo-Nazi, and Wolfgang Stremplin, the ardent philo-Semite, are then the products of well-meaning parents whose views were shaped by the doctrines of the rebellious student movement and who proved unable to prevent their offspring from embracing extreme positions because of their reluctance to engage in a genuine discussion of the taboos shrouding the past (Braese, 181; in his brief survey of *Im Krebgang,* Peter Arnds 2004b, 159, essentially agrees with Braese). While

Braese's emphasis on the transmission of the memory of expulsion is persuasive, his claim that Grass's *Novelle* does not deal ("handelt") with the sinking of the *Gustloff* at all (185) is clearly rhetorical overkill; as discussed above, this central event is the starting point of the narrative. In a more encompassing vein than Braese, Taberner establishes a framework by providing a close textual analysis of *Crabwalk* within the context of the "normalization" debate of the Berlin Republic, a debate that was reinvigorated when the governing Social Democrat-Green coalition began "promoting the Berlin Republic as rooted in values, human rights and social justice" (Taberner, 165) and positing its "'normality,'" which "avoids the hubris of nationalistic self-glorification and the calamity of revanchism" (166). In accepting "both German guilt and suffering" (167), the political and intellectual Left seeks to lay claim to a topic that had been primarily the province of intellectuals and historians on the right as demonstrated, for example, by the historians' debate about the singularity of the Holocaust in the mid-1980s. Grass, in fact, clearly states that it is a desideratum to have the Left become engaged in defining the nation so as to preempt endeavors on the part of the Right to monopolize the issue (Leitgeb and Löffler 2002, 27). The "old boy" in *Crabwalk* admits that, because of his generation's overpowering "sense of guilt," he and his generation were culpable of a failure of "staggering" proportions by abandoning the theme of "the hardships endured by the Germans fleeing East Prussia" and their unimaginable misery to "the right wing" (*CW*, 103). This admission serves Taberner (172) to plausibly propose that Grass is less interested in consensus-building about "normality" than in reasserting the Left's "interpretative sovereignty over the Hitler period." This interpretation is no longer narrowly focused on the Holocaust; rather, it admits the recognition of German agony, albeit in a "hierarchy of suffering" that establishes the primacy of the perpetrators' guilt. Yet, as Paul Pokriefke's empathy with the fates of individuals who perished during the sinking of the *Gustloff* suggests — an empathy that evolves gradually and almost against his will — the postulated hierarchy may be less rigid and impermeable or, for that matter, less obvious than Taberner seems to assume. As noted previously, critics such as Welzer and Giardano not only fail to notice the hierarchical construct but insist that Grass privileges the victims to an unconscionable degree. Nevertheless, Taberner's conclusion that once again Grass has found it necessary to intervene via literary means "in a very contemporary crisis" — albeit in a "perhaps somewhat didactic manner" (183) — by penning an "exemplary tale of the dangers of repression and, once the taboo is dismantled, over-identification" (186) seems compelling. Whether the success of the decidedly interventionist work in a "literary scene dominated by a post-ideological introspection" is indicative of the as yet deficient "normality" of the

Berlin Republic, as Taberner claims (186), may be debatable. If, as historian Robert G. Moeller (2003) assumes, "the past is alive and well," in the sense that the discourse about the "politics of memory" will solidify "the democratic bases of the Berlin Republic" (181), then the debate about *Im Krebsgang* may serve a productive end.

Moeller's primary purpose in his essay, "Sinking Ships, the Lost *Heimat* and Broken Taboos: Günter Grass and the Politics of Memory in Contemporary Germany," is to correct the misleading impressions readers and critics of the *Novelle* might gain, not about the sinking of the *Gustloff,* but about Grass's incomplete rendering of the "history of how Germans have remembered and represented" events related to the expulsion from the East (151). His contention that Nobel laureates such as Grass are "not necessarily good historians" (151) hardly does justice to the complex relationship between fiction writer and historian; evidently, works of fiction are not primarily intended to be read as historical documents and hence not subject to the stringent criteria of historiography and standards of evaluation. Actually, in explaining his method of composing the narrative, Grass claimed the superiority of his text in comparison to strictly chronological historical narratives (Jeismann and Schlögel 2002, 21; Ingo Arend 2002, confirms the role of *Im Krebsgang* as a kind of precursor of memorialization). Moeller does concede the obvious: that the *Gustloff* was indeed a taboo subject in the Soviet Occupation Zone and in the GDR because of its official founding myth, which assigned to the soldiers of the Red Army the role of liberators who defeated Fascism. Accordingly, the massacres, mass rapes, and other war crimes committed by the Red Army were suppressed. Grass's text refers to the well-documented case of the East Prussian town of Nemmersdorf (*CW,* 105–6) as a shocking case of Russian violence and carnage; Antony Beevor's *The Fall of Berlin 1945* (2002) also depicts atrocities committed by the Red Army. But Moeller charts in fairly detailed fashion the evolution of the memory culture in West Germany from the end of the Second World War to the present with regard to the expulsions and, after presenting an impressive body of evidence, concludes that, from the mid-1940s to the Berlin Republic, German victimhood had never been totally absent from the public manifestations of both individual and collective memory (180). In point of fact, Moeller contends, sometimes the supposed repression became a veritable "obsession" (159), which, as historians Konrad Jarausch and Michael Geyer suggest in their *Shattered Past: Reconstructing German Histories* (2003), was aided by the prevalence of the phenomenon of "selective perception" and the "victimization perspective." Moeller attributes Grass's alleged misrepresentation of the memory culture to his tacit assumption of "speaking for all Germans" (180); or, as Taberner (2002) states, perhaps more precisely, Grass is actually seeking to promote his leftist interpretation of German history as the only valid model. Nonetheless, Moeller justifiably attributes great significance to *Crabwalk* in that the reflections of "historians — and historical novelists — . . .on the past have significant consequences for the politics of the present" (180). Although Moeller disregards the generic distinction between novel and novella and unconvincingly categorizes Grass as a "historical novelist," his point that the debate about *Crabwalk* offers a prime example of the intertwining of "history, politics and national identity" (181) is well-taken.

Crabwalk in the United States

Even before the American translation by Krishna Winston was published in April 2003, readers in the English-speaking countries were informed about the appearance of the German original and the ensuing debate that centered on whether or not a taboo had been broken (see Beyersdorf 2006, 163); in his review of the English translation of Sebald's treatise, under the title of *On the Natural History of Destruction* in the London *Times,* Antony Beevor (2003) established German victimhood as the common denominator of *Im Krebsgang* and the works of Sebald (1999) and Friedrich (2002) mentioned above. In the United States, the blurb of the hardcover edition of *Crabwalk* displayed a bit of advertising hyperbole by announcing that "no book since *The Tin Drum* has generated as much excitement" — a statement that ignores the enormous, albeit mostly negative, response that *Ein weites Feld* generated in Germany even before it appeared. Other efforts to promote *Crabwalk* included a "Reading Guide" at publisher Harcourt's website, and a well-timed *New York Times* interview with Grass (Riding 2003) drew further attention to the publication. Presumably, the term "a novel" on the cover of *Crabwalk* — a designation accepted by most critics despite the explicit textual reference to a "novella" (*CW,* 130) — was intended to provide a literary category familiar to American readers. Similarly, the lower half of the American edition's cover features a sinking ship — possibly inspired by the cover of *Der Spiegel* — rather than Grass's drawing of a crab, which seems "to go backward but [is] actually scuttling sideways" and thereby advances "fairly rapidly" (*CW,* 3) (thus providing a good illustration of Grass's narrative technique) in the German original. However, reconstructing the *Gustloff's* history and connecting the past to the present is of less obvious and immediate appeal than the visualization of a maritime catastrophe. Although advertising claims tend to be exaggerated, *Crabwalk* attracted considerable critical notice. For example, the Web-based database *LexisNexis Academic* lists ninety-two reviews by major newspapers in the English-speaking countries through January 2004 (for a brief survey of reviews, see Beyersdorf 2006); the editors of the *San Francisco Chronicle* (14 December 2003) put Grass's text on their list of recommended reading, and the *Rocky Mountain News* (14 March 2003) reported that *Crabwalk* had attained third place on the bestseller list for fiction in Denver, Colorado, area bookstores.

American readers had been alerted to the publication of the German original; the headline of the *Los Angeles Times* (Williams 2002), "We, the Victims Too," set the tone by reiterating the prevailing consensus of German reviewers that Grass alerts readers to "a side of history mostly ignored: German suffering during WWII." *Newsweek* adopted the title of the cover story in *Der Spiegel* and informed its readers only a few weeks after the publication of the German original about "The German Titanic" (Nagorski and Theil 2002). *Crabwalk* clearly appealed to a broader segment of the reading public than those primarily interested in fiction; Robert Gerald Livingston's assessment of the "docu-novella" by Germany's "most political" postwar writer in the journal *Foreign Policy* (2003) offers a case in point.

In reviewing the American translation, the critic of *Time,* for example, echoes the commonly accepted appraisal: "Germans suffered too" (Elliott 2003) — but, unexpectedly, he attributes the "worst naval disaster ever" to the "Allies" in general rather than to the Soviets in particular. In the *Boston Globe,* Steve Dowden (2003) adopts the argument about Grass having broken a long-standing (German) taboo, but he also, somewhat contradictorily, adds the useful reminder that Kurt Vonnegut's 1969 novel *Slaughterhouse Five* deals with the firebombing of Dresden. (Keith Bullivant 2002, 95, makes the valid point that it is "non-Germans" such as Vonnegut who portray "the horrors of the bombing of Dresden.") While Dowden acknowledges the difficulties inherent in writing about "carnage on such a massive scale," as in the case of the *Gustloff,* he credits Grass with masterfully approaching his topic, as indicated in the title of the work, "from an unexpected angle." At the same time, Dowden questions Grass's premise that "repressed history" must necessarily lead to the kind of "reactionary violence" that Konrad Pokriefke engages in — a premise that is presented with a dose of "heavy-handed didacticism." Novelist and critic John Updike (2003), writing in the *New Yorker,* provides a fairly detailed description of *Crabwalk,* one that largely dispenses with evaluative comments, but in view of the war in Iraq he briefly discusses "war crimes" and raises the perhaps unanswerable question as to whether "discriminations [are] possible . . . between legitimate and atrocious ship sinkings" (87). In the case of the *Gustloff,* a ship that cannot be unambiguously classified as a non-military vessel, Grass adamantly insists in interviews that its destruction was a catastrophe but not a crime (Sandmeyer and Schönfeld 2002, 182; Boedecker 2002). In what may amount to a compliment of sorts, Updike characterizes the "crabwise narrative" as an "especially potent mix" because it draws both on the Nazi past and the "contemporary Babel of the Internet, which seethes like a global subconscious" (88). Curiously, Grass ventured into the world of the Internet without being a user of computers; he continues to type his texts on a typewriter.

Not all reviewers are prepared to grant that instigating a discussion about a "sense of national victimhood," as Richard Eder (2003) of the *New York Times* does, is called for. Eder traces this "sense" back to Germany's defeat in the First World War — which, in turn, contributed to an attitude that enabled Hitler's rise to power. Whereas the same reviewer avers in his essentially positive comments that Grass deals "far more stingingly" with the "sewer gas" of neo-Nazi resentment kindled by the fate of the *Gustloff* than with "German wartime suffering," Julia M. Klein (2003), although she singles out *Crabwalk* as "Grass's most accessible novel in years," views the bombing of Dresden in terms of "retributive justice" and professes to be unimpressed by the "latest literary cataloging of German losses." Even more categorically, Ruth Franklin (2003) of the *New Republic* deplores the fact that Grass "seems not to be charting the political current so much as swimming along with the tide" of the "new debate over German victimhood" — a debate the "falsity" of which he fails to expose. Franklin's harsh assessment appears less valid when contrasted with Grass's unambiguous statements about the causes of German suffering, which, he said, was not to be equated "with that of its victims," but simply to be acknowledged as "a terrible tragedy" (Nagorski and Theil 2002).

Jeremy Adler (2003) voices criticism of a different sort: he opines that the actual David Frankfurter "and his fellow Jews never gain our sympathy" in the same way as do the victims of the shipwreck. Furthermore, Adler claims, "Frankfurter even appears to be saddled with the guilt for having initiated the whole causal chain that sinks the ship" — a charge that is vaguely reminiscent of Dan Diner's rather far-fetched 2002 critique of Grass as catering to a new, subtle kind of anti-Semitism. Such criticism may be countered by pointing out that Frankfurter is the only genuinely Jewish character in the text, that Grass obviously considered the *Gustloff's* demise as the central event of the *Novelle* — as one of very few American critics, Adler acknowledges the generic "classic simplicity" of *Crabwalk* — and that Grass, in retelling the events leading to the maritime disaster, largely relied on historical accounts. Although Adler lauds Grass's "control" over his "scenario" as "masterly" and terms the *Novelle* a "thought-provoking book," his assumption that the unnamed "he" who is impelling Paul Pokriefke to narrate dwells in the narrator's conscience as his own "alter ego" is hard to corroborate on the basis of the text and is not shared by other critics. Apart from the generational difference, there are clear references that allow us to recognize the narrator's employer as a figure with Grass's characteristics — for example, the employer identifies himself as the author of that "mighty tome" *Dog Years* (*CW*, 79).

Grass's fellow Nobel laureate J. M. Coetzee (2003), writing in the *New York Review of Books,* offers the hitherto most comprehensive appraisal published in the United States. His appraisal includes — a rarity among critics writing in English — a brief consideration of Winston's "faithful" translation (26). While Coetzee deems Grass to be neither "a great prose stylist" — a debatable point — nor a "pioneer of fiction" and finds the "authorial device of tracking the submarine and its prey step by step" until their fateful encounter "particularly creaky," he praises his colleague as the "most enduring exemplar of democratic values in German public life" (26). In contrast to most other critics, who usually give Tulla Pokriefke poor marks — possibly on account of Paul's negative opinion of his mother — Coetzee singles her out as the "most interesting character" (25) in *Crabwalk* and, apart from Oskar Matzerath in *The Tin Drum,* perhaps in Grass's entire work. True, she is bundle of contradictions as both an unrepentant Stalinist and ardent nationalist who, in the GDR, continues to praise the Nazis' socially progressive concept of the "classless" *KdF* cruise ship (*CW,* 50) and, after the (re)unification of Germany, provides the inspiration for her grandson Konrad's research into the sinking that leads him in suspect directions. Yet as a victim who has narrowly escaped death, she is unable to repress her memories of the catastrophe that turned her hair white: "A thing like that you never forget. It never leaves you. It's not just in my dreams, that cry [of passengers sliding overboard] that spread over the water. . . . And all them little children among the ice floes . . ." (*CW,* 57–58). Tulla's "populism" may be "ugly" and unrefined; it is "deeply felt nonetheless." Hence Coetzee surmises that Grass presents a "considered argument" to his readers: Tulla and her ilk should be allowed "to have their heroes and martyrs and memorials and ceremonies of remembrance," because repression of any kind leads to "new, unpredictable" consequences (25). While, in principle, the supposition of a cause-and effect relationship between repression and the denial of an "all-inclusive national history" (Coetzee, 25) on the one hand and unintended results on the other may be correct, the concluding words of *Crabwalk,* "It doesn't end. Never will it end" (*CW,* 234), which refer to the imprisoned Konrad Pokriefke's elevation to the status of a sacrificial victim of the neo-Nazi cause by a right-wing group, suggest that proper memorialization may be impossible without appropriate safeguards to counteract the creation of sacrificial victims by right-wing extremists.

Distinctly an oddity among reviews, Irmgard Elsner Hunt's assessment (2003) inclines toward the negative in a fairly idiosyncratic fashion. Thus she considers Grass's "themes and style . . . worn" but deems the "portrait" of Tulla Pokriefke, whose dialect "will have the reader in stitches" [!], to be the "funny part" of the narrative. The only redeeming feature she grants Grass is his incorporation of the Internet. One would be hard put to find a similarly peculiar appraisal — possibly with the exception of Andrew Grimson in the London *Spectator* (2003) who similarly dismisses Grass as a writer who "long ago lost his muse" and became a "political commentator."

The *Novelle:* Narrative Strategies in the Age of Cyberspace

One of the first scholarly essays on *Im Krebsgang* is that by Anne-Marie Corbin (2003) who provides what may count as a general introduction. Although Wulf Segebrecht subtitles his essay about *Im Krebsgang,* "Aus der Geschichte lernen" (2004; Learning from History), he devotes considerable space to the distinct mode(s) of narration that characterize the representatives of three generations: Tulla, her son Paul, and Paul's son Konrad. Elizabeth Dye (2004) also notes the "three-generational structure and the narrative perspective on the past," which is complicated by the interventions of the "old man" but reveals a "family drama of absent fathers and overbearing mothers" (479–80), as evidenced by Tulla's rarely noted central role as "the driving force behind the whole narrative" (485). As Paul, the epitome of political correctness, states: "But he's not the one [the old man] forcing me to do this [the writing], it's Mother. And it's only because of her that the old man is poking his nose in; she's forcing him to force me . . ." (*CW,* 104).

Tulla, traumatized by the sinking of the ship and given to frequent "flashbacks" that are "symptomatic of post-traumatic stress disorder" (Dye, 485 n. 48), speaks, Segebrecht observes, in an emotionally charged manner that is akin to the mode of oral history, whereas Paul functions as the medium of the author and listlessly but assiduously checks sources in order to write what amounts to an "objective" history of the *Wilhelm Gustloff.* In contrast, Konrad uses his reconstruction of history for ideological purposes. However, Segebrecht suggests, Grass differentiates between the adherents of the right-wing scene, in that Konrad, who is not given to acts of mindless brutality, appears as the product of his parents' misguided education as well as of his grandmother's less than benign influence.

But it is the interventions of the aforementioned "old man," Paul's employer, that add another dimension to the story about the *Wilhelm*

Gustloff and turn it into a work of art. The "truth" of the story can not be ascertained through Paul's documentary report, Tulla's memories, or Konrad's ideological construct; rather, the combination of various perspectives, the lack of a strictly chronological narrative, and the absence of a dominant narratorial position correspond to the principle of the "crabwalk" and signify a gradual, circuitous approach to the elusive historical "truth," which, Segebrecht concludes, would seem to entail an acknowledgment of the persistence of right-wing ideologies and their sources on the one hand and the right of the victims of expulsion to be heard on the other.

Whereas Segebrecht contends that the term *Novelle* merely serves to underline the literary character of the text, which, by implication, does not conform to its generic criteria, Jill E. Twark (2004) accepts the definition of *Novelle* because of the intrinsic features of the text such as the "unerhörte Begebenheit." In accordance with Hage (2002a and b) and Beyersdorf (2006), she construes this "Begebenheit" as the (fictional) murder of the "German youth posing as David Frankfurter" (156) rather than than the (actual) sinking of the *Wilhelm Gustloff,* an event that she plausibly defines as the turning point of the *Novelle.* Less convincing is Twark's contention that the old man's interferences constitute the *Rahmen* or "external framework surrounding the narrative" (156) in that the *Rahmen* is not an obligatory but an optional feature of the *Novelle;* in fact, such framed narratives are specifically referred to as *Rahmennovellen.* (There is no unanimity concerning a potential *Rahmen;* Dye 2004, 479, perceives the "'Rahmengeschichte'" to be taking place in the present, whereas what might be called the *Binnengeschichte* [inner story] is centered "on the history of the ship.") But then Twark is reluctant to reduce *Im Krebsgang* to a conventional novella; she argues that the text also constitutes a "highly constructed metanarrative" that illuminates various options for (re)constructing German history (Twark, 147; see also Segebrecht 2004). Yet her contention that it is Paul's "narrative style" that reflects "Grass's view of history and narrative theory" (149) may be questioned in view of the interplay of the various narrative accounts discerned by Segebrecht and the dominance of the "old man" in a narrative construct that includes the Internet, with its potential to "conflate time and space as well as historical chronology" (Twark, 159).

The exploration of the function of the Internet is at the center of Kristin Veel's essay about "Virtual Memory" (2004) in *Im Krebsgang.* She proceeds from a passage in Grass's Nobel Lecture in which he laments the diminished significance of literature, as evident in its "retreat from public life" in general and young writers' use of "the Internet as a playground" in particular (*NL,* 299), in order to show that Grass's use of the Internet functions as a "contrast to the literary narrative" that is imbued with the "moral responsibility" ascribed by Grass "to the author" (Veel, 209). Touted as a "democratic forum for communication," the Internet, as the postings of both Konrad/Gustav and Wolfgang/David show, tends to blur the difference between past and present and enables them to effortlessly assume different identities "as virtual reincarnations of . . . historical characters," that is, Gustloff and Frankfurter (Veel, 210). These reincarnations ultimately lead to murder, which, however, does not signify the end of the story. Rather, "the story reproduces itself" in that Konrad, who has emancipated himself from his "idol" Gustloff, is cast in the role of martyr for right-wing causes (214). In contrast to the Internet's "collapse of the virtual and the real" (216), Grass's intricate narrative does then attempt to lay bare the roots of Konny's murder, in an attempt to promote an ongoing dialogue with "the German past," as well as being his "own contribution to cultivating the cultural memory of contemporary Germany" through his works of fiction (218).

Following Veel to some extent, David Midgley (2005) maintains that *Im Krebsgang* "deserves enduring critical attention" not primarily because it addresses "certain issues about the commemoration of the German past" — a topic that had been foregrounded in reviews and by previous critics — but rather because the text explores the function of the "media in which memories are recorded and transmitted" (56). In particular, Midgley singles out the Internet as the medium of "virtual reality" that enables Konrad as Gustloff to commit his transgression in "the world of physical reality" (60) by murdering "David." This murder, one might conclude, would not have taken place without the Internet, which, rather than fostering an entirely novel way of "thinking and communicating," appears to encourage the "uninhibited manner" of communication that leads to fatal consequences (63). Konrad commits the murder at the monument (which was destroyed after the Second World War) in honor of Wilhelm Gustloff, in the city of Schwerin, Gustloff's birthplace. Midgley cites the local paper, the *Schweriner Volkszeitung* of 30 January 1995, the fiftieth anniversary of the fateful date, in order to demonstrate the contrast between the sober, fact-based reporting of the German press and the "unreflected assertions, tendentious accounts . . ., and defamatory slogans" to be found in both the actual and Grass's fictional Internet (64). Grass's great achievement, Midgley states, is to have "evoked aspects of personal and historical memory . . . in a medium that opens them up to both contextual understanding and critical discussion" (66).

Stefania Sbarra (2005) implicitly disagrees with Midgley and stresses the assumed taboo about discussing the sinking of the *Wilhelm Gustloff,* a taboo that prevailed in both parts of Germany in the postwar period. Following Aleida and Jan Assmann, scholars in cultural studies, she distinguishes between "cultural memory," the collective knowledge of members of a society that enables later generations to reconstruct their cultural identity, and "communicative memory," which is limited to three to four generations and in which family memory plays a significant role (382). Whereas the fate of the refugees and expellees from the East was not part of their "cultural memory," the "communicative memory" relating to the *Wilhelm Gustloff* was transmitted by Tulla to her grandson, because of her son's reluctance to deal with the subject. At the meeting of the survivors of the catastrophe on the fiftieth anniversary of the ship's demise at the "Baltic seaside resort of Damp" (*CW,* 95 et passim) the Pokriefkes' family story merges with that of others and obtains a certain degree of public recognition. Moreover, Konrad's fascination with his grandmother and her tales has a precedent in Oskar's habit of seeking refuge under the skirts of his grandmother in *Die Blechtrommel,* Sbarra observes (385). Contributing to her grandson's fascination is that Tulla witnessed a tragic, catastrophic moment at the end of the Second World War, an event that she talks about obsessively; she also hails from the lost world of the Kashubians, an origin that endows her with magic features. Sbarra goes so far as to claim that Tulla is a siren who propagates the myth that the *Wilhelm Gustloff* was the realized utopia of the classless society, a utopia that, contradictorily, she also perceives to exist — at least to some extent — in the GDR (386–87). Essentially a fellow traveler, Tulla has no difficulties surviving regime changes; her obsession with the fate of the *KdF* vessel as well as her son Paul's parental failure induce Konrad to spin his tales on the Internet, tales that do not rely on well-known facts but that are motivated, his father surmises, by "the desire for an unambiguous enemy" (*CW,* 109). The consequences of Konrad's Internet activities have been repeatedly mentioned; Sbarra (388–89) perceives those consequences, following Hans Blumenberg, *Schiffbruch mit Zuschauer: Paradigma einer Daseinsmetapher* (1979; *Shipwreck with Spectator: Paradigm of a Metaphor for Existence,* 1996), as a metaphorical shipwreck of major proportions.

Although he does not refer to Blumenberg, Wolfgang Emmerich (2005) emphasizes the importance of shipwrecks in literary texts from antiquity to today. But his main focus is the representation of the fate of the *Wilhelm Gustloff* (as well as other catastrophes at sea involving German refugees) in, apart from *Im Krebsgang,* texts by Uwe Johnson, Walter Kempowski, Tanja Dückers (see also Marek Jaroszewski 2005), and Polish author Stefan Chwin. Emmerich reiterates the often posed question of whether, in view of the Holocaust, Germans should be permitted to mourn their own victims, and he traces the evolution of "cultural memory" in postwar Germany as it is expressed in literary texts. Whereas Kempowski in his monumental "collective diary" *Echolot* (1999; Echo-Sounder) provides a non-tendentious, documentary account of the sinking of the *Gustloff*, in Emmerich's opinion Grass's *Novelle* contributed significantly to a change in the discourse about German suffering because of the enormous media attention resulting from the author's status rather than the literary qualities of the work (310). In contrast to Grass, Emmerich suggests that Tanja Dückers (b. 1968) in her novel *Himmelskörper* (2003; Celestial Bodies) appears to return to what, under the influence of the student movement, was considered the politically correct attitude, that is, ignoring or downplaying German victimhood and emphasizing Nazi crimes: Dückers has her protagonists' grandparents escape almost certain death on the *Gustloff* owing to their position as staunch Nazis who were entitled to a safer mode of transportation on their flight from Danzig. One may conclude from the conflicting modes of representing the fate of the erstwhile *KdF* ship as well as the cacophonous initial critical reception of *Im Krebsgang* that the (literary) memorialization of German victims will continue to remain problematic and stimulate further discussion as well as literary texts.

Epilogue

PRECEDING THE RELEASE OF Grass's memoirs *Beim Häuten der Zwiebel,* the *Frankfurter Allgemeine Zeitung* (12 August 2006) published an interview, conducted by Frank Schirrmacher and Hubert Spiegel, in which the author for the first time publicly admitted to having been a member of the *Waffen SS* in the waning months of the Second World War. This statement caught the media and public by surprise and caused a sensation, because it radically changed what had been considered common knowledge about the author's military service. While Grass had never tried to hide his youthful belief in and commitment to Nazi doctrine until and beyond the end of the war, it was generally assumed, based on his utterances and writings, that he had spent the last months before the collapse of the Third Reich primarily as a *Flakhelfer* — a far cry indeed from his presumable role in a military unit that was declared a criminal organization during the Nuremberg trials. Although the *Waffen SS* had lost its elite status during the final phase of the war and had to rely on draftees, as was explained in an unsigned contribution accompanying the interview, Schirrmacher, in an article entitled "Das Geständnis" (2006; The Confession) expressed his great astonishment that for more than sixty years Grass had maintained his silence about a detail of his biography that seemed strangely at odds with his decade-long vociferous, stalwart opposition to any attempt to suppress or minimize German guilt about Nazi crimes. In particular, Schirrmacher singled out the highly controversial Bitburg incident as a missed opportunity for Grass to admit to his membership in the *Waffen SS.* Intended as a symbolic gesture of reconciliation forty years after the end of the Second World War, in May 1985 President Reagan and Chancellor Kohl had visited the cemetery at Bitburg, which, in addition to the graves of German soldiers, also included several burial sites of members of the *Waffen SS.* Grass, far from seizing this opportunity to acknowledge the possibility that he might have been among those buried at the cemetery, sharply attacked the visit as a media event that did not promote genuine reconciliation. While implicitly indicating his disapproval of Grass's reticence, Schirrmacher, in his judicious, non-accusatory comments, was at pains to let it be known that the author might be blamed for a youthful indiscretion but was not culpable of any crimes; rather, he suggested that the writer's belated confession provided an indication of the difficulties inherent in the concept of both collective and individual *Vergangenheitsbewältigung,* the discourse about coming to terms with the Nazi past that had played a prominent role in the postwar Federal Republic. (In his analysis of how the media seized upon the "confession" and turned it into a veritable scandal, Martin Kölbel [2007a] examines in particular the role of Schirrmacher and the *Frankfurter Allgemeine Zeitung.*)

Although the interviewers inquired about the central metaphor of the autobiography (Grass does not provide any genre classification, but the English translation by Michael Henry Heim, which became available in June 2007, displays the designation "*A Memoir*" in very small caps on the dust jacket only), the process of peeling an onion that is akin to laying bare the layers of memory, the main thrust of their questions was directed at seeking to discover what for so long had prevented Grass from acknowledging his stint in the *Waffen SS.* Before and even after the moved-up publication date of *Beim Häuten der Zwiebel* (16 August 2006), this entirely legitimate and justifiable question dominated the ensuing public debate that was carried on in the various news media — at least at the beginning — at the expense of a close analysis of the autobiographical text. (The pertinent reports, statements, comments, interviews, and caricatures, as well as reviews and letters to the editors of various print media have been collected in the two anthologies by Gorzny 2006, and the somewhat more comprehensive one by Kölbel 2007). As on previous occasions, the public persona Grass rather than the writer was at the center of the intense debate that began raging in Germany and soon spread abroad. Frank Olbert (2006), one of the first journalists to introduce the negatively connoted term "Moralapostel" (upholder of moral standards) into the debate, provided a pattern of interpretation applied by many: the professed moralist Grass had revealed a personal flaw that would seem to disqualify him from pronouncing his verdicts on public affairs and castigating others in the public realm for their assumed political and moral shortcomings. Even Grass's biographer Michael Jürgs (2006; see also below), although he did not anticipate any diminution of the writer's standing as the creator of great literature, expressed his disappointment about the author's long silence. Far more disparagingly, Hellmuth Karasek, writing in *Welt am Sonntag* (2006), insinuated that Grass might have used the astounding revelation as a marketing device in order to promote the sales of his memoir, accused him of having falsified his biography in previous accounts by misrepresenting his service in the armed forces of the Third Reich, and suggested as a potential reason for the author's non-disclosure the possibility that he might not have been awarded the Nobel Prize had his *Waffen SS* service be known. Karasek's attempt to dismantle a public icon was surpassed by those who demanded that Grass return the prize.

Speculations about the reasons for Grass's silence continued, but Tilman Krause in *Die Welt* (2006a) attributed the writer's vulnerability to his harsh condemnations of political opponents, his Manichaean world view, his hatred of those whom he considered adversaries, such as former Chancellor Konrad Adenauer, and his failure to acknowledge the role of ambivalence (see also the discussion below). The debate continued with undiminished fervor throughout the month of August and beyond; it assumed an international dimension when, for instance, Nobel Peace laureate Lech Wałęsa of *Solidarność* (Solidarity) fame, and like Grass an honorary citizen of Gdańsk, suggested that the writer relinquish the honor, and the citizens of his place of birth began discussing whether to revoke it; eventually, Grass succeeded in reassuring Wałęsa, and the citizens of Gdańsk decided by majority vote against revocation (see also Associated Press 2006). Another, somewhat belated, attempt to rebuke Grass for his assumed misdeed was more successful; as the Canadian *Globe and Mail* reported from Jerusalem (Anon. 2006d), the Israeli Netanya Academic College withdrew its "offer to award an honorary doctorate" to the Nobel laureate and implicitly followed the lead of Charlotte Knobloch, president of the Central Council of Jews in Germany, who had negated the validity of the writer's previous statements in view of his belated admission.

Conversely, international assistance was extended by both Salman Rushdie and John Irving, who affirmed their unwavering support and esteem of their (in)famous colleague. In Germany, the range of opinions extended from that of conservative historian and Hitler biographer Joachim Fest (1926–2006), who flatly stated that Grass had lost all credibility and, to add insult to injury, said that he would not even buy a used car from him, to those who defended him, such as fellow writers Martin Walser and Christa Wolf (for a brief listing of prominent opponents of Grass as well as his supporters, see Kölbel 2007b, 153–54).

Thomas Steinfeld entitled his article in the *Süddeutsche Zeitung* (2006) "Grass ist Deutschland" (Grass is Germany) in order to indicate that by virtue of his literary work, which is essentially concerned with the demise of the Third Reich and the (re)birth of a new Germany in the form of the Federal Republic, he had earned his representative role. But Steinfeld concludes ambivalently that upon publication of *Beim Häuten der Zwiebel* it will indeed become obvious that "Grass war Deutschland" (Grass was Germany) — a statement that may be read either as a confirmation of the writer's position or as a sign that he no longer occupies such eminent place. In a different, distinctly negative vein, the fairly comprehensive cover story about the "Blechtrommler" and "Moralapostel" in *Der Spiegel* (see Kurbjuweit et al. 2006) — the sixth the magazine had devoted to Grass in the course of the decades — provided a kind of interim report on the state of the debate concerning the self-appointed "moral executioner" and his latest work. Thus the writer is said to fancy himself to be the chairman of the supervisory board of the Federal Republic and to be possessed by delusions of grandeur; furthermore, he is called a Manichean and a polemicist whose concealment of his true military record offered him the advantage of being able to attack political opponents without having to fear recriminations. Grass's disclosure, the *Spiegel* authors write sardonically, toppled him from divine heights and relegated him to a place among mere fallible mortals. Moreover, they opined, the writer's so-called silence must be considered a misnomer, in that he actually engaged in deception, for example, vis-à-vis his biographer Jürgs (who, however, did not accuse Grass of having deliberately deceived him).

Notwithstanding the debate and the sometimes fierce indictment of both author and *Beim Häuten der Zwiebel,* the autobiography proved to be a bestseller: the first edition of a hundred and fifty thousand copies sold out within a few days upon publication. The reviews that began to appear tended to extend the frame of reference beyond the exploration of the presumable reasons for Grass's taciturnity. Fritz J. Raddatz in his essentially sympathetic and laudatory comments in *Die Zeit* (2006) wondered about the teenage Grass's unshakeable belief in the Nazi cause even when confronted with the devastation of Berlin and Dresden or the demoralization of the civilian population but considered the book a challenge not only for the reader but for the author himself; after all, Raddatz surmises, in the process of writing he had to summon up the courage to confront his youthful aberration, which had continued to fester.

In her review in the *Süddeutsche Zeitung,* Ijoma Mangold (2006) classifies *Beim Häuten der Zwiebel* as autobiographical literature, that is, an autobiography with fictional elements. It covers the period from 1939, the beginning of the Second World War, to 1959, the year in which *Die Blechtrommel* was published. Mangold deems Grass's extensive use of the metaphor of the onion not entirely free of vanity: although he accuses himself of having failed to ask the right questions, he prominently displays his desire to lay bare the painful truth. The onion is augmented by a piece of amber as an additional repository of the past; this functions as a *Dingsymbol* (a concrete object with symbolic significance) in the manner of the Snail in *Aus dem Tagebuch einer Schnecke,* the Flounder in *Der Butt,* the Rat in *Die Rättin,* the Toad in *Unkenrufe,* and even the Crab in *Im Krebsgang.* However, the Crab, it should be noted, has a purely metaphorical function, without any physical presence in the narrative. Although Mangold agrees with the majority of critics that Grass cannot be held responsible for the beliefs he held in his youth, she argues that the excess of metaphors obscures rather than enlightens young Grass's feelings and convictions.

In contrast to Mangold, Tilman Krause in his second article in *Die Welt* (2006b) considers the onion metaphor a stroke of genius, in that it leaves no doubt about the complexities of memory. Similarly, the amber encapsules Grass's childhood world on the shores of the Baltic and in Danzig, a world that began to crumble with the outbreak of the war. The endpoint of the autobiography in 1959, a year that also marks the beginning of the writer's virtually unparalleled success story, Krause writes, places the emphasis, following literary precedents, on the portrait of the artist as a young man rather than on the mature, accomplished novelist. It is not so much the disclosure of having been in the *Waffen SS* — the prepublication revelation of which Krause deems unfortunate — that imparts to the autobiography the attributes of a confession; rather, Grass's acknowledgment of his youthful social indifference, lack of pity, egocentrism, and inability to ask pertinent questions when, for example, his Latin teacher disappeared (he was incarcerated in the concentration camp Stutthof), constitute a far more serious self-indictment. Somewhat questioably, Krause maintains that it was entirely consistent with young Grass's attitudes as a sexually frustrated, generally insensitive youth who resented his lower-middle-class origins that he joined (or was drafted by) the *Waffen SS,* an organization that appealed precisely to young men like him. Conversely, Krause credits Grass with felicitous (fictional) passages such as the episode when he becomes separated from his unit behind the Soviet lines, gets lost in a dark forest and starts singing a children's song, whereupon another German soldier responds in kind (see *PO,* 136–41). Despite a modicum of praise, Krause rather unexpectedly, but in keeping with the tenor of his previous contribution to the debate, concludes his review with the observation that the autobiography will satisfy only those readers who share the author's simple world view, which is devoid of anything noble and elevating.

Hubert Spiegel, writing in the *Frankfurter Allgemeine Zeitung* (2006), returns to the basic question that was and continued to be at the center of the entire Grass debate: what kind of explanation Grass has to offer for his protracted silence. Spiegel finds that there is no imaginable clarification that would conclusively answer all questions. Nevertheless, he considers *Beim Häuten der Zwiebel* not an autobiography but a novel about the life of the writer, a novel, moreover, that he deems to be the writer's most important work since the *Danziger Trilogie* — surely not a universally shared opinion. But Spiegel offers a plausible elucidation, not for Grass's decade-long information deficit, but for his surprise, which bordered on incomprehension, about the violent reactions that his late confession elicited: because the writer neither forgot nor forgave himself for what kind of person he had been in his youth and what he had done then, he may have believed he was entitled to considerateness or even forgiveness — an assumption that proved to be a serious miscalculation.

It goes almost without saying that the controversy about *Beim Häuten der Zwiebel* did not go unnoticed by the press in the English-speaking countries. The *New York Times* in particular reacted rather quickly with a number of contributions, beginning with a well-reasoned editorial under the heading "The Betrayal of Memory." The editorial concluded that despite the damage to Grass's "personal probity" the revelation does not excuse or invalidate the "crimes" against which he has "railed." Even though his literary work will be "reread with an ironic eye," its "weight" will continue "unchanged." The editorial was supplemented by a brief report on the aforementioned statements of support on the part of Salman Rushdie and John Irving (van Gelder 2006), but German-Austrian writer Daniel Kehlmann (b. 1975), author of the acclaimed novel *Die Vermessung der Welt* (2005; *Measuring the World,* 2006), interprets Grass's revelation as an attempt to rescue "his life's work and the persona that he took such pains to shape." Kehlmann (2006) concedes that the "postwar German milieu" encouraged expectations that a writer engage in politics and acknowledges the *Danzig Trilogy* as one of the "masterpieces" but reiterates Karasek's charge that Grass remained silent about his *Waffen SS* involvement because he feared not being considered for the Nobel Prize. Once he had received the coveted prize, Kehlmann continues, Grass had to worry about his "posthumous reputation" in the event that curious journalists would begin digging in his past (Kehlmann does not explain why such efforts should not have been made during the author's lifetime). Hence the author attempted to "pre-empt the loss of his reputation" by going public; as a consequence, the writer's as well as "Germany's image in the world" are likely to suffer — even if Grass's early "novels will be with us for as long as people read books."

In another op-ed piece in the *New York Times* (2006), professor emeritus of history at Yale Peter Gay, a Jew who grew up in Berlin during the Nazi period, initially casts an ironic glance at the entire "Günter Grass affair" by alluding to a certain degree of hypocrisy on the part of those who consider themselves blameless and rejoice in having discovered yet "another giant with feet of clay!" But Gay is inclined to consider both Grass's activities on behalf of the SPD and his "powerful novels" positive features; in his opinion, however, they do not offer an excuse for the "uncomfortable question" of the tightly kept secret. In contrast to Kehlmann, Gay discerns profound shame as the compelling reason for the writer's silence — a shame that serves as a "reminder" of that of an entire country (or generation).

In a news release from Warsaw, the Associated Press reported in the *New York Times* on the letter, dated 20 August 2006, that Grass had written to the mayor of Gdańsk in response to calls for relinquishing his honorary citizenship; in that letter he indicated that it had taken him several decades before he had found the "right formula" to reveal his service in the *Waffen SS* during the war (Grass used similar arguments in a TV interview with Ulrich Wickert in 2006). As previously discussed, the efforts by some to rescind the honor came to naught, but the reports and comments published in the *New York Times* and other newspapers not considered here show that all aspects of the Grass controversy were deemed highly newsworthy; Neal Conan's interview with biographer Michael Jürgs on NPR's "Talk of the Nation" (17 August 2006) merely confirms this observation. In the interview, Jürgs again expressed his disappointment about Grass's secrecy, in view of his reputation as a moralist. Whereas Jens Jessen in the *Atlantic Times* (2006) informed American readers of Grass's ill-conceived "colossal spectacle of self-accusation," he opined that the author remained a "monument," albeit one that had "slightly crumbled."

John Vinocur's comments in the *New York Times* (2006), based on his reading of the "four key chapters, or first 180 pages," may count as the first review in English of *Beim Häuten der Zwiebel.* Vinocur takes issue with the onion metaphor, Grass's "dodge" intended to "blur the self-disclosure of his SS past," which might function as a "potential moral hook on his legacy." Thus Grass seeks to fob off his "selectivity . . . as memory failure" in such a fashion that the reader gains the impression that he "focused all his art at creating this subterfuge." Vinocur credits the author with "many brilliant details" such as the episode of his "urinating" into the coffee of his "drill instructors" (see *PO,* 112–13) and acknowledges him as a "great writer" who, however, "after 60 years of lying" is less than forthcoming and truthful. A similar but slightly more favorable review is that by Ben Hutchinson in *The Observer* (2006), who places the unceasing debate in the context of the tendency in the Berlin Republic to debate "its responsibilities towards the past," a debate that is characterized by memorializing the victims of the Holocaust on the one hand and German victimhood on the other. Contributing to the fierceness of the ongoing discussion is the tendency to elevate writers to the "status of moral authority" with the result that a "tsunami of self-righteousness" tends to overshadow the literary event of the publication of Grass's autobiography in which, despite his previous warnings to the contrary, he appears to distance himself from the past by "dividing himself into the first and third person, into the older 'I' and the younger 'he.'" Such a technique amounts to a stylization; the story reads "as though he were a character in one of his novels." Hence Grass's "irritating" emphasis on questioning "the very nature of memory, its gaps and distortions" in "an otherwise enjoyable book." In deviating from what may be considered the critical consensus, Hutchinson finds the early chapters with the writer's confession less interesting than the subsequent ones; for instance, the perhaps not quite "amusing intermezzo" of "lessons in 'imaginary' cooking" conducted by a former grand-hotel chef for the undernourished German soldiers in an American POW camp in Bavaria (rather than "a displaced persons' camp"; see *PO,* 177–85). In this camp the author also supposedly befriended a devout Catholic and fellow prisoner named Joseph, who may have been Joseph Ratzinger (b. 1927), the current pope Benedict XVI, whose "candor" about his military service Rafael Seligmann (2006) contrasts favorably with Grass's silence. In the final analysis, Hutchinson finds the autobiography "both entertaining and self-pitying," but he judiciously pleads for a "literary judgment, not a political witch hunt."

Whereas Neal Ascherson, writing in the *London Review of Books* (2006), confines himself essentially to a retelling of the contents, Ian Brunskill in his article in *Time Online* (2006) declares *Beim Häuten der Zwiebel* to be "one of Grass's most accessible and engaging works" on account of its "scenes of marvelous vividness," but he also notes the "difficulties involved in recalling and recounting" events — difficulties that lead to a number of "imprecisions." On the whole, the autobiography reveals the "story of a life given up to fiction," fiction that, Brunskill surmises, always entailed the "greater truth" for the author. As to Grass's claim to the position of moral authority, the reviewer refers to the writer's mentor, former Chancellor Willy Brandt, "the living embodiment of heroic resistance to Hitler," whose stature the author could never have hoped to attain.

In greater detail than others, Ian Buruma (2006) establishes the sociopolitical and cultural context that may help explain Grass's dissembling about his past, his "intent on imposing a collective guilt on his people, as if all Germans had followed Hitler as blindly as he had," and the "discrepancy" between his subtle fiction on the one hand and his fierce "public scoldings" on the other. Buruma suggests as a conceivable explanation the German propensity for "spirituality and deep culture," which entailed the rejection of "liberal democracy and capitalism, especially of the American kind," and which attracted young Grass, a "worshipper of great art," who despised his petit-bourgeois father, a man "without any tragic, mythical, or heroic qualities" (83). In the author's admission of his "recurrent sense of shame" (*PO,* 111), Buruma detects a bit of dramatization, an "element of tragic myth, if not heroism" that pervades both prewar and war-time nationalism as well as the long-neglected discussion of "German suffering" during the war (84). Actually, Buruma surmises, such a notion of myth is at the bottom of Grass's severe criticism of Adenauer's pragmatism and his "hysterical denunciations" of what to him appear to be signs of the reappearance of "Nazi ghosts." Owing to the German tradition of elevating "poets and thinkers" to the position of moral arbiters (85), Grass became the "conscience of Germany." But it is his best fiction, such as the *Danzig Trilogy*, that will continue to be read when controversies past and present will long have been forgotten.

A novel approach that largely dispenses with the separation of Grass's literary and political work, to which most commentators adhere, is that pursued by Timm Niklas Pietsch (2006). Pietsch perceives the autobiographical form, which Grass used exclusively for the first time in *Beim Häuten der Zwiebel*, not as a break with the writer's previous practice but rather as the endpoint of a development in which Grass himself gradually morphs into both narrator and actor of his prose via the use of dialogue, which in his autobiography assumes the form of a soliloquy, such as when he questions his "petrified faith" in the Nazi cause (*PO*, 285). The narrative stances with their more or less fully developed dialogic patterns between two narrator figures in *Die Rättin*, *Unkenrufe*, and *Im Krebsgang* offer further evidence of approaches to an autobiographical mode. Although the autobiography largely dispenses with fictional characters, the dialogic form has been retained in the constellation of old Grass and his youthful counterpart, in which the former seeks to approach (and understand) the latter via the unreliable medium of memory — a process that results in shame. Shame, Pietsch posits, is at the center of an unresolved guilt complex that may be said to be the leitmotif of both Grass's fictional works and his political essays. This guilt complex ultimately resulted in *Beim Häuten der Zwiebel*, a felicitous combination of autobiography and political statement. It is precisely this fusion of political and literary means of expression, Pietsch argues persuasively, that constitutes an enduring characteristic of a remarkable body of work.

Works Cited

Works by Günter Grass

Collected Works

Werkausgabe in zehn Bänden. Ed. Volker Neuhaus. Darmstadt: Luchterhand, 1987. 10 vols. (Poems, fiction, plays, essays, speeches, letters, interviews.)

Werkausgabe in 18 Bänden. Ed. Volker Neuhaus and Daniela Hermes. Göttingen: Steidl, 1997–2003. 18 vols. (An expansion of the 1987 *Werkausgabe*.)

Fiction, Diary, Memoir

Die Blechtrommel. Neuwied: Luchterhand, 1959. Trans. Ralph Manheim as *The Tin Drum*. New York: Pantheon, 1963 [c1962].

Katz und Maus. Eine Novelle. Neuwied: Luchterhand, 1961. Trans. Ralph Manheim as *Cat and Mouse*. New York: Harcourt, Brace, 1963.

Hundejahre. Roman. Neuwied: Luchterhand, 1963. Trans. Ralph Manheim as *Dog Years*. New York: Harcourt, Brace, 1965.

Örtlich betäubt. Neuwied: Luchterhand, 1969. Trans. Ralph Manheim as *Local Anaesthetic*. New York: Harcourt, Brace, 1969.

Aus dem Tagebuch einer Schnecke. Darmstadt: Luchterhand, 1972. Trans. Ralph Manheim as *From the Diary of a Snail*. New York: Harcourt, Brace, 1973.

Der Butt. Roman. Darmstadt: Luchterhand, 1977. Trans. Ralph Manheim as *The Flounder*. New York: Harcourt, Brace, 1978.

Das Treffen in Telgte. Eine Erzählung. Darmstadt: Luchterhand, 1979. Trans. Ralph Manheim as *The Meeting at Telgte*. New York: Harcourt, Brace, 1981.

Danziger Trilogie. Darmstadt: Luchterhand, 1980. Trans. as *The Danzig Trilogy: The Tin Drum, Cat and Mouse, Dog Years*. San Diego, CA: Harcourt, 1987.

Kopfgeburten oder Die Deutschen sterben aus. Darmstadt: Luchterhand, 1980. Trans. Ralph Manheim as *Headbirths or The Germans Are Dying Out*. New York: Harcourt, Brace, 1982.

Die Rättin. Darmstadt: Luchterhand, 1986. Trans. Ralph Manheim as *The Rat*. San Diego, CA: Harcourt, Brace, 1987.

Zunge zeigen. Darmstadt: Luchterhand, 1988. Also Göttingen: Steidl, 1988. Trans. John E. Woods as *Show Your Tongue*. San Diego, CA: Harcourt, Brace, 1989.

Unkenrufe. Eine Erzählung. Göttingen: Steidl, 1992. Trans. Ralph Manheim as *The Call of the Toad*. New York: Harcourt, Brace, 1992.

Ein weites Feld. Roman. Göttingen: Steidl, 1995. Trans. Krishna Winston as *Too Far Afield*. New York: Harcourt, Inc., 2000.

Mein Jahrhundert. 100 Geschichten. Göttingen: Steidl, 1999. Trans. Michael Henry Heim as *My Century*. New York: Harcourt, Inc., 1999.

Im Krebsgang. Eine Novelle. Göttingen: Steidl, 2002. Trans. Krishna Winston as *Crabwalk*. Orlando, FL: Harcourt, Inc., 2002.

Das Danzig-Sextett: Die Blechtrommel /Katz und Maus /Hundejahre /Der Butt /Unkenrufe /Im Krebsgang. 2 vols. Göttingen: Steidl, 2006.

Beim Häuten der Zwiebel. Göttingen: Steidl, 2006. Trans. Michael Henry Heim as *Peeling the Onion*. Orlando, FL: Harcourt, Inc., 2007.

Selected Other Writings

Die Plebejer proben den Aufstand. Ein deutsches Trauerspiel. Neuwied: Luchterhand, 1966. Trans. Ralph Manheim as *The Plebeians Rehearse the Uprising. A German Tragedy*. New York: Harcourt, Brace, 1966.

Selected Poems. In German with Translations by Michael Hamburger and Christopher Middleton. New York: Harcourt, 1966.

Four Plays. (*Flood. Mister, Mister. Only Ten Minutes to Buffalo. The Wicked Cooks*.) Trans. Ralph Manheim and A. Leslie Willson. Introd. Martin Esslin. New York: Harcourt, Brace, 1967.

New Poems [*Ausgefragt*]. *In German with Translations by Michael Hamburger*. New York: Harcourt, Brace, 1968.

Speak Out! Speeches, Open Letters, Commentaries. Trans. Ralph Mannheim. New York: Harcourt, Brace, 1969.

Theaterspiele. (*Hochwasser. Onkel, Onkel. Noch zehn Minuten bis Buffalo. Die bösen Köche. Die Plebejer proben den Aufstand. Davor*.) Neuwied: Luchterhand, 1970.

Max. A Play. Trans. A. Leslie Willson and Ralph Manheim. New York: Harcourt, Brace, 1972. (Trans. of *Davor*.)

In the Egg and Other Poems. In German with Translations by Michael Hamburger and Christopher Middleton. New York: Harcourt, Brace, 1977.

"Im Wettlauf mit den Utopien." (1978). Trans. Ralph Manheim as "Racing with the Utopias." In Grass, *On Writing and Politics, 1967–1983,* 51–74.

Die Vernichtung der Menschheit hat begonnen. Rede anläßlich der Verleihung des Feltrinelli-Preises am 25. Nov. 1982. Hauzenberg: Pongratz, 1983. Trans. Ralph Manheim as "The Destruction of Mankind Has Begun." In Grass, *On Writing and Politics, 1967–1983,* 137–40.

On Writing and Politics, 1967–1983. Trans. Ralph Manheim, Introd. Salman Rushdie. New York: Harcourt, Brace, 1985.

Schreiben nach Auschwitz. Frankfurter Poetik-Vorlesung. Frankfurt am Main: Luchterhand, 1990. Trans. as "Writing after Auschwitz." In Grass, *Two States — One Nation?* 94–123.

Two States — One Nation? Trans. Krishna Winston and A. S. Wensinger. New York: Harcourt, 1990.

The Future of German Democracy. With an Essay "On Loss." Ed. Robert Gerald Livingston and Volkmar Sander. New York: Continuum, 1993.

Novemberland. Selected Poems 1956–1993. Trans. Michael Hamburger. San Diego, CA: Harcourt, Inc., 1996. (German and English texts.)

Fortsetzung folgt. . . . Literatur und Geschichte. Göttingen: Steidl, 1999. ("Fortsetzung folgt," the 1999 Nobel Lecture) Trans. Michael Henry Heim as "To Be Continued. . . ." *PMLA* 115 (2000): 292–300. Repr. in *The Günter Grass Reader,* ed. Frielinghaus, 261–80.

Fünf Jahrzehnte. Ein Werkstattbuch. Göttingen: Steidl, 2004.

The Günter Grass Reader. Ed. Helmut Frielinghaus. Orlando, FL: Harcourt, Inc., 2004. (Selections from prose, poetry, essays.)

Grass Criticism

Bibliographies

Mertens, Mathias, Daniela Hermes, and Volker Neuhaus. "Günter Grass — Bibliografie." In *Das Kritische Lexikon zur deutschsprachigen Gegenwartsliteratur — KLGonline.* Ed. Heinz Ludwig Arnold. N.p. N.d. (Periodically updated.)

Neuhaus, Volker. "Literaturverzeichnis." In Neuhaus 1979, rev. ed. 1992, 217–32.

O'Neill, Patrick. *Günter Grass. A Bibliography, 1955–1975.* Toronto: U of Toronto P, 1976.

Secondary Sources

Abbé, Derek van. 1969–1970. "Metamorphoses of 'Unbewältigte Vergangenheit' in *Die Blechtrommel*." *German Life and Letters* 23:152–60.

Abbott, Scott. 1982. "Günter Grass' *Hundejahre:* A Realistic Novel about Myth." *German Quarterly* 55:212–20.

———. 1983. "The Raw and the Cooked: Claude Lévi-Strauss and Günter Grass." In Mews 1983a, 107–20.

Adams, Phoebe-Lou. 1982. "*Headbirths or The Germans Are Dying Out.*" *Atlantic* (Apr.): 110.

———. 1989. "*Show Your Tongue.*" *Atlantic* 263.6 (Jun.): 96.

Adler, Hans, and Jost Hermand, eds. 1996. *Günter Grass: Ästhetik des Engagements.* New York: Lang.

Adler, Jeremy. 2003. "Ship of State." *New York Times Book Review* (27 Apr.): 12.

Adolph, Winnifred R. 1983. "The Truth Told Differently: Myth and Irony." In Mews 1983a, 121–33.

Agee, Joel. 1982. "950 Million Germans?!" *New Republic* (14 Apr.): 30–32.

Anders, Jaroslav. 1987. "Floundering." *New Republic* (13/20 Jul.): 29–32.

Anderson, Susan C. 1987. *Grass and Grimmelshausen: Günter Grass's "Das Treffen in Telgte" and Rezeptionstheorie.* Columbia, SC: Camden House.

———. 1991. "Lies and More Lies: Fact and Fiction in Günter Grass's *Die Rättin.*" *Germanic Review* 66:106–12.

Angenendt, Thomas. 1995. *"Wenn Wörter Schatten werfen": Untersuchungen zum Prosastil von Günter Grass.* Frankfurt am Main: Lang.

Angress [Klüger], Ruth K. 1982. "*Der Butt:* A Feminist Perspective." In Pickar 1982, 43–50.

———. 1985. "A 'Jewish' Problem in German Postwar Fiction." *Modern Judaism* 5:215–33.

Annan, Gabriele. 1992. "Graveyard Utopia." *New York Review of Books* (19 Nov.): 19.

———. 2000. "Turncoats." *New York Review of Books* (30 Nov.): 39–41.

Anon. 1959. "Der Trommelbube." *Der Spiegel* (18 Nov.): 80–82.

———. 1962. "Nur mit der Zange anzufassen!" *Das Ritterkreuz* (Apr.). Repr. in Loschütz 1968, 48–50.

———. 1963a. "The Guilt of the Lambs." *Time* (4 Jan.). Repr. in White 1981 (excerpt), 2–3.

———. 1963b. "Grass: Zunge heraus." *Der Spiegel* (4 Sept.): 64–78.

———. 1963c. "Marked Man." *Newsweek* (9 Sept.). Repr. in White 1981 (excerpt), 56–57.

———. 1963d. "Günter Grass: *Hundejahre, Cat and Mouse.*" Repr. in *T.L.S.: Essays and Reviews from the "Times Literary Supplement" 1963.* London: Oxford UP, 1964, 67–71.

———. 1965. "Green Years for Grass." *Life* (4 Jun.): 51–52, 54.

———. 1969a. "Schriftsteller Grass: Sowas durchmachen." *Der Spiegel* (11 Aug.): 86–100.

———. 1969b. "Grass and His Nation's Burdens." *Times Literary Supplement* (25 Sept.): 1077–78.

———. 1970. "The Dentist's Chair as an Allegory of Life." *Time* (13 Apr.): 68–70. Repr. in O'Neill 1987c, 38–49.

———. 1972. "Dingsbums und Espede." *Der Spiegel* (21 Aug.): 101–4.

———. 1977. "Leute lechzen: Im deutschen Buchhandel grassiert das 'Butt-fieber.'" *Der Spiegel* (19 Sept.): 230–31.

———. 1979. "Film: Die Wiederkehr des frechen Oskar." *Der Spiegel* (30 Apr.): 182–92.

———, ed. 1983. *"Neue Aspekte der Grass-Forschung." Studia Germanica Posnaniensia* 12.

———. 1989. "*Show Your Tongue.*" *Publishers Weekly* (21 Apr.).

———, ed. 1990. *"Der Mensch wird an seiner Dummheit sterben": Günter-Grass-Konferenz Karpacz, 17.-23. Mai 1989. Germanica Wratislaviensia* 81.

———. 2002. "'Ein Untergang von brutaler Strenge': Wie die polnische Regisseurin Agnieszka Holland die Katastrophe der *Gustloff* verfilmen will." *Die Welt* (15 Feb.).

———, ed. 2005. *Das Literarische Quartett: Gesamtausgabe aller 77 Sendungen von 1988 bis 2001.* Berlin: Directmedia.

———. 2006a. "Von Grass bis Mika: Das große Cicero-Ranking 2006 — Die 500 Intellektuellen Deutschlands." *Cicero: Magazin für politische Kultur* (Apr.): 58–63.

———. 2006b. "The Betrayal of Memory." *New York Times* (18 Aug.).

———. 2006c. "Günter Grass: Ich war Mitglied bei der Waffen-SS." *Frankfurter Allgemeine Zeitung* (12 Aug.). Repr. in Kölbel 2006b, 25.

———. 2006d. "Israeli College Withdraws Doctorate for Grass." *Globe and Mail* (11 Nov.).

———. 2007. "Reading Guide." http://www.harcourtbooks.com/. Accessed 25 May 2007.

Arditti, Michael. 2000. "Tuesday Book: A Monument to Germany's Many Faces." *Independent* (4 Jan.).

Arend, Ingo. 1999. "Wer hat uns verraten?" *Freitag* (16 Jul.).

———. 2002. "Kraft durch Wahrheit." *Freitag* (8 Feb.).

Arendt, Dieter. 1989. "Die absurde Chiffre und die Chiffre des Absurden in Günter Grass' *Danziger Trilogie* oder: 'Was die Welt Übertage absurd nennt, schmeckt Untertage real.'" *Orbis Litterarum* 44:341–72.

———. 2001. "Günter Grass: *Der Butt.* Oder: Ein Fisch als Hegelscher Weltgeist." *Studi Germanici* 3 (2–3): 311–41.

Arens, Katherine. 1996. "John Irving, Günter Grass, and *Owen Meany:* The Gender-Sensitive *Bildungsroman.*" In Arens, *Austria and Other Margins: Reading Culture.* Columbia, SC: Camden House, 65–83.

Arker, Dieter. 1988. "*Die Blechtrommel* als Schwellenroman? Stichworte zur inneren Diskontinuität der *Danziger Trilogie.*" In H. L. Arnold 1963, 6th, rev. ed. 1988, 48–57.

———. 1989. *Nichts ist vorbei, alles kommt wieder: Untersuchungen zu Günter Grass' "Blechtrommel."* Heidelberg: Winter.

———. 2001. "Vexierbild mit Mehrfachperspektive; Zu Günter Grass: *Ein weites Feld.*" In Quéval 2001a, 253–87.

Arnds, Peter O. 2002. "On the Awful German Fairy Tale: Breaking Taboos in Representations of Nazi Euthanasia and the Holocaust in Günter Grass' *Die Blechtrommel.* Edgar Hilsenrath's *Der Nazi & der Friseur* and Anselm Kiefer's Visual Art." *German Quarterly* 75:422–39.

———. 2004a. *Representation, Subversion, and Eugenics in Günter Grass's "The Tin Drum."* Rochester, NY: Camden House.

———. 2004b. "Epilogue: Beyond *Die Blechtrommel;* Germans as Victims in *Im Krebsgang.*" In Arnds 2004a, 152–60.

Arnold, Armin. 1985. "La salade mixte du Chef: Zu *Aus dem Tagebuch einer Schnecke* und *Kopfgeburten oder Die Deutschen sterben aus.*" In Durzak 1985a, 130–41.

Arnold, Heinz Ludwig, ed. 1963. *Günter Grass.* In *Text + Kritik* 1. 4th, rev. and enl. ed. *Text + Kritik* 1/1a (1971). 5th, enl. ed. (1978). 6th, newly rev. ed. *Text + Kritik* (1988). 7th, rev. ed. (1997).

———. 1969. "Die intellektuelle Betäubung des Günter Grass: Zu seinem Roman *örtlich betäubt.*" *Text + Kritik* 4/4a (1969): 72–76. Repr. in Arnold, *Brauchen wir noch die Literatur?* Düsseldorf: Bertelsmann, 1972, 163–66. Repr. as "Zeitroman mit Auslegern: Günter Grass' *örtlich betäubt.*" In Jurgensen 1973, 97–102.

———. 1977. "Die Jagd nach dem Butt." *Vorwärts* (13 Oct.): 4.

———. 1978. "Gespräche mit Günter Grass." In H. L. Arnold 1963, 5th, rev. ed. 1978, 1–39.

———. 1986. "Literaturkritik: Hinrichtungs- oder Erkenntnisinstrument: Günter Grass' *Rättin* und das Feuilleton." *L'80: Zeitschrift für Literatur und Politik* 39:115–26.

———, ed. 1997. *Blech getrommelt: Günter Grass in der Kritik.* Göttingen: Steidl.

———. 2002. "Nachhilfeunterricht — für wen? Günter Grass' vermeintliche Novelle *Im Krebsgang* lässt mehr Fragen offen als sie zu beantworten vorgibt." *Schweizer Monatshefte* 82: 38–41.

Arnold, Heinz Ludwig, and Franz Josef Görtz, eds. 1971. *Günter Grass — Dokumente zur politischen Wirkung.* Stuttgart: Boorberg.

Ascherson, Neal. 1969. "Raw Nerves." *New York Review of Books* (20 Nov.): 16–21.

———. 1973. "Slug of Redemption." *New York Review of Books* (1 Nov.): 10.

———. 2006. "Even Now." *London Review of Books* 28.21 (2 Nov.).

Associated Press. 2006. "Grass Explains Nazi Service in Letter." *New York Times* (22 Aug.).

Atkinson, Rick. 1995. "Roar of the Literary Lion." *Washington Post* (26 Sept.).

Atlas, James. 1999. "Polemical Prize." *New York Times* (3 Oct.).

Auffenberg, Christian. 1993. *Vom Erzählen des Erzählens bei Günter Grass: Studien zur immanenten Poetik der Romane "Die Blechtrommel" und "Die Rättin."* Münster: Uni Press Hochschulschriften.

Auffermann, Verena. 2006. "Die *Cicero*-Bestenliste 2006." *Cicero: Magazin für politische Kultur* (Oct.): http://www.cicero.de/1373.php?ausgabe=10/2006.

Augstein, Rudolf. 2002. "Rückwärts krebsen, um voranzukommen." *Der Spiegel* (4 Feb.): 186–87. Repr. in *Die Flucht der Deutschen: Spiegel Spezial* 2:24–25.

Augstein, Rudolf, and Günter Grass. 1990. *Deutschland, einig Vaterland? Ein Streitgespräch.* Göttingen: Linden-Verlag.

Bach, Wolf-Dieter. 1977. "Was flach fiel: Der Butt von Grass; ein Märchen für uns Kinder alle." *Die Horen* 22 (4): 121–30.

Bader, Rudolf. 1984. "Indian *Tin Drum.*" *International Fiction Review* 11:75–83.

Balzer, Berit. 2001. "Geschichte als Wendemechanismus: *Ein weites Feld* von Günter Grass." *Monatshefte* 93:209–20.

Bancaud, Florence. 2002. "*Ein weites Feld* ou le double regard sur l'histoire." In Wellnitz 2002a, 103–28.

Bance, Alan F. 1967. "The Enigma of Oskar in Grass's *Blechtrommel.*" *Seminar* 3:147–56.

———. 1980. "*Die Blechtrommel.*" In Bance, *The German Novel, 1945–1960.* Stuttgart: Heinz, 130–46, 152–53.

Barkhoff, Jürgen. 2000. "In Grimms Wäldern wächst der Widerstand: Kulturelles Gedächtnis und Waldsterben in Günter Grass' *Die Rättin.*" In *Das schwierige neunzehnte Jahrhundert,* ed. Jürgen Barkhoff, Gilbert Carr, and Roger Paulin. Tübingen: Niemeyer, 155–68.

Barnacle, Hugo. 2000. "Snapshots of a German Way of Life." *Sunday Times* (2 Jan.).

Baron, Ulrich. 1999a. "Denn Großschriftsteller können nicht abdanken." *Die Welt* (1 Jul.).

———. 1999b. "Günter Grass und sein neues Buch *Mein Jahrhundert.*" *Die literarische Welt* (10 Jul.): 1.

———. 1999c. "Die Messe feiert Günter Grass, den Bestseller." *Die Welt* (12 Oct.): 35.

Bartl, Andrea. 1997. "'Ein weites Feld': Günter Grass und die Wende." In *Die Rezeption der deutschsprachigen Gegenwartsliteratur nach der Wende 1989,* ed. Norbert Honsza and Theo Mechtenberg. Wrocław: Verlag FRI, 141–62.

Battafarano, Italo Michele, and Hildegard Eilert. 2003. *Courage: Die starke Frau in der deutschen Literatur; Von Grimmelshausen erfunden, von Brecht und Grass variiert.* Bern: Lang.

Bauke, Joseph. 1963. "To Be Different in Danzig." *Saturday Review* (10 Aug.): 28. Repr. in White 1981 (excerpt), 43.

Baumgart, Reinhard. 1979. "300 Gramm wohlabgehangene Prosa." *Süddeutsche Zeitung* (5/6 May), 132.

Bayley, John. 1992. "A Match Made in Danzig." *New York Times Book Review* (1 Nov.): 1, 29.

Becker, Hellmut. 1969. "Lehrer und Schüler in Günter Grass' *örtlich betäubt.*" *Neue Sammlung: Zeitschrift für Erziehung und Gesellschaft* 9:503–10. Repr. in *Moderna språk* 65 (1971): 11–20.

Becker, Peter von. 1988. "Die Rache der Göttin Kali." *Der Spiegel* (22 Aug.): 154–62. Translated as "The Revenge of Goddess Kali." In Kämpchen 2001, 221–29.

Becker, Rolf. 1969. "Mäßig mit Malzbonbons." *Der Spiegel* (11 Aug.): 102–3.

Beevor, Antony. 2003. "A Nation that Was Bombed into Silence." *Times Online* (12 Feb.)

Behrendt, Johanna E. 1968. "Die Ausweglosigkeit der menschlichen Natur: Eine Interpretation von Günter Grass' *Katz und Maus*." *Zeitschrift für deutsche Philologie* 87 (4): 546–62.

———. 1969. "Auf der Suche nach dem Adamsapfel: Der Erzähler Pilenz in Günter Grass' Novelle *Katz und Maus*." *Germanisch-Romanische Monatsschrift* 19:313–26.

Bell, Pearl K. 1973. "Of Mollusks and Men." *New Leader* (29 Oct.): 15–16.

Bemis, Robert. 1963. "'Cat and Mouse' — Compact Masterpiece of Virtuoso Hero by Author of 'Tin Drum.'" Boston, MA *Globe* (7 Aug.). Repr. in White 1981 (excerpt), 42.

Benjamin, Jessica. 1978. "The Fish That Got Away." *Ms.* (Dec.): 41, 44, 78.

Benoit, Martine-Sophie. 2002. "Responsabilité et culpabilité allemandes: du citoyen à l'écrivain Günter Grass." In Wellnitz 2002a, 79–102.

Bernstein, Richard. 2000. "100 Years of Certitude: Gunter [sic] Grass's History." *New York Times* (5 Jan.).

Best, Otto F. 1983. "On the Art of Garnishing a Flounder with 'Chestnuts' and Serving It Up as Myth." In Mews 1983a, 135–49.

Beyersdorf, H[erman] E. 1980. "The Narrator as Artful Deceiver: Aspects of Narrative Perspective in *Die Blechtrommel*." *Germanic Review* 55:129–38.

———. 1992. "'. . . den Osten verloren': Das Thema der Vertreibung in Romanen von Grass, Lenz und Surminski." *Weimarer Beiträge* 38:46–67.

———. 2002. "Von der *Blechtrommel* bis zum *Krebsgang*: Günter Grass als Schriftsteller der Vertreibung." *Weimarer Beiträge* 48:568–93.

———. 2006. "Günter Grass' *Im Krebsgang* und die Vertreibungsdebatte im Spiegel der Presse." In *Wende des Erinnerns? Geschichtskonstruktionen in der deutschen Literatur nach 1989*, ed. Barbara Beßlich, Katharina Grätz, and Olaf Hildebrand. Berlin: Schmidt, 157–67.

Bielefeld, Claus-Ulrich, Günter Grass, and Dieter Stolz. 1996. "'Der Autor als verdeckter Ermittler': Ein Gespräch." *Sprache im technischen Zeitalter* 139:289–314.

Blaise, Clark. 1989. "Calcutta is the Measure of All Things." *New York Times Book Review* (21 May): 12.

Blöcker, Günter. 1959. "Rückkehr zur Nabelschnur." *Frankfurter Allgemeine Zeitung* (28 Nov.). Repr. in Loschütz 1968, 21–24. Repr. in Görtz 1984b, 71–76. Repr. (enl. version) in Blöcker, *Kritisches Lesebuch*. Hamburg, Leibniz, 1962, 208–15.

———. 1963. "Im Zeichen des Hundes." *Frankfurter Allgemeine Zeitung* (14 Sept.). Repr. in Blöcker, *Literatur als Teilhabe*. Berlin: Argon, 1966, 24–29.

———. 1972. "Wir alle sind Schnecken." *Süddeutsche Zeitung* (26/27 Aug.), 109. Repr. in Görtz, 1984b, 125–31.

Blomster, Wesley V. 1969a. "The Demonic in History: Thomas Mann and Günter Grass." *Contemporary Literature* 10:75–84.

———. 1969b. "The Documentation of a Novel: Otto Weininger and *Hundejahre* by Günter Grass." *Monatshefte* 61:122–38.

———. 1969c. "Oskar at the Zoppoter Waldoper." *Modern Language Notes* 84:467–72.

Blumenberg, Hans C. 1979. "Ein schönes Chaos: Der *Blechtrommel*-Film von Volker Schlöndorff." *Die Zeit* (North American ed.; 11 May).

Boch, Gudrun. 1992. "Weder Flagellant noch Volksdenunziant: Günter Grass in den USA." *Frankfurter Rundschau* (29 Dec.).

Boedecker, Sven. 2002. "'Eine Katastrophe, kein Verbrechen': Gespräch." *Die Woche* (8 Feb.).

Böning, Holger, Hans Wolf Jäger, Andrezj Kątny, and Marian Szczodrowski, eds. 2005. *Danzig und der Ostseeraum. Sprache, Literatur, Publizisitik.* Bremen: Edition Lumière.

Böttiger, Helmut. 1999. "Laß ma, Berta!" *Frankfurter Rundschau* (10 Jul.).

Bond, D. G., and Julian Preece. 1991/92. "Cap Arcona, 3 May 1945: History and Allegory in Novels by Uwe Johnson and Günter Grass." *Oxford German Studies* 20/21:147–63.

Bondy, François. 1972. "A Snail's Eye View." *World* (24 Oct.), 50–51. Repr. in O'Neill 1987c, 49–52.

Bosmajian, Hamida. 1979. "Günter Grass's *Dog Years:* The Dark Side of Utopia." In Bosmajian, *Metaphors of Evil: Contemporary German Literature and the Shadow of Nazism.* Iowa City: U of Iowa P, 82–114.

Boßmann, Timm. 1997. *Der Dichter im Schussfeld: Geschichte und Versagen der Literaturkritik am Beispiel Günter Grass.* Marburg: Textum.

Boston, Richard. 1982. "Elbow Room." *Punch* (21 Apr.): 668.

Boursicaut, Hélène. 2001. "Tallhover/Hoftaller/Revolat/Offtalère: réédition(s): De Hans Joachim Schädlich à Günter Grass, de *Tallhover* à *Toute une histoire.*" In Quéval 2001a, 124–46.

Boyd, Robert. 1999. "Gunter [sic] Grass Views the 20th Century in Stories with a German Perspective." *St. Louis Post-Dispatch* (26 Dec.), C14.

Boyes, Roger. 1995. "Is the Writer a Traitor?" *Times* (21 Jun.).

Brady, Philip. 1990. "'Aus einer Kürbishütte gesehen': The Poems." In Brady, McFarland, and White 1990, 203–25.

———. 1992. "A Greyer Grass." *Times Literary Supplement* (9 Oct.).

Brady, Philip, Timothy McFarland, and John J. White, eds. 1990. *Günter Grass's "Der Butt." Sexual Politics and the Male Myth of History.* Oxford: Clarendon P.

Braese, Stephan. 2003. "'Tote zahlen keine Steuern': Flucht und Vertreibung in Günter Grass' *Im Krebsgang* und Hans-Ulrich Treichels *Der Verlorene.*" *Gegenwartsliteratur* 2:171–96.

Brandes, Ute. 1998. *Günter Grass.* Berlin: Edition Colloquium.

Braun, Hugo. 1963. "Clownerien und Hundejahre." *Norddeutsche Neueste Nachrichten* (16 Dec.).

Brethomé, Jacques. 2002. "De la signification et de l'importance de certains lieux dans *Ein weites Feld* de Günter Grass." In Wellnitz 2002a, 209–38.

Breuel, Birgit. 1995. "Auferstanden aus Romanen." *Wirtschaftswoche* (7 Sept.). Repr. in Negt 1996b, 158–60.

Brode, Hanspeter. 1976. "Die Zeitgeschichte in der *Blechtrommel* von Günter Grass: Entwurf eines textinternen Kommunikationsmodells." In Geißler 1976, 86–114.

———. 1977. *Die Zeitgeschichte im erzählenden Werk von Günter Grass: Versuch einer Deutung der "Blechtrommel" und der "Danziger Trilogie."* Frankfurt am Main: Lang.

———. 1978. "Von Danzig zur Bundesrepublik." In H. L. Arnold 1963, 5th, rev. ed. 1978, 1–39.

———. 1979. *Günter Grass.* Munich: Beck.

———. 1980a. "Reisebericht. Essay. Wahlkampf: Günter Grass plädiert in den *Kopfgeburten* für eine gemeinsame deutsche Literatur." *Literatur für Leser* 4:254–59.

———. 1980b. "Kommunikationsstruktur und Erzählerposition in den Romanen von Günter Grass: *Die Blechtrommel — Aus dem Tagebuch einer Schnecke — Der Butt.*" *Germanisch-Romanische Monatsschrift* 30 (4): 438–50.

———. 1984. "'Daß du nicht enden kannst, das macht dich groß': Zur erzählerischen Kontinuität im Werk von Günter Grass." In Görtz 1984b, 75–94.

Brody, Ervin C. 1996. "The Polish-German Conflict in Günter Grass' Danzig: Pan Kishot in *The Tin Drum.*" *Polish Review* 41 (1): 79–107.

Broyard, Anatole. 1970. "Local Anaesthetic." *New York Times Book Review* (29 Mar.): 1, 15. Repr. in White 1981 (excerpt), 140.

Bruce, Allen. 1973. "*From the Diary of a Snail.*" *Library Journal Book Review:* 643–44.

Bruce, James C. 1966. "The Equivocating Narrator in Günter Grass's *Katz und Maus*." *Monatshefte* 58:139–49.

———. 1971. "The Motif of Failure and the Act of Narrating in Günter Grass's *Örtlich betäubt*." *Modern Fiction Studies* 17:45–60. Repr. in O'Neill 1987c, 144–59.

Brunkhorst-Hasenclever, Annegrit, and Martin Brunkhorst. 1981. *Materialien: Günter Grass "Die Blechtrommel," "Katz und Maus."* Stuttgart: Klett.

Brunskill, Ian. 2006. "An Added Ingredient." *Times Online* (29 Sept.).

Brunssen, Frank. 1997. *Das Absurde in Günter Grass' Literatur der achtziger Jahre*. Würzburg: Königshausen & Neumann.

———. 2006. "Tabubruch? Deutsche als Opfer des Zweiten Weltkriegs in Günter Grass' Novelle *Im Krebsgang*." *Oxford German Studies* 35 (2): 115–30.

Bucheli, Roman. 2002. "Günter Grass' Novelle im Krebsgang." *Neue Zürcher Zeitung* (9 Feb.). Repr. in *Kulturchronik* 20.2 (2002): 10–13.

Buck, Theo. 2001. "Schreibkrise eines Autors: Zur Erzählkonstruktion von Günter Grass' *Ein weites Feld*." In Lartillot 2001a, 49–59. Also in Quéval 2001a, 49–61.

Bullivant, Keith. 2003. "Germans as Victims?! Günter Grass' *Crabwise* (*Im Krebsgang*)." *South Atlantic Review* 68 (2): 91–96.

Burgess, Anthony. 1978. "A Fish among Feminists." *Times Literary Supplement* (13 Oct.), 1141.

Burkhardt, Werner. 2000. "Unterwegs und auf der Stelle." *Süddeutsche Zeitung* (9 May), 18.

Buruma, Ian. 2000. "The Tin Ear." *New Republic* (31 Jan.): 31–36.

———. 2006. "War and Remembrance." *New Yorker* (18 Sept.): 81–85.

Busche, Jürgen. 1995. "Von Glanz und Schmutz des deutschen Bürgertums." *Süddeutsche Zeitung* (19 Aug.). Repr. in Oberhammer and Ostermann 1995, 72–74. Repr. in Negt 1996b, 75–79.

Busche, Jürgen, Hellmuth Karasek, Sigrid Löffler, and Marcel Reich-Ranicki. 1988. "Günter Grass: Zunge zeigen." (30 Sept.). In Anon. 2005, 159–69.

Butler, Geoffrey P. 1979. "Grass Skirts the Issue: A Reaction to *Der Butt*." *Quinquereme: New Studies in Modern Languages* 2 (1): 23–33.

———. 1980/81. "'Übersetzt klingt alles plausibel': Some Notes on *Der Butt* and *The Flounder*." *German Life and Letters* 34 (1): 3–10.

———. 1986. "The End of the World, and After." *Times Literary Supplement* (4 April): 355.

———. 1987. "Skilful Wordiness." *Times Literary Supplement* (28 Aug.): 933.

———. 1988. "A Tall Story of Some Size: *Die Rättin* and *The Rat*." *German Life and Letters* 41:488–93.

———. 1994."*The Call of the Toad* and the Szczepan Phenomenon." *German Life and Letters* 47:94–103.

Caltvedt, Lester N. 1978. "Oskar's Account of Himself: Narrative 'Guilt' and the Relationship of Fiction to History in *Die Blechtrommel*." *Seminar* 14:284–94.

Carlsson, Anni. 1964. "Der Roman als Anschauungsform der Epoche: Bemerkungen zu Thomas Mann und Günter Grass." *Neue Zürcher Zeitung* (21 Nov.): 223.

Casanova, Nicole, and Günter Grass. 1979. *Atelier des métamorphoses: Entretiens*. Paris: Belfond.

Caspari, Martina. 2002. "Im Krebsgang gegen den Strich: Das schwierige Geschäft des Erinnerns bei Günter Grass." *Germanic Notes and Reviews* 33 (2): 106–9.

Castein, Hanne. 1990. "Grass and the Appropriation of the Fairy-Tale in the Seventies." In Brady, McFarland, and White 1990, 97–108.

Cepl-Kaufmann, Gertrude. 1975. *Günter Grass: Eine Analyse des Gesamtwerkes unter dem Aspekt von Literatur und Politik*. Kronberg im Taunus: Scriptor.

———. 1986. "Verlust oder poetische Rettung? Zum Begriff 'Heimat' in Günter Grass' *Danziger Trilogie*." In Pott 1986a, 61–83.

Chong, Jin-Sok. 2002. *Offenheit und Hermetik; Zur Möglichkeit des Schreibens nach Auschwitz: Ein Vergleich zwischen Günter Grass' Lyrik, der "Blechtrommel" und dem Spätwerk Paul Celans*. Frankfurt am Main: Lang.

Chotjewitz, Peter O. 1988. "Nichts an, aber 'n Helm auf." *Deutsche Volkszeitung/die tat* (7 Oct.), 15.

Cicora, Mary A. 1993. "Music, Myth, and Metaphysics: Wagner Reception in Günter Grass' *Hundejahre*." *German Studies Review* 16:49–60.

Clason, Synnöve. 1988a. *Der andere Blick. Studien zur deutschsprachigen Literatur der 70er Jahre*. Stockholm: Almqvist & Wiksell.

———. 1988b. "Frauenbild zwischen Tradition und Aufbruch. Am Beispiel Böll und Grass." In Clason 1988a, 85–98.

———. 1988c. "Morgner, Grass und die 'Phantastische Totale.'" In Clason 1988a, 229–37.

———. 1988d. "Uwe und Ilsebill. Zur Darstellung des anderen Geschlechts bei Morgner und Grass." In Clason 1988a, 238–44.

Clemons, Walter. 1978. "Fish Story." *Newsweek* (6 Nov.): 99.

Cloonan, William. 1979. "Günther [sic] Grass Floundering." *New Boston Review* (Sept./Oct.): 3–4.

———. 1986. "World War II in Three Contemporary Novels." *South Atlantic Review* 51 (2): 65–75.

———. 1999. "Günter Grass's *The Tin Drum:* Hiding from the Black Cook." In Cloonan, *The Writing of War. French and German Fiction and World War II.* Gainesville, FL: UP of Florida. 108–25.

Coates, Joseph. 1992. "Hypocrisies and Evasions." *Chicago Tribune* (15 Nov.): C3.

Coetzee, J. M. 2003. "Victims." *New York Review of Books* (12 Jun.), 24–26.

Conan, Neal. 2006. "Nobel Prize-Winning Novelist Admits Nazi Past." Interview with Michael Jürgs. *NPR Talk of the Nation* (17 Aug.). http://www.npr.org/templates/story/story.php?storyId=5664512.

Coogan, Daniel. 1973. "*From the Diary of a Snail.*" *America* (29 Sept.): 220.

Corbin, Anne-Marie. 2003. "Engagement und neue Distanz bei Günter Grass: Vom Wenderoman *Ein weites Feld* zur Flüchtlingsnovelle *Im Krebsgang.*" In *Deutschsprachige Erzählprosa seit 1990 im europäischen Kontext: Interpretationen, Intertextualität, Rezeption,* ed. Volker Wehdeking and Anne-Marie Corbin. Trier: Wissenschaftlicher Verlag, 79–90.

Corino, Karl, Hellmuth Karasek, Sigrid Löffler, and Marcel Reich-Ranicki. 1995. "Günter Grass: Ein weites Feld." (24 Aug.). In Anon. 2005, 2:685–717.

Cory, Mark E. 1983. "Sisyphus and the Snail: Metaphors for the Political Process in Günter Grass' *Aus dem Tagebuch einer Schnecke* and *Kopfgeburten oder Die Deutschen sterben aus.*" *German Studies Review* 6:519–33.

———. 1998. "Ein weites Feld: The Aestheticization of German Unification in Recent Works by Günter Grass." In *Politics in German Literature: Essays in Memory of Frank G. Ryder,* ed. Beth Bjorklund and Mark E. Cory. Columbia, SC: Camden House, 177–94.

Cowley, Jason. 2002. "Forgotten Victims." *The Guardian* (27 Mar.).

Crick, Joyce. 1990. "Future Imperfect: Time and the Flounder." In Brady, McFarland, and White 1990, 33–49.

Crimmann, Ralph P. 1986. "Günter Grass: *Das Treffen in Telgte:* Literaturdidaktische und literaturwissenschaftliche Beobachtungen." *Der Deutschunterricht* 38:7–22.

Croft, Helen. 1973. "Günter Grass's *Katz und Maus.*" *Seminar* 9:253–64. Repr. in O'Neill 1987c, 112–22.

Cunliffe, W. Gordon. 1969. *Günter Grass.* New York: Twayne.

Dahne, Gerhard. 1965. "Wer ist Katz und wer ist Maus?" *Neue Deutsche Literatur* (Nov.). Repr. in Loschütz 1968, 35–37. Repr. in Ritter 1977, 99–102.

Dasgupta, Subhoranjan. 2002a. "The Calcutta Connection." In Dasgupta 2002c, 75–79.

———. 2002b. "A Novel Protest against Globalisation." In Dasgupta 2002c, 60–74.

———. 2002c. *The Tin Drummer's Odyssey: Essays on Gunter [sic] Grass.* Kolkata: Dasgupta.

Da Silva, Helena. 2005. "Berlin und die historische Wende: Christa Wolfs *Kassandra* und Günter Grass' *Ein weites Feld.*" *Gegenwartsliteratur* 4:71–90.

Davenport, Guy. 1981. "Gunter [sic] Grass: Rebuilding a Ravaged Language." *Washington Post* (9 Aug.).

Delaney, Antoinette T. 2004. *Metaphors in Grass' "Die Blechtrommel."* New York: Lang.

Delius, Annette. 1977. "Einige Schwierigkeiten der Kommunikation über Literatur im Deutschunterricht: Erfahrungen mit *Katz und Maus* im Grundkurs der Studienstufe 12." *Der Deutschunterricht* 29 (2): 49–62.

Dennis, Nigel. 1978. "The One That Got Away." *New York Review of Books* (23 Nov.): 22–23.

Detje, Robin. 1999. "Du wirst es nicht glauben, Rosi." *Berliner Zeitung* (10/11 Jul.): 5.

Dickstein, Morris. 1978. "An Epic, Ribald, Miscellany." *New York Times Book Review* (12 Nov.): 12, 66. Repr. in O'Neill 1987c, 52–55.

Dideriksen, Anne-Sofie. 2001. "'Kleinmalerei und Gedächtniskrümel': Zum historischen Erzählen in *Ein weites Feld.*" In Quéval 2001a, 79–98.

Dieckmann, Christoph. 1995. "Das letzte Westpaket." *Die Zeit* (1 Dec.): 6. Repr. in Negt 1996b, 371–72.

Diederichs, Rainer. 1971. *Strukturen des Schelmischen im modernen deutschen Roman: Eine Untersuchung an den Romanen von Thomas Mann "Bekenntnisse des Hochstaplers Felix Krull" und Grass' "Die Blechtrommel."* Düsseldorf-Cologne: Diederichs.

Diersen, Inge. 1990. "'Ein Zeitgenosse, der sich einmischt': Zu Günter Grass' Roman *Die Rättin.*" *Weimarer Beiträge* 36:1821–27.

Diller, Edward. 1974. *A Mythic Journey: Günter Grass's "Tin Drum."* Lexington: U of Kentucky P.

———. 1983. "Raw and Cooked, Myth and *Märchen.*" In Mews 1983a, 91–105.

Dimler, G. Richard. 1975. "Simplicius Simplicissimus and Oskar Matzerath as Alienated Heroes: Comparison and Contrast." *Amsterdamer Beiträge zur neueren Germanistik* 4:113–34.

Di Napoli, Thomas. 1980. "In Quest of the Messiah: A Study of the Christ Figure in *The Danzig Trilogy* of Günter Grass." *Centennial Review* 24:25–42.

Diner, Dan. 2002. "Es redet aus ihnen heraus: Grass, Walser, Möllemann — über die Entstehung einer neuen Form des Antisemitismus in Deutschland." *Die literarische Welt* (15 Jun.).

Dohnanyi, Klaus von. 1995. "Du verspielst jeden Respekt als Figur des öffentlichen Dialogs." *Stern* (14 Sept.). Repr. in Negt 1996b, 161–66.

Donahue, Bruce. 1983. "The Alternative to Goethe: Markus and Fajngold in *Die Blechtrommel.*" *Germanic Review* 58:115–20.

Dowden, Steve. 2003. "Lifting a Taboo on Germany's Past." *Boston Globe* (20 Apr.).

Drabelle, Dennis. 2000. "The Full Fonty." *Washington Post* (17 Dec.).

Droste, Dietrich. 1969. "Gruppenarbeit als Mittel der Erschließung umfangreicher Romane: Grimmelshausens *Abenteuerlicher Simplicius Simplicissimus* und Grass' *Die Blechtrommel.*" *Der Deutschunterricht* 21 (6): 101–15.

Duroche, Leonard. 1994. "Günter Grass's *Cat and Mouse* and the Phenomenology of Masculinity." In *Fictions of Masculinity: Crossing Cultures, Crossing Sexualities,* ed. Peter F. Murphy. New York: New York UP, 74–95.

Durrani, Osman. 1980. "'Here Comes Everybody': An Appraisal of Narrative Technique in Günter Grass's *Der Butt.*" *Modern Language Review* 75:810–22.

Durzak, Manfred. 1970. "Abschied von der Kleinbürgerwelt: Der neue Roman von Günter Grass." *Basis* 1:224–37. Repr. as "Abschied von der Kleinbürgerwelt: *örtlich betäubt,*" in Durzak, *Der deutsche Roman der Gegenwart.* Stuttgart: Kohlhammer, 1971. 3rd, rev. and expanded ed. 1979, 289–301.

———. 1971a. "Plädoyer für eine Rezeptionsästhetik: Anmerkungen zu deutschen und amerikanischen Literaturkritik am Beispiel von Günter Grass." *Akzente* 18:487–504. Repr. as "Rezeptionsästhetik als Literaturkritik." In *Kritik der Literaturkritik,* ed. Olaf Schwencke. Stuttgart: Kohlhammer, 1973, 56–70.

———. 1971b. "Fiktion und Gesellschaftsanalyse: Die Romane von Günter Grass." In Durzak, 1979c, 247–327.

———. 1979a. "Ein märchenhafter Roman: *Der Butt.*" In Durzak, 1979c, 301–16.

———. 1979b. "Ein märchenhafter Roman: Zum *Butt* von Günter Grass." *Basis* 9:71–90 and 261.

———. 1979c. *Der deutsche Roman der Gegenwart: Entwicklungsvoraussetzungen und Tendenzen.* 3rd, rev., and enl. ed. Stuttgart: Kohlhammer.

———. 1982. "Die Zirkelschlüsse der Literaturkritik: Überlegungen zur Rezeption von Günter Grass' Roman *Der Butt*." In Pickar 1982, 63–80.

———, ed. 1985a. *Zu Günter Grass: Geschichte auf dem poetischen Prüfstand.* Stuttgart: Klett.

———. 1985b. "Der Butt im Karpfenteich: Günter Grass und die Literaturkritik." In Wolff 1985, 87–110.

———. 1985c. "Es war einmal: Zur Märchen-Struktur des Erzählens bei Günter Grass." In Durzak 1985a, 166–77.

———. 1993. "Entzauberung des Helden; Günter Grass: *Katz und Maus* (1961)." In *Deutsche Novellen: Von der Klassik bis zur Gegenwart,* ed. Winfried Freund. Munich: Fink, 265–77.

———. 2001. "Apokalyptische Szenarien in der deutschen Gegenwartsliteratur." In *Literarisches Krisenbewußtsein: Ein Perzeptions- und Produktionsmuster im 20. Jahrhundert,* ed. Keith Bullivant and Bernhard Spies. Munich: Iudicium, 184–94.

Dye, Elizabeth. 2004. "'Weil die Geschichte nicht aufhört': Günter Grass' *Im Krebsgang*." *German Life and Letters* 57 (Oct.): 472–87.

Eder, Richard. 2003. "German Angst Erupts, Dwelling on Victimhood." *New York Times* (24 Apr.).

Edschmid, Kasimir. 1962. "Gutachten." In Loschütz 1968, 60–61.

Elliott, Michael. 2003. "Germany as Mute Victim." *Time* (28 Apr.): 70.

Emmel, Hildegard. 1963. "Das Selbstgericht: Thomas Mann — Walter Jens und Edzard Schaper — Günter Grass." In Emmel, *Das Gericht in der deutschen Literatur des 20. Jahrhunderts.* Bern: Francke, 105–19.

Emmerich, Wolfgang. 2005. "Dürfen die Deutschen ihre eigenen Opfer beklagen? Schiffsuntergänge 1945 bei Uwe Johnson, Walter Kempowski, Günter Grass, Tanja Dückers und Stefan Chwin." In Böning, Jäger, Kątny, and Szczodrowski, 293–323.

Enderstein, Carl O. 1975. "Zahnsymbolik und ihre Bedeutung in Grass' Werken." *Amsterdamer Beiträge zur Neueren Germanistik* 4:133–55.

Engel, Henrik D. K. 1997. *Die Prosa von Günter Grass in Beziehung zur englischsprachigen Literatur: Rezeption, Wirkungen und Rückwirkungen bei Salman Rushdie, John Irving, Bernard Malamud u.a.* Frankfurt am Main: Lang.

———. 2000. "'Das weite Feld' — Günter Grass im angelsächsischen Sprachraum." *Neue Deutsche Literatur* 49 (1): 116–27.

Engels, Benedikt. 2005. *Das lyrische Umfeld der "Danziger Trilogie."* Würzburg: Königshausen & Neumann.

Engler, Jürgen. 2002. "Nachträglicher Vorsatz." *Neue Deutsche Literatur* 50 (6): 138–43.

Enright, D. J. 1965. "Casting Out Demons." *New York Review of Books* (3 Jun.). Repr. in White 1981 (excerpt), 86. Repr. as "*Dog Years:* Grass's Third Novel." In Enright, *Conspirators and Poets.* London: Chatto, 1966, 201–7.

———. 1970. "Always New Pains." *New York Review of Books* (4 Jun.): 20–23. Repr. in Enright, D. J. *Man is an Onion: Reviews and Essays.* London: Chatto, 1972, 96–102. Repr. in White 1981 (excerpt), 155.

———. 1982. "Hangovers." *New York Review of Books* (18 Mar.):, 46–47.

———. 1987. "Doomsday Book." *New York Review of Books* (14 Sept.): 45–46.

Enzensberger, Hans Magnus. 1959. "Wilhelm Meister auf der Blechtrommel." *Frankfurter Hefte* 14:833–36. Repr. as "Wilhelm Meister, auf Blech getrommelt," in Enzensberger, 1962a, 221–27. Repr. in Görtz 1984a, 62–69.

———. 1962a. *Einzelheiten.* Frankfurt am Main: Suhrkamp.

———. 1962b. "Gutachten." In Loschütz 1968, 61–64. Repr. in Ritter 1977, 136–39.

———. 1962c. "Zusatz: Der verständige Anarchist." In Enzensberger 1962a, 227–33.

———. 1963. "Günter Grass, *Hundejahre.*" *Der Spiegel* (4 Sept.), 70–71.

Eroms, Hans-Werner. 1993. "Ansätze zu einer linguistischen Analyse der *Unkenrufe* von Günter Grass." In *Grammatik, Wortschatz und Bauformen der Poesie in der stilistischen Analyse ausgewählter Texte,* ed. Hans Wellmann. Heidelberg: Winter, 25–41.

Eshel, Amir. 2002. "The Past Recaptured? Günter Grass's *Mein Jahrhundert* and Alexander Kluge's *Chronik der Gefühle.*" *Gegenwartsliteratur* 1:63–86.

Ewert, Michael. 1999. "Spaziergänge durch die deutsche Geschichte: *Ein weites Feld* von Günter Grass." *Sprache im technischen Zeitalter* 37:402–17. Repr. in Quéval 2001a, 31–47.

Ewert, Michael, Renate von Mangoldt, Siegfried Mews, and Julian Preece. 1999. "Der Schriftsteller als Bürger: Günter Grass zum Nobelpreis." *Sprache im technischen Zeitalter* 37 (Dec.): 402–54.

Eykmann, Christoph. 1970. "Absurde Mechanik: Die 'verunglimpfte' Geschichte in den Romanen von Günter Grass." In Eykmann, *Geschichtspessimismus in der deutschen Literatur des zwanzigsten Jahrhunderts.* Bern: Francke, 112–24.

Ezergailis, Inta M. 1974. "Günter Grass' 'Fearful Symmetry': Dialectic, Mock and Real in *Katz und Maus* and *Die Blechtrommel.*" *Texas Studies in Literature and Language* 16:221–35.

Fasel Andreas. 2005. "Wie *Das Treffen in Telgte* an die Dortmunder Oper kam." *WAMS.de* (27 Feb.). Accessed 1 Dec. 2005.

Fein, Esther B. 1992. "Günter Grass Considers the Inescapable: Politics." *New York Times* (29 Dec.), C11, C16.

Feldmann, Richard. n.d. "Kopfgeburten oder Indienfahrer: (De-)Literarisierte Indienbilder von Günter Grass und Hubert Fichte." http://parapluie.de/archiv/indien/kopfgeburt" Accessed 1 Aug. 2005.

Feng, Yalin. 2006. "'. . . durch Rückgriffe Zukunft herstellen': Ökologische Aspekte in Günter Grass' *Die Rättin;* Erinnerung als konstituierender und reflektierender Prozess." *Zeitschrift für Germanistik* 16:280–91.

Fenyves, Katalin. 1979. "Literaturgeschichte, Literatur und Leben in den neuen Romanen von Christa Wolf und Günter Grass." *Acta Litteraria Scientiarum Hungaricae* 21:432–40.

Ferber, Christian. 1979. "Wo Christoffel die Dichter bewirtete." *Die Welt* (24 Mar.).

Ferguson, Lore. 1976. *"Die Blechtrommel" von Günter Grass: Versuch einer Interpretation.* Frankfurt am Main: Lang.

Fetcher, Iring. 1999. "Kritik — Günter Grass sein Jahrhundert." *Neue Gesellschaft/ Frankfurter Hefte* 46:850–52.

Fickert, Kurt J. 1971. "The Use of Ambiguity in *Cat and Mouse.*" *German Quarterly* 44:372–78.

Fieberg, Klaus. 2003. "Günter Grass: 'Im Krebsgang.'" *Der Deutschunterricht* 55 (3): 34–42.

Filz, Walter. 1988. "Dann leben sie noch heute? Zur Rolle des Märchens in *Butt* und *Rättin.*" In H. L. Arnold 1963, 6th rev. ed. 1988, 93–100.

Fischer, André. 1992. "Ludismus und Negativitätserfahrungen in der Blechtrommel." In Fischer, *Inszenierte Naivität: Zur ästhetischen Simulation von Geschichte bei Günter Grass, Albert Drach und Walter Kempowski.* Munich: Fink, 95–213.

Flasher, John. 1983. "The Grotesque Hero in *The Tin Drum.*" In *Holding the Vision: Essays on Film; Proceedings of the First Annual Film Conference of Kent State University,* ed. Douglas Radcliff-Umstead. Kent, OH: International Film Society, Kent State U, 87–93.

Fliedl, Konstanze, Hellmuth Karasek, Sigrid Löffler, and Marcel Reich-Ranicki. 1999. "Günter Grass: Mein Jahrhundert." In Anon., 2005, 4:266–77.

Flügel, Arnd. 1995. *"Mit Wörtern das Ende aufschieben": Konzeptualisierung von Erfahrung in der "Rättin" von Günter Grass.* Frankfurt am Main: Lang.

Forster, Leonard. 1993. "Ralph Manheim, 1907–1992." *German Life and Letters* 46:104–5.

Frank, Dirk. 1998. "Zwischen Deliterarisierung und Polykontextualität: Günter Grass' *Ein weites Feld* im Literaturbetrieb." In *Baustelle Gegenwartsliteratur: Die neunziger Jahre,* ed. Andreas Erb, Hannes Krauss, and Jochen Vogt. Opladen: Westdeutscher Verlag, 72–96.

Frank, Niklas. 1992. "Der Einzelgänger." *Stern* (14 May): 214–16.

Franklin, Ruth. 2003. "The Tin Book." *New Republic* (11 Aug.): 30–33.

Franzen, Günter. 2002. "Der alte Mann und sein Meer." *Die Zeit* (7 Feb.).

Friedrichsmeyer, Erhard M. 1965. "Aspects of Myth, Parody and Obscenity in Grass's *Die Blechtrommel* and *Katz und Maus.*" *Germanic Review* 40:240–52.

———. 1970. "The Dogmatism of Pain: *Local Anaesthetic.*" *Dimension* (Special Issue): 36–49. Repr. in Willson 1971, 132–45.

———. 1983. "The Swan Song of a Male Chauvinist." In Mews 1983a, 151–61.

———. 1989. "Günter Grass's *The Rat:* Making Room for Doomsday." *South Atlantic Review* 54 (4): 21–31.

Frielinghaus, Helmut, ed. 2002. *"Der Butt" spricht viele Sprachen: Grass-Übersetzer erzählen.* Göttingen: Steidl.

Fries, Fritz Rudolf. 1992a. "Kritikerküsse, Unkenrufe: Eine Nachlese zu *Unkenrufe* von Günter Grass." *Neue Deutsche Literatur* 40 (10): 128–32.

———. 1992b. "Kröten schlucken." *Wochenpost* (7 May).

———. 1995. "Hoftaller plus IM Fonty, ein sehr weites Feld." *Neues Deutschland* (21 Aug.). Repr. in Negt 1996b, 88–90.

———. 2002. "Sprache geben." *Neues Deutschland* (14 Feb.).

Fringeli, Dieter. 1977. "Das Märchen von der dritten Brust oder: Günter Grass will abgenabelt werden." *Basler Zeitung* (3 Sept.). Repr. in Fringeli 1982, 82–92.

———. 1979. "Günter Grass in Telgte: Ein Freipass für die Sprache; Von der Gruppe (16)47." *Basler Zeitung* (14 Apr.). Repr. in Fringeli 1982, 95–100.

———. 1980. "Stört uns bitte nicht in der Vergegenkunft!" *Basler Zeitung* (7 Jun.). Repr. in Fringeli 1982, 101–5.

———. 1982. *Mein Feuilleton: Gespräche, Aufsätze, Glossen zur Literatur.* Breitenbach: Jeger-Moll.

Frizen, Werner. 1986. "*Die Blechtrommel* — ein schwarzer Roman: Grass und die Literatur des Absurden." *Arcadia* 21:166–89.

———. 1987a. "Zur Entstehungsgeschichte von Günter Grass' Roman *Die Blechtrommel.*" *Monatshefte* 79:210–22.

———. 1987b. "Matzeraths' Wohnung: Raum und Weltraum in Günter Grass' *Die Blechtrommel.*" *Text und Kontext* 15 (1): 145–74.

———. 1991. "Anna Bronskis Röcke — *Die Blechtrommel* in 'ursprünglicher Gestalt.'" In Neuhaus and Hermes, 1991, 144–69.

Frye, Lawrence O. 1993. "Günter Grass, *Katz und Maus* and Gastronarratology." *Germanic Review* 68:176–84.

Fuhr, Eckhard. 2005. "Lübeck in literarischer Hochform." *Welt.de* (8 Dec.). Accessed 8 Dec. 2005.

Füssel, Stephan, ed. 1999. "Günter Grass: *Das Treffen in Telgte.*" Stuttgart: Reclam.

Fyne, Robert. 1973. "Symbol of Progress." *Christian Century* (19 Dec.): 1258–59.

Gabler, Wolfgang. 1997. "Enttäuschende Enttäuschung: Günter Grass und das Elend der Literaturkritik." *Das Argument* 39 (3): 367–81.

Gallant, Mavis. 1973. "From the Diary of a Snail." *New York Times Book Review* (30 Sept.): 5.

Ganeshan, Vridhagiri. 1992. "Günter Grass und Indien, ein Katz-und-Maus-Spiel." In Labroisse and Stekelenburg 1992, 229–44.

Garde, Barbara. 1988. *"Selbst wenn die Welt unterginge, würden deine Weibergeschichten nicht aufhören": Zwischen "Butt" und "Rättin"; Frauen und Frauenbewegung bei Günter Grass.* Frankfurt am Main: Lang.

Gay, Peter. 1999. "A Cloud of Witness." *New York Times Book Review* (19 Dec.): 9.

———. 2006. "The Fictions of Günter Grass." *New York Times* (20 Aug.).

Geisenhanslüke, Achim. 2001. "Geschichtsbilder: Intertextualität, Allegorien und Wiederholung in *Ein weites Feld.*" In Lartillot 2001a, 157–67.

Geißler, Rolf, ed. 1976. *Günter Grass: Ein Materialienbuch.* Darmstadt: Luchterhand.

———. 1999. "Ein Ende des 'weiten Feldes'?" *Weimarer Beiträge* 45:65–81.

Gelley, Alexander. 1967. "Art and Reality in *Die Blechtrommel.*" *Forum for Modern Language Studies* 3:115–25.

Genton, François. 2002. "La critique allemande et *Ein weites Feld.*" In Wellnitz 2002a, 37–52.

Gerstenberg, Renate. 1980. *Zur Erzähltechnik von Günter Grass.* Heidelberg: Winter.

Gesche, Janina. 2003. *Aus zweierlei Perspektiven . . . Zur Rezeption der Danziger Trilogie von Günter Grass in Polen und Schweden in den Jahren 1958–1990.* Stockholm: Almqvist & Wiksell.

———. 2004. "Geographische Realität und Phantasielandschaft: Das Danzigbild in der polnischen und schwedischen Kritik zur *Danziger Trilogie* von Günter Grass." In Kątny 2004, 35–46.

Giardano, Ralph. 2002. "Der böse Geist der Charta: Ralph Giardano fürchtet, dass die Diskussion über die Grass-Novelle die Ursachen der Vertreibung vergessen macht." *Die Welt* (9 Feb.). Repr. in *Kulturchronik* 20.2 (2002): 14–15.

Gilbreath, Marvin. 1963. "Flawed Superman Totters in Fable." San Francisco, CA *News-Call Bulletin* (12 Oct.). Repr. in White 1981 (excerpt), 60.

Gillessen, Günther. 2002. "Deutschland als Opfergesellschaft?" *Neue Zürcher Zeitung* (19 Apr.).

Gilman, Richard. 1982. "On the One Hand . . ." *The Nation* (24 Apr.): 502–4.

Gilman, Sander. 1988. "Jüdische Literaten und Deutsche Literatur: Antisemitismus und die verborgene Sprache der Juden am Beispiel von Jurek Becker und Edgar Hilsenrath." *Zeitschrift für deutsche Philologie* 107:269–74.

Giroud, Françoise, and Günter Grass. 1989. *Wenn wir von Europa sprechen. Ein Dialog*. Frankfurt am Main: Luchterhand, 1989.

Gockel, Heinz. 2001. *Grass' "Blechtrommel."* Munich: Piper.

Goetze, Albrecht. 1970. "Die Hundertdritte und tiefunterste Materniade: Bemerkungen zum Roman *Hundejahre* von Günter Graß [sic] anhand des Schlußkapitels." In *Vergleichen und Verändern: Festschrift für Helmut Motekat*, ed. Albrecht Goetze and Günther Pflaum. Munich: Hueber, 273–77.

———. 1972. *Pression und Deformation: Zehn Thesen zum Roman "Hundejahre" von Günter Graß* [sic]. Göppingen: Kümmerle.

Goheen, Jutta. 1996. "Intertext — Stil — Kanon: Zur Geschichtlichkeit des Epischen in Günter Grass' *Hundejahre*." *Carleton Germanic Papers* 24:155–66.

Görtz, Franz Josef. 1978. *Günter Grass; Zur Pathogenese eines Markenbilds: Die Literaturkritik der Massenmedien, 1959–1969: Eine Untersuchung mit Hilfe datenverarbeitender Methoden*. Meisenheim: Hain.

———, ed. 1984a. *"Die Blechtrommel"; Attraktion und Ärgernis: Ein Kapitel deutscher Literaturkritik*. Darmstadt: Luchterhand,

———, ed. 1984b. *Günter Grass: Auskunft für Leser*. Darmstadt: Luchterhand.

———. 1986. "Der Poet als Poltergeist." *Frankfurter Allgemeine Zeitung* (5 Feb.): 25.

———. 1990. "Apokalypse im Roman: Günter Grass' *Die Rättin*." *German Quarterly* 63:462–70.

Görtz, Franz Josef, Randall L. Jones, and Alan F. Keele, eds. 1990. *Wortindex zur "Blechtrommel" von Günter Grass*. Frankfurt am Main: Luchterhand.

Görzel, Klaus. 1996. "Der Lustmord: *Ein weites Feld* von Günter Grass und die Kritik." *Der Deutschunterricht* 48 (5): 98–104.

Gorzny, Willi, ed. 2006. *Die Grass-Debatte. Berichte, Stellungnahmen, Kommentare, Interviews, Rezensionen, Leserbriefe*. Pullach im Isartal: Gorzny.

Graf, Andreas. 1989. "Ein leises dennoch: Zum ironischen Wechselbezug von Literatur und Wirklichkeit in Günter Grass' Erzählung *Das Treffen in Telgte*." *Deutsche Vierteljahrsschrift für Literaturwissenschaft und Geistesgeschichte* 63:281–94.

Grambow, Jürgen. 1986. "Wo die Wörter versagen." *Sinn und Form* 38:1292–1302.

———. 2002. "Tulla Pokriefkes Wiederkehr." *Neue Deutsche Literatur* 49 (4):135–39.

Grathoff, Dirk. 1970. "Schnittpunkte von Literatur und Politik: Günter Grass und die neuere deutsche Grass-Rezeption." *Basis* 1:134–52.

Graves, Peter J. 1973. "Günter Grass's *Die Blechtrommel* and *örtlich betäubt*: The Pain of Polarities." *Forum for Modern Language Studies* 9:132–42.

Gray, Paul. 1981. "Poets in Search of Peace." *Time* (18 May): 87.

———. 1987. "Sinking Ship." *Time* (20 Jul.): 73.

Greiner, Ulrich. 1995. "Streit muß sein." *Die Zeit* (13 Oct.). Repr. in Negt 1996b, 363–64.

Grimson, Andrew. 2003. "A Parable of a Lost Talent." *The Spectator* [London] (29 Mar.).

Gross, Ruth V. 1979–80. "The Narrator as Demon in Grass and Alain-Fournier." *Modern Fiction Studies* 25:625–39.

Gross, Sabine. 1996. "Soviel Wirklichkeit ermüdet: Sprache und Stil in Günter Grass' *Die Rättin*." In Adler and Hermand 1996, 111–44.

Grove, Lloyd. 1986. "Günter Grass: The Literary Giant of Germany, Pounding His Tin Drum and Cooking Up a Political Storm." *Washington Post* (23 Feb.): H1, H10.

Grub, Frank Thomas. 2003. *"Wende" und "Einheit" im Spiegel der deutschsprachigen Literatur: Ein Handbuch*. 2 vols. Berlin: de Gruyter.

Gruettner, Mark Martin. 1997. *Intertextualität und Zeitkritik in Günter Grass' "Kopfgeburten" und "Die Rättin."* Tübingen: Stauffenburg.

Guidry, Glenn A. 1991. "Theoretical Reflections on the Ideological and Social Implications of Mythic Form in Grass' *Die Blechtrommel*." *Monatshefte* 83:127–46.

Gutschke, Irmtraut. 1995. "Wann ist ein Buch publizistisch erledigt?" *Neues Deutschland* (30 Aug.): 9. Repr. in Negt 1996b, 260–62.

Haberkamm, Klaus. 1979. "'Mit allen Weisheiten Saturns geschlagen': Glosse zu einem Aspekt der Gelnhausen-Figur in Günter Grass' *Treffen in Telgte.*" *Simpliciana: Schriften der Grimmelshausen-Gesellschaft* 1:67–78.

———. 1985. "'Verspäteter Grimmelshausen aus der Kaschubei' — 'Verspätete Utopie'? Simplicianisches in Grass' *Butt.*" *Simpliciana: Schriften der Grimmelshausen-Gesellschaft* 6/7:123–38.

Hage, Volker. 1987. "*Die Blechtrommel* in der DDR — nicht länger dekadent, pubertär und provinziell?" *Die Zeit* (North American ed.; 25 Sept.).

———. 1988. "Der Mißvergnügungsreisende." *Die Zeit* (26 Aug.): 35.

———. 1999. "Das ganze Säkulum: Ein Quiz." *Der Spiegel* (5 Jul.): 160–63.

———. 2002a. "Das tausendmalige Sterben." *Der Spiegel* (4 Feb.): 184–90. Repr. in *Die Flucht der Deutschen: Spiegel Spezial* 2 (2002): 22–28.

———. 2002b. "Unter Generalverdacht." *Der Spiegel* (8 Apr.): 178–81.

Hanson, William P. 1963. "Oskar, Rasputin and Goethe." *Canadian Modern Language Review* 20 (1): 29–32.

Harris, Frederick J. 1987. "Linguistic Reality — Historical Reality: Genet, Céline, Grass." *Neohelicon* 14:257–73.

Harscheidt, Michael. 1976. *Günter Grass: Wort — Zahl — Gott; Der "phantastische Realismus" in den "Hundejahren."* Bonn: Bouvier.

Hartung, Harald. 1988. "Die schwarze Göttin." *Frankfurter Allgemeine Zeitung* (3 Sept.).

Hartung, Rudolf. 1963. "*Hundejahre.*" *Neue Rundschau* (Nov.). Repr. in Loschütz 1968, 92–98.

Harvey, Stephen. 1980. "The Beat of a Difficult Drummer." *Saturday Review* (May): 55.

Haslinger, Adolf. 1985. "Günter Grass und das Barock." In Wolff 1985, 75–86.

Hatfield, Henry. 1967. "Günter Grass: The Artist as Satirist." In *The Cotemporary Novel in German,* ed. Robert R. Heitner. Austin: U of Texas P, 115–34. Repr. in Hatfield, *Crisis and Continuity in Modern German Fiction.* Ithaca, NY: Cornell UP, 1969, 128–49.

———. 1986. "Günter Grass: *Die Rättin.*" *World Literature Today* 60 (3): 621.

Hayman, Ronald. 1985. *Günter Grass.* London: Methuen.

Head, David. 1983. "Volker Schlöndorff's *Die Blechtrommel* and the 'Literaturverfilmung' Debate." *German Life and Letters* 36:347–67.

Heilbrunn, Jacob. 1999. "Nobel Committee Is, Well, Red." *Wall Street Journal* (1 Oct.).

Heilmann, Iris. 1998. *Günter Grass und John Irving: Eine transatlantische Intertextualitätsstudie.* Frankfurt am Main: Lang.

Heinz, Jutta. 2002. "Günter Grass: *Ein weites Feld;* 'Bilderbögen' und oral history." *Gegenwartsliteratur* 1:21–38.

Helbig, Louis F. 1988. *Der ungeheure Verlust: Flucht und Vertreibung in der deutschsprachigen Belletristik der Nachkriegszeit.* Wiesbaden: Harrassowitz. 3rd, enl. ed. 1996.

Helm, Toby, and Uwe Gunther. 2002. "Grass Novel on German 'Titanic' Ends Taboo." *Daily Telegraph* (8 Feb.).

Herd, Eric W. 1987. "Blechtrommel und indische Flöte: Günter Grass' Einfluß auf Salman Rushdie." In *Zeitgenossenschaft: Zur deutschsprachigen Literatur im 20. Jahrhundert; Festschrift für Egon Schwarz zum 65. Geburtstag,* ed. Paul Michael Lützeler. Frankfurt am Main: Athenäum, 224–40.

Hermand, Jost. 1979. "Darstellungen des zweiten Weltkriegs." In *Literatur nach 1945,* ed. Jost Hermand. Wiesbaden: Athenaion, 1:11–60.

———. 1996. "Das Unpositive der kleinen Leute: Zum angeblich skandalösen 'Animalismus' in Grassens *Die Blechtrommel.*" In Adler and Hermand, 1–22.

Hermes, Daniela. 1991. "'Was mit *Katz und Maus* begann' — ein Kabinettstück Grassscher Prosakunst." In Neuhaus and Hermes 1991, 170–80.

———. 1996. "Zur Auswahl des Materials." In Negt 1996b, 481–88.

Hermes, Daniela, and Volker Neuhaus, eds. 1990. *Günter Grass im Ausland. Texte, Daten, Bilder zur Rezeption.* Frankfurt am Main: Luchterhand.

Hildesheimer, Wolfgang. 1977. "Butt und die Welt: Geburtstagsbrief an Günter Grass." *Merkur* 31:966–72.

Hille-Sandvoß, Angelika. 1987. *Überlegungen zur Bildlichkeit im Werk von Günter Grass.* Stuttgart: Heinz.

Hillgruber, Katrin. 2005. "Wer zuletzt liebt: Grass verfilmen. Robert Glinski besteht mit *Unkenrufe* die Herausforderung bravourös." *Der Tagesspiegel online* (22 Sept.).

Hilliard, K. F. 2001. "Showing, Telling, and Believing: Günter Grass's *Katz und Maus* and Narratology." *Modern Language Review* 96 (2): 420–36.

Hillmann, Heinz. 1976. "Günter Grass' *Blechtrommel:* Beispiel und Überlegungen zum Verfahren der Konfrontation von Literatur und Sozialwissenschaften." In *Der deutsche Roman im 20. Jahrhundert: Analysen und Materialien zur Theorie und Soziologie des Romans,* ed. Manfred Brauneck. Bamberg: Buchner, 2:7–30.

Hillmann, Roger. 1981. "Erzähltechnische Probleme in Günter Grass' *Katz und Maus*." In *Erzählung und Erzählforschung im 20. Jahrhundert*, ed. Rolf Kloepfer and Gisela Janetzke-Dillner. Stuttgart: Kohlhammer, 319–25.

Hinck, Walter. 2000. "Günter Grass' Hommage an Fontane: Zum Roman *Ein weites Feld*." *Sinn und Form* 52 (6): 777–87. Repr. in *Fontane-Blätter* 71 (2001): 120–31.

hlg. 1959. "Alarm auf einer Blechtrommel." *Evangelischer Literaturbeobachter* (Dec.). Repr. in Görtz 1984a, 90–96.

Höllerer, Walter. 1959a. "Roman im Kreuzfeuer." *Der Tagesspiegel* (20 Dec.). Repr. in Loschütz 1968, 15–17. Repr. in Görtz 1984a, 108–12.

———. 1959b. "Unterm Floß." *Der Monat* 131 (Aug.). Repr. in Görtz 1984a, 34–38.

———. 1960. "Letter from Germany." *Evergreen Review* 4:135–38.

Hoesterey, Ingeborg. 1981. "Aspekte einer Romanfigur: Der Butt im *Butt*." *German Quarterly* 54:461–72.

———. 1988. "Schrift und visuelle Differenz bei Günter Grass: Zur Funktion des bildkünstlerischen Intertexts in *Die Blechtrommel* und *Der Butt*." In Hoesterey, *Verschlungene Schriftzeichen: Intertextualität von Literatur und Kunst in der Moderne, Postmoderne*. Frankfurt am Main: Athenäum, 71–100.

———. 1996. "Das Literarische und das Filmische. Zur dialogischen Medialität der *Blechtrommel*." In Adler and Hermand, 23–38.

Hoffmeister, Werner. 1981. "Dach, Distel und die Dichter: Günter Grass — *Das Treffen in Telgte*." *Zeitschrift für deutsche Philologie* 100:274–87. Repr. in Füssel 1999 (excerpt), 123–26.

Hofmann, Gunter. 1995. "Die Einsamkeit des Trommlers." *Die Zeit* (25 Aug.): 1. Repr. in Oberhammer and Ostermann 1995, 150–51. Repr. in Negt 1996b, 228–29.

Hofmann, Michael. 1992. "Toad's Eye of Reunification." *The Times* (1 Oct.).

Hollington, Michael. 1980. *Günter Grass: The Writer in a Pluralist Society*. London: Boyars.

Holthusen, Hans Egon. 1966. "Günter Grass als politischer Autor." *Der Monat* 18 (216): 66–81. Repr. in Holthusen, *Plädoyer für den Einzelnen*. Munich: Piper, 1967, 40–68.

———. 1972. "Der neue Günter Grass: Deutschland, deine Schnecken." *Die Welt* (24 Aug.).

Honsza, Norbert. "Eine Welt mit vielen Möglichkeiten: *Die Blechtrommel — Der Butt — Die Rättin*." *Kwartalnik Neofilologizny* 35 (2): 163–69.

———. 1989. *Ausbrüche aus der klaustrophobischen Welt: Zum Schaffen von Günter Grass*. Wroclaw: Wydasnictwo Universytetu Wroclawskiego.

———. 1997. *Günter Grass: Skizze zum Porträt*. Wroclaw: Wydasnictwo Universytetu Wroclawskiego.

———. 2000. "Ein Zeitalter wird besichtigt: Günter Grass' *Mein Jahrhundert*." In *Literatur im interkulturellen Dialog: Festschrift zum 60. Geburtstag von Hans-Christoph Graf v. Nayhauss*, ed. Manfred Durzak and Beate Laudenberg. Bern: Lang, 179–85.

Hoock-Demarle, Marie-Claire. 1999. "L'Allemagne, la France, toute une histoire?" *Magazine Littéraire* 381 (Nov.): 53–55.

Hospital, Janette Turner. 1987. "Post Futurum Blues." *New York Times Book Review* (5 Jul.), BR 6.

Hunt, Irmgard Elsner. 1983. *Mütter und Muttermythos in Günter Grass' Roman "Der Butt."* Frankfurt am Main: Lang.

———. 1989. "Zur Ästhetik des Schwebens: Utopieentwurf und Utopieverwurf in Günter Grass' *Die Rättin*." *Monatshefte* 81:286–97.

———. 1992a. "Vom Märchenwald zum toten Wald: Ökologische Bewußtmachung aus global-ökonomischer Bewußtheit; Eine Übersicht über das Grass-Werk der 70er und 80er Jahre." In Labroisse and Stekelenburg 1992, 141–68.

———. 1992b. "Grass and the Fourth Reich." *The Nation* (16 Nov.): 580–84.

———. 1997. "Erinnerungen an die Zukunft: Über das utopische Moment in der deutschen 'Wendeliteratur.'" In *Zeitgenössische Utopieentwürfe in Literatur und Gesellschaft: Zur Kontroverse seit den achtziger Jahren*, ed. Rolf Jucker. Amsterdam: Rodopi, 191–207.

———. 2003. "Günter Grass: *Im Krebsgang*." *World Literature Today* 77 (1): 128–29.

Hutchinson, Ben. 2006. "Don't Mention the War, Gunter." *Observer* (3 Sept.).

Hutnyk, John. 1996. *The Rumour of Calcutta: Tourism, Charity, and the Poverty of Representation*. London: Zed Books.

Hyman, Stanley Edgar. 1963. "An Inept Symbolist." *New Leader* 46 (19 Aug.): 16–17. Repr. in Hyman, *Standards: A Chronicle of Books for Our Time*. New York: Horizon, 1966, 168–72.

Ide, Heinz. 1968. "Dialektisches Denken im Werk von Günter Grass." *Studium Generale* 21:608–22.

Ignée, Wolfgang. 1986. "Apokalypse als Ergebnis eines Geschäftsberichts: Günter Grass' Roman *Die Rättin*." In *Apokalypse: Weltuntergangsvisionen in der Literatur des 20. Jahrhunderts*, ed. Gunter E. Grimm, Werner Faulstich, and Peter Kuon. Frankfurt am Main: Suhrkamp, 385–401.

Ireland, Kenneth R. 1990. "Doing Very Dangerous Things: *Die Blechtrommel* and *Midnight's Children*." *Comparative Literature* 42:335–61.

Irving, John. 1982. "Günter Grass: King of the Toy Merchants." *Saturday Review* (March): 57–60. Repr. in Irving, *Trying to Save Piggy Snead*. New York: Arcade 1996, 397–409.

———. 1994. "Foreword." In Günter Grass, *Cat and Mouse and Other Writings*. New York Continuum, [vi]–x.

Ivanović, Christine. 1996. "Fonty trifft Johnson: Zur Fiktionalisierung Uwe Johnsons als Paradigma der Erzählstrategie in Günter Grass' *Ein weites Feld*." *Johnson Jahrbuch* 3:173–99.

Jacobs, Jürgen. 1983. *Der deutsche Schelmenroman*. Munich: Artemis, 11–20.

Jaggi, Maya. 2000. "After the Fall." *The Guardian* (4 Nov.).

Jahnke, Walter, and Klaus Lindemann. 1993. *Günter Grass: "Die Blechtrommel": Acht Kapitel zur Erschließung des Romans*. Paderborn: Schöningh.

Jameson, Frederic. 1996. "Prussian Blues." *London Review of Books* (17 Oct.): 3, 6–7. Repr. as "Ramblings in Old Berlin." *South Atlantic Quarterly* 96 (1997): 715–27.

Janssen-Jurreit, Marielouise. 1977. "Tragische, kaputte Endzielmänner: Günter Grass' männerkritischer (?) Roman aus feministischer Sicht." *Die Weltwoche* (17 Aug.).

Jaroszewski, Marek. 2005. "'Das leuchtende Schiff': Der Untergang der *Wilhelm Gustloff* bei Günter Grass und Tanja Dückers." In Böning, Jäger, Kątny, and Szczodrowski, 277–91.

Jaumann, Herbert. 1982. "Der Autor des *Butt* im deutschen Fernsehen: Eine empirische Fallstudie zum Image von Günter Grass und historische Aspekte der Rolle des Schriftstellers." In Pickar 1982, 91–114.

Jeismann, Michael, and Karl Schlögel. 2002. "Folklore und erfundene Volkstänze: Ein Gespräch mit dem Nobelpreisträger Günter Grass." *Literaturen* 5:21–29.

Jendrowiak, Silke. 1979a. *Günter Grass und die "Hybris" des Kleinbürgers: "Die Blechtrommel" — Bruch mit der Tradition einer irrationalistischen Kunst- und Wirklichkeitsinterpretation*. Heidelberg: Winter.

———. 1979b. "Die sogenannte *Urtrommel:* Unerwartete Einblicke in die Genese der *Blechtrommel* von Günter Grass." *Monatshefte* 71:172–86.

Jenkinson, David. 1990. "Conceptions of History." In Brady, McFarland, and White 1990, 51–68.

Jenny, Urs. 1980. "In stetiger Sorge um Deutschland." *Der Spiegel* (2 Jun.): 186–88.

Jens, Walter. 1963. "Das Pandämonium des Günter Grass." *Die* Zeit (6 Sept.). Repr. in Loschütz 1968, 85–89.

Jessen, Jens. 2006. "A Monument, Slightly Crumbled." *Atlantic Times* (Sept.): 2.

Josipovici, Gabriel. 1982. "Making Holes in the Walls." *Times Literary Supplement* (23 Apr.): 405.

Jürgs, Michael. 2002. *Bürger Grass: Biografie eines deutschen Dichters.* Munich: Bertelsmann.

———. 2006. "Wer ist Günter Grass?" *Der Tagesspiegel* (13 Aug.): 2. Repr. in Gorzny 2006, 20–21.

Jurgensen, Manfred, ed. 1973. *Grass: Kritik, Thesen, Analysen.* Bern: Francke.

Just, Georg. 1972. *Darstellung und Appell in der "Blechtrommel" von Günter Grass: Darstellungsästhetik versus Wirkungsästhetik.* Frankfurt am Main: Athenäum.

———. 1973. "Die Appellstruktur der *Blechtrommel.*" In Jurgensen, 31–43.

Kaiser, Gerhard. 1971. *Günter Grass: "Katz und Maus."* Munich: Fink.

Kaiser, Joachim. 1958. "Die Gruppe 47 lebt auf." *Süddeutsche Zeitung* (5 Nov.).

———. 1959. "Oskars getrommelte Bekenntnisse." *Süddeutsche Zeitung* (31 Oct./1 Nov.). Repr. in Görtz 1984a, 52–57.

———. 1963. "Walter Materns Hundejahre." *Süddeutsche Zeitung* (21 Sept.).

———. 1977. "Gelang Grass ein Danziger Zauberberg?" *Süddeutsche Zeitung* (13/14 Aug.). Repr. in Kaiser, *Vom "Dr. Faustus" zum "Fettfleck": Deutsche Schriftsteller in unserer Zeit.* Munich: Piper, 1988, 280–85.

———. 1980. "Kopfgeburt als Frühgeburt leider Totgeburt: Günter Grass' bescheidenes Scherflein zum Wahlkampf." *Süddeutsche Zeitung* (7 Jun.): 132.

———. 1986. "In Zukunft nur Ratten noch." *Süddeutsche Zeitung* (1/2 Mar.).

Kallin, Britta. 1997–98. "'Ist Hoftaller besser als Tallhover?' Eine vergleichende Figurenanalyse zwischen Hoftaller in Günter Grass' *Ein weites Feld* (1995) und Tallhover in Hans-Joachim Schädlichs *Tallhover* (1986)." *New German Review* 13:98–112. http://www.germanic.ucla.edu/NGR/ngr13/hoftaller.htm.

Kämpchen, Martin, ed. 2001. *My Broken Love: Günter Grass in India and Bangladesh.* New Delhi: Viking.

———. 2005. "Zum dritten Mal Kalkutta: Die Rückkehr nach achtzehn Jahren (2005)." In In Kämpchen, ed. *"'Ich will in das Herz Kalkuttas eindringen.' Günter Grass in Indien und Bangladesch.* Eggingen: Eisele, 196–204.

Kane, Martin. 2002. "In the Firing Line: Günter Grass and His Critics." In *Legacies and Identity: East and West German Responses to Unification*, ed. Martin Kane. Bern: Lang, 181–97.

Kant, Hermann. 1960. "Ein Solo in Blech." *Neue deutsche Literatur* 8 (5): 151–55.

———. 1995. "Ein Buch von stichelnder Kraft." *Facts* (24 Aug.). Repr. in Negt 1996b, 95–98.

Karasek, Hellmuth. 1969. "Zahn gezogen: Zum dritten und letzten Male: Grass' neuer Roman." *Die Zeit* (5 Sept.): 20.

———. 1977. "Nora — Ein Suppenheim." *Der Spiegel* (8 Aug.): 103–5. Repr. in Karasek 1988, 14–19.

———. 1984. "Der unermüdliche Querkopf, e.V.: Der Dauermahner Günter Grass." *Der Spiegel* (14 May): 215. Repr. in Karasek 1988, 20–22.

———. 1988. *Karaseks Kulturkritik.* Hamburg: Rosch.

———. 1999. "Grass-Jahrhundert?" *Der Tagesspiegel* (8 Jul.).

———. 2006. "Moralapostel mit Erinnerungslücken." *Welt am Sonntag* (13 Aug.): 6. Repr. in Gorzny 2006, 22.

Karasek, Hellmuth, Sigrid Löffler, Annette Mayhöfer, and Marcel Reich-Ranicki. 1992. "Günter Grass: Unkenrufe." (28 May). In *Das Literarische Quartett* 2005, 1:300–319.

Karthaus, Ulrich. 1971. "*Katz und Maus* von Günter Grass: Eine politische Dichtung." *Der Deutschunterricht* 23 (1): 74–85.

Kątny, Andrzej, ed. 2004. *Das literarische Erbe von Danzig und Gdańsk.* Frankfurt am Main: Lang.

Keele, Alan Frank. 1987. ". . . Through a (Dark) Glass Clearly: Magic Spectacles and the Motif of the Mimetic Mantic in Postwar German Literature from Borchert to Grass." *Germanic Review* 57:49–59.

———. 1988. *Understanding Günter Grass.* Columbia: U of South Carolina P.

Kehlmann, Daniel. 2006. "A Prisoner of the Nobel." Trans. from the German by Ross Benjamin. *New York Times* (20 Aug.).

Keller, Karl. 1978. "Man's Will vs. Woman's Will." *Los Angeles Times* (1 Oct.).

Kennedy, Eugene. 1987. "The Age of the Rat." *Chicago Tribune* (28 Jun.), Tribune Books 1.

Kiefer, Klaus H. 1991. "Günter Grass: *Die Rättin;* Struktur und Rezeption." *Orbis Litterarum* 46:364–82.

Kiefer, Sascha. 2002. "Frühe Polemik und späte Differenzierung: Das Heidegger-Bild von Günter Grass in *Hundejahre* (1963) und *Mein Jahrhundert* (1999)." *Weimarer Beiträge* 48:242–59.

Kielinger, Thomas. 1972. "Günter Grass: *Aus dem Tagebuch einer Schnecke.*" *Neue deutsche Hefte* 19 (3): 155–60.

Kiniery, Paul. 1970. "Review." *Best Sellers* (13 Mar.). Repr. in White 1981 (excerpt), 137.

Kinzer, Stephen. 1995. "Günter Grass: Germany's Last Heretic." *New York Times Book Review* (22 Oct.): 47.

Kirner, Florian. 1996. "Eine Welle der Kulturreaktion." *Sozialismus von unten* 5:29–33.

Klein, Julia M. 2003. "Germans as Victims of World War II." *Chronicle of Higher Education* 49.32 (18 Apr.): B16–17.

Klinge, Reinhold. 1966. "Die *Blechtrommel* im Unterricht? Ein Versuch." *Der Deutschunterricht* 18 (2): 91–103.

Kluger, Richard. 1965. "Tumultuous Indictment of Man." *Harper's* (Jun.): 110–13. Repr. in White 1981 (excerpt), 84.

Kniesche, Thomas W. 1991. *Die Genealogie der Post-Apokalypse — Günter Grass' "Die Rättin."* Vienna: Passagen.

———. 1998. "'Calcutta' oder Die Dialektik der Kolonialisierung; Günter Grass: *Zunge zeigen.*" In *Schriftsteller und Dritte Welt,* ed. Paul Michael Lützeler. Tübingen: Stauffenburg, 263–90.

———. 2001. "Fluchtpunkt Frankreich: Symbolische Topographien in *Ein weites Feld.*" In Quéval 2001a, 191–209.

———. 2002. "'Distrust the Ornament': Günter Grass and the Textual/ Visual Imagination." *Gegenwartsliteratur* 1:1–20.

Knipphals, Dirk. 2002. "Schiffskatastrophen und andere Untergänge." *taz* (20 Feb.).

Kö, Dr. 1962. "Katz und Maus." *Unser Danzig* (5 Jan.).

Koehn, Barbara. 2001. "Alfred Döblin, der Lehrer von Günter Grass." In Lartillot 2001a, 9–19.

Kölbel, Martin. 2007a. "Nachwort." In Kölbel 2007b, 335–56.

———, ed. 2007b. *Ein Buch, ein Bekenntnis: Die Debatte um Günter Grass' "Beim Häuten der Zwiebel."* Göttingen: Steidl.

Koopmann, Helmut. 1977. "Günter Grass: Der Faschismus als Kleinbürgertum und was daraus wurde." In *Gegenwartsliteratur und Drittes Reich,* ed. Hans Wagener. Stuttgart: Reclam, 163–82. Repr. (abbreviated version) in Görtz 1984b, 95–123. Repr. (abbreviated version) in Neuhaus and Hermes 1991, 200–222.

———. 1983. "Between Stone Age and Present or The Simultaneity of the Nonsimultaneous: The Time Structure." In Mews 1983a, 75–89.

Köpf, Gerhard. 1987. *Hund und Katz und Maus, Schnecke, Butt und Ratte.* Frankfurt am Main: Büchergilde Gutenberg.

Krättli, Anton. 1977. "Danziger Butt mit Zutaten: Zum neuen Roman von Günter Grass." *Schweizer Monatshefte* 57: 485–93.

———. 1979. "In Telgte und Nirgends: Literaturgeschichte als Fiktion bei Günter Grass und Christa Wolf." *Schweizer Monatshefte* 59:463–72. Repr. in Füssel 1999 (excerpt), 128–31.

———. 1986. "Herr Matzerath mit sechzig Jahren, Ultimo vorbei." *Schweizer Monatshefte* 66:333–38.

Krause, Tilman. 2006a."Ende einer Dienstzeit." *Die Welt* (14 Aug.): 3. Repr. in Gorzny 2006, 31–32.

———. 2006b. "Ich aber weinte erst später, viel später." *Die Welt* (19 Aug.). Repr. in Gorzny 2006, 143–44. Repr. in Kölbel 2007b, 300–304.

Kremer, Manfred. 1973. "Günter Grass, *Die Blechtrommel* und die pikarische Tradition." *German Quarterly* 46:381–92.

Krüger, Horst. 1969. "Das Wappentier der Republik." *Die Zeit* (25 Apr.). Repr. in Görtz 1984b, 56–62.

———. 1972. "Günter Grass: *Aus dem Tagebuch einer Schnecke.*" *Neue Rundschau* 83:741–46.

———. 1980. "Die Phantasie an die Macht: Die jüngsten *Kopfgeburten* des Dichters und Wahlkämpfers Günter Grass." *Frankfurter Allgemeine Zeitung* (14 Jun.).

Krueger, Werner. 1980. "Mystisch, barbarisch, gelangweilt: Zu Günter Grass, *Katz und Maus.*" *Acta Germanica* 12:185–96.

Krumme, Detlef. 1985. "Der suspekte Erzähler und sein suspekter Held." In Durzak 1985a, 65–79.

———. 1986. *Günter Grass: "Die Blechtrommel."* Munich: Hanser.

Kube, Lutz. 1997. "Intellektuelle Verantwortung und Schuld in Günter Grass' *Ein weites Feld.*" *Colloquia Germanica* 30:349–61.

Kügler, Hans. 1995. "'In Deutschland ist keine Bleibe mehr': Zur Zeitkritik und zur Fontanerezeption in Günter Grass' neuem Roman *Ein weites Feld* — Ein Lektürevorschlag." *Diskussion Deutsch* 144:301–4.

Kunisch, Hans-Peter. 1999. "Nichts Deutsches ist dem Dichter fremd." *Süddeutsche Zeitung* (3/4 Jul.): iv.

Kurbjuweit, Dirk, et al. 2006. "Fehlbar und verstrickt." *Der Spiegel* (21 Aug.): 46–66. Repr. in Kölbel 2007b, 53–64.

Kurz, Paul Konrad. 1964. "*Hundejahre:* Beobachtungen zu einem zeitkritischen Roman." *Stimmen der Zeit* 89 (1): 107–20. Repr. in Kurz, *Über moderne deutsche Literatur: Standorte und Deutungen.* Frankfurt am Main: Knecht, 1967, 158–76. Trans. by Mary Frances McCarthy as "*Hundejahre:* Some Remarks about a Novel of Contemporary Criticism." In Kurz, *On Modern German Literature.* University, AL: U of Alabama P, 1970, 131–48.

———. 1969. "Das verunsicherte Wappentier: Zu *Davor* und *Örtlich betäubt* von Günter Grass." *Stimmen der Zeit* 184:374–89. Repr. in Kurz, *Über moderne Literatur: Standorte.* Frankfurt am Main: Knecht, 1971, 3:89–112.

———. 1974. "Exempla politica im Roman: Die episierte Wahlreise." In Kurz, *Über moderne Literatur IV: Standorte und Deutungen.* Frankfurt am Main: Knecht, 69–78.

———. 1977. "The Insecure Heraldic Animal: On Günter Grass's *Uptight* and *Local Anaesthetic.*" Trans. of Kurz 1969 by Sister Mary Frances McCarthy. In Kurz, *On Modern German Literature.* University, AL: U of Alabama P, 4:73–95, 252–53.

Labroisse, Gerd. 1999. "Zur Sprach-Bildlichkeit in Günter Grass' *Ein weites Feld.*" In *Das Sprachbild als textuelle Interaktion,* ed. Labroisse and Stekelenburg. *Amsterdamer Beiträge zur neueren Germanistik.* Amsterdam: Rodopi, 347–79.

Labroisse, Gerd, and Dick van Stekelenburg, eds. 1992. *Günter Grass, ein europäischer Autor?* Amsterdam: Rodopi.

Lane, Margery. 1963. "Günter Grass' Morality Tale." Greensboro, NC *Daily News* (1 Sept.). Repr. in White 1981 (excerpt), 54–55.

Larsen, Thor A. 1983. "'Die Geschichte will weiblich geprägt werden': Zum Feminismus im Roman *Der Butt* von Günter Grass." In *Frauen und Frauenbilder: Dokumentiert durch 2000 Jahre,* ed. Jorunn Valgard and Elsbeth Wessel. Oslo: Germanistisches Institut der Universität Oslo, 94–100.

———. 1985. "'Das ist die Wahrheit jedesmal anders erzählt': Zum Roman *Der Butt.*" In Durzak 1985a, 115–29.

Lartillot, Françoise, ed. 2001a. *Günter Grass "Ein weites Feld": Aspects politiques, historique et littéraires.* Nancy: Presses Universitaires de Nancy.

———. 2001b. "Avant-propos." In Lartillot 2001a, 5–7.

———. 2001c. "La fonction des images dans *Ein weites Feld.*" In Lartillot 2001a, 133–55.

———. 2002. "Le sort des Lumières dans Ein weites Feld." In Wellnitz 2002a, 151–84.

Lawson, Richard H. 1985. *Günter Grass.* New York: Ungar.

Lehmann-Haupt, Christopher. 1987. "Books of the Times." *New York Times* (29 Jun.): C18.

Lehnemann, Widar. 2001. "Günter Grass: *Katz und Maus.*" Paderborn: Schöningh.

Leitgeb, Hanna, and Sigrid Löffler. 2002. "'Falsche Folklore und erfundene Volkstänze.' Gespräch mit Michael Jeismann und Karl Schlögel." *Literaturen* 5:20–29.

Leonard, Irene. 1974. *Günter Grass.* Edinburgh: Oliver & Boyd.

Leonard, John. 1970. "Books of the Times." *New York Times* (26 Mar.). Repr. in White 1981 (excerpt), 138–39.

———. 1978. "Books of the Times." *New York Times* (9 Nov.), C24.

———. 1981. "*The Meeting at Telgte.*" *Books of the Times* (Jul. 1981): 314–16.

———. 1982. "Consider a Billion Germans." *New York Times Book Review* (14 Mar.): 11, 20.

Leroy, Robert. 1973. *"Die Blechtrommel" von Günter Grass: Eine Interpretation.* Paris: Les Belles Lettres.

Lewis, Flora. 1980. "Before *The Tin Drum* He Had Never Acted; Now He Is a Star." *New York Times* (17 Apr.): C23.

Lichtenberg, Johannes. 1969. "Die Leere eines Literaten." *Nürnberger Nachrichten* (6 Aug.).

Lietzmann, Sabine. 1970. "Grass gewinnt Statur." *Frankfurter Allgemeine Zeitung* (27 Apr.): 24.

Liewerscheidt, Ute. 1976. *Günter Grass: "Die Blechtrommel": Kommentare, Diskussionsaspekte und Anregungen für produktionsorientiertes Lesen.* 5th, rev. ed. Hollfeld/Obfr.: Beyer, 2000.

Lilienthal, Volker. 1988. "Nur verhaltener Beifall für die zahme *Rättin:* Ein Fall von politischer Gesinnungskritik? Zur literaturkritischen Rezeption von Günter Grass." *LiLi: Zeitschrift für Literaturwissenschaft und Linguistik* 18:103–13.

Lindquist, Wayne P. 1989. "The Materniads: Grass's Paradoxical Conclusion to the *Danzig Trilogy.*" *Critique* 30:179–92.

Livingston, Robert Gerald. 2003. "Germany's Sunken Memories." *Foreign Policy* (1 Mar): 80–82.

Locke, Richard. 1987. "Gunter [sic] Grass' Book of Revelation." *Washington Post* (19 Jul.): x5.

Löffler, Sigrid. 1995. "Heißgeredet, totgeschrieben." *Süddeutsche Zeitung* (26/27 Aug.). Repr. in Oberhammer and Ostermann 1995, 180. Repr. in Negt 1996b, 251–53.

Lorou, Richard Blé. 2003. *"Erinnerung entsteht auf neue Weise": Wende und Vereinigung in der deutschen Romanliteratur.* Kiel: Ludwig.

Lorrain, Sophie. 2001a. "Histoire et mémoire dans *Ein weites Feld.*" In Lartillot 2001a, 95–114.

———. 2001b. "Topographie et écriture: Du nord au sud, d'est en ouest: ligne droite, cercle et croix." In Quéval 2001a, 147–68.

Loschütz, Gert, ed. 1968. *Von Buch zu Buch; Günter Grass in der Kritik: Eine Dokumentation.* Neuwied: Luchterhand.

Lottmann, Joachim. 2005. "Ultimativer Trash für die Generation 50 plus." *WAMS.de* (18. Sept.).

Lubich, Frederick Alfred. 1985. "Günter Grass' *Kopfgeburten:* Deutsche Zukunftsbewältigung oder Wie wird sich Sisyphos in Orwells Jahrzehnt verhalten?" *German Quarterly* 58:394–408.

Lucke, Hans. 1969. "Günter Grass' Novelle *Katz und Maus* im Unterricht." *Der Deutschunterricht* 21 (2): 86–95.

Lüdke, Martin. 1988. "Halb zog es ihn, halb floh er hin." *Frankfurter Rundschau* (4 Oct.), VB5.

———. 1995. "Der Meister ist wieder da!" *Die Woche* (5 May). Repr. in Negt 1996b, 381–83.

M., J. M. 1978. "*Der Butt* und der *Osservatore.*" *Bayernkurier* (4 Feb.).

Macpherson, Hugh. 2000. "Walking with Fonty." *Times Literary Supplement* (8 Dec.), 22.

Maddocks, Melvin. 1973. "Hesitation Waltz." *Time* (8 Oct.): 109–12.

Mahrdt, Helgard. 2000. "Essen. Trinken. Dichten: Zur Bedeutung des Symposiums in Günter Grass' Erzählung *Das Treffen in Telgte.*" *Text & Kontext* 22 (2/1): 195–211.

Maier, Wolfgang. 1961. "Moderne Novelle." *Sprache im technischen Zeitalter* 1:68–71.

Malik, Amita. 1989. "A Touch of Grass." *Indian Express Magazine* (22 Oct.).

Mangold, Ijoma. 2006. "Seht, wie meine Augen tränen." *Süddeutsche Zeitung* (19 Aug), 11. Repr. in Gorzny 2006, 142–43. Repr. in Kölbel 2007b, 322–24.

Mannack, Eberhard. 1982. "Oskars Lektüre: Zum Verweisungszusammenhang in Günter Grass' *Blechtrommel.*" In *From Wolfram and Petrarch to Goethe and Grass: Studies in Literature in Honour of Leonard Forster,* ed. D. H. Green, L. P. Johnson, and Dieter Wuttke. Baden: Koerner, 587–600.

———. 1991. "G. Grass' *Das Treffen in Telgte:* Literarische und wissenschaftliche Rezeption." In Mannack, *Barock in der Moderne: Deutsche Schriftsteller des 20. Jh. als Rezipienten deutscher Barockliteratur.* Frankfurt am Main: Lang, 109–14.

Mannoni, Olivier. 1996. *Un écrivain à abattre: l'Allemagne contre Günter Grass.* Paris: Ramsay.

———. 2000. *Günter Grass: L'honneur d'un homme.* Paris: Bayard.

———. 2001. "Grass, le roman et léternel retour du même." In Quéval 2001a, 169–76.

Martini, Fritz. 1962. "Gutachten." In Loschütz 1968, 58–60. Repr. in Ritter 1977, 133–36.

Marx, Bill. 1999. "Speaking in German an Array of Voices Witness the Century in Tales of Nobel Laureate Gunter [sic] Grass." *Boston Globe* (28 Nov.).

Mason, Ann L. 1973. "Günter Grass and the Artist in History." *Contemporary Literature* 14:347–62.

———. 1974. *The Skeptical Muse: A Study of Günter Grass' Conception of the Artist.* Bern: Lang.

———. 1976. "The Artist and Politics in Günter Grass's *Aus dem Tagebuch einer Schnecke.*" *Germanic Review* 51:105–20. Repr. in O'Neill 1987c, 159–74.

Matt, Beatrice von. 1986. "Nur Ratten noch." *Neue Zürcher Zeitung* (28 Feb.).

Maurer, Robert. 1968. "The End of Innocence: Günter Grass's *The Tin Drum.*" *Bucknell Review* 16 (2): 516–23. Repr. in O'Neill 1987c, 96–112.

Mayer, Hans. 1967. "Felix Krull und Oskar Matzerath: Aspekte des Romans." *Süddeutsche Zeitung* (14 Oct.). Repr. in Mayer, *Das Geschehen und das Schweigen: Aspekte der Literatur.* Frankfurt am Main: Suhrkamp, 1969, 35–67. Repr. in *Positionen des Erzählens: Analysen und Theorien zur Literatur der Bundesrepublik,* ed. Heinz Ludwig Arnold and Theo Buck. Munich: Beck, 1976, 49–67.

———. 1971. "Günter Grass and Thomas Mann: Aspects of the Novel." Translation of Mayer 1967 by Jack D. Zipes. In Mayer, *Steppenwolf and Everyman.* New York: Crowell, 1971, 181–99.

———. 1988. "Grass und seine Tiere." In H. L. Arnold 1963, 6th rev. ed. 1988, 76–83.

Mayer, Sigrid. 1978. "Grüne Jahre für Grass: Die Rezeption in den Vereinigten Staaten." In H. L. Arnold 1963, 5th, rev. ed. 1978, 151–61.

———. 1982. "*Der Butt:* Lyrische und graphische Quellen." In Pickar 1982, 16–23.

———. 1983. "The Critical Reception of *The Flounder* in the United States: Epic and Graphic Aspects." In Mews 1983a, 179–95.

———. 1988. "Zwischen Utopie und Apokalypse: Der Schriftsteller als 'Seher' im neueren Werk von Günter Grass." *Amsterdamer Beiträge zur neueren Germanistik* 24:79–116.

———. 1992. "Günter Grass in Calcutta: Der interkulturelle Diskurs in *Zunge zeigen.*" In Labroisse and Stekelenburg, 245–66.

———. 1993a. "Günter Grass in Calcutta and the Aesthetics of Poverty." In *Intertextuality,* ed. Ingeborg Hoesterey and Ulrich Weisstein. Columbia, SC: Camden House, 142–58.

———. 1993b. "Politische Aktualität nach 1989: Die Polnisch-Deutsch-Litauische Friedhofsgesellschaft oder *Unkenrufe* von Günter Grass." In *Literatur und politische Aktualität,* ed. Elrud Ibsch and Ferdinand van Ingen. Amsterdam: Rodopi, 213–23.

Mayer[-Iswandy], Claudia. 1988. "Von 'Unterbrechungen' und 'Engführungen': Lyrik und Prosa in *Butt* und *Rättin.*" In H. L. Arnold 1963, 6th, rev. ed. 1988, 84–92.

———. 1991. *"Vom Glück der Zwitter": Geschlechterrolle und Geschlechterverhältnis bei Günter Grass.* Frankfurt am Main: Lang.

———. 2002. *Günter Grass.* Munich: Deutscher Taschenbuch Verlag.

McElvoy, Anne. 1992. "High Priests or Nut-Cases?" *Times Literary Supplement* (19 Jun.): 14.

McFarland, Timothy. 1990. "The Transformation of Historical Material: The Case of Dorothea von Montau." In Brady, McFarland, and White 1990, 69–96.

McGoniggle, Thomas. 2000. "Ink with Spit." *Los Angeles Times* (26 Nov.).

McLaughlin, Richard. 1963. "'Cat and Mouse' by Günter Grass Shows War Folly." Springfield, MA *Republican* (25 Aug.). Repr. in White 1981 (excerpt), 51.

McPherson, William. 1978. "A Fish Story." *Washington Post* (5 Nov.), G1, G4.

Meffre, Liliane. 2002. "Les paysages dans le roman de Günter Grass *Ein weites Feld.*" In Wellnitz 2002a, 199–208.

Menne-Haritz, Angelika. 1981. "Der Westfälische Friede und die Gruppe 47." *Literatur für Leser* 1:237–45. Repr. in Füssel 1999 (excerpt), 131–33.

Merivale, Patricia. 1990. "Saleem Fathered by Oskar: Intertextual Strategies in *Midnight's Children* and *The Tin Drum.*" *Ariel* 21 (3): 5–21. Repr. in *Magical Realism: Theory, History, Community,* ed. Lois Parkinson Zamora and Wendy B. Faris. Durham, NC: Duke UP, 1995, 328–45.

Mertens, Mathias, Daniela Hermes, and Volker Neuhaus. n.d. "Günter Grass." *Kritisches Lexikon der Gegenwartsliteratur (KLG) online*. http://www.klgonline.de.

Metken, Günter. 1988. "Fluchtpunkt Kalkutta." *Süddeutsche Zeitung* (10 Sept.).

Mews, Siegfried. 1982. "Der Butt als Germanist: Zur Rolle der Literatur in Günter Grass' Roman." In Pickar 1982, 24–31.

———, ed. 1983a. *"The Fisherman and His Wife": Günter Grass's "The Flounder" in Critical Perspective*. New York: AMS P.

———. 1983b. "Grass' *Kopfgeburten:* The Writer in Orwell's Decade." *German Studies Review* 6:501–17.

———. 1983c. "The 'Professorial' Flounder: Reflections on Grass's Use of Literary History." In Mews 1983a, 163–78.

———1989. "From Admiration to Confrontation: Günter Grass and the United States." In *Amerika! New Images in German Literature*. ed. Heinz D. Osterle. New York: Lang, 315–34.

———. 1994. "Günter Grass und das Problem der deutschen Nation." In *Zwischen Traum und Trauma — Die Nation,* ed. Claudia Mayer-Iswandy. Tübingen: Stauffenburg, 111–27.

———. 1997. "A Farewell to the Letters of the Federal Republic? — F. Schirrmacher's Postwall Assessment of Postwar German Literature." In *Beyond 1989: Re-reading German Literature since 1945,* ed. Keith Bullivant. Providence, RI: Berghahn, 21–33.

———. 1999. "'Im Ausland geschätzt?' — Zur Grass-Rezeption in den USA." *Sprache im technischen Zeitalter* 37 (152): 423–37.

———. 2001. "Günter Grass. Review Article." *German Quarterly* 74:201–5.

Meyer-Gosau, Frauke. 1997. "Ende der Geschichte: Günter Grass' Roman *Ein weites Feld* — drei Lehrstücke." In H. L. Arnold 1963, 7th, rev. ed. 1997, 3–18.

Michaelis, Rolf. 1972. "Das Prinzip Zweifel." *Frankfurter Allgemeine Zeitung* (2 Sept.).

———. 1977. "Mit dem Kopf auch den Gaumen aufklären." *Die Zeit* (12 Aug.).

Michelsen, Peter. 1972. "Oskar oder Das Monstrum: Reflexionen über *Die Blechtrommel* von Günter Grass." *Neue Rundschau* 83:722–40.

Midgley, David. 2005. "Günter Grass, *Im Krebsgang:* Memory, Medium and Message." *Seminar* 41:55–67.

Mieder, Wolfgang. 1978. "Kulinarische und emanzipatorische Redensartverwendung in Günter Grass' Roman *Der Butt.*" *Sprachspiegel* 34:4–11. Repr in Mieder, *Sprichwort, Redensart, Zitat: Tradierte Formelsprache in der Moderne.* Frankfurt am Main: Lang, 1985, 27–35.

Miles, Keith. 1975. *Günter Grass.* New York: Barnes & Noble.

Miller, Eldon. 1963. "A Simple but Disturbing Story." Raleigh, NC *News and Observer* (18 Aug.). Repr. in White 1981 (excerpt), 49–50.

Millot, Cécile. 2001. "*Ein weites Feld* est-il un roman de la *Wende*? Ou comment raconter l'histoire?" In Lartillot 2001a, 61–75.

Minden, Michael. 1990. "Implications of the Narrative Technique in *Der Butt.*" In Brady, McFarland, and White 1990, 187–202.

———. 1993. "A Post-realist Aesthetic: Günter Grass, *Die Blechtrommel.*" In *The German Novel in the Twentieth Century: Beyond Realism,* ed. David Midgley. Edinburgh: Edinburgh UP, 149–63.

Misch, Manfred. 1997. "'. . . eine Fülle von Zitaten auf Abruf': Anspielungen und Zitate in Günter Grass' *Ein weites Feld.*" In *Deutschsprachige Gegenwartsliteratur,* ed. Hans-Jörg Knobloch and Helmut Koopmann. Tübingen, Stauffenburg, 153–62.

Mitchell, Breon. 1973. "The Demonic Comedy: Dante and Grass's *Hundejahre.*" *Papers on Language and Literature* 9:65–77.

Mitgang, Herbert. 1978. "Grass: on Men, Women and 'Flounder.'" *New York Times* (25 Nov.): 15.

———. 1992."Germany and Poland as War-Crossed Lovers." *New York Times* (18 Dec.): C25.

Moeller, Robert G. 2003. "Sinking Ships, the Lost *Heimat* and Broken Taboos: Günter Grass and the Politics of Memory in Contemporary Germany." *Contemporary European History* 12 (2): 147–82.

Moennighoff, Burkhard. 2001. "Sichausdenken und Nichtreisenmüssen: Texte des Barocks in Günter Grass' *Der Butt.*" In *Ach, Neigung zur Fülle . . . Zur Rezeption "barocker" Literatur im Nachkriegsdeutschland,* ed. Christiane Caemmerer and Walter Delabar. Würzburg: Königshausen & Neumann, 83–94.

Morris-Keitel, Peter. 1996. "Anleitung zum Engagement: Über das ökologische Bewußtsein in Grass' Werk." In Adler and Hermand, 145–68.

Morrison, Blake. 1992. "Super Grass." *The Independent* (27 Sept.).

Moser, Sabine. 2000. *Günter Grass: Romane und Erzählungen.* Berlin: Schmidt.

———. 2001. "'Du bildest dir wieder was ein': Die Imagination historischer 'Realitäten' in *Ein weites Feld.*" In Quéval 2001a, 63–77.

———. 2002. *Dieses Volk, unter dem es zu leiden galt: Die deutsche Frage bei Günter Grass*. Frankfurt am Main: Lang.

Müller, Jan-Werner. 2000. "Günter Grass and His Critics: The Metaphysics of Auschwitz." In Müller, *Another Country: German Intellectuals, Unification, and National Identity*. New Haven, CT: Yale UP, 64–89.

Müller, Ulrich. 1985. "Frauen aus dem Mittelalter, Frauen im mittleren Alter: Günter Grass: *Der Butt*." In Wolff 1985, 111–35.

Müller, W. J. 1978. *Der Butt* und der *Osservatore*." *Bayernkurier* (4 Feb.): 17.

Müller-Eckhard, H. 1959. "Die Brechtrommel." *Kölnische Rundschau* (13 Dec.). Repr. in Görtz 1984a, 96–99.

Mundt, Hannelore. 1989. *"Dr. Faustus" und die Folgen: Kunstkritik als Gesellschaftskritik im deutschen Roman seit 1947*. Bonn: Bouvier.

Murti, Kamakshi P. 2001. *India: The Seductive and Seduced "Other" of German Orientalism*. Westport, CT: Greenwood.

Nagorski, Andrew, and Stefan Theil. 2002. "The German Titanic." *Newsweek* (11 Mar.): www.keepmedia.com.

Nayhauss, Hans-Christoph Graf von. 1990. "Günter Grass' *Rättin* im Spiegel der Rezensionen." In Anon. *Der Mensch wird an seiner Dummheit sterben (Günter-Grass-Konferenz Karpacz 17.-23. Mai 1987): Acta Universitatis Wratislaviensis* 116:81–115.

———. 2000. "*Unkenrufe* in fünf Gängen zur deutsch-polnischen Versöhnung: Vom Krötenschlucken eines Dichters angesichts neuer Wirklichkeiten nach der Wende." In *Zeitbewußtsein und Zeitkonzeption*. ed. Norbert Honsza. Wroclaw: Wydawnictwo Uniwersytetu Wroclawskiego, 37–55.

Negt, Oskar. 1996a. "Über die literarische Öffentlichkeit und den Verlust ihrer kritischen Substanz." In Negt 1996b, 7–28.

———, ed. 1996b. *Der Fall Fonty. "Ein weites Feld" von Günter Grass im Spiegel der Kritik*. Göttingen: Steidl.

Neis, Edgar. 1970. *Erläuterungen zu Günter Grass, "Die Blechtrommel."* 9th, rev. ed. Hollfeld/Obfr.: Bange.

Neubauer, Martin. 1998. *Günter Grass: "Katz und Maus."* Munich: Mentor.

Neuhaus, Stefan. 2002. "'Zweifel ist immer richtig!' Günter Grass' *Ein weites Feld*." In S. Neuhaus, *Literatur und nationale Einheit in Deutschland*. Tübingen: Francke. 437–70.

Neuhaus, Volker. 1970. "Belle Tulla sans merci." *Arcadia* 5:278–95. Repr. in Neuhaus and Hermes 1991, 181–99.

———. 1979. *Günter Grass*. Stuttgart: Metzler. 2nd, rev. and enl. ed., 1992.

———. 1982. *Günter Grass. "Die Blechtrommel."* Munich: Oldenbourg, 1988. 2nd, rev. and enl. ed. 3rd, rev. ed. 1992.

———. 1988. "Das christliche Erbe bei Günter Grass." In H. L. Arnold 1963, 6th, rev. ed. 1988, 108–19.

———. 1991a. "Vorwort." In Neuhaus and Hermes, 7–9.

———. 1991b. "'Das biedermeierliche Babel' — Günter Grass und Düsseldorf." In Neuhaus and Hermes, 133–43.

———. 1992. "Günter Grass' *Die Rättin* und die jüdisch-christliche Gattung der Apokalypse." In Labroisse and Stekelenburg, 123–39.

———. 1993a. "The Rat-Motif in the Works of Günter Grass." In *Crisis and Culture in Post-Enlightenment Germany,* ed. Hans Schulte and David Richards. Lanham, MD: UP of America, 453–67.

———. 1993b. "Günter Grass: *Die Blechtrommel.*" In *Interpretationen: Romane des 20. Jahrhunderts.* Stuttgart: Reclam, 2:120–42.

———. 1997. *Schreiben gegen die verstreichende Zeit: Zu Leben und Werk von Günter Grass.* Munich: Deutscher Taschenbuch Verlag.

———. 1999. "Das Motiv der Ratte in den Werken von Günter Grass." In *Die Zoologie der Träume,* ed. Dorothee Römhild. Opladen: Westdeutscher Verlag, 170–84.

———. 2001a. "Die Erzähler und ihre Funktion in *Ein weites Feld.*" In Lartillot 2001a, 77–83.

———. 2001b. "*Ein weites Feld* als historischer Roman." In Quéval 2001a, 23–30.

———, ed. 2007. *Günter Grass — "Katz und Maus": Kommentar und Materialien.* Göttingen: Steidl.

Neuhaus, Volker, and Daniela Hermes, eds. 1991. *Die Danziger Trilogie: Texte, Daten, Bilder.* Darmstadt: Luchterhand, 1991.

Neumann, Bernd. 1985. "Konturen ästhetischer Opposition in den fünfziger Jahren: Zu Günter Grass' *Die Blechtrommel* (Erscheinungsjahr 1959)." In Durzak 1985a, 46–64.

Newlove, Donald. 1981. "*The Meeting at Telgte.*" *Saturday Review* (May): 71.

Noerr, Gunzelin Schmid. 1978. "Über den *Butt.*" In H. L. Arnold 1963, 5th, rev. ed. 1978, 90–93.

Nolte, Jost. 1963. "Der Zeit in den schmutzigen Rachen gegriffen." *Die Welt* (7 Sept.).

Oberhammer, Georg, and Georg Ostermann, eds. *Zerreissprobe: Der neue Roman von Günter Grass "Ein weites Feld" und die Literaturkritik. Eine Dokumentation.* Innsbruck: Innsbrucker Zeitungsarchiv, 1995.

Øhrgaard, Per. 1983. "'He, Butt! Das ist deine andere Wahrheit': Die Romantik als Bezugspunkt in der deutschen Gegenwartsliteratur." In *Aspekte der Romantik: Vorträge des Kolloquiums am 25./26. 4. 1983,* ed. Sven-Aage Jørgensen, Per Øhrgaard, and Friedrich Schmöe. Munich: Fink, 128–45.

———. 2005. *Günter Grass: Ein deutscher Schriftsteller wird besichtigt.* Trans. from the Danish by Christoph Bartmann. Vienna: Zsolnay.

Olbert, Frank. 2006. "Der Moralapostel steigt vom Sockel." *Kölner Stadt-Anzeiger* (12 Aug.): 4. Repr. in Gorzny 2006, 18.

Onderdelinden, Sjaak. 1992. "*Zunge zeigen* in den Zeitungen." In Labroisse and Stekelenburg, 205–28.

O'Neill, Patrick. 1974. "Musical Form and the Pauline Message in a Key Chapter of Grass's *Blechtrommel.*" *Seminar* 10:298–307.

———. 1982. "The Scheherazade Syndrome: Günter Grass' Meganovel *Der Butt.*" In Pickar 1982, 1–15.

———. 1987a. "Grass's Doomsday Book: *Die Rättin.*" In O'Neill 1987c. 213–24.

———. 1987b. "Introduction." In O'Neill 1987c, 1–20.

———, ed. 1987c. *Critical Essays on Günter Grass.* Boston: Hall.

———. 1990. "Prophecy as Process: Reconstructing the Future in Grass's *Die Rättin.*" *University of Dayton Review* 20 (3): 15–20.

———. 1992. "A Different Drummer: The American Reception of Günter Grass." In *The Fortunes of German Writers in America: Studies in Literary Reception,* ed. Wolfgang Elfe, James Hardin, and Gunther Holst. Columbia: U of South Carolina P, 277–85.

———. 1999. *Günter Grass Revisited.* New York: Twayne.

Osinski, Jutta. 1996. "Aspekte der Fontane-Rezeption bei Günter Grass." *Fontane Blätter* 62:112–26.

Osterle, Heinz. 1985. "An Orwellian Decade? Günter Grass Between Hope and Despair." *German Studies Review* 8:481–507.

Ottinger, Emil. 1962. "Zur mehrdimensionalen Erklärung von Straftaten Jugendlicher am Beispiel der Novelle *Katz und Maus* von Günter Grass." *Monatsschrift für Kriminologie und Strafrechtsreform* 5/6:231–37. Repr. in Loschütz 1968, 38–48. Repr. in Ritter 1977, 112–27.

Pakendorf, Gunther. 1980. "Günter Grass: *Der Butt* oder das Märchen von der Emanzipation." *Acta Germanica* 13:175–87.

Palencia-Roth, Michael. 1979. "The Anti-Faustian Ethos of *Die Blechtrommel.*" *Journal of European Studies* 9:174–84.

Parry, Idris. 1967. "Aspects of Günter Grass's Narrative Technique." *Forum for Modern Language Studies* 3:99–114.

Paver, Chloe E. M. 1997. "Lois Lane, Donald Duck, and Joan Baez: Popular Culture and Protest Culture in Günter Grass's *örtlich betäubt*." *German Life and Letters* 50:53–64.

———. 1999. "Günter Grass: örtlich betäubt." In Paver, *Narrative and Fantasy: A Study of Novels by Johnson, Frisch, Wolf, Becker, and Grass*. Oxford: Clarendon P, 164–95.

———. 2000. "Jesus in the Market Place: Ethical Capitalism in Günter Grass's *Unkenrufe*." In *Literature, Markets and Media in Germany and Austria Today*, ed. Arthur Williams, Stuart Parkes, and Julian Preece. Oxford: Lang, 71–83.

Pelster, Theodor. 1999. *Günter Grass*. Stuttgart: Reclam.

———. 2004. *Günter Grass: "Im Krebsgang."* Stuttgart: Reclam.

Perels, Christoph. 1978. "Über den *Butt*." In H. L. Arnold 1963, 5th, rev. ed. 1978, 88–90.

Petz, Beatrice. 2000. "Günter Grass since the Wende: German and International." In *German-Language Literature Today: International and Popular?* Ed. Arthur Williams, Stuart Parkes, and Julian Preece. Oxford: Lang, 67–84.

Petzold, Klaus, ed. 2003. *Günter Grass: Simmen aus dem Leseland*. Leipzig: Militzke.

Pflanz, Elisabeth. 1976. *Sexualität und Sexualideologie des Ich-Erzählers in Günter Grass' Roman "Die Blechtrommel."* Munich: UNI-Druck.

Phelan, Anthony. 1990. "Rabelais's Sister: Food, Writing, and Power." In Brady, McFarland, and White 1990, 133–52.

Pickar, Gertrud Bauer. 1970. "The Aspect of Colour in Günter Grass's *Katz und Maus*." *German Life and Letters* 23:304–9.

———. 1971. "Intentional Ambiguity in Günter Grass' *Katz und Maus*." *Orbis Litterarum* 26:232–45.

———. 1977. "Günter Grass's *örtlich betäubt*: The Fiction of Fact and Fantasy." *Germanic Review* 52:289–303.

———, ed. 1982. *Adventures of a Founder: Critical Essays on Günter Grass' "Der Butt."* Munich: Fink, 1982.

———. 1983. "The Prismatic Narrator: Postulate and Practice." In Mews 1983a, 55–74.

———. 1985. "Spielfreiheit und Selbstbefangenheit — Das Porträt eines Versagers." In Durzak 1985a, 96–114.

———. 1989. "Starusch im Felde mit den Frauen: Zum Frauenbild in Grass' *örtlich betäubt*." *Colloquia Germanica* 22:260–82.

Pietsch, Timm Niklas. 2006. *"Wer hört noch zu?" Günter Grass als politischer Redner und Essayist.* Essen: Klartext.

Pinfold, Debbie. 2001. *The Child's View of the Third Reich in German Literature.* Oxford: Clarendon P.

Plagwitz, Frank F. 1996. "Die Crux des Heldentums: Zur Deutung des Ritterkreuzes in Günter Grass' *Katz und Maus*." *Seminar* 32:1–14.

Plard, Henri. 1963. "Verteidigung der *Blechtrommel*." In H. L. Arnold 1963, 1–8. Repr. as "Über die *Blechtrommel*" in Arnold 4th, rev. ed. 1971, 27–37. Repr. in Arnold 5th, rev. ed. 1978, 40–50.

Platen, Edgar. 2000. "Kein 'Danach' und kein 'Anderswo': Literatur mit Auschwitz; Bemerkungen zur ethischen Dimension literarischen Erinnerns und Darstellens (am Beispiel von Günter Grass' *Ein weites Feld*)." In *Erinnerte und erfundene Erfahrung: Zur Darstellung von Zeitgeschichte in deutschsprachiger Gegenwartsliteratur,* ed. Edgar Platen. Munich: Iudicium, 130–45.

Porterfield, Waldon R. 1970. "Psychedelic Novocain." Milwaukee, WI *Journal* (29 Mar.). Repr. in White 1981 (excerpt), 141.

Pott, Hans-Georg, ed. 1986a. *Literatur und Provinz: Das Konzept 'Heimat' in der neueren deutschen Literatur.* Paderborn: Schöningh.

———. 1986b. "Der 'neue Heimatroman'? Zum Konzept Heimat in der neueren Literatur." In Pott 1986a, 7–21.

Prawer, Sigbert. 1981. "Rising from the Rubble." *Times Literary Supplement* (26 Jun.), 717. Repr. in Füssel 1999, 119–23.

———. 1985. "The Death of Sigismund Markus. The Jews of Danzig in the Fiction of Günter Grass." In *Danzig; Between East and West: Aspects of Modern Jewish History.* Cambridge, MA: Harvard UP, 95–108.

Preece, Julian. 1990. "Literature and the End of the World: Günter Grass's *Die Rättin*." In *Literature on the Threshold: The German Novel in the 1980s,* ed. Arthur Williams, Stuart Parkes, and Roland Smith. New York: Berg, 321–34.

———. 1994. "'Die Schlacht, die schon dagewesen, die immer wieder kommt': Barocke Geschichte im *Butt* von Günter Grass." *Simpliciana: Schriften der Grimmelshausen-Gesellschaft* 16:311–22.

———. 2000a. "Günter Grass, His Jews and Their Critics: From Klüger and Gilman to Sebald and Prawer." In *German Monitor: Jews in German Literature since 1945,* ed. Pól O'Dochartaigh. Amsterdam: Rodopi, 609–24.

———. 2000b. "Seven Theses on 'Der Fall Fonty.'" In *Cultural Perspectives on Division and Unity in East and West 1949/1989,* ed. Clare Flanagan and Stuart Taberner. Amsterdam: Rodopi, 215–30.

———. 2001a. "Ein allzu deutscher Roman?" In Quéval 2001a, 211–26.

———. 2001b. *The Life and Work of Günter Grass: Literature, History, Politics.* Houndmills, Basingstoke, Hampshire, UK: Palgrave.

Preisendörfer, Bruno. 1999. "Im Füllhorn der Anekdoten." *Der Tagesspiegel* (8 Aug.).

Prescott, Orville. 1963. "Books of the Times." *New York Times* (8 Feb.). Repr. in White 1981 (excerpt), 4.

Prescott, Peter S. 1992. "Return of the Natives." *Los Angeles Times* (29 Nov.), Book Reviews 2.

Prochnik, Peter. 1990. "Male and Female Violence in *Der Butt.*" In Brady, McFarland, and White 1990, 153–67.

Pusch, Louise. 1988. "Die Kätzin, die Rättin und die Feminismaus." *Women in German Yearbook* 4:15–16. Repr. in Pusch, *Alle Menschen werden Schwestern.* Frankfurt am Main: Suhrkamp, 203–4.

Quéval, Marie-Hélène, ed. 2001a. *Lectures d'une oeuvre. "Ein weites Feld." Günter Grass.* Paris: Editions du temps.

———. 2001b. "Avant-propos." In Quéval 2001a, 7–10.

Quinn, John S. 1963. "Review." *Best Sellers* (15 Aug.). Repr. in White 1981 (excerpt), 48.

Raab, Bob. 1970. "Review." San Rafael, CA *Independent Journal* (4 Apr.). Repr. in White 1981 (excerpt), 143.

Raddatz, Fritz J. 1973. "Der Weltgeist als berittene Schnecke: Günter Grass' kleine Hoffnung — aus großer Melancholie." In Jurgensen 1973, 191–97.

———. 1977a. "'Heute lüge ich lieber gedruckt.' ZEIT-Gespräch über den 'Butt' mit Günter Grass." *Die Zeit* (12 Aug.), 29–30.

———. 1977b. "'Wirklich bin ich nur in meinen Geschichten.' *Der Butt* von Günter Grass — Erste Annäherung." *Merkur* 31:892–901. Repr. in Raddatz 2002b. 43–63.

———. 1979. "Günter Grass, die Wörter und der Dreißigjährige Krieg: Kein Treffen in Telgte." *Die Zeit* (30 Mar.): 57. Repr. in Füssel 1999, 110–11. Repr. in Raddatz 2002a, 64–68.

———. 1980. "Der neue Grass: Heitere Groteske, ernster Nonsense." *Die Zeit* (16 May).

———. 1985. "In Zukunft nur Ratten noch." *Die Zeit* (29 Nov.): 105–6. Repr. in Raddatz 2002a, 69–72.

———. 1988. "Literatur und Lüge." *Natur: Das Umweltmagazin* (Oct.): 50–51. Repr. in Raddatz 2002a, 73–81.

———. 2002a. *Günter Grass: Unerbittliche Freunde; ein Kritiker, ein Autor.* Zurich: Arche.

———. 2002b. "*Im Krebsgang.* Gespräch zwischen Fritz J. Raddatz und Mike Albath." In Raddatz 2002a, 123–34.

———. 2006. "'Ich habe mich verführen lassen.'" *Die Zeit* (17 Aug.): 41–42. Repr. in Gorzny 2006, 135–36. Repr. in Kölbel 2007b, 304–6.

Raddatz, Fritz J., and Ulrich Greiner. 1999. "Grass: Eine Kontroverse über das Buch *Mein Jahrhundert.*" *Die Zeit* (15 Jul.): 47. Raddatz's contribution repr. in Raddatz 2002a, 82–85.

Radisch, Iris. 1992. "Der Tod und ein Meister aus Danzig." *Die Zeit* (8 May), Literatur 1–2.

———. 1995. "Die Bitterfelder Sackgasse." *Die Zeit* (25 Aug.). Repr. in Oberhammer and Ostermann 1995, 152–55. Repr. in Negt 1996b, 111–14.

Rahner, Thomas. 2005. *Die Blechtrommel, Günter Grass: Inhalt, Hintergrund, Interpretation.* Munich: Mentor.

Ratte, Günter. 1986. *Der Grass.* Frankfurt am Main: Eichborn.

Rebhandl, Bert. 2005. "Unterm Rock: Die *Unkenrufe* im Kino." *Frankfurter Allgemeine Zeitung* (24 Sept.): 37.

Reddick, John. 1971. "Eine epische Trilogie des Leidens? *Die Blechtrommel. Katz und Maus. Hundejahre.*" In H. L. Arnold 1963, 4th, rev. ed. 1971, 38–51. Repr. in Arnold, 5th, rev. ed. 1978, 60–73.

———. 1972. "Action and Impotence: Günter Grass' *örtlich betäubt.*" *Modern Language Review* 67:563–78.

———. 1974. "Vom Pferdekopf zur Schnecke: Die Prosawerke von Günter Grass zwischen Beinahe-Verzweiflung und zweifelnder Hoffnung." In *Positionen des deutschen Romans der 60er Jahre,* ed. Heinz Ludwig Arnold and Theo Buck. Munich: Beck, 39–54.

———. 1975. *The "Danzig Trilogy" of Günter Grass.* New York: Harcourt.

———. 1981. "Vergangenheit und Gegenwart in Günter Grass' *Die Blechtrommel.*" In *"Die Mühen der Ebenen": Kontinuität und Wandel in der deutschen Literatur und Gesellschaft 1945–1949,* ed. Bernd Hüppauf. Heidelberg: Winter, 373–97.

———. 1983. "Günter Grass's *Der Butt* and the 'Vatertag' Chapter." *Oxford German Studies* 14:143–58.

———-. 1999. "Still Banging the Tin Drum German Giant." *The Independent Online* (3 Oct.).

Reed, Donna K. 1985. *The Novel and the Nazi Past.* New York: Lang.

Reed, John. 1973. "The Anatomy of Progress." *Christian Science Monitor* (26 Sept.): 11.

Reich-Ranicki, Marcel. 1958. "Eine Diktatur, die wir befürworten." *Die Kultur* (15 Nov.).

———. 1960. "Auf gut Glück getrommelt." *Die Zeit* (1 Jan.). Repr. in Görtz 1984a, 116–21. Repr. in Reich-Ranicki 1992a, 13–18. Repr. in Reich-Ranicki 2003, 13–18.

———. 1963a. "Selbstkritik eines Kritikers." Broadcast Westdeutscher Rundfunk (22 May). Repr. in Görtz 1984a, 151–57. Repr. as "Selbstkritik des *Blechtrommel*-Kritikers" in Reich-Ranicki 1992a, 21–28. Repr. in Reich-Ranicki 2003, 19–26.

———. 1963b "Unser grimmiger Idylliker." In Reich-Ranicki, *Deutsche Literatur in Ost und West.* Munich: Piper, 216–50. Repr. in Reich-Ranicki 1992a, 28–48. Repr. in Reich-Ranicki 2003, 27–44.

———. 1967. "Günter Grass: *Hundejahre.*" In Reich-Ranicki, *Literatur der kleinen Schritte.* Munich: Piper, 22–33. Repr. as "Bilderbogen mit Marionetten und Vogelscheuchen." In Jurgensen 1973, 21–30. Repr. in Reich-Ranicki 1992a, 51–65. Repr. in Reich-Ranicki 2003, 45–65.

———. 1969. "Eine müde Heldensoße." *Die Zeit* (29 August 1969): 16. Repr. in Reich-Ranicki, *Lauter Verrisse.* Munich: Piper, 1970, 84–92. Repr. in Reich-Ranicki, *Entgegnung: Zur Literatur der siebziger Jahre.* Stuttgart: Deutsche Verlags-Anstalt, 1979, 173–81. New, enl. ed. 1981, 173–81. Repr. in Reich-Ranicki 1992a, 91–101. Repr. in Reich-Ranicki 2003, 77–87.

———. 1977. "Von im und synen Fruen." *Frankfurter Allgemeine Zeitung* (13 Aug.). Repr. in Reich-Ranicki 1992a. 105–17. Repr. in Reich-Ranicki 2003, 89–101.

———. 1979. "Gruppe 1647." *Frankfurter Allgemeine Zeitung* (31 Mar.). Repr. in Reich-Ranicki, *Entgegnung: Zur deutschen Literatur der siebziger Jahre.* Stuttgart: Deutsche Verlags-Anstalt, 1981, 209–17. Repr. in Reich-Ranicki 1992a, 119–32. Repr in Füssel 1999 (excerpt), 91–101. Repr. in Reich-Ranicki 2003, 77–87.

———. 1986. "Ein katastrophales Buch." *Frankfurter Allgemeine Zeitung* (10 May). Repr. in Reich-Ranicki 1992a, 131–42. Repr. in Reich-Ranicki 2003, 113–22.

———. 1992a. *Günter Grass: Aufsätze.* Zurich: Ammann. [Enl. ed.] as *Unser Grass.* Munich: Deutsche Verlags-Anstalt, 2003.

———. 1992b. "Wie konnte das passieren?" *Der Spiegel* (4 May): 254–63. Repr. in Reich-Ranicki 1992a as "Der Einfaltspinsel in der Rumpelkammer," 145–53. Repr. in Reich-Ranicki 2003, 133–41.

———. 1995. ". . . und es muß gesagt werden." *Der Spiegel* (21 Aug.): 162–69. Repr. in Reich-Ranicki 2003, 151–65.

Reinhold, Ursula. 1986. "Günter Grass: *Die Blechtrommel* — eine literarische Provokation." *Weimarer Beiträge* 32:1667–86.

———. 2000. "Die Stadt Berlin in Romanen der 90er Jahre." In *Mentalitätswandel in der deutschen Literatur zur Einheit (1990–2000),* ed. Volker Wehdeking. Berlin: Schmidt, 57–68.

Rempe-Thiemann, Norbert. 1992. *Günter Grass und seine Erzählweise: Zum Verhältnis von Mythos und literarischer Struktur.* Bochum: Brockmeyer.

Reynolds, Daniel. 2003. "Blinded by the Enlightenment: Günter Grass in Calcutta." *German Life and Letters* 56:244–60.

Rhodes, Richard. 1963. "But Kafka Was Convincing." Kansas City, MO *Star* (11 Aug.). Repr. in White 1981 (excerpt), 46–47.

Richard, Lionel, ed. 1999. "Günter Grass." *Magazine Littéraire* 381 (Nov.).

Richter, David H. 1982. "The Problem: No Problems." *Commonweal* (16 Jul.): 409–10.

Richter, Frank-Raymund. 1977. *Die zerschlagene Wirklichkeit: Überlegungen zur Form der "Danzig-Trilogie" von Günter Grass.* Bonn: Bouvier.

———. 1979. *Günter Grass: Die Vergangenheitsbewältigung in der "Danzig-Trilogie."* Bonn: Bouvier.

Richter, Hans Werner. 1986. *Im Etablissement der Schmetterlinge: Einundzwanzig Portraits der Gruppe 47.* Munich: Hanser.

Richter, Sabine. 2004. "Das Kaleidoskop des Günter Grass: Jüdische Karikaturen aus der Kaschubei." In Kątny, 47–54.

Rickels, Laurence A. 1985–86. "*Die Blechtrommel* zwischen Schelmen- und Bildungsroman." In *Der moderne deutsche Schelmenroman: Interpretationen,* ed. Gerhart Hoffmeister. *Amsterdamer Beiträge zur neueren Germanistik* 20, 109–32.

Riding, Alan. 2003. "Günter Grass Worries about the Effects of War, Then and Now." *New York Times* (8 Apr.).

Rifkind, Donna. 1992. "Reunion in the City of the Dead." *Washington Post* (8 Nov.): X6.

Rimmon-Kenan, Shlomith. 1987. "Narration as Repetition: The Case of *Cat and Mouse.*" In *Discourse in Psychoanalysis and Literature,* ed. Shlomith Rimmon-Kenan. London: Methuen, 176–87.

Ritter, Alexander. 1977. *Günter Grass: "Katz und Maus."* Stuttgart: Reclam. Enl. ed. 2001.

Roberts, David. 1972. "Tom Thumb and the Imitation of Christ: Towards a Psycho-Mythological Interpretation of the 'Hero' Oskar and His Symbolic Function." In *Proceedings and Papers of the Fourteenth Congress of the Australasian Universities Language and Literature Association Held 19–26 January 1972 at the University of Otago, Dunedin, New Zealand,* ed. K. I. D. Maslen. Dunedin: AULLA, 160–74. Repr. as "Aspects of Psychology and Mythology in *Die Blechtrommel.*" In Jurgensen 1973, 45–74.

———. 1976. "The Cult of the Hero: An Interpretation of *Katz und Maus.*" *German Life and Letters* 29:307–22.

Roehm, Klaus-Jürgen. 1992. *Polyphonie und Improvisation: Zur offenen Form in Günter Grass' "Die Rättin."* Frankfurt am Main: Lang.

Rohlfs, Jochen W. 1982. "Chaos or Order? Günter Grass's *Kopfgeburten.*" *Modern Language Review* 77:886–93.

Rollfinke, Dieter, and Jacqueline Rollfinke. 1986. "The Excremental Wheel of Fortune." In D. and J. Rollfinke, *The Call of Human Nature: The Role of Scatology in Modern German Literature.* Amherst: U of Massachusetts P, 1986, 160–90.

Rothenberg, Jürgen. 1975. "Anpassung oder Widerstand? Über den 'Blechtrommler' Günter Grass und sein Verhältnis zur Zeitgeschichte." *Germanisch-Romanische Monatsschrift* 25:176–98.

———. 1976a. *Günter Grass: Das Chaos in verbesserter Ausführung: Zeitgeschichte als Thema und Aufgabe des Prosawerks.* Heidelberg: Winter.

———. 1976b. "Großes 'Nein' und kleines 'ja': *Aus dem Tagebuch einer Schnecke.*" In Geißler 1976, 136–53.

Rovit, Earl. 1965. "The Holy Ghost and the Dog." *American Scholar* 34:676–84.

Rüdiger, Bernhardt. 2001. *Erläuterungen zu Günter Grass, "Die Blechtrommel."* Hollfeld/Obfr.: Bange.

Rühle, Arnd. 1979. "Was macht die Gruppe 47 im Dreißigjährigen Krieg?" *Münchner Merkur* (7/8 Apr.). Repr. in Füssel 1999, 108–9.

Ruhleder, Karl H. 1966. "A Pattern of Messianic Thought in Günter Grass' *Cat and Mouse.*" *German Quarterly* 39:599–612.

Rushdie, Salman. 1981. "Günter Grass. *The Meeting at Telgte.*" In Rushdie 1991. 273–75.

———. 1985. "Salman Rushdie on Günter Grass." *Granta* 15:179–85. Repr. as "Introduction" in Grass, *On Writing and Politics, 1967–1983.* ix–xv. Repr. in Rushdie, *Imaginary Homelands: Essays and Criticism, 1981–1991.* London: Granta/Viking, 1991, 276–81.

Russell, Peter. 1979/80. "Floundering on Feminism: The Meaning of Günter Grass's *Der Butt.*" *German Life and Letters* 33:245–56.

Ryan, Judith. 1977. "Resistance and Resignation: A Re-Interpretation of Günter Grass' *Katz und Maus.*" *Germanic Review* 52:148–65.

———. 1981. "'Into the Orwell Decade': Günter Grass's Dystopian Trilogy." *World Literature Today* 55:564–67. Repr. in O'Neill 1987c, 189–96.

———. 1983a. "Beyond *The Flounder:* Narrative Dialectic in *The Meeting at Telgte.*" In Mews 1983a, 39–53.

———. 1983b."The Revocation of Melancholy: Günter Grass' *The Tin Drum.*" In Ryan, *The Uncompleted Past: Postwar German Novels and the Third Reich.* Detroit, MI: Wayne State UP, 56–69, 170–71.

———. 1995. "The Office of the Red, Black, and Gold." *German Politics and Society* 13 (3): 43–48.

Sandford, John. 1990. "Men, Women, and the 'Third Way.'" In Brady, McFarland, and White 1990, 169–86.

Sandmeyer, Peter, and Gerda Marie Schönfeld. "'Eine Katastrophe, aber kein Verbrechen': Interview mit Günter Grass." *Der Stern* (14 Feb.): 181–86.

Sbarra, Stefania. 2005. "Die Entkonkretisierung der Zeitgeschichte im Familienalbum: Günter Grass' *Im Krebsgang.*" *Weimarer Beiträge* 51:376–90.

Schäble, Günter. 1986. "Vorbereitungen zur Weltbaisse." *Der Spiegel* (24 Feb.): 255–58.

Schade, Richard Erich. 1982. "Poet and Artist — Iconography in Grass' *Treffen in Telgte.*" *German Quarterly* 55:200–211. Repr. in Füssel 1999 (excerpt), 133–36.

———. 2004. "Günter Grass's *Mein Jahrhundert:* Histories, Paintings, and Performance." *Monatshefte* 96:409–21.

Schädlich, Hans-Joachim. 1998. "Tallhover — ein weites Feld: Autobiographische Notiz." In *Spuren gehen . . ." Festschrift für Helmut Koopmann,* ed. Andrea Bartl, Jürgen Eder, Harry Fröhlich, Klaus-Dieter Post, and Ursula Regener. Tübingen: Niemeyer, 41–50. Repr. in Quéval 2001a, 11–22.

Schaller, Thomas. 1988. *Die Rezeption von Heinrich Böll und Günter Grass in den U.S.A.: Böll und Grass im Spiegel der Unterrichtspraxis an höheren amerikanischen Bildungsinstitutionen.* Frankfurt am Main: Lang.

Scherf, Rainer. 1987. "Günter Grass: *Die Rättin* und der Tod der Literatur." *Wirkendes Wort* 37:382–98.

———. 1995. "*Katz und Maus" von Günter Grass: Literarische Ironie nach Auschwitz und der unausgesprochene Appell zu politischem Engagement.* Marburg: Tectum.

———. 2000. *Das Herz der Blechtrommel und andere Aufsätze zum Werk von Günter Grass.* Marburg: Tectum.

———. 2002. "Grundlagen für eine Interpretation von *Ein weites Feld.*" In Wellnitz 2002a, 129–50.

Scherman, David E. 1965. "His World of Worms, Eels and A Mad Dwarf." *Life* (4 Jun.): 56.

Scheub, Ute. 2006. *Das falsche Leben: Eine Vatersuche.* Munich: Piper.

Schilling, Klaus von. 2002. *Schuldmotoren: Artistisches Erzählen in Günter Grass' "Danziger Trilogie."* Bielefeld: Aisthesis.

Schirrmacher, Frank. 1990. "Abschied von der Literatur der Bundesrepublik." *Frankfurter Allgemeine Zeitung* (2–3 Oct.).

———. 1992. "Das Danziger Versöhnungswerk." *Frankfurter Allgemeine Zeitung* (6 May).

———. 2006. "Das Geständnis." *Frankfurter Allgemeine Zeitung* (12 Aug.): 1. Repr. in Gorzny 2006, 17. Repr. in Kölbel 2007b, 27–36.

Schirrmacher, Frank, and Hubert Spiegel. 2006. "Warum ich nach sechzig Jahren mein Schweigen breche: Eine deutsche Jugend; Günter Grass spricht zum ersten Mal über sein Erinnerungsbuch und seine Mitgliedschaft in der Waffen-SS." *Frankfurter Allgemeine Zeitung* (12 Aug.), 1. Repr. in Gorzny 2006, 15–16. Repr. in Kölbel 2007b, 26–27.

Schlant, Ernestine. 1999. *The Language of Silence: West German Literature and the Holocaust.* New York: Routledge.

Schlöndorff, Volker, and Günter Grass. 1979. *Die Blechtrommel als Film.* Frankfurt am Main: Zweitausendeins.

Schloz, Günther. 1972. "Schnecken, Zweifel und Espede." *Deutsche Zeitung/ Christ und Welt* (8 Sept.), 11.

Schmidt, Josef. 1985. "Parodistisches Schreiben und Utopie in *Das Treffen in Telgte.*" In Durzak 1985a, 142–54.

Schmidt, Thomas E. 2002. "Ostpreußischer Totentanz." *Die Zeit* (14 Feb.).

Schmitt, Evelyne. 2001. "Temps et littérature dans *Ein weites Feld.*" In Lartillot 2001a, 85–93.

Schneider, Irmela. 1975. *Kritische Rezeption: Die "Blechtrommmel" als Modell.* Frankfurt am Main: Lang.

Schneider, Peter. 2002. "Alles reimt sich auf Faschist." *Frankfurter Allgemeine Zeitung* (26 Mar.).

Schneider, Rolf. 1979. "Eine barocke Gruppe 47." *Der Spiegel* (2 Apr.): 217–18. Repr. in Füssel 1999, 111–13.

———. 1995. "Vom Vergnügen, Grass zu lesen." *Berliner Zeitung* (1 Sept.), 4. Repr. in Negt 1996b, 278.

———. 2002. "Der beste Grass seit Jahren." *Die Welt* (5 Feb.).

Schneider, Ronald. 1981. "Ästhetische Opposition gegen die 'Restaurationsgesellschaft': Günter Grass' *Die Blechtrommel* und Martin Walsers *Halbzeit* als Paradigmen westdeutscher Nachkriegsliteratur." *Der Deutschunterricht* 33 (3): 82–95.

Schnell, Josef. 1975. "Irritation und Wirklichkeitserfahrung: Die Funktion des Erzählens in Günter Grass' *Die Blechtrommel*." *Der Deutschunterricht* 27 (3): 33–43.

Scholz, Hans. 1979. "'Für die teutsche Poeterey': Günter Grass' *Treffen in Telgte*." *Der Tagesspiegel* (6 May): 51. Repr. in Füssel 1999, 115–19.

Schönau, Walter. 1974. "Zur Wirkung der *Blechtrommel* von Günter Grass." *Psyche* 28 (7): 573–99.

Schott, Webster. 1970. "The Dog Is Not for Burning." *Life* (15 Mar.). Repr. in White 1981 (excerpt), 137.

Schreiber, Jürgen. 1986. "Der Herr der Ratte." *Natur: Das Umweltmagazin* (Apr.): 38–45.

Schreiber, Mathias. 1992. "'Lust an der Vernichtung.'" *Der Spiegel* (18 May): 296–97.

Schröder, Susanne. 1986. *Erzählerfiguren und Erzählperspektive in Günter Grass' "Danziger Trilogie."* Frankfurt am Main: Lang.

Schütt, Hans-Dieter. 1999. "'Ich, ausgetauscht gegen mich, bin Jahr für Jahr dabeigewesen.'" *Neues Deutschland* (10/11 Jul.): 16.

Schütte, Wolfram. 1972. "Schneckenwindungen, behutsam nachgegangen." *Frankfurter Rundschau* (26 Aug.).

———. 1979. "Unter einem Dach: *Das Treffen in Telgte*." *Frankfurter Rundschau* (31 Mar.). Repr. in Görtz 1984b, 141–45.

———. 1980. "Egotrip oder Der alltägliche Sisyphus." *Frankfurter Rundschau* (21 Jun.).

———. 1986. "Futsch midde Minscher (oder: Alles für die Katz)." *Frankfurter Rundschau* (1 Mar.).

———. 1995. "'Wie aus der Zeit gefallen: Zwei alte Männer.'" *Frankfurter Rundschau* (26 Aug.). Repr. in Neg.

Schulz, Andrej. 1997. *Chancen tätiger Resignation: Zur "melancholischen Struktur" in Günter Grass' Roman "Die Rättin."* Bern: Lang.

Schumann, Willy. 1966. "Die Wiederkehr der Schelme." *PMLA* 81:467–74.

Schurr, Monika Elisa. 2001. "Ein Doppelportrait — Symbiotische Beziehungen in Grass' *Hundejahre* und *Ein weites Feld*." In Queval 2001a, 243–52.

Schwab-Felisch, Hans. 1958. "Talente und Stilfragen bei der 'Gruppe 47.'" *Frankfurter Allgemeine Zeitung* (7 Nov.). Repr. in Görtz 1984a, 29–34.

———. 1972. "Melancholische Variationen: Zu Günter Grass' *Aus dem Tagebuch einer Schnecke.*" *Merkur* 26:1025–30.

Schwan, Werner. 1990. *"Ich bin doch kein Unmensch"; Kriegs- und Nachkriegszeit im deutschen Roman: Grass, "Blechtrommel" — Lenz, "Deutschstunde" — Böll, "Gruppenbild mit Dame" — Meckel, "Suchbild."* Freiburg im Breisgau: Rombach.

———. 1996. "Günter Grass, 'Ein weites Feld': mit Neugier und Geduld erkundet." *Poetica* 28:432–64.

Schwarz, Wilhelm Johannes. 1969. *Der Erzähler Günter Grass.* Bern: Francke. 2nd, enl. ed., 1971.

Schweckendiek, Adolf. 1970. "Joachim Mahlke in Günter Grass' *Katz und Maus.*" In Schweckendiek, *Könnt ich Magie von meinem Pfad entfernen: Neurosenkundliche Studien an Gestalten der Dichtung.* Leimen: Marx, 42–47.

Sebald, Winfried Georg. 1983. "Konstruktionen der Trauer: Zu Günter Grass, *Tagebuch einer Schnecke* und Wolfgang Hildesheimer, *Tynset.*" *Der Deutschunterricht* 35.5 (Oct.): 32–46.

Segebrecht, Wulf. 2004. "Günter Grass' Novelle *Im Krebsgang* oder: Aus der Geschichte lernen." In Kątny 2004, 23–34.

Seibt, Gustav. 1995. "Die Uhr schlägt, das Käuzchen ruft." *Frankfurter Allgemeine Zeitung* (19 Aug.). Repr. in Oberhammer and Ostermann 1995, 67–69. Repr. in Negt 1996b, 71–75.

Seligmann, Rafael. 2006. "The Pope Chose the Truth." *Atlantic Times* (Sept.): 5.

Sera, Manfred. 1977. "Der Erzähler als Verfolger und Verfolgter in der Novelle *Katz und Maus* von Günter Grass." *Zeitschrift für deutsche Philologie* 94:586–604.

Serrier, Thomas. 2001. "D'une unification à l'autre: comment sortir de la Nation? Toute une histoire de Günter Grass." In Quéval 2001a, 177–89.

Shafi, Monika. 1993. "'Dir hat es die Sprache verschlagen': Günter Grass' *Zunge zeigen* als postmoderner Reisebericht." *German Quarterly* 66:339–49.

———. 1997. "Gazing at India: Representations of Alterity in Travelogues by Ingeborg Drewitz, Günter Grass, and Hubert Fichte." *German Quarterly* 70:39–56. Repr. in Shafi, *Balancing Acts: Intercultural Encounters in Contemporary German and Austrian Literature.* Tübingen: Stauffenburg, 2001, 1–38.

———. 2002. "'*Gezz will ich ma erzähln*': Narrative and History in Günter Grass's *Mein Jahrhundert.*" *Gegenwartsliteratur* 1:39–62.

———. 2006. "*Talkin' 'Bout My Generation:* Memories of 1968 in Recent German Novels." *German Life and Letters* 59 (2): 201–216. **Cf.**

Sheehan, James. 2000. "The German Question." *New York Times Book Review* (5 Nov.).

Sheppard, R. Z. 1978. "A Turbot de Force." *Time* (23 Oct.): 104–5.

———. 1989. "The Message Is the Message: *A Prayer for Owen Meany*." *Time* (3 Apr.): 80.

Siehr, Karl-Heinz. 1997. "'Abwickeln' — *Ein weites Feld* — Der Fall Fonty: Notizen aus linguistischer Sicht." In *Sprachsystem-Text-Stil: Festschrift für Georg Michel und Gunter Starke zum 70. Geburtstag*, ed. Christine Kessler and Karl Ernst Sommerfeldt. Frankfurt am Main: Lang, 275–95.

Siemes, Christof. 2005a. "Bis die Augen überlaufen." *Die Zeit* (3 Feb.).

———. 2005b. "'Was ich nicht ausstehen kann, sind Genies': Gespräch mit Günter Grass." *Zeit.de* (1 Dec. 2005). Accessed 1 Dec. 2005.

Silberman, Marc. 1985. "Schreiben als öffentliche Angelegenheit: Lesestrategien des Romans *Hundejahre*." In Durzak 1985a, 80–95.

Simon, John. 1963. "The Drummer of Danzig." *Partisan Review* 30 (Fall): 446–53. Repr. in O'Neill 1987c, 21–27.

———. 1965. "And Man Created Dog." *Book World* (23 May): 12–13. Repr. in White 1981 (excerpt), 70–71.

———. 1978. "What's Cooking?" *Saturday Review* (11 Nov.): 57–59.

———. 1999. "Sturm und Drang." *Washington Post* (19 Dec.), 2–3.

Simon, Sven. 1977. "A Literary Interlude with Grass." *Christian Science Monitor* (22 Sept.).

Simonsen, Sofus. 1979. "*The Flounder*." *Magill's Literary Annual; Books of 1978*. Englewood Cliffs, NJ: Salem P, 226–30.

Slaymaker, William. 1981. "Who Cooks, Winds Up: The Dilemma of Freedom in Grass' *Die Blechtrommel* and *Hundejahre*." *Colloquia Germanica* 14: 48–68.

Šliažas, Rimvydas. 1973. "Elements of Old Prussian Mythology in Günter Grass' *Dog Years*." *Lituanus: Baltic States Quarterly of Arts and Sciences* 19 (1): 39–48.

Smith, Lyle H., Jr. 1978. "Volk, Jew, and Devil: Ironic Inversion in Günter Grass's *Dog Years*." *Studies in Twentieth Century Literature* 3:85–96.

Solères, Isabelle. 2001a. "Chronologie succincte — 1819–1898." In Lartillot 2001a, 43–48.

———. 2001b. "Theodore Fontane et l'unification allemande." In Lartillot 2001a, 21–42.

Sosnoski, M. K. 1971. "Oskar's Hungry Witch." *Modern Fiction Studies* 17 (3): 61–77.

Spaethling, Robert H. 1970. "Günter Grass: *Cat and Mouse.*" *Monatshefte* 62:141–53.

Speicher, Stephan. 2005. "Lurchs Abenteuer: *Unkenrufe,* ein Film von Robert Glinski nach Grass." *Berliner Zeitung* (22 Sept.).

Speirs, Ronald. 1990. "The Dualistic Unity of *Der Butt.*" In Brady, McFarland, and White 1990, 11–32.

Spender, Stephen. 1963. "Beneath the Adam's Apple, the Tin Drum Beats On." *New York Times Book Review* (11 Aug.): 5. Repr. in White 1981 (excerpt), 57.

———. 1965. "Scarecrows and Swastika." *New York Times Book Review* (23 May): 1, 32. Repr. in White 1981 (excerpt), 71–72.

———. 1981. "Elbe Swans and Other Poets." *New York Review of Books* (11 Jun.): 35–36. Repr. in O'Neill 1987c, 56–60.

Spiegel, Hubert. 2006. "Ist die schwarze Köchin da?" *Frankfurter Allgemeine Zeitung* (26 Aug.). Repr. in Gorzny 2006, 151–52. Repr. in Kölbel 2007b, 308–10.

Spreckelsen, Wolfgang. 2001. *Günter Grass: "Katz und Maus."* Stuttgart: Reclam.

Staiber, Maryse. 2001a. "Diese ewigen Spaziergänge und seine endlosen Dialoge." In Quéval 2001a, 227–42.

———. 2001b. "Fontys Geburtstagsfeier bei Mac Donald's: Zu einer Episode in *Ein weites Feld.*" In Lartillot 2001a, 115–26.

———. 2002. "'Wir vom Archiv nannten ihn Fonty': Zu Günter Grass, *Ein weites Feld.*" In Wellnitz 2002a, 239–56.

Stallbaum, Klaus. 1989. *Kunst und Künstlerexistenz im Frühwerk von Günter Grass.* Cologne: Lingen.

Steiner, George. 1964. "The Nerve of Günter Grass." *Commentary* 37 (May): 77–80. Repr. as "A Note on Günter Grass." In Steiner, *Language and Silence.* New York: Atheneum, 1967, 110–17. Repr. in O'Neill 1987c, 30–36.

Steinfeld, Thomas. 2006. "Grass ist Deutschland." *Süddeutsche Zeitung* (19 Aug.). Repr. in Gorzny 2006, 81–82. Repr. in Kölbel, 2007b, 186–87.

Steinig, Swenta. 1992. "Günter Grass: *Das Treffen in Telgte.*" In *Erzählen, Erinnern: Deutsche Prosa der Gegenwart,* ed. Herbert Kaiser and Gerhard Kopf. Frankfurt am Main: Diesterweg, 188–210.

Stern, Guy. 1982. "*Der Butt* as an Experiment in the Structure of the Novel." In Pickar 1982, 51–55.

Steuer, Pernilla Rosell. 2004. *— ein allzu weites Feld? — Zu Übersetzungstheorie und Übersetzungspraxis anhand der Kulturspezifika in fünf Übersetzungen des Romans "Ein weites Feld" von Günter Grass.* Stockholm: Almqvist & Wiksell.

Stolz, Dieter. 1994. *Vom privaten Motivkomplex zum poetischen Weltentwurf: Konstanten und Entwicklungen im literarischen Werk von Günter Grass (1956–1986).* Würzburg: Königshausen & Neumann.

———. 1997. "Nomen est omen: *Ein weites Feld* von Günter Grass." *Zeitschrift für Germanistik* 7:321–35.

———. 1998 "Nomen est omen: *Ein weites Feld* by Günter Grass." Translation of Stolz 1997 by Julian Preece. In *"Whose Story?" Continuities in Contemporary German-Language Literature,* ed. Arthur Williams, Stuart Parkes, and Julian Preece. Bern: Lang, 1998, 149–66.

———. 1999. *Günter Grass zur Einführung.* Hamburg: Junius. Rev. and enl. ed. as *Günter Grass, der Schriftsteller: Eine Einführung.* Göttingen: Steidl, 2005.

———. 2002. "Günter Grass: *Ein weites Feld* und kein Ende . . ." In Wellnitz 2002a, 11–36.

Stowell, H. Peter. 1979. "Grass's *Dog Years:* Apocalypse, the Old and the New." *Perspectives on Contemporary Literature* 5:79–96.

Streitfeld, David. 1989. "Working Up a Sweat." *Washington Post* (14 May): X14.

———. 1993. "Gunter [sic] Grass, Unrelenting." *Washington Post* (15 Feb.): C1–C6.

Streul, Charlotte Irene. 1988. *Westdeutsche Literatur in der DDR: Böll, Grass und andere in der offiziellen Rezeption, 1949–1985.* Stuttgart: Metzler.

Sturm, Daniel. n.d. "Literatur am laufenden Bändel — Günter Grass in der Zensur." http:*//parapluie.de/archiv/indien/grass.* Accessed 1 Aug. 2005.

Sutherland, John. 1982. "Nationalities." *London Review of Books* (6–19 May): 18.

Swedish Academy. 1999. "Press Release; Nobel Prize for Literature 1999: Günter Grass." (30 Sept.).

Symons, Morwenna. 2005. *Room for Manoeuvre: The Role of Intertext in Elfriede Jelinek's "Die Klavierspielerin," Günter Grass's "Ein weites Feld," and Herta Müller's "Niederungen" and "Reisende auf einem Bein."* Leeds, UK: Maney.

Szczypiorski, Andrzej. 1992. "Fröschegequak und Krähengekrächz." *Der Spiegel* (4 May): 263–64.

T., D. "The Wild Imagination of Günter Grass Returns." Washington, DC *Star* (22 March). Repr. in White 1981 (excerpt), 138.

Taberner, Stuart. 1998. "Feigning the Anaesthetisation of Literary Inventiveness: Günter Grass's *örtlich betäubt* and the Public Responsibility of the Politically Engaged Author. *Forum for Modern Language Studies* 31:69–81.

———. 1999. "'sowas läuft nur im Dritten Programm': Winning Over the Audience for Political Engagement in Günter Grass's *Kopfgeburten oder Die Deutschen sterben aus.*" *Monatshefte* 91:84–100.

———. 2002. "'Normalization' and the New Consensus on the Nazi Past: Günter Grass's *Im Krebsgang* and the Problem of German Wartime Suffering." *Oxford German Studies* 31:161–86.

Talgeri, Pramod. 1988. "A Voyeuristic Look at Slums and Burning Corpses." *The Times of India* (20 Oct.).

Tambarin, Marcel. 2002. "'Deutsche Einheit, reine Spekulation!': L'unification et ses conséquences à travers *Ein weites Feld* de Günter Grass." In Wellnitz 2002a, 55–78.

Tank, Kurt Lothar. 1959. "Der Blechtrommler schrieb Memoiren." *Welt am Sonntag* (4 Oct.). Repr. in Görtz 1984a, 39–42.

———. 1965. *Günter Grass.* Berlin: Colloquium. 5th, rev. ed. 1974. Trans. John Conway as *Günter Grass.* New York: Ungar, 1969.

———. 1973. "Deutsche Politik im literarischen Werk von Günter Grass." In Jurgensen 1973, 167–89.

Taylor, D. J. 1992. "Stranger than Fact." *Sunday Times* (11 Oct.).

Taylor, Robert. 1992. "The Doleful, Dreary *Call of the Toad.*" *Boston Globe* (21 Oct.): 84.

Thomas, Noel L. 1973. "An Analysis of Günter Grass' *Katz und Maus* with Particular Reference to the Religious Themes." *German Life and Letters* 26:227–38.

———. 1979. "Günter Grass's *Der Butt:* History and Significance of the Eighth Chapter ('Vatertag')." *German Life and Letters* 33:75–85.

———. 1980. "Simon Dach und Günter Grass's *Das Treffen in Telgte.*" *New German Studies* 8:91–108.

———. 1982. *The Narrative Works of Günter Grass: A Critical Interpretation.* Amsterdam: Benjamins.

———. 1985. *Grass: "Die Blechtrommel."* London: Grant & Cutler.

———. 1988. "Food Poisoning, Cooking, and Historiography in the Works of Günter Grass." In *Literary Gastronomy,* ed. David Bevan. Amsterdam: Rodopi, 9–17.

Thomson, Philip. 1991. "History-writing as Hybrid Form: Günter Grass's *From the Diary of a Snail.*" In *The Modern German Historical Novel,* ed. David Roberts and Philip Thomson. New York: Berg, 181–90.

Tiesler [Hasselbach], Ingrid. 1971. *Günter Grass: "Katz und Maus."* Munich: Oldenbourg. New ed. 1990.

Tournier, Michel. 1975. "*Le Tambour* relu par *Le Roi des aulnes.*" *Le Monde* (17 Jan.). Repr. (enl. version), "Günther [sic] Grass et son tambour de tôle," in Tournier, *Le vol du vampire: Notes de lecture.* Paris: Mercure de France, 1981, 320–28.

Triller, Anneliese. 1977. "Grobe Verzeichnung: Die Darstellung der Dorothea von Montau durch Günter Grass." *Rheinischer Merkur* (19 Aug.): 20.

Tschapke, Reinhard. 1985. "Rummel um Grass: Wenn der Lärm die Literatur übertrifft." *Die Welt* (19 Aug.). Repr. in Oberhammer and Ostermann 1995, 77–78. Repr. in Negt 1996b, 69–71.

Twark, Jill E. 2004. "Landscape, Seascape, Cyberscape: Narrative Strategies to Dredge up the Past in Günter Grass's Novella *Im Krebsgang.*" *Gegenwartsliteratur* 3:143–68.

Ubben, Helmut, ed. 2001. "Günter Grass lädt Auricher Schüler zum Gespräch." (16 Nov.). http://www.auricher-wissenschaftstage.de/grassint.htm. Accessed 15 Feb 2006.

Ulfers, Friedrich. 1982. "Myth and History in Günter Grass' *Der Butt.*" In Pickar 1982, 32–42.

Ulrich, Carmen. 2004. *Sinn und Sinnlichkeit des Reisens: Indien(be)schreibungen von Hubert Fichte, Günter Grass und Josef Winkler.* Munich: Iudicium.

Umbach, Silke. 1992. "Die Wirtin vom Brückenhof; Die Libuschka in Grass' *Das Treffen in Telgte* und ihr Vorbild bei Grimmelshausen: *Die Landstörtzerin Courasche.*" *Simpliciana: Schriften der Grimmelshausen-Gesellschaft* 14:105–30.

Ungureit, Heinz. 1963. "Da wären die *Hundejahre.*" *Frankfurter Rundschau* (31 Aug.).

Updike, John. 1970. "Books." *New Yorker* (25 Apr.). Repr. in White 1981 (excerpt), 149–50.

———. 1973. "Snail on the Stump." *New Yorker* (15 Oct.): 182–85.

———. 1978. "Fish Story." *New Yorker* (27 Nov.): 203–4, 206. Repr. in Updike, *Hugging the Shore: Essays and Criticism.* New York: Knopf, 1983, 477–82.

———. 1981. "Readers and Writers." *New Yorker* (3 Aug.): 90–93.

———. 1982. "The Squeeze Is On." *New Yorker* (14 Jun.): 129–34.

———. 2003. "Suppressed Atrocities: A New Book by Gunter [sic] Grass." *New Yorker* (21/28 Apr.): 186–88.

Valentin, Jean-Marie. 1982. "Les orgies de Raspoutine: Günter Grass, lecteur de R. Fülop-Miller." *Revue d'Allemagne* 14:683–402.

Vanasten, Stéphanie. 2006. "'Kleine Ausbrüche in die Freiheit': Zum Günter Grass'schen Signifikat des Berliner Tiergartens." In *Literarische Mikrokosmen/ Les microcosmes littéraires: Begrenzung und Entgrenzung/Limites et ouvertures; Festschrift für Ernst Leonardy/Hommage à Ernst Leonardy,* ed. Christian Drösch, Hubert Roland, and Stéphanie Vanasten. Bruxelles: Lang, 179–91.

Van der Will, Wilfried. 1967. *Pikaro heute: Metamorphosen des Schelms bei Thomas Mann, Döblin, Brecht, Grass.* Stuttgart: Kohlhammer.

Van Gelder, Lawrence. 2006. "Authors Support Günter Grass." *New York Times* (18 Aug.).

Veel, Kristin. 2004. "Virtual Memory in Günter Grass' *Im Krebsgang.*" *German Life and Letters* 57:206–18.

Verdofsky, Jürgen. 1992. "*Unkenrufe* vielsprachig: Übersetzertreffen bei Günter Grass." *Frankfurter Rundschau* (3 February): 10.

Verweyen, Theodor, and Gunther Witting. 1980. "Polyhistors neues Glück: Zu Günter Grass' Erzählung *Das Treffen in Telgte* und ihrer Kritik." *Germanisch-Romanische Monatsschrift* 30:451–65. Repr. in Füssel 1999 (excerpt), 137–41.

Vester, Heinz-Günter. 1997. "Postmodern Emotions: *Ein weites Feld.*" In *Emotion in Postmodernism,* ed. Gerhard Hoffmann and Alfred Hornung. Heidelberg: Winter, 237–45.

Vinocur, John. 1980. "After 20 Years: *The Tin Drum* Marches to the Screen." *New York Times* (6 Apr.), sect. 2: 1, 17.

———. 2006. "Grass's Lapses in Recalling the Past Are Puzzling." *New York Times* (29 Aug.).

Vormweg, Heinrich. 1963. "Apokalypse mit Vogelscheuchen." *Deutsche Zeitung* (31 Aug.). Repr. in Loschütz 1968, 70–75.

———. 1978. "Eine phantastische Totale: Nachtrag zur *Butt* Kritik." In H. L. Arnold 1963, 5th, rev. ed. 1978, 94–100.

———. 1986. *Günter Grass.* Reinbek: Rowohlt. 2nd, enl. and rev. ed. 1993. 3rd enl. ed. 1996. 4th ed. 1998. Rev., new ed. 2002.

———. 1988. "Die Scham und die Würde." *Der Tagesspiegel* (5 Oct.).

Wagenbach, Klaus. 1963. "Jens tadelt zu unrecht." Repr. in Loschütz 1968, 89–92.

Wagener, Hans. 1988. "Simplex, Felix, Oskar und andere — Zur barocken Tradition im zeitgenössischen Schelmenroman." In *Literarische Tradition heute: Deutschsprachige Gegenwartsliteratur in ihrem Verhältnis zur Tradition,* ed. Gerd Labroisse and Gerhard P. Knapp. *Amsterdamer Beiträge zur neueren Germanistik* 24. Amsterdam: Rodopi, 1988, 117–58.

Wandor, Michelene. 1987. "To End Them All." *New Statesman* (26 Jun.): 26.

Webb, W. L. 1992. "What Maisie Wants to Know." *Guardian* (13 Oct.): 11.

Weber, Alexander. 1986. "Johann Matthias Schneuber: Der Ich-Erzähler in Günter Grass' *Das Treffen in Telgte;* Entschlüsselungsversuch eines poetisch-emblematischen Rätsels." *Daphnis* 15:95–122.

———. 1995. *Günter Grass's Use of Baroque Literature.* Leeds, UK: Maney.

Weber, Hans. 2001. "Geschichte durch Geschichten: Überlegungen zu Günter Grass *Mein Jahrhundert* im DaF-Unterricht." *Unterrichtspraxis* 34 (1): 34–41.

Weber, Wolfgang. 1999. "Mein Jahrhundert? Anmerkungen zu Günter Grass und seinem jüngsten Buch." *World Socialist Web Site www.wsws.org* (30 Nov.).

Weisberg, Richard. 2000. "Why Grass Won the Nobel Prize (Review)." *Tikkun: A Quarterly Jewish Critique of Politics, Culture & Society* 15:93.

Wellnitz, Philippe. 2001. "'Fonty hielt im Vorbeigehen einen Vortrag über die Macht des Ridikülen': Aspects du comique dans *Ein weites Feld.*" In Lartillot 2001a, 127–32.

———, ed. 2002a. *Günter Grass: "Ein weites Feld/Toute une histoire."* Strasbourg: Presses Universitaires.

———. 2002b."Avant-Propos." In Wellnitz 2002a, 5–10.

———. 2002c. "*Ein weites Feld/Toute une histoire* de Günter Grass: Un roman picaresque?" In Wellnitz 2002a, 185–98.

Welzer, Harald. 2002. "Zeitzeichen: Zurück zur Opfergesellschaft." *Neue Zürcher Zeitung* (3 Apr.).

Weninger, Robert. 2004. "Mediale Kannibalen und 'die gefräßige Wirklichkeit >Politik<': Vom ewigen Streit um Günter Grass.'" In Weninger, *Streitbare Literaten: Kontroversen und Eklats in der deutschen Literatur von Adorno bis Walser.* Munich: Beck, 208–29.

Wertheimer, Jürgen. 1983. "Das Treffen in Telgte: Die Doppelzeitigkeit von Geschichten und Geschichte." *Arbitrium* 1:92–100.

West, Anthony. 1965a. "The Hound of Hitler." *Newsweek* (24 May): 117–18. Repr. in White 1981 (excerpt), 74–75.

———. 1965b."Making Scarecrows." *New Yorker* (20 Nov.): 236, 238, 241. Repr. in White 1981 (excerpt), 100–101.

West, Paul. 1965. "The Grotesque Purgation." *The Nation* (16 Aug.): 81–84. Repr. in White 1981 (excerpt), 99.

White, John J. 1990. "'Wir hängen nicht vom Gehänge ab': The Body as Battleground in *Der Butt.*" In Brady, McFarland, and White 1990, 109–31.

White, Ray Lewis. 1981. *Günter Grass in America: The Early Years*. Hildesheim: Olms.

Wickert, Ulrich. 2006. "Ja, ich hätte es sagen können." [Excerpts of Interview with Günter Grass.] *Frankfurter Rundschau* (19 Aug.). Repr. in Gorzny 2006, 77–78. Repr. in Kölbel 2007b, 81–85.

Wiegenstein, Roland H. 1963. "*Hundejahre*." Broadcast Westdeutscher Rundfunk (28 Oct.). Repr. in Loschütz 1968, 75–79.

Wierlacher, Alois. 1987. *Vom Essen in der deutschen Literatur: Mahlzeiten in Erzähltexten von Goethe bis Grass*. Stuttgart: Kohlhammer.

Wildman, Eugene. 1989. "Gunter [sic] Grass' Love-Hate Relationship with Calcutta." *Chicago Tribune* (21 May): C7.

Williams, Carol J. 2002. "We, the Victims Too." *Los Angeles Times* (18 Mar.).

Williams, Gerhild S. 1980. "Es war einmal, ist und wird wieder sein: Geschichte und Geschichten in Günter Grass' *Der Butt*." In *Deutsche Literatur in der Bundesrepublik seit 1965: Untersuchungen und Berichte*. ed. Paul Michael Lützeler and Egon Schwarz. Königstein im Taunus: Athenäum, 182–94.

Willson, A. Leslie. 1966. "The Grotesque Everyman in Günter Grass's *Die Blechtrommel*." *Monatshefte* 58:131–38.

———, ed. 1971. *A Günter Grass Symposium*. Austin: U of Texas P.

Wimmer, Ruprecht. 1983. "'I, Down through the Ages': Reflections of the Poetics of Günter Grass." In Mews 1983a, 23–38.

———. 1985. "'Ich jederzeit': Zur Gestaltung der Perspektiven in Günter Grass' *Treffen in Telgte*." *Simpliciana: Schriften der Grimmelshausen-Gesellschaft* 6/7:139–50.

Winkler, Willi. 1992. "Frau gefunden, Friedhof geleast." *taz* (7 May).

Winston, Krishna. 2002. "Wacken und Klötze aus dem Weg geräumt." In Frielinghaus 2002, 72–81.

Wisskirchen, Hans. 2001. "Der Zahnarzt als Erzähler in Günter Grass' Roman *örtlich betäubt*." In *Medizin und Kultur*, ed. Giovanni Maio and Volker Roelcke. Stuttgart: Schattauer, 201–12.

———, ed. 2002. *Die Vorträge des 1. Internationalen Günter Grass Kolloquiums im Rathaus zu Lübeck*. Lübeck: Kulturstiftung Hansestadt Lübeck.

Wistoff, Andreas. 1996. "Marcel Reich-Ranicki und der Geist der Spätaufklärung." *Zeitschrift für deutsche Philologie* 115. Sonderheft, 197–214.

Wittek, Bernd. 1997. *Der Literaturstreit im sich vereinigenden Deutschland*. Marburg: Tectum.

Wittmann, Jochen. 1989. "*Urtrommel* und *Säulenheiliger*: Zur Genese der *Blechtrommel*." *Germanica Wratislaviensia* 88:200–229.

——— 1991. "The GDR and Günter Grass: East German Reception of the Literary Works and Public Persona." In *German Literature at a Time of Change, 1989–1990: German Unity and German Identity in Literary Perspective*, ed. Arthur Williams, Stuart Parkes, and Roland Smith. Bern: Lang, 273–84.

Wittstock, Uwe. 2002. "Die weit offen stehende Tabu-Tür." *Die Welt* (15 Feb.).

Wolff, Rudolf, ed. 1985. *Günter Grass: Werk und Wirkung*. Bonn: Bouvier.

Yates, Norris W. 1967. *Günter Grass: A Critical Essay*. [Grand Rapids, MI]: Eerdmans.

Zehm, Günter. 1986. "Einer träumt vom Großen Blitz." *Die Welt* (1 Mar.).

———. 1988. "Die indische Reise des Johann Wolfgang Grass." *Die Welt* (27 Aug.).

Ziltener, Walter. 1982. *Heinrich Böll und Günter Grass in den USA: Tendenzen der Rezeption*. Bern: Lang.

Zimmer, Dieter E. 1972. "*Aus dem Tagebuch einer Schnecke.*" *Die Zeit* (29 Sept.).

Zimmermann, Hans Dieter. 1982. "Der Butt und der Weltgeist: Zu dem Roman *Der Butt* von Günter Grass." *Diskussion Deutsch* 13:460–69.

———. 1983. "Günter Grass: *Die Blechtrommel* (1959)." In *Deutsche Romane des 20. Jahrhunderts: Neue Interpretationen*, ed. Paul Michael Lützeler. Königstein im Taunus: Athenäum, 324–39.

———. 1985. "Spielzeughändler Markus, Lehrer Zweifel und die Vogelscheuchen: Die Verfolgung der Juden im Werk von Günter Grass." In *Juden und Judentum in der Literatur*, ed. Herbert A. Strauss and Christhard Hoffmann. Munich: Deutscher Taschenbuch Verlag, 295–306.

Zimmermann, Harro. 1999. "Im Bergwald der Sprache." *Die Zeit* (15 Apr.): 53.

———. 2006. *Günter Grass unter den Deutschen: Chronik eines Verhältnisses*. Göttingen: Steidl.

Zimmermann, Werner. 1965. "Von Ernst Wiechert zu Günter Grass: Probleme der Auswahl zeitgenössischer Literatur im Deutschunterricht des Gymnasiums." *Wirkendes Wort* 5:316–27.

———. 1969. "Günter Grass: Katz und Maus (1961)." In Zimmermann, *Deutsche Prosadichtungen unseres Jahrhunderts: Interpretationen für Lehrende und Lernende*. Düsseldorf: Schwann, 2:267–300.

———. 1988. "Günter Grass: *Das Treffen in Telgte;* Eine Erzählung (1979)." In *Deutsche Prosadichtungen des 20. Jahrhunderts: Interpretationen*, ed. Werner Zimmermann and Klaus Lindemann. Düsseldorf: Schwann, 3:141–67.

Ziolkowski, Theodore. 1967. “Der Blick von der Irrenanstalt: Verrückung der Perspektive in der modernen deutschen Prosa.” *Neophilologus* 51:42–54.

———. 1969. “The View from the Madhouse.” Translation of Ziolkowski, 1967. In Ziolkowski, *Dimensions of the Modern Novel: German Texts and European Contexts.* Princeton, NJ: Princeton UP, 332–61.

———. 1976. “The Telltale Teeth: Psychodontia to Sociodontia.” *PMLA* 91:9–21.

———. 1981. “Historical Analogy: *The Meeting at Telgte.*” *New York Times Book Review* (17 May): 7, 22.

Zschachlitz, Ralf. 2001. “Allegorien des Erzählens in *Ein weites Feld.*” In Lartillot 2001a, 169–85.

Zweig, Paul. 1973. “Failure of Nerve.” *New Republic* (1 Dec.): 28–29.

Index